American Public Opinion

Ninth Edition

American Public Opinion

Robert S. Erikson

Columbia University

Kent L. Tedin

University of Houston

PEARSON

Boston   Columbus   Indianapolis   New York   San Francisco   Upper Saddle River
Amsterdam   CapeTown   Dubai   London   Madrid   Milan   Munich   Paris   Montréal   Toronto
Delhi   Mexico City   São Paulo   Sydney   Hong Kong   Seoul   Singapore   Taipei   Tokyo

Editor in Chief: Ashley Dodge
Editorial Assistant: Stephanie Ruland
Marketing Coordinator: Jessica Warren
Managing Editor: Denise Forlow
Program Manager: Carly Czech
Project Manager: Doug Bell/Lumina Datamatics, Inc.
Senior Operations Supervisor: Mary Fischer
Operations Specialist: Mary Ann Gloriande
Art Director: Maria Lange

Cover Image: Christian Mueller/Shutterstock
Digital Media Project Manager: Tina Gagliostro
Full-Service Project Management and Composition: Sneha Pant/
 Lumina Datamatics, Inc.
Printer/Binder: RR Donnelley
Cover Printer: RR Donnelley
Text Font: Sabon LT Std 10/12

Credits and acknowledgments borrowed from other sources and reproduced, with permission, in this textbook appear on appropriate page within the text.

Library of Congress Control Number:
2014939905

10 9 8 7 6 5 4 3 2 1

ISBN 10: 0-13-386267-4
ISBN 13: 978-0-13-386267-6

DEDICATION

Dedicated to the memory of Maggie Banks Tedin (1947–2008), companion and wife of Kent Tedin for 32 years, and friend of Bob Erikson and his family.

BRIEF CONTENTS

CONTENTS

3   Microlevel Opinion: The Psychology of Opinion-Holding   55

4   Macrolevel Opinion: The Flow of Political Sentiment   90

LIST OF FIGURES AND TABLES

Figures

Tables

PREFACE

In this ninth edition of *American Public Opinion*, we present an accounting of the role of public opinion in the democratic politics of the United States. As with previous editions, this book discusses the contemporary literature on public opinion, supplementing it with our own illustrations and analyses of contemporary public opinion data. It provides an in-depth analysis of public opinion, beginning with its origins in political socialization, the impact of the media, the extent and breadth of democratic values, and the role of public opinion in the electoral process. *American Public Opinion* is unique in that it goes beyond a simple presentation of data and discussion of the formation of opinion, to include a critical analysis of the role of public opinion in American democracy. As in previous editions, the ninth edition examines the relationship between public opinion and policy.

Readers familiar with the earlier eighth edition will notice few changes in format. The chapter titles are identical to those from the eighth edition. The within-chapter headings have changed little. Yet, because public opinion and electoral politics are always changing, each edition of this book requires extensive revision of content. In this ninth edition, we strive to keep the discussion as current as possible.

New to This Edition

- The ninth edition includes extensive discussion of public opinion on contemporary issues such as the Affordable Care Act (Obamacare) and gay marriage.
- The ninth edition expands the discussion of whether the representation of public opinion is equal for all income groups.
- The discussion of voters and elections is updated to focus on the 2012 presidential election, Obama vs. Romney.
- The discussion of mass media and politics is revamped to offer more material on the influence of the Internet and social media.
- The contemporary growth of political polarization and its causes is a theme weaved throughout the chapters of the ninth edition.
- The ninth edition is updated to include both recent polls (through 2013) and the findings of the latest research on public opinion.

As this book has evolved through multiple editions, so too has the list of authors. The first edition (1973) was authored by Robert S. Erikson and Norman L. Luttbeg. With the second edition, Kent L. Tedin joined the team as a third author. That triumvirate held through three editions. By the time of the fifth edition, Luttbeg left the team to pursue other scholarly pursuits. This is the third edition solely authored by Erikson and Tedin. But Luttbeg's contribution to the book remains, most notably in the five linkage models, which he originated.

The preparation of this volume relies heavily on the survey data of the National Election Studies, conducted by the University of Michigan, supported by grants from the National Science Foundation, and made available by the Interuniversity

Consortium for Political and Social Research. We also relied extensively on the General Social Survey (also funded by the National Science Foundation) and the data available online from the Roper Center Data Archive at the University of Connecticut. These organizations bear no responsibility for the analysis or interpretations presented here. We are greatly indebted to them for making their data available to us and to other scholars on whose research we depend.

Acknowledgments

We benefit from the assistance provided by our editor, Melissa Mashburn, and to colleagues, students, and staff at Columbia University and the University of Houston. We are indebted to Prof. Kathleen Knight of Columbia University for her helpful advice. Special thanks go to Matthew Kantrowitz and David Llanos, for their invaluable research assistance.

Robert S. Erikson
Kent L. Tedin

CHAPTER 1

Public Opinion in Democratic Societies

LEARNING OBJECTIVES

- **Explain the historical development of the concept *public opinion***
- **Explain the evolution of the modern public opinion poll**
- **Identify the main criticisms of the modern public opinion poll**
- **Identify the political consequences of the modern public opinion poll**

Few Americans in the twenty-first century can remember a time when public opinion polls—like television, shopping malls, and eight-lane freeways—were not part of the popular landscape. Polls tell us which television shows are the most popular, how frequently people attend church, what person Americans most admire, plus a myriad of opinions on current political topics. We shall see, however, that the study of public opinion is much broader than simply gauging popular reaction to recent events. It is, for example, also concerned with how people learn about government, their trust in existing political institutions, their support for the political rules of the game, the interrelationships among their opinions, and the trend toward political polarization that began more than fifteen years ago. The list could go on. But more than anything else, the study of public opinion is justified by the simple notion that democratic institutions should result in government decisions that reflect the views of everyday people. In the words of Robert Dahl, the most eminent political theorist of the post–World War II era, "I assume that a key characteristic of a democracy is the continued responsiveness of the government to the preferences of its citizens, considered as political equals" (1971, 1). It is this presumption, and its implications, that guides the systematic analysis of mass opinion.

1-1 Public Opinion and Government

Rousseau, in 1744, was among the first to use the term *public opinion* (*l'opinion publique*), meaning the customs and manners of all members of society (as opposed to some elite). By 1780, French writers were using the term interchangeably with *common will*, *public spirit*, and *public conscience* to refer to the political aspects of mass opinion (Price 1992, 8). *Public opinion* soon came into common usage among those writing about government.

However, long before scientific methods were developed to measure attitudes or the term *public opinion* gained currency, political theorists speculated about the "group mind" or the "general will" and how it might influence the political order. Writers beginning with Plato and Aristotle, through Locke and Hobbes as well as Rousseau, did not see public opinion as an aggregation of individual opinions, as is common today. Rather, they saw the whole as greater than the sum of its parts, much in the way a mob with a united purpose behaves in a fashion that would be foreign to any individual member. To these predemocratic theorists, public opinion was a mass entity, which if brought to bear on public affairs had potential for enormous influence. It was like a force of nature, constrained perhaps by certain regularities, but a unified whole that changed continually, like the currents in the ocean (Palmer 1936; Spitz 1984; Cress and Wootton 2011).

It was not until the rise of popular sovereignty that thinking about public opinion began to consider individual or group characteristics. By the eighteenth century, no Western political regime could afford to ignore the views of the masses. This change was brought about by the construction of electoral institutions and parliamentary bodies for regular consultation with the public and the gradual extension of the franchise to the lower classes. Henceforth, governments would find it necessary to take account of public opinion and its distribution throughout the polity. This accounting was not simply a question of government responsiveness to mass policy desires. Government also had to take account of popular support for the ongoing political order. A strong argument can be made that only when the political status quo was threatened did political elites, in an act of self-preservation, grudgingly extend the franchise to portions of the mass public (Ginsberg 1982). But with the granting of the franchise, there soon developed an ethical imperative that governments are morally obligated to heed public opinion in formulating policies.

In the early years of the American republic, to speak of "public opinion" was mostly to speak about the thin layer of the educated, affluent public in a position to communicate their views to government. While the nation's founders agreed on the principle of popular government, they greatly distrusted the wisdom and judgment of the masses on matters political. To Alexander Hamilton,

> The voice of the people has been said to be the voice of God; and however generally this maxim has been quoted and believed, it is not true in fact. The people are turbulent and changing; they seldom judge or determine right.
> (Farrand 1961, 299–300)

While not all took such an uncharitable position, it was generally thought that public opinion was easily swayed and subject to fits of passion. Thus, institutions were developed, such as the Electoral College and the indirect election of senators, to distance political leaders from the opinions of everyday citizens.

Nevertheless, by the mid-nineteenth century, many who followed the American political scene voiced concern about an excess of influence on political decision making by public opinion. One reason was the integration of the working class into the electorate via the universal franchise. By the 1850s, it became impossible to argue that the public's opinion could be ignored. Writing in 1848, Alexis de Tocqueville, perhaps the most astute observer of nineteenth-century America, thought "there was no country in which . . . there is less independence of mind and true freedom of discussion than in America" (1966, 254). He felt the numerical majority intimidated the minority so that only a narrow range of opinion could be expressed. In the end, he feared that the views of the majority could result in either social or governmental tyranny (Spitz 1984, 70). History was, of course, to prove him wrong. But those writing later agreed with his assessment of the importance of public opinion. In 1888, the perceptive British journalist and author James Bryce would claim that "in no country is public opinion so powerful as in the United States" (1900). He also noted, "the obvious weakness of government by opinion is the difficulty of ascertaining it."

Of those writing before the development of the modern opinion poll, perhaps the most influential critic of public opinion was Walter Lippmann (1922, 1925). Like many of the founders, Lippmann believed mass opinion was subject to passions that could be induced by elite propaganda. He was convinced that the manipulation of public opinion by those opposed to the League of Nations was responsible for the tragedy of America's failure to join after World War I. Famously, Lippmann perceptively observed that the images of politics received by the public are not direct pictures of events, immediate experiences of action, or provable economic and social theories. Rather, they are "pictures in people's heads" generated by political interests to benefit their cause. In a prescient analysis of major findings by modern survey research, Lippmann challenged traditional democratic theory and its notion of an informed and rational public basing opinions on a considered judgment of the facts. He argued that the average person had little time for affairs of state and would rather read the comics than consider the pros and cons of weighty political issues. It should not be expected, therefore, that the mass public be competent in matters of state. Lippmann's prescription for democracy was for the public to choose leaders but for public policy to be developed and implemented by scientifically oriented experts.

The debate over the role of public opinion in democracy was given a new focus by the appearance of scientific polling in 1935 (Fried 2012). Among the most outspoken proponents of polls as a guide to government decision making was George Gallup, a pioneer of the new technology (Gallup and Rae 1940). Gallup was a prairie populist with a Ph.D. in psychology, who believed in the collective wisdom of everyday citizens. He distrusted intellectuals and experts, and he thought that elite rule and democratic government were incompatible. The challenge for democracy, as he saw it, was, "Shall the common people be free to express their basic needs and purposes, or shall they be dominated by a small ruling clique?" In other words, how does one make those holding high public office responsive to the needs and wishes of the public?

Poll results, Gallup argued, could be considered a "mandate from the people," a concrete expression of the policies the public desires the government to enact. No longer would elected officials have to rely on the ambiguities of elections, claims by self-serving interest groups, newspaper stories, communications from constituents, or other nonrepresentative channels of public sentiment. Rather, they could turn to the latest opinion poll. In the past, claims that elected officials should heed popular preferences directly when formulating policy could always be countered with arguments like those of sixteenth-century political theorist Michel de Montaigne (1967), who wrote that "public opinion is a powerful, bold, and unmeasurable party."

Gallup saw the modern opinion poll as the high-tech equivalent of the New England town meeting—an opportunity for all citizens (or at least a representative sample) to voice their opinions. The scientific poll gave crispness, clarity, and reliability to mass opinion. Gallup and his supporters argued that through polls, the will of the people could accurately be determined. No longer could failure to take seriously popular preferences when enacting public policy be justified by claims that public opinion is unknowable. With the aid of the modern opinion poll, it was the moral responsibility of elected officials to convert the public will into public policy.

Not all were enthusiastic about the new polling technology and George Gallup's prescriptions for it. Sociologist Herbert Blumer and political scientist Lindsay Rogers soon launched frontal assaults on the opinion poll and its implications. Blumer (1948) asserted the "one person, one vote" definition of public opinion inherent in polls was precisely what public opinion was not. Public opinion could not be reduced to a nose count of citizens. Rather, it was the interactions and communications among functional groups that percolated through society and came to the attention of government. These interactions and communications were not aggregations of individual opinions but "an organic whole of interacting, interrelated parts." To Blumer, not all opinions counted equally. They merited the label *public opinion* only to the extent opinions surfaced in a public forum and were taken seriously by those in government with power and influence. This view, of course, clashed directly with the populist inclinations of Gallup and other early pollsters.[1]

Lindsay Rogers, on the other hand, was convinced that the public was not intellectually or emotionally fit to play the role Gallup's opinion-poll democracy required of it (Fried 2006). In any case, polls were not technically able to ascertain the public's message. Rogers (1949) reformulated the position of the English philosopher Edmund Burke that it is the duty of elected representatives to follow their conscience and best judgment and not be slaves to moments of popular passion.[2] Only in this fashion, argued Rogers, could the true public interest be served. Rogers was also one of the first to raise serious methodological questions about polls—that is, to challenge pollsters on their own turf. He addressed questions of measurement, opinion aggregation, intensity, and framing effects that occupy a great deal of attention among contemporary students of public opinion. In essence, he claimed that polls of public opinion did not really measure "public opinion." Notably, polls do not allow for the deliberation of issues, and a sophisticated understanding of issues requires deliberation. Deliberation, in turn, requires group discussion and analysis. Rogers argued that "Dr. Gallup does not make the public more articulate. He only estimates how in replying to certain questions it would say 'yes,' 'no,' or 'don't know.' Instead of feeling the pulse of democracy, Dr. Gallup listens to its baby talk" (1949, 17).

Rogers' perspective on public opinion has intellectual roots in the writings of Founding Father James Madison. According to Colleen Sheehan (2004, 406), Madison rejected the notion of public opinion as simply an aggregation of public sentiments. Rather, he saw it as a process of community conversation and deliberation, with citizens influencing each other through public and private discourse, ultimately influencing political decisions through an "enlightened public voice" (406).

The critiques of Blumer and Rogers helped spawn the development of an important methodological innovation in public opinion—the deliberative poll (Delli Carpini, Cook, and Jacobs 2004). Gastil (2000, 22) defines public deliberation as the careful examination of a political problem, identification of solutions to that problem, and debate over the merits of proposed solutions. Lindeman (2002, 119) sees deliberation as "a cognitive process in which individuals form, alter, or reinforce their opinions as they weigh evidence and arguments from various points of view." Luskin, Fishkin, and Jowell (2002, 456) assert that "Now several decades' experience the wiser, we know that opinion polls . . . have not been the great boon to democracy that Gallup envisioned." The problem, in their view, is responses to conventional opinion questions are mostly ill-considered and barren of information (see also Bartels 2008). A somewhat different critique is offered by Scott Althaus (2003, 278), who argues that fair representation is undermined by the uneven distribution of political knowledge. In particular, the poorly informed is less likely to have opinions than the better informed.

The general idea behind deliberation is that individuals will revise, modify, or change their opinions in light of new information and the force of argument made by fellow discussants. A by-product of deliberation is that the policy preferences are more "informed, enlightened, and authentic" (Page 1996, 1).

The deliberative poll, pioneered by James Fishkin (1997), combines the strength of the representative sample survey with the internal validity of the experimental design, which allows for comparison of deliberate polls with traditional polling methods. In national deliberative polls, a representative sample of 600 or so participants is selected by a telephone survey and transported to a single site. They are broken into small groups, given detailed information on key issues facing the nation, and engaged in two to four days of deliberation. As we shall see shortly, everyday citizens found in their normal environment bear little resemblance to the democratic ideal often caricatured by the New England town meeting. The purpose of the deliberative poll is to create the conditions, whereby a representative sample of Americans can express informed and thoughtful opinions—a situation unlike the 1935 polling innovation of George Gallup (at least according to critics like Lindsay Rogers).

There have now been a number of studies involving the deliberative poll (Luskin, Fishkin, and Jowell 2002; Barabas 2004; Sturgis, Roberts, and Allum 2005; Jackman and Sniderman 2006; Hilmer 2011). The research is decided a mixed bag, with many conflicting results. Compared to traditional polling, participants in deliberative polls are (sometimes) better informed, have stronger interrelationships among their opinions (constraints), and are more politically efficacious (more likely to participate in the political process). However, deliberative polls rarely change opinions. An exception is on low visibility, low information issues (Farrar et al. 2010). Those participating in deliberative polls, while they gain information, tend to retain their predeliberative opinions (Visser, Hobrook, and Krosnick 2008).

Critics of deliberative polls claim that the dynamics of small groups show that even when opinion moves, it generally moves in the direction of the group majority. Also, better-educated, higher status deliberators tend to be disproportionately vocal and persuasive in group discussions (Mendelberg 2002). In addition, Hibbing and Theiss-Morse (2002) show many citizens recoil from the discord and disagreement that naturally accompanies open political deliberation. Many citizens don't like to argue about politics, and when placed in that situation they develop feelings of frustration and powerlessness, rather than the more positive consequences attributed to deliberation by its advocates. Finally, critics note the artificial laboratory setting employed in studies of deliberate polling. Subjects are transported, often at considerable distance, to a central site. They then engage in a prearranged discussion of issues chosen by the project investigators. There are, of course, nontrivial differences between this methodology and the ideal of the New England town meeting.

A different argument flowing from the critique of Lindsay Rogers holds that public opinion changes in a capricious fashion—that is, over short periods of time, policy preferences shift rapidly, frequently, and arbitrarily. This belief was used by the author of Federalist Paper No. 63 to argue for an indirectly elected Senate, which would serve as "an anchor against popular fluctuations" and protect the people against their own "temporary errors and delusions." This argument has been advanced most notably in the realm of foreign affairs—where public interest and information tend to be lower than for domestic matters. In 1950, political scientist Gabriel Almond argued that on matters of foreign policy, the public reacts with "formless and plastic moods which undergo frequent alteration in response to changes in events" (53).[3] This view of public opinion was used to buttress arguments about limiting the role of mass opinion in policy decisions and is still a touchstone of the "realist" school of foreign policy (Mearsheimer 2001). Recently, however, scholars have "rehabilitated" the public on matters of foreign policy. According to the revisionist approach, citizens make decisions about foreign affairs based on the principle of "low information rationality" (Brewer et al. 2004). While not possessing extensive knowledge of world events, they are nevertheless able to use informational shortcuts to form stable and reasonable reactions to international events (Page and Shapiro 1992; Holsti 2004, 2011). Among these shortcuts are the images they hold of foreign countries as allies or threats to American security, or isolationist versus internationalist perspectives on America's proper role in the world (Drezner 2008). We shall elaborate on these points in Chapter 4.

The liberal democracy school of thought (Dahl 1989) holds that an essential element of democracy is the creation of institutions and practices that allow for meaningful public input into the governing process. Democratic government works best when elected officeholders and appointed officials respond to the popular will. Citizens are more likely to comply with government decisions when they are backed by the moral force of popular approval. In addition, advocates of liberal democracy argue that decisions based on popular will are most likely to be the correct decisions. This idea traces its heritage to Aristotle's view that the pooled judgments of the many are likely to contain more wisdom than the judgments of the few.[4] The liberal democratic model does not hold that public policy must be driven only by the engine of public opinion. Rather, public opinion must count for something of consequence in government decision making.

The arguments we have just outlined are still occasionally elaborated upon today. However, most current research on public opinion does not address normative issues about the proper role of opinion in the governmental process. Rather, empirical questions dominate the field—that is, questions about "what really is" as opposed to "what ought to be." But empirical questions often have important normative implications. Clearly of consequences are "How much does the public know about public affairs, and how is that knowledge organized?" "How is public opinion articulated?" "Whose voices are heard?" "Are some segments of society (presumably the more affluent) better able to communicate their opinions to political decision makers than those with fewer economic resources?" The answers to these questions are important for theories of how the just polity should be structured.

1-2 Public Opinion Defined

Public opinion is notoriously difficult to define. There are scores, if not hundreds, of variations on a definition (see Childs 1965 for a sampling). V.O. Key, Jr., famously defined public opinion as "those opinions held by private persons which governments finds it prudent to heed" (1961b, 14). But what if government does not find it prudent to heed a particular opinion held by the public? Is it then not a "public opinion"?

We take a somewhat different approach. A standard definition of *public* is a group that has something in common. Some argue that there is no such thing as a single public; rather, there are many publics (MacDougall 1966). Thus, one can refer to the tennis-playing public, the snowmobiling public, or the television-watching public. Others, however, take a broader view. For political scientists, what members of the "public" in *public opinion* have in common is a connection to government. At a minimum, all citizens aged eighteen and older have the right to vote. That binds them together with a common interest, even if they choose not to exercise the right. And, of course, everyone is affected in some way by government. That creates a common interest as well. Students of government also regularly speak of several specialized publics. They talk of the "attentive public," those persons who generally pay close attention to politics, and "issue publics," those persons who focus on specific issues while paying less attention to others. It is perhaps helpful to think of these as "subpublics" of the overall public (i.e., the adult population).

We may first describe an opinion as a verbal expression of an attitude.[5] There are, of course, other ways in which attitudes can be expressed, such as marches, demonstrations, or riots. But we reserve the term *opinion* as the manifestation of attitudes in words or writing.[6] Attitudes are latent; they cannot be directly observed. Social psychologists typically define an attitude as an enduring predisposition to respond. Normally, attitudes do not change weekly or monthly. Although change is clearly possible, attitudes are mostly stable over extended periods. Opinions are imperfect indicators of the underlying, unobserved attitude. Because opinions are imperfect measures, we sometimes find they are inconsistent or display contradictions. We deal with this problem at length in Chapter 3.

Second, opinions are disagreements about matters of preference, which cannot be resolved using the rules of science. Thus, when it comes to music, I may prefer opera. You may prefer hard rock. But there is no systematic way of demonstrating the virtue or goodness of one over the other. The same is true for opinions about welfare policy, foreign aid, or same-sex marriage. Disagreements about questions of fact are not opinions but beliefs.[7] There was once disagreement about whether the earth circled the sun. Some believed the reverse—that the sun revolved around the earth. That disagreement has been resolved by scientific methods. There is still disagreement over whether massive doses of vitamin C will prevent colds and other illness. Some believe this notion is nothing more than a hoax; others take large doses of the vitamin daily. But one's position on this issue is a belief, not an opinion, because in principle the question may someday be resolved with finality. Disagreements over classical versus rock music will not be resolved.

No one has yet advanced a definition of *public opinion* that satisfies a substantial number of students in the field. We prefer to keep our definition short and simple. We define *public opinion* as the preferences of the adult population on matters of relevance to government. The first implication is that not all opinions are public opinion. Thus, one's preference for computer operating systems—Windows, Linux, OS X—is excluded from our definition because it has nothing to do with government. The second implication is that while in the broadest sense we are talking about all adults, that does not exclude the possibility of referencing subgroups, such as the attentive public. A third point is that by the term *preferences*, we mean more than simply the affective component of an opinion. *Affect* refers to feelings—like or dislike, approve or disapprove. However, we must also be concerned with the cognitive component of an opinion. *Cognition* refers to the process of knowing, to the intellectual sophistication one brings to the ordering of political opinions. Obviously, the amount of political information one has affects the ability to link one political concept with another and is important for our understanding of public opinion. Finally, while we have defined *opinions* as verbal manifestations of attitudes, events such as riots, demonstrations, and marches are also indicators of public opinion for certain attentive publics.

In the recent era, the meaning of *public opinion* sometimes seems to have evolved into whatever opinion polls show public opinion to be. In the opinion of CBS News Poll director Kathleen Frankovic, "Polls are not only part of the news today, they are news. They not only sample public opinion, they define it" (1998, 150). In many ways, the findings of public opinion polls (or survey research in general) should inspire trust. Counterintuitive though it may seem, mathematical statistics and decades of experience reveal that one *can* generalize from a random sample of 1,000 or so individuals to the nation as a whole. And one rarely has reason to believe that survey respondents systematically lie to pollsters.

We must be careful, however, not to reify. Public opinion and the results of public opinion polls are not the same thing. A public opinion poll is an indirect measure of "public opinion," much like an IQ test is an indirect measure of "intelligence." As shown in later chapters, the results of opinion polls must be interpreted with great care. Findings can vary considerably with different question wordings or different shadings of how issues are presented to respondents. Also, survey respondents sometimes tend to give socially desirable responses. For this reason, opinion polls sometimes inaccurately report attitudes and behaviors such as nonvoting, racist feelings, and tolerance for pornography because of a tendency for respondents to give a favorable accounting of themselves.

1-3 The Evolution of the Public Opinion Poll

Before the appearance of the modern public opinion poll in 1935, popular sentiment was assessed by newspapers and magazines through a variety of informal and haphazard soundings called *straw polls*.[8] The *Harrisburg Pennsylvanian* is credited with conducting the first of these polls in the summer of 1824. It showed presidential candidate Andrew Jackson, with 63 percent of the vote, an easy winner over John Quincy Adams and Henry Clay.[9]

But it was not until 1896 that straw polling became a serious business. In that year, the *Chicago Record* conducted an elaborate and expensive straw poll to tap voter preferences in the bitterly fought presidential contest between William McKinley and William Jennings Bryan. It sent out postcard ballots to every eighth voter in twelve Midwestern states, as well as ballots to every registered voter in Chicago.[10] The owner of the *Chicago Record* had clear Republican sympathies, and the Democratic Party feared the poll was nothing more than a Republican trick. The party urged Democrats not to return the ballots. Nevertheless, with the aid of a team of eminent mathematicians, the *Record* predicted in October that McKinley would win Chicago with 57.95 percent of the vote. Amazingly, he received 57.91 percent on Election Day. Outside of Chicago, however, the *Record*'s predictive record was a failure (Jensen 1968).

With the dawn of the twentieth century, straw polls were becoming a regular feature in many magazines and newspapers. Like today, the poll results were "newsworthy." Approximately eighty-four straw polls were conducted during the 1928 presidential election, of which six were national. The straw polls occupied thousands of column inches in the print media. If anything, they were featured even more prominently than is currently the case.[11] The polls were of major importance to their sponsors as a promotional gimmick. They created interest in the publication. Also, those publishers using mail-out ballots usually included a special subscription offer along with the ballot. By all indications, the scheme worked remarkably well to boost circulation (Robinson 1932).

Like current opinion polls, the straw polls did not limit themselves simply to electoral contests. They polled on the issues as well, most notably the burning issue of the 1920s: Prohibition. The wet–dry controversy was as emotion laden as any issue to surface in American politics. If popular sentiment on the issue were to be measured by a cutout ballot from a newspaper, one side would sometimes attempt to secure a monopoly on that issue and send in all the ballots. Or one side would urge its people not to participate in a straw poll when the sponsor's sentiments on the issue were known. Thus, a poll in Delaware sponsored by Pierre du Pont, a well-known wet, was boycotted by drys. It wound up showing 97 percent of its respondents in favor of repeal. Mr. du Pont wisely decided against publishing the poll results as an indicator of public opinion. Rather, he submitted the returned ballots as a petition to the Delaware legislature urging the repeal of Prohibition (Robinson 1932).

The straw polls were a public relations disaster waiting to happen. By the 1930s, considerable advances had been made by market researchers in the field of applied sampling. However, the magazines and newspapers sponsoring the straw polls were oblivious. Their major concern with straw polls was how they contributed to profitability, not the technical quality of the poll itself. Methodologically, straw polls stayed in the rear guard, learning nothing from the advances in sampling methods, using the same outdated methods year after year.

Straw polls were, in fact, known to be notoriously unreliable. In 1932, Claude Robinson published an analysis of the state-by-state error margins of the major straw polls of the day.[12] The average error of the polls conducted by the Hearst newspapers was 12 percent in 1924. The poll by *The Pathfinder*, a weekly magazine, was off by an average error of 14 percent in 1928. The *Farm-Journal* poll of thirty-six states in 1928 had an average error of 17 percent. Even the best known and most professionally operated of the straw polls—the *Literary Digest* poll—was off the mark by an average error of 12 percent in both 1924 and 1928.

It was the 1936 election and the notorious misprediction of its outcome by the *Literary Digest* that brought an end to the era of straw polls. The *Literary Digest* was the largest circulation general magazine of its time, with over 2 million subscribers. Much of this success could be traced directly to its straw poll, a regular feature since 1916. While the *Digest* poll experienced more than its share of mispredictions, it had managed each time to get the winner of the presidential election right. And it was not modest. The *Digest* claimed "uncanny accuracy" for its poll, congratulating itself frequently on its amazing record. But in the 1936 presidential election, the *Digest* poll wildly mispredicted the outcome, giving Alf Landon 57 percent of the vote and Franklin Roosevelt 43 percent. Roosevelt won handily with 62.5 percent of the vote. The *Digest* was off the mark by almost 20 percentage points. Its credibility shattered, the *Digest* went bankrupt a year later.[13]

In that same year, three young pollsters with backgrounds in market research, using "scientific" methods of sampling, did correctly predict the win by Roosevelt. The three were Archibald Crossley, Elmo Roper, and George Gallup, each of whom went on to found his own poll. The best known of these was, of course, George Gallup, founder of the Gallup Poll.

Gallup was a talented self-promoter. In the 1936 election season, he taunted the *Literary Digest*, offering clients a money-back guarantee that his poll would be closer to the actual vote on Election Day than the *Digest*'s.[14] He urged newspapers and magazines to run the two polls side by side (J. Converse 1987, 116–20).

Gallup used in-person interviews as opposed to mail questionnaires, and he employed "quotas" to ensure that his samples looked demographically like the overall population. His 1936 poll forecast Roosevelt with 55.7 percent of the vote— 6.8 percent off the mark. But he got the winner right, and he used that fact, along with the *Digest*'s disaster, to quickly become the nation's preeminent pollster.

But all was not right with the Gallup Poll. While Gallup continued to forecast the correct winner in the 1940 and 1944 presidential contests, his surveys consistently overestimated the Republican vote (Moore 1992, 66–68). Then, in 1948, the Gallup Poll incorrectly forecast that Republican Thomas Dewey would defeat Democrat Harry Truman by a margin of 49.5 to 44.5 percent. It is important to note that the Crossley Poll and the Roper Poll also predicted a win by Dewey. Roper had the margin at 52.2 percent Dewey and 37.1 percent Truman. Something was clearly wrong with the sampling methodology used by all three of these polls. That something was quota sampling. In a comprehensive study of the failure of the polls in 1948, the Social Science Research Council recommended the abandonment of quota samples and their replacement with probability samples (Fried 2012). Probability sampling is the method used in "scientific" public opinion polls (see Chapter 2).

Gallup, Crossley, and Roper were commercial pollsters. They did polls for clients and by necessity were concerned with costs and profitability. They had little incentive for pure research or for the lengthy surveys necessary to answer complex academic questions.[15] Those topics would be addressed by the major academic survey organizations, most notably the National Opinion Research Center (NORC) at the University of Chicago and the Survey Research Center (SRC)[16] at the University of Michigan. NORC was founded in 1941, and its associates produced several classics in the field of public opinion, including *The American Soldier* (Stouffer 1949) and *Communism, Conformity, and Civil Liberties* (Stouffer 1955). The SRC, founded in 1946, has focused on studies of the American electorate. Perhaps the most influential book to date on public opinion and voting, *The American Voter* (Campbell et al. 1960), was published by a group associated with the SRC.

Both the NORC and the SRC devote considerable resources to technical issues involving sampling and question wording. The NORC pioneered the split-ballot technique, in which different forms of a question are asked of random halves of a sample to investigate the effects of question wording. Researchers associated with the SRC have also devoted extensive time and energy to problems of question wording (Schuman and Presser 1996). But most important are the periodic surveys conducted by each of these institutions.

Every other year since 1948, the SRC and the Center for Political Studies have conducted the American National Election Studies (ANES).[17] These are large, in-person national surveys of issues relevant to elections. In presidential years, respondents are interviewed in the autumn before the election and then reinterviewed after the election. The total interview time is often three to five hours, and hundreds of questions are asked. The ANES surveys voters in midterm election years as well, with shorter interviews usually conducted only after the election.

Since 1971, the NORC has sponsored the General Social Survey (GSS), conducted on an annual or a biennial basis. The GSS has a general set of questions, often repeated from one survey to the next, and a topical module that addresses a specific substantive concern at considerable length. Both the ANES and the GSS are publicly available, formatted and ready for analysis with common computer statistical packages. Much of the data presented in this book come from these two sources.

While both the ANES and the GSS interview people in their homes, this is an expensive undertaking. By the early 1970s, techniques were being developed to scientifically sample telephone numbers using a random-digit-dialing methodology. This greatly reduced the cost of surveys and encouraged the media to conduct their own public opinion polls, much as they did in the days of the straw polls. In 1976, CBS News and the *New York Times* went into partnership to conduct their own polls. They were soon followed by the NBC/*Wall Street Journal*, the ABC/*Washington Post* polls, and CNN.[18] The principal advantage to the media of in-house polls is that they can decide on the topics and timing of the surveys rather than being confined to the topics and timing of independent pollsters like Gallup. In-house polls also free the media from reliance on leaks from political campaigns about how candidates are faring with the voters. They can find out for themselves on an impartial, firsthand basis. The most significant nonprofit, nonpartisan organization that polls on a regular basis is the Pew Research Center. Unlike media polls that usually address topical issues with an abbreviated number of questions, Pew conducts episodic polls that treat specific topics (e.g., political trust) in considerable depth.

A relatively new innovation is the Election Day exit poll, developed by CBS News in the late 1960s. It did not, however, gain prominence until the 1980 election, when it was first used to forecast the outcome of a presidential election. With an exit poll, one chooses a representative sample of precincts in a state and interviews voters as they leave the polling place. The networks usually know by 3:00 P.M. who has won the election, although they do not reveal this information for any one state until the polls have closed in that state. Beyond forecasting, exit polls have proved extremely valuable for understanding why people voted for specific candidates. Prior to 1990, each network conducted its own exit polls.

In 1990, the major networks, along with CNN and the Associated Press, formed a consortium, Voter News Service (VNS), to conduct common exit polls and share the information. This worked well until the 2000 presidential election, when VNS prematurely forecast a Gore victory in Florida. Then, in 2002, VNS exit polls were not reported on election night due to concerns over unreliability. As a consequence, VNS was dissolved and replaced by a new consortium called the National Election Pool (NEP). All the networks and other subscribers get from the NEP the same data at the same time. However, each has their own set of experts who analyze the data and draw conclusions (Best and Krueger 2012).

The most recent innovation in polling is measuring public opinion using the Internet. Respondents are recruited by a variety of methods. Most often they are recruited directly over the Internet and are offered an incentive to participate in online polls. The resulting sample is then adjusted for self-selection and weighted based on Census data. Of course, those lacking an Internet connection cannot be included in the sample (19 percent as of February 2013).[19] Another method is to recruit respondents by telephone, give those lacking Internet access the necessary equipment, and provide everyone with an incentive to participate in the vendor's surveys.

One further innovation in polling worth mentioning is the development of a code of standards for those in the field of public opinion. Unlike physicians, lawyers, and morticians, pollsters are not subject to government regulation. On occasion there have been calls by some in Congress for regulation. The first of these came in 1948, with many Democrats charging that the polls were biased in favor of Republicans. Another came in response to using exit polls to call the winner of the presidential election in 1980 before the voting booths had closed on the West Coast. It was argued that many Democrats failed to vote once they learned that President Carter had been defeated. However, virtually all attempts by the government to regulate opinion polls have run afoul of the First Amendment's guarantee of the right of free speech.

In 1986, the American Association for Public Opinion Research (AAPOR) adopted a code of ethics and practices for the profession.[20] Among the major features of this code are full disclosure, confidentiality, and responsibility to those being interviewed. Pollsters must make available full information about who sponsored the survey and give details of relevant methodology, such as how the sample was selected. They must hold as confidential the responses to questions by specific individuals. They must avoid any practice that would harm or mislead a respondent. While the AAPOR has a standards committee, its only power of sanction is the glare of adverse publicity.

1-4 The Modern Public Opinion Poll and Its Political Consequences

Prior to 1940, politicians judged public sentiment mainly from newspapers (Herbst 1993; Kernell 2006). For example, William McKinley kept tabs on "public opinion" by compiling a scrapbook, called *Current Comment*, of newspaper articles from every section of the country (Hilderbrand 1981). Herbert Hoover followed a similar practice. His staff classified newspaper articles and editorials by point of view and by state (Fried 2012, 29). Contemporary political leaders clearly have much better information on the content of public opinion than they did prior to the advent of scientific polling. John Geer (1996) argues that politicians well informed about public opinion use a qualitatively different leadership style than those without reliable opinion information. In particular, he argues certain skills historically associated with leadership are found less frequently in today's political leaders. They include the ability to craft good arguments and a willingness to remain committed to a stand.

According to Geer, before polling, politicians were uncertain if the electorate was on their side, and a premium was placed on the ability to convince both citizens and other politicians of the merits of an argument. Today, this skill is less essential because more certainty exists about the electorate's preferences. For example, staff disputes on issues are often resolved by reference to public opinion rather than nuanced argument. Modern politicians are also less likely to remain committed to issue positions if the polls show them to be electoral losers. William Jennings Bryan ran for president in 1896 on the "free silver" platform. Despite being soundly defeated, he showcased the same issue in his 1900 presidential bid. Bryan remained convinced that public opinion was on his side (Anderson 1981). Geer argues that in the absence of reliable opinion data as a reality check, politicians' estimate of public opinion is driven by their personal views and reinforced by those around them, who often think as they do. On the other hand, Ronald Reagan in the 1960s and early 1970s was a strong proponent of a voluntary social security program. Because polls showed a large proportion of the public disagreed, it is probably no accident that he dropped the issue when he ran for the presidency.[21] Finally, the modern opinion poll has likely forever changed the standard by which political leadership is judged. Every decision is now evaluated in reference to public opinion. How, for example, would history treat Lincoln's Emancipation Proclamation if a Gallup Poll in June 1862 showed 72 percent of Northerners wanted to abolish slavery (Geer 1996)?

Change is not neutral. Innovations benefit some at the expense of others. The modern public opinion poll is no exception. Benjamin Ginsberg (1986) makes the counterintuitive argument that replacement by the modern opinion poll of traditional methods of expressing public opinion has served to "domesticate" public opinion. In other words, public opinion is a less potent force in American politics now than it was prior to scientific polling. Public opinion polls may serve to reassure people that their opinions are being heeded, when in fact they may be ignored by powerful elites who set public policy mainly with regard to their own interests.

"Traditional" methods of expressing public opinion refers to letters to newspapers and public officials, personal contact, elections, advocacy group activity, marches, demonstrations, and riots—to list the more obvious. Such methods are still available, but when these indicators of public opinion differ from those reported in polls, it is universally assumed that polls are more representative. If one conceives of public opinion as an aggregation of equally weighted preferences, that assumption is almost certainly correct. However, polling by simply totaling individual opinions has, according to Ginsberg, changed some important aspects of "public opinion" as expressed by methods commonly employed before the advent of the scientific survey.

For example, public opinion was once largely a group phenomenon. At election time, elected officials would consult closely with the leaders of advocacy groups, such as farmers and organized labor, to be informed of membership opinion. Opinion polls have undermined the ability of group leaders to speak for their membership, as the members can now be polled directly. Any difference between the polls and the characterization of group opinion by leaders is usually resolved in favor of the polls. During the Nixon administration, wage and price controls were strongly opposed by organized labor. However, polls showed Nixon was popular with the rank and file, thus undercutting the ability of union leaders to threaten reprisals at the voting booth.

Where it had once been a behavior (letter writing, marches, etc.), public opinion is now mostly a summation of attitudes. In fact, the citizen is relieved of all initiative whatsoever. Pollsters contact respondents, determine worthwhile questions, analyze the results, and publicize them. If a citizen feels strongly about an issue, one mode of expression not available is to call a survey house and demand to be included in the next opinion poll.

Polls weaken the connection between opinion and intensity. It requires little effort to "strongly agree" with a statement proffered by an interviewer. Converse, Clausen, and Miller (1965) have demonstrated that public opinion as measured in surveys is much less intense than that offered in voluntary modes of popular expression. Polls, in practice, submerge intense opinions with those held by the much larger, more apathetic population. This characteristic of opinion surveys can be employed by elected officials to promote their policy choices. Both Lyndon Johnson and Richard Nixon used evidence from polls to publicly justify their policies in Vietnam as being in step with majority preferences, despite widespread public protests. Ginsberg claims a good argument could be made that if decision makers had accepted the more intense behavioral indicators of sentiment about the Vietnam War, as opposed to the evidence from polls, the Vietnam War would have ended much sooner. However, recent empirical research casts doubt on that assertion. Rottinghaus (2007) demonstrates that as the White House mail turned more "hawkish" on Vietnam, so did the Johnson administration's Vietnam policy, regardless of what the polls were showing.

Finally, modern opinion polls have changed the character of public opinion from an assertion to a response. Before polling, citizens themselves chose the topics on which to express their opinions. Now, as Ginsberg points out, these subjects are chosen mostly by polling technocrats. Most publicly expressed opinion is based less on the concerns of citizens than on the concerns of whomever is paying for the poll. Thus, in 1970, a year of both racial strife and antiwar protest, the Gallup Poll devoted 5 percent of its questions to American policy in Vietnam, devoted less than 1 percent to race relations, and had no questions on student protests. On the other hand, 26 percent of its questions (in a nonpresidential year) concerned the electoral horse race.

Whatever the merit of Ginsberg's arguments, they suffer from the same problem as those of Lippmann, Blumer, and Rogers—a rejection of the normative view that all opinions ought to count equally. According to Sidney Verba, whatever its faults, the modern scientific opinion survey best approximates just what democracy is supposed to produce—an equal voice for all citizens. The sample survey is "rigorously egalitarian" (Verba 1996). Citizens participate equally; their voices are counted equally. However, not everyone agrees with this position. Adam Berinsky (2004) claims some opinion items suffer from "exclusion bias." Those with fewer cognitive resources are most likely to give "don't know" answers on relatively demanding questions such as those concerning social welfare. Were they able to give voice to their concerns, their opinions would be predominantly liberal. A similar point is made by Scott Althaus (2003), who argues that political knowledge is crucial for the expression of rational, self-interested opinions. Of course, political knowledge is very unevenly distributed across the electorate (Delli Carpini and Keeter 1996; Althaus 2003). Finally, some critics such as Martin Gilens (2012) and Larry Bartels (2008) claim that it is the preferences of the most affluent Americans that are mostly enacted into public policy, with the opinions of poor and middle-income Americans having little influence on policy outcomes.

In the beginning of the twenty-first century, there are few who endorse less democratic input into the political system as opposed to more democratic input, whatever might be the imperfections of the latter. Polls may have shortcomings, but as measures of public opinion they are clearly more representative of all opinion than are the traditional measures. In fact, the traditional measures may be even less representative today than they were in the past. In recent years, paid political consultants have become sophisticated at marshaling local interest groups on issues of importance to their clients, raining letters, faxes, e-mails, and phone calls on Congress and the White House, as well as newspapers and talk shows (Chadwick 2005; Baker 2006). It is often difficult to distinguish between these mobilized outbursts of public sentiment and those that are genuinely spontaneous.

Implicit in Ginsberg's analysis is an assumption that modern opinion polling has discouraged the communication of public opinion by other methods. However, all the means available to express public opinion prior to 1936 are still available and are often used effectively. One need only witness the controversies over abortion, same-sex marriage, or the emergence of the Tea Party movement. Explicit in the analysis is a claim that public opinion polls have domesticated public opinion—that it is not as powerful a force in political decision making as it once was. There is, however, no systematic, hard evidence to support this assertion. The simple truth is that poll results are brought forcefully to the attention of government authorities at all levels (Converse 1987, 14). The relationship of public opinion to public policy in the modern era is an empirical question, about which we have much to say in this book.

1-5 Sources of Information on Public Opinion

Since the 1930s, tens of thousands of surveys have been conducted, hundreds of thousands of questions have been asked, and millions of respondents have been interviewed. Much of these data have been housed in several data libraries or archives. In addition, a great deal of public opinion information can be accessed through the Internet. (A list of useful Internet addresses is presented in the section that follows.)

The most comprehensive and up-to-date method for finding particular public opinion items is a computerized database called iPOLL (Public Opinion Location Library), located at the Roper Center in Storrs, Connecticut. The Roper archive contains more than 600,000 items, which can be accessed through the Internet. For some questions, demographic breakdowns are available as well as the actual data. Many colleges have an iPOLL subscription. By simply entering one or more keywords, such as *gun control*, users can obtain question wording, item frequencies, and basic documentation for questions housed at the archive. The survey data are also sometimes available and can be directly downloaded. The Institute for Research in Social Science at the University of North Carolina houses the surveys conducted by Lou Harris and Associates, plus more than 350 statewide-level polls. An excellent multipurpose site for public opinion data and other social data is Data on the Net, maintained by the University of California at San Diego. It serves as a gateway to almost 100 data archives throughout the world. Finally, World Associates for Public Opinion Research is a source for public opinion data across a range of subjects. This site tends to focus on market research, but it also archives political surveys. In addition, there are often short feature stories about polling and research methods.

For academic students of public opinion, including undergraduate and graduate students, the most valuable data archive is the Inter-University Consortium for Political and Social Research (ICPSR) at the University of Michigan. Many colleges and universities are members of the Consortium, while membership in other data archives is less frequent. The Consortium publishes annually a complete catalog of its holdings and distributes a newsletter informing members of new acquisitions. This information as well as the frequencies for some of its data sets can be accessed at its Web site. The Consortium also disseminates the American National Election Studies, the General Social Survey, and the World Values Survey. These are three of the most important nonproprietary academic surveys available for secondary analysis, and we rely on them extensively in this book. Each of these studies comes with a completely documented codebook. Both the codebooks and the data sets are routinely received by universities that are Consortium members. In addition, a number of journals regularly publish opinion data. Each issue of the *Public Opinion Quarterly* has a section called *The Polls* in which survey data on a specific topic are reviewed.

Current Polling Data

The Internet is now an important resource for monitoring polls. The following sites make available the latest public opinion polling data on a wide range of topics—from public reaction to an event recently in the news to the latest reading on presidential popularity or the current poll data on a high-profile election.

www.fivethirtyeight.com: First-rate analysis of polling data by Nate Silver, who expertly combines statistical analysis and popular politics.

www.pollster.com: Thorough site for commentary on polling that is now hosted by the *Huffington Post*. The editors received an excellence award in 2007 from the American Association for Public Opinion Research.

www.imediaethics.org: Critical commentary on contemporary polling by David Moore, an academic and long-time associate of the Gallup Organization.

www.pollingreport.com: A service of the Polling Report, a nonpartisan clearinghouse for public opinion data; provides reports on current opinion on politics, the economy, and popular culture.

www.pollsandvotes.com. A nonpartisan site developed by the academic political scientist Charles Franklin. It mostly covers the link between public opinion polls and elections.

polltracker.talkingpointsmemo.com: A web-based news organization that follows polls in addition to other newsworthy subjects.

www.hsph.harvard.edu/horp: Surveys conducted and collected by the Harvard School of Public Health. Provides public opinion information on health issues and related public policy issues.

www.gallup.com: The site for the Gallup Poll.

www.americanprogress.org: Contains an "experts" site, one of which is public opinion. It contains insightful commentary and analysis on current polls and polling issues by Ruy Teixeira and others.

www.pipa.org: This site reports original polling and discussion on international issues, conducted by the Program on International Policy Attitudes at the University of Maryland.

www.publicagenda.org: A site that presents opinion data and commentary on domestic policy issues.

www.people-press.org: The site for the Pew Research Center for the People and the Press; an independent research group that conducts surveys in some depth about current issues, regularly conducts polls on public attentiveness to news stories, and charts trends in fundamental social and political values.

www.democracycorps.com: Conducts regular polls on current political matters.

www.harrisinteractive.com: Home of the Harris Poll, which does predominantly Internet surveys.

www.ipsos-na.com: Conducts polls for the Reuters news service in the United States and Canada.

Polling Data Archives   Earlier in this chapter, we discussed a number of data libraries. The Web sites for these archives are listed below.

www.icpsr.umich.edu: The site for the Inter-University Consortium for Political and Social Research, home to the American National Election Studies. It archives the General Social Survey and others.

www.norc.uchicago.edu: The site for the National Opinion Research Center (NORC), home to the General Social Survey and other NORC studies.

www.ipoll.com: The site for the Roper Center archive, which houses the Gallup Poll, media polls, and many others. iPOLL contains more than 600,000 questions, which can be accessed by keywords.

www.odum.unc.edu/odum/home2.jsp: The Odum Institute archive, associated with the University of North Carolina, home to the Harris Poll and the National Association of State Polls, which houses more than 350 state-level studies.

http://libraries.ucsd.edu/ssds: Data on the Net, maintained by the University of California at San Diego; also provides links to other social data bases.

http://ucdata.berkeley.edu/data_record.php?recid=3: The archive for the Field Poll, devoted to political and social issues in California.

http://sda.berkeley.edu: Houses the American National Election Studies and the General Social Survey, plus others. It has easy-to-use software that allows for the analysis of these data.

Data Archives for Non-American Surveys Survey research now occurs regularly all over the world. The best of the archives and their Web sites are listed below.

> www.worldvaluessurvey.org: The World Values Survey. The most recent project contains data using many of the same questions in more than fifty counties. Easy-to-use software allows for the analysis of these data.
> www.issp.org: The archive for the International Social Survey.
> http://ec.europa.eu/public_opinion/index_en.htm: This site is for archives for the Eurobarometer and the Central and Eastern Eurobarometer.
> www.mori.com: A British-based opinion research firm and archive. MORI holds mostly British opinion data but also conducts and archives occasional cross-national studies.

Polling Organizations A number of professional polling organizations offer useful and interesting information on survey research.

> www.aapor.org: The site for the American Association for Public Opinion Research, the oldest and most prestigious of the polling organizations; includes a complete index to articles published in the *Public Opinion Quarterly*.
> www.wapor.org: The site for the World Association for Public Opinion Research; often contains useful articles about opinion research.
> www.casro.org: The site for the Council of American Survey Research Organizations, the primary organization for those doing commercial survey research.
> www.ncpp.org: The site for the National Council on Public Polls; contains information on national standards and how to conduct and interpret polls.

1-6 Linkage Models Between Public Opinion and Public Policies

In a democracy, public opinion is supposed to influence the decisions by the elected leaders. But how effective, in practice, is the public at controlling what its government does? This book attempts to answer this important question. The mechanisms of popular control are more complicated than one might think. (For a sampling of contemporary perspectives, see Fearon 1999; Ferejohn 1999; Manin, Przeworski, and Stokes 1999; Erikson, MacKuen, and Stimson 2002; Hutchings 2003; Mansbridge 2003; Stimson 2004.) Here, we sketch five models, drawn from Luttbeg (1968), by which public opinion can get reflected by public policy.

The Rational-Activist Model

This model is the basis for the widely accepted concept of the ideal citizen's role in a democracy. Voting on the basis of issues is at the heart of the rational-activist model. By the standards of this model, individual citizens are expected to be informed politically, involved, rational, and, above all, active. On the basis of an informed and carefully reasoned set of personal preferences and an accurate perception of the various candidates' positions, voters are expected to cast a ballot for those candidates who best reflect their issue preferences. In this way, the victorious candidates in elections will be the ones who best represent constituency policy views.

This model places a burden on citizens, who are expected to hold informed and enlightened views about the policy positions of candidates and vote accordingly. As we have noted, politics does not play a salient role in the lives of most Americans. Many people rarely or never vote. Those who do are often inattentive to policy issues, particularly in low-salience elections.

Certainly, issue voting allows for some influence of public opinion on government policy. But in our search for methods by which political leaders can be held accountable, we must look beyond the rational-activist model.

The Political Parties Model

The political parties model greatly reduces the political demands placed on the citizen. The model depends on the desire of political parties to win elections as a mechanism for achieving popular control. According to the model, a party states its positions on the issues of the day in its platform. Because of their interest in winning elections, parties can be counted on to take stands that appeal to large segments of the electorate. Voters then select among platforms, giving support to the candidate of the party whose platform most conforms to their personal preference. Instead of facing multiple decisions for the numerous offices up for election, voters need only make a single decision among the available choice of parties.

A number of questions are raised by a consideration of this model. For example, to what extent do parties take distinct positions, and to what extent do voters recognize them? Does a party's electoral fortunes reflect the degree of public support for its policies, or is a party's vote largely independent of the policies it advocates?

The Interest Groups Model

In the preceding models, we emphasized the central importance of communication between elected officials and their constituents. For representatives to respond to public demands, they need to know what these demands are. For the public to achieve accountability from representatives, they need to know what the representatives have done and what alternatives were available. Interest groups can perform this function. They can serve as a link between people and their representatives.

Numerous organized groups in society claim to speak for various segments of the electorate—the Sierra Club, the National Organization for Women, and the National Rifle Association, to mention just three. At one extreme, these groups could be so inclusive of individuals in society and could so accurately represent their members' opinions that representatives could achieve accountability merely by recording the choice of each group, weighing them by the number of voters they represent, and voting with the largest group. This would be in accord with what might be called the interest groups model of popular control.

Under ideal circumstances, interest groups might succeed in communicating public opinion to officials between elections and with greater clarity than can be communicated through election outcomes. Interest groups, like political parties, could simplify the choices for the individual voter, making it possible for an electorate that is largely disinterested in politics to nevertheless achieve accountability.

Several questions arise out of the interest groups model. Does group opinion, the somehow combined opinions of all those persons in all the relevant interest groups, coincide with public opinion? Or, do the opinions carried to government by interest groups reflect only the opinions of the wealthy or the business sector of society? Who among everyday citizens belongs to interest groups? Are some segments of society overrepresented and others mostly uninvolved in any type of group activity?

The Delegate Model

When voters are doing their job (via the rational-activist model), elections are decided by policy issues. To win elections under such circumstances, politicians must cater to the views of their prospective voters, and to stay elected, elected officials must anticipate voter preferences in advance of the next election. When politicians take voter preferences seriously in this way, acting as the voters' agent, we say they are behaving as the voters' delegates. This is the delegate model at work.[22] By this model, representation of public opinion can be enhanced simply because elected leaders believe they will be voted out of office if they do not attend to voter opinion—whether or not the voters would actually do so.

Several questions are raised by the delegate model: Can elected officials accurately learn public opinion, or do they receive a distorted view? To what extent do elected officials actually heed public opinion as they perceive it? What do elected leaders view as the consequences of ignoring public opinion? Finally, how often do elected officials see their role as representing constituency preferences as opposed to their (possibly conflicting) personal views of the constituency's best interests?

The Sharing Model

Because as a society we do not designate leaders early in life and hold them as a class apart from then on, it is unlikely that the personal opinions held by elected officials on the issues of the day differ diametrically from those held by the rest of the electorate. This possibility is the final model of political linkage: the sharing model. This model simply states that because many attitudes are broadly held throughout the public, elected leaders cannot help but satisfy public opinion to some degree, even if the public is totally apathetic. Unilateral disarmament, total government takeover of the economy, a termination of public education, a complete disregard for the preservation of the environment—all are examples of actions so contrary to broadly held American attitudes that they would be rejected by any set of government leaders. Even on issues that provoke substantial disagreement, the distribution of opinion among political leaders may be similar to that among the public. If so, even when leaders act according to personal preference and are ignored by disinterested citizens, their actions would often correspond to citizen preferences. For this model, we need to consider how broadly opinions on national issues are shared and how similar the views of elected officials are to those of the public at large.

1-7 Plan of This Book

We have by necessity ordered facts into chapters that strike us as convenient. Chapter 2 discusses the science of assessing public opinion. Chapter 3 is concerned with the psychology of opinion-holding and focuses on the role of political ideology and party identification. Chapter 4 chronicles trends in public opinion over time. Chapter 5 discusses the formation of political attitudes. Chapter 6 evaluates data on broad public acceptance of certain attitudes that may be necessary for a stable democratic government. Chapter 7 delves into the group basis of public opinion. Chapter 8 analyzes the effect of the media on those attitudes. Chapter 9 is an analysis of public opinion and elections. Chapter 10 views the reverse aspect of political linkage—how elected officials respond to the views of their constituents. Chapter 11 assesses the linkage models and draws conclusions about public opinion in the United States based on the data presented throughout this book.

Critical Thinking Questions

1. Some critics claim that public opinion surveys allow politicians to become overly dependent on polls for decision making. Do you think the modern public opinion poll has improved the quality of decision making by elected officials?
2. The authors propose five mechanisms by which public opinion can influence government decisions. Do you think this list is complete, or would you add additional mechanisms? Which of these do you think is most crucial for democratic government?
3. Some scholars like Benjamin Ginsberg say that the modern public opinion poll has discouraged other outlets for expressing public opinion, such as petitions and demonstrations. Do you do think the modern public opinion poll has "domesticated" public opinion, as Ginsberg claims?

Endnotes

1. The term *pollster* was coined by political scientist Lindsay Rogers in his book *The Pollsters: Public Opinion, Politics, and Democratic Leadership* (1949) to evoke in the minds of readers the word *huckster* (Hitchens 1992, 46).
2. Or, as Winston Churchill put it, "Nothing is more dangerous than to live in the temperamental atmosphere of a Gallup Poll, always feeling one's pulse and taking one's temperature. . . . There is only one duty, only one safe course, and that is to try to be right and not to fear to do or waver in what you believe to be right" (quoted in Bogart 1972, 47).
3. For a recent review of the volatility of public opinion on foreign policy, see Drezner (2008).
4. The eighteenth-century French mathematician Marquis de Condorcet, using jury decisions as an example, was able to demonstrate mathematically a greater probability that the majority would come to the right decision than the probability the minority would come to the right decision. For a popular rendition of this idea, see Surowiecki (2004).
5. It also includes the functional equivalent of verbal expressions, such as filling out a written questionnaire.
6. One ambiguity inherent in this conceptualization is that some people may never express orally or in writing some of their opinions. We could possibly conceptualize such opinions as internal, but that has the unhappy consequence of muddying the distinction between attitudes and opinions. Our simple solution for unexpressed opinions is to assert

that, if expressed, they would have the same characteristics and qualities of expressed opinion.

7. It should be noted that our distinction between opinions and beliefs is not common to all fields. In a court of law, for example, an expert witness is frequently asked to give an "expert opinion" on a matter of fact. In everyday conversation, it is quite frequent that someone asserts, "It is my opinion that . . . ," followed by some assertion of factual truth.

8. The name apparently comes from a practice in rural areas of throwing straw into the air to see which way the wind is blowing. Presumably, a "straw poll" is a method for determining the direction of the political winds. Pioneer pollster Claude Robinson (1932, 6) defined a *straw poll* as "an unofficial canvass of an electorate to determine the division of popular sentiment on public issues or on candidates for public office." Today, the term generally refers to any assessment of public opinion based on nonscientific sampling methods.

9. The sample consisted of 532 respondents from Wilmington, Delaware, selected "without discrimination of parties" (Gallup and Rae 1940, 35).

10. Straw polls used three methods to gather data. One was the ballot-in-the-paper method, in which the reader filled out the ballot, cut it out of the paper, and mailed it to the sponsoring organization. The second was the personal canvass, in which solicitors took ballots to crowded locations such as theaters, hotels, and trolleys and got willing citizens to complete them. Sometimes ballots were simply left in a crowded area in the morning, and those completed were retrieved in the evening. The third method was to send ballots by mail to a specified list of people and ask that they send them back by return mail.

11. The *Chicago Record* featured daily straw-poll updates on its front page from September 1896 through Election Day. It was typical for newspapers and magazines to publish regular updates of their straw-poll findings.

12. The sample sizes for the straw polls were so large that they typically made projections on a state-by-state basis.

13. Straw polls were not the only method used to handicap the "horse race" of presidential campaigns in the prepoll era. One source for many years was a Wall Street betting market on the election outcome. Market prices on the candidates' chances of winning were followed much the same that poll numbers are followed today. Early in the twentieth century, these markets predicted presidential vote outcomes with roughly the accuracy of that polls do in the modern era. However, most elections during this period were one-sided. In the one close race (1916), the election markets predicted the wrong winner. See Rohde and Strumpf (2004).

14. Gallup marketed to newspapers a column, "America Speaks," from 1935 to 1971 which was based on his polls.

15. Although early on, Gallup did do split-ballot question-wording experiments. These were not, however, publicly released.

16. Now a division of the Institute for Social Research.

17. Over the years, these University of Michigan–based surveys have undergone a number of name changes. In the early years, they were dubbed the SRC surveys, after the Survey Research Center. Then they became the CPS surveys, named after the Center for Political Studies, a division of the Institute for Social Research. Currently, they are referred to as the American National Election Studies.

18. However, only the CBS News/*New York Times* has its own in-house polling operation. ABC, NBC, and CNN contract with outside commercial polling houses for their opinion surveys.

19. Survey by Pew Internet and American Life Project and Princeton Survey Research Associates International, January–February 2013.

20. A copy of the code of ethics can be obtained from the AAPOR Web site at www.aapor .org.

21. Early in his second term, George W. Bush revised the idea of privatizing social security. He engaged in a highly publicized sixty stops in sixty days national campaign. However, the more he campaigned, the more the public came to disapprove of the proposal to privatize social security. By the summer of 2005, he dropped the idea for lack of public support (Jacobson 2007).

22. In first through sixth edition, we labeled this model *the role-playing model*, following Luttbeg's original formulation. For the politician, an alternative to the delegate role is the role of the trustee who, rather than following constituency preferences, acts according to the politician's conception of the constituents' best interests. See Wahlke et al. (1962) for various formulations of legislator roles.

CHAPTER 2

Polling: The Scientific Assessment of Public Opinion

LEARNING OBJECTIVES

- Identify ways that polls affect politicians
- Explain probability sampling, sampling error, and confidence level
- Identify potential biases in the wording of public opinion questions
- Explain how preelection polls are conducted and describe the accuracy of those polls

---

The use of scientific polling to gauge and analyze public opinion and elections has now been part of the political landscape for over seventy years. And it continues to grow. This growth is evident in the media's obsession with campaigns as horse races, where journalists' interest lies more in forecasting the outcome than the substance of the campaign. During the presidential election season, the news media is saturated with polling reports. In recent presidential campaigns, one finds national polls being reported at a rate of greater than one per day (Moore 2013), with even more state polls reported on a daily basis (Wlezien and Erikson 2002; Cohen 2008).[1] Perhaps as many as two-thirds of the election stories that are reported on the network news in recent years are supported by polling data (Hess 2000). The news media's preoccupation with the polls appears to agree with public demand. In 2012, 20 percent of all the traffic to the *New York Times* Internet site went to Nate Silver's blog on election polling (Owen 2013).

2-1 The Value of Polls

Of course, polling is not confined to election polls and the prediction of the next election outcome. As discussed in Chapter 1, academic polls advance our knowledge of public opinion. Commercial pollsters (e.g., Gallup) satisfy the public's (and private clients') curiosity regarding trends in public opinion. Although not as highly publicized as the pollsters' election forecasts, polls routinely ascertain public preferences on a variety of policy issues and monitor the public pulse regarding such indicators as party identification, ideological identification, and the approval rating of the current president. This is the stuff of public opinion analysis and the subject of subsequent chapters.

Politicians and the Polls

Politicians have a particularly strong interest in the polls, as their professional careers may depend on reading public opinion accurately. Like the rest of us, politicians have access to commercial opinion polls such as the Gallup Poll. But the politicians often seek further intelligence regarding public opinion by commissioning their own polls. The first president to poll the public was Franklin Roosevelt, who did so in the late 1930s. While his next two successors, Truman and Eisenhower, had little use for private polling, presidential polling picked up in earnest with John Kennedy. Since then, virtually every major presidential decision has been made with the benefit of private polls. Presidents seek updates of public attitudes toward current policies, public reactions to future policy options, and especially information on their own standing with the voters (Jacobs and Shapiro 2000; Fried 2012).

Politicians below the presidential level also do their own polling, as do the major political parties. Senate and House members spend about 3 percent of their sizable campaign war chests on polling their states or districts (Fritz and Morris 1992). Although the general purpose of this polling is to monitor their electoral standing against current or future opponents, private constituency polls can also register signals regarding shifts in constituency concerns.

A candidate's poor showing in preelection polls makes fund-raising difficult and dampens volunteer enthusiasm. As observed by Mike Murphy and Mark Mellman (2007), two leading political consultants (one a Republican and the other a Democrat), "Early national polling is used to declare winners and losers. Those declarations affect the flow of money and [media] coverage." Good poll numbers result in more media attention (Traugott and Lavrakas 2008). A strong showing in the polls can legitimize a candidate, ensuring that he or she is taken seriously, and being taken seriously is necessary to raise money.

Polls create expectations about who is the likely election winner. In presidential primaries with a number of more or less unknown candidates, expectations about who will win in the preelection polls help to frame the postelection spin. Sometimes losers manufacture "wins" by beating expectations even when they fail to win the most votes. A classic example occurred in the New Hampshire Democratic primary of 1992, when Bill Clinton came in second (to Paul Tsongas) and hailed himself as the "comeback kid." In the 2004 election, this pattern was repeated when John Edwards received a bonanza of favorable press coverage when he beat expectations in the Wisconsin primary, even though he lost to John Kerry by 6 percent of the vote (Ruttenberg 2005). Thomas Patterson (2002, 2005) makes a compelling argument that the standing in the polls of a presidential candidate determines the way the candidate's personal qualities are described by the media. When poll numbers are good, news stories are positive; when poll numbers are bad, stories turn negative (see also Farnsworth and Lichter 2011). For example, in an analysis of *Newsweek*'s reporting of the 1988 presidential campaign, Patterson demonstrates that when polls showed Michael Dukakis doing well in the 1988 presidential race, he was described as "relentless in his attack" and "a credible candidate." As he later dropped in the polls, *Newsweek* described him as "reluctant to attack" and "trying to present himself as a credible candidate." Interestingly, the change in descriptors coincided quite closely with the point he fell behind George H.W. Bush in the polls (Patterson 1989, 104–6). Finally, standing in the polls can determine whether or not a candidate is invited to participate in the presidential debates. For example, while Ross Perot's poll numbers justified his appearance in the 1992 debates, his poll support was deemed insufficient for his inclusion in the 1996 presidential debates.

Presidential popularity, now gauged virtually daily, is the public opinion indicator watched with perhaps the most interest by members of Congress, others in the political community, and the media. Arguably, one important aspect of presidential power, including influence over Congress, is the chief executive's personal standing with the public (Canes-Wrone and de Marchi 2002; Bond, Fleisher, and Wood 2003; Canes-Wrone and Shotts 2004; Lebo and O'Green 2011). While it is debatable how much a president can leverage popular approval into public support for his favored projects, there is little doubt that members of Congress and Washington insiders believe that a popular president holds the power to persuade public opinion. It was the high job approval enjoyed by President Clinton (about 70 percent) that in the opinion of many (including Clinton) saved his presidency after he was impeached by the House of Representatives.[2] President George W. Bush's surge in popularity following 9/11 smoothed the passage of the Patriot Act and other items from his conservative agenda through the Congress.

The Public Looks at the Polls

More and more people say they are paying attention to the polls. In 1944, only 19 percent of the public said they regularly or occasionally followed poll results; by 1985, it was 41 percent, and in 2000, the figure had risen to 65 percent. In 2008, 89 percent said they had read or heard about the latest polls in the presidential election contest.[3] Yet few citizens have even a rudimentary understanding of how a public opinion poll works. In September 2005, the Gallup organization asked a national sample whether interviews with 1,500 or 2,000 people (typical sample sizes for national polls) "can accurately reflect the views of the nation's population" or whether "it's not possible with so few people." Only 30 percent said a sample of that size could yield accurate results, 68 percent said it was not possible, and the remaining 2 percent had no opinion. While the public may not understand the technicalities of polling, a sizable majority nevertheless believes polls are important guides for public officials (Traugott and Kang 2000). In 2011, 68 percent said the nation would be better off if political leaders followed the views expressed in public opinion polls more closely.[4]

However, in recent years polling methodology has drawn far more than the usual public attention, thanks to the Internet. Bloggers from both the political left and right complain about alleged biases in favor of one candidate or another. Perhaps that is the reason why confidence in the polling community has shown a recent decline. In 1998, 55 percent of the public said they "generally trust [pollsters] to tell them the truth." By 2006, trust in pollsters had dropped to 34 percent, about the same level (at the time) as trust in Congress (Gershenson, Glaser, and Smith 2011). On the positive side, access to the Internet has allowed interested members of the public to learn more about the ins and outs of polling methodology than ever before.[5]

2-2 Sampling

Public opinion polls are based on samples. When the Gallup Poll reports that 50 percent of adult Americans approve of the way the president is handling his job, it is obvious that the Gallup organization has not gone out and interviewed 225 million American adults. Instead, it has taken a sample. The reasons for sampling are fairly straightforward. First, to interview everyone would be prohibitively expensive. The Census for 2010 is estimated to cost $11.8 billion. Second, to interview the entire population would take a very long time. Months might pass between the first and last interviews. Public opinion might, in that period, undergo real change.

Sampling provides a practical alternative to interviewing the whole population—be it national, state, or local. Furthermore, when done correctly, sampling can provide accurate estimates of the political opinions of a larger population. The theory of sampling is a branch of the mathematics of probability, and the error involved in going from the sample to the population can be known with precision. However, as the polling environment changes, many surveys of public opinion are challenged by the demanding requirements of sampling theory.

The history of scientific sampling can be divided into three eras (Goidel 2011). In the first era, between 1935 and 1974, almost all surveys were done in person, usually at the home of the respondent. Telephone penetration was not sufficiently widespread to allow for the selection of representative telephone samples. In 1936, 33 percent of the population had landline telephones, by 1946 it raised to 50 percent, and by 1974 it was 95 percent.[6]

In the second era, beginning around 1974, the near universal penetration of landline telephones plus the development of statistical methods to select a representative sample of telephone numbers, along with much lower cost, led to a dramatic increase in telephone surveys. For the media, this method mostly supplanted in-person surveys, although government agencies and major academic survey units continued to use them.

The third era began around the onset of the twenty-first century with the rise of Internet surveys. One benefit of Internet surveys is the increase in penetration. According to the U.S. Census, in 2012, 80 percent of Americans had Internet access.[7] With the parallel rise in cell phone–only households, telephone surveys became more expensive and response rates plummeted. Most reputable survey firms now use a mix of landline and cell phone numbers. But with the development of sophisticated statistical adjustment routines, proponents of Internet surveys began to proclaim them as differing little in accuracy from other survey modes—and again often much less expensive.

Sampling Theory

The *population* is that unit about which we want information. In most political surveys, the population is one of the following: (1) those aged eighteen and older, (2) registered voters, or (3) those who will (or do) vote in the next election. These are three quite different groups. It is important that the population be clearly specified. When one sees a poll addressing abortion, presidential popularity, or voter intent in an upcoming election, those reporting the poll should provide a clear description of the population about which they speak. The *sample* is that part of the population selected for analysis. Usually, the sample is considerably smaller than the population. National telephone surveys conducted by reputable firms employ samples of 1,000 to 1,500 respondents, although smaller samples are sometimes used in state and local contests. But as samples get smaller, the probability of error increases. Sample size should always be reported along with the results of a survey. If that information is missing, the alleged findings should be treated with a great deal of caution.

When samples accurately mirror the population, they are said to be *representative*. The term *randomness* refers to the only method by which a representative sample can be scientifically drawn. In a simple random sample, each unit of the population has exactly the same chance of being drawn as any other unit. If the population is American attorneys, each attorney is required to have exactly the same probability of being selected in order for the sample to be random. Attorneys in big cities could not have a greater likelihood of getting into the sample than those from rural areas. This situation obviously requires a detailed knowledge of the population. In the case of attorneys, one could get a list from the American Bar Association and then sample from that list. But suppose the population was unemployed adults. To specify the population in a fashion to be able to draw a random sample would be difficult. As a consequence, obtaining a representative sample of the unemployed is not easy.

A *probability sample* is a variant of the principle of random sampling. Instead of each unit having exactly the same probability of being drawn, some units are more likely to be drawn than would others—but this is a known probability. For example, if one were sampling voter precincts in a state, it is of consequence that some precincts contain more people than do others. To make the sample of people in those precincts representative, the larger precincts must have a greater likelihood of being selected than smaller ones.

At this point, we need to introduce the concepts of *confidence level* and *sampling error*. A sample rarely hits the true population value right on the nose. The confidence level tells us the probability that the population value will fall within a specified range. The sampling error specifies that range. A commonly used confidence level is 95 percent (it is sometimes higher, but almost never lower). For a sample of 600, the sampling error is 4 percent. What all this means is that if we took 100 samples from our population, and each of these samples consisted of 600 marbles randomly drawn, then 95 out of 100 times we would be plus or minus 4 percent of the true population value. Our sample came up 65 percent red. While this figure may not be exactly correct, we at least know that 95 out of 100 times (our 95 percent confidence level) we are going to be within four points—one way or the other—of the true proportion of red marbles in the barrel. This much can be proved mathematically.

Let us turn to a political example. The Gallup Poll reported that President Barack Obama's approval rating after his first 100 days in office was 69 percent (*Washington Post/ABC News Poll*, April 26, 2009). Since the sample size in this survey was 1,072, we know that if the poll were repeated 100 times, 95 of the 100 repetitions (the 95 percent confidence level) would produce results that are plus or minus 3 percent (the sampling error) of what we would find if we interviewed all American adults.[8] Thus, Obama's popularity on or about April 29, 2009, could have been as high as 72 percent or as low as 66 percent. The best estimate (according to the central limit theorem) is 69 percent. Sampling error decreases as we move away from a 50/50 split, and it increases as the population has more heterogeneous political attitudes. But by far the most important factor is the size of the sample.

The importance of sample size for sampling accuracy can be easily demonstrated by flipping a coin. We know that, in theory, if a coin is flipped honestly, a large number of times it should come up about equal proportions of heads and tails. Suppose we flipped a coin ten times. Given a large number of repetitions of ten flips, we might frequently get seven heads, eight tails, and so on. But if instead of flipping the coin ten times, we flipped it 100 times, our large number of repetitions would only occasionally yield 70 heads or 80 tails, and if we flipped it 1,000 times, our repetitions would tend to cluster around 500 heads and 500 tails, with 700 heads or 800 tails being rare events indeed. The larger the size of the sample (i.e., the number of times the coin is flipped), the closer we will come to the theoretical expectation of one-half heads and one-half tails.

Unlike the size of the sample, the size of the population is of little consequence for the accuracy of the survey.[9] That is, it does not make much difference if we are surveying the city of Houston or the entire United States. With a sample size of 600, the sampling error would be identical for both the city and the nation—all other things being equal. Table 2.1 presents the sampling errors associated with specific sample sizes.

Using a large barrel of marbles and a table of random numbers, we drew a "perfect" sample—that is, the sampling method fit perfectly with the mathematics of sampling theory. When we sample humans, we cannot draw a perfect sample.

TABLE 2.1	Sampling Error and Sample Size Employing Simple Random Sampling*	
Sample Size	**Sampling Error (plus or minus)***
2,430	2.0
1,536	2.5
1,067	3.0
784	3.5
600	4.0
474	4.5
384	5.0
267	6.0
196	7.0
150	8.0

* This computation is based on the assumptions of a simple random sampling with a dichotomous opinion that splits 50/50 and a 95 percent confidence level.

Source: Compiled by the authors.

Although a marble cannot refuse to tell us if it is red or green, a person may refuse to be interviewed. Sampling theory does not allow for refusals. Consequently, surveys of public opinion only approximate the underlying theory of sampling.

One way to compensate for the workings of chance in probability surveys and for survey nonresponse is through poststratification weighting. We know from the Census the distribution of key demographic factors among the American population. If the sample does not match the Census, it can be weighted to bring it into line. For example, we know 12 percent of the American population is African-American. If a sample of 1,000 contained just 8 percent African-Americans, it can be weighted to bring the total up to 12 percent. If this were the only weighting consideration, we would multiply African-Americans by 1.50 and everyone else by .957. This would raise the percent of African-Americans in the sample to 12 percent but still keep the sample size at 1,000. The demographics normally used for weighting include age, gender, education, race/ethnicity, and homeownership, although the choice of weight factors varies among survey professionals. Weighting is an effective, but still imperfect, solution for adjusting samples that depart from known demographics. Those who refuse to be interviewed may be different from those who consent, and weighting cannot correct for this difference.[10]

Bad Sampling: Two Historical Examples

Historically, there are many instances in which sampling theory was ignored or those conducting the polls were ignorant. If the poll simply concerns political opinions (favor/oppose abortion, approve/disapprove of tax reform, favor/oppose the registration of handguns, etc.), there is no reality test. The survey may have been done badly and be considerably off the mark, but how would one know?[11] On the other hand, pre–Election Day surveys have a reality test: Election Day. In these surveys, sampling mistakes have, in several dramatic cases, cast opinion pollsters in a highly unfavorable light.

To see how not to sample, it is worth reviewing two classic polling mistakes from the past. One, discussed in Chapter 1, was the *Literary Digest* fiasco of 1936. The other was when the seemingly scientific polls all failed in the presidential election of 1948.

The Literary Digest, 1936　Chapter 1 discussed the prescientific straw polls that were used to gauge candidate fortunes prior to 1936. The best known of the commercial publications conducting straw polls was the *Literary Digest*. The *Digest* accurately forecast the winner (if not the exact percentage points) of each presidential election between 1920 and 1932. In 1936, as in previous years, it sent out some 10 million postcard ballots "drawn from every telephone book in the United States, from the rosters of clubs and associations, from city directories, lists of registered voters, [and] classified mail order and occupational data" (*Literary Digest*, August 1936, 3). About 2.2 million returned their postal ballots. The result was 1,293,699 (57 percent) for Republican Alf Landon and 972,867 (43 percent) for President Franklin Roosevelt. On Election Day, Roosevelt not only won but also won by a landslide, receiving 62.5 percent of the vote and carrying every state except Maine and Vermont. The *Literary Digest* was not only wrong; it was also wrong by 19.5 percent. On November 14, 1936, the *Literary Digest* published the following commentary:

What Went Wrong with the Polls?

None of Straw Votes Got Exactly the Right Answer—Why?

In 1920, 1924, 1928 and 1932, the *Literary Digest* Polls were right. Not only right in the sense they showed the winner; they forecast the actual popular vote and with such a small percentage of error (less than 1 percent in 1932) that newspapers and individuals everywhere heaped such phrases as "uncannily accurate" and "amazingly right" upon us. . . . Well this year we used precisely the same method that had scored four bull's eyes in four previous tries. And we were far from correct. Why? We ask that question in all sincerity, because *we want to know*.

Why *did* the poll fare so badly? One reason that can be discounted is sample size. The *Literary Digest* claims to have polled 10 million people (and received 2.2 million responses). Thus, a large sample is no guarantee for accuracy. Rather, their sampling procedure had four fundamental defects. First, the sample was drawn in a biased fashion. The *Digest* clearly did not use random selection or anything approaching it. Even though questionnaires were sent out to 10 million people, a large part of the sample was drawn from telephone directories and lists of automobile owners—during the Depression, a decidedly upper-middle-class group, predominantly Republican in its political sentiments. In other words, the *Digest* did not correctly specify the population. A second factor contributing to the *Digest*'s mistake was time. The questionnaires were sent out in early September, making impossible the detection of any late trend favoring one candidate or the other. Third, 1936 marked the emergence of the New Deal Coalition. The *Digest* had picked the winner correctly since 1920 using the same methods as in 1936, but in 1936 voting became polarized along class lines. The working class and the poor voted overwhelmingly Democratic, while the more affluent classes voted predominantly Republican. Since the *Digest*'s sample was heavily biased in the direction of the more affluent, it is not surprising that their sample tended to favor the Republican, Alf Landon.

Finally, there was the problem of self-selection. The *Literary Digest* sent out its questionnaires by mail. Of the 10 million they mailed, only a little over 2 million were returned—about 22 percent. Those people who self-select to respond to mail surveys are often quite different in their political outlook from those who do not respond. They tend to be better educated, to have higher incomes, and to feel more strongly about the topics dealt with in the questionnaire (Dillman 2008). So even if the sample of 10 million had been drawn in an unbiased fashion, the poll probably still would have been in error due to the self-selection factor (Squire 1988). A fundamental principle of survey sampling is that one cannot allow the respondents to select themselves into the sample.

Despite the failure of the *Literary Digest*, several public opinion analysts did pick Franklin Roosevelt as the winner. Among them was George Gallup, who built his reputation on a correct forecast in 1936. In terms of percentage, Gallup did not get particularly close. He missed by almost 7 percent. But he got the winner right, and that is what most people remember.

"Dewey Defeats Truman": The 1948 Polling Debacle   Following Gallup's success at predicting the 1936 election, "scientific" polling surged in popularity and became perceived within the political class as almost infallible. Gallup and other pollsters predicted the winners of the presidential elections of 1940 and 1944. Then, in 1948 the pollsters all predicted that the Republican presidential candidate, Tom Dewey, would defeat Truman. The pollsters were so confident of Dewey's victory that they did not even poll during the last few weeks of the campaign, seeing it as a waste of time. Virtually all politically knowledgeable observers saw the outcome as certain. Famously, Dewey began to name his cabinet.

The 1948 presidential election jarred the pollsters from their complacency. President Truman defeated Dewey in an upset. Gallup's prediction of Truman's vote was off by 5 percentage points. While this error was actually smaller than that in 1936, the crucial fact was that Gallup got the winner wrong.[12]

Why were Gallup and the other pollsters wrong in 1948? The technique used by Gallup in 1936 and up until the Dewey–Truman disaster is called *quota sampling*. This technique employs the Census to determine the percentage of certain relevant groups in the population. Importantly, quota sampling is not scientific sampling. Respondents are not randomly chosen. For quota sampling, the pollster determines, for example, what percentage of the likely voters are male, Catholic, white, and college educated. Within these groups, interviewers are then assigned quotas. They must interview a certain percentage of women, a certain percentage with less than high school education, a certain percentage of blacks, and so on. But there are few, if any, constraints as to which individuals in these groups are to be interviewed.

The principal problem with quota sampling is a variation on the problem of self-selection. The interviewer has too much opportunity to determine who is selected for the sample. An interviewer who must, for instance, get a specified number of females and a specified number of blacks may avoid certain areas of town or may get the entire quota from a single block. Experience with quota samples demonstrates that they systematically tend to underrepresent the poor, the less educated, and racial minorities.

Research on Gallup's misprediction in 1948 reveals he had too many middle- and high-income voters. One irony in Gallup's misprediction is that two years before the *Literary Digest* fiasco, a Polish statistician named Jerzy Neyman (1934) published a landmark article demonstrating the superiority of random sampling to quota samples in survey work. So powerful was his mathematical demonstration that quota samples became an object of ridicule in scientific circles. During World War II, virtually all the voluminous government survey work was based on some variant of random sampling. The problems with quota samples had been known for some time. However, for reasons of cost, Gallup did not think he could abandon the quota method. After the 1948 election, he changed his mind, or his mind was changed for him. A blue ribbon panel of statistical experts very publically criticized the quota samples used by Gallup and other commercial pollsters (notably Archibald Crossley and Elmo Roper) as being scientifically indefensible (Frankel and Frankel 1987; Fried 2012).

Sampling Methods for In-Person Surveys

From the 1930s into the 1980s, the predominant survey methodology was to interview respondents in person, in their own homes. Earlier we described simple random sampling (SRS) to illustrate the principles involved in drawing a scientific sample. However, in-person surveys rarely employ SRS. There is no master list of all Americans who could be sampled. Even if there were, the persons selected would be widely scattered throughout the country, making in-person interviews prohibitively expensive. For example, an interviewer might have to travel to Kerrville, Texas, just to talk to one respondent. Rather, polls where respondents are personally inter-viewed use *multistage cluster samples*.

The first step in drawing a multistage cluster sample of the American elector-ate is to divide the country into four geographic regions. Within each region, a set of counties and standard metropolitan statistical areas (SMSAs) is randomly se-lected. To ensure a representative selection of the national population, each county or SMSA is given a chance to be selected proportional to its population (proba-bility sampling). National surveys typically include about eighty primary sampling units (PSUs). Once selected, the PSUs are often used several years before they are replaced. The reason is economic: Compact geographic areas save time and money. Interviewers are expensive to train, but once trained they can be used over and over.

About twenty respondents are chosen within each PSU. First, four or five city blocks (or their rural equivalents) are randomly selected. Then, four or five house-holds are sampled within each block. It is at the household level that the continued use of probability methods becomes most difficult. Ideally, the interviewer obtains a list of all persons living in the household and samples randomly from the list. And indeed, some academic polls (e.g., the General Social Survey [GSS] and the American National Election Studies [ANES]) attempt to meet this ideal. Many sur-vey organizations, however, abandon probability methods at the block level and rely on some type of systematic method for respondent selection. The problem is that specific individuals are hard to locate. Interviewers are given a randomly drawn starting point and then instructed to stop at every *n*th household. The interviewer first asks to speak to the youngest man of voting age; if no man is at home, the interviewer asks to speak to the youngest woman. If both refuse, or if no one is at home, the interviewer goes to the next adjacent dwelling. Each interviewer has a male/female quota and an age quota, but this is not a quota sample because the in-terviewer cannot choose who gets into the sample.

Multistage cluster samples work well and are an efficient compromise, given the expense involved in a simple random sample approach. The drawback is that cluster samples have a greater sampling error than SRS, as would be expected be-cause the respondents are clustered into 75 to 100 small geographic areas. A simple random sample of 1,000 has a 3 percent sampling error. Gallup reports that its in-person national samples (multistage cluster samples) of 1,500 have a 4 percent sampling error.

Telephone Surveys

Today, most surveys are conducted by telephone (or over the Internet, see later) rather than in person. The principal advantages are the speed with which telephone (and Internet) surveys can be completed and their low costs. They also free one from having to use clusters, as the physical location of a respondent is irrelevant in tele-phone and Internet surveys. However, there are disadvantages as well.

Nationwide, as many as a third of all telephone numbers may be unlisted. Those most likely to have unlisted numbers are younger, lower income, renters, and non-white households with children. A solution to this problem is random digit dialing (RDD). A ten-digit telephone number is composed of an area code (the first three numbers), an exchange (the next three), a cluster (the next two), and the two final digits. Since the geographic assignment of area codes, exchanges, and clusters is publicly available, one can define and sample a national population. The following is an example:

713-496-78 __ __

The first eight digits are randomly sampled from the population of 72,000 digital residential codes. Then the last two digits are chosen by a computer program that generates random digits. These methods bring persons with unlisted numbers into the sample.[13] On the negative side, some calls are made to nonworking numbers. But the sample of households is representative. Once the household is selected, it is then necessary to sample residents within it. Sophisticated methods to ensure random selection have been developed by statisticians, but they require an enumeration of all household members by age and sex—information many respondents are unwilling to provide over the telephone. One simple alternative is the last birthday method. Interviewers ask to speak to the person in the household who had the last—that is, the most recent—birthday. Another technique is to ask to speak to the youngest male, and if not at home, to the youngest female. Both these techniques give a good approximation of random sampling within the household (Daniel 2012). The latter has the advantage of always having an eligible respondent at home (the person with the last birthday may not be at home).

The Cell Phone Challenge   Telephone surveys only interview people with telephones. Until recently, almost all households had landline telephones. This is not so today. Many potential survey respondents rely solely on cell phones, and the number is growing. According to the National Health Interview Survey (a government-funded in-person survey), more than one out of three households (34 percent) had only wireless telephones in 2012. Those adults most likely to rely only on cell phones are between eighteen and twenty-four years old, renters, attending school, and living with unrelated roommates (Blumberg and Luke 2012).

Cell phone–only households are now so prevalent that most survey organizations use "dual frame" samples based on a mix of cell phone–only households and households with a landline (the occupants of which may also have cell phones).[14] The percent cell phone in any sample varies by survey organization, but it can be as many as one-third.[15] However, this "dual frame" strategy is expensive. Sometimes cell phone respondents are offered a monetary incentive to participate in the survey (Link and Lai 2011; Peytchev and Neely 2013). Also, the Telephone Consumer Protection Act of 1991 prohibits the use of auto dialers when calling cell phones. The numbers have to be dialed manually, which further adds to the expense. In January 2008, Gallup announced its national polls would be based on dual frame samples (Moore 2008, 133). Among the 2012 presidential preelection polls, all eleven national telephone polls that were included in *New York Times* columnist Nate Silver's analysis of poll accuracy were dual frame surveys.[16]

Refusals and Nonresponse   A significant problem with telephone surveys, although it applies to in-person surveys as well, is refusal. The telephone, however, particularly lends itself to abuse, as persons selling aluminum siding, upholstery, or can't-miss real-estate deals sometimes attempt to gain a respondent's confidence by posing as a pollster. The sales pitch comes later. A study by the Roper Organization showed that 27 percent of a national sample had experienced these sales tactics (Turner and Martin 1984, 73). People, especially those in large cities, are becoming wary of callers claiming to be taking polls. However, by 2005 both the state and federal government had instituted "do not call" lists, which bar telemarketers from calling telephone numbers registered on the lists. The national list contains millions of telephone numbers. However, the effect of these lists on survey response rates appears to be inconsequential. Response rates have continued to drop since 2005.

Nonresponse involves more than refusals. It includes any reason why the designated respondent is not interviewed, such as ring–no answer or contacting an answering machine. The response rate is computed as a percentage. In simple terms, it is the number of people successfully interviewed divided by the total number of people called.[17] In the 1960s and earlier, it was common to find response rates in the 80 percent range (Moore 2008, 121).

Most pollsters believe that survey nonresponse is a serious problem and seems to be getting worse (Berinsky 2009; Keeter 2011; Peytchev 2013). Holbrook, Krosnick, and Pfent (2008), analyzing over a hundred surveys conducted by major field services between 1996 and 2005, found that the response rate declined by a rate of two tenths of a percent each month. The highly regarded Pew Research Center surveys saw response rates for their standard five-day telephone surveys drop from 36 percent in 1997 to 9 percent in 2012.[18] Even well-funded and highly influential government surveys, such as the University of Michigan's Survey of Consumer Attitudes, have experienced a significant drop in response rates for its monthly telephone survey of consumer confidence. In 1978, the responses rate was 72 percent; by 2003, it had dropped to 48 percent. Even maintaining a 48 percent response rate has come at the cost of more time in the field, more interviewer training, more calls to ring–no answer numbers, and sophisticated attempts to convert refusals into successful interviews by calling respondents a second time.[19] The principal cause of the drop has been an increase in refusals, but there was also a significant increase in noncontacts beginning around the mid-1990s. For surveys where resources are not abundant and time windows are short (as is often the case in media surveys), response rates are significantly lower than for the Pew Center or for the Survey of Consumer Attitudes (Curtin, Presser, and Singer 2005; Peytchev 2013).

To many, therefore, it comes as a surprise that in the face of declining responses rates there has been no commensurate decline in the accuracy of public opinion surveys. The reason is that those sampled but not interviewed differ little on social and political opinions than those sampled *and* interviewed. A great deal of research demonstrates that low response rates do not bias survey results. Since 2000 the Pew Research Center has been conducting studies of the consequence of low response rates. Even with a response rate of just 9 percent in its 2012 study, the survey data matched up well with reliable benchmarks provided by the Census and other government agencies. For instance, there was no significant difference in home ownership, having children in the household, being a current smoker, receiving food stamps, unemployment benefits, or being married.[20]

Still, it begs the question of how can polls with a 9 percent response rate be essentially accurate? The answer is that the decision to respond to a poll is probabilistic. It is not the case that potential survey respondents can be divided into two discrete class—those willing and those never willing to participate. Rather, nearly everyone has some probability of consenting to an interview, which is dependent on mostly idiosyncratic circumstances at the time the call is made. If a potential respondent is watching a closely contested athletic event, the probability that he or she would decline the interview is quite high. On the other hand, if the athletic event is a blowout by one team, the probability of consenting to the interview increases. But these circumstances at the time of the call are random.

In an analysis of the research on nonresponse, Groves (2006) found little evidence of any direct link between response rates and biased survey results. Groves found occasional bias but, crucially, that its degree was not predictable from the response rate. Rather, it was predicted by other factors that were unique to each survey, such as the correlation between the survey subject matter and the willingness of people to participate. Groves concluded that "blind pursuit of high response rates in probability sample is probably unwise" (668). Still, there is a limit as to how far we can take this principle, with response rates now hovering in single digits.

Interactive Voice Response (Robotic) Telephone Polls

Given the rising cost of high-quality telephone surveys, some have turned to still new methods of polling that reach more respondents for less money. One innovation is robotic polling, whereby respondents punch buttons on their telephone in response to the instructions of automated voices (robots).

Robotic polls are most prevalent at the state or local level, where they are typically conducted for media clients who wish to acquire fast and cheap information about where the public is leaning in the next election. In robotic polls (or as their sponsors prefer to call them, "interactive voice response" polls), the survey research firm samples telephone numbers by RDD with an auto dialer. The person who answers the telephone hears the recorded voice of a professional announcer describing the poll and receives instructions for answering questions via punching numbers on the telephone. The key difference from regular polling—but a big difference—is that there is no human being at the controls on the pollster's side of the communication.

The allure of automatic polls is the ability to obtain many interviews at low cost. There are no interviewers to train or hire. A robotic poll can readily conduct over a thousand surveys within three days or even sooner upon demand. At least one robotic poll firm—Survey USA—claims a record of considerable accuracy with only about 2.33 percent as the average error for general election surveys. For the 2012 presidential election, Survey USA missed the true vote division by 2.2 percent.[21] Still, considerable controversy follows robotic polls. Their most obvious challenge is that they offer no control over the person in the household (a child? a visitor?), who actually answers the telephone and punches a set of replies. And it is not in every-body's nature to respond to automated surveys. Response rates are at best in single digits and may even fall below 1 percent. And, as previously noted, federal law for-bids the use of auto dialers for cell phone numbers. Another problem is the inability of robotic polls to gather much contextual data on the respondent. Vote choice and a couple of demographics are usually the best these polls can provide. Therefore, robotic polls are mostly limited to the horse-race question and not much else. Also, one should not conclude simply because robotic polls have shown some success in predicting election outcomes that they provide unbiased estimates in other public opinion domains. Many political observers who follow the polls closely are reluctant to treat robotic polls seriously, preferring to focus on those conducted by humans.[22]

Internet Polls

As noted earlier, the 2012 Census reports that 80 percent of adult Americans have access to the Internet. Of course, one cannot simply send out a survey over the Internet and expect to get meaningful results. Still, given that level of Internet penetration, polls over the Internet are a booming business, in both the com-mercial world and the academic world. According to Gary Langer, a public opin-ion consultant and former director of polling for the ABC television network, in 2009 there were about as many polls done over Internet as done by telephone.[23] The ratio favoring the Internet is only likely to rise, given the increasing cost of telephone surveys and the often quite inexpensive cost of some Internet surveys.[24]

Polling via the Internet allows for a certain degree of sophistication, as com-plex questions can be combined with visuals. However, Internet polls have a num-ber of drawbacks when compared to in-person and telephone polls. First, there is the problem of coverage error. The 20 percent of Americans without Internet access have a zero probability of getting into the sample. These 20 percent are quite dif-ferent from those with Internet access, and the problem cannot be solved by simply weighting the data to Census benchmarks (Moore 2008). Second, Internet samples are not probability (or random) samples. Unlike RDD, there is no finite master list of e-mail addresses from which to draw a sample. Consequently, Internet samples are not scientific. Thus, strictly speaking, it is not permissible to report sampling error or associated measures like "statistical significance." Third, most recruiting for Internet surveys is done over the Internet. This method introduces the prob-lem of self-selection, the same problem that occurred with the *Literary Digest* in 1936. In the case of polls about politics, those with an interest in politics are more likely to "self-select" to participate in an Internet survey than are those with little or no interest. An extensive analysis of Internet polling methods by the American Association for Public Opinion Research reached the conclusion that "researchers should avoid nonprobability online panels when the one of the research objec-tives is to estimate population values."[25] Because they are not scientific, reputable organizations like the Pew Research Center refuse to use them, and the *New York Times* refuses to publish the results of any survey based on Internet polling that is not probability based.

There have, however, been some serious attempts to use the Internet apply-ing either scientific methods or methods that while not being strictly scientific, proponents claim are sufficiently rigorous as to yield reliable results. We shall review two of these methods. The first of these is the Internet probability panel.[26] Address-based sampling is used to select a representative sample of respondents (Link and Lai 2011). That is, a sample of tens of thousands is scientifically drawn from all mailing addresses housed by the post office, which is then randomly sampled to form the Internet panel. Those selected for the sample are contacted by telephone or mail and offered payment to participate in the Internet surveys (usually about one survey a week). Those without Internet access, who agree to participate, are given web–TV connections and equipment so they too are part of the sample. The sample is, therefore, scientific. The principal downsides are first the method is expensive. It is as expensive as or more expensive than dual frame telephone surveys. Second, critics claim there is a problem with "panel conditioning." Respondents are interviewed up to fifty times a year. After numerous interviews, it is alleged that panel respondents differ significantly from the general population (Dillman 2008).

A second approach, which is not scientific, but employs a rigorous statistical methodology to minimize bias, is an opt-in Internet survey using "sample matching."[27] A large number of people (a million plus) are nonscientifically recruited for an online panel through a variety of methods, including online advertising (pop-up ads) as well as targeted advertising to recruit people typically underrepresented in opt-in Internet surveys (Groves et al. 2009). Respondents are offered an incentive to participate. From this million-plus member database, a sample for an individual study of public opinion is randomly drawn so that it matches the characteristics of the target population—such as age, race, gender, education, and region.[28] This methodology works well in predicting the presidential vote. Based on surveys conducted twenty-one days before the election, one vendor (UGOV) was off the mark by 2.6 percent in 2012.[29] Data from Internet surveys have now essentially replaced telephone surveys in the most prestigious peer-reviewed journals in political science. Between 2010 and 2012, thirty-nine articles using Internet data were published in the *American Political Science Review*, the *American Journal of Political Science*, and the *Journal Politics*.[30]

2-3 Question Wording

It should surprise no one that in survey research, as in everyday life, the answers received are often dependent on the questions asked. This reality has both an upside and a downside for opinion polling. The upside is that people are sensitive to the way survey questions are phrased. That means they are paying reasonably close attention to what they are being asked, and their answers can be taken seriously. If changes in question wording had no impact, the opinion poll would likely be too blunt an instrument to be of much use. The downside is that because the distribution of public opinion can be a function of question wording, incorrect or inappropriate inferences about its true nature are easily possible. Not all variations in question phrasing affect the distribution of responses, but in some cases they clearly do. In this section, we review some of the aspects of question wording that can affect the distribution of public opinion.

Question Asymmetries

Two questions that seem logically equivalent can sometimes yield diametrically opposite results. The best known example is greater support for free speech when respondents are asked if the United States should "forbid" speeches against democracy versus should the United States "allow" speeches against democracy. Although to support free speech means answering "no" to the forbid question and "yes" to the allow question, the two are logically equivalent. Typically, 25 percent or more say "yes" to the allow option than "no" to the forbid option (Hippler and Schwarz 1986). In 2012, Gallup found 51 percent of Americans disapproved of the "financial bailout" of the banks, while in the same week Pew reported 66 percent of the public thought the "government loans" to the banks were mostly "good" for the economy. The difference is likely due to the harshness of the terms—*forbid* and *bailout* are more likely to grate on the ears than are *allow* and *government loans*.

Multiple Stimuli

Many questions have more than one stimulus to which respondents may react. Sometimes these are just bad questions. Take, for instance, the following question from a 2007 *Newsweek* Poll: "Do you think the scientific theory of evolution is well-supported by evidence and widely accepted in the scientific community?"[31] How does the substantial number of people who believe the theory of evolution *is not* well supported by the evidence but *is* widely accepted by the scientific community respond to this question?

In other instances, such questions are not faulty but are often a necessary requirement for measuring opinions on complex topics. Examples of commonly used single-stimulus questions are "Generally speaking, do you consider yourself a Democrat, an Independent, a Republican, or what?" or "Do you approve or disapprove of the way the president is handling his job?" But suppose we were interested in public support for the First Amendment right of free speech. We could ask people to agree or disagree with the statement, "I believe in free speech for all, no matter what their views might be." In 1978, 89 percent of opinion-holders agreed (Sullivan, Piereson, and Marcus 1982). But that tells us little other than in the abstract there is near consensus on a fundamental principle of the American creed. However, real controversies over free speech do not occur in the abstract but in concrete circumstances. Thus, we might ask, "Suppose an admitted Communist wanted to make a speech in your community. Should he be allowed to speak or not?" In 2008, only 66 percent of the public said the person should be allowed to speak. If the admitted Communist was teaching in a college, 37 percent said he should be fired. It is quite clear that in specific circumstances, people are responding to both the free speech stimulus and the Communist stimulus. As we shall see, the level of support for free speech is a matter of considerable controversy (see Chapter 6).

Many less obvious instances of multiple stimuli can affect the distribution of public opinion. One way is to preface the question with the name of an authoritative or admired person or institution. Consider the responses of white Americans to different phrasings of a question about the controversial policy of minority set-asides (Sniderman and Piazza 1993, 113).

Form A		Form B	
Sometimes you hear it said there should be a law to ensure that a certain number of federal contracts go to minority contractors. Do you favor or oppose such a law?		The Congress of the United States—both the House of Representatives and the Senate—has passed a law to ensure that a certain number of federal contracts go to minority contractors. Do you favor or oppose such a law?	
Favor law	43%	Favor law	57%
Oppose law	57%	Oppose law	43%
	100%		100%

Invoking the symbol of the law in this question transforms the policy of set-asides from one backed by a minority of white respondents to one backed by a clear majority—a change that may not be trivial in the politics of affirmative action. The use of authoritative symbols also provides a cue for the uncertain, decreases the don't-knows, and raises the percentage of those favorable and unfavorable among those who know little or nothing about the issue in question (Smith and Squire 1990; Bishop 2005, 33–36).

Question Order Effects

By *order effects*, we mean the effect the previous content of the interview might have on a specific question. For example, respondents usually desire to be consistent in their answers. When asked back in 1980 if "the United States should let Communist newspaper reporters from other countries come here and send back to their papers the news as they see it," 55 percent said yes. But when the question was preceded by one that asks whether "a Communist country like Russia should allow American newspaper reporters to come in and send back the news as they see it," then 75 percent favored letting Communist reporters into the United States (Schuman and Presser 1996, 27; Schuman 2008). Since most answered yes to allowing American reporters into (Communist) Russia, it was obviously inconsistent to bar Communist reporters from the United States. With respect to the abortion issue, general support for abortion will increase if a specific item with a high level of support is asked first. Thus, if respondents are asked if abortion should be permitted "if there is a strong chance of serious defect in the baby" (84 percent say yes), general support for abortion is 13 percent greater than if the specific abortion item is not asked first (Schuman and Presser 1996, 37).

Other examples of order effects include the questionnaire placement of presidential popularity or presidential vote items. Incumbent presidents do worse on both if the question comes late in a survey as opposed to early. The reason is that content of the interview reminds respondents of troublesome aspects of the incumbent's presidency (Sigelman 1981). Pocketbook voting (i.e., voting on the basis of changes in one's personal finances) can be induced by asking questions about finances immediately before ascertaining vote choice (Sears and Lau 1983). Finally, pollsters sometimes provide information on somewhat obscure topics before asking opinions about the topic. Suffice it to say that the content of the information provided in the stem of the question can easily affect the answer given (Bishop 2005).

Balanced Arguments

If a question mentions only one side of a controversy, that side will often get a disproportionate number of responses. An example is, "Do you favor the death penalty?" Because only one option ("favor") is given, we might expect that option would be more frequently chosen than if the question is balanced, as in "Do you favor or oppose the death penalty?" The same is true for questions that use an agree/disagree format (called *Likert scales*). The common practice is to inform the respondent of both agree and disagree options in the stem of the question.

At best, however, agree/disagree questions present only one side of the issue. Respondents must construct the other side of the issue themselves. In the following example, providing balanced alternatives on a question about unemployment yields quite different results compared to an agree/disagree alternative (Cantril 1991, 126).

Form A		Form B	
Do you agree or disagree with this statement: "Any able-bodied person can find a job and make ends meet."		Some people feel that any able-bodied person can find a job and make ends meet. Others feel there are times when it is hard to get along and some able-bodied people may not be able to find work. Whom do you agree with most?	
Agree	65%	Can make ends meet	43%
No opinion	10%	No opinion	18%
Disagree	25%	Sometimes to get along	39%
	100%		100%

The Middle Position

The public seldom splits into polar camps on any issue, and even when a middle position is not offered, many will volunteer an intermediate alternative. With no middle position offered, a respondent might claim "no opinion," a response that might actually mean that the respondent has thought about the matter but is cross-pressured and is conflicted between the two sides of the issue (Treier and Hillygus 2009).

When the question wording explicitly includes a middle position, many respondents seize this middle response as the safe alternative. In one study, Schuman and Presser (1996, 166) found that when respondents are asked on political issues if they "are on the liberal side or the conservative side," 16 percent volunteer that they are "middle of the road." But if the "middle of the road" option is offered, it is taken by 54 percent. While there is little doubt about the consequence of offering a middle position (or an "unsure" or "undecided" option for issue questions), there is no consensus about the desirability of doing so. Some argue that most respondents do have a preference, albeit in some cases a weak one. Offering the middle alternative as an in-between sort of response encourages respondents not to express their opinion (Gilljam and Granberg 1993; Schuman 2008).

When questions are framed to offer a middle or compromise position, public opinion can appear in a different light than when they are presented with only a pair of two stark alternatives. For instance, Gallup asked two questions about the death penalty in May 2003, less than three weeks apart. When the public was asked if it favored the death penalty, 70 percent said yes. But when Gallup presented an option of life in prison without the possibility of parole, support for the death penalty dropped to 53 percent. Similar patterns are found, for instance, on the issue of school prayer. When asked about the matter, the vast majority of respondents voice favor for official prayers in public schools, despite their unconstitutionality. But when respondents are given the added option of moments of silence (which could be used for private prayer), much of the support for official prayer moves to this new alternative.

Response Acquiescence

Often when people are asked whether they agree or disagree with an abstract statement, or one about which they know little, they tend to agree rather than disagree. This tendency is called *response acquiescence*. It arises mostly because the public is ill informed and may not have genuine opinions on many issues (see Chapter 3). We can illustrate this with a 1986 study of attitudes about pornography. Respondents were asked whether they agreed or disagreed that "people should have the right to purchase a sexually explicit book, magazine, or movie, if that's what they want to do." Evidently, people saw this statement as a referendum on individual rights, since an overwhelming 80 percent agreed with the statement. However, in the same poll respondents were also asked whether they agreed or disagreed with the opposite statement that "community authorities should be able to prohibit the selling of magazines or movies they consider to be pornographic." Sixty-five percent agreed with this opposite view as well.[32] Overall, a large number of respondents agreed that the public had a right to purchase pornographic materials *and* also agreed that the community has the right to stop people from purchasing the same material. The most likely explanation of this contradiction is response acquiescence. These examples indicate the danger of using single Likert-type items to measure the level of public opinion. The best strategy for dealing with response acquiescence is to use two or more items where half are worded positively and half negatively—that is, to support free speech the respondent must agree with one statement and disagree with another.

Filter Questions

Most people believe that good citizens should have opinions on current political topics. Thus, when interviewed by polling organizations, they tend to offer opinions on subjects about which they know little or nothing. In an otherwise conventional survey of the Cincinnati area, Bishop and his colleagues (1980) included a question asking respondents whether the nonexistent "Public Affairs Act" should be kept or repealed. Eighteen percent thought it should be kept; 16 percent favored its repeal. Given these findings on a fictitious issue, it should not be surprising that on real but somewhat obscure issues many will offer opinions on matters about which they have no true attitude.

One way to reduce this problem is by using filter questions. Respondents are read a question and response alternatives and then asked, "Where would you place yourself on this scale, or haven't you thought much about this?" Using the 2004 NES question that asks people to indicate on a 1–7 scale if they feel more or less money should be spent on defense, 13 percent of the sample indicated they had not thought enough about the issue to have an opinion. But that does not mean that all the remaining 87 percent have a true attitude. Another 23 percent took the middle position on the scale. It seems likely some taking this position have either no attitude or one that is poorly developed.

One danger in using screening questions is that some people with real attitudes, but who are hesitant to express them, may be filtered out of surveys (Berinsky 1999). An alternative is to use branching questions, where those who say they are undecided or unsure are encouraged in follow-up probes to make a choice (Smith 1984; Krosnick and Kerent 1993). But, of course, this strategy runs the risk of eliciting opinions where no true underlying attitude exists.

Open-Ended Questions

Most survey questions are "closed ended," asking the respondent to choose from a fixed menu of options. Sometimes, however, survey researchers ask "open-ended" questions, without the prompt of a fixed set of alternatives. With open-ended questions, classifying the responses is a multistep process with the interviewer recording the answer, and then coders classifying the answers according to predetermined categories. With the closed-ended version, almost all respondents choose one of the options that are offered. The open-ended version generates a wide range of responses, often with a high percentage offering no opinion due to the difficulty of instant recall required by surveys.

One frequently used open-ended question asks: "What is the most important problem facing the country today?" Schuman and Presser (1996) compared this open-ended format to an identical closed-ended format, where the latter respondents were given a choice among seven possible options. For alternatives such as "inflation," the open and closed formats yielded the same results. But twice as many people mentioned "crime and violence" in the closed-ended format (35 percent) as in the open-ended format (16 percent). The authors claim that listing "crime and violence" in the closed-ended format legitimized the option, if only because the words "facing the country today" used in the stem of the question imply national problems. Many think of crime as a local problem. In this instance, the extent to which crime and violence was seen by the public as the most important problem facing the country is very much dependent on how the question was asked.

Naturally, any option that is offered in a closed-ended question is likely to be chosen more frequently than from the comparable open-ended question. One illuminating example is how the format affects the responses following 9/11 regarding who was responsible for the attacks. Few Americans *volunteered* that Saddam was behind the 9/11 attacks when asked the open-ended version. But when explicitly presented with this possibility as an item from the menu of choices in a closed-ended format, a surprisingly large percentage—often more than 50 percent—saw Saddam as being personally involved (Althaus and Largio 2004). For some, being specifically given the option that Saddam may have been involved allowed for a more efficient search of "considerations" in memory needed to construct an opinion.

Social Desirability

Respondents want to make a good impression on those who interview them. Even though the interviewer is a total stranger, survey respondents often feel pressured to give answers that conform to widely held social norms. This phenomenon, often called *social desirability* (or impression management), results in reported answers that are more socially acceptable than the respondent's true attitude or belief. For example, people overreport voting. The 2008 election provides one example. Although only 62 percent of eligible citizens cast votes, over 80 percent claimed to have voted in NBC News/*Wall Street Journal* polls after the election. Good citizens vote, and to avoid a negative impression, some nonvoters "recall" having voted.

Other examples abound of possible survey contamination from social desirability. Respondents often approach questions about religion as if the survey were a referendum on their faith and overreport the extent to which they attend church (Bishop 2005). During the 2008 Democratic presidential primary campaign, pollsters worried about respondents overreporting a voting preference for Obama on the grounds that it would appear socially undesirable to vote against a plausible black candidate. This concern was shown to be unfounded (Hopkins 2009). And survey respondents may overreport their enthusiasm for platitudes such as free speech, a concern we address in Chapter 6.

One way to overcome social desirability bias and gain an accurate reading of public sentiment is via the "list experiment." By this procedure, respondents are randomly assigned to two groups. The baseline group gets a list of statements and is asked the number of statements on the list that it agrees with. The experimental group gets the same list plus one more representing the sensitive item of interest. The idea is that the differential between the two groups in the mean number of statements they agree with unobtrusively measures the proportion who endorses the sensitive statement. The reason this works is that respondents know that the survey investigator can only know the number of statements agreed with, and not their views about any one actual statement (Glynn 2013).

Here is one example. A list experiment was conducted to ascertain what proportion would accept a woman as president. It turns out that support plummeted 20 percent compared to the results of the usual question directly asking people whether they would accept a woman president (Streb et al. 2008). Evidently, the usual survey support for a woman president is boosted somewhat by social desirability.

The Question Wording Experiment

For scientific research, the gold standard is the experimental design. Average citizens most frequently encounter this method when the media reports on trials involving the effectiveness of a new drug. Half of the sample randomly gets the drug; the other half randomly gets a placebo (sugar pill). If the half that gets the drug differs significantly on key indicators from the half that gets the placebo, the drug is deemed effective—at least in the case of this one trial. While question wording experiments have been around for a long time (J. Converse 1987), it is only with the advent of computer-assisted telephone interviewing (CATI) that the potential of this method has been fully realized. In a simple survey experiment, half of the sample might randomly get a question on affirmative action for "blacks" and the other half would get exactly the same question, but "women" would be substituted for blacks (Sniderman and Piazza 1993). This would allow the investigator insight into whether opposition to affirmative action was based on principle or on racial resentment. CATI and Internet surveys allow for much more complex experiments, where respondents are assigned multiple different versions of an interview (Feldman and Huddy 2005; Huber, Hill, and Lenz 2012). The survey experiment is a strong design because (1) the experiment is invisible to the respondent, (2) there is the capacity to make strong causal inferences owing to the experimental design, and (3) there is the ability to generalize from a sample to a population (Tedin and Weiher 2004).

Summary: The Pitfalls of Question Wording

Variations in question wording can clearly influence the distribution of public opinion. That fact should be recognized and considered when using opinion data. Some questions are obviously biased (see next section). Read the questions carefully. What are the stimuli? Are authorities being invoked? Are inferences being made about the level of opinion from single Likert items? Are "no opinion" screens used on obscure issues? Are balanced questions truly presenting both options in a fair manner? Is the format open ended or closed ended? Are there reasons to think answers are influenced by impression management? All these possibilities are cause for concern. Some types of inferences are more reliable than others. Multiple questions on the same issue can give insight into the range of opinion. But the most reliable strategy is to compare responses to the same question. Thus, subgroup differences on the same question are usually quite meaningful, as are differences when groups are randomly assigned different questions. Also effective is comparing change over time in response to the same question. Because the stimulus is identical, variation is likely due to a change in the public's view.

2-4 Polls and Predicting Elections

How accurate are public opinion polls? The one good test occurs on Election Day. Only when comparing the polls to actual election outcomes can the accuracy of the polls be tested objectively. Predicting elections presents the pollsters with the usual challenges to polling accuracy, plus more. Like all other public opinion polls, election polls must deal with the problem of frequent refusals. What if, for instance, supporters of one candidate or party were more likely to agree to be interviewed? And election polls are not immune from even the problem of question wording. There are many ways to ask respondents whom they will vote for, and these sometimes have consequences (McDermott and Frankovic 2003). When trying to predict elections, pollsters face one further challenge that does not arise when simply trying to predict general opinion. That challenge is that pollsters must take into account who votes and who does not. And voters are always prone to overestimate their likelihood of voting.

We will see below that preelection polls have a strong record of accuracy. Yet even polls that are correctly executed do not always predict the actual Election Day winner. Different polls administered during the same time interval sometimes show conflicting numbers. Occasionally poll numbers swing wildly over a short period. These characteristics do not necessarily mean the polls are defective, but they do require explanation.

The media tends to attribute more accuracy to preelection polls than even the best designed polls can possibly deliver. First, an obvious point. Preelection polls refer to sentiment at the time they are conducted, not on Election Day. The horse-race analogy commonly used to discuss elections is, in this case, appropriate. The horse that is ahead going into the stretch is not always the horse (or the candidate) that wins. But even given the overall trend, there are still "house effects"—variations in survey results due to idiosyncratic ways in which survey organizations conduct their polling. For example, there is surprisingly great variation in the way the candidate-choice question is asked in presidential elections.[33] Survey "houses" vary further in such matters as their frequency of callbacks to elicit responses from refusers, how they poststratify and weight their respondents, how they allocate "undecideds," and how they measure and adjust for the respondent's likelihood of voting. Thus, polls from different firms can be at some variance with one another during the campaign for a variety of reasons.

Most importantly, we should remember that polls will inevitably vary because of ordinary sampling error. Commentators during election campaigns have a tendency to overinterpret shifts in the polls as meaningful when they actually represent house effects or sampling error. One study of the preelection polls during the fall of 1996 showed that the evident movement of the polls, a subject of much interpretation by the popular media, was no greater than would be expected from chance alone, given routine sampling error (Erikson and Wlezien 1999). Preferences undoubtedly did shift back and forth during the 2000 Bush–Gore campaign. But in the Bush–Kerry campaign of 2004, the polls were so stable within a narrow range where, arguably, virtually all the "changes" from one poll to the next could have been due to nothing more than sampling error. Even in 2008, when the presidential campaign was conducted during an economic storm, the horse race changed surprisingly little.

Allocating Undecideds

Typically, surveys show 15 percent or more of the electorate to be undecided at any point during a presidential campaign (the figure is much higher for lower-level races), winding down to 5 to 8 percent a few days before the balloting. Survey houses differ in the way they handle these undecideds. While common sense might dictate a simple reporting of candidate preferences plus undecideds, most media polls do not follow that strategy. If voters claim to be unsure, they are pressed in a follow-up question to indicate which candidate they "lean to." Voters who maintain they are really undecided must be quite firm in their conviction in the face of pressure to make a choice. The inevitable result of this strategy is a sizable swing in candidate preferences, mostly accounted for by those forced to make a choice when their initial reaction was undecided (Crespi 1988; Moore 1992).

Late movement by undecided voters can determine the election, yet go undetected if polling ceases before Election Day. The flow of the undecideds was one reason Truman beat Dewey (the final Gallup Poll showed that 19 percent of the electorate was undecided). And it is the reason Ronald Reagan soundly defeated Jimmy Carter in 1980, when polls showed the contest to be very close, and why Ross Perot performed better in 1992 than almost all preelection polls indicated.

If undecideds in preelection polls do not split evenly on Election Day, how, then, is one to allocate them before the election? There is no one correct answer for all circumstances. Sometimes the undecideds are reported as just that—"undecided." However, the poll will then underestimate the percentage of the vote going to a candidate who has momentum. Sometimes undecided respondents are asked to rate candidates on a 0–10 scale. The undecideds are then allocated to the candidate they like best. If there is a tie on that question, party identification is used to assign the undecideds to a candidate. Other polls exclude the undecideds altogether and base their preelection forecasts only on those voters willing to make a choice.

Deciphering Who Votes

Undoubtedly, the most fundamental problem with pre–Election Day polls as predictors is an inability to define the population properly. Recall that a random sample must be drawn from a finite population. However, it is impossible to precisely define the Election Day population. Only about one-half of adult Americans vote in presidential elections. No one has yet determined a method that predicts with great accuracy who will vote. Yet it is those Election Day voters who constitute the population, not adult Americans or even registered voters. In a preelection survey in 1996, the Pew Research Center asked a national sample of those over age eighteen if they were "absolutely certain," "fairly certain," or "not certain" to vote in the upcoming election for president.[34] Here are the results:

Absolutely certain	69%
Fairly certain	18%
Not certain/unsure	13%
	100%

Actual turnout in 1996 was about 49 percent.

Since respondents' self-reports greatly inflate their likelihood of voting, survey researchers try to screen voters by objectively assessing their likelihood of voting. If all respondents who claimed they would vote were allowed through the screen, the projected election results would be distorted in favor of the party whose supporters are least likely to vote. Historically, the poor and the less educated are the least likely to vote, and these people tend to support Democratic candidates. Election results are also affected by the level of excitement of each party's supporters, which can vary from election to election. Pollsters seem to do a good job of screening in the days leading up to election, when voter interest in the election is fairly easy to ascertain. But screening becomes a challenge to pollsters in the early days of the campaign. The danger is that shifts in the polls of likely voters are often due not to people changing their mind but rather to change in the composition of who counts as a likely voter. Democrats' and Republicans' relative excitement varies in the short term so that first one party and then the next will be overrepresented among likely voters in a way that has little bearing on the vote later on Election Day, when their level of excitement matters (Erikson, Panagopoulos, and Wlezien 2004).

To screen their preelection samples for nonvoting, pollsters first ask respondents whether they are registered and then ignore the choices of the unregistered. Registered respondents are asked a set of questions designed to measure their likelihood of voting. Pollsters use one of two methods at this stage. By the cutoff method, they divide registered respondents into those more and less likely to vote (above or below the cutoff value of voting likelihood) and then count the preferences only of the most likely. (For instance, if they anticipate a 60 percent turnout, they count the preferences of the 60 percent most likely to vote.) By the probable electorate method, the pollster weights registered respondents by their likelihood of voting. For instance, the preferences of a voter estimated at 30 percent likely to vote would be weighted only 0.30 as much as a certain voter. Which method is better is a matter of debate (Erikson 1993; Ferree 1993; Hugick and Molyneux 1993; Daves 2000). The important point is that the type of screen and its application can have an important consequence for a poll result.

How Accurate Are the Polls?

Given the daunting challenges that pollsters face, one might expect that polls do a poor job of predicting elections. But that would be wrong. Polls conducted early in campaigns often give a misleading view of what will transpire on Election Day. But that is because events change beyond the pollsters' control. Similarly, primary elections are difficult to poll accurately even in the final week of the campaign, as preferences leading up to primary elections are historically volatile. (Voters focus late, and they choose within their party rather than between parties.) But general election polls conducted late in the campaign, such as in the final week, show an excellent record of accuracy. This is reassuring not just because we might sometimes want to know outcomes in advance. It assures us that opinion polls should also be reasonably accurate as snapshots of public opinion at the moment, even when we lack the feedback of an election to verify.

Figure 2.1 summarizes the accuracy of presidential polls over sixteen elections, from 1952 to 2012. This graph shows the actual vote (measured as the Democratic percent of the two-party vote) as a function of the Democratic share of the two-party vote in the polls during the final week of the campaign. (The Republican vote in the polls or on Election Day is 100 percent minus the Democratic percent.) The vote in the polls is measured by pooling all polls available where the middate of the polling period is within one week of Election Day.

In Figure 2.1, the polls would be perfectly accurate if the sixteen annual observations all fell on the diagonal line. They do not of course, since polls are not perfect. Rather, the late polls tend to be accurate within about 1.5 percentage points.

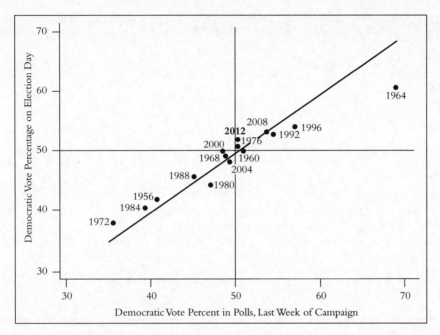

FIGURE 2.1 Democratic vote for president (as share of two-party vote) by Democratic strength (as share of two-party vote) in all polls (combined) in the final week of the campaign, 1952–2012. The 2012 result is highlighted.

Source: Compiled by Robert S. Erikson and Christopher Wlezien.

This is less than one would expect by chance from sampling error alone, but we must keep in mind that the polls cannot register the late movement in the very final days of the campaign. Historically, the late polls show no bias in favor of one party's candidates or the others. And, contrary to some claims, they do not inflate support for incumbents. One can see from Figure 2.1 that polls tend to exaggerate the sizes of large leads in landslide elections (e.g., 1964, 1972).[35] But when elections are close, presidential polls tend to be quite accurate.

Presidential polls have been remarkably accurate in this century—in 2000, 2004, 2008, and 2012. In 2000, the late polls revealed Gore's late advancement that led to a virtual tie in the popular vote. (Gore, of course, won the popular vote, whereas Bush won the contested and decisive electoral vote.) In 2004, the polls correctly predicted another close election with most tilting toward Bush, the winner. In 2008, the late polls correctly predicted Obama's win and reported the vote margin with impressive accuracy. In 2012, most polls predicted Obama's victory while slightly underestimating its size.

Table 2.2 details the record of the final polls of the 2012 race. Here, the vote is measured as the relative strengths of candidates Obama and Romney, allowing votes for undecideds (in the polls) and votes for minor-party candidates (in the polls and the election), so that the sum of Obama and Romney support does not add quite up to 100 percent. The margin is measured as Obama's lead over Romney. The national polls did vary but in a range that is more than acceptable in terms of sampling error.

TABLE 2.2   Accuracy of Final Polls in the 2012 Presidential Election

Poll	Obama	Romney	Obama Margin
ABC/*Washington Post*	50	47	+3
Politico/GWU/Battleground	47	47	+0
CBS/*New York Times*	48	47	+1
CNN	49	49	+0
Fox	46	46	+0
Gallup	48	49	−1
IBD/Tipp	50	49	+1
NBC/*Wall Street Journal*	48	47	+1
Pew	48	45	+3
Average (Poll of Polls)	*48.7*	*47.7*	*+1.0*
Actual Vote	**51.1**	**47.2**	**+3.9**

Source: Based on data from 2012 General Election: Romney vs. Obama, Huffington Post, November 2012, http://elections .huffingtonpost.com/pollster/2012-general-election-romney-vs-obama. Selected polls are prominent likely voter polls based on live telephone interviewers.

As the table reveals, the polls underestimated the size of Obama's lead by about 3 percentage points, probably because of a modest last-minute trend toward the president and also because some pollsters underestimated turnout among racial minorities loyal to Obama. Meanwhile, the pollsters did very well at predicting the results in the key battleground states. Of the ten states deemed to be the battleground states of 2012, Obama defeated Romney in all but North Carolina. And indeed the averages of the polls had the winner right in all ten states.[36] Over recent election years, state-level polls have a strong record of accuracy, for predicting not only how the state will vote for president but also the important offices of senator and governor.

Given the handicaps that pollsters face and the fact that they do not always converge toward a common solution to their common problems, it is remarkable that the polls perform as well as they do. The pollsters' best defense is that, despite possible criticisms of specific procedures, their polls do predict with considerable accuracy. What keeps the pollsters on their toes is the knowledge that if they were systematically off the mark, they would be out of business.

Election Day Exit Polls

Now over a quarter century old, the *exit poll* is an important if sometimes controversial innovation in opinion polling. Representative precincts are selected, and voters are interviewed immediately after leaving the voting booth. Questions go beyond vote choice to include demographic and attitudinal information. Exit polls are commissioned by the news media to help them to project the winner soon after the polls close on Election Day and report on the demographic and issue correlates of the vote choice. While the National Election Pool (NEP) provides data to television networks and other news outlets, each news sources hires its own experts to analyze the data and ultimately call the election night winners (Best and Krueger 2012).

When networks and other news organizations call elections, exit poll results actually play only a partial role compared to such techniques as getting early returns from sample precincts and comparing reported election results with past voting patterns from the same geographic area. The major purpose of exit polls is to provide background data on which types of voters prefer which candidates. As raw data from exit polls stream in throughout Election Day, they are unreliable as indicators of the vote margins in the states and the nation.

There are several reasons why raw exit results are unreliable. There is a small but consistent partisan skew. The "raw data" tend to overstate the Democratic vote and understate the Republican vote. The reason is that Democrats are more willing to cooperate with exit pollsters than are Republicans (Best and Krueger 2012). Compounding the problem is that the large number of polling places that need to be monitored requires that many interviewers must be hired on a temporary basis. They are often inexperienced and poorly trained. With mostly young interviewers seeking interviews outside polling places, older voters are more likely to refuse cooperation, which (currently) contributes to the Democratic skew in the raw data.

Early voting provides a further hurdle. As of 2012, about 37 percent of all voters cast their vote in presidential elections before the first Tuesday in November.[37] These early voters tend to be more partisan, ideological, and politically interested than Election Day voters. Election night analysts must estimate this early vote and factor that along with the exit poll data and other considerations when making their Election Day projections (Biemer et al. 2003; Frankovic 2003; Stein and Vonnahme 2008).[38]

Although by themselves, the data from exit polls comprise at best only a rough indicator for predicting elections results, they are useful for postelection analysis of the vote. After the election outcomes are known, exit poll data can be properly weighted to adjust for such factors as precinct voting and certain demographic patterns to the refusals. Processed in this way, long after the election, exit polls become among the best sources for investigating the variables that affect the vote in different elections. For analytical purposes, exit polls have two advantages to offset their disadvantages. The respondents include only voters, and their responses reflect their thinking on Election Day.

2-5 Conclusion

For more than sixty years, public opinion polls have been part of the political landscape, and there is every sign that their influence is growing. While the scientific pollsters have an admirable track record, it must be recognized that polls are imperfect predictors. Even the best preelection poll is based on a probability model that on rare occasions can go wrong due to an unlucky dose of sampling error. Preelection polls can also go wrong when the behavior they are sampling changes underneath their feet. The electorate's choice is often volatile in the days before an election, and the pollsters race to catch up by means of polling until the last minute. Polls can go wrong because people are increasingly likely to refuse requests to be interviewed. And polls can go wrong when they miscalculate which eligible voters will actually show up to vote. Under the circumstances, contemporary polls do a surprisingly good job at predicting elections. One reason may be that pollsters know they must do a good job because they lose credibility and their jobs if they do not.

In this book, our central interest is in polls regarding public opinion, not election outcomes. A challenge is that unlike with election polls, we do not know for sure how close opinion polls are to the correct result. Unless the target opinion is the outcome of an initiative or referendum election, opinion polls lack direct validation. And opinion polls are sensitive to matters of question framing and question wording. The key to understanding polls is a realization that the numbers do not speak for themselves; they require interpretation. Among the keys to that interpretation are how the sample was selected, how the questions were phrased, an appreciation for the context in which the survey was conducted, and a comparison to other surveys taken at the same time or an analysis of trends over time.

Critical Thinking Questions

1. Since a poll's exact question wording can affect the answers people give about political issues, what cautions should one employ when interpreting the latest public opinion polls?
2. Some people express doubts about the accuracy of polls because they often only interview a few hundred people. How would you defend scientific polling against this criticism?
3. While pollsters have made disastrous mispredictions about the outcome of some past elections, the polls have been quite accurate lately. But what kinds of dangers might lurk that could possibly cause major polling errors again?

Endnotes

1. According to David Moore (2013), in the last twenty-one days before voting in 2012, ninety survey organizations conducted 550 polls on the upcoming presidential election.
2. Following the Senate's failure to convict Clinton on impeachment charges, he is reported to have said, "Thank God for public opinion" (Edwards 2003, 4).
3. Pew Research Center and Opinion Research Corporation, October 24–27, 2008.
4. Gallup Poll, September 8–11, 2011.
5. The best source for informed commentary on contemporary poll practices is www .pollster.com.
6. https://www.census.gov/hhes/www/housing/census/historic/phone.html.
7. Internet World Stats, www.internetworldstats.com/stats.htm.
8. Strictly speaking, in terms of statistical theory, if the poll were repeated an infinite number of times, in 95 percent of the trials the result would be between 54 and 60 percentage points. We are assuming simple random sampling, which is a useful simplification of Gallup's sampling procedure.
9. The exception is when the population itself is quite small (e.g., less than 10,000). With a small population, a correction can be made to properly lower the sampling error. Table 2.1 shows that a sample of 384 drawn from a very large population has a sampling error of 5 percent. However, if our barrel contained only 1,000 marbles and we randomly drew 384, then, instead of a sampling error of 5 percent, the true sampling error would be 0.785×5.0 percent, or 3.9 percent. The sampling error correction for small populations is the square root of $N - n/N - 1$, where N is the population size and n is the sample size.
10. Some pollsters extend poststratification to weight by party identification. The idea is that the public is reasonably stable in partisanship, so that when one interviews, say, more Republicans than normal, then Republicans should be weighted down to adjust for the distorted sample. This procedure, designed to add precision to the sample

estimates, is controversial. The danger is that, unlike with demographics, partisanship can change in the short run. An unexpected surge of Republican respondents might indicate sampling error, but it could also mean more people decide to call themselves Republicans.

11. One's suspicions are aroused, however, if polls on the same topic at about the same time with similarly worded questions show quite different results.

12. In 1948, Gallup had Dewey at 49.5 percent and Truman at 44.5 percent (with 6 percent going to minor-party candidates). The vote, in fact, was Truman 49.5 percent and Dewey 45.1 percent, with others getting 5.4 percent. The Roper Poll in 1948 was further off the mark than Gallup. Roper had Dewey at 52.2 percent and Truman at 37.1 percent (with 10.7 percent going to minor-party candidates).

13. This description is somewhat of an oversimplification of modern RDD methods. For a detailed explanation, see Lepkowski et al. (2008).

14. Thus, each sample has (1) cell phone–only households, (2) households with cell phones and landlines, and (3) households with landlines only. Complex statistical weights must be used to ensure that this mix is representative of the adult population (Daniel 2012).

15. Recently, Peytchev and Neely (2013) have suggested that survey accuracy could be optimized by going to cell phone–only sampling frame, and not calling landlines at all.

16. fivethirtyeight.blogs.nytimes.com/2012/11/10.

17. Actual formulas, however, are a good deal more complex. Not every unanswered call is included in the denominator, depending on the survey. A detailed discussion of methods for computing response rates can be found at the Web site for the American Association for Public Opinion Research, www.aapor.org.

18. www.people-press.org/2012/05/15/assessing-the-representativeness-of-public-opinion-surveys.

19. While the overall response rate for the Survey of Consumer Attitudes between 1977 and 1999 was 70 percent, it dropped to 66 percent in the period between 1995 and 1999.

20. The one significant difference was a tendency for survey respondents to be more engaged in civic activity than nonsurvey respondents. The reason is likely that people who are civic volunteers are also predisposed to be survey volunteers. Thus, the standard telephone survey may be inappropriate for studies of volunteer activities and more generally for studies of social capital.

21. Based on likely voters in the last twenty-one days of the campaign. fivethirtyeight.blogs.nytimes.com/2012/11/10.

22. Joshua Clinton and Steven Rogers (2013) present evidence that robotic polls are most accurate when the election they are polling is also being polled by conventional pollsters. The inference is that robotic poll results may sometimes be adjusted to be consistent with the pack.

23. Gary Langer, "Study Finds Trouble for Opt-in Internet Surveys," *The Numbers*, September 1, 2009, http://abcnews.go.com/blogs/politics/2009/09/study-finds-trouble-for-internet-surveys/.

24. One can in fact do Internet surveys essentially for free. See www.surveymonkey.com. However, the data one gets for free at this site may be worth exactly what was paid for it.

25. For the full report, see *Public Opinion Quarterly* 74 (Winter 2010): 711–81. For a rebuttal of this position, see Doug Rivers, "Second Thoughts about Internet Surveys," www.huffingtonpost.com/guest-pollster/doug_rivers_b_724621.html.

26. For an example of this methodology, see www.knowledgenetworks.com.

27. Among the best known users of this methodology are Harris Online and UGOV/Polimetrix. The Web site for the latter can be found at http://research.yougov.com. The methodology described in this section for the opt-in, sample matching methodology is the one used by UGOV/Polimetrix.

28. This is a simple example, as other information from the target population may be known as well, such as voter registration, being a born-again Christian, and party identification. This information can be obtained from the American Community Survey conducted by the U.S. Census.

29. fivethirtyeight.blogs.nytimes.com/2012/11/10.

30. Many of these articles were based on data collected by UGOV/Polimetrix for the Comparative Congressional Elections Project. UGOV/Polimetrix uses opt-in, sample matching Internet surveys. The statistics employed in these studies assume probability sampling, even though UGOV/Polimetrix samples are not probability samples.

31. *Newsweek* Poll conducted by Princeton Survey Research Associates, March 28–29, 2007.

32. A 1986 *Time*/Yankelovich Survey, cited in "Opinion Roundup," *Public Opinion* (September/October 1986): 32.

33. For a list of the way the major polling firms ask this question, see Crespi (1988, Ch. 5).

34. The Pew Research Center for the People and the Public. News Release, August 2, 1996.

35. Note that Figure 2.1 effectively assigns the undecideds as either staying home or voting Democratic or Republican in proportion to the choices among those who make a choice in the final poll. Allocating the undecideds as voting, say, 50–50, would lead to slightly lower predictions in landslide elections.

36. Mark Blumenthal, "2012 Poll Accuracy: After Obama, Models and Survey Science Won the Day," http://www.huffingtonpost.com/2012/11/07/2012-poll-accuracy-obama-models-survey_n_2087117.html.

37. http://www.people-press.org/2012/11/15/section-3-the-voting-process-and-the-accuracy-of-the-vote/.

38. While the analysts at television networks and other news organizations use exit polls as one tool for predicting state-level races and winners for president and important statewide offices, they have learned to predict cautiously. The most notorious misprediction was the early call that Gore had won Florida in 2000 (and by implication an Electoral College majority). Faulty exit polls played a part in this misprediction. Since the 2000 fiasco, network analysts have made no serious errors in prematurely calling state winners. It may be said that network analysts know more about forecasting elections than they used to, including knowing more about the limits of what they know.

CHAPTER 3

Microlevel Opinion: The Psychology of Opinion-Holding

LEARNING OBJECTIVES

- Explain the term *microlevel opinion*
- Describe the level of political knowledge among the American public

- Explain the causes of attitude instability at the microlevel
- Explain the difference between liberal and conservative political ideology

In theory, democracy works best when people actively attend to public affairs—ideally, when they direct policymakers toward the problems most deserving of attention and actively monitor their deliberations. In this best-of-all worlds, people might disagree with one another, but their opinions are soundly reasoned and logically consistent. Their preferences transcend conflict among self-interested parties to reflect a concern for the general welfare.

In actuality, public opinion falls considerably short of this ideal. As early survey researchers explored the nature of public opinion, they found several reasons for pessimism. For instance, respondents often express preferences so thoughtless as to be arguably too shallow for consideration as meaningful opinions. The opinions that people do hold sometimes seem like unconnected preferences with no logical relationship to one another. Where predictability exists, opinions often flow from disturbing prejudices rather than thoughtful consideration. Often it appears that political leaders or powerful interest groups find it all too easy to manipulate political symbols so as to fool a politically gullible mass public.

Although recent discussions of the capabilities of mass opinion vary in theoretical perspectives, they find some significant reason for optimism (compare Popkin 1991; Page and Shapiro 1992; Delli Carpini and Keeter 1996; Stimson 2004; Dalton 2008; Lewis-Beck et al. 2008; Arceneaux and Kolodny 2009; Boudreau 2009; Bullock 2011). Many ordinary people stay politically informed and can be considered politically sophisticated. Actually, it may seem remarkable that people hold political opinions at all. Why, we might ask, do people bother to develop and maintain political opinions when the time spent on politics might be better devoted to dealing with matters that affect their private lives? As most of our political involvement is as passive spectators watching helplessly on the sidelines, why do we not only pay attention but invest time and effort developing opinions? Indeed, a strong argument can be made that if the main purpose of following politics is to affect policy outcomes, staying informed and thinking about politics is, from a cost–benefit perspective, an irrational investment (Downs 1958).

Because many people are sufficiently political to have ignored such advice, political opinions must be of some benefit to the people who hold them. It has long been recognized that holding political opinions serves several positive psychological functions (Smith, Bruner, and White 1956). Opinions can serve a social function—for instance, when people learn to agree with the prevailing views within their preferred social groups. Opinions can serve a direct psychological function—when political opinions follow as an extension of personality. A frequently cited example is the person who seeks an ordered and disciplined personal environment being more susceptible to authoritarian political ideologies (Altemeyer 1997; Hetherington and Weiler 2009). Opinions can also promote economic self-interest—when people develop political opinions consistent with their economic standing. Sometimes people develop elaborate ideologies to rationalize their economic status, as when rich people adopt a conservative economic ideology to justify the wealth they have accumulated (Page and Jacobs, 2009).

As one would expect, opinions often reflect economic self-interest—for example, when the rich adopt more conservative economic positions than the poor (see Chapter 7). But the pull of self-interest is far from universal. People often derive opinions from values that have little if anything to do with obvious self-interest (Sears and Funk 1990). One example is when prosperous citizens concern themselves with the economic plight of others. Another very different example is when people express racial animosity in circumstances that lack an obvious economic motive (de Figueiredo and Elkins 2003; Kinder and Kam 2010). Even obvious economic interests are sometimes overridden by alternative calculations. In a study of school districts affected differently by court-ordered financial equalization, property-rich districts had to pay more school taxes and property-poor districts had to pay less. While attitudes toward this decision generally reflected how one's district was affected, many liberals who had to pay more taxes favored the equalization and many conservatives who had to pay less opposed the measure—contrary to their economic self-interest (Tedin 1994b).

While sometimes it seems that people arbitrarily generate opinions, those opinions usually have reasons behind them.[1] Abstract values such as authoritarianism, egalitarianism, and liberal/conservative ideology are important to politics because they cause people to have opinions when they have no direct stake in a particular issue (Bawn 1999; Stenner 2005; Gerber, Huber et al., 2011). For example, many Americans living in small, homogeneous Midwestern farming communities have opinions about bilingual education. These opinions have political consequences, even though the lives of the opinion-holders are almost certainly not touched by the issue.

This chapter examines public opinion at the microlevel of the individual citizen, usually when observed as a survey respondent. We first examine the extent of political knowledge and the depth of opinion-holding. We then explore the core values and beliefs that sometimes hold opinions together, typically in terms of the liberal–conservative ideological spectrum. Then, we explore party identification or relative allegiance to the Democratic or Republican Party as a source of political orientation. Finally, we summarize some of the issues involved regarding the growing polarization of American politics.

3-1 Political Attention and Opinion-Holding

When public opinion is reported on some issue, the underlying division of opinion often shows considerable diversity in terms of attention and caring about the matter at hand. At one extreme we find highly attentive citizens who follow public affairs closely and hold informed (if diverse) opinions regarding even complicated questions of public policy. These citizens vote regularly, and their votes are based on issue preferences that have been well thought out. Moreover, they make their views known to elected leaders, even during the time intervals between political campaigns.

At the other extreme we find citizens who can be best described as "apolitical." Virtually disengaged from politics, they ordinarily pay no attention to the political happenings reported in newspapers and on television, and they do not vote. Their interests in politics are perked up only by unusual events, such as the threat of war or a political sex scandal. But by being passive, they collectively forfeit their influence on policy outcomes.

Most people fall between these two extremes, and their attention to the world of government and politics varies considerably. Cognitive ability or general intelligence is certainly an important factor for understanding politics and holding political opinions (Delli Carpini and Keeter 1996; Althaus 2003; Joslyn 2003). But we should not assume that when people are politically inattentive they lack the mental capacity to follow public affairs, or that politics is too complicated for ordinary folks to figure out. Whether one follows politics closely is largely a matter of personal taste, similar to the choice of whether to follow certain sports, like football and baseball. And just as sporting events are more fascinating and comprehensible to regular followers, so too is following politics easier for those who have invested time and effort learning about the political world. For those who choose not to invest in an understanding of politics, following political events and holding informed opinions is a considerably more difficult task (Zaller 1992; Barabas and Jerit 2009).

Just as it is misleading to describe public opinion by focusing on the typical citizen, it can be misleading to assume that a citizen's attention level regarding one aspect of politics extends to all others. People vary not only in their taste for public affairs but also in the aspects of public affairs that engage their interest most. For instance, some people focus on national politics but ignore their local political environment, while others do the reverse. Some people are issue serialists, who become members of the attentive public only when issues dear to their interests enter the public agenda. On some issues, they hold strong opinions and make their views known; on others, they react with indifference. We must also recognize that interest in public affairs is seasonal, peaking during election campaigns as people become more informed when preparing to vote.

Levels of Political Knowledge

Since the 1930s, more than 2,000 factual pop quiz political knowledge questions have been asked of the American public. Table 3.1 presents a sampling of factual knowledge across a variety of issue domains from a number of polling sources. The table suggests a surprising level of public ignorance.

TABLE 3.1	Level of Information Among the Adult U.S. Population		
Percentage		**Year**	**Source**
96	Know United States is a member of the United Nations	1985	D&K
96	Know president's term is four years	1989	D&K
88	Know Cuba is communist	1988	D&K
86	Know Democrats have a House majority	2009	Pew
85	Know Joe Biden is vice president	2012	Pew
77	Know George W. Bush has a plan to privatize Social Security	2005	CBS
74	Know governor of home state	1989	D&K
74	Know "Obamacare" has an individual mandate	2013	Kaiser
72	Can name one right guaranteed by First Amendment	2013	Stats
71	Know Republican Party is more conservative than Democrats	2012	Pew
69	Know Pakistan and Afghanistan share a common border	2009	Pew
66	Know Supreme Court justices service a life term	2005	G&C
66	Know if Obama/McCain won their state in the 2008 election	2012	Pew
65	Know donkey is the Democratic mascot	2012	Pew
62	Know Mitt Romney is a Mormon	2012	Pew
63	Know party of congressional representative	1995	IRC
62	Know *Row v. Wade* is about abortion rights	2013	Pew
61	Know Nancy Pelosi is a Democrat	2102	Pew
55	Know Supreme Court upheld most of "Obamacare"	2012	Pew
57	Know Supreme Court has the "last say" on the Constitution	2005	G&C
52	Know unemployment is 8 percent (from a list of four choices)	2012	Pew
50	Can locate Syria on a map	2013	Pew
47	Know congressman's vote on Clinton impeachment	1999	WP
46	Know Republicans won a majority in the U.S. House	2010	Pew

Percentage		Year	Source
43	Recognize name of Speaker of the House (John Boehner)	2011	Pew
44	Know Auschwitz/Dachau/Treblinka were Nazi concentration camps	2005	TNS
40	Know Republicans have a House majority	2012	Pew
36	Can name the president (Putin) of Russia	2007	Pew
35	Know name of their U.S. Congressional Representative	2013	Gallup
35	Can name at least one Supreme Court justice	2003	Find Law
34	Can name the secretary of treasury (Geithner)	2012	ANES
31	Know what affirmative action is	1985	D&K
27	Know that more is spent on Medicare than foreign aid	1995	IRC
21	Know House and Senate raised the minimum wage	2007	Pew
19	Know political office held by William Rehnquist (chief justice)	2004	IPSOS
15	Can identify office held by Harry Reid (majority leader)	2007	Pew
14	Know name of secretary general of the United Nations	2012	ANES
12	Know who presided over Clinton *impeachment* trial	1999	Pew

Source: ANES (American National Election Studies); D&K (Delli Carpini and Keeter 1996); IRC (IRC Survey Research Group); WP (*Washington Post*); Pew (Pew Center for People and the Press); CBS/NYT (CBS News/New York Times); GSS (General Social Survey); Ipsos (Ipsos Public Affairs); TNS (TNS Intersearch); G&C (Gibson and Caldeira 2009); Stats (Stats Group); Kaiser (Kaiser Center, Harvard University); Gallup (Gallup Poll).

Although the items presented in Table 3.1 are taken from a range of years, there has been little change over time in the level of political knowledge. Americans appear no better informed about political matters today than they were twenty years ago (according to Pew polling in 2007) or fifty years ago (Delli Carpini and Keeter 1996). Given the rise in levels of education and the greater availability of political media, many find this lack of improvement puzzling. Perhaps there are counter-trends that cancel out improvements in education and technology, or there may be inherent limits to how much political information the public can absorb.

The most disconcerting aspect of the public's ignorance during normal times may be people's inability to recall the names of leading political officeholders. Some examples are included in Table 3.1. Over two-thirds of the public can name their state's governor, but few can immediately recall the name of key Washington leaders. When the Republicans gained control of the House of Representatives in 1995, Speaker Newt Gingrich became a rival to the president for the center of the political stage—but he became no household name. At the height of his political power in 1995, only 54 percent could identify him as House Speaker. In 2011 just 41 percent could recognize the name John Boehner as House Speaker from a list of four.

Political Misinformation   Just as alarming as evidence of public ignorance of political facts is the willingness of some to claim beliefs that are decidedly not true. Two examples are the sizeable proportions of the electorate, who claimed (well into the late 2000s) that the United States found weapons of mass destruction (WMD) in Iraq or that Saddam Hussein had something to do with the 9/11 attacks even though both claims are clearly false. Similarly, contrary to all evidence, in 2012 a stubborn minority of 18 percent insisted that Obama is a Muslim, and in that same year, 39 percent claimed he was born in some country other than the United States and is thus constitutionally ineligible for the presidency. (Both claims are absurd.)[2]

Why do people persist in asserting belief in things that any sophisticated person would know to be false? The explanations are multifaceted. First of all, unlike political leaders who act on their beliefs, ordinary citizens bear no cost for holding erroneous beliefs; to utter an erroneous political statement brings no cost to a survey respondent (Caplan 2007). And it can provide psychic benefits. By a process called "motivated reasoning," people can persist in maintaining a misbelief because it is convenient to their worldview or ideological position (Lodge and Tabor 2013). It is no coincidence that Republicans in 2012 were more likely to believe that Barak Obama is a Muslim (30 percent) than were Democrats (8 percent). Stereotypes are often associated with misinformation. Those holding negative group stereotypes are also prone to hold incorrect (and unflattering) information about that group (Bobo and Johnson 2004). Or misinformation can serve certain personality needs (Stenner 2005). Finally, in an era of polarized politics and a fragmented media, people frequently encounter false information from seemingly reliable sources. These encounters are not always without effect (Gilliam and Iyenger 2000; Jerit and Barabas 2006).

Context and Political Information

In March 1999, armed forces of the North Atlantic Treaty Organization conducted an intensive bombing raid on the nation of Serbia in an attempt to halt "ethnic cleansing" by Serbs in the predominantly Albanian province of Kosovo. Prior to the bombing, it is safe to say, most Americans had never heard of Kosovo. However, within a few days of the bombing, a Pew Research Center poll (March 29, 1999) found that 43 percent of Americans were able to identify Kosovo as a province of Yugoslavia located in Central Europe. This was a remarkable amount of learning for a nation often scolded for its lack of geographical knowledge.

But of course this event was understandable. People begin to pay attention to political events that are in the news. Indeed political events can attract near universal attention, but only if they contain the necessary elements of drama—a terrorist attack, a hostage drama, or a sex scandal.

Public knowledge improves in the face of threat, which is a powerful motivator for people to learn about politics (Marcus, Neuman, and MacKuen 2000; Brooks and Manza 2013). Closely following 9/11, public knowledge of issues related to terrorism stood at levels quite unexpected during normal times. In November 2001,

84 percent of the public knew the Northern Alliance was the ally of the United States in Afghanistan, 85 percent knew that Pakistan had a common border with Afghanistan, and 67 percent knew Colin Powell was secretary of state (Prior 2002). However, as the threat receded, political knowledge retreated to levels found during normal times. Less than a year after 9/11, fewer than half of American adults could name Colin Powell as secretary of state, and fewer than a third could name Donald Rumsfeld as secretary of defense.

Measuring Political Knowledge

In assessing the political knowledge of the public, we must contend with numerous methodological considerations. The context of the interview and the way the knowledge question is asked can affect the assessment of information levels. One problem is that the survey format is not conducive to searching long-term memory for answers, as an expectation develops during the interview process that answers should be provided in a matter of seconds. When respondents are given extra time, they are significantly more likely to provide correct answers (Prior and Lupia 2008).

In addition, assessment of the public's level of political knowledge is sensitive to question format. We can distinguish between open-ended questions which require fairy demanding *recall* ("What is the name of the vice president?") versus less demanding recall ("What is the job of Joe Biden?"). Still different are closed-ended multiple-choice questions that measure *recognition*. These items present the respondents with a list of possibilities and ask them to identify which on the list holds the office (e.g., "Which of the following people is the vice president of the United States?")

This latter type of closed-ended question has its adherents. If asked in an open-ended format "What is the name of your congressional representative?" about 40 percent can give the correct answer. Using a closed-ended format where a list of possibilities is offered, close to 90 percent can often correctly identify their congressional representative (Tedin and Murray 1979; McDermott and Frankovic 2003; Pew 2007).

Gibson and Caldeira (2009, 439) make a similar argument about the judicial branch. When using appropriately crafted closed-ended questions, they find "respondents demonstrate relatively high knowledge about the Supreme Court." For instance, when asked what job or political office the late William Rehnquist held, only 12 percent identified the former chief justice by his title. But when asked to choose among Rehnquist and two plausible ringers from a list of three names, 71 percent answered correctly.

Knowledge and Opinions

One concern about the public's low attention to politics is that policy preferences of the informed public may differ substantially from the uninformed majority. There are two ways of looking at this problem. On the one hand, those who believe that informed opinion should carry greater weight can argue that poll results are contaminated by the counting of passive, uninformed opinions. On the other hand, those who believe that people should have equal influence can argue that disproportionate weight should not be given to the perhaps one-sided views of the assertive minority who make their views known (Berinsky 2004). The differences between informed and uninformed opinion that are known to exist are generally attributed to the greater education and income of those who are more knowledgeable.

Converting Information into Opinions

We present examples of the relationship between information and opinions based on the 2012 American National Election Studies (ANES) survey.[3] For this task, we introduce a summary index of political information. We score respondents on the basis of their knowledge of candidate policy differences, which past research has shown to be a good measure of relevant political information (Luskin 1987; Zaller 1992). Details of this index are presented in the Appendix. When we use this index, we compare voters at two information extremes. High-information respondents are the 27 percent (34 percent of voters) who correctly saw Romney to the right of Obama on all seven issues. Low-information respondents are the bottom 37 percent (27 percent of voters) whose knowledge of candidate differences on issues appears to be so impoverished that their evaluation of candidate positions approached the "guess" range.

Table 3.2 shows differences in opinion-holding by knowledge level in the 2012 ANES survey. High-information respondents tend to be more liberal on cultural and social issues like abortion rights and gay marriage but more conservative on social

TABLE 3.2   Opinion by Level of Political Information, 2012

Opinion	High Information (%)	Low Information (%)	Difference (%)
Legalize all abortions	55	36	+19
Reduce defense spending	48	31	+17
Oppose torture to fight terrorism	68	68	0
Oppose death penalty	35	32	+3
Legalize gay marriage*	70	60	+10
Favor more gun control	36	48	−12
Support preferential hiring of blacks	14	25	−1
More government aid to blacks	23	26	−3
Support Obamacare	47	60	−13
Favor guaranteed standard of living	23	48	−25
Increase domestic spending	32	63	−31
Liberal (of ideological identifiers)	37	40	−3
Democratic (of party identifiers)	44	71	−28

*On gay marriage question, proportions are of those preferring legal marriage or no recognition, excluding responses favoring civil unions.

Source: American National Election Studies, 2012. Cell numbers represent percentages among opinion-holders. For measure of high- and low-income respondents, see the Appendix.

welfare (redistributive) issues like taxing the rich or Obamacare. Overall, the least informed are more likely to select the liberal label to describe themselves and, notably, to call themselves Democrats rather than Republicans.

Information is the basis for (most) opinions about politics. But what is the process by which information becomes converted into opinions? One interpretation holds that citizens translate information into opinions using the rules of *instrumental rationality*—that is, for the issue at hand, citizens form opinions based on the personal costs and benefits that accrue to them. For example, farmers favor free trade because it opens more markets for their products. In short, by this view, people form opinions based on personal self-interest.

As we have mentioned, while it obviously plays a role in shaping political opinions, self-interest is far from dominant. One can readily find people whose political opinions defy their economic circumstances, such as rich people who are advocates for the poor, or chronically ill individuals who oppose national health care. As we discuss in this and subsequent chapters, people's opinions on specific issues are shaped by their broader political predispositions such as their party identification and core political values (e.g., Feldman 1988; Alvarez and Brehm 2002; Goren 2004; Haidt 2012), which may differ greatly among individuals. For some, these political predispositions take on the status of an ideological worldview. Political predispositions tend to be stable, even over a lifetime. While these predispositions might be influenced by personal circumstance and certainly are subject to change, they have their origin in early political learning or political socialization.

Political psychologists stress the mechanisms by which political opinions are shaped by the way information is processed. The two variations are called online and memory-based processing. Suppose one is asked his or her opinion about a political issue. With *online* processing, individuals are able to immediately recall their position, which can be updated as new information arrives. Updated opinions are then stored in long-term memory and recalled when needed (Lodge, Steenbergen, and Brau 1995). Memory-based processors lack this immediate recall but instead consult their memory for relevant considerations that favor one side of the issue or the other. Online processing is particularly applicable to political campaigns, where information is relatively abundant and attitudes are accessed with some frequency. When survey respondents are asked their opinions about policies or politicians, the more politically sophisticated are most prone to online processing, as they readily access their updated information and attitudes without needing to think the matter through. The memory-based approach helps us understand opinions where information is less plentiful, and it may be more appropriate for attitudes not accessed regularly.

Low Information Rationality

How informed must citizens be in order to make rational decisions? Research on "low information rationality" (Popkin 1991; Lupia and McCubbins 1998) contends that even unsophisticated citizens, mostly barren of political knowledge, can make political choices as if they were much better informed, or perhaps even fully informed. In voting or forming opinions, people can rely on shortcuts or heuristics. The most obvious of these is party identification. In congressional elections, one can be certain to vote for the most ideologically conservative candidate by simply voting Republican. No further information is needed—not even the name of the candidates. The same holds for the formation of political opinions.

One key is the "likeability heuristic" (Brady and Sniderman 1985). Citizens with little political information can take cues from sources they like and trust, such as Rush Limbaugh, Planned Parenthood, or any other issue advocacy group, and simply adopt the same issue position. All that is necessary is for the individual to like or dislike the source in order to form the equivalent of a well-informed political opinion (Arceneaux and Kolodny 2009; Boudreau 2009). Of course, low information does not mean no information. At a minimum, one needs to know where the liked (or disliked) group stands on a particular issue.

Depth of Opinion-Holding

Chapter 2 presented examples of how seemingly minor variations in the framing and wording of survey questions can provoke major variations in survey results. Such phenomena could occur only if people were often ambivalent about their political convictions. On a given political issue, some survey respondents can recall from memory long-term convictions that they have held on the particular subject. Many, however, can offer no more than the top-of-the-head casual opinions of the kind sometimes known as *doorstep opinions*. One consequence is a disturbing degree of response instability when people are interviewed more than once, in what is called a *panel survey*. Many panelists who offer opinions in successive interviews change their position from one side to the other—which is seemingly inconsistent with the traditional notion of an attitude as an enduring predisposition. The implications are important for understanding public opinion.

Table 3.3 shows examples of response turnover from a special (pilot) ANES survey back in 1989. The issues varied from the hotly debated (abortion, death penalty) to the technical and obscure (funding the Stealth bomber, building a new Alaska pipeline). Respondent views were measured in the summer and again in the fall of 1989. Respondents received no filter to encourage nonresponses, and over 90 percent offered opinions to each question.[4]

The table shows from 13 to 22 percent switching sides between interviews just a few months apart. As discussed later, analysts agree that almost all of such switching represents not true opinion change but rather some sort of response error. As one would expect, more response error appears for obscure issues such as Alaska pipelines and Stealth bombers, about which people typically do not think much, than for salient moral issues like abortion and the death penalty.

The setup of Table 3.3 enhances the observed stability because multiple respondent choices are collapsed into two alternatives. Responses appear less stable when a middle ground is included. Table 3.4 presents the abortion example again, this time with three alternatives.

Whereas in Table 3.3 the choices for restrictions on abortion were combined as one, for Table 3.4 we separate out the extreme "right-to-life" position that abortions should never be permitted or permitted only under exceptional circumstances from the more moderate or middle position that abortions "should be permitted, but only after the need has been clearly established." The turnover table now shows

TABLE 3.3 Turnover of Opinion Response on Selected Issues, 1989 ANES Pilot Study

		Death Penalty				Stealth Bomber	
		Summer 1989				Summer 1989	
		Oppose	Favor			Oppose	Favor
Fall 1989	Oppose	19%	5%	Fall 1989	Oppose	41%	8%
	Favor	5%	73%		Favor	9%	42%

		Abortion				More Welfare Spending	
		Summer 1989				Summer 1989	
		Legal	Restricted			Favor	Oppose
Fall 1989	Legal	34%	5%	Fall 1989	Favor	35%	11%
	Restricted	6%	53%		Oppose	11%	43%

		Affirmative Action				New Alaska Oil Pipeline	
		Summer 1989				Summer 1989	
		Favor	Oppose			Oppose	Favor
Fall 1989	Favor	13%	8%	Fall 1989	Oppose	36%	10%
	Oppose	5%	74%		Favor	12%	42%

		More Gun Control				More Cooperation with Russia	
		Summer 1989				Summer 1989	
		Favor	Oppose			Favor	Oppose
Fall 1989	Favor	59%	7%	Fall 1989	Favor	38%	10%
	Oppose	13%	21%		Oppose	13%	39%

		More Spending to Fight AIDS				More Aid to Nicaraguan Contras	
		Summer 1989				Summer 1989	
		Favor	Oppose			Oppose	Favor
Fall 1989	Favor	48%	8%	Fall 1989	Oppose	49%	11%
	Oppose	15%	29%		Favor	10%	30%

Source: Based on National Election Studies, 1989 pilot study data. In some instances, framing of question varied with respondent and with wave.

25 percent changing their position from one survey to the next, with many respondents finding the middle position attractive. Notably, however, virtually no respondent switched from pro-choice to pro-life or vice versa.[5]

If the amount of turnover of responses to the abortion question seems high, consider that abortion positions are probably the most stable of political attitude responses, rivaled perhaps only by party identification (Converse and Markus 1979; Wetstein 1993; Green, Palmquist, and Schickler 2002). Less morally charged issues show considerably less response stability. Typical is the turnover of responses to the

TABLE 3.4   Opinion Consistency on Abortion, 1989

	Summer 1989		
	Never permitted, or only if rape, incest, or woman's life in danger	Other than if rape, incest, or woman's life in danger, after need established	Always permitted as a matter of personal choice
Fall 1989			
Never permitted, or only if rape, incest, or woman's life in danger	31%	6%	1%
Other than if rape, incest, or woman's life in danger, after need established	6%	12%	4%
Always permitted as a matter of personal choice	2%	5%	34%

Source: Based on National Election Studies, 1989 pilot study.

TABLE 3.5   Opinion Consistency on Whether Government Should Provide Fewer or More Services, 2004

	Preelection Response, 2004		
	Government should provide many fewer services	In between, no opinion	Government should provide many more services
Postelection Response, 2004			
Government should provide many fewer services	14%	6%	4%
In between, no opinion	5%	21%	16%
Government should provide many more services	2%	9%	23%

Source: Based on National Election Studies, 2004 election data.

ANES's "spending and services" question between the preelection and postelection surveys in 2004, shown in Table 3.5.

Only a minority of the respondents (37 percent) had a sufficiently firm attitude to take the same side consistently (pro/pro or con/con) in both interviews. A few (6 percent) changed sides completely from one interview to the next, and others

(21 percent) took no position in either interview. The remainder (36 percent) took sides in one interview but not in the other.

The most studied patterns of response instability are from several four-year, three-wave panels as part of the ANES (Converse 1964; Converse and Markus 1979). In a 1950s panel, the same respondents were interviewed at two-year intervals—in 1956, 1958, and 1960. The ANES 1970s panel interviewed the same respondents in 1972, 1974, and 1976. In the 1990s, ANES conducted a small panel with the same respondents interviewed in 1992, 1994, and again in 1996. The most recent multiyear ANES panel study followed a set of respondents from the 2000 election to the end of the 2004 campaign.

One important fact learned from the ANES panel studies is that the time interval between panel waves has little bearing on the observed amount of response stability. For instance, the degrees of response turnover to questions on abortion and guaranteed living standards asked four years apart in the ANES 1970s, 1990s, and 2000s panels are only slightly larger than the amount of response turnover shown in Tables 3.3 and 3.4 for the same issues when the same question was asked only a few months apart.

This evidence suggests that most response change does not represent true change in underlying attitudes. If people were really changing their minds frequently, long time intervals would produce greater decay of initial positions. While scholars agree that response instability generally does not indicate true attitude conversion, they disagree in what the unstable responses mean. One position, developed by Philip E. Converse, holds that people who change positions usually have no position but instead respond randomly. This "nonattitude" explanation has been challenged by other scholars, who prefer a "measurement error" explanation. While the details of the opposing interpretations are too complicated to receive full treatment here, we can present brief sketches of the competing points of view.

The "Nonattitudes" Explanation

After analyzing turnover patterns from the 1950s panel, Converse (1964) proposed that virtually all respondents who change their position over time hold no true convictions but instead express random responses or "nonattitudes." The strong evidence for infrequent true change is that response instability varies little with the time between surveys. Surveys four months and four years apart yield about the same amount of response turnover. If people were actually changing their minds, observed opinions would be more stable over the briefer time interval.

If the nonattitude thesis is correct, most observed response change is random error, as if changers are simply flipping coins. Just as coins can be flipped heads one time and tails the next, they can also be flipped consistently heads or tails both times. Thus a further implication of the nonattitudes thesis is that many consistent responses are random responses that appear stable only by chance. On one notorious issue from the 1950s panel, the abstract "power and housing" question (whether "the government should leave things like electric power and housing for private businessmen to handle"), Converse (1964, 293) reached a startling conclusion. He estimated that less than 20 percent of the adult public held meaningful attitudes on this issue even though about two-thirds ventured a viewpoint on the matter when asked in a survey.

Many have found the implications of the nonattitudes explanation quite disturbing. In a democracy, public officials presumably respond to the policy preferences of the public, enacting these preferences into law. But if large segments of the public do not really have coherent preferences or preferences at all, why should elected officials heed their views? Indeed, if survey responses are largely nonattitudes, why should anyone take public opinion polls seriously? Fortunately, there are ways to avoid such a pessimistic assessment.

The "Measurement Error" Explanation

An obvious implication of the nonattitudes explanation is that the seemingly random element to survey responses is the fault of the respondents themselves, as if their lack of political sophistication is to blame. That is, the assumption is that when people give unstable responses to opinion questions, the reason is a lack of the political sophistication necessary to form crystallized opinions. But if, instead, response instability is largely unrelated to political sophistication, then we can hardly place blame on the public for its lack of sophistication.

In fact, contrary to this prediction of nonattitude theory, response instability varies little if at all with measures of political sophistication or political knowledge (Achen 1975; Erikson 1979; Feldman 1989). The disturbing level of instability found for surveys of the general public is also found for subsamples representing the sophisticated and informed. If even politically sophisticated individuals respond with a seeming random component, what is to blame? It probably is not a lack of capability on the part of those being interviewed.

For this reason, a measurement error explanation has been proposed to account for response error (Achen 1975; Erikson 1979; Ansolabehere, Rodden, and Synder 2008). This explanation does not challenge the evidence that most response instability represents error rather than true change. However, by the measurement error explanation, the "blame" for the response instability is placed not so much on the capabilities of the respondents as on the survey questions themselves. Even the best survey questions produce some instability from respondents who hold weak or ambivalent attitudes about policy issues. Some inherent limitations in the survey enterprise make measuring attitudes an imprecise task. These include ambiguities in question wording, single-item indicators, the problem of investigator-defined responses to closed-ended questions that may not be congruent with the way respondents think about issues, and the problem of respondents having to give immediate answers to perhaps 100 or more questions with virtually no opportunity for reflection or considered judgment. Thus it is the inherent limitations of the survey method that mostly explain response instability, not the inherent limitations of the respondent.

An Explanation Based on Response Probability

John Zaller and Stanley Feldman offer a "theory of the survey response" that provides a more general explanation for response instability and incorporates the findings of both the nonattitudes and measurement approaches (Zaller 1992; Zaller and Feldman 1992; see also Alvarez and Brehm 2002). From this perspective, respondents do not hold fixed, stable attitudes on many issues, but they *do* have propensities to respond one way or another. The answer they give, however, depends on the considerations that come to mind when a question is asked. A consideration is simply anything that affects how someone decides on a political issue, one way or another. For example, when one is asked for an opinion on universal health insurance, considerations may include higher taxes, sick people unable to get medical care, and big government. The actual survey response depends on the considerations that are accessible when the question is asked. Assuming the considerations listed were of equal importance, the respondent would oppose universal health insurance as two considerations point in that direction versus one that points to support.

But the considerations that come to mind at one point in time may not be the same as at another. Usually, for our hypothetical respondent, the considerations that come to mind induce opposition to universal health care. But perhaps the respondent recently saw a television news story about a hardworking man paid poverty-level wages who could not afford medical treatment for his bedridden wife. When asked the universal health care question, that consideration may be at the top of the head and induce support for universal health care. But the news story will eventually be forgotten, and considerations that induce opposition will again predominate. Thus, for many issues, responses are probabilistic. There is a propensity to come down on one side of an issue, but the probability is something greater than 0 and less than 1.0.

Even though the opinions expressed on an issue may vary, the underlying attitudes that give rise to them may be quite stable. Suppose our hypothetical individual has a 70 percent probability of choosing the conservative response on national health insurance, and further assume that this places her at the eightieth percentile of conservatism on the issue (the respondent is more conservative than 80 percent of citizens). Within a period of two to four years, our respondent should still be near the same eightieth percentile. Stimuli in the environment might cause minor variations in probabilistic responses—for example, a liberal national mood swing might lower everybody's probability of a conservative response. But our hypothetical respondent would still be more conservative than 80 percent of citizens.

We have a paradox. Peoples' *latent* attitudes tend to be stable over time as described earlier. Yet any particular survey response is problematical. Given this dilemma, how can we improve the measurement of political opinion? One solution is to ask multiple questions of respondents on similar issues and record their average response. When using multiple items to measure a concept, response stability increases significantly (Ansolabehere, Rodden, and Synder 2008).

If people's attitudes are as stable as just described at the microlevel, should we expect opinion trends at the macrolevel? We show in the next chapter that net public opinion on an issue is often very stable over time. However, we observe interesting exceptions where public opinion moves in a unidirectional fashion in response to one-sided environmental stimuli (Page and Shapiro 1992; Zaller 1992). An example is the first few months of the Iraq war, where both Republicans and Democrats in Congress mostly supported the president, and belief that the "cost of the war" was worth it hovered around 60 percent or more (Holsti 2012).

3-2 Liberal–Conservative Ideology and the Organization of Opinions

When a person expresses viewpoints on a number of political subjects, we might expect that these opinions are connected to each other in some pattern. One expectation is that opinions are connected by logical consistency with core political values. For instance, a person who believes strongly in individual responsibility would be inclined to respond negatively toward government help for the inner cities or toward the government guaranteeing a job and a good standard of living. A person with strong egalitarian values would be expected to respond in an opposite fashion. To take another example, a person committed to traditional social values probably would oppose abortion rights and oppose people who are gay serving in the military. A person with a strong belief in individual choice would take the opposite view.

We could try to account for opinions in terms of how people weigh political values such as individual responsibility, equality, tradition, and individual freedom. When we describe a person's core political values in this way, we begin to describe his or her political ideology. In the broadest sense, a person's ideology is any set of beliefs about the proper order of society and how it can be achieved. People with strong ideologies use their personal ideology as a guide for understanding the political world.

As a convenient shorthand, observers often prefer to reduce ideology to the single dimension of the left–right ideological continuum, classifying political values simply according to their relative liberalism versus conservatism. This classification permeates discussions of American politics by the media and political partisans. The left–right ideological distinction between liberals and conservatives contains considerable useful political content when describing the opinions of political elites or politically active people. For instance, delegates to national political conventions clearly understand ideological labels and tend to polarize as consistent liberals or conservatives (Herrera 1992; Jennings 1992). Because the ideological liberal–conservative continuum holds less meaning to those near the bottom of the sophistication ladder, the importance of liberal–conservative ideology within the mass public is a matter of uncertainty and controversy.[6]

A standard poll question asks respondents their ideological identification, usually with the three choices of liberal, moderate, or conservative. As many as one-fourth decline to classify themselves ideologically given the choice of "no opinion." Of those who choose, almost half choose the "moderate" or "middle-of-the-road" alternative when it is offered.

Ideally, ideological classification is a convenient way to measure individuals' core political values and to summarize their political views on a variety of issues. In practice, the result is mixed. The most politically sophisticated segment of the public approximates the ideal. For them, ideological identification goes a long way toward describing their political convictions. But when less sophisticated people respond to the ideological identification question with a response of liberal, moderate, or conservative, we can be less sure of what the response means. At worst, the response represents some idiosyncratic meaning known only to the respondent, or perhaps a doorstep opinion made up on the spot.

Liberal and Conservative Terminology

What do the terms *liberal* and *conservative* actually mean? At the philosophical level, political thinkers with reputations as liberals and conservatives differ in several ways. Conservatives view society as a control for humanity's worst impulses; liberals view the human condition as relative to the quality of society. Conservatives consider people inherently unequal and worthy of unequal rewards; liberals are egalitarian. Conservatives venerate tradition, order, and authority; liberals believe planned change brings the possibility of improvement.[7]

Of course, people who are liberal or conservative in their practical politics need not strictly adhere to the philosophy associated with their ideological label. Nevertheless, we can see the implications of these philosophic distinctions at work in the common applications of the ideological labels to political points of view. Conservatives are more afraid than liberals of "big government," except on matters of law and order and national security. In foreign policy preferences, conservatives are more aggressive; liberals are more cooperative or yielding. Conservatives are more likely to see harmful consequences of government help for the disadvantaged, while liberals see the benefits. Conservatives tend to be moralistic; liberals are more permissive.

These kinds of relative distinctions are familiar to people who follow politics closely. But the language of ideology holds less meaning for the public as a whole. One test is whether the individual can both identify the Republican as the more conservative party and offer a plausible definition of the term *conservative*. Throughout the years roughly half the public passes this test of understanding of ideological labels (Converse 1964; Lewis-Beck et al. 2008).

What do people think of when they hear the terms *liberal* and *conservative*? Table 3.6 summarizes the responses from a 1994 ANES study of how people describe liberals and conservatives. Respondents were asked, "What sorts of things do you have in mind when you say that someone's political views are liberal?" and similarly, "What sorts of things do you have in mind when you say that someone's political views are conservative?" They were allowed up to three responses to each question, six overall. Seventy-eight percent of the sample gave at least one response.

As in other years, economic distinctions were used most often to explain the difference between liberals and conservatives. Liberals spend; conservatives save. Liberals are seen as favoring the welfare state and give away programs; conservatives are seen as favoring free enterprise and opposing big spending social programs. Liberals were also seen as being more change oriented and innovative, while conservatives were viewed as more status quo-oriented and rigid. All these are reasonably broad distinctions. But the public also sees differences between liberals and conservatives on narrower issues. Conservatives are seen as moralistic and religious, while liberals are seen as having more flexible moral standards and not as religious. The contemporary issues of abortion and gay rights show up in the expected fashion. However, with the end of the Cold War, fewer respondents mention defense and national security issues than in the past. In addition, a number of responses deal with peripheral matters such as liberal and conservative positions on narrow policy issues (see also Lewis-Beck et al. 2008, ch. 9).

TABLE 3.6 Perceived Meaning of Ideological Labels, 1994

Question:	What sorts of things do you have in mind when you say someone's political views are liberal?
	What sorts of things do you have in mind when you say someone's political views are conservative?

Type of Mention	Example	Percentage Mentioning
Change	L's accept change/new ideas/innovative.	23
	C's resist change/protect status quo/rigid.	
Fiscal	L's for socialism/welfare state/give-away programs.	24
	C's for free enterprise/capitalism/oppose social programs.	
Personality	L's are open-minded/not concerned with consequences.	14
	C's are moralists/concerned with consequences.	
Morality	L's not interested in setting moral standards/not religious.	13
	C's have definite moral standards/religious.	
Spend/save	L's free spenders/favor government spending.	24
	C's thrifty/economize on government spending.	
Civil liberties	L's support upholding of Bill of Rights/human rights.	5
	C's want to limit Bill of Rights/human rights.	
Class	L's for little people/working people/unions.	12
	C's for big business/the rich.	
Abortion	L's are pro-choice.	15
	C's are pro-life.	
Gay rights	L's favor gay rights.	9
	C's oppose gay rights.	
Defense	L's weak on defense/national security.	4
	C's strong on defense/national security.	
People	L's identify label with prominent national figures.	5
	C's identify label with prominent national figures.	

$N = 595$.

Source: Based on American National Election Studies, 1994. The questions allow for multiple responses.

TABLE 3.7	Ideological Preferences and Opinions on Selected Policy Issues, 2012*		

Belief	Support Among Self-Declared Liberals	Support Among Self-Declared Conservatives
The government should provide "more services even if it means an increase in spending"	78	20
The government should guarantee "that every person has a job and good standard of living"	62	11
Favor 2010 Health Care Law (Obamacare)	83	28
The government "should make every effort to improve the social and economic position of blacks"	26	9
Permit abortion "always" or "if needed"	67	31
The government "should make it more difficult to buy a gun"	60	27
Oppose torture to fight terrorism	81	54
Legalize gay marriage**	90	37
Oppose "death penalty for persons convicted of murder"	45	22
The United States "should spend less on defense"	65	20

*Reported figures are percentage of opinion-holders only.

**On gay marriage question, proportions are of those preferring legal marriage or no recognition, excluding responses favoring civil unions.

Source: American National Election Studies, 2012.

When survey respondents are asked to classify themselves on the liberal–conservative spectrum, their answers tend to correspond to their policy positions. Examples of the relationships and positions on specific issues are shown in Table 3.7. Self-declared liberals take issue positions considerably more liberal than do self-declared conservatives.

This tendency is even clearer when issue positions are summed over several issues. Table 3.8 compares people's liberalism and conservatism as measured by their composite stands over the ten issues shown in Table 3.7 with their self-declared ideology. People who are very liberal on the ten issues identify as liberals, and people who are very conservative on the ten issues overwhelmingly identify themselves as conservatives. It may also be noted that people who cannot identify themselves as liberal, moderate, or conservative tend to cluster in the center of the political spectrum as measured by their stands on specific issues.

TABLE 3.8   Correspondence of Ideological Self-Ratings and Summary of Positions on Ten Issues, 2012

Ideological Self-Rating	Summary Position on Ten Issues*				
	Very Liberal	Liberal	Center	Conservative	Very Conservative
Liberal	53%	32%	17%	8%	1%
Moderate	20	27	29	27	12
Conservative	8	15	22	41	80
Don't know	19	26	32	25	7
	100%	100%	100%	100%	100%
(Percentage of total sample)	(14)	(22)	(27)	(18)	(20)

*See the Appendix for construction of ten-item summary scores. The full distribution of scores is shown in Figure 3.1. The categories here are as follows: Very Liberal −10 to −5, Liberal −4 to −2, Center −1 to +1, Conservative +2 to +4, and Very Conservative +5 to +10.

Source: Based on National Election Studies, 2012 election data.

Use of Ideological Language

Although ideological terms are within the vocabularies of a large share of the American public, few actually employ them to defend their choices of party or candidates. For each American National Election Study, respondents are asked what they like and dislike about each major party and presidential candidate. Starting with *The American Voter* (Campbell et al. 1960, 216–49), responses have been recorded according to their "levels of conceptualization."

Table 3.9 enumerates the electorate by these levels based on ANES surveys for presidential year from 1956 to 2000 (data are not available for 1992 and 1996 or beyond 2000). The researchers were interested in the conceptual sophistication of the responses. To what extent is the public motivated in evaluating parties and candidates by a reasonably rigorous use of the ideological concepts of liberal and conservative, and what types of thinking motivates others in their vote choice?

Respondents who spontaneously and knowledgeably evaluated the parties and candidates in terms of their placement on the liberal–conservative spectrum were labeled as "ideologues" (meaning political sophisticates, and not as the term is sometimes used, an ideology-driven fanatic). Ideologues evaluate candidates and parties in broad abstract terms consistent with our understanding of liberalism and conservatism.

As can be seen in Table 3.9, only a small portion of the electorate is classed as ideologues, 20 percent in 2000. A typical ideologue in the 2000 election responded as follows when asked: "Is there anything you like about Al Gore?" (Lewis-Beck et al. 2008, 262).

TABLE 3.9   Levels of Political Conceptualization, 1956–2000

	1956	1960	1964	1968	1972	1976	1980	1984	1988	2000
Ideologues	12%	19%	27%	26%	22%	21%	21%	19%	18%	20%
Group benefits	42	31	27	24	27	26	31	26	36	28
Nature of the times	24	26	20	29	34	30	30	35	25	28
No issue content	22	23	26	21	17	24	19	19	21	24
	100%	99%	100%	100%	100%	101%	101%	99%	99%	100%
Number of cases	1,749	1,701	1,431	1,319	1,372	2,870	1,612	2,257	2,040	1,807

Source: 1956–1976: Paul R. Hagner and John C. Pierce, "Correlative Characteristics of Levels of Conceptualization in the American Public, 1956–1976," *Journal of Politics* 44 (August 1982), pp. 779–809, 1980–1988; compiled by Paul Hagner and Kathleen Knight; (2000); Lewis-Beck et al. (2008): 279.

Yes, I definitely like his stand on Social Security. He'll keep it and improve it. (Anything else?) His strong protection of the environment and stand against drilling oil in Alaska. (Anything else?) He is trying to work on the health program, which will be slow going. (Anything else?) I love his pro-choice stand and his program for schools.

An added 28 percent of the 2000 sample expressed their likes and dislikes about the candidates (Bush and Gore) and parties in terms of "group benefits," They tend to think in terms of identifiable interests like labor unions or environmental groups rather than along an abstract liberal–conservative continuum. How do the parties and candidates reward or punish favored citizen groups? Seniors, for example, frequently expressed their political likes and dislikes in terms of group benefits—for example, mentions of government health insurance were a common topic when asked about Al Gore. One citizen responded, "His health care, so that senior citizens will not have any out-of-pocket expenses; that is the direction we need to heed" (Lewis-Beck et al. 2000, 269). Many group-benefit responses were class-related, evoking the notion that Republicans favor big business while the Democrats favor the "little person."

Moving down the conceptual ladder, another 28 percent of the 2000 respondents referred to the "nature of the times" when evaluating candidates and parties. Nature-of-the-times voters were guided by perceptions of past performance, such as which candidate or party brought economic prosperity or which party kept its promises (or vice versa). A typical nature-of-the-times respondent, when asked what he disliked about the Democrats, said, "They promise too much giveaway at taxpayer expense." The same respondent when asked "Is there anything you like about the Republican Party?" offered, "They are willing to help you so you can work out your needs. People should not remain on welfare all their lives."

The lowest level of conceptualization, with 24 percent, is "no issue content." About a third of this group in 2000 expressed no likes or dislikes at all about the parties or candidates. Their comments tended to focus on the candidates' personal characteristics. This group evidenced no cognitive organization to their thinking and often simply fell back on party identification. Typical was the following exchange:

(Anything you like about the Democratic Party?)	"No."
(Anything you dislike about the Democratic Party?)	"The scandal that went on in the Oval Office. It was mockery."
(Anything you like about the Republican Party?)	"They do a good job in general, like the Reagan years, which is why we are doing good now. Beyond that, nothing specific."
(Anything you dislike about the Republican Party?)	"No" (Lewis-Beck et al. 2008, 278).

As we might expect, a variety of factors are related to the level of conceptualization, but none of these move the percentage of ideologues above one-third. There are slightly more ideologues among voters than nonvoters, but only by 4 percent. Education is also a strong determinant, with just 3 percent with less than a high school degree being ideologues compared to 31 percent with a college degree (Lewis-Beck et al. 2008, 281–8).

The distribution of how people conceptualize partisan politics may be interpreted to mean that Americans are not very ideological, and in one sense this is correct. The authors of *The American Voter* accounted for the scarcity of ideologues in terms of the public's "cognitive limitations," particularly a lack of intellectual ability to think in terms of ideological abstractions (Campbell et al. 1960, 253). Now many political scientists see *The American Voter* judgment as overly harsh. Although the authors did not realize it at the time, the 1956 presidential election was probably the least ideological of all modern campaigns, conducted essentially as a referendum on President Eisenhower's first term. Because the 1956 campaign was not conducted at an ideological level, respondents in that year were not apt to explain their likes and dislikes about parties and candidates in terms of ideological nuances. They chose the easier criteria of group representation and the nature of the times. Subsequent elections, starting with 1964, focused more sharply on issue differences among the candidates and parties, with the percentage of ideologues increasing noticeably over the percentage reported in 1956.

There are four lessons to be learned about the levels of conceptualization. First, at best one-fifth of the electorate pay meaningful attention to ideological themes. As we have seen, a greater proportion of the electorate can utilize the ideological language than are classifiable as ideologues. One explanation is that many individuals can use ideological labels without pursuing much ideology. For instance, many at the "group-interest" level identify with liberals or conservatives as a group with which they share a common interest, much as some may feel about teachers or labor unions (Tedin 1987).

Second, ideologues have distinctive background attributes. They are among the best educated, most knowledgeable, and most politically active segments of the electorate. Third, ideologues are among the most likely to vote (typically 90 percent of ideologues cast their ballot in presidential elections) and tend to be the most partisan segments of the electorate. They are likely to vote consistently for the same party from one election to the next. Fourth, the paucity of ideologues raise serious questions about the extent to which elections can reasonably be interpreted as mandates for policy change, since only about a fifth of the electorate is engaging in sophisticated ideological thinking about parties and candidates (Lewis-Beck et al. 2008, 289).

Ideology as Liberal–Conservative Consistency

Suppose we array the American public on a scale from most liberal to most conservative. What would this distribution look like? Would most people be at the liberal or conservative pole? Or would they cluster in the middle? Figure 3.1 displays the distribution of the American public's liberal–conservative "scores" as measured by their cumulative responses to ten opinion questions in the 2012 ANES survey. A person with all liberal opinions would score at minus 10, whereas a person who expresses conservative outlooks on all ten issues would score at plus 10. (For details of the index construction, see the Appendix.) Most respondents were near the midpoint of the scale (0), indicating that their liberal and conservative viewpoints balanced each other out.

Because over a series of issues most people give some liberal and some conservative positions, there is a temptation to label the public as political moderates. But these voters in the center cannot be grouped as sharing the same moderate ideology because they differ greatly in their pattern of responses on individual issues. For instance, one voter with balanced liberal and conservative views may be liberal on social welfare issues and civil rights but conservative on foreign policy and law

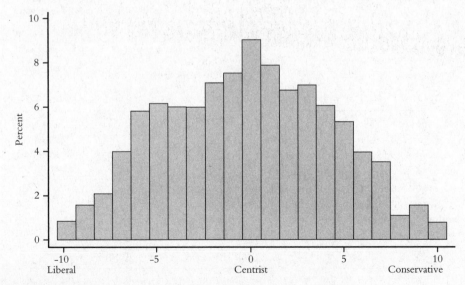

FIGURE 3.1 Distribution of composite opinion scores, 2012.

Source: Based on National Election Studies, 2012 election data.

and order, while another with equally balanced views professes exactly the opposite opinions. Still a third person may have an overall score that is neither very conservative nor very liberal for the reason that he or she expresses few opinions at all (a point emphasized by Treier and Hillygus 2009).

If ideology influences people's opinions, opinions on two separate issues should be predictable from one another because both are "constrained" by the opinion-holder's ideological perspective. If a conservative ideology binds some to oppose spending programs for example, their conservatism should compel them to support the death penalty or perhaps to oppose abortion rights. Table 3.10 shows examples of the search for ideological constraint.

For a pair of issues, an individual is more likely to offer consistently liberal or conservative positions if the issues are logically related or share content. Table 3.10 (a)

TABLE 3.10	**Correlations Between Opinions on Selected Issues, 2012**						
		(a) Increase Domestic Spending				**(b)** Ban Torture of Terror Suspects	
		Pro	*Con*			*Pro*	*Con*
Affordable Care Act (Obamacare)	Pro	33%	15%	**Cut military spending**	Pro	33%	7%
	Con	11%	41%		Con	30%	30%
	Gamma = .78				Gamma = .65		
		(c) Legalize All Abortions				**(d)** Legalize All Abortions	
		Pro	*Con*			*Pro*	*Con*
Legalize gay marriage	Pro	39%	25%	**Affordable Care Act (Obamacare)**	Pro	31%	23%
	Con	7%	28%		Con	14%	32%
	Gamma = .72				Gamma = .51		
		(e) More Gun Control Legislation				**(f)** More Domestic Spending	
		Pro	*Con*			*Pro*	*Con*
More aid to blacks	Pro	14%	10%	**Cut military spending**	Pro	19%	15%
	Con	27%	48%		Con	25%	40%
	Gamma = .44				Gamma = .34		

Source: Based on American National Election Studies, 2012 election data.

presents one such example. People's opinions regarding government involvement in health care are rather predictable from their general views on domestic government spending. We find a certain tough versus tenderminded consistency on defense spending and torture, as people tend to either resist more defense spending and oppose torture or do the reverse. We also find some consistency of views on paired cultural issues like abortion and gay marriage, and we see that in Table 3.10(c).

When issues are not closely related in content, liberal–conservative consistency tends to fade, but not entirely. The next two examples in Table 3.10(d) and (e) compare opinions on pairs of issues that are only remotely related—Obamacare and abortion, guns and aid to blacks. We definitely see a pattern of correlation for these issue pairs, but to a lesser degree. In these instances, while each issue has a liberal and a conservative side as these ideological terms are used, there is no compelling argument why a person could not simultaneously hold a liberal belief on one issue and a conservative belief on the other. Consider also the relationship between "more" domestic spending and "less" military spending, shown in Table 3.10(f). Arguably, people should gravitate toward one side of the trade-off of either more domestic spending and less military spending (liberal) or less domestic spending and more military spending (conservative). Table 3.10(f) shows only a modest correlation. Favoring spending in one domain does not offer a sound prediction of less appetite for spending in the other.

Actually, ideological constraint has clearly increased over the years. Since Converse (1964) pioneered research on constraint in the 1960s, Americans have become more consistently liberal or conservative on pairs of issues. We continue this discussion in Section 3.4 on growing polarization.

Liberal–conservative opinion consistency is highest among those most knowledgeable about politics, such as people identified as "ideologues" (Stimson 1975; Knight 1985). We can illustrate this point by comparing the respondents classified as least knowledgeable and most knowledgeable in the 2012 ANES survey. Among the select "high-information" group, opinions on different issues are highly correlated, while for the "low-information" group there is essentially no correlation at all. Our illustration is for the 2012 relationship between opinion on the Affordable Care Act (Obamacare) and opinion on abortion.

		Low Information Legal Abortions		High Information Legal Abortions	
		Pro	*Con*	*Pro*	*Con*
Affordable Care Act	*Pro*	20%	37%	37%	12%
	Con	14%	29%	14%	35%
		Gamma = .06		Gamma = .76	

We see that with the accumulation of a high level of political information, people tend toward consistently liberal or consistently conservative positions, while we see no relationship at all for those with low levels of information. A broader illustration compares the high-information, medium-information, and low-information groups in terms of their distributions on the composite ten-item liberal–conservative

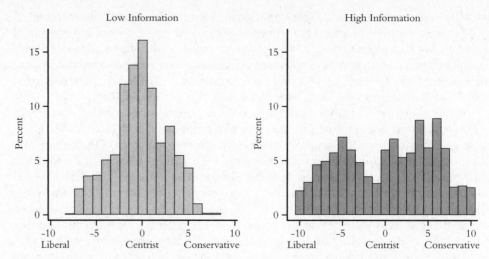

FIGURE 3.2 Composite opinion by information level. Information levels are for the highest and lowest third on information about candidate positions.

Source: Based on National Election Studies, 2012 election data.

scale. Figure 3.2 shows the results. Low-information voters cluster toward the center of the spectrum, as one would expect. Medium-information voters show a more even, almost flat density of opinion across the spectrum. High-information voters cluster more toward opinion on the left or right, with a bimodal distribution showing surprisingly few in the center.

Ideological Thinking: A Summary

The public is mixed in its understanding and usage of ideological language and thinking. Most citizens do not engage in the ideological thinking of the sort found among political elites. But ordinary citizens often use ideological labels in at least a limited way as part of their political vocabulary. Many, however, do not do even this. For perhaps as much as half the electorate, the liberal versus conservative component of political discourse is nothing more than a confusion of background noise. The fact that there is little ideological consistency to people's issue positions demonstrates that few people use their ideological position as a cuing device to arrange their responses to the political world. The kind of attitudinal constraint that motivates people toward consistently liberal, conservative, or moderate political viewpoints is reserved for a relatively small, politically active segment of the public.

In our effort to understand public opinion, we should not ignore this politically sophisticated segment of the American public, which does follow government and politics in terms of the liberal–conservative continuum. Thinking about politics in liberal versus conservative terms is sophisticated not because it is preferable to hold ideologically extreme convictions or to view the political world through a distorted lens. Rather, having the liberal–conservative spectrum as a political frame of reference is necessary to understand the language of politics as it is practiced by political elites. Many ordinary Americans do follow this ideological discussion.

3-3 Party Identification and the Organization of Political Opinions

So far, we have ignored partisanship as a way of organizing political opinions. More than on the basis of ideology, Americans' political opinions are structured by party identification. Whereas ideological identification may be of particular relevance for a select segment of the public, people at all levels of sophistication appear to hold meaningful party identifications. Whereas ideological identification and questions about core values are intended to summarize a person's political predispositions, party identification represents a person's net evaluation of the Republican and Democratic parties. It is relatively easy to prefer one party over the other while holding little political information or giving even modest thought to most political issues.

For most people, party identification is a central aspect of political identity. Compared to ordinary political opinions, people's party identifications are quite stable over time, both before and after adjustment for measurement error (Green, Palmquist, and Schickler 2002). For instance, when interviewed during two successive presidential campaigns four years apart, most respondents persist with their original basic identification as a Democrat, Independent, or Republican. Only a small percentage of respondents switch party identification from Democratic to Republican or vice versa. Those who switch generally move in and out of the Independent category rather than "convert" from one side to the other.

As discussed in Chapter 5, the source of one's party identification is often the political values that were transmitted in the family during childhood. At the other end of the causal chain, party identification is the best predictor of how people vote. Following the sequence through, we find that people tend to vote for the party with which their parents identified.

Survey researchers normally ascertain party identification by asking respondents whether they consider themselves Democrats, Independents, or Republicans. Partisans may then be asked whether they consider themselves "strong" or "not so strong" (often translated as "weak") Republicans or Democrats. Classifying on strength plus partisan direction makes four categories of partisans. Meanwhile, Independents are sometimes asked whether they "lean" toward one of the parties. The Independents can be classified as Republican leaners, Democratic leaners, and pure Independents. Pure Independents typically make up no more than about 10 percent of a national sample, suggesting that few citizens are purely neutral when it comes to partisanship. Altogether, there are seven potential categories of party identification, on a scale from "strong Democrat" to "strong Republican." Usually, however, the three-category classification is sufficient. Except where otherwise indicated, this book employs the simple three-category division of party identification as Republicans (strong plus weak), Democrats (strong plus weak), and Independents (pure plus partisan leaners).

Party identification can be a handy cue by which to orient the remainder of one's political beliefs. An alert Republican, for example, learns that a good Republican is supposed to subscribe to conservative positions on certain issues and responds accordingly. At the same time, we might expect that the rare event of a partisan conversion results when a person becomes aware that his or her ideological views are out of alignment with his or her partisan heritage. These causal processes could not occur, however, unless people were aware of the Democratic versus Republican differences on the issues of the day.

Perceptions of Party Differences

As we show in Chapter 10, Democratic and Republican leaders are ideologically different, with the Republicans generally conservative and Democrats generally liberal. Here we can ask: To what extent does the public perceive these party differences?

The American National Election Studies have regularly asked their respondents to place the major parties' positions on selected issues of the day, typically on a seven-point scale from liberal to conservative. We can classify response patterns as either placing the Democrats to the left of the Republicans (correct), the Republicans to the left of the Democrats, rate them tied at the identical position, or declare no interest in the issue. Table 3.11 presents the perceptions of the parties' relative positions on various issues in recent ANES surveys. Typically, from one-half to two-thirds rate the Democrats as the more liberal (left) party. Few guess incorrectly and identify the Republican Party with the liberal position.

Over the years, the public has increasingly seen party differences on the issues. As recently as the early 1960s, the public saw party differences only in terms of social welfare issues. The public image of the parties as distinct on social welfare issues goes back to the New Deal era of the 1930s, when the parties began to develop opposite philosophies toward the role of the federal government in the economy. Until about 1964, party differences on issues outside the social welfare sphere were not sharply focused at the leadership level, such as congressional and presidential politics. It is no surprise, therefore, that before the 1960s people generally did not see either party as liberal or conservative on civil rights or foreign policy issues.

TABLE 3.11 Public Perceptions of Party Differences on Issues, 1996–2012

Perceptions of Which Party Is More in Favor of. . . .	Democrats (%)	Republicans (%)	No Difference, Don't Know, No Interest (%)
More domestic spending (2012)	72	9	19
Reducing defense spending (2012)	59	16	26
Guaranteed living standard (2012)	71	6	22
Aid to blacks (2004)	56	8	36
Equal role for women (2004)	42	9	49
National health insurance (2012)	74	7	18
Abortion rights (2012)	73	7	20
Regulating the environment (1996)	48	9	44

Source: Based on National Election Studies data.

Nowadays, Americans generally perceive the Democrats as the more liberal party not only on social welfare issues but also on civil rights, foreign policy, plus social issues like gay rights. Arguably, this happened largely because the parties became more polarized at the elite level (Poole and Rosenthal 2007; Abramowitz 2010). Public perceptions simply followed the behavior and the rhetoric of party leaders. The biggest change occurred with the ideological Goldwater election of 1964 (Carmines and Stimson 1989). Senator Goldwater, the 1964 Republican candidate, campaigned as a forthright conservative. By opposing the Civil Rights Act of 1964, he altered the Republican image on civil rights. By his tough posturing about the Soviet Union, he made the Republicans appear to be the most belligerent on foreign policy. His Democratic opponent, President Lyndon Johnson, was able to exploit Goldwater's image as an extreme conservative. Goldwater lost the election in a landslide, but he and his supporters moved the Republican Party sharply to the right in a manner that has lasted into the twenty-first century.

Events after 1964 added to the growing perceptions of party differences, as growing polarization of Democratic and Republican elites fueled a further division between Republican and Democratic identifiers in the mass public (Hetherington 2006). By the 1980s, public perceptions of the parties began to seriously diverge on "social issues" such as abortion, "toughness" on crime, and gay rights, with Republicans seen as moralistic and Democrats as permissive. Today, on virtually all national issues that divide Americans, the two major parties are seen as taking quite different sides. While there was once a time when critics complained that the parties did not offer meaningful policy choices, the more typical complaint today is that the chasm has become too wide. As we show in Chapter 10, a sharpening of divisions between congressional Democrats and Republicans maintains the liberal–conservative party polarization among everyday citizens that began in 1964.

Party Identification and Policy Preferences

Increasingly over the years, Americans have become polarized along partisan and ideological lines, clustering as liberal Democrats or conservative Republicans. Table 3.12 displays some examples of partisan divergence on specific issues from the 2012 ANES study. Figure 3.3 displays the difference between Democrats and Republicans in terms of scores on the composite ten-item index of liberalism–conservatism. In terms of their net ideological direction, most Democrats are left of center and most Republicans are right of center. But there are some conservative Democrats and liberal Republicans. Clearly, ideology and partisanship are not the same thing.

The correlation between partisanship and ideological direction sharpens if we isolate informed citizens. Figure 3.4 repeats the ideological comparison of Democrats and Republicans, this time separately, for voters at the low and high ends of the information scale. Among low-information voters there exists almost no correlation between partisanship and ideology; in this set, Democrats are only barely to the left of Republicans on average, with considerable overlap. But among high-information voters, virtually all Democrats are to the left of center, and virtually all Republicans to the right. In other words, find an informed voter and partisanship follows ideology, or perhaps it is the other way around.

TABLE 3.12   Party Identification and Policy Opinions, 2012

	Percent Liberal Among				
Issue	**Strong Dem.**	**Weak Dem.**	**Ind.**	**Weak Repub.**	**Strong Repub.**
More domestic spending	91	73	36	12	18
Job guarantee	59	53	33	15	9
Less defense spending	57	48	39	21	9
Preferential hiring of blacks	37	21	15	2	6
Obamacare	93	77	47	28	10
Ban torture of terror suspects	80	73	68	59	45
Legalize gay marriage	75	82	69	51	20
Raise taxes on wealthy	91	91	78	68	62
Favor more gun control	64	57	44	24	18
Favor abortion rights	61	56	41	35	21
Mean	*70*	*61*	*48*	*31*	*20*
Liberal identifiers*	78	85	34	6	2

*Percent liberal among liberal and conservative identifiers.

Source: Based on National Election Studies, 2012 data.

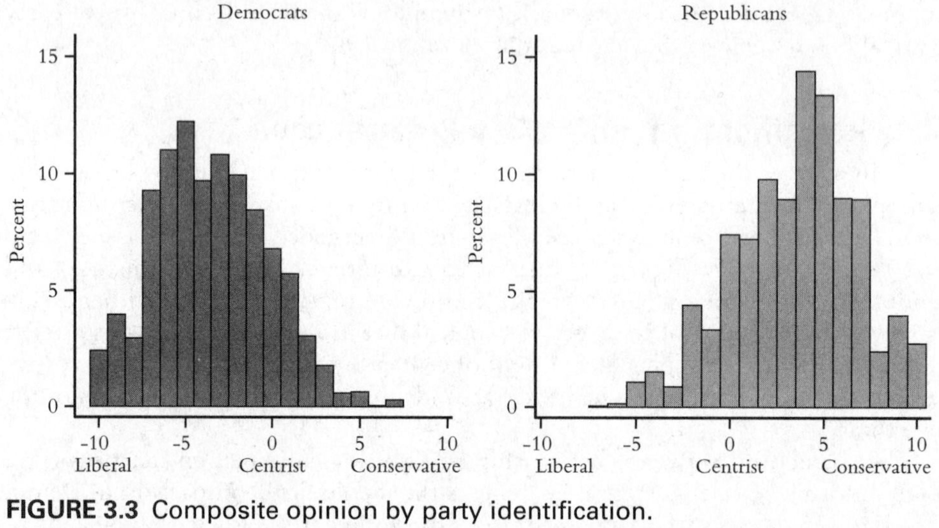

FIGURE 3.3 Composite opinion by party identification.

Source: Based on National Election Studies, 2012 election data.

While Democratic identifiers have been somewhat more liberal than Republicans on social welfare issues since the 1930s, Democrats and Republicans did not separate on other types of issues until the 1960s, starting with the ideological 1964 election. Before that time, Democrats in the electorate were not identifiably more

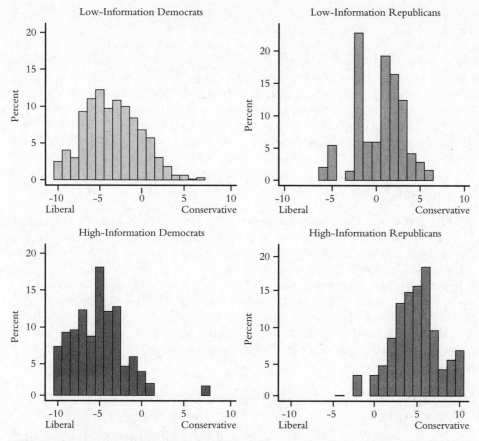

FIGURE 3.4 Democratic and Republican composite opinion, by information level.

Source: Based on National Election Studies, 2012 election data.

liberal on civil rights, foreign policy, or social issues. Of course, they had no reason to be, as people saw the two parties as differing only on the social welfare dimension.

What causes the consistency between political opinions and party identification? Do people learn their political opinions from their party identifications, or do political opinions shape party identifications? Undoubtedly both causal processes are at work, but their relative contributions can be only roughly estimated.

Because party identification can be such a strong and stable attitude, partisanship often drives policy opinions more than the reverse (Campbell et al. 1960; Goren 2005; Levendusky 2009); parties realign their positions on an issue, and their supporters follow. A classic example occurred among partisans after Republican President Nixon initiated the thaw in U.S. relations with the People's Republic of China in the early 1970s. Republicans abandoned their hostility to "Red China" faster than Democrats did.[8] Similarly, when President Reagan initiated a new friendship with the Soviet Union, Republicans were quicker to think the Cold War was over.[9] When in early 1991 many congressional Democrats balked at supporting President Bush's intervention in the Persian Gulf, the Democratic rank and file became more dovish and the Republican rank and file became more hawkish (Zaller 1992, 104–5).

Partisanship can influence not only attitudes and opinions, but also beliefs about the state of the world. Following the Iraq invasion of 2003, it was soon evident that no weapons of mass destruction were found, contrary to the claim that had become the Bush administration's chief justification for the war. Well into 2004, most Republicans in surveys (but few Democrats) continued to insist not only that WMD had been discovered but also that Saddam Hussein had been allied with the terrorist group Al-Qaeda (Kull, Ramsey, and Stewart 2003–2004; Bloch-Elkon and Shapiro 2005; Nacos, Bloch-Elkon, and Shapiro 2011). Similarly, when asked in surveys, Republican identifiers claimed U.S. casualty rates in Iraq that were lower than Democratic identifiers' estimates (Berinsky 2009; see also Gaines et al. 2007).

While partisanship influences people's perceptions of the world and shapes their opinions, sometimes it is party identification that changes when initial partisanship and issue positions get out of alignment (Markus and Converse 1979; Franklin and Jackson 1983; Jacoby 1988; Abramowitz and Saunders 1998; Putz 2002; Carsey and Layman 2006; Campbell, Green, and Layman 2011). The gradual conversion of conservative white southerners from the Democratic to the Republican Party is a case in point. Some people who become ideologically disaffected by their home party become Independents. Those who go all the way and shift from one party to the other often display the ideological zeal of true converts.

Party Identification: Psychological Identification or Running Tally?

Political scientists still do not fully understand party identification. *The American Voter* (Campbell et al. 1960) presented one influential interpretation—that one's party identification is essentially a psychological attachment or "affective orientation" to one's favorite party. By this view, party identification can approach blind loyalty, as when people find reason to support their party's position and vote for its candidates long after they have rational reasons for doing so.

Some scholars, however, emphasize the more rational aspects of party identification. By this view, people learn a party identification based on what Morris Fiorina (1977) calls a "running tally" of their partisan decisions. For example, voters who find repeated reason to vote Republican begin to call themselves Republican—not so much out of psychological attachment as by way of learning a convenient shorthand rule for deciding how to vote. If reasons develop for such voters to vote Democratic instead, they do not blindly continue down the Republican path in the face of contrary evidence. Instead, they vote Democratic or even change partisanship in response to the new running tally.

Both interpretations of partisanship carry some validity. For example, many partisans persist in voting loyally for their party even when it no longer represents their views on issues. But many partisans casually change allegiance when circumstances seem to warrant it. Perhaps our question should be whether by forming a standing decision to vote Democratic or Republican, people enhance or detract from their ability to vote rationally.

3-4 Political Polarization

In several places, this chapter has alluded to an ongoing change in the structure and organization people bring to their political opinions. The public shows a growing ideological awakening, with Democrats and Republicans becoming increasingly distinct from each other. These changes mirror shifts among political leaders such as members of Congress, who have become polarized into warring camps of liberal Democrats and conservative Republicans. Is it correct to say that the American public has also become politically polarized? Scholars debate the nature of the change, its severity, why it has occurred, and its consequences. (See Fiorina and Abrams 2009; Levendusky, 2009; Abramowitz·2010; Fiorina, Abrams, and Pope 2011; Sniderman and Stiglitz 2012.)

While the degree to which people have moved to the ideological extremes can be debated, liberals and conservatives are more at odds with each other than has existed for a very long time. The most politically active citizens line up as liberals or conservatives, with fewer and fewer in the middle. Importantly, their ideological alignments increasingly correspond to their partisan alignment. Among politically active citizens, liberal Republicans and conservative Democrats have become virtually extinct.

Some of this change is in response to the hardening of party positions at the elite level. The term *sorting* is often used to describe the dynamics by which people align their ideology and their partisanship—for example, become liberal Democrats or conservative Republicans. Some (e.g., Levendusky 2009) see the "sort" arising from citizens passively adopting the positions of their favorite party, as if party identification is the primary motivator. Undoubtedly, as discussed in Section 3.3, people often take party cues when they develop their issue positions. But the reverse process, whereby people select their partisanship based on issue positions, must also play an important role, especially when ideology is involved. For instance, following the Democratic Party leadership's support for civil rights legislation in the 1960s, southern white conservatives began their march away from the Democrats toward the Republican Party. The Republicans' general ideological positioning generated this partisan change (offset by liberals moving the opposite direction). Southern whites did not convert from conservative Democrats to liberal Democrats.

Subsequent chapters continue the discussion of political polarization. Chapter 5 addresses the circumstances that can activate ideological political behavior. Chapter 6 addresses the possible consequences of polarization for democratic functioning. Chapter 7 addresses the extent to which the United States has divided geographically into "red" (Republican) and "blue" (Democratic) states. Chapter 8 discusses how changes in the mass media environment facilitate polarization. Chapter 9 shows how ideological voting has increased in recent elections, including 2012. Chapter 10 addresses the effect of public opinion on elite polarization, as politicians can polarize into liberal and conservative camps in response to the demands of their party's ideological base.

We should also recognize the risk that talk of a polarized public can get exaggerated. A vast swath of the public eschews identification with either political party, preferring to call themselves "Independent." It is probably a stretch to claim that the majority of Americans are ideologically engaged. Many citizens rarely participate in politics at all, even to vote. For better or worse, the Americans who are normally on the ideological sidelines can act as referees in the ideological debate.

Critical Thinking Questions

1. Many people are ill-informed and uninterested in politics. Is this a problem for assessing public opinion?
2. It is often said that Americans have become increasingly polarized in their political opinions as they divide more into liberal Democrat versus conservative Republican camps. Would it be better for democracy if Americans were not so divided along ideological lines?
3. When people are interviewed at two different points in time, they often give different answers to the same survey question. What are the implications of this inconsistency for understanding public opinion?

Endnotes

1. Analysts must be sensitive to the accuracy of the reasons people give for their opinions. For instance, people can recall their position on some matters, but not the original reasons for it, and then rationalize their choice with new reasons that may not have had any bearing on their choice. A lengthy literature exists on how people store and retrieve political information when making or remembering political judgments. For examples, see Lodge and Stroh (1993) and Wyer and Ottati (1993).
2. *Source*: Associated Press/GiF Knowledge Networks Poll, August 2012. Another arguable example of people persisting in incorrect beliefs, not directly in the realm of politics, is the division of opinion between scientists, the presumed experts, and the mass public on issues like Darwin's theory of evolution and that human behavior contributes to global warming. Scientists are in near consensus that evolution and human responsibility are correct, yet the public is considerably skeptical. See Pew 2009 (July 9, 2009, Pew Survey Reports: "Public Praises Science; Scientists Fault Public, Media," http://people-press.org/report/528/).
3. We use only the Face-to-Face sample for the 2012 ANES (which also has an Internet Supplement) to both maintain consistency with past editions, and eliminate mode effects when we are looking at ANES data over time.
4. Although the responses shown in Table 3.3 are part of a framing experiment, this is not a source of serious distortion. In some instances, different framing in the two waves enhances response turnover. Yet this contamination appears slight. For issues in which some respondents were given variable framings and others the same framing, the effect of this difference in stimulus appears to have been but a few percentage points. Where some respondents repeatedly received an elaborate framing of the underlying arguments for the two points of view while a control group got none, responses were no more stable when respondents received framing.
5. The abortion question was actually asked three times in the 1989 ANES pilot study. The pilot respondents were first asked their abortion views in late 1988 as part of the regular ANES 1988 election survey. Over three waves, only 26 percent took a consistent pro-life position and only 27 percent took a consistent pro-choice position. An even smaller 5 percent were consistently in the middle, but 42 percent took a middle position in at least one wave.
6. As a practical matter, the single dimension of liberal–conservative ideology is a better measure of underlying political values than specific values measured individually. Zaller (1992, 26) states the case nicely: "There is . . . a tendency for people to be fairly consistently 'left,' 'right,' or 'centrist' on such disparate value dimensions as economic individualism, opinions toward Communists, tolerance of nonconformists, racial issues, sexual

freedom, and religious authority. The correlations among these different value dimensions are never so strong as to suggest that there is one and only one basic value dimension, but they are always at least moderately strong, and among highly aware persons, the correlations are sometimes quite strong. And, of course, there are also moderately strong correlations between people's self-descriptions as liberal or conservative and their scores on the various value measures."

7. For discussions of the origins of liberal–conservative terminology, see Kerlinger (1984) and Rotunda (1986).

8. For instance, between 1966 and 1971, the percentage of Democratic opinion-holders who told Gallup they favored U.N. admission for China rose from one-third to nearly half. Meanwhile, Republican support rose from 1 in 4 to a clear plurality in favor of admission.

9. For instance, in 1984 (pre-Gorbachev) and 1988, "strong Democrats" (with opinions) increased their support for cooperation with Russia by four percentage points. "Strong Republicans" (with opinions) increased their support by 24 points (1984 and 1988 ANES data).

CHAPTER 4

Macrolevel Opinion: The Flow of Political Sentiment

LEARNING OBJECTIVES

- Explain what it means to be ideologically conservative but pragmatically liberal
- Describe the trend over time in attitudes toward health care, affirmative action and defense spending, and major cultural issues

- What is the public mood?
- Describe the predictors of presidential approval

Public opinion specialists begin their investigations of survey data by analyzing the *frequencies*, or the percentagized divisions, of opinion for the sample. The frequency distributions reflect the content of public opinion at the moment of the poll. When a particular survey question has been repeatedly asked in the past, the latest frequencies also provide information about opinion trends.

Frequency distributions must be interpreted with caution because, as we saw in Chapter 2, responses are often influenced by question wording. When the polls show a certain percentage favoring a particular response to a question, we need some anchor, a reference point, by which to measure the significance of the finding. One way is to compare the frequencies for one question with those for slightly different but related questions. This comparison allows us to see what distinctions the mass public makes in the kinds of policies it is willing to support. A particularly useful anchor is to compare answers to the same question over time. If the public displays a different level of support for some policy today than one year ago or five years ago, then we may have located a potentially important change in public opinion.

Unfortunately, the data that would allow for the accurate assessment of trends in public opinion are often not as available as one might expect. Commercial pollsters naturally ask questions of current interest to their media clients. As popular interest fades, those questions are often not repeated. Academic polling units are more concerned with the continuity and comparability of questions over time, but even they are not immune to the wax and wane of topical issues. Thus, questions dealing with civil liberties were frequently asked in the McCarthy era of the early 1950s, when many people thought their basic personal liberties were threatened, but not asked again until the early 1970s. Before the 1960s, questions about race relations were seldom asked; the aspirations of the black minority were given little thought by white politicians, press, and public. Even when the polls monitor opinions on the same issue over time, they often vary question wording, making it difficult to separate real change from question-wording effects.

In the following sections we present an overview of macrolevel public opinion, or what polls tell us about the content of public opinion both today and in the past. We begin by examining opinion on specific policy issues that have been polled over the years, searching for liberal or conservative trends. Second, we consider the possibility of general ideological movement. Poll trends are often described in ideological terms, as if the public's frame of reference is shifting on the liberal–conservative continuum. Third, we examine changes in the distribution of party identification over the years. And finally, we consider one important partisan question well known for its volatility: the president's approval rating.

4-1 The Micro Foundations of Macro Opinion

Chapter 3 showed that the survey response tends to be erratic. When survey respondents are asked their opinion on more than one occasion and change their answers, the chances are that the shift represents error (or at best a shift in short-term influences) rather than true opinion change. When it comes to basic political predispositions, true opinion change is incremental if it occurs at all. We might ask, therefore, whether it is meaningful to assess survey responses in the aggregate. Would we expect to find real (statistically significant) changes in opinion, given that responses may contain more randomness than real change? The fact is that observable changes in the aggregate responses at the macrolevel are far more orderly than the individual responses at the microlevel of which they are comprised. This is the "miracle of aggregation." Survey error that is so mischievous at the microlevel, when one analyzes individual responses, tends to cancel out at the macrolevel. Although people rarely change their true opinions, when they do, the shifts tend to be uniform. When macrolevel change occurs, a shift by only a small portion of the public can have important political consequences.

For a useful illustration, we turn not to a survey question about politics but instead about economics. In the 1996 ANES panel, 520 respondents were asked whether their personal family economic circumstances had improved, stayed the same, or gotten worse over the previous year. The same respondents had been interviewed two years earlier in 1994. In both 1994 and 1996, the ANES asked respondents about their family income for the past year. Although the interviews were two years apart, we might expect considerable correspondence between respondents' recall of family income change in 1996 and the *actual* change in their reported income from the 1994 to the 1996 survey. We get:

	Change in Reported Income, 1996 minus 1994		
	Worse	Same	Improved
Recall of Previous Year's Change in Family Income, 1996			
Worse	28%	20%	21% (118)
Same	36	37	30 (174)
Improved	36	43	49 (228)
	100%	100%	100%
N	(134)	(139)	(247) **(520)**

We might expect strong consistency between actual income growth (as reported in separate interviews) and the 1994 recall of income change. But that is not what we see in the table cells. Respondents with a rising family income were only slightly more likely to report an income rise than those whose family income was falling. We could interpret the table to mean that people are no more than dimly aware of their own economic circumstances. But a better explanation is survey noise.

Looking at the "macro" level data we get a different picture. In 1996, at a time when national income levels were rising (including for our ANES respondents), the proportion of ANES respondents who claimed their circumstances were improving was roughly twice that of those who claimed a decline. Although individual survey responses to the family income question are not very accurate measures of actual family income growth, the aggregate measure is. The errors cancel out so that aggregate results of polls on economic conditions (and other matters) are often accurate even if individual responses are not. We could interpret the table to mean that people are no more than dimly aware of their own economic circumstances. But a better explanation is survey noise. For instance, people have different reference points for "improved" and "worse" in terms of family income, making it seem as if people often respond randomly. But apart from illustrating survey error, the table provides meaningful information about aggregate opinion change. We see that the proportion who claimed their circumstances were improving (228/520 or 44 percent) was roughly twice that of those who claimed a decline (118/520 or 23 percent). These numbers are very similar to the income reported in 1996 minus the income reported in 1994 (48 percent versus 26 percent). On average, people saw improvement during a time when family income was indeed growing, and growing at a faster rate than inflation. The macrolevel signal peeking through the noise was indeed accurate.

As an aggregate measure, the mean report of family income growth is a useful measure of net economic satisfaction. It has its political uses, as changes in family income help to account for changes in party identification as the electorate gradually shifts its net partisanship in response to how well the presidential party maintains prosperity (Erikson, MacKuen, and Stimson 2002). Other economic survey questions tap respondents' perception of the national economy, both past and future. At any one time, survey respondents will disagree about whether the national economy has improved or worsened over the past year. But their mean perception tends to be accurate. And in the aggregate, survey respondents can predict short-term changes in the national economy, even if most individual responses are vague guesses. In fact, the mean responses regarding whether the economy will improve or worsen form one of the key components of the economists' index of leading economic indicators.

With these economic examples, we can readily understand that the aggregate information contains a signal about the aggregate economy plus random noise. The noise of uninformed respondents, being random, cancels out in the aggregate and the signal remains.[1] In politics, the shifts of attentive citizens provide the signals that overcome the error in individual survey responses. (See Converse 1990 for an excellent exposition.) When public opinion changes beyond the realm of what we would expect by sampling error, the change is real even if most individuals may not be undergoing conversions.

4-2 Trends in Policy Opinions

For convenience, most policy questions can be divided into four general domains: (1) social welfare, (2) civil rights, (3) foreign policy, and (4) cultural issues. Social welfare controversies pertain to the distribution of wealth and government efforts to help the disadvantaged; civil rights refer to the quest for equality under the law; foreign policy, obviously, refers to views about the U.S. role abroad; and cultural issues usually involve differences over lifestyles or "moral values" such as abortion, prayer in the public schools, and capital punishment.

Social Welfare Issues

From the New Deal to the present, the American public has been receptive to government programs to accomplish economic welfare objectives. In fact, on social welfare legislation, mass opinion has often been well ahead of congressional action. For example, the earliest polls revealed an overwhelming majority (89 percent) in favor of "old age pensions" prior to the adoption of the Social Security Act in 1936 (Cantril 1951, 521). A majority also supported the right of workers to organize and bargain collectively before the 1941 Wagner Act transformed these principles into law (Page and Shapiro 1992, 136). Majority approval has continually been found prior to each increase in the federal minimum wage (Erskine 1962b; Gallup Poll Index 1985, 17; Saad 2013).

It has long been noted that the American public is ideologically conservative but operationally liberal (Free and Cantril 1967; Cantril and Cantril 1999). Polls persistently show self-identified conservatives outnumbering self-identified liberals. When it comes to specific social welfare programs, however, only a minority of the public are opposed to liberal spending. Table 4.1 shows levels of support for federal spending on a variety of federal programs. Program by program, few Americans want reductions in social spending. The most frequent preference, in fact, is not to reduce spending or even to keep spending the same but rather to *increase spending* across a wide variety of social programs such as health, education, and alternative energy. While it is easy to say "spend more" without appreciating the tax consequences,

TABLE 4.1	Opinion About Spending Too Little, About Right, or Too Much on Selected Federal Programs		
	Spend Too Little (%)	About Right (%)	Spend Too Much (%)
Health care	59	21	16
The environment	52	30	12
Police and law enforcement	47	39	11
Social Security	53	35	07
Education	73	17	08
Military and defense	24	40	32
Childcare	45	38	09
Aid to blacks	49	63	01
Alternative energy	60	26	10
Welfare programs	20	33	43
Poor people	63	27	10
Foreign aid	08	26	60
Space exploration	20	40	30

Source: Based on data from General Social Survey, 2012.

respondents in the 2012 General Social Survey were told that if they say "spend more," "it might require a tax increase to pay for it." Still, we see majorities saying "spend more" for health care, the environment, education, and social security. Few people want to spend less on these programs. The most notable exception is a lack of enthusiasm for increased spending on foreign aid (just 8 percent)—a program which few people feel benefits them directly. Also, more spending on the space program generates little enthusiasm. Despite occasional rhetoric to the contrary, the domestic services provided by government to its citizens are popular.

Of course, there are limits to the public's enthusiasm for social welfare programs. Most notably, Americans clearly make the classic distinction between the "deserving poor" (those who have fallen on hard times through no fault of their own) and the "shiftless poor," who would rather receive a government handout than hold a job. Thus, in the mid-1980s one poll showed that 88 percent of people with opinions agreed that the government ought to help those "who are unable to support themselves," while at the same time 91 percent agreed that "too many people on welfare could be working" and 94 percent said "too many people on welfare get money to which they are not entitled" (Page and Shapiro 1992, 125).

This distinction can be seen most graphically by large changes in poll numbers when slight changes are made in the way questions are phrased. For example, in a question-wording experiment (shown in Table 4.1), the 2012 GSS asked in random order if too little, about right, or too much is spent on the poor; 61 percent said "too little." But when asked the same question about "people on welfare," just 20 percent said "too little" was being spent.

More than a mere illustration of question-wording effects, this experiment reflects a belief among Americans that the government should help those who cannot help themselves—the deserving poor. But Americans see people on welfare as able but unwilling to work, and thus meriting little sympathy. There is a widespread belief among the American public that people who receive financial assistance ought to work for their money, even if the work they do is of little use. Even spending more on "unemployment benefits" generates only modest support among the public.

But this may not be all to the story about Americans' hostility toward people on welfare. Race, regrettably, is an important part of the explanation. Many whites harbor the belief that blacks are lazy; they tend to exaggerate the extent to which blacks populate the welfare rolls. The effect of this belief on support for welfare can be seen in the fact that those whites who believe (mistakenly) that most welfare recipients are black are also those who are most opposed to welfare (Gilens 1999; Kuklinski et al. 2001).

Sometimes polls ask a general question about the ideal balance between spending more or less tax money on domestic programs. Answers to these questions tend to cycle, depending on current political context, perhaps as a "thermostatic" response to current policies (Wlezien 1995a). When Republicans are in charge, survey respondents tend to support more spending. For example, when the ANES asked in 2008, at the end of the Bush presidency and at the onset of the recession, if the government should "provide fewer services, even in areas such as health and education, in order to reduce spending" or instead "provide more services and spending," 49 percent chose more services and spending, 23 percent took a neutral position, with 28 percent choosing fewer services and less spending. But in 2012 at the end of Obama's first term, opinion turned more cautious about further spending, 38 to 33 percent preferring fewer services over more services.

Health Care   As we noted earlier, the public has frequently been out in front of elected officials on many innovations in social welfare policy. This has certainly been the case with regard to health care. Since the 1930s, opinion polls have consistently shown the public favors some form of government-subsidized health insurance. In 1937, a Gallup poll showed that over 70 percent favored the notion that "the federal government should provide free medical and dental care for those who cannot pay." During the 1950s and 1960s, 60 to 65 percent supported the principle of the government paying the medical bills of the elderly, which was enacted into law in 1965 with Medicare (Erskine 1975).

Since 1970, the ANES has asked its national samples the same question on the politics of health care, where the liberal choice is "government health insurance plan which would cover all medical and hospital expenses," and the conservative alternative is that medical expenses would be "paid to individuals through private insurance."[2] In the first twenty years this question was asked, the preferences for the two differing approaches were about equal as shown in Figure 4.1. Then in 1992, when health care reform was a prominent theme in Clinton's successful presidential campaign, preference for a government plan rose to 51 percent, and preference for a private plan dropped to 28 percent. As Congress was poised to act on the Clinton plan, the health care industry mounted a major counterattack and Clinton's health care plan was abandoned without a vote in Congress; by 1994, a slight plurality

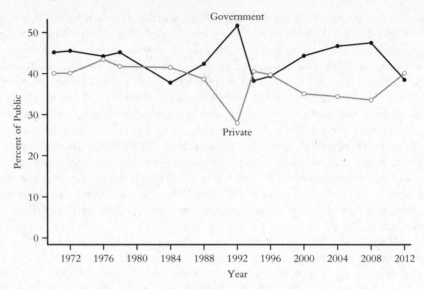

FIGURE 4.1 Private versus government health insurance.

Source: American National Election Studies, 1970–2012.

opposed the government plan. Subsequently, growing pluralities began favoring the public plan once again. In 2008, support for a government health program rose to an all-time high of 46 percent, with 33 percent preferring a private health plan. After a long struggle, the Affordable Health Care Act (Obamacare) passed Congress in 2010, but in the process it took a beating in the polls; in the case of the government versus private question shown in Figure 4.1, the "government" plan was opposed 43 to 39 percent.

Throughout the 2009–2010 health care debate, there was widespread support for requiring insurers to cover people with preexisting conditions, paying for it by increasing taxes on the rich, and employer-mandated participation in health care insurance. But still the circumstances for passage of health care reform were not easy. Powerful interest groups opposed significant change from the status quo and there was a strong public relations campaign against Obama's plan, striking at people's understandable fear of change. Even if concerned about medical costs under the status quo, insured Americans generally were satisfied with the quality of their health care.[3] Americans had questions about three issues: Would reform really improve health care? Would their own health care get better or worse? Would costs significantly increase?

The Affordable Care Act (ACA) was the rare act of Congress that seemingly was opposed by a plurality of those with opinions on the matter. Virtually no poll from 2010 through 2013 shows plurality support. At the same time, many who opposed the act did so because the act did not go far enough (in their view) to offer health insurance, not that it went too far. (Ultimately, the ACA was based on private insurance, not a government program.) If those who oppose because it does not go far enough are combined with those who support the ACA, they outnumber those who oppose it because it goes too far, for example, opponents of big government. For instance, in one CNN survey (September 2013), opponents of

ACA outnumbered supporters by a resounding 57 to 38 percent. But when those who opposed the act because it was "not liberal enough" were combined with ACA supporters, those who opposed the act as "too liberal" were outnumbered by a convincing 49 to 39 percent.

Some opponents were against the ACA out of seeming ignorance. The one provision that drew widespread opposition is the mandate that everyone have health insurance or pay a fine. In one survey, the opposition to the mandate provision was an overwhelming 65 to 33. However, when these respondents were reminded that under ACA "most Americans would still have coverage through their employers and automatically satisfy the [mandate] requirement without having to buy any new insurance," opinion flipped to 61 percent in favor and 34 percent against (Kaiser Tracking Poll, 2012).[4]

As Obamacare enters its first phase of implementation, it remains unpopular with the public. Most, however, resist the idea of defunding it or entirely repealing it. With the polarized political climate and strong Republican Tea Party opposition, the level of support is unlikely to change in the short run.

Taxes   Compared to European countries, taxes in the United States take a smaller share of Gross National Product and are less progressive (Alesina and Glaeser 2004). Nevertheless, polls on taxes often portray extreme antitax sentiment by the public. In 2001, 62 percent said the income taxes they "currently pay" were too high (Associated Press). In 2003, 66 percent told the Harris Poll that high taxes had pushed their family to the breaking point. In 2012, 68 percent said they would "not" be willing to pay more taxes to reduce the deficit (CBS News).

The seemingly inconsistent poll data on spending and taxes appear to demonstrate that the public irrationally expects to have its cake and eat it too. Citizens want a plethora of public services (as shown in Table 4.1), but they do not want to pay for them. Of course, survey questions about taxing and spending usually are asked in a vacuum as if spending required no new revenue or as if taxes provided no benefits. When the views of the public are assessed with realistic questions designed to measure the trade-offs between different types of services and the taxes to pay for them, the public appears quite rational. When pressed to make choices with budget constraints, respondents tend to recognize that they cannot have it both ways—more government spending and lower taxes (see also Page and Shapiro 1992; Hansen 1998).

Antitax sentiment has fluctuated over time, partially in response to shifts in the actual tax bite. Since 1947, Gallup has regularly asked its respondents whether federal income taxes are "too high." Antitax sentiment has been at its highest (about 70 percent) following wartime increases from the Korean and the Vietnam Wars, as well as in the late 1970s as part of an overall antigovernment right turn. At other times, only about half complain about the income tax being too high. One such period of lesser concern about taxes was during the George W. Bush administration, when taxes were cut and stayed cut even though the Iraq War was being fought. By the time of Obama's presidency in 2009, only 46 percent claimed their federal income taxes were "too high" (Gallup).

The most relevant question might not be attitudes toward taxes, but rather the fairness of the tax burden. In general, people see the middle class paying too much while the rich do not pay their fair share (Campbell 2010).[5] Still people tend to not give the redistributive aspects of tax policy much thought.

Public opinion on tax policy took on special relevance during the debate in 2001 over the massive tax cuts benefiting the wealthy that President George W. Bush ultimately pushed through Congress. According to estimates by Citizens for Tax Justice, over the ten-year life of the legislation, the top 1 percent of households would receive an average tax break of $32,247 per household per year, while the bottom 60 percent would get an average annual tax break of only $325.

Bush's tax cuts could probably not have passed without considerable consent among the public. Indeed, the public was polled twenty-five times during the debate over the 2001 Bush tax cut, and on average 56 percent supported it and 33 percent opposed it (Hacker and Pierson 2005). The obvious question is, why did the public seem to support a tax cut that served to promote economic inequality?

One answer is question wording. Hacker and Pierson (2005) contend that the apparent support for the Bush tax cuts was an illusion since respondents were simply asked whether or not they favored a tax cut. There was no mention of costs or trade-offs. Since a majority typically respond that taxes are too high, it is not surprising that when presented with a simple *yes–no* on lower taxes, people tend to say *yes*. The authors present examples of instances where tax questions also include trade-offs and find support for tax cuts is noticeably lower.

Another answer is that a favorable opinion about the Bush tax cuts stemmed from an unenlightened sense of self-interest. According to Bartels (2005, 2008), most people disapprove of growing economic inequality but fail to connect this phenomenon to the tax issue, mostly out of simple ignorance. Proponents of the tax cut played on citizen perceptions that their own personal taxes are "too high" and took advantage of the generally low levels of citizen information. The least informed citizens were the ones most likely to favor the tax cuts. Meanwhile, well-informed partisans gravitated to the position of their party. The best-informed Republicans were 14 percentage points more likely to favor the tax cuts than the lesser informed. The best-informed Democrats were 19 percentage points more likely to oppose the tax cuts than the lesser informed (Lupia et al. 2007).

In any event, the seeming public support for Bush's tax cut that helped it become law seems to have been short lived. In 2009 when asked whether Bush's tax cuts for those making over $250,000 a year should expire, a national survey reported that 49 percent were in favor, 42 percent opposed (Democracy Corps). By 2012 sentiment had increased by a margin of 57 to 40 percent for letting the tax cuts expire (Marist College Institute).

Civil Rights

Discerning the true attitudes held by white Americans on civil rights issues has proved a difficult and controversial task. Taking easy issues first, polls clearly show at a minimum that Americans have rejected the prevalent white supremacist ideology ("old fashioned racism") that pervaded mass attitudes as recently as a few decades ago. Poll data from the 1930s and 1940s suggest that perhaps a majority of white Americans once believed blacks to be intellectually inferior and undeserving of equal status with whites. In 1939, a Roper poll found 76 percent of white respondents agreeing that "Negroes" had generally "lower" intelligence than white people (Page and Shapiro 1992). As late as 1944, just 44 percent believed that "Negroes are as intelligent as white people" (Erskine 1962a). By 1994, according to a Harris survey, only 12 percent of whites agreed with the stereotype that blacks have less native intelligence than other races. The decline in overt racism is evident from the following trend. In 1944, 45 percent said, "Negroes should have as good a chance as whites to get a job"; by 1972, a near consensus of 97 percent shared that belief (Page and Shapiro 1992, 69).

In the analysis of public opinion on racial issues, it is common to distinguish between questions concerning the goals or ideals of the civil rights movement and government action to actually implement those goals into public policy. The public is more supportive of the abstract goals of the civil rights movement than their implementation (Frankenberg and Jacobsen 2011). For example, when asked in 2007 if black and white children should go to the same or separate schools, 95 percent of whites preferred the ideal of both races "going to the same schools" (Pew). But when asked as late as 2000 if the government in Washington "should see to it" that black and white children attend the same schools or if this is "not the government's business," just 47 percent of whites supported implementation of the ideal by federal government action (ANES).

Figure 4.2 presents trends in white support for integrated schools, in terms of both principle and implementation. First, consider the question of whether white and black children should attend the same or separate schools. In 1942, just 30 percent (of whites) said "same school" and 66 percent said "separate schools." Figure 4.2 picks up the series in 1956, when the percent saying "same school" had grown to 49 percent. By 1996, 96 percent of the white public said they favored black and white children attending the same school. From 1942 to 1996, there was a 65 percentage

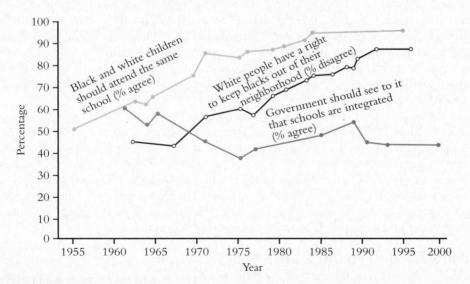

FIGURE 4.2 Support for school integration and open housing.

Source: Based on National Opinion Research Center, Gallup, and General Social Survey.

point increase in white support for integrated schools, perhaps the largest change in public opinion for which we have data.

Figure 4.2 shows a different trend, however, on the question of whether the "government in Washington should see to it" that black and white children go to the same schools. When framed in terms of possible federal action, there is less support for the integration positions, with white Americans more in favor of government action in the 1960s than in the 1970s and later. While opposition to racial discrimination is almost universal, attitudes about government intervention are anything but consensual.

Still, not all implementation trends are conservative. Figure 4.2 shows that whites became increasingly opposed to "a right" to keep blacks from their neighborhoods. By 1996, the number disagreeing that white people "had a right" to keep blacks out of their neighborhood had grown to 87 percent.

Affirmative Action   One of the most contentious civil rights issue in contemporary politics is "affirmative action" to help blacks (plus other racial minorities and women) advance in the education system and the workplace. While surveys show considerable white opposition to affirmative action programs, the extent of this opposition depends heavily on how the question is framed. Let us look first at a more or less generic question. In September 2013 Gallup asked a sample of white respondents if they "generally favored or opposed affirmative action for racial minorities." Fifty-one percent were in favor; 37 percent were opposed.

If the survey question simply addresses helping the advancement of the disadvantaged, we get about the same result as for the generic question. A 2007 Pew survey randomly asked half its sample, "In order to overcome past discrimination, do you favor or oppose affirmative action programs designed to help blacks, women, and other minorities to get better jobs and education?" 52 percent of whites supported affirmative action, while 37 percent opposed—about like the generic question. But when the question emphasizes "preferences" for minorities, support for affirmative action plunges. The other half of the Pew sample was asked, "In order to overcome past discrimination, do you favor or oppose affirmative action programs which give special preferences to qualified blacks in hiring and education?" Support among whites drops to 39 percent, while a plurality of 47 percent said they oppose affirmative action.

Public reaction to existing affirmative action policies can be interpreted as mixed. When asked about the pace of affirmative action, 36 percent in a 2003 *Los Angeles Times* poll (all races) said affirmative action programs had "gone too far," while 18 percent said they "had not gone far enough." Thirty-six percent saw these programs as "just about adequate now." A CBS poll in 2006 (all races) shows essentially the same results. When asked if affirmative action programs should be ended now, phased out, or continued for the foreseeable future, 12 percent said "end now," 33 percent said "phase out," and 36 percent said "continue."[6]

Whites and Racial Attitudes Today   Some claim that in the twenty-first century, *implicit* racial messages are more likely to elicit negative stereotypes about African-Americans than are *explicit* racial messages (Mendelberg 2001, 2008). The distinction can be best illustrated with an example. A random half of a sample got the question: "Some people want to increase spending for new prisons to lock up violent inner city criminals. Others would rather spend this money for anti-poverty programs to prevent crime. What about you?" In the other half of the sample the word *inner city* is deleted (Hurwitz and Peffley 2005). The mention of "inner city" yields more support for building prisons. Differences as illustrated by this example suggest that significant racial resentment still exists, but it takes on an increasingly sophisticated guise, sometimes through the use of code words like "inner city." Mendelberg claims that implicit racial messages actually work better than explicit racial messages to ignite racial animosity, although other research suggests the matter is still not settled (Huber and Lapinski 2006, 2008; Hutchings and Jardina 2009).

How does one explain the tepid support among whites for specific remedies to solve the problem of racial discrimination in the face of their overwhelming support for the ideals of racial integration Two explanations are commonly debated: race per se and the politics of race. The first of these, the "racial resentment" argument (Sears and Kinder 1971; Kinder and Sanders 1996), holds that many whites maintain but disguise negative views about African-Americans. They learn the norm of racial equality but resist laws to enforce equality because they see them as unde-served and are thus resentful. Over the years that public expression of racist sentiment has become increasingly unfashionable. Outright racial discrimination also became illegal. Consequently, people learned it is socially unacceptable to express overtly racist opinions. Instead, racial resentment is expressed indirectly by a glorification of traditional values such as "the work ethic" and "economic individualism" in which blacks and some other minorities are seen as deficient (Tarman and Sears 2005; Banks and Valentino 2012). Federico (2006) finds that the most educated whites are the most likely (or best able) to mask their racial attitudes in nontrans-parent ways. Some of the apparent liberal trend in racial attitudes is not real change but rather reflects the need to express increasingly sophisticated "socially desirable" opinions. Opposition to implementation, usually on grounds other than race, is simply disingenuous.[7]

A rival explanation for white resistance to civil rights legislation is that it is ideological, not racial: the claim is that conservative ideology is driving responses and not racial animus. Sniderman and Piazza (1993, 107) argue that "the central problem of racial politics is *not* the problem of prejudice" (italics in the original). The agenda of the civil rights movement has changed from one of equal opportunity to equal outcomes. No fair-minded person could find consistency between the American Creed and denial of voting rights; segregated universities, workplaces, and lunch counters; and confinement to the back of the bus. But in the eyes of many, the new civil rights agenda of affirmative action very much clashes with the principle of equal treatment for all. Its implementation also requires an activist, expansion-ist government. Antigovernment ideology is a long-standing tradition in American politics, preventing many whites (particularly conservative whites) from translating an abstract commitment to racial equality into support for specific federal policies (Sniderman and Carmines 1997; Sniderman, Crosby, and Howell 2000).[8]

Recent research has shown support for both schools of thought. Feldman and Huddy (2005) looked at support for a college scholarship program where both the race and economic status of the recipient were experimentally manipulated. With the economic class of the hypothetical recipients held constant while their race varied, white respondents were more eager to offer scholarships when the recipient was identified as white rather than black. Feldman and Huddy also applied a measure of "racial resentment," defined as a belief that blacks are not deserving of special treatment. It was the racially resentful respondents who mainly differentiated by race, more willing to offer scholarships to white children than to black children. This is consistent with the "racial resentment" thesis. However, complicating matters, self-identified "conservatives" tended to oppose scholarships regardless of the recipient's race, a finding consistent with the ideological explanation.

To summarize, white racism has been declining, but we should keep in mind that survey respondents have become hesitant to share overtly racist views. Government policies to induce further equality among the races are often opposed. In part, this is due to hidden racial animosity as described earlier. In part, it can be attributed to principled conservatism.

Foreign Policy

Scholars often depict public opinion on questions of foreign policy as being particularly shallow and without meaningful content. Typical is the observation by Light and Lake (1985, 94) that "public opinion polls show that people do not follow foreign affairs closely and often do not know enough about the specifics of a particular issue to form opinions." As applied to most citizens on most foreign policy issues, one cannot easily object to this statement. However, an important foreign policy matter can easily grab public attention and profoundly affect the popularity of the president or the outcome of the next election.

Foreign policy opinions are subject to more abrupt changes than are domestic policy opinions. If *abrupt change* is defined as ten or more percentage points over a single year, abrupt changes are twice as likely on foreign policy as on domestic issues (Page and Shapiro 1989). The explanation is straightforward: There are more dramatic events on the international scene than on the domestic scene. Few domestic occurrences have the impact of the Cuban missile crisis, the Iran hostage crisis, 9/11 and subsequent U.S. involvement in Afghanistan, and the two wars involving Iraq.

Internationalism Versus Isolationism   One indicator of foreign policy sentiment is one's preference for an internationalist versus an isolationist posture in foreign policy. For many people, this dimension serves as a core value that structures other foreign policy opinions. An internationalist, for example, is more likely to favor foreign aid, trade pacts, humanitarian aid, military intervention, and defense spending (Brewer et al. 2004).

Prior to World War II, American opinion was strongly isolationist. In 1937, 70 percent of opinion-holders said U.S. entry into World War I had been a mistake (Free and Cantril 1967, 62). That same year, 94 percent of opinion-holders said the United States should "do everything possible to keep out of foreign wars." But once the United States was involved in World War II, internationalist sentiment increased sharply. By June 1943, 83 percent said the United States would have to play a larger part in world affairs than before the war (Page and Shapiro 1992, 176).

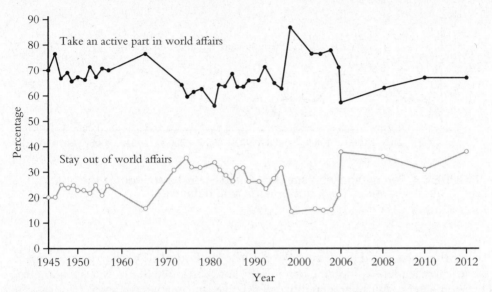

FIGURE 4.3 Do you think it would be best for the future of this country if we take an active part in world affairs, or if we stayed out of world affairs?

Source: The U.S. Role in the World Poll, 1996: University of Maryland; Gallup; National Opinion Research Center; General Social Survey; Transatlantic Trends Survey; 2008–2012, The Chicago Council on Global Affairs Poll.

Figure 4.3 tracks post–World War II internationalist versus isolationist sentiment as monitored by the question of whether the United States should "take an active part" or "stay out" of world affairs. Support for internationalism has risen steadily over the years, with one true spike following 9/11. But there have also been two periods of gradual decline, corresponding to the prolonged Vietnam and Iraq Wars, as opposition mounted. Since about 2005 there has been a decrease in support for the United States taking an active role and an increase for the "staying out" option. For instance, when in September 2013 the Obama administration proposed unilateral missile strikes against Syria, 59 percent of the public opposed the strikes (ABC/*Washington Post*).

Still, as Figure 4.3 shows, Americans have mostly favored an internationalist position in foreign affairs. A majority of Americans have historically favored U.S. participation in the United Nations—despite a minority of vocal critics. In 2011, just 15 percent of the population said we "should give up" our membership in the UN versus 82 percent who said we should not (Pew).

Defense Spending   One source of frequently shifting opinion is public perception of the adequacy of defense spending. Figure 4.4 shows a roller coaster of changing beliefs regarding whether the United States is spending "too little on the military, armaments, and defense."

Beginning in 1978, large segments of the public began to believe that U.S. defenses were underfunded. This conservative trend resulted in part from the Soviet Union's invasion of Afghanistan in 1979, which President Carter denounced as "the

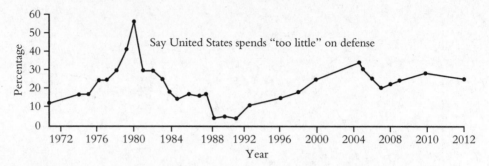

FIGURE 4.4 Percentage who say the United States is spending "too little" on the military, armaments, and defense.

Source: Based on Roper, General Social Survey, and Gallup.

worst threat to world peace since World War II." Both the Democratic and Republican Party leadership became convinced that the United States was spending too little on defense. Without a credible alternative elite counterargument, public opinion quickly fell into line. Belief that we are spending "too little" on defense reached an all-time high of 56 percent in February 1980 (GSS).

Following the renewed military buildup under both Carter and Reagan, the citizenry became reassured that America's defenses were again strong. As the 1980s progressed, support for increased defense spending retreated to the level of the early 1970s. With the collapse of the Soviet Union in the early 1990s, support for increases in defense spending fell to record lows. With the advent of war in the Persian Gulf and then the Iraq War, belief that the United States is spending too little on defense began a slow but steady rise. As the war in Iraq bogged down and costs mounted, the belief that "too little" was being spent on defense began a predictable decline, standing at 24 percent in February 2012 (Gallup).

Statistical analysis of trends in public attitudes toward defense spending shows that it follows a rational course. It is not just that spending attitudes respond to the severity of the perceived threat (or the threat people are told to believe). In addition, support for defense spending responds to the waxing and waning of the actual defense buildup. When spending goes up, demand for further spending goes down, and vice versa (Wlezien 1995a).

Foreign Interventions and War   As we observed in Chapter 3, when the United States gets militarily involved in foreign conflicts in remote corners of the world—for example, Iraq or Afghanistan—the public rises from its slumber and begins to pay attention. When the United States gets involved in actual war—from World War II to Iraq—the initial public response has been widespread support. But as wars become prolonged, with an uncertain verdict—Korea, Vietnam, and Iraq—initial support decays.

An important question is, what are the conditions under which the public will support a war effort or cease to do so? The scholarly consensus is that the crucial ingredient for obtaining the public's support for a war effort is the encouragement of political elites from whom the public gets its signals (Zaller 1992; Berinsky 2009;

Holsti 2011). When politicians of all stripes support the war effort, the public generally goes along as well as it happened at the initial stages of the Iraq War. At the onset of the conflict in Iraq in March 2003, 76 percent of the public said "it was right to take military action." Ninety-three percent of Republicans said "it was right" and even a majority of Democrats, 59 percent, said it was the right thing to do. When elite support divides, as when the parties split over the Iraq War, public support declines—mainly among supporters of the dissenting party. In 2008, the last year of the Bush administration, 73 percent of Republicans still maintained that "it was right to take military action," compared to only 17 percent of Democrats.[9]

Although the public takes its cues about foreign policy matters from elites, there are limits to elite influence. And when events influence the views of foreign policy elites in Washington, these changing events are often visible to ordinary citizens as well. When political leaders and the general public are changing their opinion in the same direction, the leaders and the public may be responding to the same flow of events, without one set of individuals necessarily influencing the other.

One obvious source of eroding support for war is a steady mounting of casualties (Mueller 1973, 1996, 2005; Gartner and Segura 1998). Some claim that casualties can be tolerated when the war is perceived to be just or making progress toward victory (Feaver and Gelp, 2004; Gelpi, Feaver, and Reifler 2005–2006). The United States suffered far more casualties in World War II than in succeeding wars; yet, public opinion polls showed widespread support for continuing toward unconditional victory rather than attempting a negotiated settlement (Berinsky 2009). Others claim it is realities on the ground that matter most (Holsti 2011). For instance, people who read news stories about home-state causalities in Afghanistan were more likely to oppose the war than when the home state was not mentioned in the news story about causalities (Kriner and Shen 2012). While perceptions of the "justness" of a war matters, so do consequences for the home front.

Cultural Issues

In the first half of the twentieth century, the only types of policy issues that drew strong national attention, including those from pollsters, were social welfare matters involving spending and taxing and foreign affairs. Starting in the 1950s, civil rights pushed toward center stage. Soon after, a new set of concerns called *cultural issues* arrived and never left. In their broadest context, these issues involve conflicts between forces of social change and forces committed to maintaining "traditional moral values." Examples of cultural issues include prayer in public schools, immigration, decriminalization of marijuana use, gun control, and tolerance for gay lifestyles.

On many cultural issues, the public is thought to be rather conservative. That is less true today than in the past. Notably, over a relatively short period of time the public has moved sharply more favorable of gay rights (Bowman, Rugg, and Marsico 2013) and the legalization of marijuana. Figure 4.5 shows the sharp increase in support for gay marriage and the legalization of marijuana between 1996 and 2013. In both instances, preference for the liberal option has doubled or more over this time period.

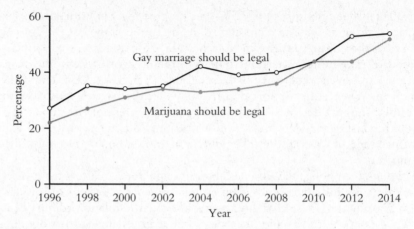

FIGURE 4.5 Should gay marriage and marijuana be legal?

Source: Based on General Social Survey; ABC Poll; Gallup Poll; Pew Research Center.

The underlying dynamics of these dramatic changes have certain similarities, but also noticeable differences. The major driving force behind the increase in support for gay marriage is generational change. In 2013, 66 percent of the millennial generation (born after 1981) favored gay marriage versus 36 percent of the silent generation (born between 1928 and 1945). As the older generation passes from the electorate, support for gay marriage will certainly increase. Still there has been notable nongenerational liberal opinion change on gay marriage as well, with the most cited reason mentioned having family members or friends who are gay.[10] Support for the legalization of marijuana likewise shows significant generational differences, with 65 percent of the millennial generation supporting legalization compared to 32 percent for the silent generation. But there has also been significant change within age cohorts, much more so than the data shown for gay marriage. Among the "baby boom" generation, support for the legalization of marijuana increased from 24 percent to 50 percent between 1994 and 2013.[11]

Table 4.2 shows current opinion on other issues that make up the cultural domain. Despite fierce opposition from some social conservatives, the public has long believed the schools are a proper forum for teaching the biology of human reproduction. Seventy-four percent favored sex education as far back as 1974, rising to 89 percent in 2012. A stable dynamic clearly holds in the case of pornography laws, where the trend has been mostly unchanged at least since 1973, with those opposing laws against its distribution to anyone over the age of 18 ranging between 37 and 42 percent.

Most opinion items show the public favors prayer in the public schools when offered a choice between prayer and no prayer. For instance, in 2012, 59 percent disapproved of the Supreme Court decision outlawing prayer in the public schools. But consider responses to a 2005 Gallup survey in which respondents were offered a choice between a spoken prayer or a moment of silence in the public schools. Sixty-nine percent said they preferred a moment of silence.

When it comes to evolution, a literal interpretation of the Bible holds sway with the public over the views of establishment science. A sizable plurality favors the

TABLE 4.2   Opinion Distributions on Social Issues (Percentage of Opinion-Holders)

		Liberal	Conservative
Pornography[*]	Should there be laws against the distribution of pornography to adults?	63 (no)	37 (yes)
Sex education[*]	Do you favor sex education in the public schools?	89 (yes)	11 (no)
Prayer in schools[*]	Should prayer be permitted in public schools?	41 (no)	59 (yes)
Gun ownership[*]	Right to own guns more important than controlling gun ownership	48 (no)	52 (yes)
Evolution[**]	God created man in present form	51 (no)	49 (yes)

Source: Based on a) *GSS (2012); b) **Pew (2013); c) Gallup.

creationist theory over evolution to account for the origin of human life. Gallup first asked in 1982 which statement came closest to the views of how life began on earth: (1) evolution only, (2) evolution guided by God, or (3) creation by God in the last 10,000 years. In eighteen survey repetitions through 2012, "creation by God in the last 10,000 years" had either a plurality or an outright majority. Evolution becomes a political issue when school boards decide what is to be taught in public schools. When asked by CBS in 2008, 56 percent of Americas favored teaching "creation science" in the public schools along with evolution. In a 2005 Pew poll, 38 percent insisted on teaching creationism *instead* of evolution (Plutzer and Berkman 2008).

Immigration has been a long-standing issue throughout American history. The recent controversy over immigration has mostly focused on Hispanic immigrants from the south of the U.S. border. It is now estimated that there are more than 11 million immigrants in the United States who are not in the country legally. Public opinion toward current immigration-related issues has been subject to much analysis (Hainmueller and Hiscox 2010; Segovia and Defever 2010; Freeman, Hansen, and Leal 2012; Strauss 2012; Masuoka and Junn 2013). A review shows Americans' attitudes are clearly mixed, and opinions are very much a function of the questions that are asked. When a generic question is posed, such as "Is immigration a good thing or bad thing for this country today," a majority since 2001, when the question was first asked, has answered it is "good thing" (Gallup). As of July 2013, "good thing" stands at an all-time high of 72 percent. Despite the sometimes heated rhetoric, a 2013 study by the Pew Research Center found overall attitudes about immigrants were more positive than negative, but negative sentiment is not trivial.[12]

Most polls show majority sentiment for finding some way to allow immigrants living in the country illegally to gain legal status. Pew (2013) reports that 71 percent believe there should be some way for those in the country illegally to gain some sort of legal status, although just 43 percent say that method should be U.S. citizenship.[13] On the other hand, polls show many Americans are concerned about immigrants assimilating and not learning English, and there is overwhelming support for tighter security at U.S. borders. Still, the overall trend regarding opinion about immigrants has shown a perceptible move in a liberal or more tolerant direction since 2000 (Segovia and Defever 2010). Perhaps one reason is the net flow of immigrants to the United States from Mexico since 2005 has been near zero, or perhaps even negative. That is, more people of Hispanic heritage are leaving the United States for Mexico than are leaving Mexico for the United States. If this pattern continues, any percentage point increase in the American Hispanic population will be due solely to population replacement.[14]

Not all cultural issues show declining conservatism among the American public. Despite several highly visible attacks at schools by gun-wielding assassins resulting in the deaths of students, teachers, and staff, opposition to gun control seems to have actually increased in the twenty-first century. As of 2012, more people opposed the banning of handgun ownership—74 percent—than at any time in the past fifty years. When asked what is more important, protecting the right of Americans to own guns or to control gun ownership, the percentage saying "right to own guns" was at its lowest point of 32 percent in 1999 followed shortly after the shootings of twelve students at Columbine High School by two of their classmates.[15] Since that date, support for the right to own a gun has risen dramatically. The high point of 54 percent occurred in May 2009, dropping only slightly to 49 percent in May 2013 (Pew).

Even though in the abstract a majority appears to endorse the right to own guns, a substantial majority also favors a variety of specific government actions to control the availability of firearms. Surveys conducted in 2013 show 86 percent favored background checks on all potential gun buyers, 54 percent favored a ban on assault-style weapons, 68 percent favored creating a federal data bank to keep track of all gun sales, 58 percent favored a ban on semi-automatic weapons, and 61 percent favored a ban on high-capacity ammunition clips.[16] Of course, all these measures could be implemented and people could still retain the "right to own guns" for hunting and other recreation. Still, legislation proposing these fairly mild restrictions has never been able to pass Congress. One reason is effective lobbying by the National Rifle Association. Also, the Pew Center reports that 15 percent of gun control opponents have contacted a public official versus 8 percent of those favoring gun control. In addition, gun control supporters are more likely to contribute money to the cause (12 percent) than are gun control opponents (3 percent).[17] Currently, gun control legislation of any is sort is stalled in Congress.

Law and Order   As can be seen in Figure 4.6, opinions about law and order issues roughly follow changes in the rate of violent crime. In the case of the view that courts do not deal harshly enough with criminals, opinion shows a decided conservative trend starting in the mid-1960s through 1995. Then it begins to move in a liberal direction. The data show support for the view that courts do not deal harshly enough with criminals. In 2006, this position was endorsed by 65 percent of the public, up 20 percentage points from 1965, but down from its all-time high of

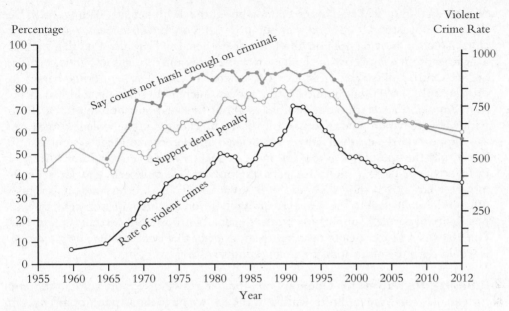

FIGURE 4.6 Law-and-order opinion and the rate of violent crime.

Source: Richard G. Niemi, John Mueller, and Tom W. Smith, *Trends in Public Opinion* (New York: Greenwood, 1989); General Social Survey (1989–2006); Harold W. Stanley and Richard G. Niemi, *Vital Statistics of American Politics, 2011–2012* (Washington, DC: Congressional Quarterly, 2012); FBI Uniform Crime Reports.

80 percent in 1998. Interestingly, the public's apparent taste for greater punitiveness has not caught up with the actual trend toward longer criminal sentences. Conceivably some respondents confront the survey question about harshness toward criminals in a factual vacuum about criminal sentencing and respond simply as if it were a referendum on the goodness or badness of crime. Still, punitive sentiment is trending downward following the downward trend in violent crime. In 2012, only 57 percent favored harsher sentences, lowest in forty years.

Public opinion about the death penalty is particularly important. Compared to other issues, citizens have firmer opinions on the death penalty. The public is also aware of the positions on this issue taken by political candidates and tell pollsters that it is important for their vote decision.[18] Further, public opinion on the death penalty figures prominently into many Supreme Court decisions on the issue. In both *Furman v. Georgia*, a decision in 1972 banning the death penalty, and *Gregg v. Georgia*, reinstating it in 1976, the court in defining cruel and usual punishment said, using the same words in both cases, that the death penalty "is not fastened to the absolute but may acquire meaning as public opinion becomes enlightened by a humane justice" (Baumgartner, De Boef, and Boydstun 2008). When Gallup first asked about the death penalty in 1936, 59 percent were in favor. The all-time low came in 1966 when, for the first time, those opposing the death penalty outnumbered those favoring it by a margin of 47 to 42 percent. Support peaked in 1996 at 78 percent and has declined steadily since.

There is some debate over whether punitive opinion changes in reaction to changes in the crime rate (as would appear from Figure 4.6), media coverage of crime, or both. In a statistical analysis of opinion about the death penalty, Baumgartner, De Boef, and Boydstun (2008) find that homicide rates and media coverage have about equal effects in moving opinion about the death penalty. They also find that there is a significant time lag between changes in crime rates and changes in public opinion. We see that lag illustrated in Figure 4.6, where the rate of violent crime begins to drop sharply in 1990 but public opinion moves much more slowly in a liberal direction. Baumgartner et al. estimate it takes about five years for opinion to catch up with what we would predict statistically based on changes in the violent crime rate.

Support for the death penalty for convicted murderers is influenced significantly by the way the question is asked. The most frequently asked version states, "Are you in favor of the death penalty for persons convicted of murder?" The latest reading (February 2013) shows 64 percent in favor (NYT/CBS). If respondents are also offered (in additional to the death penalty) an option of "life imprisonment with no possibility of parole," support for the death penalty drops to 48 percent (Quinnipiac Poll 2013). Since forty-eight of the fifty states offer this latter sentencing alterative, it would seem the more appropriate question to ask.

Equality for Women   Opinion polls show a growing support across the years for equality for women. From Gallup and GSS, we have data spanning fifty years on the question of whether or not the public would vote for a qualified woman for president—the ultimate nontraditional role. Figure 4.7 shows growth in support, from a minority view in the 1930s to near unanimity in the 1990s, only to drop off somewhat in the twenty-first century.

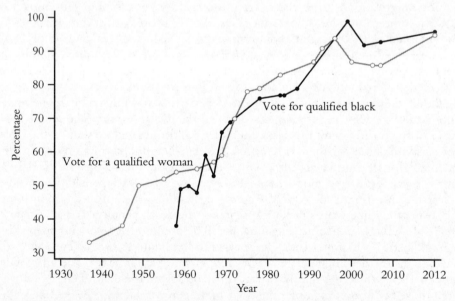

FIGURE 4.7 Would vote for a qualified woman or a qualified black for president.

Source: Based on Gallup, General Social Survey.

Over the decades, the public shifted from general opposition to the idea of a woman president to a general accepting the idea in principle.[19] Other opinion indicators on the role of women show a similar pattern. Since 1972, the ANES has been asking respondents if women should have "an equal role with men in running business, industry, and government" or whether a "woman's place is in the home." In 1972, a mere 59 percent (of opinion-holders) chose the "equal role" option. By 1980, 75 percent did. By 2008 (the most recent year the question was asked), the division among opinion-holders was 93 to 7 in favor of women having an active role rather than saying women should stay home.

Abortion   The most salient of the social issues from the 1970s on into the twenty-first century has been abortion. In 2011, slightly over 1.2 million abortions took place in the United States, down from the high point in 1996 when there were 1.36 million abortions.[20] Americans tend to oppose abortion on moral grounds while supporting the right to abortion as a matter of public policy. In 2013, for example, 50 percent of respondents said they "personally believe that abortion is wrong" (Gallup), while also in 2013, 54 percent said abortion should be legal in most cases (Pew). Even for the hot button issue of abortion, many Americans have ambivalent feelings.

The public debate on abortion tends to stress the extremes, with the "pro-life" advocates demanding an end to all abortions and the "pro-choice" advocates demanding abortion on request. But most Americans favor neither polar position. In a 2013 Gallup survey, 26 percent said that "abortion should be legal in any circumstances" and 20 percent said that "abortion should be illegal under all circumstances." The majority, 58 percent, said abortion should be legal, but only under certain circumstances (3 percent had no opinion).

We can discover the circumstances under which the public feels abortion should be allowed. Since 1972, the General Social Survey has been asking respondents if "you think it should be possible for a pregnant woman to obtain a legal abortion" and then specifying six different circumstances. We can group these circumstances into "traumatic" and "elective," with traumatic being external circumstances beyond the woman's control including danger to her health, damage to the fetus, and rape or incest. Elective reasons include personal and economic considerations—for example, if a married woman wants no more children, the family cannot afford more children, or if an unmarried pregnant woman does not wish to marry the father. Opinion on these items has been remarkably stable since the *Roe v. Wade* decision in 1973 (Fiorina, Abrams, and Pope 2010; GSS, 1972–2012). Public support for abortion rights in traumatic and elective circumstances in the 2012 General Social Survey was

Traumatic Abortion		Elective Abortion	
Defective fetus	70%	Married, does not want children	43%
Health danger	83%	Cannot afford children	41%
Rape/incest	72%	Does not want to marry	40%

Most Americans favor some restrictions on abortion rights. According to a 2003 Gallup survey, 88 percent of the public favored a law requiring physicians to inform patients about alternatives to abortion before performing the procedure, and in the same survey 72 percent favored a law requiring "the husband of a married woman be notified" if a woman wants an abortion. In 2005, a Pew Research Poll showed that 73 percent favored a law requiring parental notification before a pregnant teenager under eighteen could get an abortion; also in 2005, a Quinnipiac poll found that 70 percent favored a 24-hour waiting period before an abortion took place.

Despite majorities favoring some restrictions, Americans oppose a total ban on abortion rights, as only a minority of the public favors reversing *Roe v. Wade* (which in most states would effectively outlaw all abortions). When the public was asked in 2013 if the *Roe* decision should be overturned, 63 percent said *no* compared with 29 percent who wanted the ruling overturned (Pew). At the same time, those who want a total ban seem to hold the most intense opinions. Of the 18 percent in the 2008 ANES survey who said their views on abortion were "extremely important" in terms of casting their vote, 34 percent favored banning all abortions. For everyone else, only 11 percent favored a total ban.

It seems clear that the public wants abortion kept legal, but with some restrictions. Measured by Gallup's standard abortion question, asked every year since 1975, pro-choice support peaked in 1994, when 33 percent said "abortion should be legal under any circumstances." By 2013, 26 percent took this position. The slight decline since then is probably in part due to the highly charged debate over pro-life issues such as "partial birth abortions." When the question is framed simply as "pro-life" versus "pro-choice," the division is close to an even split. In May 2013, 48 percent identified as pro-choice and 45 percent identified as pro-life (Gallup). Also, there is some evidence that younger voters in recent years are less supportive of abortion rights than previous generations (Wilcox and Carr 2010).[21]

4-3 General Ideological Movement

The preceding sections have shown trends on specific survey items. For a particular issue, opinion might become more conservative over time, or more liberal—or, as is often the case, it may just stay the same from one survey reading to the next. If there is a general ideological trend from the data we have examined, it would seem to be lost in the details. A challenging question is whether the public regularly undergoes changes in its "ideological mood." Conceivably, one could detect broad currents of opinion that sometimes flow in the liberal direction and sometimes in the conservative direction. We do know that any general ideological movement cannot be large. From one year to the next, net opinion on any issue rarely changes more than a few percentage points. And large movements generally are responses to events unique to the issue, such as when defense spending preferences once fluctuated in response to the momentary intensity of the Cold War.

One way to locate trends in liberalism or conservatism on the part of the public is simply to record changes in the degree to which people call themselves liberals or conservatives. However, as shown in Chapter 3, self-ranking as liberal or conservative is sometimes questionable for the reason that many people lack adequate understanding of these terms. At a minimum, though, changes in how people describe themselves ideologically should reveal shifts in how fashionable are the terms *liberal* and *conservative*.

In polls taken between the late 1930s and the mid-1960s, respondents remained about evenly divided between self-declared liberals and self-declared conservatives. But then a conservative shift began so that by 1970, conservatives clearly outnumbered liberals, typically by a ratio of about 3 to 2. This change is puzzling, as the public's stands on issues did not obviously become more conservative at the same time. Why did the liberal label go into disfavor so suddenly in the late 1960s?

To some extent, the sudden shift toward "conservatism" reflected an increased public concern about issues on which people saw themselves as conservative (e.g., law-and-order issues) and less public concern about issues on which people saw themselves as liberal (e.g., New Deal social welfare issues). Also, in the changing 1960s, opponents of civil rights legislation frequently justified their position in terms of conservative ideology rather than opposition to the equal-opportunity goals of the civil rights movement. Finally, the mid-1960s were a time when much liberal legislation (such as Medicare, federal aid to education, and major civil rights protection) was enacted. As policy became more liberal, people's ideological frame of reference changed. To be a liberal was to seek even more liberal policies rather than simply to support the new status quo.

In any case, the growth of conservative self-identification in the late 1960s was a one-time event. Over the past thirty-plus years, people have preferred the "conservative" label to the "liberal" label by a ratio that sometimes approaches 2 to 1, with a plurality choosing the moderate category over both extremes. Figure 4.8 shows the distribution of the electorate's ideological self-identification from 1976 to 2012. The

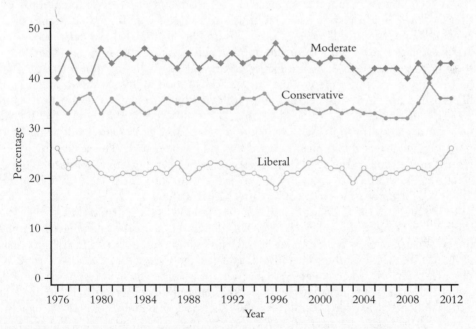

FIGURE 4.8 Ideological identification of the U.S. Public, 1976–2012.
Question: "How would you describe your views on most political matters? Generally, do you think of yourself as liberal, moderate, or conservative?"

Source: Based on CBS/NYT Polls averaged yearly.

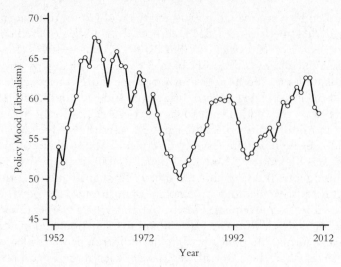

FIGURE 4.9 The public's policy "mood," 1952–2011.

Source: Reprinted by permission from James A. Stimson, University of North Carolina. http://www.unc.edu/~jstimson/Data.html.

figure is notable for the absence of any trend. In terms of ideological identification, the electorate shows essentially the same distribution for the thirty-five-year span.[22]

A second way to monitor changes in liberalism/conservatism is to carefully estimate movement in responses to multiple survey items containing left–right policy content. James Stimson (1999; see also Ellis and Stimson 2012) has performed such an investigation, averaging trends in opinion across a range of subject matter. Stimson's updated findings, shown in Figure 4.9, reveal an oscillating movement of what he calls the electorate's ideological "mood." His mood index shows an increase in liberalism in the 1950s and early 1960s, followed by a decline in the late 1960s and 1970s, followed again by a liberal surge in the 1980s, leveling off in the 1990s. The new century saw Stimson's measure of mood swing more conservative following 9/11, only to swing toward liberalism toward the end of the decade. The scale shown represents movement on the scale of the percentage of liberal (among opinion-holders). Thus, the maximum difference in "mood" is a seventeen-point range from the liberal "high" of the early 1960s to a conservative "low" around 1979.[23]

One can read the fluctuation in the national mood as the ebb and flow of the electorate's net demand for policy change. This demand is sensitive to changes in public policy. When Congress passes major liberal legislation in response to a liberal mood, as in the 1960s, the demand for liberalism is satisfied and the electorate's mood turns conservative. Similarly, when congressional action turns conservative in response to mood, as under Reagan's presidency in the 1980s, the demand for conservatism is satiated and national mood turns more liberal (Erikson, MacKuen, and Stimson 2002). The conservative policies under the presidency of George W. Bush seemingly created a liberal turn in mood. A recent more conservative shift according to the index can be accounted for as a reaction to the liberalism of the Obama administration. Policy that pushes in one ideological direction induces the public to favor change in the opposite direction.

4-4 General Partisan Movement

From an electoral standpoint, one of the most important indicators is the distribution of party identification among the categories of Democrat, Republican, and Independent. The conventional view among political scientists regarding trends in party identification is that macrolevel partisanship is quite stable except for the rare shock of a "partisan realignment." Partisan realignments are precipitated by political parties making major changes in their policy orientations. As parties' policy images change in fundamental ways, the electorate responds with surprisingly large shifts in party identification.

The classic example of a realignment was the New Deal of the 1930s, when the electorate transformed from predominantly Republican to Democrat (Burnham 1970, 119–20; Sundquist 1973, 183–217). This change came in response to the Great Depression under a Republican president and Democratic president Franklin Roosevelt's response. Roosevelt was first elected in 1932, as the electorate demanded change with the onset of the Great Depression. Once in office, Roosevelt's policies, known as the New Deal, greatly expanded the role of the federal government to deal with the national emergency. People tended to align their partisanship anew based on their preferences for or against Roosevelt's economic liberalism. Although no polls were available until 1936, trends in election outcomes and voter registration clearly showed a major electoral shift in favor of the Democratic Party (Ladd 1970; Sundquist 1973, 183–217). To some extent, the electorate's division into Democrats and Republicans even today can be traced to the New Deal realignment.

If there had been polls in the 1920s, they would have shown a Republican dominance in partisanship. By 1937, when a national poll asked the party identification question for the first time, the Democrats predominated. In 99 percent of national polls conducted between 1937 and the present, Democrats outnumbered Republicans. On paper at least, the Democratic Party has had a decisive edge in identification.

In theory, the party system is stable for long periods punctuated only by realignment shocks such as the New Deal. Looking back on a half-century of political history, some scholars see signs of a more recent realignment (or something like it) in the 1960s, when issues like civil rights and social policy began to divide the parties nationally (Aldrich and Niemi 1995; Aldrich 2003). Others question the value of conceiving partisan history as equilibrium punctuated by sharp realignments (Mayhew 2002). In any case, it is now clear that the net direction of partisanship within the electorate is constantly moving over time.

As discussed in Chapter 3, individual-level party identification is quite stable over time, as individuals rarely change their party preference. Still, when people do change partisanship (even if momentarily), they move in one-sided fashion in response to events. Figure 4.10 shows the annual reading of party identification in the Gallup poll since 1945. Measured as the percentage of Democrats among combined Democrat and Republican identifiers, this macrolevel index has been dubbed "macropartisanship" (MacKuen, Erikson, and Stimson 1989). The graph shows palpable movement, with what usually is a Democratic edge that is sometimes quite narrow but at other times a hefty two to one advantage in the count of partisan identifiers. The partisan landscape changes via gradual evolution as well as realignment shock.

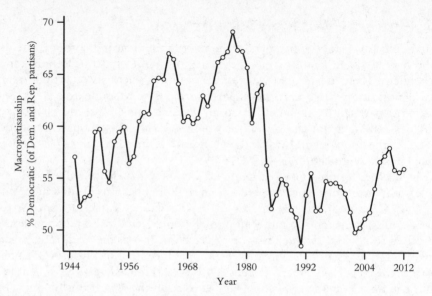

FIGURE 4.10 Macropartisanship, 1945–2012.

Source: Author created table based on data compiled from Gallup Polls.

There were several changes in U.S. party identification over the last half of the twentieth century. The Democrats generally gained from World War II to a peak of support around 1964. Then the Republicans rebounded, only to show precipitous losses following the Watergate revelations of 1973 and 1974. The Democratic gain was followed by a strong Republican trend in the 1980s. Around the turn of the century, the electorate became almost evenly divided between Democrats and Republicans. Then, toward the end of the George W. Bush administration, the Democrats more than recovered their losses.

Close investigation of partisan trends shows that macropartisanship tracks both presidential approval (or, more accurately, the causes of approval) and economic conditions (MacKuen, Erikson, and Stimson 1989; Erikson, MacKuen, and Stimson 1998, 2002; but see Green, Palmquist, and Schickler 1998, 2002 for another view). For instance, the combination of economic recovery and the positive appeal of President Reagan helped the Republicans gain in the 1980s. The George W. Bush presidency presents a mixed story. Following 9/11, the Republicans surged to a temporary lead, followed by substantial losses as Bush's popularity declined during his second term.

Interestingly, movement of party identification bears no resemblance to the movement of ideological mood or ideological identification previously discussed. The electorate's relative favor for Republicans or Democrats is totally unrelated to the electorate's swings between conservatism and liberalism. Although many people choose their partisanship based on ideology, the macrolevel movement of partisanship responds more to perceptions of party performance in office than to ideological preference.

One further trend of note in party identification is the growth in the proportion of the electorate who reject each major party, preferring to call themselves Independents. From World War II to about 1966, only between 22 and 25 percent of the public typically called themselves Independents. Then, as the United States faced the Vietnam War, youth unrest, and the peak of the civil rights revolution, a major rejection of the parties began. Since the late 1960s, about one-third of the electorate has called itself Independent. There is no general trend toward weakened partisanship, however. Recent decades have seen a resurgence in partisan strength, with a majority of those identifying with one of the major parties calling themselves a "strong" Democrat or "strong" Republican (Bartels 2000).

4-5 Presidential Approval

Without a doubt, the most closely watched political indicator in the United States is the president's approval rating. Unlike the other macro level attitudinal indicators we have discussed, presidential approval shows fluctuations so large as to attract attention from both politicians and the general public. The president's approval rating takes on importance because it is widely believed to measure the president's degree of political support at the moment. Congress may be more likely to enact the policy proposals of a president who shows popular support (Canes-Wrone and de Marchi 2002; Bond, Fleisher, and Wood 2003). Presidential approval also provides a guide to reelection prospects (Lewis-Beck and Rice 1982; Brody and Sigelman 1983; Wlezien and Erikson 2000).

While many polling organizations ask some variant of the presidential approval question, the standard measure is Gallup's question, asked regularly for over fifty years. When the Gallup Organization polls the American public, it regularly asks its respondents whether they "approve" of the president's performance, "disapprove" of the president's performance, or have no opinion. Attention generally focuses on the percentage (of all respondents) who approve of the president's current performance.

Gallup's sampling of presidential approval began with sporadic monitoring of Franklin Roosevelt in the late 1930s, when public opinion polling was in its infancy. However, regular readings of Roosevelt's approval rating were interrupted by World War II. Beginning with Harry Truman, presidents have been monitored in terms of public approval on virtually a continuous monthly basis. This database provides enough information that, in general terms at least, we now know which kinds of circumstances increase a president's popularity and which lead to its decline. In condensed form, Figure 4.11 depicts the history of presidential approval polling over sixty-eight years, from Truman to Obama (in 2013).

All presidents enjoy some time above 50 percent approval, and most have unhappily spent some time below the 50 percent baseline. Presidents Truman, Nixon, Carter, and both Bushes all spent time near or below the 30 percent approval level. Three sources account for most variation in a president's approval rating: (1) the honeymoon effect, (2) the rally-round-the-flag effect, and (3) the economy.

The Honeymoon

Every president starts the term with a rather high level of political support, with approval ratings in the 70 percent range not unusual. Then, as the term unfolds, the approval rating undergoes a gradual but inevitable decline. It is not surprising to find that presidents start out with an aura of goodwill, with even supporters of the defeated

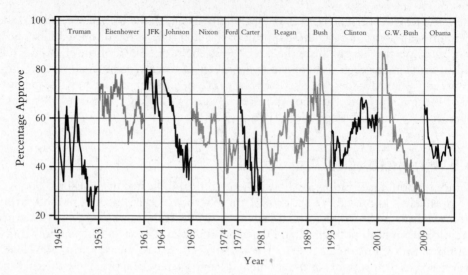

FIGURE 4.11 Presidential approval from Truman to Obama, 1945–2013, quarterly.

Source: Author created table based on data compiled from Gallup Polls.

opponent offering their approval. The more interesting question is why this honeymoon eventually fades. Some say the reason presidents lose support over time is that they cannot please all segments of society all the time. Eventually, so this theory goes, the president must upset the expectations of some supporters, and this disillusionment creates a spiral of declining approval (Mueller 1973). Indeed, one might imagine a general rule that political support decays over time, with leaders inevitably becoming less popular the longer they govern. The implication is that no matter what presidents do to solve national problems, their political support will continue to erode.

A second interpretation is more optimistic. A president's early loss of popularity is best considered a retreat from an artificially high starting point rather than the erosion of a natural base (Kernell 1978). About a year into a presidency, the president's popularity reaches its natural, lower equilibrium level. By the second year, a president's popularity level stabilizes at about 50 percent. From this point on, approval is as likely to rise as it is to fall. The approval rating continues to vary around the usual average of about 50 percent—a function of events that reflect sometimes positively and sometimes negatively on the president's stewardship.

The basic reason presidents begin with an artificially high approval rating is that newly elected presidents start out free of criticism—either from other politicians or from the media. This grace period arises in part because the president has just proved his popularity at the ballot box. It also arises because the new president is a blank slate; he has conducted few official acts to be second-guessed. Instead of criticizing a new president, politicians and the media respond with words of support. Ordinary citizens take their cue from these expressions of goodwill—they, too, express approval (Brody 1991).

As the term evolves, however, the president must take actions that are subject to second-guessing and criticism from the media and from political opponents. The result is a natural decline in support. But after the first year, a new president's popularity generally stabilizes at a more natural level. Still, popularity continues to move in response to perceptions of how the president copes with events and the task of national leadership. We examine next some sources in this variation.

Rally-Round-the-Flag Effect

From time to time, public attention focuses on some foreign policy event—perhaps an unexpected crisis or a major treaty or U.S. intervention abroad. In the past, most of these were related to the Cold War. Early examples include the Soviet shooting-down of a U.S. spy plane (the Francis Gary Powers U-2 incident) in 1960, the Cuban missile crisis in 1962, and seizures of U.S. ships by communist foreign governments in 1968 (the U.S.S. *Pueblo* by the North Koreans) and in 1975 (the *Mayaguez* by the Cambodians). However, not all salient foreign policy events are anxiety provoking. Examples include events such as major treaties (e.g., Nixon's Moscow Treaty of 1972), summits (starting with Eisenhower's Geneva summit conference with Soviet leaders in 1955), and peace efforts such as Johnson's bombing halt (1968) and Carter's Camp David accords (1978) establishing the foundation for peaceful relations between Israel and Egypt.

What these events have in common is a focus on foreign policy. Generally, major foreign policy events are followed by a short-term surge in support for the president—what is called the rally-round-the-flag effect. These are special moments when eyes turn to the president, and the media and national politicians are seen to unite behind the chief executive.

Going to war is a special case. In the short term, wars traditionally result in the showering of approval on the president. One example comes from the early days of polling. While Roosevelt's approval ratings in the late 1930s were no more than respectable (typically in the mid-50s), entry into World War II saw his numbers rise into the 1970s. More recent wars show similar patterns. Truman gained 9 points following the start of the Korean War in 1950. Johnson gained 8 points following a major escalation of the Vietnam War in 1966. Lesser conflicts, such as Johnson's 1965 invasion of the Dominican Republic and Reagan's invasion of Grenada, were also followed by surges in presidential popularity. At one time, the record for the biggest gain from a war was the first President Bush's popularity surge to Gallup's record high of 87 percent in March 1991 following the brief first Gulf War against Iraq. The record was eclipsed by George W. Bush's even greater surge in popularity to 90 percent in some polls following 9/11.

But the political rewards from wars and invasions can be short lived (Mueller 1973, 1994; Berinsky 2009). Bush's popularity decline following the protraction of the Iraq War is fresh in memory. Vietnam provides the prime example. The Johnson administration miscalculated the American public's taste for a prolonged war in Vietnam. Johnson's approval fell in a few short years from the 70s to the low 30s. During the Korean conflict, Truman's approval declined even further—into the 20s—as did Carter's approval during the Iran hostage crisis. Both Truman and Johnson declined to seek reelection, and Carter was defeated in 1980. The first Bush's unique popularity after the first Gulf War shows what a short successful war can do to presidential popularity. But his approval decline in the war's aftermath (from 67 percent in August 1991 to 46 percent by January 1992) provides another lesson—that the political benefit from any presidential success may be short-lived.

The Economy

It is common knowledge that the president's approval rating rises and falls with the state of the economy. When unemployment or inflation rises, the president is blamed. When these indicators of economic gloom decline, the president is praised. Naturally, approval ratings reflect these tendencies. It is as if the electorate reads the state of the economy as a sign of the president's competence.

The exact mechanism by which the electorate converts economic perceptions into presidential approval has been the subject of considerable scholarly investigation. The simplest mechanism would be the straightforward response of personal pocketbook considerations—that when people face good economic times they support the president, and when they face hard times they do not. Consider, however, that most people, most of the time, know that they do not owe their current economic fortune to the president. If the economy is thriving, a person who just got fired or laid off is not likely to blame the president for his or her personal misfortune. Similarly, if the economy is clearly troubled, a person who earns a big raise and promotion is not likely to attribute this good fortune to the president.

But people *do* recognize the state of the general economy as having some relevance to their personal economic well-being. Consequently, citizens reward or punish the president not on the basis of their personal circumstances but rather their perceptions of the national economy. Such responses are called *sociotropic*, as people respond to how *society* is faring rather than how they personally are doing economically (Kinder and Kiewiet 1979). But the motive is still largely personal. People care about the national economy because they personally can be affected.

Evaluations of economic performance tend to be prospective rather than retrospective—that is, people update their evaluations based on prospects for the economy's future rather than evaluating its recent performance. We know this because, statistically, presidential approval tracks consumer expectations about the nation's economic future rather than consumer evaluations of current conditions (MacKuen, Erikson, and Stimson 1992; Erikson, MacKuen, and Stimson 2002). In sum, when people evaluate the president based on the economy, they do not wait until they feel the good or bad times directly in their pocketbook. Rather, they evaluate the president based on economic conditions generally, including the consensus of opinion regarding the economic future.

Presidential Approval and Presidential Success

Each president's record of approval follows its own arc, reflecting the public's often changing judgment of his performance. Approval is more volatile than other indicators of public opinion—one would not want to predict a president's approval numbers a year ahead from the president's numbers today. Approval is distinct for each president—one would not want to predict a new president's approval numbers based on those of his predecessor. And a president's approval numbers are not always a measure of his actual level of success, objectively measured.

A useful lesson is the approval record of President Harry Truman. Based on Gallup's numbers, Truman was one of the least popular presidents. But historians judge (and the public feels in retrospect) that Truman was among the most successful.

4-6 Conclusion: What Moves Public Opinion?

We have seen that public opinion has changed dramatically on many issues over the seventy years or so since the advent of reliable public opinion polling. Large shifts have sometimes occurred over short periods, or incremental moves have aggregated over the years to a fundamental reversal in American political sentiment.

Abrupt changes in public opinion normally can be traced to the public's reaction to current events. Explaining incremental change is more complex. Cohort replacement is certainly one factor. Almost 50 percent of the American electorate is replaced every twenty years (Abramson 1983, 54). When we see dramatic change in support for the ideals of the civil rights movement between 1960 and 1980, it is important to understand that only about half of those comprising the adult population in 1960 were still part of that population in 1980. The new 50 percent enter the electorate often socialized to a different set of political values. Thus, the change that appears in support for the ideas of the civil rights movement does not necessarily mean that people have changed their minds, although that may have happened as well.

Finally, the effects of modernization have certainly affected the political opinions of the American public. Included here are demographic trends such as rising levels of education, movement from rural to urban areas, the growth of the nonwhite population (especially Hispanics), and the increasing penetration of the national mass media to all sectors of society. These advances of education, urbanization, racial diversity, and media penetration have undoubtedly played a role in the public's changing political attitudes and preferences.

Critical Thinking Questions

1. There has been a lot of polling on a wide range of issues over many years. So can we gauge the public as getting either more liberal or more conservative over time? Why is answering this question complicated?
2. Assessing whites' attitudes toward African-Americans is complicated by such factors as social desirability. How might these measurement problems be overcome? Can we really know the public's opinions on matters involving race?
3. To what extent do you think a president's popularity as measured in the polls will match the conclusions of future historians?

Endnotes

1. Not everyone agrees that the "noise" in surveys is random. Althaus (2003) argues this noise is mostly not random and often serves to the disadvantage of those in the lower economic strata as they are less likely to express opinions.
2. On the 7-point scale, points 1, 2, and 3 are collapsed to indicate preference for a government health plan, and points 5, 6, and 7 are collapsed to indicate preference for a private plan.

3. In one poll, 93 percent with health insurance said they were very satisfied with the quality of their care. ABC News/USA Today/Kaiser Family Foundation Health Care Poll (September 7–12, 2006).

4. http://kff.org/health-reform/poll-finding/kaiser-health-tracking-poll-march-2012/.

5. In 2009, 16 percent said "lower income people" paid too little in taxes. Only 5 percent of the same sample said "middle income" people paid too little, while 60 percent said "upper income people" paid too little.

6. For more on trends in affirmative action attitudes, see Steeh and Krysan (1996), Sharp (1999), and Stoker (2001). Questions about affirmative action were rarely asked by pollsters in the 1960s and early 1970s, when affirmative action policies were pioneered.

7. According to this view, the racially prejudiced find a respectable outlet for expressing their views on symbolic issues such as the busing of school children for racial balance. It has been demonstrated, for example, that the most vocal opponents of busing are often nonparents with little direct stake in the matter (Sears, Hensler, and Speer 1979).

8. White racial attitudes are difficult to measure (Kuklinski, Cobb, and Gilens 1997) because racial appeals are often subtle. See Mendelberg (2001) regarding racial appeals to whites during election campaigns.

9. www.people-press.org/2011/11/11/17/section-4-views-of-Iraq/.

10. www.people-press.org/2013/03/20/growing support for gay marriage.

11. http://www.people-press.org/2013/04/04/majority-now-supports-legalizing-marijuana.

12. http://www.people-press.org/2006/03/30/section-iv-views-and-perceptions-of-immigrants/.

13. http://www.people-press.org/2006/03/30/section-iv-views-and-perceptions-of-immigrants/.

14. http://www.pewhispanic.org/2012/04/23/net-migration-from-mexico-falls-to-zero-and-perhaps-less/.

15. The question was first asked in 1993.

16. www.pollingreport.com/guns.htm.

17. http://www.people-press.org/2013/05/23/broad-support-for-renewed-background-checks-bill-skepticism-about-its-chances/.

18. A 2000 ABC News/*Washington Post* Poll found 72 percent of respondents saying the death penalty issue was either "very" or "somewhat" important to them in deciding how to vote in the 2000 presidential election.

19. See Streb et al. (2008) for a significant qualification. They argue that the high level of support for a woman for president has a significant social desirability component and present evidence to support their contention.

20. Data from the Alan Guttmacher Institute at www.guttmacher.org, downloaded September 23, 2013.

21. Using the GSS data, Wilcox and Carr merged 2000–2006 data and divided the sample into four age groups. The group from eighteen to twenty-nine was the least pro-choice of these age groups, in contrast to previous GSS readings where the oldest age group was least pro-choice. Gallup also aggregated data from 2006 to 2010 and found little difference between age groups except for those over 65 years which were notably more pro-life than other age groups (http://www.gallup.com/poll/9259/Generational-Gulf-Moral-Views-Vary-Age.aspx).

22. Ellis and Stimson (2012) provide an up-to-date discussion of trends in ideological identification. For an earlier discussion of trends in ideological identification and whether or not they can be explained, see Box-Steffensmeier, Knight, and Sigelman (1998).

23. For still another analysis of ideological trends using multiple survey items, see Smith (1990).

CHAPTER 5

Political Socialization
and Political Learning

LEARNING OBJECTIVES

- Describe the influence of the family on political predispositions
- Describe how schooling affects political opinions

- Describe how personality and our genes influence political predispositions
- Identify life-cycle and generational effects on political opinions

Just as one learns to read and write and identify fashionable clothing, one learns about politics. A considerable portion of this learning occurs before one is old enough to enter the voting booth. Adults, for example, tend to generalize from their idealization of childhood family authority structure to their preferred authority structure for the state (Barker and Tinnick 2006). Even adult party identification and ideological orientations can be traced back to childhood. A central premise in the study of childhood socialization to politics, called "the primary principle," holds that what one learns as a preadult affects one's later political life. This assumption is crucial, for there is little reason for interest in the reaction of preadults to their political environment except insofar as it affects their adult attitudes and behaviors (Stoker and Bass 2011).

To *socialize* is commonly defined as the older generation teaching the younger generation its culture and values. Thus, one perspective on political socialization focuses on the learning of attitudes, values, and acceptable forms of behavior necessary to fit into the established political and social order. It is the learning or failure to learn the lessons of being a good citizen, as defined by the political status quo (Easton and Dennis 1969). Another perspective sees the field as more akin to generic political learning. The emphasis is on individual political change throughout the life cycle rather than on molding the person to fit the political community (Jennings 2004).

This chapter presents a journey through the political life cycle, starting with the formative years. We first trace the evolution of political learning from earliest childhood up to the approach of adult life, evaluating the agents of socialization along the way. We then analyze aspects of political socialization during adulthood.

5-1 The Preadult Years: Socialization to Citizenship

In every political system, children are indoctrinated from a young age to accept the ongoing political order. According to David Easton and Jack Dennis (1969, 5), pioneers in the study of political socialization, the persistence of the political system "may in part be dependent upon the success of a society in producing children most of whom acquire positive feelings about it." Childhood socialization involves encouraging the young to identify with the regime and inculcating a sense of loyalty and belonging to the political order. More than that, it also involves the transmission of the political culture from one generation to the next.

A good deal of what we know about early childhood socialization comes from studies conducted decades ago of children from preschool through the eighth grade, conducted as early as the 1950s and repeatedly replicated (Carter and Teten 2002; Block and Block 2006). The dawn of political awakening begins before children commence their formal education. Perhaps the most important lesson children learn at this early stage is a sense of national identity. Preschoolers frequently confuse political authority with religious authority. In a study of kindergarten children in California, Moore, Lare, and Wagner (1985) report that when asked "Who does the most to run the country?" 30 percent responded "God" or "Jesus." The most significant public figures for the young child are the president and the police officer. One school of thought contends that both officials play a major role in promoting the child's attachment to and identification with the political order. Schwartz (1975) found that 90 percent of her preschool sample were able to recognize the "man in the picture" as being "the policeman," and 75 percent were able to answer correctly when asked "What does the policeman do?" The responses most frequently given concerned regulating traffic, helping lost children, and "catching bad people." The children, for the most part, saw the police officer as a benevolent authority figure symbolizing the State.

Unlike adults, who tend to be cynical about politics, the young child sees the president and the police officer as trustworthy, helpful, and benevolent. According to the "benevolent leader hypothesis" (Greenstein 1965), a positive image of the president (the most visible symbol of political authority) formed in early childhood has a direct effect on the formation of attitudes and beliefs about other political figures and institutions. There is a hypothesized "spillover effect" from this early view of the president to later perceptions of other political authorities. Because the president is favorably viewed, they too tend to be viewed favorably. Later in life, when the individual is able to make critical judgments about politics, this early idealization builds what David Easton (1965) refers to as "diffuse support"—a reservoir of goodwill toward the political system that is independent of any benefit the individual might receive. It helps legitimize the political order and, in times of political stress, the residue of this early idealization helps maintain a positive attitude toward government.

Beginning about the age of ten or eleven, children start moving away from a personalized view of government to one based on a more sophisticated understanding. By late grade school, children can distinguish between the office of the presidency and the person holding that office. That is, while still holding positive view of the office, they were more likely to be critical of the person holding that office (Carter and Teten 2002).

However, definitions of democracy in late childhood and even through adolescence seldom include the right to criticize government. Only 54 percent of the eighth graders in Hess and Torney's (1967) sample checked the option "you can say things against the government" as one possible definition of democracy. And 84 percent of eighth graders agreed that "the government usually knows what is best for the people."

The major spurt in a child's political learning usually comes during adolescence, when the individual is in many ways beginning to politically resemble an adult. In a study of fifteen-year-old high school students, Conover and Searing (2000) found that almost all developed a sense of their identity as citizens of the United States. When asked to define basic citizens' rights, most students answered with a core set of rights, such as those of speech, religion, and privacy. However, learning of basic rights and tolerance for others does not grow much further during the high school years. Conover and Searing (2000), for example, found levels of political tolerance among their sample of adolescents to be "disappointing low."

The Consequences of Preadult Socialization to Citizenship

The most dramatic findings in the literature on early socialization of citizenship are the extent to which young children (kindergarten through eighth grade) personalize government and the remarkable degree to which they idealize political authority. But do these findings really mean anything for adult behavior? The theory of diffuse support, born of childhood idealization, has a certain appeal but is difficult to verify empirically.

First, the theory seems not to be general, as not all children idealize authority. African-American (Greenberg 1970; Gimpel, Lay, and Schuknecht 2003), Mexican-American (Garcia 1973), Native American (Fridkin, Kenney, and Crittenden 2006), and poor, isolated, rural white Appalachian children (Jaros, Hirsch, and Fleron 1968) are much more cynical about political authority than are middle-class white children. In fact, Jaros, Hirsch, and Fleron (1968) termed views of the president by Appalachian children as outright "malevolent."

When major political events arise, children can react as well as adults. One such event is the "Watergate" scandal of 1972–1974. Studies that investigated the impact of Watergate on children found that the dramatic negative shift in the portrayal of President Nixon deeply impacted their image of the president. The benevolent leader was transformed by Watergate into someone malevolent (Arterton 1974).

However, at least in the case of Watergate, there is no evidence that the drastic swing in preadult views of the president had any effect in later life. For instance, ANES data shows that as adults those who would have been in grade school during Watergate have been no more or less trusting of government than other age cohorts. Similarly, the benevolent view of political authorities found among the children in the early socialization studies of the early 1960s must be reconciled with later radical protestors from the same age cohort. One possible explanation is that the samples chosen by the early researchers (eighth grade and younger) were not yet of impressionable age. We now know that political experiences have the most lasting long-term effect on people between the ages of seventeen and twenty-six ("the impressionable years thesis").

5-2 The Agents of Preadult Socialization

Having traced the development of political attitudes through the preadult years, we now attempt to sort out the agents most responsible for this development. The family seems to be the most influential source of preadult attitudes, but it certainly is not the only source. Schools make an effort to mold future citizens, and it seems probable that effort meets with at least some success. Other possible agents of early political socialization include childhood friends and the mass media. Finally, when important historical events occur, it seems likely that they leave an imprint on the young of impressionable age.

The Family

Political influence within the family is a function of numerous factors, but among the most important are communication and receptivity (Sears and Levy 2003). Parents score high on both these dimensions. First, children, particularly young children, spend a large amount of time with their parents. The opportunities for children to learn parental attitudes and for parents to exert influence on children are considerable. Second, in terms of receptivity, few bonds are as strong as the affective tie between parents and children. The stronger this tie and the more personal the relationship, the greater the parents' ability to exert influence.

A common assumption is that the political attitudes of family members are highly similar, with the presumed causal flow being from parents to children (rather than from sources outside the family that affect all family members alike).[1] However, recent research has shown that socialization can sometimes be reciprocal—with children influencing parents. For instance, immigrant school children may socialize their first-generation parents based on political information learned in the classroom (Wong and Tesng 2007; Fitzgerald 2011). Much of what we know about the family and political socialization comes from the longitudinal Youth-Parent Socialization Panel study spanning the years from 1965 to 1997. A national sample of high school seniors and their parents were first interviewed in 1965. The students were then reinterviewed in 1973, 1982, and 1997. The parents were reinterviewed in 1973 and 1982. In 1997, children over the age of fifteen born to the original 1965 seniors were interviewed. Thus, we have an incredibly rich data set for understanding a wide range of social influences on political opinions over three generations.

Shown in Table 5.1 is the relationship in 1965 between the attitudes of seniors and their parents on four policy issues. Reading across the rows in the table, we can see that the students are much more likely to be pro-school integration and pro-school prayer when their parents favor these positions. For example, 83 percent of the children with pro-integration parents also favored school integration, but when parents opposed integration, the percent favoring integration dropped to 45 percent—a difference of 38 percentage points.[2]

Table 5.1 shows for 1965 that the relationship between parents and their children weakens considerably for the question of an elected Communist being allowed to hold office and virtually disappears on the question of allowing atheists to give speeches against churches. The best explanation is that these civil libertarian issues are of little importance to most families. In general, affect-laden issues with relatively

TABLE 5.1 Relationship Between High School Students and Parent Opinions on Four Policy Issues, 1965

Students	Federal Role in School Integration[a] (Parents)			Prayers in Public Schools[b] (Parents)			Elected Communist Can Hold Office (Parents)			Allow Speeches Against Churches (Parents)		
	Pro	Depends	Con	Pro	Depends	Con	Pro	Depends[b]	Con	Pro	Depends[b]	Con
Pro	83%	64%	45%	74%	62%	34%	45%		32%	88%		82%
Depends	07	17	14	03	08	07	01		00	0		0
Con	10	18	41	23	30	59	53		67	12		18
Total	100%	100%	100%	100%	100%	100%	100%		100%	100%		100%
N	(961)	(202)	(453)	(1,253)	(68)	(238)	(1,337)		(222)	(1,376)		(523)

[a]Based on pairs in which both parents were "interested enough" to give a pro or con response.

[b]Ten or fewer cases.

Source: M. Kent Jennings, Student-Parent Socialization Study, 1965 (data obtained through the Inter-University Consortium for Political and Social research).

long lives on the political agenda are most effectively transmitted from parents to children, regardless of the generation (Jennings, Stoker, and Bowers 2009). In 1997, for instance, a strong correlation was found again between parental and filial attitudes about whether prayers belong in the public schools. The strongest relationship between the 1997 parents and their children was on abortion, an issue not on the political agenda in 1965. In fact, in 1997 the correspondence between parents and children on abortion was stronger than for party identification (Jennings, Stoker, and Bowers 2009).

The most thoroughly documented successful long-term transmission of an attitude from parent to child involves partisanship. Again using the 1965 wave of the Youth-Parent Socialization Panel, Table 5.2 documents the widespread agreement between parents and children on the question of party preference. For instance, reading across the rows of the table, when we move from parents who are Democratic to those who are Independent to those who are Republican, the percentage of Democratic children drops dramatically and the percentage who say they are Republicans increases. When parents agree between themselves on partisanship (74 percent do agree), 76 percent of the adolescents follow the preferences of their parents. This pattern was also reflected in the 1997 data. Interestingly, when parents disagree on partisanship (one is a Democrat, the other a Republican), the child is more likely to adopt the mother's partisanship than the father's. Also, with parental divergence on partisanship, the number of Independent children rises substantially, as one would expect given the cross-pressures (Jennings and Langton 1969; Kroh and Selb 2009).

The success with which parents are able to transmit their partisanship to their children seems to have remained essentially static over the generations, despite vast changes in the family social structure. To generalize, the relationship between the partisanship of parents in 1997 (the 1965 high school seniors) and their own

TABLE 5.2 High School Senior Party Identification by Parent Party Identification, 1965

Students	Parents			
	Democrat	**Independent**	**Republican**	**Frequencies***
Democrat	66%	29%	13%	(43%)
Independent	27	55	36	(36%)
Republican	07	17	51	(21%)
Total	100%	100%	100%	
Frequencies*	(49%)	(24%)	(27%)	100%

*The frequency totals present the proportion of parents and students holding a particular party preference. For example, looking at the column frequencies we can see that 49 percent of the parents call themselves Democrats. Looking at the row frequencies we can see that 43 percent of the students in the sample call themselves Democrats.

Source: Based on M. Kent Jennings, Student-Parent Socialization Study, 1965 (data obtained through the Inter-University Consortium for Political and Social research).

children is similar to that between parents and children in 1965 (Jennings, Stoker, and Bowers 2009). This generational continuity is important because it helps perpetuate existing party divisions across generations.

What is the mechanism by which parental transmission of political attitudes works? There are at least three possible explanations. One explanation is the simple matter of communication within the home. Children need to be aware of their parents' opinions. Second, the most politicized parents are likely to be most successful in socializing their children, since politics is important to those parents. Looking over the long haul (thirty-plus years), we expect those high school seniors who were most successfully socialized to their parents' political views will be those most likely to maintain those political attitudes over the life cycle. Third, transmission might not entirely be due to socialization. Genetics may play a role, as will be discussed shortly. The idea is not that there is a gene for partisanship or for particular political viewpoints. That is obviously not the case. Rather, the argument is that genetic transmission from parents to children includes genetic traits that predispose people toward particular views.

Communication   Party identification is passed from parent to child with much more success than other political orientations. One explanation grounded in social psychology is that most political questions are remote from the day-to-day concerns of the family. Few parents hold their political opinions strongly, and few children have an accurate perception of those opinions. In this regard, party identification is unique. At election time, young children often ask if "we" are Democrats or Republicans. In a study of high school seniors, Tedin (1974) found that while 72 percent were aware of parental party identification, no more than 36 percent were aware of parent attitudes on any one issue. But when issue attitudes were about as salient and well perceived as partisanship, parent–child correspondence approached that for partisanship. If children accurately perceive the political attitudes of their parents, socialization is quite successful. But misperception is frequent.

Politicization   We would expect the more politicized the parents, the more success they would have influencing their children. However, the politicization hypothesis is only partially borne out for political opinions (Beck and Jennings 1991; Jennings, Stoker, and Bowers 2009). Data from the Youth-Parent Panel show the most politicized families in 1965 successfully transmitted their partisanship, vote choice, and political trust, but for most other issues politicized parents were often less successful in transmitting political attitudes than nonpoliticized parents. The reason was the greater sensitivity to powerful environmental factors in the 1960s among politicized adolescents, such as the civil rights movement. On the other hand, in the less politically volatile 1990s, the 1997 parents were a good deal more successful in transmitting their issue preferences than were their own parents back in 1965. As before, partisanship and vote choice were successfully transmitted. However, in the case of issues, some of the correspondence between politicized parents and their children in 1997 is spectacularly higher than for nonpoliticized parents (Jennings, Stoker and Browers 2009). The reason is a lack of conflicting environmental counter influences in the 1990s that could push politically savvy adolescents away from the politics embraced by their parents.

By exploiting the Youth-Parent Panel's 1997 wave, it is possible to observe the successful parental socialization of 1965 high school students some thirty-two years later at the age of fifty. For each issue, Jennings, Stoker, and Bowers (2009) divided the 1965 high school seniors into two groups. One group agreed with their parents' position on the issue (giving identical responses to the question); the other did not. The authors then analyzed the extent to which these two groups (one "successfully" socialized and the other "unsuccessfully") retained in 1997 the political opinions they first inherited from their parents as found in the 1965 survey. In almost every instance, the continuity of political opinions was greater among those who acquired their parents' orientations back in 1965 than those who did not. For instance, 54 percent who adopted their parents' exact party identification in 1965 (as a Democrat, Republican, or Independent) retained that exact identification in 1997, compared to 33 percent among those who differed from their parents back in 1965. The inference is that early acquisition of parental political views has lifelong consequences (see also Kroh and Selb 2009).

Parents, of course, are not the only members of the family. There are often brothers and sisters. Sibling gender is randomly assigned, so a study of family gender structure has the virtue of comprising a natural experiment. Healy and Malhotra (2013) have found that when males have sisters instead of brothers, they are more likely to identify as Republicans and hold conservative values. The reason, the authors claim, is that in families composed of both male and female children, traditional gender role tasks tend to be assigned, with boys assimilating this division of family labor as the norm. For females, it should be noted, sibling gender has no evident effect.

The Peer Group

Like parents, the peer group enjoys considerable opportunity to influence attitudes and behavior. Strong affective ties are involved, and young people normally spend a substantial part of their time with friends. Parents and peers differ, however, at the point in the preadult's life when influence is greatest. Parents dominate the lives of their offspring until adolescence, at which point peers become increasingly important (Beck 1977). Despite the considerable attention paid to peer groups in the United States, there is relatively little research and (perhaps as a logical consequence) little agreement on the role of peers as an agent of political socialization. Some scholars argue that peer groups are the most important of all adolescent socialization agencies, while others assert that the influence of peers is largely redundant.[3] Peers are seen as simply reinforcing the lessons learned in the family and school. It is clear, however, that adolescent peers can be influential in areas involving the individual's status in the group. But these areas usually involve matters of taste in music, clothing, and hairstyles and "deviant" social practices rather than politics. For instance, numerous studies have demonstrated that peer influence (versus self-selection) is highly predictive of adolescent decisions to smoke—a practice discouraged by most parents (Kobus 2003; Hoffman et al. 2007).

In the Youth-Parent Socialization Panel, a subset of the 1965 students were asked to indicate their best friend of the same sex, who was then included in the sample. As expected, for party identification the correlation between students and parents greatly exceeded that between students and peers. On the other hand, in the case of changing the voting age from twenty-one to eighteen (one had to be twenty-one to vote at the time of the survey), the student–peer correlation exceeded the student–parent correlation. This is the pattern one would expect. Partisanship is learned during early childhood and is not a particularly youth-oriented issue. On the other hand, preadults were more likely to become aware of the eighteen-year-old vote issue during adolescence, and the issue is particularly relevant to high school seniors (Jennings and Niemi 1974). We would therefore expect more peer influence in the latter instance. In situations in which parents and peers disagree on partisanship, the student is more likely to follow the parent. But when parent and peer disagree on voting age, the student is more likely to follow his or her best friend (Sebert, Jennings, and Niemi 1974). Thus, peer versus parent influence seems to be issue-specific.

It is difficult to make any absolute assessment of peer influence, but it seems certain that even in adolescence, peers are not as important as parents. When politics is remote from one's day-to-day concerns, and when family social harmony as well as one's status in the peer group is only slightly affected by politics, parents probably have an advantage over peers in the socialization process. If one assumes all other things are equal, adolescents are more likely to be aware of and receptive to parent attitudes simply because most contemporary political issues are more important to parents than to their peers (Tedin 1980).[4] Of course, when a matter is important to the esteem with which an adolescent is held by the peer group, parents usually cannot compete with peer influence. But for most American youth, everyday political issues are rarely of consequence for their standing in the peer group.

The Primary and Secondary School

Many political theorists, practical politicians, political reformers, and political revolutionaries believe or have believed that the school is an instrumental agent in the political training of the young. Examples abound. After the 1917 Russian revolution, children were removed from the family (presumably still attached to the old order and unsympathetic to Communist values) and required to spend long periods in school for political retraining. The Allied Powers followed a similar policy after the defeat of the Nazis in World War II. The schools were "de-Nazified," and German youths were instructed in the principles of democratic government as defined by the West. The same perspective on socialization is reflected in the fierce debate over a multicultural curriculum in American schools, or the teaching of "intelligent design" in the classroom along with the theory of evolution. The school is seen as an effective vehicle for instructing students in the values necessary for life in adult society.

Virtually all nations charge the public schools with the responsibility of teaching obedience to political authority. The practice is nearly universal, and from the standpoint of maintaining political stability and continuity, many believe it is a necessity. It is commonly believed that political stability is highly dependent on the ability of the agents of socialization to produce in children feelings as to the rightness, the oughtness, and the legitimacy of the political order. In all nations with an effective national government, this task is assigned to the schools. They are the one agent of political socialization over which the government has considerable control.

There can be little doubt, as we noted in the section on childhood political development, that preadults in the United States generally learn the lessons of patriotism and obedience. Most readers are undoubtedly aware of the patriotic rituals that characterize most classrooms—pictures of American heroes, the display of the American flag and proclaiming one's allegiance to it, singing patriotic songs, "young citizens leagues," and the emphasis on obedience to authority. Teaching methods change periodically in response to changes in thinking about what is and is not effective for student learning, but the goal of socializing the young to be loyal citizens is never divorced from changes in the curriculum (Ross 2004; Westheimer 2007). As Richard Merelman (1997, 56) observes, "the proposed national civics standards are mainly a symbolic ritual masked as educational policy for reinforcing cultural hegemony." In other words, the curriculum is focused on teaching a common American culture and values as opposed to teaching individual and group differences. More recently, political scientist Ian MacMullen (2011) makes the case for a status quo bias in education, arguing that if the overwhelming consensus among adults favors existing political institutions and practices, these should be taught positively in the schools in the interests of maintaining a stable polity. Others see this as stagnating critical thinking and political innovation (Hand 2011).

Regardless, students of political education agree that teaching loyalty and obedience is only one aspect of political education. There are other goals as well, such as teaching political knowledge, political participation skills, tolerance of competing political views, and acceptance and support for democratic values. An invigorated role for the schools in these areas would seem even more important in the twenty-first century than in the past, given the recent decline in young adult interest and participation (Campbell 2005; Wattenberg 2011). One disappointment is that political education does not seem to generate much political enthusiasm or eagerness to participate in adult citizenship. For example, in a 2012 poll of high school seniors just 26 percent said they had "a lot" or a "great deal" of interest in current events.[5]

As political knowledge increases, people support democratic values and express faith in the political system (Dudley and Gitelson 2003; Galston 2004, but see Green et al. 2011). Unfortunately, high school students' factual knowledge about politics is notoriously low. Niemi and Junn (1998) report that fewer than two-thirds of twelfth graders were aware that it is legal to participate in a boycott, organize a recall election, or impeach legislators. According to the National Assessment of Educational Progress, often called "the nation's report card," only 24 percent of high school seniors in 2010 had a "proficient" knowledge of how the government worked, and 37 percent failed the national civics test (Coley and Sum 2012).

Finally, surveys of high school youth suggest that support for democratic values is limited and fragile. Niemi and Junn's (1998) study from the 1990s finds that only 52 percent of high school seniors knew the right to religious freedom is part of the Bill of Rights and only 47 percent knew there is a constitutional ban on double jeopardy. In a 2004 survey of high school students, 75 percent said flag burning was illegal, 50 percent said the government could censor the Internet, and more than a third said the First Amendment goes too far in guaranteeing individual rights.[6] With similar findings persisting over many decades, the inescapable conclusion is that adolescent youth typically are little interested in politics, possess little factual foundation, and are slow to learn democratic norms (Bennett 1997, 1998; Mann 1999).

The poor performance of adolescents on political quizzes and the desire of educational professionals to prepare adolescents for their adult role as citizens have engendered a lively debate over possible remedies. First, we need to note that almost all high school students take civics courses, usually in the twelfth grade (Coley and Sum 2012). So any shortcomings are not due to lack of exposure to content. We need to begin by asking the extent to which traditional high school civics courses add an incremental improvement to commonly accepted standards for democratic citizenship. A detailed study of data from the National Assessment of Education Progress by Richard Niemi and Jane Junn (1998) turned up modest effects of the civics curriculum on trust in government—the more courses taken, the more trust in government—and stronger effects on political knowledge.[7] Moreover, Niemi and Junn find that if one looks at all factors relevant to civics instruction beyond simply hours in the classroom—the amount and recentness of coursework, variety of topics studied, and discussion of current events—the estimated effects increase. These findings are supported in an experimental study by Green et al. (2011). Across a variety of schools, one randomly selected set of civics classes received enhanced instruction on the constitutional protections of civil liberties while a control group did not. The authors report significant and lasting gains in knowledge about civil liberties (but no increased *support* for civil liberties). These studies serve to rehabilitate the often-maligned civics curriculum as a contributor to political learning.

It is not entirely clear how the curriculum in high school contributes to levels of political knowledge or support for democratic values. There is, however, no doubt that those with a high school degree are more politically tolerant than those without. Consider the following. The 2012 GSS shows that while only 56 percent of those with a grade school education support free speech for an atheist, 74 percent of those with a high school degree are supportive. Similarly, while only 67 percent of those with a grade school education would allow a homosexual to teach in college, 79 percent of those with a high school degree would be willing. Numerous other examples can be offered.

It may be that a high school education simply slots people into social, economic, and political positions in which they have a greater opportunity to learn and absorb democratic norms. Or it may be that the type of civics curriculum makes a significant difference. The evidence is mixed. A study by Avery (2002) showed a link between classroom discussion of civil liberties issues and the development of tolerant attitudes. On the other hand, the study by Green et al. (2011) found no relationship between an experimentally induced increase in knowledge about civil liberties (see earlier) and actual support for civil liberties. Elevated levels of information alone may not be sufficient to raise levels of political tolerance. On the other hand, studies contrasting an "open classroom" where high school students freely engage in discourse and debate on controversial real-world political problems, as opposed to the traditional "citizenship transmission" model, show that the former substantially elevates knowledge of democratic processes (based on response to a 49-item scale) and that students are more accepting of conflict as a normal part of the political process (Campbell, D.E. 2008).

Perhaps ominously, overall rates of extracurricular activities among high school students dropped substantially between the mid-1960s and the late 1990s. High school students at the dawn of the twenty-first century simply did not participate in civic activities to the same extent as their parents did a generation earlier (Jennings and Stoker 2004). The pattern for high school students is consistent with (and may be a precursor to the decline) an adult communal participation described by Robert Putnam in *Bowling Alone* (2000).

One solution may be encouraging those in high school to participate in community activities. If the effect of formal civic education remains mixed, there is little doubt that participating in community activities in high school leads to higher rates of political activity in adult life. These activities, even when required by schools, are thought to foster a sense of civic identity that eventually results in elevated adult political participation. Metz and Youniss (2003) analyzed data from a school comparing the 1998–1999 graduating class, which had no community service requirement, to the 2001–2003 class, which had a forty-hour community service requirement. The students required to perform community service continued to do so at an even higher rate once the requirement was completed and expressed an intention to volunteer in the future at significantly higher levels than the 1998–1999 cohort of students who had no community service requirement. Dietz and Boeckelman (2012) showed participation by students in a presidential election simulation significantly boosted political interest and political knowledge. A follow up one year later found lasting effects (see also Jennings 2002; Andolina et al. 2003; Torney-Purta and Amadeo 2003; McFarland and Thomas 2006; Zukin et al. 2006).

5-3 College: Higher Education and Its Impact

Although most students are legally adult when they enter college, the college experience is for many a transition period between life with the family and being on one's own. Today almost one of every two high school graduates goes to college. At the turn of the twentieth century, most young people did not even graduate from high school, let alone contemplate attaining a college degree.[8] Consequently, the proportion of the adult population with college experience has been rising steadily. For example, in the short period between 1972 and 2012, the proportion of adults over twenty-five with college degrees rose from 13 to 31 percent (GSS).

This increase is a combination of two factors. First, older, less-educated citizens are departing the electorate and being replaced by a better-educated younger age cohort. Second, young adults today are more likely to get a college degree than was the case for the same age cohort some 40 plus years ago.

The College Years

What are the political implications of the growth in the college-educated public? As a starting point, let us follow the evolution of the political attitudes of college freshmen, as monitored continually by the University of California at Los Angeles CIRP annual surveys and shown in Figure 5.1. Although the current crop of college students is slightly more conservative in self-identification than students of the 1960s and 1970s, the popularity of the liberal label among college freshmen has been increasing in recent years. In terms of self-identification, college freshmen are slightly more conservative in the second decade of the twenty-first century than in 1970.

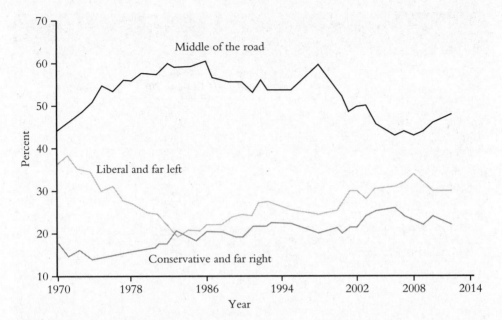

FIGURE 5.1 Ideological self-identification of college freshman, 1970–2012.

Source: Based on data from CIRP Freshman Study, Higher Education Research Institute, University of California, Los Angeles.

Among freshmen in 1970, liberals outnumbered conservatives by about a 2 to 1 margin. By 1985, perhaps due to the Reagan Revolution, conservatives slightly outnumbered liberals. Since then, however, liberals have been gaining. In 2012 they outnumbered conservatives by 30 to 23 percent. This trend toward self-identified liberalism has been accompanied by an increasing liberalism on issues such as the death penalty, legalization of marijuana, and gay marriage.

Notable in Figure 5.1 is a move away from the political middle ground, consistent with the recent trend toward political polarization. The move, however, does not seem to coincide with any long-term increase in political interest among college freshmen. In 1966, 58 percent of freshmen said that "keeping up to date with political affairs" is very important; it fell to an all-time low of 26 percent in 1998, then dramatically jumped to 51 percent in 2002—a likely consequence of the 9/11 terrorist attack—but falling back to just 35 percent in 2012.

Acknowledging that students start their college experience somewhat more liberal than the adult population, the next question is how the four years (or so) of the college experience shapes their attitudes. As we discuss at greater length in Chapter 6, education is strongly correlated with political tolerance and support for democratic values. As the population has become better educated, its expression of support for these values has also increased. In addition, college generally has a liberalizing effect on noneconomic political opinions. Evidence in support of this view can be traced back to the 1920s. College seniors are consistently found to be less conservative than entering freshmen (Gross 2013).[9]

Drawing on data from surveys from UCLA's CIRP, Table 5.3 nicely illustrates the likely liberalizing effect of the college experience with some recent data. The

TABLE 5.3	College Student Political Attitudes as Freshmen in 2004 and Seniors in 2008		
	At College Entry 2004	At End of College 2008	Change
Liberal or far left	30	39	+9
Middle of the road	42	39	−3
Conservative or far right	29	23	−6
Legalize marijuana	30	44	+14
Support same-sex marriage	57	69	+12
Abortion should be legal	49	61	+12
Abolish death penalty	40	46	+6

Source: Based on Amy Liu, Sylvia Ruiz, Linda DeAngelo, and John Pryor. 2009. "Findings from the 2008 Administration of the College Senior Survey (CSS); National Aggregates." Report from the Higher Education Research Institute, UCLA, Table 42.

table compares attitudes of college freshmen in 2004 with the comparable attitudes of college seniors in 2008 when they would be graduating from college. In terms of ideological preference and on specific issues, this 2004 cohort of college freshmen (the class of 2008) becomes more liberal over time. The obvious inference is that something about the college experience caused attitude change. The interesting question is, what were the factors that may have been responsible?[10]

Three explanations are commonly advanced for these gains in liberalism: increased awareness, enlightenment, and indoctrination. None of these standing alone is entirely convincing. The awareness explanation is predicated on the fact that two of the stronger correlates of education are political knowledge and use of the media. Being informed about innovations and current events is directly related to education. For example, in a study of support for the civil rights of women, one investigator found a large increase in support for women's rights occurring among the educated shortly after the media began devoting considerable attention to the issue. Early in the 1990s this same pattern appeared for "black" as opposed to "African-American" in terms of the preferred identifier for members of this racial group. Among blacks in the mass public, the college educated were the most likely to prefer "African-American" (Sigelman, Tuch, and Martin 2005).

A second argument asserts that education leads to "enlightenment," which in turn leads to liberalism. According to Lottes and Kuriloff (1994, 33) "during college, attitudes and values tend to become more open, humanitarian, altruistic, tolerant and liberal." However, as we demonstrate in Chapter 7, education is not always a correlate of liberalism. On economic issues, the better educated tend to be more conservative. But as education increases, so does one's ability to think analytically and critically. The consequence is likely to be the rejection of stereotypes and prejudice, an increased tolerance of diverse lifestyles, and an increased liberalism across a variety of social issues.

TABLE 5.4   Political Orientations of College Faculty and College Seniors

Year	Liberal (%)	Middle of Road (%)	Conservative (%)	
Faculty				
1984	42	27	31	100%
1999	45	37	18	100%
2004	48	31	21	100%
Students				
1984	35	39	26	100%
1999	36	31	33	100%
2012	37	39	24	100%

Source: For 1984 students and faculty, Ernest Boyer and Mary Jean Whitelaw, The Condition of the Professoriate: Attitudes and Trends, 1989 (New York: Harper, 1989); for 1999 faculty, Denise E. Magner, "Faculty Attitudes and Characteristics: Results of a 1998–1999 Survey," Chronicle of Higher Education (Sept. 3, 1999), pp. A20–A21; the 1999 college seniors data are courtesy of Dr. Jerry Jacobs, Department of Sociology, University of Pennsylvania, 2004 Faculty data Lindholm, Szelenyi, Hurtado and Korn (2005); 2012 students data: UCLA HERI Institute.

A third explanation holds that the "liberal" college faculty indoctrinates students in the direction of their own political views. As Table 5.4 shows, college faculty members are more liberal than college seniors. But whether there is cause and effect is an open question. Woessner and Kelly-Woessner (2009a)found that even in political science courses, students had at best only a hazy idea of the ideological orientation of their professors. Note also in Table 5.4 that while between 1984 and 1999, the percentage of conservative faculty dropped from 31 to 18 percent, conservative students over the same period increased from 26 to 33 percent. Zipp and Fenwick (2006), analyzing the faculty data from 1989 through 1997, found centrists increasing at the expense of ideological extremes, with the social sciences faculty showing a modest drift in the conservative direction. It is also important to understand that there is a significant ideological variation across academic disciplines. For the social sciences, the professoriate in 1997 were 67 percent liberal, 15 percent center, and 18 percent conservative. For the business schools, 32 percent were liberal, 20 percent were center, and 48 percent were conservative (Zipp and Fenwick 2006, 310). While the data for all faculty show liberals outnumber conservatives, the data show no ideological hegemony dominating the academy, and little evidence of faculty politically "indoctrinating" their students (Woessner and Kelly-Woessner 2009a).

However, the data still beg the question as to why college faculty are decidedly more liberal than those in other professions requiring advanced degrees. In the most thorough investigation to date, Neil Gross (2013), based on the analysis of an extensive database, offers an explanation—self-selection. The professoriate have long had a reputation for being liberal,[11] much like bankers have long been thought of as being conservative. According to Gross (2013), an atypical number of smart young liberals tend to be attracted to the professorate just as an atypical number of smart young conservatives tend to be attracted to investment banking. One reason is a desire to be in a profession with like-minded colleagues. The UCLA CIRP survey shows supporting data for this thesis exist as early as the first year of college. Among freshmen who aspired to be college professors, 53 percent described themselves as liberal, while just 17 percent described themselves as conservatives. Other research shows that among those enrolled in graduate school seeking a Ph.D., 49 percent identified as liberals and just 18 percent as conservative (Woessner and Kelly-Woessner 2009b). The bottom line is that college faculty trend liberal, but students are mostly influenced while in college by their peers (Pascarella and Terenzini 2005).

College Students Compared to Noncollege Youth

Most observers would agree that college has an impact on student political views. Not only do college students become more liberal with increased years of college exposure (as noted earlier), but also there are substantial differences between young people in college and young people who do not attend college.[12] However, not all these differences can be attributed to the college experience. We know from panel studies (where respondents are reinterviewed over time) that many of the differences between those who go to college and those who do not already existed when the two groups were still in high school. The Youth-Parent Socialization Panel show that for some opinion differences, particularly those on civic tolerance, the large differences between college seniors and their counterparts who did not attend college were already apparent in high school (Highton 2009). The college-bound were already more liberal than their noncollege age cohorts. In this instance, a self-selection factor was evident in addition to the effect of going to college. The effect of college was clearly evident in the Youth-Parent Socialization Panel data on questions of prayer in the public schools and support for racial integration. After high school, in 1965, there were no differences between the college-bound and the noncollege bound. However, by 1973 there were substantial differences between those with a college degree and those who had not been to college, leading to an inference that college had caused opinion change in a liberal direction (Jennings and Niemi 1982, 257–60).

5-4 Personal Predispositions and Political Attitudes

So far, this chapter has discussed the various environmental factors from the formative years that shape political attitudes. But people are more than the sum of their environmental influences. They also contribute their personal dispositions to the mix. Ignoring politics for the moment, everybody knows that people vary considerably in terms of their unique personalities. These psychological differences are only partially traceable to socialization. They may also be determined by one's genetic makeup, much like weight and height.[13] Psychologists believe that people form unique personalities at an early age, which are mostly stable throughout the life cycle.

Substantial research suggests that to some extent many of our political beliefs can be traced to our personalities and perhaps back to the genes with which we were born.

Personality and Political Attitudes

Social psychologists generally define *personality* as a set of mental traits or dispositions that govern cognitions and behavior. But how might they affect political opinions? Current thinking is that political predispositions are a function of environmental factors as they interact with personality traits (Gerber et al. 2010; McCrae and Costa 2012). As people become aware of political issues, they form political opinions or, more broadly, political ideologies. The process of forming political predispositions is significantly influenced by personality traits originating early in life.

Today, most social psychologists see five major traits as defining individual differences in personality—these are sometimes called the big five. The measurement of the big five has the virtue of being free from political content, a problem that has rendered many other personality measures (e.g., authoritarianism) often unsuitable for the study of political orientations. The big five are shown here.

1. *Openness:* open to new experiences versus conforming and preferring routine
2. *Conscientious:* organized, disciplined versus careless and impulsive
3. *Extraversion:* sociable and affectionate versus somber and reserved
4. *Agreeableness:* trusting and helpful versus suspicious and uncooperative
5. *Emotional stability:* calm and secure versus anxious and self-pitying

These personality types are easily recognizable. For each trait we might hypothesize some pattern where people at the polar ends of the trait might differ politically. Traits 3, 4, and 5 have occasionally been linked to political opinions (notably extroversion), but it is the first two traits—openness and conscientiousness—that are time-tested, consistent predictors of political opinions in exactly the way we would expect.

Openness to new experiences means a willingness to seriously entertain new, sometimes unconventional, ideas—like gay marriage. According to psychologist John Jost (2009), those whose personalities that embrace change become liberals; those nervous about change become conservatives. We would predict, therefore, that those with a dominant openness personality trait would tend to be liberal. On the other hand, conscientiousness implies a personality that is organized, hard working, and inclined to follow prevailing social norms. If this trait is dominant, we would expect individuals to be conservative. Numerous studies have documented exactly these patterns (Barbaranelli, Capara, and Vecchione 2007; Schoen and Schumann 2007; Mondak 2010; Gerber et al. 2010; Gerber et al. 2012).

Other studies have measured personality observationally and come to the same conclusion. For instance, consistent with theory and common intuition, students who keep messy dorm rooms or workers who maintain messy offices tend to be liberals, while those who display their tidiness tend to be conservatives politically (see Carney et al. 2009 for a review of recent evidence).

Of course, the most important political predisposition is party identification. The data show a mixed picture, but at best personality is a weak or perhaps non-existent determinant of the direction of partisanship. Once we account for ideology, personality is usually not a factor (Mondak 2010; Gerber, Huber, et al. 2010; Gerber et al. 2012). On the other hand, Gerber et al. (2012) have shown that the personality traits of extraversion, agreeableness, and openness are determinants of whether people affiliate with *any* party and the strength of that affiliation. Personality simply may not determine the direction of that affiliation, but it does determine if people affiliate at all and, if so, how strongly.

One of the most provocative big five studies involved an Internet survey of thousands of volunteers who took the personality inventory test as part of their interview. Respondents came from across the United States, including every state of the union. The researchers found that state-level personality helps to predict manifestations of liberalism–conservatism, such as the state's presidential voting (Rentfrow et al. 2009). The study showed that the divide between red states and blue states (in terms of recent presidential voting) is due in part to a geographical divide in terms of personality. Residents of red (Republican) states tend to be conforming and favoring order to their lives, while residents of blue (Democratic) states tend to be open to new ideas and impulsive. This result may be surprising because we might think that when comparing large groups like U.S. states, individual differences in personality would cancel out, particularly when considering the indirect impact on politics. But this is not the case. States may recruit residents based on who might be attracted to the type of people who already live there. Or, it could be variation in state culture. Or, it could be genetic differences among the populations who comprise the various states. The possibilities are intriguing.

Genetic and Political Attitudes

At its most basic, people share the genetic makeup of their biological parents. The study of genetics has been prominent in the behavioral sciences, and for decades scholars have been trying to figure out how genetic and social influences contribute to a variety of personal characteristics such as simple happiness (Plomin 1997).

One way to answer questions about genetic versus social influence is through the study of identical (monozygotic or MZ) twins and fraternal (dizygotic or DZ) twins. MZ twins share identical genes, while DZ twins share 50 percent of their genes. DZ twins are no more genetically alike than any siblings. The hypothesis is that MZ twins should be more similar than DZ twins to the extent genetics determines behavior.

Several political scientists have recently advanced the notion that the parents not only influence political opinions through social interaction with their children but add a genetic component as well. It is not that specific opinions are genetically based, but that genes determine deep-seated personality traits, which in turn influence political opinions. Genes may prime people to respond openly or cautiously to contemporary political issues. Thus, someone genetically programmed with an open disposition would be more likely to favor same-sex marriage than someone programmed with a cautious disposition.

The effect of genetic inheritance can be estimated by analyzing the difference in the rate that identical twins agree on political issues compared to the rate of fraternal twins. The idea is that the two types of twins share environmental factors so that the surplus political similarity within pairs of identical twins is genetically determined. Indeed, by comparing identical and nonidentical twins in terms of their political attitudes, researchers have found differences of the sort that on statistical grounds must be of genetic rather than environmental origin (Alford, Funk, and Hibbing 2005; Smith et al. 2013).

One attitude that appears fairly resistant to genetic influence is party identification (Alford, Funk, and Hibbing 2005; Hatemi et al. 2009). Socialization exerts a particularly strong effect on the formation of partisanship and apparently overwhelms genetic factors. At the same time, genes may influence more than simply political opinions. The degree to which people participate in politics appears to be influenced by their genetic makeup. Fowler, Baker, and Dawes (2008) show this effect from their careful analysis of voting participation records of identical and nonidentical twins. Pairs of identical twins were more alike in their frequency of voting than were pairs of nonidentical twins, and by an amount that suggested that genetic makeup was a contributing factor.

Still, not everyone is convinced (Beckwith and Morris 2008; Charney 2008; Shultziner 2013). For the data to be compelling, one must accept the assumption of equal environments; that is, the assumption that MZ and DZ twins share their twin's environment to the same extent, and not only in childhood but also in adulthood when political attitudes or behavior is measured. Differential environmental factors could account for the greater similarity we see in the political opinions and behavior of identical twins versus fraternal twins rather than genetics.[14] The question of how much genes matter for political beliefs and behavior remains a matter of study and lively controversy.[15]

Discussion

Clearly, when it comes to politics, people are more than blank slates to be shaped by their environment. Even within the family, not all brothers and sisters are alike in politics just like they differ from each other in so many ways. Nor will any two adults in similar life environments (or even sharing a marriage) necessarily think alike politically. These differences are part of our unique political dispositions, which sometimes are traceable to our different personalities, which were largely in place by early childhood. They might also be traceable to factors in place at the time of our birth.

To speak of genetic variation accounting for political behavior does not of course mean that there are specific genes for specific political thoughts or acts. One plausible theory is that certain aspects of our genetic variation affect broad personality characteristics, which have ramifications for political orientations.[16] Perhaps genes affect ideological dispositions by affecting how people rate on the personality traits of openness and conscientiousness, as we discussed earlier. It is also possible that genetic and personality influences, while quite real, amount to only a trace compared to the full range of influences on political attitudes.

5-5 Socialization During Adulthood

Preadult (and college-age) socialization is important because it influences the values and beliefs people hold at the outset of their adult political experience.

But this takes the story only to the threshold of adulthood. What about subsequent socialization? In the nonpolitical realm, habits formed in youth are the reason that commercial advertisers will pay higher rates for media programs that attract younger viewers. They believe ads can convert the product preferences of a younger audience, but are less effective with an older audience. The political predispositions acquired by one's mid-to-late twenties persist to what might seem a surprising extent throughout adulthood. This fact only accentuates the importance of the early socialization experience.

Early adulthood is also an important time of political awakening, as the political environment exerts a particularly strong pull during the first years of adult life. The implication is that generations (or birth cohorts) differ politically based on the collective experiences around the onset of their adulthood in what are called *generation effects*. Another aspect of adult socialization is that people *do* change politically as they grow older. When these changes are age-dependent, we call them *life-cycle effects*. An example is when people gradually get more politically conservative as they age (see Table 5.5). Finally, like children, mature adults change in response to commonly shared experiences, such as the turbulent 1960s, the end of the Cold War, and the tragedy of 9/11. These time-dependent changes are called *period effects*. By definition, period effects exert a common influence on people at all ages in the life cycle. They are responsible for the bulk of the short-term movement in opinion discussed in Chapter 4.

A life-cycle effect exists when people's political views are influenced by maturation. As a reference point, assume each new political generation enters political life with identical political attitudes. Then, any difference across generations would be due to aging. When we find, as we often do, that the young are more liberal than their elders, these age differences are explained by life-cycle effects. The implication is that the young, having few responsibilities, can afford to be idealistic. As they age, however, they take on the responsibility of raising a family, paying a mortgage, and holding down a full-time job. The effect is nicely captured in an old satirical comment about European partisan politics: "Those at 18 who are not socialist have no heart; those at 40 who are still socialist have no head." In addition, it is often noted that learning continues throughout life, but reevaluation seems more frequent early in life than later (Sapiro 2004). Certain predispositions are reinforced over time, as people are more likely to expose themselves selectively to political stimuli with which they agree than to those with which they disagree (Stroud 2011). The life-cycle concept assumes a process that is similar for all age groups over time. It has been asserted, for example, that as people get older, political parties of the right become more attractive. This assertion (which we investigate later) posits an independent effect of aging on partisan predispositions.

A generational effect exists when a specific age cohort is uniquely socialized by a set of historical events. The logic of generational analysis dictates an interaction between age and experience. The usual assumption is that certain events in history make an indelible imprint on the young (defined approximately as the cohort of people aged seventeen to twenty-six). It is argued that a generation's singular personality is shaped when its members leave the family and step out into the world on their own. Those who are younger remain shielded, to a certain extent, from the trauma of external events by the family. Those who are older are better equipped to resist its influence by their previous life experiences. For a distinct political generation to exist, something of historical consequence must have happened during their "impressionable years" (about the ages seventeen to twenty-six). It is difficult to imagine anything occurring in the 1950s that would have distinctively stamped a generational cohort. On the other hand, one can easily conceive of the Vietnam War era (1965–1972) or the Great Depression of the 1930s as defining unique generations.

Period effects complicate matters further. Strong political shocks can affect young and old alike; for example, when the Cold War ended, all age groups relaxed their interest in further defense spending. After 9/11, trust in government increased across all age groups. When changes occur among all age cohorts simultaneously and in same direction, they are "period effects." They are change due to a common shared experience affecting everyone in the same way, regardless of age.[17]

The Life Cycle, Generations, and Party Identification

Much research on generational politics has focused on change in party identification. Generational effects are most important in the direction of party identification (Republican, Independent, or Democrat), but variation in the strength of partisanship (strong partisan, weak partisan, or Independent) responds most to movement through the life cycle.

Any survey will show that young adults have weaker partisan attachments than their elders due to life-cycle effects. For example, the 2012 ANES data show 42 percent of those over age fifty-five claiming to be "strong" partisans, compared to only 23 percent under thirty. Similarly, only 32 percent of those over fifty-five are Independents, compared to 47 percent of those under thirty. With figures such as these, one might forecast a general decline in partisanship as older cohorts with firm partisanship exit the electorate and are replaced by younger cohorts with weaker partisan attachments. But this does not happen—at least under equilibrium conditions—because each new generation acquires stronger partisan attachments as it ages. Under equilibrium conditions, the electorate's net partisan strength is stable, with each age cohort showing the same strength of partisanship as previous cohorts at the same point in the life cycle.

Maturation brings about a hardening of partisan commitment. Young adults start out disproportionately Independent in partisan choice, unsure of both parties. With age, they harden their choices. When they become senior citizens, the proportion calling themselves Independent is reduced by half. By the time it is necessary to enter a nursing home, most Americans have figured out whether they are Democrats or Republicans.[18]

Alternatively, the direction of partisanship is often imprinted on a political generation by historical events. We can see examples in Figure 5.2, which displays the relationship between age and the direction of party identification for an accumulation of Gallup polls. We use data from 1990 and 1998 so we can see the sliver of

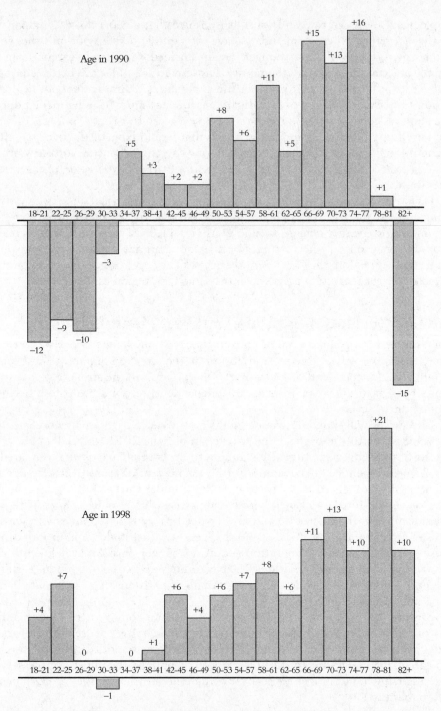

FIGURE 5.2 Party identification by age in 1990 and 1998 (percentage Democratic minus percentage Republican).

Source: Based on "America's Views and Mood 1998," Public Perspective (Dec./Jan. 1999), p. 65.

those who were in their impressible years during the Roaring Twenties, as well as a much larger group who were in their impressible years during the Great Depression. Comparing age groups at these points in history reveals clear generation effects.[19]

Let us look first at the data collected in 1990. We see that those citizens who were in their impressionable years during the 1930s depression (those between sixty-six and seventy-seven) were the most Democratic age cohort in the electorate. But note also the partisanship of those in their impressionable years during the boom times of the 1920s, when Republicans were ascendant. These citizens, in their eighties in 1990, were the most Republican age cohort. The difference in partisanship between those seventy-four to seventy-seven in 1990 and those eighty-two and over illustrates the profound effect of being socialized in the Roaring Twenties versus the Great Depression of the 1930s. The gap in partisan preference between these groups, who differ only modestly in chronological age, is quite startling, especially considering that the differentiation in the two groups' experiences had occurred decades earlier.[20]

At the other end of the age spectrum, the youngest cohorts in 1990 were more Republican than their elders (save those over eighty), having been socialized under the beleaguered President Carter and the optimistic years of the early Reagan administration. Moving forward to 1998, the youthful Republicans in 1990 were now between twenty-six and thirty-seven years old. They were still the most Republican cohort in the electorate as of 1998, but the fact that they experienced the good times of the 1990s during the Clinton presidency while still in their impressionable years undercut their earlier, more Republican leanings. The most Republican cohort in 1990—those eighty-two years old and over and socialized under Presidents Harding, Coolidge, and Hoover—had now exited the electorate. The Great Depression generation has also now largely exited the electorate, and the age differences within today's electorate on the direction of partisanship are leveling off.

The responses of new generations of young voters are particularly relevant to the understanding of partisan realignments. As discussed in earlier chapters, the United States has periodically undergone a partisan realignment. During realignments, the pace of partisan change quickens, with unusual numbers of voters changing their partisanship in response to new issues and events. The classic realignment occurred during the 1930s in response to the depression and New Deal, and it featured dramatic gains for the Democratic Party. Since the 1960s, pundits have occasionally forecast a massive new partisan realignment around the corner. If one arrives, what will it look like?

There is reason to believe that the vanguard of any new realignment will be young voters. Young voters lack strong partisan attachments, so they are particularly susceptible to political trends. For example, in 2008 with Bush's exit and Obama's election, the political winds favored the Democrats. Based on a merged set of Pew Research Center polls from 2008 polls, totaling 17,543 respondents, the largest partisan difference by age group was for those between eighteen and twenty-nine, where the Democrats had a 14 percentage point advantage over Republicans.

The idea that young voters lead realignments is labeled the *mobilization theory* of realignment because it involves the mobilization of new voters. However, period effects also contribute to realignments, with both new voters and old voters showing equal rates of partisan conversion. If events are strong enough to cause a realignment, they may be strong enough to convert both old and young from one party to another. This view is known as the *conversion theory*.

Will young voters lead the next realignment? Predictions based on the 1930s realignment are difficult because that realignment happened just as public opinion polling began. We saw, however, that the depression cohort, which began voting in the 1930s, even in the late 1990s led other age groups in allegiance to the Democratic Party. But young voters in the 1930s were not numerous enough to account for a massive realignment by themselves. Examining early Gallup polls and *Literary Digest* polls (see Chapter 2), Erikson and Tedin (1981) found evidence of considerable voter conversion during the realignment era. Realignments, it seems, are events of such force that even older generations of voters find the pressures difficult to resist.

Today it is recognized that partisan change occurs constantly, even without realignment-level shocks. The electorate's net party identification (or macropartisanship) constantly undergoes small changes, largely in response to whether the political and economic news favors the presidential party (Erikson, MacKuen, and Stimson 1998, 2002). In the short run, almost all the changes are due to period effects, as all age groups (generations) shift their partisanship more or less in tandem.

Generations and Political Polarization

As discussed in previous chapters, there has been much commentary that like political elites the electorate also is becoming polarized. First, it is important to spell out what polarization does and does not mean. It *does not* mean that citizens are taking wholesale more ideologically extreme positions on political issues. What it *does mean* is that Americans holding liberal positions are increasingly identifying themselves with the Democrat Party, and those holding conservative positions are increasingly identifying themselves with the Republican Party (Abramowitz 2010). For instance, in 1972 the correlation between party identification and liberal conservative ideology was just .32; by 2012 the correlation had risen to .61 (ANES).

An analysis by Stoker and Jennings (2008) shows one key driving force behind the increased mass polarization is generational replacement. New entrants into the electorate evidence a greater level of polarization than those exiting the electorate. This pattern is consistent with the impressionable years thesis, where the recent increase in elite polarization affects the opinions of seventeen- to twenty-six-year-olds but does not much affect the older generations, whose opinions have now hardened. To the extent elite polarization continues, new generations will be socialized to a more polarized party system. As the electorate changes and the younger more polarized generations replace the older less polarized generations, party polarization of the electorate will increase until it reaches some new equilibrium point.

Generations, the Life Cycle, and Policy Issues

Understanding of generation and life-cycle effects is far less advanced when we turn from partisanship to policy issues. For one thing, policy issues are many, with a likelihood that each tells a different story. In Chapter 4 we saw a variety of trends (often stationary) in opinion on many issues. The presumption is that these trends are mainly due to period effects, as all birth cohorts move in tandem to the ethos of the times. In rare cases there may be generational effects, as each new batch of adult citizens brings a new perspective to old problems like taxing and spending or the death penalty. We might expect to find life-cycle effects, with people starting out liberal but becoming more conservative as they age. But in some instances, such as the rise of white acceptance of racial integration in the 1960s and 1970s, change is so fast that the liberalism of the times must offset any conservative life-cycle effect, making specific birth cohorts become more liberal with age.

The supposedly liberalizing (or radicalizing) effect of the 1960s on the generation that came of age in that decade has been the focus of much analysis. Delli Carpini (1986) and Davis (2005) have made intensive studies of the 1960s generation and isolated a number of instances in which this generation differed from surrounding age cohorts. What we would expect among this generation, of course, is a leftist bent to their political ideology. For the most part, these authors found that the generation of the 1960s was more supportive than other cohorts of government involvement in the issues of race, civil liberties, economics, and social concerns. As the generation aged, however, its distinctiveness began to erode. Society exerts a pull toward the political center as one moves through the life cycle (Delli Carpini 1986, 120–38).

The Case of the Vietnam War and Political Attitudes   If lasting effects of the 1960s generation are to be located, they would most likely be found among the subcohort of antiwar activists. The Youth-Parent Socialization Panel provides an ideal vehicle for this analysis. From the group that started out in 1965 as high school seniors, Jennings (1987) compared in 1973 those college graduates who protested the Vietnam War with a matching sample of those college graduates who were not protesters. An advantage of the panel approach is that one can look back at the sample in high school and see if the later differences go beyond what could be explained by self-selection.

On partisanship, protestors and their counterparts started out alike. In 1965, protesters-to-be were 39 percent Democratic; nonprotesters were 38 percent Democratic. By 1973, the two groups had shifted in opposite directions, with the protesters 48 percent Democratic and the nonprotesters 27 percent. By 1982, these percentages had changed little.

On policy issues there appeared to be substantial effects. In 1965, while in high school, the (future) protesters were 8 percent less favorable to prayer in the public schools than the nonprotesters, but seventeen years later they were 30 percent less favorable than the nonprotesters. The protesters were 13 percent more supportive of a federal role in school integration in 1965, but 43 percent more supportive in 1982. However, with the passage of time the once liberal protesters began to move in a conservative direction. While 83 percent of the protesters considered themselves liberals in 1973, only 63 percent did so in 1982. Declines of at least 20 percent also occurred on questions of government responsibility for providing jobs, legalization of marijuana, rights of accused, helping minorities, and equality for women. The protesters were still considerably more liberal than the nonprotesters in 1982, but they had lost at least some of their distinctiveness.

By 1982, the protesters' attitudes had been shaped by both generational and life-cycle effects. Their experience as antiwar protesters stamped them with an indelible liberal print, while life-cycle effects pushed them back in a conservative direction. Furthermore, their liberalism had been eroded by a period effect—exposure to the conservative ethos of the 1980s. In an interesting follow-up, Jennings (2002) showed that the offspring of the protestors were also a good deal more liberal than were the offspring of the nonprotestors. The experience as war protestors shaped not only the protestors' politics years later but also those of their children.

In a different analysis of the Youth-Parent Socialization Panel, Erikson and Stoker (2011) examined the effect of the first Vietnam draft lottery on political attitudes of male respondents who went off to college and upon graduation became eligible for the draft. In 1969, for the first time, a lottery was held to determine who would be drafted and possibly sent off to war. Recent college graduates either got a low (unsafe) or a high (safe) lottery number. Those with low numbers, facing the possibility of being sent to serve in war, became more opposed to the war, a stance that persisted through the last wave of the panel in 1997. Another effect was that the risk of a draft notice precipitated a rethinking of party identification. Unlike others in the Youth Panel, male collegians who drew a high draft number generally abandoned their earlier (1965) partisan preference when interviewed in 1973. In later interviews (1982, 1997), these once at-risk men maintained their attitudes from 1973 rather than reverting to their beliefs in 1965 when they were seniors in high school. Remarkably, these attitude changes (first observed in the 1973 panel wave) persisted long after the initial anxiety over the 1969 draft had been resolved, and regardless of whether the person actually underwent military service or not.

These examples from long ago show how it is possible for major events to shape one's political attitudes and partisanship. When life-altering events occur, it is not only that they can change partisan behavior in the short run. The change can be permanent.

Ideology and the Life Cycle   Thanks to extensive collection of data on the ideological preferences of Americans, ideological identification (as a liberal, moderate, or conservative) is the one issue-related variable for which we have strong evidence to document the nature of change and stability over time. Opposite the pattern for party identification, with its clear generational effects but no certain life-cycle effects, ideological identification shows clear life-cycle effects and no generational effects. As one might expect, each new generation starts out more liberal than average but then drifts toward the conservative with age. Moreover, each generation starts out with the same level of liberalism and drifts rightward at about the same rate. A regular pattern of newly entering liberals who then turn conservative works to keep the electorate's net division of ideological identification constant, at least under equilibrium conditions. We saw this in Chapter 4, where unlike party identification, the division of ideological identification has been remarkably stable for over a quarter of a century.[21]

Table 5.5 illustrates the combination of birth cohorts and age cohorts for respondents in cumulated CBS/*New York Times* surveys for four years at eight-year intervals: 1984, 1992, 2000, and 2008. In each year, conservatism increases with age (read down the column). Showing life-cycle effects, each "generation" changes with the time. For instance, the youngest group (age twenty-five and under) in 1984 was only 4 percentage points more conservative than liberal in self-identification.

TABLE 5.5 Ideological Identification (% Conservative Minus % Liberal) by Birth Cohort, 1984, 1992, 2000, and 2008

Birth Year	1984	1992	2000	2008
1983–1990				2 (18–25)
1975–1982			−2 (18–25)	9
1967–1974		0 (18–25)	4	11
1959–1966	4 (18–25)	10	9	11
1951–1958	4	10	9	9
1943–1950	10	12	13	10
1935–1942	17	19	17	16
1927–1934	19	20	20	21
1919–1926	21	22	16	11 (82–89)
1911–1918	19	19	17 (82–89)	
1903–1910	29	25 (82–89)		
1895–1902	22 (82–89)			

Source: Based on CBS News/*New York Times* polls. Birth years are approximated from respondents' reported age.

Eight years later, when they became twenty-six to thirty-three, they were 10 percentage points more conservative than liberal. The cycle of entry by the new and exits among the old kept the balance of liberals and conservatives more or less at a constant level.

5-6 The Persistence of Political Orientations

At the outset of this chapter, we noted that a key assumption justifying the study of political socialization is that orientations formed early persist over time. There is a good deal of evidence that many important political predispositions do endure over a considerable span. There is also a good deal of evidence that people continue to learn and adjust their political perspective in response to their adult environment and the events in their lives. When we speak of long-term persistence, it is helpful to think of persistence as relative to one's peers rather than as an immunity from period effects—the impact of commonly shared events. Consider the mental experiment of imagining a group of young people at the onset of adulthood. Some are Democrats and some are Republicans, some are liberal and some are conservative, with further variation in other attitudes and opinions as well. The mental experiment is to ask whether or not the relative political positions of these young people stay the same throughout their lifetime. For instance, would the young liberals still be the most liberal and the young conservatives still be the most conservative during their old age? Obviously people can change, but the answer to this mental experiment is *yes*. The young conservatives remain the most conservative among their peers in old age (likewise for liberals).

It is important to understand that when we speak of persistence, what mostly persist are core values and predispositions rather than specific opinions on issues of the day. Thus, overarching values such as partisanship, liberal–conservative orientation, and racial attitudes tend to persist, while trust in government or attitudes about defense spending tend to be more fleeting. Regarding persistence, two major points merit elaboration. First, political attitudes are malleable through the impressionable years. Second, after the impressionable years, political orientations harden considerably. Change still occurs, but stability markedly increases.

Once the impressionable years leading up to adulthood end, the stability of core political values increases greatly. There now exist three long-term panel surveys, all of which demonstrate this same point. The longest of these, and the most dramatic example of persistence, is the Bennington study originated by Theodore Newcomb. Young women (sixteen to twenty years old), mostly from conservative homes, matriculated at Bennington College, which at the time (in the 1930s) had an avowedly liberal faculty. Students were first interviewed between 1935 and 1938 and then re-interviewed in 1960 and again in 1984. The data thus stretch over almost fifty years. Using a number of items to create a scale of liberal–conservative political orientations, Alwin, Cohen, and Newcomb (1991) found a high level of persistence over the fifty-year period. The authors concluded that 60 percent of the variance in the 1984 political predispositions could be predicted from the predispositions in the 1930s when the students were attending Bennington, whereas the remaining 40 percent reflected attitude change (Alwin, Cohen, and Newcomb 1991, 265). A second long-term panel survey (spanning thirty-seven years) is the Terman study of gifted children (Terman and Oden 1959). Respondents were interviewed four times, beginning in 1940 and ending in 1977 (when they were about thirty and sixty-seven years old). A reanalysis of these data by Sears and Funk (1999) showed that 65 percent held the same party preference and 54 percent held the same political ideology in 1977 that they had in 1940. (See also Green and Palmquist 1994.) One conclusion is that socialization to core values for many people is largely complete by the late twenties.

Strong evidence for the persistence thesis comes from the Youth-Parent Socialization Panel data. These data clearly support the impressionable years–later persistence hypothesis. Attitudes were subject to considerable change between eighteen and twenty-six years of age but became considerably more stable in the years following (Jennings and Stoker 1999). In Figure 5.3 we used the Socialization Panel data for an even stronger test of persistence. We divided the 1965 high school seniors into Democrats and Republicans. We then looked at their reported vote choice for president between 1968 and 1996 based on their 1965 partisanship. The figure shows the 1965 Democrats consistently voted for Democratic presidential candidates and 1965 Republicans consistently voted for Republican presidential candidates over the following eight presidential elections for which we have data.[22] The foundation upon which the study of political socialization is based—what is learned young has a lifetime effect—is solidly supported by the evidence.

A Note on Marriage

Of course when people change their adult environment, change in political views sometimes follows. When one loses a job or gets a new one, moves to a new

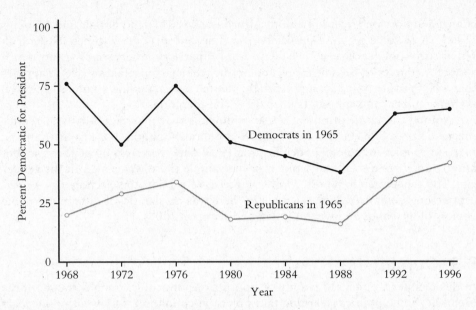

FIGURE 5.3 Vote for president as adults, by party identification as high school youth in 1965.

Source: Based on University of Michigan Political Socialization Study Data. Recalls of vote decisions are from 1973, 1982, and 1997 survey waves.

community, or joins a new circle of friends, the new political environment can change his or her political views. It should be no surprise that the biggest life change for most is marriage.

When people visit Internet dating sites, they are likely to choose dating partners with similar beliefs, including political opinions (Huber and Malhortra 2012). The same is true when choosing marital partners; those who choose each other tend to share political opinions. This relationship between spousal partners is at least as strong as we find among parents and their children for partisanship, and stronger when it comes to many specific issues. In fact, the similarity of martial partners on politics exceeds or equals that found on any other social or biological dimension (Stoker and Jennings 2005; Alford et al. 2011).

The obvious question is, "what is the cause?" Marital political correspondence could be a product of (1) assortive mating, that is self-selection as we saw in the dating example earlier; (2) stratified mating, that is choosing mates from the same social strata, or (3) persuasion. Over the course, the married spousal couples could progressively become more and more alike politically, even if they do not begin the marriage with many overlapping political values.

The data point strongly toward the self-selection explanation, with a modest amount of movement toward similarity over the course of the marriage. Using a sample of almost 4,000 married couples, Alford et al. broke length of the marriage down using a scale starting at one year or less and ending at 46 years or more. On a twenty-eight-item battery of political opinions, the husband–wife correlations changed almost imperceptibly. Both Alford et al. (2011) and Stoker and Jennings (2005) show some growing similarity over time, but it is overwhelmed by the high initial correspondence seen in the first year of marriage. There simply is not much room for couples to become more similar after the marriage takes place. It appears that when people are seeking potentially lifetime mates, finding a kindred spirit on matters political and cultural trumps other considerations.

Among the implications of these findings is that marriage serves to reduce the gender gap in partisanship, voting, and political opinion. For instance, among married couples in the 1997 Socialization Panel data there was no gender gap, but among unmarried men and women in the sample there was a significant gender gap. The gender gap in reported votes in the 1996 presidential election was 41 percent among unmarried respondents. But there was no significant difference in vote choices of husbands and wives (Stoker and Jennings 2005).

5-7 Conclusion

In this chapter we focused mainly on sources of political learning throughout the life cycle. Some political learning takes place in childhood, followed by the years seventeen to twenty-six when people are most politically impressionable. While attitudes crystallize in later adulthood, political learning still takes place as individuals respond to their environment and life events. Even partisanship, the most stable of political predispositions, responds in adulthood to issues and political personalities (Fiorina 1981; Erikson and Stoker 2011). But generally speaking, political change in adulthood is incremental. It is the early years that offer the greatest potential for a radical break from the past.

Critical Thinking Questions

1. Successful political socialization means the younger generation comes to accept the political values of the older generation. Could you imagine what would happen if political socialization was not successful?
2. Evidence now indicates that genes play a partial role in determining political opinions. Why might we want to be cautious in linking people's political opinions to their genetic makeup?
3. Polling data show that major events, like the Great Depression of the 1930s, can have a long-lasting effect on public opinion. What sort of events might occur in the future that would leave a similar unique mark on a political generation?

Endnotes

1. The earliest evidence to support this belief came from a number of early studies (pre-1960) in which parents and children were not independently interviewed. Children (normally students) were interviewed and then asked to report the political attitudes of their parents. The parents themselves were not actually interviewed. We now know that this methodology grossly overestimates the amount of parent–child similarity on most political issues. In reporting parent attitudes, children tend to project their own attitudes onto parents, artificially inflating attitude correspondence.

2. Note in Table 5.1 there was 83 percent agreement between parents and high school seniors when parents favored a federal role in school integration, but only 41 percent agreement when parents were opposed. There were clearly some strong pro-integration environmental effects acting on the high school seniors in 1965 as well as the influence of their parents.

3. The former point is made by Harvey (1972, 601); the latter point is made by Silbiger (1977, 174).

4. Moreover, there is strong evidence that adolescents today have become less interested in politics over time than adolescents in the 1970s and 1980s, according to the finding from the "Monitoring the Future" surveys of high school seniors conducted yearly since 1975 by the University of Michigan (see also Wattenberg 2011).

5. Monitoring the Future: A Continuing Study of American Youth; 2012 data downloaded from www.monitoringthefuture.org.

6. The survey was sponsored by the John S. and James L. Knight Foundation and conducted by the Survey Research Center at the University of Connecticut. www.knightfdn.org, downloaded May 10, 2005.

7. The principal difference is between little or no civics education to any degree (Niemi and Junn 1998, 72).

8. It is important to appreciate that the meaning of a college education is quite different in the twenty-first century from the 1930s or earlier. Prior to World War II, someone with a college education was a rarity. Now such education is an everyday part of the social landscape. Thus the impact of a college degree today is quite different than fifty years ago, particularly when it comes to slotting people into social and economic networks. For an extended discussion of this point, see Nie, Juhnn, and Stehlik-Barry (1998, ch. 6).

9. For a summary of the extensive literature on education and liberalism, see Feldman and Newcomb (1969). See also Nie, Junn, and Stehlik-Barry (1998). The most recent comprehensive analysis can be found in Gross (2013).

10. Similarly, the 2006 nationwide *Youth Survey on Politics* shows that among college freshmen 51 percent called themselves "liberal" or "moderate leaning to liberal," rising to 69 percent among college seniors (Fall 2006 Biannual Youth Survey on Politics and Public Service, Institute for Politics, John F. Kennedy School of Government, Harvard University). See also Sidanius et al. (2008).

11. Gross (2013, 105) reports a recent survey that shows when respondents are asked to guess the political ideology of college professors, 52 percent say the "average professor" is liberal on economic issues and 59 percent say the "average professor" is liberal on social issues. Gross argues the perception of the professoriate as being liberal goes back to the early twentieth century.

12. See the 2006 Biannual Youth Survey on Politics and Public Service, Institute for Politics, John F. Kennedy School Government, Harvard University.

13. Psychologists posit that heredity accounts for about .25 to .50 in the formation and development of the big five personality traits (Mondak 2010, 40).

14. One study with original data specifically designed to test the common environment thesis finds little support, and lends confirmatory evidence to the thesis of a genetic influence on political predispositions, albeit that influence may work indirectly through personality (Smith et al. 2013).

15. Some researchers claim that specific genes contribute to specific political behavior, like voting (Fowler, Banker, and Dawes 2008; Fowler and Dawes 2013). Critics contend, however, that such correlations are often spurious (Charney and English, 2012,2013). For instance, people of different ethnic ancestry (e.g., national origin) have different genetic makeup and sometimes differ in rates of political participation. Differences in voter participation rates across nationality groups are not necessarily genetically induced.

16. But the causal flow may not be as imagined. Perhaps political attitudes and personality traits are each propelled independently from genes without one affecting the other. Or could political attitudes drive personality? See Verhulst, Eaves, and Hatemi (2012). And when personality affects attitudes on specific issues, the effect might be direct rather than via the person's ideological leaning as an intermediate linkage. See Mondak (2010).

17. The alert reader of this section will learn, correctly, that the accounting of change in terms of generation, life-cycle, and period effects is fraught with more difficulties and ambiguities than one might think at first glance. When scholars study generation and life-cycle effects, they divide survey respondents by birth date or age. Dividing by birth date yields a set of birth cohorts, or people born during specific spans of years, like 1940–1944. Dividing by age yields "age cohorts," or people of specific age segments, like people fifty-six to sixty years old. Suppose we check the survey responses of a birth cohort over time as it goes through the political life cycle. Any change that is observed could be a manifestation of either a life-cycle effect due to people changing as they grow older or a period effect due to people of all cohorts changing due to common experiences. Suppose we compare the survey responses of different age groups in a survey conducted at one specific period. Any observed variation by age could be a manifestation of life-cycle effects due to respondents at different stages of the cycle or to generation effects whereby respondents of different ages are affected by different experiences.

18. The Socialization Panel study provides a clue to why strength of partisanship increases throughout the life cycle. In the later life of the 1965 high school seniors, an increase in partisanship was found—but mainly among those who voted. Those who did not vote tended to remain Independents. Thus, one aspect of age that may lead to the acquisition of partisanship is simple learning based on experience (Jennings and Markus 1984).

19. The 1990 data are a compilation of Gallup polls from 1989 to 1991 that contain 12,600 cases. The 1998 data are based on a single year. The exact number of cases was not reported in the original source.

20. A slightly different interpretation of differences between generations is in terms of the unique events occurring as different generations came of age; they emphasize the extra experience of the older generation. For instance, the more experienced predepression generation differed from the postdepression generation mainly due to their added years of exposure to the "good" Republican years of the 1920s, before the depression. Both groups moved Democratic during the depression, but the older group's starting point was more Republican (Erikson, MacKuen, and Stimson, 2002, ch. 5).

21. The current steady state of ideological identification was preceded by a surge in conservative identification in the late 1960s and 1970s, contrary to the atmosphere of societal change at the time (see Chapter 4). The possible role of different generations in this shift has not been systematically explored.

22. It is important to distinguish between absolute and relative continuity. By *absolute continuity* we mean those who were strong liberals at Time 1 remain strong liberals at Time 2. By *relative continuity* we mean those who were most liberal at Time 1 are the most liberal at Time 2, but they may not have maintained their exact position on the scale. Correlation coefficients measure relative continuity, so what we are referring to in this section is the tendency, over time, for the most liberal respondents at Time 1 to be the most liberal at Time 2, not that they maintain the exact position on issues between time points. It would be unreasonable, for example, to think that in the Bennington study respondents would maintain the same issue position over a fifty-year period.

CHAPTER 6

Public Opinion and Democratic Stability

LEARNING OBJECTIVES

- Explain democratic values in the context of public opinion
- Explain the theories of democratic elitism and pluralistic intolerance
- Describe how differing levels of political trust affect specific political opinions
- Explain the authoritarian personality and its importance for political opinions

In a democracy, public opinion is important because it can influence the decisions political leaders make. Certain aspects of public opinion take on special importance because they can influence the functioning of democratic government. In this chapter we analyze those attitudes and predispositions generally thought necessary to maintain a democracy and examine the degrees to which Americans appear to hold these attitudes.

Ideas about what is vital for the functioning of a democratic government can be divided into four groups. First, there should be widespread tolerance of opposing points of view and support for the rules of democracy. An apt analogy here is the rules of the road for driving an automobile. If most people did not accept the rule that one must stop when the light is red, chaos would ensue. The rules of democracy involve guarantees that the civil liberties of all shall be protected—that majorities rule, but minorities have rights.

Second, democracy's stability may rest on a social consensus regarding values and goals. Disagreements must not be so fundamental that neither resolution nor compromise can be gained by institutionalized procedures. Too great a division may overtax even the best procedures for resolving conflict. Contemporary examples include the Hutu–Tutsi division in Rwanda, the Serb–Croat–Muslim division in Bosnia, and the division among the Shun, Kachin, and Karen peoples of Myanmar (formerly Burma), each of whom want an independent state. Strong cultural divisions are particularly vexing for the design of new democracies, as in Iraq, with its divisions between Shiites, Sunnis, and Kurds.

Third, it is important that people find reasons to trust their fellow citizens, trust government, and believe that democratic participation is meaningful. For people to accept government decisions, they must believe their political actions can be effective.

155

They should feel that they can trust the government to respond to their interests. Should they be on the losing side in an electoral contest, they should believe that while government officials will change, there will be no retribution against ordinary citizens. Widespread and intense distrust (political alienation) could threaten the stability of a democratic system.

Fourth, democracy is often thought to work best when people have certain kinds of what might be called *political personalities*. For instance, people should be open-minded rather than seek comfort for their problems by blaming others. They should accept the complexity of democratic decision making rather than seek solutions from a strong leader to override democratic discussion. When antidemocratic personalities are common, so the theory goes, minority rights become fragile and the stability of democracy is threatened.

6-1 Support for Democratic Values

One of the great threats to any political system, democracies included, is the desire on the part of those who hold political power to maintain it and to work their will free from constraints imposed by others. Ambition in political leaders is not, in and of itself, an undesirable trait. But history is strewn with examples of people in government warding off competition by the expeditious route of eliminating it. Consequently, democracies must anticipate that leaders may not suffer criticism gladly and may not want to share or give up political power if there is a way to avoid it. One solution to this problem, developed by the framers of the U.S. Constitution, was to build in a series of mechanisms designed to protect the rights of people outside government who aspire to political influence from those on the inside who hold political power. But constitutions can only go so far in making good on these protections. As Judge Learned Hand (1959, 144) once observed, "Liberty lies in the hearts and minds of men and women; when it dies there, no constitution, no laws, no court can save it." Some commitment to democratic values on the part of both political leaders and the public is essential.

In using the term *democratic values*, we are referring to procedural norms. These norms do not refer to the substance of legitimate political conflict, such as the desirable trade-off between inflation and unemployment or the merits of government-paid health coverage versus private health insurance, but to the rules of the game in which that conflict takes place. One important set of procedural norms is found in the Bill of Rights. Here Americans are guaranteed the right to freedom of expression, freedom from unreasonable search and seizure, protection from self-incrimination, a speedy and public trial, free exercise of religion, and so on. Two related democratic values of great importance are majority rule and minority rights. At regular intervals, the population is mobilized into opposing camps. Each camp proclaims its own virtue and criticizes the opposition. An election is then held, and the winners take control of the government. The losers remain free to rouse popular hostility toward the new leaders in the hope of embarrassing them and ultimately replacing them in office. This procedure is normally the way decision makers are chosen in the United States. One therefore hopes to find an understanding among the electorate that these are the methods that should be employed to select public officials.

TABLE 6.1 Support for Democratic Values Stated in the Abstract			
Statement	**Democratic Response (%)**	**Uncertain Response (%)**	**Undemocratic Response (%)**
People in the minority should be free to try to win majority support for their opinions.	89	9	2
Public officials should be chosen by majority vote.	95	3	2
I believe in free speech for all, no matter what their views might be.	85	7	9
No matter what a person's political views are, he is entitled to the same legal protections as anyone else.	93	4	3
Important that people should be allowed to express unpopular opinions without fear of punishment*	96	0	4

*PIPA/Knowledge Networks (2009).

Source: John L. Sullivan, James Piereson, and George E. Marcus, *Political Tolerance and American Democracy* (Chicago: University of Chicago Press, 1982), p. 203.

As shown in Table 6.1, survey evidence does in fact demonstrate overwhelming support for democratic values when stated in the abstract. For instance, in 2009, 96 percent of the public agreed that "people should be allowed to express unpopular opinions without fear of being harassed or punished." But note that these assertions are very general, with no reference to any specific person or group. These statements basically constitute an official American political ideology—the sort of lessons that are taught in a variety of both political and nonpolitical contexts by the family and the school and reinforced by the mass media.[1]

However, when statements about the rules of the game have a double stimulus, with references both to democratic principles and to unpopular groups, support for these rules declines. Relevant evidence is presented in Table 6.2, in which the statements are two-pronged. Each refers to a democratic norm plus some specific group or activity. For example, in the statement "Members of the Ku Klux Klan should be banned from running for public office," individuals are asked to respond to both the norm of free elections and feelings about the Klan. In this instance, 70 percent of the public would ban someone from the Klan from running for public office (Gibson 1987). In a more contemporary example, the 2012 GSS shows that 50 percent of the public supports removing a book from the public library authored by a Muslim clergyman who preaches hatred of the United States.

One interpretation of these data is that public support for procedural rights is less than ideal. The pattern in Table 6.2 is clearly one of a lack of enthusiasm for the values of democracy when items refer to protests, demonstrations, or unpopular groups. Of course, we might avoid getting overly alarmed if we keep in mind that this evidence is not drawn from actual behavior and may simply represent ill-considered survey responses to hypothetical situations. However, when ordinary citizens are given the power to directly legislate using the ballot box, they often use that power to deprive unpopular minorities of their civil liberties and rights. Barbara Gamble (1997) looked at seventy-four ballot initiatives on public accommodations for minorities, school desegregation, gay rights, English language laws, and AIDS policies. She found that more than three-quarters of these elections resulted in the defeat of policies designed to protect minority rights.

A Growth in Democratic Tolerance?

There is a good deal of evidence that Americans are more tolerant of unpopular ideas today than in the past. Back in 1942, just 30 percent said that they believed "in free speech to the extent of allowing radicals to hold meetings and express their views in this community."[2] More recently, Table 6.3 shows the change in Americans' tolerance of selected unpopular groups from 1954 to 2012. One point attracts immediate attention: the appearance of a substantial increase in political tolerance over more than a half-century of polling. For example, note that tolerance for someone "speaking out against churches and religion" rose from 38 percent in 1954 to 75 percent in 2012. A simple conclusion is that the American public has become more tolerant of opposing points of view. A common explanation for this change is based on social learning theory. The assumption is that increases in exposure to social and cultural diversity lead to increases in support for democratic norms. Two changes of consequence for this explanation are rising levels of education and the move from rural to urban areas. The proportion of people who have been to college has more than doubled since the 1950s (U.S. Census). Educated people are more likely to understand the importance of protecting democratic liberties, if only in their own self-interest. Also, social and cultural diversity, such as that found in the city, bring individuals into contact with people who are not like them. They learn that those who are different are not always dangerous (Williams, Nunn, and St. Peter 1976; Hillygus 2005).

A less obvious explanation for the rise in support for democratic values holds that there has been little real change between 1954 and 2012; rather, what we see is nothing more than an artifact of the question—that is, the groups used in 2012 to elicit tolerant or intolerant responses are not as threatening as they were in 1954. One undisputed conclusion from the research on democratic values is that perceived threat to the nation is the most powerful determinant of political intolerance (Davis 2007; Brooks and Manza 2013). In 1954 the Cold War with the Soviet Union was hitting its stride. The climate of opinion in the United States was strongly influenced by the scare tactics of the ultra-right-wing junior senator from Wisconsin, Joseph

TABLE 6.2 Support for Democratic Values by Specific Applications

	Democratic Response (%)	Undecided (%)	Undemocratic Response (%)
[Should] people who want to overthrow the government by revolution be allowed to hold public meetings to express their views (GSS 2006)	69	1	30
[Should] books that contain dangerous ideas be banned from public libraries (Pew 2012)	40	5	55
Freedom of speech should not extend to groups sympathetic to terrorists (Pew 2012)	47	4	49
The American press has too much freedom to do what it wants (First Amendment Center 2005)	57	4	39
The police should be allowed to search houses of people who might be sympathetic to terrorists without a court order (Pew 2009)	64	3	33
Approve/disapprove of racial or ethnic profiling in combatting terrorism (NBC/WSJ 2010)	43	6	51
In the event of a national emergency should government be allowed to take control of the Internet and limit access of social media (First Amendment Center 2012)	59	9	33
Approve/disapprove of holding suspected terrorists without access to lawyers and without a trial (Time/SRBI 2006)	47	4	49
If a person takes the Fifth Amendment and refuses to testify, the person is probably guilty of a crime (Fox News 2002)	36	4	48
If a person is suspected of a serious crime, do you think the police should be allowed to hold him in jail until they can get enough evidence to charge him (CBS 2006)	48	4	48
The government should be allowed to access records of books people check out from the library (First Amendment Center 2005)	51	9	40
Government should be able to restrict media broadcasts that might be offensive to racial groups (First Amendment Center)	48	N/A	52
Approve/disapprove of the government intercepting your e-mails as part of a broad effort to combat terrorism (Time/SRBI 2011)	57	2	41
Members of the Ku Klux Klan should be banned from running for public office (Gibson 1987)	25	5	70
[It is] a good idea for the government to keep a list of people who take part in demonstrations (Harris and Weston 1979)	25	26	50

Source: American National Election Studies (1958–2012).

McCarthy. He claimed to have proof that communists had infiltrated the American government, and more than a few people believed him (Goldstein 1978). People were terminated from their jobs and blacklisted because they were presumed to harbor communist sympathies. At a minimum, low levels of support for democratic values among the public during the McCarthy era dissuaded many Americans from speaking out against these indefensible practices. The groups identified in the 1954 survey are those usually associated with the left—communists, atheists, and socialists. Tolerance may appear to have gone up simply because these groups no longer appear to pose the danger many once thought.[3]

In an ambitious project, Sullivan, Piereson, and Marcus (1982) devised a test to determine if the increased tolerance one sees in Table 6.3 is real or simply an illusion. They suspected that support for the civil liberties of a specific group was largely driven by emotion rather than considered judgment. If someone liked atheists, that person would have no problem allowing them the right of free speech. It takes no tolerance to put up with someone with whom one agrees or someone who is promoting a political agenda with which one concurs. On the other hand, the same person might heartily dislike members of the Ku Klux Klan and be quite willing to deny them free expression. The acid test for tolerance, according to Sullivan and his colleagues, is putting up with those whose ideas one finds repugnant. In other words, they suspected that support for procedural rights depended on whose ox was being gored.

TABLE 6.3 Public Tolerance for Unpopular Ideas, 1945–2012

	Person Should Be Allowed to Make a Speech			Person Should Be Allowed to Teach in College			Person's Book Should Remain in the Library		
	1954 (%)	1972 (%)	2012 (%)	1954 (%)	1972 (%)	2012 (%)	1954 (%)	1974 (%)	2012 (%)
An admitted communist	28	52	65	6	39	61	29	53	71
Someone against churches and religion	38	65	76	12	40	63	37	60	75
Someone who favors government ownership of all railroads and large industries	65	77	*	38	56	*	60	67	*
Someone who believes that blacks are genetically inferior	*	61**	57	*	41	46	*	62	63

*Question not asked.
**GSS (1976).

Source: General Social Survey; Samuel Stouffer, *Communism Conformity and Civil Liberties* (New York: Wiley 1954).

Sullivan, Pierson, and Marcus (1982, 60–63) devised a "content-controlled" question in which respondents were given a list of groups and asked which one they liked least (with an option to supply a group not on the list). Respondents were then queried as to whether they would "put up with" (i.e., be tolerant of the procedural rights of) their least-liked group.

As Table 6.4 indicates, tolerance using a least-liked approach from surveys between 1985 and 2005 does not seem to have improved much since 1954.[4] For instance, only 43 percent would allow a member of their least-liked group to make a speech in their city. It is, therefore, not surprising that 53 percent in 2012 said that they would not allow a Muslim clergyman who preaches hatred of the United States to make a speech in their community (GSS).

These levels of tolerance are not much different from the 1950s. For instance, in 2005 only 30 percent of the public believe members of its least-liked group should be allowed to run for public office. If this dismal level of support for democratic values is true, it has thought-provoking implications. The data call into question the inherent willingness of Americans to embrace one of the pillars of democratic thought: tolerance. It also seems to offer little hope for improvement. Most studies show a strong relationship between education and support for democratic values. One might suppose as aggregate levels of education increased, so would political tolerance. However, the revisionist thesis holds this is not the case, as Americans seem little if any more tolerant now than they were during the McCarthy era of the 1950s. Thus improvements in the general level of education, according to this viewpoint, are not the answer to what is seen by some as a dangerously low level of support for democratic values.[5]

TABLE 6.4   Levels of Tolerance Using Content-Controlled Items (1985 and 2005)

	Percent Tolerant of Least-Liked Group
Members of the [least liked group] should be allowed to teach in public schools (1985)*	19
The [least liked group] should not be outlawed (1985)*	31
The [least liked group] should be allowed to hold public rallies in our city (1985)*	32
Members of the [least liked group] should be allowed to make a speech in this city (2005)**	36
Members of the [least liked group] should be allowed to run for public office. (2005)**	30
Members of the [least liked group] should be allowed to hold public rallies in our city. (2005)**	29

Source: *James Gibson, *Freedom and Tolerance in the United States* (National Opinion Research Center, unpublished codebook, 1987); **Gibson (2008).

Not surprisingly, this line of research has been subject to substantial criticism. Among the most telling critiques is a claim that the questions used are inherently incapable of determining the true level of support for democratic values. The questions are flawed because by their very nature they have double stimuli—support for a general principle and reactions to an unpopular group or political act. Further, these stimuli are not balanced. A strong stimulus (one's single most disliked group) is contrasted to a much weaker stimulus (abstract democratic values).

In the typical survey setting, in which respondents must give answers in a few seconds, it is not unexpected that the strong stimulus frequently overwhelms the weak one (or first comes to mind). Most people know whom they do and do not like, and whom they do not like they often find threatening. Coming to grips with an abstract principle is more difficult. Thus, initially, the strong stimulus dominates. But importantly, several studies show that people can often be talked out of—or talked into—antidemocratic positions (Chong 1993; Cobb and Kuklinski 1997). Gibson (1996) demonstrates that of Americans who initially gave an intolerant response, 38 percent changed their minds when given subsequent counterarguments for the tolerant alternative. But counterarguments were even more effective among those initially giving a tolerant response. Sixty-three percent changed their minds and gave the intolerant response. It seems quite clear that people have great difficulty reconciling their desire to support the principles of democratic procedures with their fears and apprehensions about unpopular and perhaps threatening groups.

Still, the data shown in Table 6.3 show the importance of the target group when assessing change in tolerance over time. Note the difference in change in the tolerance for "an admitted communist" and for "someone who believes blacks are genetically inferior." Between 1972 and 2012, the public moved from 52 percent saying an admitted communist should be allowed to speak to 65 percent. But for the race and genetics question, the change was slightly in the other direction moving from 61 percent down to 57 percent saying a person holding racist views should be allowed to speak. There are strong social pressures against appearing to endorse the "old fashioned racism" queried in this question.

9/11: The Trade-Off Between Civil Liberties and Protecting National Security

So far we have focused on democratic values and public toleration for the activities of unpopular groups. In this section we take a somewhat different approach and analyze the extent to which the American public would restrict civil liberties in exchange for greater national security. It is real and not hypothetical circumstances that provide the acid test for citizen commitment to democratic values. In everyday life, concerns over civil liberties are usually remote. In that regard, the 9/11 terrorist attack on the World Trade Center in New York and the Pentagon near Washington, D.C., provides a unique circumstance to test the willingness of citizens to trade off liberties protected by the Bill of Rights for more domestic security. In the wake of 9/11, the government proposed and enacted a number of measures, such as the "Patriot Act," to increase national security, but at a cost in terms of personal liberty.

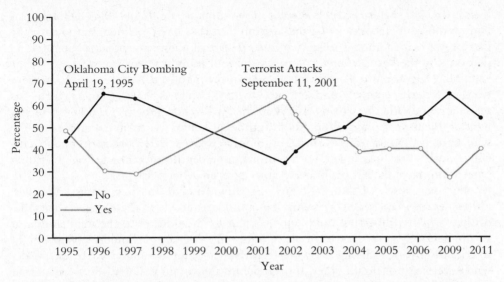

FIGURE 6.1 Question: "In order to curb terrorism in this country, do you think it will be necessary for the average person to give up some civil liberties, or not?"

Source: Based on surveys by *Los Angeles Times, Newsweek,* Pew Center.

The public debate has turned on the need to protect civil liberties as the government seeks greater powers to defeat a mostly foreign enemy, but one that also poses risks to domestic security.

To properly test for the effect of 9/11, we must examine data both before and after the terrorist attack. As shown in Figure 6.1, starting with the Oklahoma City bombing in 1995, the public has been repeatedly asked, "In order to curb terrorism in this country, do you think it will be necessary for the average person to give up some civil liberties, or not?" Immediately following the Oklahoma City bombing, 49 percent thought it would be necessary to give up some civil liberties. As time passed, the percentage taking this position declined. However, shortly after 9/11, 63 percent thought it would be necessary to give up some personal liberties to fight terror, but again these percentages declined over time. As of July 2005, 40 percent believed we may have to give up some civil liberties to fight terrorism, which was just a single percentage point lower than just after the bombing of the Murrah Federal Building in Oklahoma City on April 19, 1995. However, by 2009 just 27 percent thought we might have to give up some civil liberties to fight terrorism, the lowest percentage point in the time series.

The data in Figure 6.1 underscore the persistent finding in the literature on democratic values that the perception of threat against society or cherished beliefs is the single most important factor that drives people to cede fundamental liberties to government (Huddy et al. 2005; Davis 2007; Brooks and Manza 2013). Public perceptions of this threat have varied considerably since 9/11, 2001. In October 2001, 53 percent said there would likely be another terrorism attack in the next few months. That figure bottomed out at just 5 percent during the 2009 economic meltdown, and then rose to 19 percent in the summer of 2013 (CBS/NYT). Interestingly, although perceptions of a threat from terrorists have declined, support for the Patriot Act (which unquestionably infringed on civil liberties) increased. In 2004, 33 percent said the Patriot Act was a necessary tool to fight terrorism; by 2011 public sentiment had risen to 42 percent (Pew). Unfortunately, the precursors to perceptions of threat are poorly understood. One possibility is that "ethnocentrism" (as tendency to divide the world sharply in the "us" versus "them") is a key determinant of threat perception. While some authors link ethnocentrism to support for the war on terror (Kinder and Kam 2010; Sides and Gross 2013), they do not specifically address how it is linked to variations in perceptions of threat. Perhaps threat perceptions have their roots in personality or even genetic origins.

For their study of post-9/11 attitudes toward civil liberties, Davis and Silver (2004; see also Davis 2007) constructed a nine-item scale that addressed the trade-off between civil liberties and personal security. In addition to the item shown in Figure 6.1, they asked, for example, if high school teachers should "have the right to criticize America's policies toward terrorism" or should high school teachers "defend America's policies in order to promote loyalty to our country." Sixty percent of a national sample said teachers should promote loyalty. On the other hand, 77 percent opposed the government being able to search a suspected terrorist's property without a warrant. Davis and Silver conclude that on the whole Americans are not unreasonable on these matters. Among the best predictors of a willingness to yield liberties to the government was the perception of threat and trust in government. The more people feared the possibility of another terrorist attack in the next three months and the more they trusted government, the more likely they were willing to cede fundamental liberties to the government in order to fight terror.

The Theory of Democratic Elitism

If the public is as equivocal about or nonsupportive of democratic values as many believe, how does democracy in the United States survive? American colleges and universities contain substantial numbers of atheists (Gibson and Bingham 1985, 15). In 2012, 34 percent of the public would not allow atheists to teach in these institutions (GSS). Why has there been no mass movement to root out the nonbelievers? Beyond the obvious observation that what people say has no one-to-one link with actual behavior, one influential accounting for this circumstance is "the theory of democratic elitism" (Stouffer 1955; McCloskey 1964; Rose 1964).

The starting point for the theory of democratic elitism is the observation that support for democratic values is not evenly spread throughout the population. Perhaps not surprisingly, surveys show the least commitment to democratic values among the least educated and the politically inactive. Conversely, surveys show the most support for democratic values among the highly educated and politically alert, and especially among public officials. For example, Nunn, Crockett, and Williams (1978) classified 83 percent of a community leader as "more tolerant" compared to only 56 percent of a comparable mass sample. Even today, the mass public is not as verbally supportive of democratic values as political elites in the late 1970s or even the mid-1950s. The 2012 General Social Survey shows 71 percent of the public favors free speech for a communist and 52 percent favors free speech for a militarist.

Comparable figures for elites show greater verbal support going back as far as 1954 (Stouffer 1955; McClosky and Brill 1983; Gibson and Bingham 1985).

Perhaps the most important predictor of support for democratic values is education. Several investigators have presented data showing people who are better educated tend to be more supportive of democratic procedures than those with less education (Stouffer 1955; Nunn, Crockett, and Williams 1978; Nie, Junn, and Stehlik-Barry 1998). The 2012 General Social Survey shows that 61 percent of those with a grade-school education would allow a homosexual to teach at a college or university, while 88 percent of those with a college degree would do so. Most now believe that the causal link between education and support for democratic values runs through verbal cognitive proficiency—the ability to gather, analyze, and comprehend information and discover where one's self-interest truly lies (Nie, Junn, and Stehlik-Barry 1998; Hillygus 2005).

In addition, some go even further and argue that within categories of education, political elites are more tolerant than the public. One author inferred from the Stouffer data (part of which is presented in Table 6.3) that the "differences between leaders and the community at large does not seem due simply to education, since 79 percent of the college-educated leaders are among the more tolerant as compared to 66 percent for the general college-educated population" (Kornhauser 1970, 67). According to the theory of democratic elitism, political leaders are more tolerant than their education alone would predict because of their exposure to the democratic values that permeate the American elite political culture (McCloskey 1964; McClosky and Brill 1983). The system works, therefore, because those who are least attached to democratic values are unlikely to be active or influential in politics. On the other hand, those most committed to democratic tolerance are the ones who have the most influence on actual political outcomes because of their high interest and high levels of political participation. Proponents of democratic elitism can point to countries like Argentina, where government had historically been unstable, and find confirmation of their theory in the fact that educated political activists in that nation are very low in their support for democratic values (Dahl 1971, 139; Stevens, Bishin, and Barr 2006). That American political elites score high on these values is then interpreted as an explanation for democratic stability in the United States.

In the words of one of the pioneer scholars on the subject, "Democratic viability is ... saved by the fact that those who are the most confused about democratic ideas are also most likely to be politically apathetic" (McCloskey 1964, 365). The implication would seem to be a cautionary note that too much democracy is a bad thing if, once actively engaged, the masses can pose a substantial threat to democratic values. Democracy works best, it would seem, when people are content to passively vote for competing sets of elites who control the political parties but to otherwise leave political decisions to elected leaders.

Considerable criticism has been directed at this theory. Any explanation of democratic stability that portrays political activists and officeholders as saviors and common people as potential saboteurs of democratic government will be found immediately suspect by many. Reanalysis of the Stouffer data by Robert Jackman (1972), for example, casts considerable doubt on the claim that political elites are more supportive of democratic values than are others who share their education, gender, region of origin, and other distinguishing characteristics. The Sullivan,

Piereson, and Marcus (1982) least-liked-group analysis found that the differences in tolerance between political activists and nonactivists were spurious, caused by other factors related to both support for democratic values and tolerance. Sniderman et al. (1989) found that conservative elites were particularly less tolerant than the conservative mass public, and much less tolerant than the liberal mass public. In their study of post-9/11 attitudes, Davis and Silver (2004) found that even liberals, who in normal times are the strongest defenders of civil liberties, are, under perception of threat, willing to make concessions on civil liberties.

Elite support for democratic values is most crucial when these values face an actual threat. One can point to examples in U.S. history when most elites—regardless of their political persuasions—failed to come to the rescue when democratic values were actually under siege. One instance was the lack of elite opposition to the internment of Japanese Americans during World War II. Another was the failure of elites to respond critically to violations of traditional norms of free speech and due process during the persecution of alleged communists in the McCarthy era of the early 1950s.

In the case of the McCarthy era, James Gibson (1988) has correlated the tolerance scores of the mass and elite samples from the 1954 Stouffer survey, aggregated by state, with an index measuring repressive legislation passed by the states during that period. He found no evidence of demands for the repression of American communists emanating from the mass public. But he did find evidence of a link between intolerant state elites and repressive state legislation, with the role of the public perhaps being best described as acquiescence.

We should not make too much of the educated elite's greater support for civil liberties when confronted with attitudinal surveys on the matter. The better educated may simply learn what are socially desirable and "appropriate" answers to questions about tolerance (Berinsky 1999). Doubts about the tolerance-inducing effect of education can be drawn from the often-noted pressure for "political correctness" within certain provinces of society. In the 2012 GSS, a surprisingly high 23 percent of college-educated whites would not allow someone who believed blacks are genetically inferior to give a speech in their community. Using this same item, Chong (2006) breaks the GSS data into pre– and post–political correctness eras (which he pegs as before and after 1986) and examines the willingness of eighteen-to twenty-three-year-old college students to allow someone who believes blacks are genetically inferior to speak freely. Among the college students, there is a 6 percent *decrease* in tolerance post-1986, compared to an overall gain of 3 percent for the sample as a whole. Chong argues that the change in political culture condemning "hate speech" that peaked in colleges in the mid-1980s had the effect of lowering tolerance for free expression, particularly among self-identified liberal students. In some instances, the norms transmitted in the education process can provide the intellectual rationale for rejecting the right to express controversial ideas.

In a similar vein, when it comes to endorsing the ideals of the civil rights movement, well-educated whites are considerably more supportive of these ideals than those with less education. However, in demanding applied situations (such as government action to benefit racial minorities), the well educated are no more likely to be supportive than are the less educated. (For details, see Chapter 7.) Jackman and Mulha (1984) stress that education does not so much increase tolerance as it increases awareness of the socially acceptable and the ability of those in the privileged class to develop sophisticated rationales for their privileged position. Of course, not everyone agrees with this interpretation.

Pluralistic Intolerance

In another approach to reconciling an intolerant public with continuing democratic government, Sullivan, Piereson, and Marcus (1982) offer a theory of "pluralistic intolerance." While the public may be quite intolerant, their data show no consensus as to what group should be suppressed. There was a great deal of diversity among the groups Americans like least. In the Sullivan, Piereson, and Marcus (1982) survey, the least-liked group was American communists at 29 percent, followed by the Ku Klux Klan at 24 percent. Because there is no agreement on what groups to suppress, elites receive mixed signals and consequently have the freedom to act on the basis of their own (presumably democratic) preferences. In other words, with no intolerant consensus, there is no demand for political repression of any particular group.[6]

The most recent survey in 2005 (Gibson 2008) shows the most disliked group is the Klan at 44 percent, followed by radical Muslims at 13 percent, Nazis at 12 percent, and atheists at 6 percent. On a list of the three most disliked, only the Klan and Nazis garnered mention by a majority of Americans. But one in five (21 percent) listed atheists as one of their three most disliked groups (more than for communists). Is this most current distribution "pluralistic"? Since no group gathers a "least liked" 50 percent majority, a defensible answer is *yes*, particularly since in the twenty-first century the Klan and Nazis are fringe groups with virtually no political impact and just a smattering of followers. Their current status as the most disliked in 2005 seems a relic of the past and leads one to question whether their selection as "least liked" simply indicates ritualistic responses to now toothless bogymen.

The theory of pluralistic intolerance implies that when one vulnerable group is very unpopular among the general public, political repression will occur. In the 1950s, intolerance was focused on communists and people of the political left. Repression of those persons has been amply documented (Goldstein 1978). Following the decline and fall of McCarthyism in the mid-1950s, intolerance became unfocused and repression was much less evident. The post-9/11 atmosphere presents concern about a new focus on public intolerance of Muslims and people of Arab extraction. The 2005 survey shows that 13 percent of Americans mentioned radical Muslims as their most disliked group, and 37 percent mentioned them as one of their three most disliked groups (Gibson 2008). Further, other survey data show respondents do not distinguish between "Muslims" and "Muslim-Americans" when it comes to stereotypes about violence and trustworthiness (Sides and Gross 2013).[7]

But is public hysteria over outgroups the major factor when repression occurs? The direction of causation here is very much open to question. It is possible that both the policy of repressing the left during the McCarthy era and mass public opinion opposing communists and the like were determined by political elites.[8] In fact, a common interpretation of mass–elite linkage is that independent of any effect of opinion on policy, elite opinion and behavior shape mass opinion (e.g., Zaller 1992; Jacobs and Shapiro 2000; Page 2002). The danger in focused intolerance at the mass level may be that demagogic elites can find a receptive audience to fuel an antidemocratic political movement.

Intolerant Beliefs and Intolerant Behavior

How much significance should we allot to responses to survey questions about tolerance and civil liberties? Intolerant beliefs may be of consequence only if they lead to intolerant behavior, and there is little evidence of any meaningful link. It is important to realize that behavior has multiple causes, of which attitudes are only one (Deutscher 1973). For example, a person would probably look for group support before attempting to prevent an atheist from speaking or before removing books by a communist from the public library. The opinions measured in studies of political tolerance are so uniquely distant from intolerant behavior as to render them little more than hypothetical (Weissberg 1998). For instance, do the expressed fears of some citizens in an opinion survey about libraries stocking their shelves with inflammatory books by Marxists really capture an enduring predisposition for antidemocratic behavior? Translating antidemocratic beliefs into behavior is likely to be a much less frequent occurrence than translating a preference for a political candidate into the behavior of casting a vote for that candidate.

6-2 Political Consensus

Clearly, a democracy is more stable if citizens agree, or are in consensus, on basic values and goals. Some conflict over issues is inevitable in a democracy because public policies generally cannot benefit or penalize all persons or groups equally. Intense or severe political conflict, however, is undesirable because it may threaten the stability of democracy. Robert Dahl (1971, 335) defines *intensity of conflict* as a function of the extent to which each side sees the other as an enemy to be destroyed by whatever means necessary. As issues become more intensely debated, the language of conflict becomes harsher; opponents are accused of acting out of less than honorable motives, and tactics that were once regarded as illegitimate are given serious consideration. The Hutu–Tutsi split in Rwanda, the Muslim–Christian split in Lebanon and, of course, the Sunni–Shi'ite hostility in Iraq are classic examples of political divisions that make democratic government and the protection of civil liberties extremely difficult.

The United States has clearly experienced political conflict in its history. Now, in the twenty-first century, some even see the growing polarization of public opinion leading to a "culture war" over basic values. But unlike many other countries, there has not been significant controversy over a number of fundamental issues. Evidence from several surveys indicates the following: (1) The broad elements of the constitutional order are widely endorsed; 90 percent agree that America is unique because it is founded on the ideals of freedom, equality, and opportunity[9]; (2) there is a consensus that defects should be remedied by legal processes of change; (3) most people are satisfied with the economic order, with 94 percent agreeing that we "must be ready to make sacrifices if necessary ... to preserve the free enterprise system"; few want to nationalize large corporations; big business is widely accepted; labor unions are less popular, but few want to see them eliminated; (4) Americans believe that opportunities exist for personal achievement—the doors of success are open for those willing to work; and (5) most people are content with their lot.[10] When asked recently, 87 percent said they felt extremely or very patriotic (ANES 2012); 94 percent professed loving or liking their country (ANES 2012); 76 said they felt extremely good or very good when they see the American flag fly (ANES 2012); 85 percent are extremely or very proud to be an American (Gallup 2013), and 89 percent say they would rather be a citizen of the United States than of any other country (GSS 2004).

Traditional sources of cleavage that have posed problems in other countries have, for the most part, been moderate in the United States. Among the most important of these are class, regionalism, and religion. Particularly important is the fact that political attitudes are only weakly related to these divisions (see Chapter 7). Regional differences (at least currently) also tend not to be intense. The American public is mobile. The Bureau of the Census reports that in a typical year, 20 percent of the population moves, with about one-third moving a considerable distance. Even the South, on the question of race, is beginning to lose some of its uniqueness. Religious antagonisms, too, do not lead to severe issue conflicts. One reason is that religious preference is only slightly related to social class. One's religion does not determine one's opportunities or economic well-being. The low salience of these conflicts is evidenced by data showing that 91 percent in 2012 said they would vote for a Jew for president, 96 percent said they would vote for a black (and of course Barack Obama was elected president in 2008 and reelected in 2012), 94 percent said they would vote for a Catholic, 92 percent would vote for a Hispanic, 95 percent would vote for a woman, and 80 percent would vote for a Mormon (Gallup 2012). Despite these observations, there have been important divisions within American society.

Race and Ethnicity

Racial divisions have existed since the beginning of the republic. The historic struggles to end slavery, racial segregation, and racial discrimination are well known. Today, there still exists a wide gap between the opinions of white Americans and African-Americans on a substantial range of issues. These differences are most pronounced on questions of what constitutes fair treatment for blacks (again, see Chapter 7), but exist in other domains as well. The possibility for conflict between the races is intensified by the fact that socioeconomic differences reinforce issue disagreements. Compared to whites, blacks are disproportionately working class and unemployed.

While blacks clearly have specific policy grievances and tend to view partisan politics from a different perspective than whites, they do not reject the central tenets underlying the American political system. In 1981, 76 percent of a national sample of black respondents thought the United States had a special role to play in the world; 86 percent said the United States was the best place in the world to live (Gallup 1986); in 2009, 88 percent of blacks agreed "I am very patriotic" (Pew), and in 2012, 91 percent of blacks said they were extremely or very patriotic and 94 percent claimed to love or like their country (ANES).

Today, the fastest-growing minority group is Hispanic Americans, who have already overtaken African-Americans as the largest minority group in the United States. Like previous waves of immigrants when they came to the United States, newcomers from Mexico and elsewhere in Latin America have been seen as threats by many Americans fearful of change. One prominent social scientist, the late

Samuel Huntington (2004), even expressed concern that Hispanic Americans differ from previous immigrant groups by resisting assimilation into the mainstream American culture. However, studies of Hispanic Americans (themselves a culturally diverse group of different national origins and races) suggest such fears to be unfounded. For instance, when asked questions about pride in the United States and American citizenship, Hispanic Americans answer affirmatively at rates similar to non-Hispanic whites and African-Americans (de la Garza, Falcon, and Garcia 1996). Hispanics differ little from whites and blacks on the 2012 ANES patriotism questions; 88 percent of Hispanics said they were extremely or very patriotic and 89 percent said they either loved or liked the United States.

But should we even be singling out minorities as if to ask whether they pass the test of democratic citizenship or American patriotism? If a danger to democracy exists, it may come not from minorities rejecting mainstream American values or resisting assimilation, but rather from some members of the dominant white majority who resist their aspirations. At the fringe are white "super patriots" who though low in number have shown a willingness to engage in unlawful acts including violence. They may offer the greatest threat of civil disorder today.

6-3 Political Support: Trust and Efficacy

A common assumption is that political systems work better when citizens both trust their fellow citizens and trust their government. Social trust (trusting fellow citizens) is a key component of *social capital*, often cited as the lubricant that makes democracy work. *Political trust* (trusting government) is the affective component of support. Those high in political trust are satisfied with the procedures and products of government. The opposite of trust is *political cynicism*, or the evaluation that the political system is not producing policies according to expectations. *Efficacy* is the cognitive or belief component of support; it is the extent to which a person believes his or her political activities will influence government.

Political Trust

The performance of government drives political trust. No government, of course, ever has the complete trust of all its citizens. However, many argue that it is important for democratic government to maintain some minimal (usually unspecified) level of trust among its citizens. One argument is pitched at the normative level. If the distinctive character of democracy is the substitution of voluntary consent for coercion, it is no small moral shortcoming when citizens withdraw trust out of a conviction that the government is not acting in their best interests (Nye 1997). Others make claims of a more practical bent. Levels of trust are thought to affect the leadership strategies available to political decision makers. Leaders must be able to make decisions and commit resources without first consulting those persons who will be affected by the decisions and called upon to supply the resource materials. As William Gamson (1968, 45–46) wrote, when trust is high, "the authorities are able to make new commitments on the basis of it and, if successful, increase support even more. When it is low or declining, authorities may find it difficult to meet existing commitments and govern effectively." Thus, when trust was high in 1964, the government could draw on its credit rating with the electorate and send troops to fight an overseas police action in Vietnam with little public debate. That sort of freedom was considerably constrained after 1972.

Levels of trust are particularly important in the economic area, where the government needs maneuvering room to pursue long-term policy goals. For example, if inflation becomes entrenched, the government must sometimes call upon citizens to endure the pain of recession for the promise of stable prices at a point in the indeterminate future. Citizens must have faith in the fairness and competence of government and not demand a premature accounting based on a short-term appraisal of cost and benefits (Weatherford 1984, 1987; Hetherington and Rudolph 2008). More concretely, low trust among citizens can undermine the willingness of bright people to go into government and the willingness to voluntarily comply with the law (Nye 1997). It has also been shown that political trust influences support for redistributive policies—that is, a willingness to make financial sacrifices to help minorities and the poor or provide foreign aid. According to Hetherington (2005), when trust is high, Americans are more willing to approve the spending of dollars necessary for these programs. The effect of trust on willingness to spend on redistribution may be particularly important for conservatives, who see redistribution of tax money as a sacrifice rather than a benefit. When trust in government is high, conservatives are more willing to support government spending programs; when trust is low, they are likely to oppose them (Rudolph and Evans 2005; Hetherington and Rudolph 2008).

If political trust drops sufficiently low, the result can be social disruption. Disruption may serve as an impetus to needed reform, or it may threaten the stability of an existing regime. At the very least, a portion of state resources must be diverted to cope with the disturbances. Lack of trust is particularly dangerous when the system is not performing in an adequate fashion—as, for example, in an economic depression. During the worldwide depression of the 1930s, many democratic governments ceased to be effective. Those with a reservoir of trust among their citizens were able to withstand the strain, while those not so advantaged (such as Austria, Germany, and Spain) succumbed to severe antidemocratic movements. To those who remember that era and its consequences, concern about trust is more than an academic exercise. See the pathbreaking work of Lipset (1960) and Almond and Verba (1963).

The level of political trust serves as a barometer, indicating how well government is performing. It is, therefore, no surprise that scholars have paid considerable attention to the fluctuations in trust over time.[11] Figure 6.2 presents the trend in political trust between 1958 and 2012 taken from the American National Election Studies. The data from 1958 to 1966 reflect the tranquility of the Eisenhower years, the Camelot years of Kennedy, and the landslide election of Lyndon Johnson. After 1966 trust began to decrease at a steady pace until 1980. Common explanations include the government's handling of the civil rights movement, the Vietnam War, Watergate, the pardon of Richard Nixon, and the economic and foreign policy problems associated with the Carter administration.

Trust did not rebound until Ronald Reagan took office and proclaimed it was "morning in America." The Reagan administration's attack on big government and an improving economy helped boost the level of trust. By 1984, trust had rebounded considerably, although it was nowhere close to the levels of the late 1950s and early 1960s.

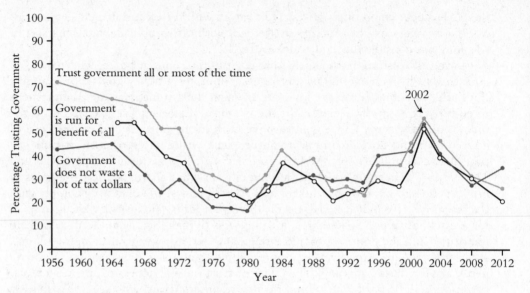

FIGURE 6.2 Trends in public trust by item.

Source: American National Election Studies (1958–2012).

With the events of 9/11, trust in government skyrocketed. In January 2001, a CBS/*New York Times* poll showed a mere 31 percent of Americans claiming to trust the government in Washington to do what is right "most of the time" or "just about always." Two weeks after 9/11, an ABC News/*Washington Post* poll showed 64 percent trusted government "most of the time" or "just about always." A CBS/*New York Times* poll in early October 2001 found 55 percent trusted government. The *New York Times* proclaimed "Suddenly Americans Trust Uncle Sam" (Langer 2002). One had to go back to the presidency of Lyndon Johnson in 1966 to see trust at this elevated level. However, the surge in trust was not to last. CBS/*New York Times* polls showed trust in government at 46 percent in January 2002, falling to 36 percent in July 2003—about where it stood before 9/11. By September 2005, trust in government "all" or "most of the time" had fallen to just 29 percent, holding at 24 percent in late 2012 (ANES).

Reconsidering Political Trust   The rapid surge and decline in trust following 9/11 forced students of public opinion to reconsider the theoretical underpinnings of political trust. The long decline in trust starting in 1966 already had been subject to a good deal of speculation. Inglehart (1997a) saw the decline simply as part of an overall decline in confidence in all major institutions due to a rise in postmaterialist values, which encourage the denigration of authority. For instance, over the three decades prior to 2000, confidence had plunged in such institutions as American business (55 to 21 percent), universities (61 to 30 percent), and medicine (73 to 29 percent.)[12] Growing distrust of government is simply part of this overall pattern.

But it is not that simple. Many parts of government are quite popular. In a survey experiment just after 9/11, half the respondents were asked the conventional question about trust in government where trust specifically referred to "handling national security and the war on terrorism." In the other random half sample trust referred to "handling issues like the economy, health care, Social Security and education." In the case or terrorism, 68 percent trusted government; for domestic issues 38 percent gave a trusting response (ABC News). In addition, some parts of government are well liked. A Pew Research survey (2013) shows that while just 19 percent trusted the government to do the right thing "almost always or most of the time" (the conventional question), more than 60 percent had a favorable view of the Food and Drug Administration, the Department of Education, Health, and Human Services as well as "federal workers."[13]

Trust in government may well be a function of what facet of government the public is primed to see as important at the time of the survey. Like the "rally around the flag" spike in presidential approval during an international crisis, political trust increases when the media focus on international events, such as 9/11. When the priming focuses on domestic events, trust tends to decline (Bishop 2005). Hetherington and Rudolph (2008) claim priming provides one explanation for the high level of political trust in the 1950s, as the public was primed to view the Soviet threat as a major problem facing America. Paradoxically, when the Soviet empire collapsed in 1989, trust in government actually declined. Hetherington and Husser (2012) asserts the current measure of political trust is too general. People trust some parts of the government, but not others. More informative would be a battery of questions relating to trust in government across key segments of government activity.

Today's low level of trust of course does not approach the depths that lead to rejection of the political order. Nevertheless, there may still be worrisome consequences. Orren (1997) argues that people low in political trust turn to quick, simpleminded fixes—for example, direct legislation, third parties, and term limits—as fixes for perceived problems. In two-party presidential elections, the distrustful are more likely to vote for the challenger than the incumbent. In three-party contests, the distrustful are more inclined to vote for third-party candidates than the Republican or the Democrat. In voting for president, those low in trust opt for candidates promising the most far-reaching change (Hetherington 1999). A similar pattern appears on the issue of term limits for elected officials. The strongest predictor of those voting for term limits in state referenda is low political trust (Karp 1995). Scholz and Lubell (1998) show trust in government significantly influences compliance with tax laws. Those scoring low on trust in government tended to underreport their taxable income. And, as is no surprise, just 3 percent of those who identify with the Tea Party trust the government (Pew 2013).

None of the possible consequences listed earlier, however, threatens democratic stability. How low, then, must political trust fall before it makes a difference? One obvious observation is that in the mid-1970s, when trust was at its nadir, the process of government did not operate with any appreciable difference from the 1950s. The weapons of war were still being built, pensions were paid, and the garbage was collected. The survival of democracy and the functioning of government were not threatened. Further, one could argue that if there had *not* been a plunge in trust in the wake of Watergate, it would have been the more disturbing outcome. Leaders (e.g., Nixon) whose actions threaten the democratic fabric presumably deserve the distrust of "small d" democrats.

Finally, we note that in monitoring the level of public trust, the location of trust within groups is important. In the United States, support is highest among the white, non-Southern, non-Jewish, middle-aged upper middle class. In other words, trust is concentrated in people who are most rewarded by the existing system. Extending broad trust beyond this group may be a key to democratic stability. We should also be mindful that one's trust in government at the moment is partially a function of whether one's preferred political party is in power. Everything else being equal, partisans are most likely to trust their government when their own party controls Congress and the presidency (Keele 2005). However, among members of the out party, those who are high in trust are most likely to go along with proposals offered by the incumbent administration, rather than digging in their heels in opposition (Hetherington and Husser 2012).

Political Efficacy

The concept of *political efficacy* was originally developed in the early 1950s to explain variations in voting turnout. The four questions used to measure it have been repeated frequently and over a longer period than almost any other survey indicator. Efficacy can be best described as a belief that one can influence the political process. It is a feeling that an active citizen can play a part in bringing about social and political change and that one's input counts (Campbell, Gurin, and Miller 1954, 187). Since it was first developed, the concept has been generalized to account for a wide variety of political activities including online political participation (Kenski and Stroud 2006).

Data from two large-scale studies of political participation show a strong relationship between political efficacy and many types of political activity (Verba and Nie 1972; Verba, Schlozman, and Brady 1995). Beyond its relationship to voting, these studies generally show that the higher the sense of political efficacy, the greater the likelihood that one will participate in political activities of a relatively demanding sort. Conversely, a low sense of efficacy is one of the factors normally associated with political apathy (Verba and Nie 1972; Lewis-Beck et al. 2008). Some current research is directed toward how to increase young people's sense of political efficacy through the school curriculum and extracurricular activities (Pinkleton, Austin, and Fortman 1998; Bowler and Donovan 2002; Kahne and Westheimer 2006). However, the best predictor of efficacy remains the one identified back in the 1950s—years of formal education (Campbell, Gurin, and Miller 1954). Recently, like many other political predispositions, political efficacy has been linked to genetics (Klemmersen et al. 2012).

It should come as no surprise that political efficacy and trust are related—that those who feel they can influence government also tend to trust it. According to the 2012 ANES, only about 10 percent of the American public scored in the top 25 percent in efficacy but also in the bottom 25 percent in political trust.[14] Thus, there seems to be a nontrivial segment of the population that could be mobilized for active opposition to the status quo given the appropriate circumstances. It might be noted, for example, that the low-trust/high-efficacy group voted at almost twice the rate for third-party candidate Ross Perot in 1992 than did the rest of the population.

Considerable research has been conducted on the behavior patterns of those low on trust but high on efficacy. Shingles (1981) finds that the combination of low trust and high efficacy overcomes the disadvantages of low income and low education in motivating political participation. This combination was a particularly important antecedent of political activity among African-Americans. Jennings and Andersen (1996) find the same pattern in support for the confrontational tactics used by the AIDS Coalition to Unleash Power (ACT-UP), which demanded that the Food and Drug Administration release experimental AIDS drugs.[15] In a variety of research settings, Edward Muller and his colleagues (Muller and Jukam 1983; Muller and Opp 1986; Muller and Seligson 1987) demonstrated that nontraditional political activity is most likely to occur among people who are distrustful of and alienated from government and who also believe that their actions (sometimes violent) will get them what they want.[16] More recently, Skocpol and Williams (2013) find those drawn to the Tea Party tended not to trust government, but score high in a belief they could be politically effective.

Social Trust

Social trust can be differentiated from political trust. Social trust is generalized trust in others. It is trust in other people, people you have never met. It is often measured with the question, "Do you believe that most people can be trusted or that you can't be too careful in dealing with people?" Social trust has little in common with political trust, as the two have different origins (Uslaner 2002; Delhey and Newton 2003; Mishler and Rose 2005). Looking across a variety of nations, the level of social trust is strongly related to the existence of democratic institutions. The higher the level of interpersonal trust among citizens, the more likely a nation will have democratic institutions and the more likely a nation is able to maintain long-term democratic stability (Newton 2007; Jamal and Noorudin 2010). Among the reasons for this are that democratic institutions depend on a trust among citizens that those voted into power will not use extralegal methods to stay there or use the power of state to suppress political opposition. People who trust others tend to be tolerant, appreciate democracy, participate in politics, contribute to charity, serve on juries, have high levels of confidence in political institutions such as Congress and the Supreme Court, and generally display the hallmarks of civic virtue (Putnam 2000). According to some, generalized trust is the oil that lubricates democracy (Warren 1999; Uslaner 2002; Zmerli and Newton 2008).

Like political trust, social trust has been declining. In 1960, 57 percent of the public said they trusted most people (Almond and Verba 1963). By 1978, social trust had dropped to 40 percent and by 1994 to 33 percent, a range where it has more or less stayed (GSS 1972–2012). Almost all of this decline can be attributed to generational replacement (Putnam 2000, 140; Jennings and Stoker 2004). Trusting seniors are being replaced in the electorate by less trusting new entrants. With the events of 9/11 came an increase in social trust, but it did not skyrocket like political trust. In November 2001, 42 percent said they trusted most people (Pew), but by February 2002 social trust had dropped to 34 percent, and stood at 32 percent in 2012 (GSS). Still, compared to other nations, Americans tend generally to trust others. Only the Scandinavian countries routinely exceed the United States when it comes to generalized social trust.

Social trust also matters because it can influence public opinion. Brewer and colleagues (2004) show that social trust influences the level of trust in the benign intentions of most foreign countries, which in turn promotes an internationalist perspective in foreign affairs. More famously, social trust matters because it is an essential component of social capital. Many students of democracy believe that the development and maintenance of a civic culture is greatly aided by high levels of social capital.[17] Robert Putnam (1995a, 182) writes that "democratic government is strengthened, not weakened, when it faces a vigorous civil society." Social capital involves membership in voluntary associations and networks that create a sense of political efficacy. It allows people to work together effectively to influence government, which in turn mitigates the intensity of conflict that can threaten democratic government (Fukuyama 1995; Verba, Schlozman, and Brady 1995). Associational life in civil society, in the words of Verba and his colleagues, "operates as the school of democracy" (Brady, Verba, and Schlozman 1995, 285).

Levels of social capital have attracted much attention in recent years because of the provocative claim by Putnam (1995a, 1995b, 2000) that civic engagement in the United States has undergone a serious decline. As evidence, Putnam notes that membership in voluntary associations ranging from the Red Cross to bowling leagues has declined appreciably over the last three decades. The primary culprit, according to Putman, is the widespread appeal of television beginning in the mid-1950s.[18] The more one watches television, the less time one has for life in voluntary associations.[19] In addition, data show that the more one watches television, the lower one's level of interpersonal trust. Television emphasizes violence, crime, and duplicitous personal relationships. According to the "mean world" thesis of George Gerbner (1998), heavy television users confuse its content with the real world. They see the world as unrealistically mean and dangerous, which has a negative effect on social trust. Not everyone, however, is convinced by the decline-in-social-capital thesis. Some have challenged the evidence of a decline (Pettinico 1996; Ladd 1998; Shapiro 2002); others doubt its connection to democratic stability (Jackman and Miller 1996; Tarrow 1996) or at least hold its effect is inconsistent across nation states (Jamal and Nooruddin 2010).

6-4 Personality and Democratic Citizenship

In Chapter 5 we discussed certain personality traits that can affect political opinions—such as why some people are liberals and others are conservatives. In this chapter we discuss those personality traits that are sometimes posited as making one more or less conducive to democratic citizenship. Could it be that certain personality types are attracted to authoritarian leadership, whereas other personality types make healthy democratic citizens?

The Authoritarian Personality

Influenced by events in Germany during Hitler's rule, a group of scholars from the University of California at Berkeley began a systematic investigation into the personality structure of individuals particularly susceptible to anti-Semitic and fascist political appeals. Was there something about the personality of some individuals that led them to actively support or passively sympathize with a program of genocide against Jews, homosexuals, and gypsies, and the replacement of democratic government by dictatorship (as happened in Germany between 1932 and 1945)? The study (Adorno et al. 1950) has had a profound influence on all branches of the social sciences.

The thesis of the book is straightforward. Prejudice, suspicion, distrust, and hostility are manifestations of attempts to resolve deep-seated psychological conflicts. At the heart of these conflicts is a highly ambivalent orientation toward authority. To compensate for feelings of personal weakness, authoritarians present a tough façade. They are critical of those they see as beneath them, particularly those who are different, such as members of minority groups or those living "deviant" lifestyles such as gays and lesbians. Authoritarians are submissive to those above them in the social order and condescending toward those below. As depicted in German folklore, they are like a person on a bicycle—above they bow, below they kick. While such persons are outwardly deferential, they in fact harbor considerable hostility toward authority. This hostility, however, is mostly unconscious, and authoritarians are only intermittently aware of the hate side of this love–hate amalgam. Rather, negative feelings are repressed by primitive ego defensive mechanisms. Authoritarians are extremely servile toward authority, driving from consciousness the malice they feel toward those above them. Other characteristics of authoritarian syndrome include (1) conventionalism—a rigid adherence to conventional middle-class values; (2) anti-intraception—opposition to the tenderhearted, subjective, and imaginative; (3) superstition—a belief in mystical determinants influencing one's fate; and (4) ethnocentrism—a strong attachment to one's own group and hostility to outgroups (Kirscht and Dillehay 1967, 5–6).

Authoritarianism is thought to originate primarily with childhood family relationships, with recent research suggesting a possible genetic component as well (Ludeke and Krueger 2013).[20] Peterson, Smirles, and Wentworth (1997) demonstrate a strong tendency for authoritarian parents to have authoritarian children.[21] Persons displaying the authoritarian syndrome often describe parental affection as being given only as a reward for good behavior. Their parents employed rigid, punishment-oriented disciplinary practices, as opposed to discipline based on love withdrawal. Family roles were clearly defined in terms of dominance and submission (Milburn, Conrad, and Carberry 1995). The implications of *The Authoritarian Personality* for public opinion and democratic stability became obvious to students of politics soon after its publication. One of the first tasks investigators set for themselves was to determine the political correlates of authoritarianism. (Are authoritarians prejudiced toward minorities? Do they hold antidemocratic political beliefs? and so on.) This undertaking was greatly aided by the fact that *The Authoritarian Personality*, unlike other such studies, provided a ready-made paper-and-pencil test to measure the extent to which the syndrome exists. This instrument, the *California F-scale* (the *F* is for fascism), early after its publication, became virtually synonymous with authoritarianism. Typical agree/disagree items from the original F-scale include the following (Adorno et al. 1950, 167):

- What young people need most of all is strict discipline by their parents.
- Most people who don't get ahead just don't have enough willpower.
- Sex criminals deserve more than prison; they should be whipped in public or worse.

Investigators soon discovered severe methodological problems with the F-scale. Among the most difficult to resolve was response set. All twenty items in the original F-scale were worded in a positive direction (to agree was authoritarian). The obvious solution is to reverse some of the items so that to disagree is the authoritarian response. However, this strategy compromises the reliability of the scale. Also, one essential requirement of a personality measure is that it not be contaminated by political content. It is now generally agreed that the F-scale is biased in the direction of right-wing authoritarianism. For example, one agree/disagree item from the F-scale states: "Homosexuals are hardly better than criminals and ought to be severely punished." Such a question may tap both personality traits and right-wing political outlooks. Consequently, the F-scale is not sensitive to authoritarians of the left (such as American communists) and is likely overly sensitive to authoritarians on the right (such as neo-Nazis or skinheads).

Because of these problems, the original F-scale is no longer used. However, there have been three important attempts to measure authoritarianism in a more scientific fashion. The first, by Milton Rokeach (1960), was the development of a new measure—the *dogmatism scale*—which Rokeach claimed could tap authoritarianism of both the left and the right. Currently, the four-item dogmatism scale is one of the most frequently used measures of authoritarian tendencies (although it suffers from response set, because to be "dogmatic" is to agree with scale items). It also is better able to predict extreme conservative opinion than extreme liberal opinion. Typical dogmatism agree–disagree items state, "there are two types of people in the world—those who are for the truth and those against it," or "most of ideas that get printed today are not worth the paper they are written on."

The second solution was simply to recognize the ideological problem and reformulate the concept. Bob Altemeyer (1981, 1988, 1997) developed a highly reliable scale of thirty-four items free from response set, which he labels "Right Wing Authoritarianism" (RWA). He argues that authoritarianism naturally leads to right-wing political views. Unfortunately, since much of what is to be explained by authoritarianism contains conservative political content, this approach runs the risk of being tautological. He reorganizes the concept into three domains: submission to established authorities, aggression toward outgroups, and adherence to traditional social conventions. Typical agree–disagree items from Altemeyer's RWA scale are "Once our government leaders and authorities condemn the dangerous elements in our society, it will be the duty of every patriotic citizen to help stomp out the rot that is poisoning our country from within" and "It is best to treat dissenters with leniency and open mind, since new ideas are the lifeblood of progressive change." Altemeyer (1988, 329) found no evidence of authoritarianism on the political left, even among those holding extreme opinions. Authoritarianism, in his studies, was limited to those on the political right.

Karen Stenner (2005) offers a third solution. She uses a scale consisting only of items that ask respondents about the qualities they think are most important for childrearing. For instance, do people believe it is more important for a child to be obedient or self-reliant; considerate or well-behaved? Stenner argues that attitudes about childrearing are independent of political content and are a valid measure of authoritarian tendencies, that is, tendencies to desire society to be structured in a way to maximize sameness and minimize diversity among people, beliefs, and behavior. Her scale proves to be a robust predictor of racial intolerance, political intolerance, and moral intolerance. In addition, she finds over time that authoritarianism is becoming a more, not less, powerful predictor of these forms of intolerance (Stenner 2005, 190).

Regardless of approach, one consistent finding for authoritarianism is its clear association with social conformity (Altemeyer 1997; Feldman 2003; Stenner 2005). For instance, in a typical study, a persuasive message was presented (from a variety of sources) to a number of different groups. Those scoring high on the F-scale were particularly likely to change their attitude when the message was delivered by a high-status source (Harvey and Beverly 1961, 125–30). Interestingly, authoritarians generally claim to hold their political opinions strongly, even though they tend not to be particularly informed politically (Peterson, Duncan, and Pang 2002; Lavine, Lodge, and Freitas 2005).

Researchers studying democratic values have found authoritarianism—measured in a variety of fashions—to consistently be related to political intolerance. Sullivan, Piereson, and Marcus (1982) found "large and significant" differences (in the predicted direction) between those scoring high and those scoring low on the dogmatism (D) scale with regard to the toleration of respondents' least-liked group, as did McClosky and Brill (1983, 342) using the traditional F-scale. Gibson and Tedin (1988) report similar findings in a study of tolerance for gay rights. They found that dogmatism contributed to an intolerance for gays by reducing support for norms of democracy (see also Mirels and Dean 2006). Feldman and Stenner (1997; Stenner 2005) find authoritarianism contributes to intolerance by increasing the perceived threat of disliked groups. Lavine, Lodge, and Freitas (2005) find a difference between authoritarians and others in how they solve problems under threat.

Where nonauthoritarians tend to be open to new information to solve the problem, authoritarians are more likely to seek new information to reinforce their existing opinions. It is on this basis that Hetherington and Weiler (2009) argue that the current polarization in politics is exacerbated (and increasingly so) by authoritarianism. The elite-driven issues that define contemporary politics are the same "high heat" issues that structure and activate the authoritarian personality (race relations, gay rights, crime, the war on terror, the use of military force). It is not so much how partisans disagree, but what they disagree on— "notions of the proper societal order and threats to it." Among authoritarians, these issues lead to a perception of threat, and a bitter visceral reaction. Authoritarian sentiment is not so much associated with a belief in a competitive world as it is closely associated with a belief in a dangerous world (Duckitt and Sibley 2009). One consequence is a drive toward ideology conformity, and interestingly, the drive is strongest among those who know the most about politics and have the firmest grasp on abstract political principles (Federico, Fisher and Deason 2011).

We see the same manifestations of the authoritarian personality in studies of the trade-off between protection of civil liberties and desire for greater national security. A number of studies claim there in an interaction between authoritarianism and threat. Threat activates authoritarianism (Feldman and Stenner 2003; Stenner 2005), which results in "harsh" policy preferences. Even with extensive statistical controls, those scoring high on authoritarianism are more likely to trade civil liberties for national security than are those scoring low (Davis 2007).

Huddy and Khatib (2007) report a strong relationship between authoritarianism and "uncritical patriotism." Huddy et al. (2005) found authoritarians more likely to endorse government surveillance, extended security checks, and visa restrictions on Arab-Americans than did nonauthoritarians. Kam and Kinder (2007) show that authoritarians are more likely to favor increased spending on homeland security, border control, support the war in Iraq, and approve of President George W. Bush's response to 9/11. Stevens, Bishin, and Barr (2006) find authoritarianism related to greater confidence in order-maintaining institutions.

Decades of research have also found a substantial linkage between authoritarianism and racism. The correlation between these constructs is one of the most enduring in the social science literature. John Ray (1988, 673), one of the most trenchant critics of the authoritarianism concept, concedes that "despite all the other failures of their theory, Adorno et al. would appear to have succeeded in at last one of their basic aims—to find something that would predict who is a racist and who is not." Meloen, van der Linden, and de Witte (1996) have demonstrated strong relationships between authoritarianism and voting for political parties with a racist agenda. Sniderman and Piazza (1993) have shown that authoritarian values among whites lead to the negative stereotyping of both Jews and African-Americans, two groups that are alike only in their joint history as outgroups. It is not the actual characteristics of blacks, any more than it is the actual characteristics of Jews, that evoke prejudice and dislike. Rather, it is the ethnocentric dimension of the authoritarian personality—the generalized hostility to outgroups—that is part of the syndrome.

One particularly interesting study on authoritarianism involved the classic experiment developed by Stanley Milgram (1969) to measure obedience to authority. In this experiment, a naive subject ("the teacher") is required by the study director ("the authority figure") to administer an electrical shock each time "the learner" fails to perform a rote memorization task satisfactorily. The teacher is not aware that the learner is in league with the person running the experiment and is in fact receiving no shock at all. However, each time the learner fails the task, the authority figure (the experimenter) orders the teacher to shock the learner at an ever higher level of voltage. As the shocks presumably become stronger, the learner cries out in pain. The object is to see how long the teacher will obey the authority figure and continue to administer the shocks. One disturbing feature of this study is that many subjects continue to administer the shocks until the learner is in an apparent state of unconsciousness. It is important to appreciate that Milgram's studies go beyond a simple pencil-and-paper approach and are a measure of how people really act in a highly realistic setting. Milgram's work was in fact so realistic that it could not be conducted today due to human-subjects considerations.

Is There a Democratic Personality?

Considerably less attention has been paid to the possibility that certain personality traits might promote support for democratic principles. Much of the older literature was either speculative or consisted of inferences based on intensive interviews with small samples. Authors like Lasswell (1951), Lane (1962), Inkeles (1961), and

Sniderman (1975) write about the democratic character as being warm, outgoing, high in self-esteem and ego strength, flexible, and tolerant of ambiguity. The more recent research focuses on the building of social capital and its key component social trust. There is ample evidence that trust in others correlates with support for democracy, as does a rejection of authoritarian perspectives on the world. But context matters as well. For instance, how much does social trust encourage democracy and how much does the existence of democracy encourage the creation of social trust.

It is misleading to talk about "the democratic personality" as if it were a distinct psychological type, impervious to environmental circumstances. The emphasis on environment is important because personality traits that encourage support for democratic principles (the accepted norm) among citizens of the United States probably encouraged support of totalitarian communism (the accepted norm) among citizens of the former Soviet Union. In other words, some personality types work well within the given rules of the political game—whatever those rules might be. It is not surprising, therefore, that many politicians who were successful when communism was the accepted norm in the Soviet Union are also successful under the norms of democracy in Russia and the independent states. For example, Russian prime minister Vladimir Putin is a former colonel in the Soviet KGB (the intelligence agency).

6-5 Conclusion

There seem to be two fundamental prerequisites for the existence and maintenance of democratic rights and freedoms. One is economic and the other is psychological. In the former, considerable research indicates that some minimal level of economic affluence and development is necessary before a democracy can operate successfully. If people must worry about feeding themselves and their children, concern about democratic government will be a low priority for most (Inglehart 1990; Huntington 1991). Beyond simple sustenance, the most relevant factor associated with democratic development is communication networks. Without sufficiently developed channels of communication, interests cannot be articulated and aggregated, and conflicting groups cannot exchange information on goals and desires (Lipset 1959). But once a minimal level of economic development has occurred in tandem with associated communication networks, psychological and cultural factors become important (Inglehart 1997b).

This chapter has analyzed a number of political attitudes commonly thought to affect the stability of democracy. All may be of consequence, but none alone, or even in combination, provides a total explanation for the continued protection of democratic values in the United States. America has perhaps been most fortunate in that it has experienced few intense group or issue cleavages dividing the population. As long as a modest consensus exists and most of the population has a minimal degree of economic security, the system seems able to tolerate a wide variety of personality types, a relatively low level of trust in government, and considerable lack of enthusiasm (although perhaps not outright hostility) for procedural democratic norms.

Critical Thinking Questions

1. Public opinion polls show that support for democratic values is shallow. What might be done to improve this support among the American public?
2. Democratic theorists say we should tolerate political speech of all kinds, no matter how much we might dislike its content. The polls show the public often disagrees. Are there conditions which justify placing limits on political speech?
3. Public opinion polls show that political trust in the United States has plunged since the 1960s. Do Americans really not trust their government? Besides reading poll results, how else might one determine the extent to which the public trusts the government in Washington?

Endnotes

1. For a review of trends in political tolerance see Schafer and Shaw (2009).
2. Data are from the U.S. Office of Public Opinion Research and were downloaded from iPOLL. Thirty percent responded *yes*, 63 percent said *no*, and 6 percent had no opinion.
3. One bit of evidence for this thesis is the rather substantial increase in support for the civil rights of communists that occurred between 1988 and 1993, the period surrounding the fall of the communist Soviet Union. According to the GSS, in 1988, 60 percent would allow an admitted communist to speak; in 1993, 71 percent would. In 1988, 59 percent would allow an admitted communist's book to remain in the library; by 1993, 70 percent would. Increases in tolerance for other groups addressed in this battery of questions (e.g., atheists and militarists) were not nearly as large, so the explanation must be that with the fall of the Soviet Union, communists do not seem so dangerous.
4. Sullivan, Piereson, and Marcus (1982, 67) concede that tolerance may have increased somewhat between 1954 and 1978, but not as much as the items in Table 6.3 would lead one to believe.
5. See also Green et al. (2011), showing a disconnect between levels of information about civil liberties and support for civil liberties.
6. A point first noted by Herson and Hofstetter (1975).
7. And, as we noted earlier, the 2012 GSS shows a high level of intolerance for a Muslim clergyman preaching hatred of the United States.
8. For additional critiques of the theory of pluralistic intolerance, see Gibson (1986) and Sniderman et al. (1989).
9. Greenberg, Quinlan, Rosner Research (August 2007; from IPOLL).
10. Surveys reported in Dahl (1982) and Ladd (1989), Freedom Forum (August 16–26, 2007; from IPOLL).
11. The literature on trust is voluminous. Among the better, more recent studies are Craig (1993), Nye, Zelikow, and King (1997), and Hetherington (2005).
12. Based on Harris Polls, cited in Nye (1997, 283).
13. In fact, of 14 federal agencies mentioned, only the Internal Revenue Service had a favorability rating of less than 50 percent.
14. The ANES efficacy scale is based on three agree/disagree core items: "Sometimes politics and government seem so complicated that a person like me can't really understand what's going on"; "People like me have no say in what government does"; and "I don't think public officials care much what people like me think." For each, to disagree is to give the efficacious response. The trust scale is based on the items in Figure 6.2.

15. The tactics used by ACT-UP members included stopping trading on the floor of the New York Stock Exchange, disrupting political speeches, locking themselves inside the offices of major pharmaceutical companies, and conducting "die-ins" on streets with heavy traffic (Jennings and Andersen 1996, 313).
16. The best statement of this perspective can be found in Finkel, Muller, and Opp (1989).
17. Although there is conflicting evidence, it appears that high levels of trust lead to greater community involvement, not the reverse (Brehm and Rahn 1997; Uslaner 2002; Jennings and Stoker 2004).
18. In 1950, only 10 percent of all households had television. By 1960, 90 percent of all households had television. Americans typically watch three to four hours of television a day. The more television they watch, the less active they are in voluntary associations (Putnam 1995a).
19. We might infer something similar in the case of the extensive use of the Internet.
20. For an argument that the authoritarian syndrome originates in Darwinian evolution, see Somit and Peterson (1997).
21. Peterson, Smirles, and Wentworth (1997) report a significant path coefficient ($r = .47$) between authoritarianism in parents and authoritarianism in children. Altemeyer (1997) finds a similar relationship ($r = .40$).

CHAPTER 7

Group Differences in Political Opinions

LEARNING OBJECTIVES

- Describe the effect of differences in social class on political opinions
- Describe how racial and ethnic groups differ on their political opinions

- Describe how differing religious orientations affect partisanship and public opinion
- Explain the gender gap

People often think of themselves as belonging to a specific group. This group identification may influence political opinions, as people see certain policies as being beneficial to the group with which they identify. Thus, we are not surprised if blacks are more favorable to affirmative action than whites, or people with high incomes more opposed to social welfare programs than those living near the poverty line. However, not all group differences are the result of calculated self-interest. Many political opinions are based on sociotropic considerations—that is, on the well-being of the nation as a whole rather than on that of the individual or the group (Kinder and Kiewiet 1981). Life experiences can also shape political outlooks. For instance, individuals with a college education differ sharply from those without on a variety of cultural or social issues, such as abortion. Growing up as a white person in the South once virtually ensured an allegiance to the Democratic Party, although obviously no longer.

In this chapter we explore the validity of generalizations made about group differences in public opinion. In earlier chapters, we observed that Americans are becoming more polarized—with ideology increasingly driving party attachments and vote choice. Here we examine the degree to which group differences contribute to this polarization. For example, do we see increasing political divisions between the rich and the poor? Is the nation becoming more divided by geography, as if a political gulf exists between Democratic "blue" states and Republican "red" states? Do differences in education, age, and religion divide people more than before, especially on cultural issues? On some group dimensions, are Americans becoming more alike rather than different? Long-standing racial and ethnic divisions may now be less distinct than in the past.

7-1 Socioeconomic Class and Political Opinions

Because a great many issues in political life concern the distribution of benefits within society, the rich and the poor often seem to have quite different economic interests. The haves and the have-nots are expected to disagree, for example, on questions involving taxation and government services. In most European democracies, the major political battle lines are drawn between working-class parties and parties of the middle class. As indicated by the fact that the United States has never had an appreciable socialist movement, America has escaped the more extreme forms of class polarization and conflict. There are, nevertheless, class differences on many political issues.

How do we measure economic or social class? One approach, called *subjective social class*, is simply to ask people into which social class they fall—the lower class, working class, middle class, or upper class. When asked, almost everyone is willing to place himself in one of these classes. In the 2012 General Social Survey, 8 percent identified themselves with the lower class, 44 percent with the working class, 43 percent with the middle class, and 4 percent with the upper class. This division has remained virtually unchanged since the GSS first asked the question in 1972.

An alternative to the subjective approach is to use the objective indicators of occupation, income, and education. Each indicator has its problems. The connections among the three are often far from perfect. Many blue-collar workers have greater incomes than white-collar workers. Also, education is an imperfect predictor of income because many college graduates often have lower incomes than skilled manual workers. We could focus on income, but the same dollar amounts buy distinctly different lifestyles in various parts of the country. A $50,000 annual income in rural Montana might allow a pleasant middle-class lifestyle, while a family would have to struggle to live on that amount in New York City. Subjective class identifications are actually quite predictable from education, income, and occupation (Jackman and Jackman 1983).

Class Differences on Economic Issues

Income is more concentrated at the upper levels of society in the United States than it is in any other Western democracy save Russia and Mexico (Rector and Hederman 2004). Today, about 35 percent of all wealth in the United States is in the hands of the top 1 percent (Wolff 2012). In terms of annual income, over 20 percent goes to those in the top 1 percent. Rather than decreasing, the level of income concentration has been increasing, fueled significantly by wealth generated through the technology revolution. From 1992 to 2013, real (inflation-adjusted) income of the top 1 percent grew by 86 percent (almost doubled), while income for the remaining 99 percent grew by only 6 percent. Doing the math differently, 68 percent of the income growth went to the top 1 percent. The recovery from the Great Recession has been even more unequal. Ninety-five percent of the income growth in 2009–2013 went to the top 1 percent (statistics from Saez 2013).

The public is not blind to this accelerated inequality (for a review, see Shaw and Gaffey 2012). An increasing number of Americans see society as divided by class. In 1988, just 26 percent thought the nation was divided into the "haves" and the "have-nots"; by 2011, 45 percent thought it was so divided (Pew). In 2012, 80 percent of the public said the difference between rich people and poor people was larger now than it was twenty years ago (ANES). Yet by European standards, political cleavages along class lines in the United States are rather muted. Perhaps one reason is a belief among Americans that the opportunity to succeed financially is readily available to those with the energy and ability. For example, one poll found only 12 percent saying there is little or no chance of becoming rich in the United States if one is willing to work hard. When a British sample was asked a similar question, 63 percent said they did not think they had a chance to become rich if they really wanted to.[1]

Table 7.1 shows the relationship between subjective social class and beliefs regarding whether the government should spend more money on programs such as health care, education, retirement benefits, aid to cities, and science and technology. For most of these programs, the working class is the group most likely to favor increased government spending. The greatest opinion difference among the classes is on Social Security benefits, aid to poor people, child care, and AIDS research. Obviously, the working class has real concerns about the well-being of their children when they are away from home, for their own financial security after retirement, and the AIDS epidemic. On the other hand, there is no meaningful difference in opinion on spending for roads and bridges, which benefits all classes. The opinions on these spending increases seem predictable from one's station in life. Social Security and unemployment are of much more concern to the working class than the more affluent classes. On the other hand, the most affluent class is a potential beneficiary of increasing spending on science and technology, and its members tend to support such spending increases. There is virtually no constituency for an increase in spending on foreign aid.

TABLE 7.1 Subjective Social Class and Opinions About Spending on Selected Government Programs			
Percentage Wanting to Spend More on	Working Class	Middle Class	Upper Middle/ Upper Class
AIDS research*	60	51	38
Education**	80	70	60
Aid to poor people**	51	42	22
Space program†	11	14	22
Social security**	68	51	32
Child care**	57	49	39
Health care†	63	58	39
Helping large cities†	49	36	25
Roads and bridges†	42	45	42
Science and technology**	20	23	40
Foreign aid†	11	07	08

*ANES, 2000.

**ANES, 2012.

†GSS, 2012.

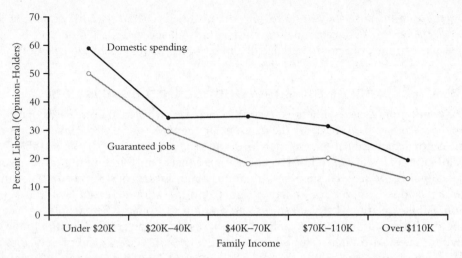

FIGURE 7.1 Social welfare opinions by family income (whites only).

Source: American National Election Studies, 2012.

For the 2012 ANES, Figure 7.1 shows how family income, an objective indicator of social class, is related to opinion on the issues of increasing domestic spending and services and support for a government-guaranteed job and good standard of living. (Nonwhites are excluded here in order to show the effect of income independent of race.) We would expect for reasons of simple economic self-interest that people in the lower-income categories would support public policies designed to promote employment and fund social programs, with a commensurate lack of support among the more financially secure. As one goes from poor to affluent, one does in fact see a decline in the percentage of people holding liberal positions on these economic issues. Despite the repeated findings that rich and poor divide on redistributive issues like taxing and spending, it may seem puzzling that this class division is not stronger than shown in surveys. Clearly, more than direct self-interest is at work. Many wealthy individuals support government programs, paid for by their tax dollars, for which the direct benefits go to those less fortunate, while many of the less fortunate oppose programs for which they pay little tax but receive benefits.

One instance of this puzzle was the general public acceptance of President George W. Bush's tax cuts in 2001 and 2003, even though the cuts predominantly benefited the wealthy. According to polls, a plurality accepted Bush's tax cuts, including even repeal of the estate tax, which benefits only the wealthiest 2 percent. Why did ordinary people not object? One reason is that those of modest income often do not understand the complexities of the tax code. Also taxes are unpopular. It is of no small psychological importance that while the Bush tax cuts put the most dollars in the pockets of the wealthy, everyone got a tax cut, however small. It was apparently of little consequence that the primary beneficiaries were the rich. The results raise intriguing questions. Would more voters oppose tax cuts for the rich if they were better informed? Or, as some say, is it simply that citizens favor benefits for the rich because they hope to join them someday (Bartels 2005; Lupia et al. 2007)? Americans are economic optimists. One poll showed that 76 percent believe that one can start out poor, work hard, and become rich (Page and Jacobs 2009, 51).

Class Differences on Noneconomic Domestic Issues

On noneconomic issues, liberalism tends to increase rather than decrease as one goes up the status ladder. Typical are the relationships between social class and opinions on the death penalty, abortion, gay marriage, and legal immigration, shown in Table 7.2. While the differences are not large, they are consistent. Reading the table across the columns, we see that support for gay marriage rises as one moves up the status ladder, as does support for abortion rights, and favoring increased legal immigration. Similar relations between status and opinion are found when people are asked about whether communists, socialists, or atheists should be granted the full range of civil liberties. Also high-status white respondents express less racial prejudice than their low-status counterparts (Kinder and Sanders 1996; Sniderman and Carmines 1997; Gomez and Wilson 2006).

Those with higher incomes tend to be conservative on economic issues, but on issues outside the economic realm status differences are complicated by the role of education. We saw in Chapters 5 and 6 that educational achievement promotes political tolerance and political liberalism. This liberalizing effect of education is, however, almost entirely limited to noneconomic issues. If we separate the effects of income and education on political attitudes, we find different patterns for economic and noneconomic issues. On noneconomic issues, high education but not high income is associated with liberalism. On economic issues, high income is negatively related to liberalism, but education is not.

Table 7.3 shows relevant examples. This table indicates that within low- and high-income categories, liberal opinions on the noneconomic issue of gay marriage increase with educational attainment. Note, for instance, the increase in support

---

TABLE 7.2   Opinions on Noneconomic Domestic Issues by Subjective Social Class (Whites Only)

Percent with Opinion	Working Class	Middle Class	Upper Class
Oppose death penalty*	15	30	35
Favor/allow abortion for any reason**	18	38	49
Allow gay marriage*	60	64	68
Allow books by homosexual in library**	37	77	82
Increase legal immigration*	7	15	29

Note: Opinion-holders include only those with a clear pro or con opinion. Those with a middle response, for example, "4s" on ANES seven-point scales, are excluded.

*ANES, 2012.

**GSS, 2008.

TABLE 7.3   Joint Effect of Income and Education on Selected Issues (Whites Only)

		Education		
		High School Only	Some College	College Graduate
For gay marriage (%)				
	Low	57	69	76
Income	Medium	62	62	67
	High	57	62	83
For more domestic spending (%)				
	Low	50	47	41
Income	Medium	40	36	35
	High	17	35	21

Source: American National Election Studies, 2012 election data. Percentages are based on opinion-holders (pro or con) only. For the full texts of the opinion questions, see the Appendix.

for gay marriage in the high-income group when we compare those with a high school education to those with some college to those with a college education. We see 57 percent of those with high income and only a high school education favor gay marriage compared to 83 percent with high income and a college degree.

The reverse pattern is apparent on the economic issue of domestic spending. As family income goes up, individuals become more conservative on domestic spending within categories of education. Thus, 41 percent of college graduates with low incomes want increased spending, compared to only 21 percent of college graduates with high incomes.

Class Differences on Foreign Policy

The major class difference on foreign policy attitudes is that people in the lower educational strata more readily take the isolationist position than the more internationally minded, better-educated strata. These sorts of class differences can be traced to the 1930s and 1940s, when isolationism had great appeal to the working class, while the middle and upper classes favored an active role for the United States in world affairs (Mueller 1977). In 1948, for example, 92 percent of the college educated favored an active role for the United States compared to only 59 percent with less than a high school education (Page and Shapiro 1992). As shown by the more contemporary data in Table 7.4, the better educated continue to favor an active role for the United States in world affairs, want a more powerful United Nations, are more willing to normalize relations with Cuba, believe that diplomacy is a better approach to international problems than military threats, and did not (back in 1993) view communism as harshly as those with less education.

TABLE 7.4   Education and Internationalism

Percent with Opinion	Less Than High School	High School Graduate	College Graduate
U.S. should take an active role in world affairs (2006)*	49	57	76
United Nations has too little power (2004)*	15	25	36
United States should reestablish relations with Cuba (2008)**	40	53	73
Communism worst kind of government (1993)*	63	49	36
Diplomacy better than use of threats in foreign relations (2004)†	39	53	62

*General Social Survey.

**Gallup.

†ANES.

We might expect that high-status people would be more willing to support military action abroad, as it is in some ways a logical extension of internationalism, just as isolationism implies keeping the troops at home. The accumulation of survey evidence presented in Table 7.5 shows a modest tendency on the part of those with higher levels of education to support American military adventures. In the case of Vietnam, support for the war in 1968 among the college educated may seem surprising because the most visible war opponents were found on college campuses. Only if we refine the educational index to isolate the small segment of people with graduate degrees or four-year degrees from the most prestigious universities was there disproportionate anti-Vietnam War sentiment at the top of the educational ladder (Rosenberg, Converse, and Schuman 1970, 54–65). Regarding the Gulf War of 1991, the education differences are considerable when respondents were asked if they agree that "all things considered, the [1991 Persian] Gulf War was worth the cost." We also see those with higher education were more likely to approve the handling of the later war in Iraq and the war in Afghanistan. However, as of 2012, the more educated citizens were *less* likely to support a military adventure in Iran.

Class Differences in Voting and Party Preference

Ever since the 1930s, socioeconomic class has been the principal factor dividing people into Republicans and Democrats. We can see this division persisting into the twenty-first century, using data from the 2012 American National Election Study. Figure 7.2 divides white respondents into five income groups from low to high, arranged as quintiles, with each group representing roughly one-fifth of whites in

Issue	Less Than High School (%)	High School Graduate (%)	College Graduate (%)
United States should expand the Vietnam War (1968)*	24	21	25
United States should be more involved in Central America (1986)*	19	21	25
The Persian Gulf War was worth it (1992)*	48	56	61
United States should commit peacekeeping troops to Kosovo (1999)**	44	49	63
Approve government handing of Iraq War (2008)*	17	24	28
Approve government handling of Afghanistan War (2008)*	16	23	26
Invade Iran to stop nuclear threat* (2012)	36	26	12

TABLE 7.5 Education and Opinion on U.S. Involvement in Foreign Countries

*American National Election Studies.

**Gallup.

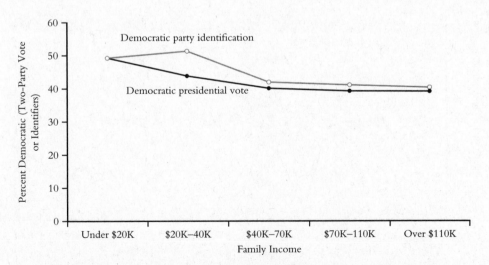

FIGURE 7.2 Democratic party identification and Democratic presidential vote by family income, 2012 (whites only).

Source: American National Election Studies, 2012 election data.

the sample. As one would expect, the figure shows that as one moves up the income ladder, the frequency of Democratic Party identification and frequency of Democratic presidential voting both decrease, although to only a modest degree. (There are many poor Republicans and rich Democrats.) Among the poorest fifth of white citizens, about half the partisans call themselves Democrats and about half the voters chose Obama. Among the richest fifth of white voters, Republicans outnumber Democrats 60 to 40 percent in party identification, while Romney outpolled Obama by about the same amount.

As measured by family income, class differences in politics have actually grown. Figure 7.3 shows the trend, with a comparison of the voting behavior of the top and bottom thirds of family income (for whites only) from 1952 through 2012. Although class voting receded somewhat in 2012 compared to 2008, as a general trend the rich and poor have grown farther apart politically.[2] Even as cultural issues have become more salient to voters, the partisan polarization of the rich and poor has increased (see also Stonecash 2000; Bartels 2008; Abramowitz 2010).

The growth in class voting may appear counterintuitive. It is sometimes presumed that the increased salience of cultural issues trumps economic issues to push working-class voters into the arms of the Republican Party. But this is not generally the case. It is true that the Democrats are challenged to win working-class votes if the working class is (awkwardly) defined as those without a college education. Education cuts differently than income. At one time, Republicans drew their strongest support from the best educated, just as they do now from the most affluent. But this trend has eroded so that in some surveys the most educated—particularly professionals with advanced university degrees—are the most Democratic. (Educated business leaders continue to lean Republican.) While the increased importance of cultural issues is largely responsible for the attraction of educated citizens to the Democrats, the poor as a group are decidedly more Democratic than the rich.[3]

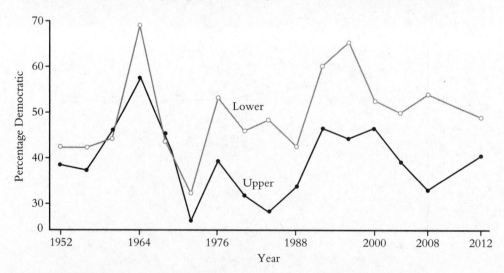

FIGURE 7.3 Major party Democratic presidential vote (whites only) by upper third and lower third of family income, 1952–2012.

Source: National Election Studies data.

7-2 Race and Political Opinions

The most profound political division between groups in the United States is between blacks and whites. While progress has surely been made, there is a wide gulf between blacks and whites on most political issues, particularly on those involving discrimination and its remedies. Of course, African-Americans are not the only racial or ethnic minority in America. The proportion of Latinos (Hispanics) and Asians is growing at a rapid rate, and the former now outnumber blacks as the largest minority group in the United States. However, neither group has the distinctive political opinions that characterize the black population.

Blacks, Whites, and Civil Rights

Until the late 1970s, the central division of opinion in the United States concerning the role of African-Americans was the very issue of a racially integrated society. In a 1964 ANES, respondents were asked if they favored "strict segregation" of the races, "desegregation," or "something in between." Not surprisingly, 73 percent of blacks favored desegregation, while only 6 percent favored segregation, with 21 percent favoring something in between. Among whites, about equal numbers chose strict segregation (25 percent) as desegregation (27 percent), with the remainder choosing something in between. But by 1978 (the last year this question was asked), only 5 percent of whites favored strict segregation—about the same as among blacks (6 percent). In 1964, the ANES shows 74 percent of whites thought civil rights leaders were "pushing too fast" compared to 11 percent among blacks. But by 1980 the percentage had dropped to 40 percent among whites, with blacks remaining essentially unchanged.

By the late 1970s, the political agenda on race shifted to the question of whether the government should actively help blacks move into the economic mainstream through preferences in education and employment or whether blacks themselves were responsible for their economic well-being. We can compare the distribution of these sentiments among blacks and whites using an ANES question asked in 1974, 1988, and 2012 as to whether the government should "make every effort to improve the economic and social condition of blacks and other minorities" or whether they should help themselves.

	Whites			Blacks		
	1974	**1988**	**2012**	**1974**	**1988**	**2012**
Government should help blacks	25%	25%	14%	63%	58%	42%
Unsure	26	24	24	25	21	28
Blacks should help themselves	50	51	62	12	21	30
	101%	100%	100%	100%	100%	100%

These are substantial differences between blacks and whites, with both racial groups now seeing less need for government action than they had before. There has been either a declining belief in the ability of government to solve racial problems or an increasing belief that such assistance is not as necessary as was once the case.

In recent years, much of the debate over racial policies has shifted to the arena of affirmative action. Given the dual emphasis in the American political tradition on equality and individualism, many well-intentioned citizens appear caught in a dilemma. First, there is a recognition that blacks historically have not had the same opportunities as whites, but there is also a belief that educational opportunities and jobs should be filled on merit, without reference to race, sex, or religion.

As one would expect, blacks are more supportive of affirmative action than whites. In 2012, the GSS asked if due to past discrimination blacks should be given preferences in hiring and promotion, or whether such preference is wrong because it discriminates against whites. The data are shown as follows:

	Whites (%)	Blacks (%)
Favor preferences for blacks in hiring and promotion	15	42
Oppose preferences for blacks in hiring and promotion	85	58
	100	100

As seen here, programs that imply preferences or quotas for minorities are highly unpopular with whites, while dividing blacks.[4] A majority of blacks, in fact, oppose affirmative action in this instance. As noted in Chapter 4, questions on affirmative action are sensitive to question-wording effects, as many of the terms employed, such as *quotas* and *racial preferences*, are politically charged. We can see this from the divisions in responses to a very similar question to the one earlier (this one from the NBC News/*Wall Street Journal* poll, 2010), where the affirmative action alternative rejects "rigid quotas."

	Whites (%)	Blacks (%)
Affirmative action programs needed "as long as there are no rigid quotas"	45	78
Not sure	5	7
Affirmative action programs "should be ended because they unfairly discriminate against whites"	50	15
	100	100

In this instance, whites are divided while blacks are one-sidedly favorable.[5] These opinion gaps are rooted in differences between blacks and whites concerning perceptions of the continued existence of racial discrimination. However, these differences, while not trivial, are declining. In 1996 ABC Polls found 70 percent of blacks calling racism "a big problem," compared to 44 percent in 2009. Among whites, the figures were 52 percent in 1996, declining to 22 percent in 2009.

But still there are vast differences in the extent to which blacks and whites see discrimination in their own communities. Among whites, in 2009, 83 percent believed blacks receive equal treatment in employment, compared to just 38 percent of blacks. Eighty-one percent of whites see equal opportunity in housing compared to 47 percent of blacks. Whites are less optimistic about blacks receiving equal treatment from the police (43 percent), but only 9 percent of blacks believe the police afford them equal treatment (ABC News, 2012). On a more upbeat note, 56 percent of blacks believe they have achieved racial equality or will do so soon; just 18 percent said it will never occur (ABC News, 2009).

Race and Political Opinions Generally

Next, we consider differences among racial groups in terms of political opinions generally. How do blacks and whites differ on issues that are tangential to civil rights? What about other racial groups, mainly Hispanics and Asian-Americans, whose shares of the U.S. public are growing?

Extending beyond matters of civil rights, members of nonwhite racial groups tend to be more liberal than the white majority on most issues (Harris 2011; de la Garza and Jang 2011; Junn et al. 2011; Abrajano and Alvarez 2012). Some examples are shown in Table 7.6, comparing African-Americans and Hispanics with whites in the 2012 ANES. (The ANES includes too few Asian-Americans for a separate analysis.)

Overall, racial minorities are more liberal than whites, except that variation is minimal on the cultural issues of gay marriage and abortion. In general we

TABLE 7.6   Race and Opinion on Selected Noncivil Rights Issues, 2012

Percent of Opinion-Holders	White	Hispanic	African-American
More domestic spending	35	71	84
Less defense spending	35	45	42
For Affordable Care Act (Obamacare)	45	70	89
Allow undocumented immigrants to stay in the United States	60	81	78
For guaranteed job, standard of living	27	54	68
Favor abortion rights	51	50	56
Allow gay marriage	65	67	56
For more gun control	39	68	61
Against death penalty	25	36	52
Liberal (of ideological identifiers)	34	61	53

Source: 2012 ANES data.

see Hispanics more liberal than whites and African-Americans more liberal than Hispanics. Hispanics appear as the most liberal group only on immigration (no surprise) and (mild surprise) in terms of ideological self-identification. Despite the fact that blacks are overwhelming Democratic, they tend on many social issues to be conservative. If Asian-Americans could be included in this table, they would be between whites and Hispanics on the liberalism scale (Junn et al. 2011). The sharpest distinction is the substantial black–white difference on economic issues such as the pace of domestic spending and whether or not the government should guarantee everyone a good standard of living. For whites, social class is a consistent correlate of opinion on these social welfare issues. However, for blacks there is no relationship. Upper-income blacks are about as supportive as lower-income blacks. The mostly likely explanation is the "linked fate" hypothesis (Dawson 1994). Most blacks believe their own economic well-being is linked to the overall progress of blacks as a group—a position most strongly held by upper-income blacks (Tate 1993). In 2012, 56 percent of blacks said their personal life is affected by what happens to blacks as a group (ANES). Upper-income blacks are more likely to identify with their race than with their social class. Upper-class whites, on the other hand, are more likely to identify with their social class.

Racial Groups and the Vote

In terms of the vote and party identification, there are major differences between blacks and whites. According to the 2012 National Election Pool exit poll, 93 percent of African-Americans, but only 39 percent of whites, cast their vote for Barack Obama. Latinos and Asian-Americans voted predominantly Democratic, although not nearly to the same extent as blacks. The 2012 vote choice for the four major ethnic groups in the United States is as follows:

2012 Vote	Asian-Americans (%)	Blacks (%)	Latinos (%)	Whites (%)
Obama	73	93	71	39
McCain	26	06	27	59
Percent of electorate	(3)	(13)	(10)	(72)

In Obama's two presidential victorious elections, minorities not only voted more Democratic than usual but also turned out at a greater rate than usual. In fact, according to the U.S. Census, in 2012 eligible African-Americans for the first time turned out to vote at a higher rate than eligible whites (Wheaton 2013). It can be argued that if blacks had voted at the same frequency in 2008 as in 2004, and had they voted Democratic at the slightly lower 2004 rate, Obama would have lost the presidential election to McCain (Ansolabehere, Persily, and Stewart 2010).

The voting differences we see among the races are also found in terms of the underlying attitude of party identification. Following are the racial divisions in party identification from pooled Pew surveys (N = 31,201) over the 2008 presidential campaign:

Party Identification	Asians (%)	Blacks (%)	Latinos (%)	Whites (%)
Democrat	38	77	45	31
Independent	42	20	35	35
Republican	20	4	21	34
	100	100	100	100

Whites as a group are slightly more likely to identify with the Republican Party than with the Democrats. In contrast, within each of the three minority groups, the Democrats hold solid pluralities in terms of party allegiance.

Once, between the Civil War and Franklin Roosevelt's presidency, most blacks who could vote opted for the Republican Party because it was the party of Lincoln. From the 1930s to the present, however, most blacks have supported the Democratic Party. Initially this shift was a response to economic issues rather than any consequential attempt on the part of the Democratic Party to remove racial barriers or explicitly appeal to blacks. Only in recent decades could the Democratic Party be identified as the party with clearly greater sympathy for the civil rights cause. As a result of the Democrats' increasing image as the more pro–civil rights party, Democratic voting among blacks at the presidential level has changed from a tendency to near unanimity. The change over time is shown in Figure 7.4. Clearly the black vote is a pivotal factor for the Democratic Party in presidential elections. In only one such election since World War II (1964) has the Democratic candidate received a majority of the *total* white vote.

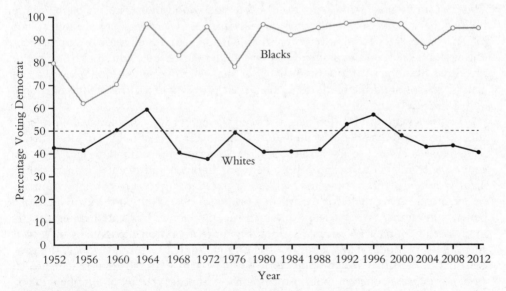

FIGURE 7.4 Race and the two-party presidential vote, 1952–2012.

Source: Gallup Poll, 1952–1976; American National Election Studies, 1980–1992; Voter News Service, 1996–2000; National Election Pool, 2004–2012.

Over the years, the share of the votes that are cast by racial minorities has steadily increased. By the middle of the twenty-first century, the majority of citizens (if not voters) is projected to be nonwhite. We see that nonwhites comprise a major share of the Democratic constituency. Not only are they growing, but black, Hispanic, and Asian-Americans are also becoming more Democratic in their voting behavior. A central question of American politics is whether the Republican Party can find ways to appeal to racial minorities and perhaps reverse their trend toward support for the Democrats.[6]

7-3 Age and Political Opinions

When we examine the breakdowns by age on the scores of political issues found in polls, we find instances of three possible patterns. On the majority of issues there are no meaningful age-group differences; on a sizable minority of issues, those older are more conservative than those younger; rarely are the young more conservative than their elders. As discussed in Chapter 5, there are two major reasons why older cohorts might differ from younger ones. First, there may be life-cycle effects in which the process of maturation results in changes throughout adulthood. People do generally grow more conservative with age. Second, there may be generational effects, with each group of young voters differing from those in the past. While increasing conservatism with age creates an age gap in opinions, so could generational differences of the type where each cohort of new citizens is more liberal than those that came before.[7]

The Politics of Age

This section focuses mainly on issues where young and older citizens have unique political perspectives on some issues, perhaps because of competing self-interest. For instance, advocates for children often blame inadequate funding for programs benefiting youngsters on the political power of older Americans, whom they accuse of greedily siphoning off more than their fair share of government dollars, or voting against school bond referendums to keep their property taxes low (Tedin, Matland, and Weiher 2001).

We see meaningful differences between the age groups on many economic issues. Younger adults are more likely to feel the government should provide a variety of increased services to its citizens, and are generally more likely to endorse new economic trends. For instance, those between eighteen and twenty-five are significantly more acceptant than their elders of outsourcing jobs to foreign countries rather than keeping them for American workers, and believe that the growing number of immigrants "strengthens American society" (Pew 2013). Reflecting its self-interest, the younger cohort is considerably more liberal on the issue of increased spending for student loans. On the issue of government health insurance, the generational differences are complicated. Senior citizens endorse government health care, but express concern about reform when it appears that extending benefits to others besides seniors, such as with Obamacare. When we turn to cultural issues, we find younger cohorts consistently more liberal than older ones. The young are more receptive to new ideas since they are, for the most part, not committed to old ones.

TABLE 7.7 Age and Opinion on Selected Issues

	Percentage Support Among Opinion-Holders		
	Under Thirty	Fifty-Five and Over	Difference
Economic Issues			
Government should provide more services and increase spending (2012)*	56	38	18
Approve of Affordable Care Act (Obamacare) (2012)*	62	47	15
Favor allowing Social Security funds invested in stock market (2012)*	72	46	26
Increase spending on student loans (1996)*	70	42	28
Social Issues			
Homeowners cannot discriminate on the basis of race when selling their home (2008).**	78	66	12
Oppose death penalty for murder (2012)*	32	29	3
Allow same-sex marriage (2012)*	77	48	29
Allow abortion for any reason (2012)*	37	40	3
Foreign Policy/Military Issues			
United States should decrease military spending (2012)*	45	33	12
Has Iraq War been worth fighting (2008)?†	26	35	09
Against invading Iran to stop nuclear threat (2012)*	77	75	2
Civic Orientations			
Follow political campaigns "always" or "most of the time" (2012)*	28	66	−38
Read newspapers about campaign (2012)*	28	64	−36
View Internet information about presidential campaign (2012)*	60	41	19
Liberal/Conservative Ideological Identification (2012)*			
Liberal	35	26	9
Moderate	36	25	11
Conservative	29	45	−16

*American National Election Studies.

**General Social Survey.

†ABC News.

This point can be illustrated using the 29 percentage point gap between those under thirty and those over fifty-five on the issue of gay marriage in Table 7.7 For those over fifty-five, it was inconceivable during most of their lives that this item would even be on the political agenda. Alternatively, those over thirty have heard dialog on the issue much of their lives.

On the issue of racial discrimination in housing, a once-robust generation gap has now largely disappeared. The reasons are instructive. For the 2008 GSS, there is just an 11-point gap between those under twenty-five and those over fifty-five who say they would allow homeowners to discriminate based on race when selling their property. This age gap was much greater in the past, for instance, 25 percentage points in 1996 and 32 points in 1988 (GSS). The age gap shrunk because those who grew up when it was commonplace to believe people could discriminate based on race are from an older generation that is rapidly departing the electorate and being replaced by a younger generation who reject discrimination.

On foreign affairs, it is often thought that the young are more wary of foreign intervention than their elders. However, the truth of that claim often depends on circumstances. In past conflicts, including World War II, Korea, and even Vietnam, the younger cohort has in fact been more supportive of U.S. involvement than those over fifty-five were (see Wittkopf 1990; Berinsky 2009). Currently, however, the younger generation is slightly more dovish on defense issues and military intervention.

Importantly, younger Americans in general are less interested and involved in politics than older generations (Wattenberg 2011). These differences are reflected in Table 7.7. For instance, in 2008 those over fifty-five were 11 percentage points more interested in the national campaign than those under thirty. Strikingly, in the 2012 ANES, oldsters were 36 percentage points more likely to read about the campaign in the newspaper. On the other hand, following politics on the Internet was far more common among the young.

The lack of political involvement among the young is clearest when it comes to voting participation. According to the Current Population Survey conducted by the U.S. Census, in the 2012 presidential election only 41 percent of eligible voters under twenty-five cast a ballot compared to 70 percent of those sixty-five and above. This is part of the political life cycle. Young people are preoccupied with other things besides politics—school, social life, learning to make a living, and so on—and often lack attachments to their local community. As they mature, they pay more attention to the world of politics, an interest that often does not reach its peak until well into old age. Especially in low-turnout elections, seniors greatly outweigh young people at the polls.

Of course an event such as Obama's campaign can temporarily arouse young people toward greater activity. According to the Bureau of the Census, the only group to show a significant increase in turnout between 2004 and 2008 were those between eighteen and twenty-four, who voted at a 49 percent rate, up 2 percentage points from 2004. Seniors sixty-five and older, by contrast, voted at a 70 percent rate,[8] the same as in 2012. In casting their votes, the young surged toward Obama to a degree not found among their elders. Exit polls show that in 2008 those under thirty gave 67 percent of their vote to Obama compared to 51 percent by the rest of the electorate, a percentage which decreased only slightly in 2012 (60 percent Obama, 37 percent Romney). Similarly, in terms of party identification, youth in 2008 and again in 2012 were almost twice as likely to call themselves Democratic than Republican, whereas as recently as 1992 the allegiance of young voters (under thirty) was virtually evenly divided between the two parties (Keeter, Horowitz, and Tyson 2008; Mellow 2013). Whether the recent cohort of young voters will continue to vote more often and more Democratic as they age remains to be seen, as does the voting behavior of the generation that will enter the electorate upon turning eighteen.

7-4 Religion and Political Opinions

Compared with other nations, Americans are religious (Norris and Inglehart 2004). In 2005 respondents in the World Values Survey were asked if they were or were not a religious person.[9] As we can see from the following table, the United States stands out in the high proportion of its citizens who find religion important in their lives.

	Am a Religious Person (%)	Am Not Religious (%)	Other/Don't Know* (%)
United States	72	24	04
Canada	66	27	07
Australia	52	38	10
Britain	49	41	10
Spain	46	47	07
France	47	36	17
Germany	43	38	19
Sweden	33	49	17
Japan	24	62	14
China	22	60	18

*Volunteered.

Most Americans belong to churches, although that was not always the case. At the time of the American Revolution, only 17 percent were church members. By the end of the Civil War the number had doubled to 35 percent, then increased to 53 percent by 1916, to 63 percent in the 1990s (Finke and Stark 1994), dropping slightly to 59 percent in 2012 (Gallup).[10]

Protestants, Catholics, Mormons, Jews, and "Nones"

Table 7.8 presents a basic inventory of religious preferences in the United States, drawn from the authoritative 2004 National Survey of Religion and Politics, with a large sample of 4,000 respondents.[11] The table shows 53 percent of American adults are Protestant, 22 percent are Catholic, 2 percent are Jewish, 6 percent are "other," and 17 percent profess no religious preference ("Nones").[12] Some major religious streams are further broken into subgroups. Protestants are divided into evangelical and mainline denominations, with evangelicals being the largest of the various religious subgroups. Churches considered to be evangelical are theologically conservative, stress being "born again," and believe in the inerrancy of the Bible, although this characterization is somewhat of an oversimplification. Predominantly, black and Hispanic denominations are considered separately. Catholics are divided into Anglo (white non-Hispanic) and Hispanic. The table treats Jews as a single group, as well as the "nones."

Table 7.8 shows Mormons are the most Republican and conservative followed by evangelical Protestant denominations. These two groups are also the most pro-life on abortion. At the other end, atheists/agnostics are generally the most liberal (although black Protestants are the most Democratic). "Nones" in general tend to be liberal. To be unchurched is to be outside the American cultural mainstream, and

TABLE 7.8   Religious Denomination and Political Opinions, 2004 (Percent)

	Party Identification		Political Ideology		Abortion	Size of Group
	Republican	Democrat	Conservative	Liberal	"Pro-Life"	
All respondents	38	42	40	28	48	100
Protestant	48	39	47	22	56	(53)
Evangelical	58	26	58	16	70	25
Mainline	44	40	41	30	35	16
Black	11	71	31	26	54	9
Hispanic	38	44	35	25	63	3
Catholic	36	47	39	31	50	(22)
Anglo	41	44	40	29	48	18
Hispanic	15	62	35	36	56	5
Jewish	22	68	22	57	16	2
Mormon	65	22	60	10	70	2
Other	27	38	28	32	46	5
None	26	43	25	39	27	17

Source: Adapted from Corwin Smidt, Lyman Kellsteadt, and James Guth, "The Role of Religion in American Politics," In Corwin Smidt (ed.), *Oxford Handbook of Religion and American Politics* (Oxford: Oxford Press, 2009); Mormon data is from the 2007 Pew Research Center study of Religion and American Life.

such marginality tends to result in a liberal political outlook. Mainline Protestants tend to be Republican and conservative, but less pro-life on abortion than the sample as a whole. Despite the doctrinal position of the Catholic Church on abortion, Anglo Catholics are no more pro-life than the sample as a whole. Hispanic Catholics tend to be Democratic and liberal, but are decided pro-life on the abortion issue. Only evangelicals and Mormons exceed them. Thus, it possible that both major parties can appeal to the growing Hispanic population—the Democrats on economic issues and the Republicans on cultural issues. Jews are notably Democratic, liberal, and pro-choice.[13]

Historically, politically relevant cleavages between Protestants, Catholics, and Jews were at their pinnacle in 1960, when Democrats broke with tradition and nominated a Catholic, John F. Kennedy, for president. The following table shows the presidential vote by religion (among Northern whites) in 1960 (ANES).[14]

Northern Whites	Protestant (%)	Catholic (%)	Jewish (%)
Voting Democratic (Kennedy)	28	83	83
Voting Republican (Nixon)	72	17	17
	100	100	100

Almost three-fourths of the Protestant vote among Northern whites was for Nixon, while over 80 percent of the Catholic and Jewish vote went for Kennedy. In more typical elections, without a Catholic candidate, the same ordering exists, but the differences are smaller. The following table shows the presidential vote divisions among (Northern white) Protestants, Catholics, and other (including "Nones") in the 2012 ANES. Among Northern whites, Protestants tilted more than two-thirds for Romney while Catholics almost divided equally. The remainder (Jews, members of other religions, and "Nones") were the most strongly for Obama. Two takeaways are that Protestants remain noticeably more Republican than Catholics and that non-Christians are the most Democratic of all.

Northern Whites	Protestant (%)	Catholic (%)	Other or None (%)
Voting Democratic (Obama)	31	46	64
Voting Republican (Romney)	69	53	36
	100	100	100

The temporal stability of partisan differences between Protestants, Catholics, and Jews is shown in Figure 7.5. For Northern whites, the figure displays the party identification (as percent Democrat of partisan identifiers) for the three religious groups between 1956 and 2012. The relative ordering of the three religious groups has been stable over the half century of polling: Jews most Democratic, followed by Catholics and then Protestants. Historically, Catholics have been more Democratic than Protestants, although this gap has noticeably narrowed in recent years.

One explanation for this once persistent Democratic voting among Catholics is that in the past American Catholics were less affluent than their Protestant

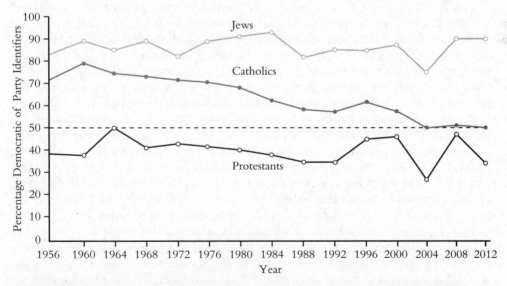

FIGURE 7.5 Religion and party identification (Northern whites only), 1956–2012 (2012 percent Jewish is for all religious non-Christians.)

Source: National Election Studies.

neighbors—a condition that would naturally cause them to gravitate to the Democratic Party for economic reasons. But there is more than economics at work, because during the 1940s, surveys showed that even affluent Catholics tended to be Democratic, much as affluent blacks are today (Berelson, Lazarsfeld, and McPhee 1954, 64–6). Besides, the Protestant–Catholic gap in income closed decades ago. The Democrats had traditionally wooed immigrant voters, most of whom were Catholic. The payoff of this policy for the Democratic Party has been the continued allegiance of many members of Catholic ethnic groups—the Irish, Italians, Polish, East Europeans, Filipinos, and Mexicans—who continue to identify and vote more consistently Democratic than Protestants, despite having incomes that place them solidly in the middle class. Perhaps the best explanation for the Democratic allegiance of Catholics is simply the socialization of partisanship from one generation to the next. Even though the social and economic reasons for remaining Democratic no longer exist, there is a family tradition of Democratic partisanship among Catholics that keeps them from turning Republican in spite of the erosion of the once firm Catholic allegiance to the Democratic Party.

Evangelicals, Mainline Protestants, Catholics, and Seculars

Of course to talk about religion and politics today, more is involved than the historical division between Protestants and Catholics. As discussed earlier, an important division today is between evangelical and mainline Protestants. Another is between those who regularly attend religious services and those who do not. This suggests the classification (Catholic churchgoers, evangelical churchgoers, mainline Protestant churchgoers, and "seculars" who do not go to church) shown in Table 7.9.

In Table 7.9, the four groups are compared in terms of their partisanship and opinion in the 2012 American National Election Study. We distinguish evangelical Protestants from mainline Protestants by the shorthand of whether they claim to be "born again."[15] Seculars include those who either claim no religion or if they do, say they "never" attend services, as one would not expect religion to have much sway over people who ignore their professed religion. To facilitate the estimation of religion's effects on political views, the table compares white respondents only. Basically, the table reveals seculars to be (relatively) on the left, evangelical churchgoers on the right, with Catholic and mainline Protestant churchgoers in the middle.

First, we look once again at partisan differences by religion. Among white voters, the group that most strongly supported Romney and opposed Obama was evangelicals. Seculars (nonreligious) were the group most strongly supporting Obama. This pattern is consistent with other recent elections (Smidt, Kellstedt, and Guth 2009).

The one set of political issues that divide religious groups more than any other is, of course, the cultural issues. Historically, people of strong religious faith tend to hold to traditional moral values, while seculars hold more modernistic values. Thus, the seculars are the most liberal on cultural issues, such as abortion and gay rights, and evangelicals stand out uniquely for their conservatism. This is not only true for abortion, as we saw in Table 7.8, but also for allowing gay marriage (as shown in Table 7.9).

TABLE 7.9   Religious Divisions and Political Views Among Whites, 2012

Percent of Opinion-Holders	Secular [Not a Church Goer] (43%)	Catholic Church Goer (16%)	Mainline Protestant Church Goer (16%)	Evangelical Protestant Church Goer (25%)
More domestic spending	46	32	37	29
Less defense spending	42	29	39	21
For Affordable Care Act (Obamacare)	51	51	52	35
Government should help blacks	23	18	21	10
For guaranteed job, standard of living	34	24	23	25
Favor abortion rights	60	43	52	27
Allow gay marriage	80	63	68	34
For more gun control	43	47	43	24
Against death penalty	24	36	24	19
Democrat (of party identifiers)	61	55	43	29
Liberal (of ideological identifiers)	52	30	34	20
Vote for Obama, 2008	57	50	52	23

Note: Opinion-holders include only those with a clear pro or con opinion. Those with a middle response, for example, "4s" on ANES seven-point scales, are excluded.

Source: 2012 American National Election Studies. Seculars include those with no religion and those who claim a religious denomination but do not attend services. Evangelical church attenders claim membership in a Protestant church and to be "born again." Mainline church attenders are all other members of Protestant faiths. Religiously observant members of the Jewish faith and non-Judeo-Christian faiths are omitted from the analysis.

Further differences by religious orientation can be found on domestic spending and foreign policy issues. Wilson (2009) analyzes the three survey questions on government spending programs used consistently in the ANES time series (services/spending, job guarantee, and health care). Over the years, the most consistently economically conservative have been evangelical Protestants. Table 7.9 shows this once again to be true in 2012. The most likely explanation is distrust of government, commitment to the Protestant notion of personal self-reliance, reinforced by messages from the pulpit (Wald, Owen, and Hill 1989; Jelen 1992; Djupe and Gilbert 2002). Closely following evangelicals are mainline Protestants, who are only slightly less conservative. Catholics have a history of liberalism on economic issues.

While some studies tend to find little linkage in general between religion and foreign policy opinion (Holsti 2004; Kohut and Stokes 2006; Pew 2007), evangelical Protestants do stand out as distinct. They tend to distrust the UN, favor increases in defense funding, support Israel and oppose a Palestinian state, and favor combating terrorism through military action (Page 2006).[16] Some current research focuses on the link between religion and support for U.S. engagement in preemptive military action such as in Iraq. The data from a variety of sources point to evangelicals as key supporters of this doctrine (Barker, Hurwitz, and Nelson 2008; Guth 2009).

The political differences we see between evangelicals and others—and to a lesser extent between the religious and the secular—are relatively new to American politics. Fifty years ago, evangelical churches rarely got involved in politics and one's religiosity had little bearing on one's political views. But back then there were few cultural issues on the political agenda to spur some religious people to defend traditional values and others, usually less religious, to push for change. At the same time, we should be cautious about stereotyping people politically from their religious beliefs. A significant minority of seculars are conservative just as a significant minority of evangelicals are on the liberal side of the political spectrum (Putnam and Campbell 2010).

To some extent, religion has contributed to today's polarization, as politics can sometimes seem like ideological combat between strident conservative and liberal political foes. Campbell, Green, and Layman (2011), for instance, demonstrate in an experiment that if a voter is informed that a candidate is an evangelical Christian, it increases support among Republicans and undercuts support among Democrats. On the other hand, identifying a candidate with a less polarizing denominational preference ("Catholic") has no effect.

7-5 Geography and Political Opinions

People commonly think of American public opinion as differing along regional lines. The South stands out in particular for its political conservatism, particularly on civil rights and cultural issues. Outlandish fads (political and otherwise) are thought to start in the West, most notably in California. The East is often characterized as being liberal (every New England congressional district elected a Democrat in 2008). There have been other regional stereotypes that once may have been valid but seem less so today. The South, for example, was once the most international-minded region in foreign policy, largely because of the cotton growers' interest in free trade with other nations. The Midwest at one time had the reputation, seemingly deserved on the basis of poll results, for being the most isolationist (least internationalist) region of the country (Hero 1973).[17] The long-term trend shows little loss of regional distinctiveness in party preference.

Several factors, however, serve to undermine the impact of region. Americans are mobile (20 percent move each year) and dilute the native citizenry. Only 40 percent of adults say they currently live in the same locale as they did when they were sixteen years old (GSS 2012). The near-universal penetration of the national media would seem to have a homogenizing effect on regionalism. But we should not overstate the case. On many issues, meaningful regional differences persist, especially between the South and the remainder of the country.

In the twenty-first century, the media introduced a new set of geographic terms to the political lexicon. It became common to identify states as "red" (Republican) or "blue" (Democrat) based on their presidential voting. Fiorina et al. (2011) analyzed differences in public opinion between blue and red states using the 2000 and 2004 ANES. They found surprisingly small opinion differences and no evidence of a "culture war." (See also Levendusky and Pope 2011.)

Using data from the 2012 ANES, we compare residents of "red" states which went Republican in 2012 with those of "blue" states which went Democrat. For comparison, we use the summary 21-point ten-issue scale of liberalism–conservatism introduced in Chapter 3. With a possible range of +10 to −10, the red states lean slightly to the right and the blue states to the left. The differences are shown in Figure 7.6 Out of ten issue questions, the average citizen in a Republican state will give the conservative response to about 5.5 questions compared to 4.5 for the average citizen in a Democratic state. While this is a real difference, it is hard to make argument for severe issue polarization based on how states cast their electoral college vote (for a somewhat different take on polarization, see Abramowitz 2010).

It is only recently that commentators have been talking about red and blue states. The most common way to divide the country has been by region (Northeast, Midwest, South, and West) and by urban/rural. Taking region first, analysis of public opinion

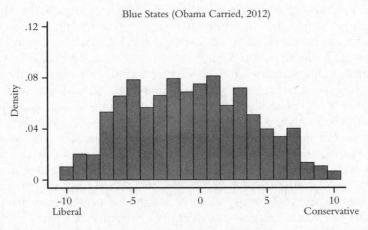

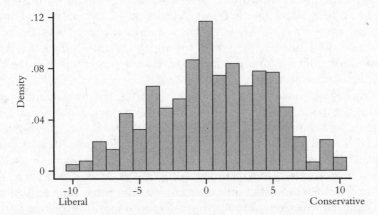

FIGURE 7.6 Liberalism–conservatism of public opinion in "red" states (won by Romney, 2012) and "blue" states (won by Obama, 2012).

Source: Data from 2012 ANES. See the Appendix for the derivation of the index.

data from the millennium forward shows that on virtually all cultural issues—such as school prayer, gay rights, allowing communists to speak in one's community, abortion, and gun control—the South is markedly conservative. The South is also markedly conservative on foreign policy issues. Its residents want to spend more on defense and are more likely to endorse the use of military force to settle international conflicts. These distinctive opinions represent the cultural conservatism of the South.

Just as on some issues the South is uniquely conservative, the Northeast is uniquely liberal. We illustrate with some examples from a 2009 Pew poll. For example, 67 percent in the Northeast favor legal abortions in all or most cases, compared to 49 percent in the South, and 59 percent in the West.[18] Similar patterns can be found for civil liberties, prayer in the schools, and gun control. For instance, 60 percent of people in the Northeast favor allowing gay marriage versus just 30 percent in the South. The other two regions fall in between. Fifty-eight percent in the South believe books with dangerous ideas should be banned, compared to 41 percent for the rest of the country. Those in the South are also most likely to favor protecting gun ownership over gun control (52 percent) versus just 35 percent in the Northeast. Again, the Midwest and the West fall in the middle. The South also stands out as having citizens most likely to believe that the best way to insure peace is through military strength (64 percent). For the rest of the country, it is 52 percent. In the South, 58 percent say torture is often justified against suspected terrorists, compared to 43 percent in the West, with the other two regions falling in between. On immigration, the West is unique in that 78 percent favor providing illegal immigrants with a route to citizens, while a lesser 62 percent of the South and Midwest favor this position. One area where there is almost no difference among regions is attitudes toward business. In terms of ideological self-identification, 46 percent in the South call themselves conservative, compared to 40 percent in the Midwest, 37 percent in the Northeast, and 34 percent in the West.

But are regional differences in fact related to a regional culture, or are they simply compositional effects? For instance, the South's cultural conservatism is at least partially due to its adherence to evangelical Christianity. While composition does account for much of the observed regional differences, there is certainly some truth to this view; individual state culture does make some contribution to one's partisanship and political ideology (Erikson, Wright, and McIver 1994). For example, even with demographic factors held constant, residents of, say, Minnesota are more liberal than, say, Oklahoma. There is something about state culture that affects partisanship and ideology beyond the fact that residents may differ in their religion, income, education, or race.

Other than state residence and regional groupings, the most common geographical division is between cities, suburbs, small towns, and rural areas. It is generally thought that urban areas are sources of liberal and nonconventional political attitudes, with rural and small-town America being the bastions of conservatism. This is the pattern we see in the 2008 Pew merged data set, where (for whites only) among rural respondents, 38 percent identify as conservatives, compared to 23 percent classified as living in urban places. Earlier analyses by Yang and Alba (1992), using GSS data and focusing on nonconventional opinions, show that residents of urban areas are much more liberal on these domains than are those living in small towns and rural areas. A study by Wilson (1985) shows urban residence has a positive association with political tolerance.

At least part of this variation is due to composition effects. City residents show up as more liberal in surveys because they have a large proportion of people with liberal group characteristics, such as blacks, gays, Jews, and secular nonchurchgoers. Small towns and rural areas are conservative because they are disproportionately evangelical and, outside the South, contain few blacks. But not all these urban/rural differences disappear when controls for composition effects are introduced. In fact, most remain statistically significant, although reduced in magnitude. Fischer (1975, 428) advances an "urban subculture" theory, which holds that urban residents are more nonconventional in their political opinions because urban life provides a *critical mass*, meaning "the congregation of numbers of persons sufficient to maintain viable unconventional subcultures." In other words, there is something about urban life—perhaps social diversity or the existence of support groups—independent of the social background of the residents that attracts liberals to move there and influences residents to become more liberal or nonconventional than those living in small towns and rural areas.

The Changing American South

The once distinctive South (the old Confederacy) is gradually losing its unique political character. The reasons are complex but certainly involve the economic boom that began after World War II, migration (many blacks left the region in search of jobs, while many Northern whites moved into the region for the same reason), plus rapid industrialization of the region with attendant liberalizing consequences.

The South's original distinctiveness spans many elements of opinion and political behavior. We have discussed the South's conservatism on cultural issues. The uniqueness of the South was associated even more with a conservative stance on racial questions and overwhelming support for the Democratic Party. In recent years, surveys show only small differences between white Southerners and the rest of the nation on race. In terms of partisanship, white Southerners have shifted from being predominantly Democratic (but conservative) to overwhelmingly Republican.

Over the past half century, the white South has adapted to the end of racial segregation. Table 7.10 shows the dramatic decline in the difference between Southern and non-Southern whites in response to the question of whether or not one favors the principle of black and white children attending the same school. In 1956, the differences between the South and the rest of the nation were substantial. By 1985 (the last year the question was asked), there was almost no difference of consequence between the whites in the South and whites in the rest of the nation on whether black and white children should attend the same schools.[19] For the 1994 ANES question on whether "the federal government should see to it" that blacks and whites attend the same schools, there was no difference between whites in the South and the rest of the nation (38 percent in both regions favored government action).

Not all are convinced by the New South argument. Measuring racial hostility is difficult, given the social norms that surround the race issue. The most racially prejudiced may in fact be the most likely to hide their true feelings. Using a method

TABLE 7.10   School Integration Opinion Among Whites by Region and Education, 1956 and 1985

	Favor Blacks and Whites Attending the Same School	
Non-South	*1956 (%)*	*1985 (%)*
Less than high school	58	86
High school	67	98
Some college or more	79	99
South		
Less than high school	8	67
High school	20	93
Some college or more	30	98

Source: 1956 data adapted from Howard Schuman, Charlotte Steeh, and Lawrence Bobo, Racial Attitudes in America (Cambridge, MA: Harvard University Press, 1985), p. 78; the 1985 data are from the General Social Survey.

to disguise racially sensitive questions, Kuklinski, Cobb, and Gilens (1997) report considerably more racial resentment among white Southerners than among whites outside the South.[20] For example, 42 percent of white Southerners expressed anger at the thought of a black family moving in next door, compared to 10 percent of non-Southern whites (Kuklinski, Cobb, and Gilens 1997, 329–30). Their conclusion is that many white Southerners are giving insincere answers when asked directly about racial issues.

The initial attachment of the South to the Democratic Party goes back, of course, to the Civil War, but it was reinforced by economics. The South was long the poorest region of the country—a plus for the Democratic Party, given its image of providing jobs and benefits to the average person. Until the Voting Rights Act of 1965, blacks were effectively disenfranchised in much of the South, meaning that the Democratic Party of the South was largely a white party. Strategically, the white South had gained by staying with the Democrats because its prominent position stymied the party's Northern liberal wing to act on blacks' pressing demands for civil rights legislation. Then, the parties began to diverge on civil rights at about the moment that blacks began voting in heavier numbers. The next forty years or so saw a rapid decline in the white South's allegiance to the Democratic Party. Today, whites are more Republican in the South than in any other region, and the South has become the most dependably Republican region in terms of voting, first only for president but now more generally for other offices as well.

Figure 7.7 documents Republican gains in the white South in terms of party identification. In 1952, Democrats outnumbered Republicans by an 8 to 1 ratio in the white South. By 2012 Republicans outnumbered Democrats by more than 2 to 1 (with an even greater Republican tilt in voting behavior).

The survey evidence regarding the white South's growing Republicanism reveals the importance of long-standing party attachments. Older Southern whites who

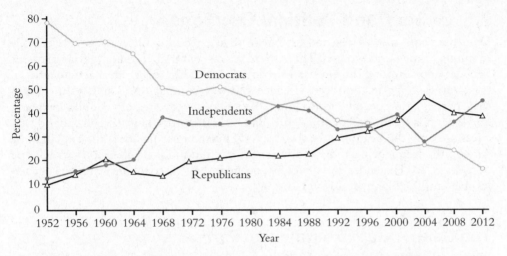

FIGURE 7.7 Party identification among white Southerners, 1952–2012.

Source: National Election Studies.

grew up during the Democratic era have been more resistant to Republicanism than young Southerners, who flock to the Republican Party unburdened by the habits of lifelong Democratic identification (Green, Palmquist, and Schickler 2002). We can see this pattern even today in the following table, based on pooling multiple Pew surveys from 2008. Among whites outside the South, it is older partisans who are the most likely to call themselves Republicans, as expected. Among white Southerners, however, age makes little difference, with one exception: It is the very oldest partisans, who (as of 2008) were eighty-five years of age or older, who are the most resistant to the Republican label. The gradual exit of this older generation of Southern whites has contributed to the growing Republicanism in the South.[21]

	Percent Republican Identifiers				
2008	**18–24**	**25–44**	**45–64**	**65–85**	**85–**
Southern whites	63	63	63	59	51
Non-Southern whites	45	49	45	48	52

It is not just that young white Southerners have become more Republican; they are now considerably more Republican than their white counterparts in the North. It is paradoxical that younger Southerners show the most movement to the Republican Party even though polls have shown them to be more liberal on racial and cultural issues than their elders. The nature of this attraction has been debated by scholars. Some emphasize a latent racism among Southern whites as the cause (Carmines and Stimson 1980; Valentino and Sears 2004). Others insist that the source is the white South's cultural conservatism on social issues and foreign policy (Abramowitz 1994). The matter remains unresolved.

7-6 Gender and Political Opinions

Over the years, survey researchers began to see growing differences between the opinions of men and women. This difference has entered common parlance as the "gender gap." Among the consistently documented differences are party identification, voting, opinions on force, violence and war, compassion issues, political efficacy, participation beyond voting, and political knowledge (Kanthak and Norrander 2004; Mondak and Anderson 2004; Dolan 2011). However, observed gender differences are only the beginning of the story. Of much consequence is the explanation. Among the frequently cited are differences in childhood socialization (Wolak and McDervitt 2011), gender roles, biology, occupations (Norris 2006), and even genetics (Hatemi, Medland, and Eaves 2009).

The Gender Gap in Voting and Partisanship

In the early days of survey research, it was thought that there were few differences between men and women in partisanship, voting, and political opinions. Although women participated less than men, they were thought to be indistinguishable from them on questions of party and voting, with perhaps a few minor differences on issue positions. In fact, according to ANES data, between 1952 and 1964 women voted more Republican than men, with the largest gap being 6 percent in 1956. Had the 1960 election been decided by women only, Richard Nixon would have defeated John F. Kennedy—despite the lore about Kennedy's boyish good looks being an asset among female voters.

In 1968, women began voting more Democratic than men, but it was not until the 1980 election that considerable media attention were devoted to the gap between male and female voting for president. In 1980 the gap between male and female vote choice was 8 percent. The gender gap weakened somewhat between 1984 and 1994, but emerged again strongly in 1996, when women voted 13 percent more Democratic than did men—currently the largest gap (in terms of presidential voting) for which we have data. In 2012, the gender gap was 10 percent, with 55 percent of women voting for Obama compared to 45 percent of men (NEP).

The pattern we see for voting also appears for party identification. Since 1988 women have been about 10 percentage points more Democratic than men (ANES). This Democratic tendency in identification is particularly noticeable among unmarried and well-educated women, but disappears when comparisons are made between male and female married respondents. For instance, the 1997 wave of the Michigan socialization panel shows that for the 1996 presidential election unmarried men were 41 percent points more likely to vote Republican than unmarried women, but there was no difference between husbands and wives (Stoker and Jennings 2005).

The conventional wisdom about the gender gap is that over the years women became more Democratic as greater numbers entered college and the workforce, and became more attuned to their own political agenda. However, the notion that the gender gap was created by women becoming more Democratic in their partisan preference and vote choice is wrong. The data show just the opposite. The voting behavior and partisan behavior of women has remained within a narrow band since 1980. Meanwhile, men moved decidedly in the Republican direction. It is this decisive movement among men that accounts for most of the gender gap in partisanship and vote choice (Kaufmann and Petrocik 1999; Kaufman 2006).

Still the gender gap expands and shrinks. We might initially conclude that this shifting around has to do with the candidates and issues in particular elections. Mostly, that is not the case. Rather, the gender gap is a dynamic process that exists independently of elections. Box-Steffensmeier, De Boef, and Lin (2004) use CBS polls aggregated quarterly between 1977 and 2004 to study the gender gap in partisanship between elections. Poor economic conditions hurt women more than men. In periods of high unemployment, women are more likely to gravitate to the Democratic Party than are men—increasing the gender gap. As economic conditions improve, the gender gap in partisanship shrinks.

The Gender Gap in Political Knowledge

One of the largest and most analyzed gender gaps occurs between men and women on political knowledge (Kenski and Jamieson 2000; Dolan 2011; Wolak and McDervitt 2011). Media polls frequently report large knowledge gaps between men and women. For instance, in 2007 Pew queried the political knowledge of the public using a twenty-three-item test. Forty-five percent of men scored in the "high" knowledge category compared to 25 percent of women.[22] Holding key background factors constant (such as education, age, and race) has only a modest effect in reducing these differences.

However, men and women respond differently to multiple-choice questions, creating the illusion of a larger gender gap than really exists. Given a multiple-choice knowledge test, men are more likely than women to guess at the correct answer than say "don't know" (Rapoport 1982, 1985). Perhaps this gap is a residual of childhood socialization where boys are taught to be aggressive and girls to be more nurturing. Obviously, if men are guessing more than women, some of the guesses are going to be right, while "don't know" answers can never be right. The consequence is that men score higher on measures of political knowledge. Mondak and Anderson (2004) estimate that this different propensity to guess accounts for as much as half the gender gap in political knowledge. Still, even with background controls and corrections for guessing, there exists a nontrivial political knowledge gap between men and women that has yet to be fully explained. It is, however, worth noting that when men and women are quizzed on gender-relevant political information items, the gender gap disappears (Dolan 2011).

The Gender Gap in Issue Opinions

Women and men often differ in their opinion on issues. Table 7.11 presents gender differences in selected issue domains. Since the 1930s, surveys have shown that women are less prone to endorse violence and aggression in any form, be it at the personal level, regarding capital punishment, or in foreign affairs regarding matters such as war (Berinsky 2009). The table shows the same 18 percentage point gender gap in 2004 regarding the war in Iraq as it does for 2009 regarding the war in Afghanistan. These gender differences have also appeared in other conflicts. Women were 12 percent more likely than men to say it was wrong for the United States to

TABLE 7.11   Gender and Political Opinions

Opinion	Percent Among Opinion-Holders		
	Men	Women	Difference
Force, Violence, and Aggression			
Government should decrease defense spending (2012)*	36	38	+2
Want stricter gun control laws (2008)*	36	52	+16
Oppose death penalty over life in prison for capital murder (2009)**	38	54	+16
Iraq War not worth fighting (2004)†	38	46	+18
Oppose Afghanistan War (2009)**	40	58	+18
Oppose invading Iran to combat nuclear threat (2012)*	76	74	−2
Compassion			
Spend budget surplus on social programs, not tax cut (1999)*	49	64	+15
Government should provide health insurance (2008)*	46	54	+8
Government should provide more spending and services (2012)*	40	49	+9
Increase spending on the poor (2012)*	40	48	+8
Civil Liberties/Civil Rights			
Legalize same-sex marriage (2012)*	62	67	+5
Favor legalization of marijuana (2012)*	44	38	−6
Allow communists to speak (2008)††	72	64	−8
Reduce crime by solving social problems (1996)**	27	33	+6
Favor government aid to blacks (2008)*	24	24	0
Gender-Related Issues			
Abortion should be available for any reason (2012)*	45	41	−4
Men and women equally suited for politics (2008)*·†	63	67	+4
Increase spending for child care (2008)†	49	54	+6

Note: Opinion-holders include only those with a clear pro or con opinion. Those with a middle response, for example, "4s" on ANES seven-point scales, are excluded. But note exception on the women's role question.

*American National Election Studies.

**CNN/ORC

†Strong agreers opt for "1"—the most pro-equality option on the ANES 1–7 scale.

††General Social Survey.

get involved in the 2001 Gulf War (ANES 1992). There was a similar gender difference in support of the Korean War and the Vietnam War, with women typically being 8 to 10 percent less enthusiastic than men. This gender difference on foreign affairs has important electoral consequences. When elections tend to turn on questions of human rights and issues of war and peace, the gender gap in voting increases, with women moving to favor Democratic candidates.

These differences on violence and aggression are probably due to the interplay of socialization and biology. There is a large body of research showing that men have a greater predisposition than women do to use force (Schlesinger and Heldman 2001). The socialization of young boys frequently emphasizes aggression (witness playground games), while such aggression is discouraged in young girls. Another possible explanation is that women are more risk averse than men (Tedin and Yap 1993). For example, 31 percent of men but only 5 percent of women favor building more nuclear power plants (ANES Pilot 1991).

Women are generally more supportive of a compassionate approach to political issues than are men, but the differences are not as large as the gap for the use of force and violence. Still, there are meaningful gender differences on spending for social programs, health insurance, and assisting the poor, as seen in Table 7.11. When large differences appear, they are usually on issues that address specific hazards rather than more general society-wide problems. For example, in addition to differences in support for building nuclear power plants, substantial gaps have been documented in support for the 55-mile-per-hour speed limit, for state laws requiring seatbelts, and for stiff jail terms for drunk drivers.

On civil liberties issues, men and women usually do not differ. One exception is that women have historically been more supportive of gay rights than men, although the 2012 ANES shows a modest 4 percentage point difference on same-sex marriage. Note the 9 percent difference favoring men on willingness to allow a communist to "speak in your neighborhood." These differences are not limited to the United States but show up in Western Europe and the former Soviet Union as well (Norris 1988; Tedin and Yap 1993; Tedin 1994a). Controls for background factors reduce, but do not eliminate, these differences. In the case of civil rights, even though women sometimes benefit from affirmative action programs, they generally differ little from men in their opinions. Table 7.11 shows no gender difference on aid to blacks and a 1 percent difference on affirmative action for minorities.

Perhaps surprisingly, on most gender-related issues the gender gap is small to nonexistent. Women are more in favor of increased spending for child care, but on most other gender issues there are either quite modest gender differences or, occasionally, differences that seem to run counter to self-interest. In twenty-one successive readings of the General Social Survey, men have been at least as supportive of abortion "for any reason" as have women. In some early GSS surveys, men were as much as 10 percentage points more supportive, although the gender gap on abortion has essentially disappeared in recent years (as shown in Table 7.11).

One reason for this pattern is that on many issues that directly concern women there is a greater gap among women themselves than between women and men. Take, for instance, the label *feminist*. Women accepting this label tend to be highly educated and affluent. Their voting patterns are as we might except. In the 2012 ANES, the roughly one-quarter of women who rejected the feminist label voted almost 3 to 1 for Romney over Obama, 77 to 23 percent. Meanwhile the roughly half who favored the feminist label voted for Obama by two to one (66 to 34).[23]

We see clearly the class division among women by looking at the 2008 ANES question that asks if "women should have an equal role with men in running business, industry, and government," or whether "women's place is in the home." Women disagree among themselves on the answer to this question more than they disagree with men. The line of stratification divides working women and home-makers and divides on level of education. Sixty-seven percent of working women chose the most equalitarian category (option 1 on a seven-point scale), compared to only 44 percent of the homemakers. Among working women with a college degree, 71 percent chose the most egalitarian option. Only 36 percent of homemakers with no more than a high school education chose this option. Although support for women in the workforce continues to increase as full-time working women have become commonplace, there are lifestyle distinctions about what makes one an important and worthwhile person that split the political opinions of women.

7-7 Conclusion

Group characteristics can clearly make a difference in how people see the political world. Belonging to a group is part of one's self-identification. Many groups have a vested political interest. Being prosperous and economically secure encourages one to believe that through one's own effort success can be achieved, and government should be limited in its ability to spend tax money to aid those who have not been successful in life's competition. Being poor encourages the opposite perspective. Race, religion, gender, region, and age also intrude on one's life in a fashion not entirely neutral, consequently coloring the way one sees the desirable organization and ends of the polity.

Over time, certain group distinctions may increase or decrease in importance. Some see cultural differences in terms of religion leading to further political polarization. Group distinctions that may increase in political relevance are those between the young and the old, the Sun Belt and the Frost Belt, and the technologically skilled and unskilled. These potential cleavages may at some point replace traditional sources of voting alignments, such as partisanship or class. If that happens, the benefits that government bestows on its citizens, as well as the obligations it demands, may also change.

Critical Thinking Questions

1. People of differing social classes often have differing political opinions. Are these class differences simply due to one's personal self-interest?
2. People with differing religious orientations often have markedly differing political opinions. Why do you think religion affects people's political views?
3. Polls demonstrate that men and women often have differing political views, with women being more liberal and democratic than men. Why do you think this gender gap has arisen?

Endnotes

1. "Public Opinion and Demographic Report," *Public Perspective* 4 (May/June 1993): 85.
2. The increased partisan divide based on income is also found when party identification is substituted for the vote. Even occupational class has held its own as a predictor of the vote when multivariate controls are imposed (Manza and Brooks 1999).

3. It can also be observed that the richest states tend to vote more Democratic than the poor states. While the reasons for this are complex, it is also true that within each state, the rich vote more Republican than the poor. The poorer the state, the more the rich vote Republican (Gelman et al. 2008).

4. There is greater racial division on questions involving racial preferences in education than on jobs, with blacks more one-sidedly favorable to affirmative action in the realm of education opportunities. More blacks, as well as more whites, are likely to endorse programs that create equality of opportunity rather than equality of outcomes.

5. Sigelman and Welch (1991) analyzed answers to a large number of affirmative action questions and found that depending on question wording, as many as 96 percent of blacks and 76 percent of whites were favorable, or as few as 23 percent of blacks and 9 percent of whites were favorable. They also found that those affirmative action programs that get the most support from blacks also get the most support from whites.

6. Within the category of Hispanic (Latino) or Asian-American, there are further variations in political viewpoint, based on national origin. Given that they were exiled from Castro's Cuba, Cuban-Americans tend to be Republicans, unlike Hispanics generally (Abrajano and Alvarez 2012). As a legacy of the Vietnam War and its aftermath, most Vietnamese-Americans tend Republican, unlike Asian-Americans generally (Junn et al. 2011). African-Americans also can differ politically based on national origin, since many are recent immigrants from the Caribbean or from Africa. See Greer 2013.

7. Generational differences can be a function of compositional effects, as when more recent political generations hold opinions different from their elders because of their greater levels of education.

8. The ratio of the senior voting rate to the youth voting rate, which approaches 3 to 1 in midterm years, drops to about 3 to 2 in presidential elections.

9. Data available at www.worldvaluessurvey.org.

10. The Gallup questions is, "Do you happen to be a member of a church or synagogue?"

11. For a detailed description of the survey, see Green (2007).

12. These proportions belonging to different religious groupings have changed little over the decade since the survey.

13. Smidt et al. (2010, 52) finds that Republican support among all religious groups declined by the time of the 2008 election.

14. We use only northern whites so as not to confuse the effect of denominational preference with race and region. The South is largely Protestant and conservative; blacks are largely Protestant and liberal.

15. In Table 7.8, recall, the division between mainline versus evangelical Protestants was based on the denomination. Smidt (2009) offers a thoughtful discussion of alternative ways of measuring the politically relevant divisions within American Protestantism.

16. Page (2006) argues these links are indirect, a function of partisanship and political ideology.

17. To take an example of one-time regional differences in foreign policy isolationism, Southerners, when asked in 1945 whether the United States and Russia "should make a permanent military alliance," responded favorably by a ratio greater than 2 to 1. At the other extreme, a slight majority of Midwesterners opposed such an alliance (Cantril 1951, 961). By the late 1950s, such disparities had largely disappeared (Key 1961a, 134).

18. Pews Values Survey conducted April 14–20, 2009. Data set downloaded June 11, 2009, data analysis by authors.

19. As almost everyone now endorses the principle of white and black students attending the same school, the question has not been asked by the GSS since 1985.

20. Kuklinski and colleagues randomly gave one-half of the sample a list of three nonracial items and asked how many of the items make them angry—importantly, not which one,

just how many. The other half of the sample got the same three items plus an additional item addressing race, such as "a black family moving in next door." Again, the respondents were asked how many make them angry. Only the additional item for half of the sample getting four options addresses race. Thus, respondents saying two of four items anger them assume the interviewer cannot know which two—which indeed he or she cannot. However, statistical methods can be used to determine the level of anger about "a black family moving in next door" among Southerners and non-Southerners as a group.

21. Even as the oldest generation of white southerners resisted the Republican label, they still voted Republican for president at a rate similar to their younger counterparts.

22. Pew Research Center, "Public Knowledge of Current Affairs Little Changed by News and Information Revolutions" (Released April 15, 2007).

23. Women were defined as "feminists" or "nonfeminists" using the ANES 100 point feeling thermometer. Those rating feminists higher than 50 were classified as "feminists"; those rating them below 50 points were classified as "nonfeminists."

CHAPTER 8

The News Media
and Political Opinions

LEARNING OBJECTIVES

- Explain the difference between the *new media* and what went before
- Analyze the claims that there is bias in the news

- Describe *agenda setting* and *priming*
- Describe the *Fox News effect*

Our political beliefs are shaped by the political information we receive, and most of this information is transmitted through the mass media. In totalitarian political systems, the regime attempts to shape this information by controlling outlets for the news. In democracies, the mass media are relatively free of government control. Indeed, it is difficult to imagine free democratic elections without a free flow of competing information in the mass media.

However, the proper flow of political information requires more than the government simply allowing an unfettered mass media to print or broadcast free from political interference. Much of what we read, see, or hear in the mass media comes from newspapers, magazines, television, radio, and Internet outlets that are owned by large private conglomerates, such as Comcast, Disney, and News Corp. Within these institutions, individuals with complex motives and incentives decide what to print, broadcast, or post. These motives and incentives range from a commitment to report the news thoroughly and objectively, to packaging the news for profit like any other commercial product, to using corporate power over the media to preserve the economic and political status quo or to press for a unique ideological agenda.

Defined most broadly, the content of the mass media extends beyond matters of politics to include all aspects of information and entertainment. Although it can be tempting to read political implications in the entertainment portions of media content, that is not our concern here. Our focus is on political news and commentary in newspapers and on the radio, television, and the Internet. In this chapter we discuss the nature of the news media, their possible biases, and the effect of the media on public opinion.

8-1 The Evolution of the American Media

The evolution of the media can be divided into five eras (West 2001).[1] The first is the Era of the Partisan Press (1787–1832). During this period, the press was simply an arm of the political parties, with parties or factions reaching out to their supporters via newspapers. At one time, the newspaper of the Federalists, the party of Alexander Hamilton, was the *Gazette of the United States*. For the Democratic-Republicans, the party of Thomas Jefferson, it was the *National Intelligencer*. It was the parties that arranged financial support and appointed the editors. The job of each newspaper was to promote the party's issue positions and criticize opponents. The *Gazette*, for example, ran numerous stories about sexual misconduct between Thomas Jefferson and his slave Sally Hemmings. Due to limited population literacy and high subscription costs, these were not mass circulation newspapers. Rather, they were directed at the elite of each party, providing some news and instructing the faithful about the issue positions the party championed. It was fully understood that objectivity was not a goal in reporting the news.

The Era of the Commercial Media began in 1833 with the advent of the penny press. Newspapers now sold for a penny (vs. 6 cents in the earlier era), which—along with rising literacy—allowed for mass circulation. With the invention of the telegraph, in 1848 newspapers organized the Associated Press, which gathered information from around the world. Political news could be delivered to newspaper editorial desks from all parts of the country hours or even minutes after it happened.

The penny press also entertained its readers with human interest stories and sensational reports of crimes and disasters. Importantly, the press now made a profit—often a substantial profit. This financial success allowed the press to free itself from control by the political parties and gave rise to powerful independent editors who could package news stories as they saw fit. However, this packaging was often strongly partisan and sensationalistic, a practice referred to as *yellow journalism*. Among the most flamboyant practitioners of yellow journalism was William Randolph Hearst. He used his newspapers to promote his politics. By claiming that the explosion that sunk the U.S. battleship *Maine* in Havana harbor was the work of Spanish agents, he provoked a public outcry for a war between the United States and Spain.[2] The practice of yellow journalism tended to undermine the credibility of the press. The media would have to transform themselves yet another time before gaining the confidence and respect of the public (Bettig and Hall 2003).

The new century (1900) saw the dawning of the Era of the Objective Media. Previously, reporters were not professionals; they had no specialized training or professional values that guided their work. Recognizing a need, newspaper magnate Joseph Pulitzer provided funding to establish a school for journalism at Columbia University. Other schools soon followed. Journalists were trained to be *objective*, defined by the American Society of Newspaper Editors as "free of opinion or bias of any kind." Commensurate with their new status, reporters now had bylines—that is, the reporter's name appeared along with the story. This innovation allowed the public to hold reporters accountable for what they wrote.

The coverage of the Vietnam War and Watergate represented the high point for the objective press. The glaring light of publicity was brought to bear on matters of the highest importance by investigative journalists. Woodward and Bernstein became household names for investigations that ultimately brought down the Nixon White House. Walter Cronkite, anchor of the CBS evening news, was once cited as the most trusted man in the United States. Public confidence in the media was at an all-time high. There was talk of the media establishment as a coequal "fourth branch of government" (Cook 2007).

The fourth Era of Interpretive Journalism began about 1980 and soon cascaded into a fifth, which can be labeled the Era of Fragmented Media. The Era of Interpretive Media ushered in a rejection of the ideal of objective journalism for a more interpretive style. This trend accelerated with the new availability of cable/satellite TV and the Internet, which fragmented the market for news considerably. With the two trends of interpretative journalism and fragmentation, media sources have become increasingly diverse and often partisan, allowing people to seek out media outlets fitting their political perspective. A feedback process commenced, leading the current state of affairs where one can easily find media outlets that cater to any partisan political taste.

Interpretive Journalism

The trend toward interpretative journalism reflects a general skepticism about the possibility of holding to a standard of strict objectivity that arose in intellectual circles in the 1980s. Facts do not speak for themselves; rather, they need to be understood in context. This development coincided with the career aspirations of journalists, who want to add their independent and unique contribution to the political debate—their "journalistic voice." They do not simply want to report the news; they want to analyze it. Reporters became less inclined to behave as lapdogs for politicians, as some have characterized their role during the Era of the Objective Press (Sabato 1993).

This shift to interpretive journalism is not simply a changing taste on the part of working reporters; it reflects a change in how editors and executive producers see the market for news. In the realm of politics, news consumers demand more than hearing and reading what the politicians have to say (Iyengar, Norpoth, and Hahn 2004). Journalists today do not see their job as helping politicians get their story out directly to the public. Rather, journalists see themselves as standing between politicians and the public. Politicians do not talk to citizens; politicians talk to journalists. It is the journalists who talk to the public. They see their job as analyzing and interpreting for the public the often ambiguous or misleading messages being delivered by political leaders. Thomas Patterson (1996) argues that this interpretative style empowers journalists by giving them significant control over the news message. It places the journalist at the center of the news story.

There are substantial empirical data to document this change. For example, journalists increasingly speak for candidates rather than candidates speaking for themselves. The average length of the candidate sound bite (candidates speaking for themselves) on the network news has decreased dramatically. In 1968 these sound bites averaged 43.1 seconds. By 2008 they averaged only 8.9 seconds (Farnsworth and Lichter 2011). Any glimpse of cable news channels would show the speaking time allotted to journalists dominates the broadcast. Presidential candidates often get more speaking time on late-night television (like the *Tonight Show*) than they do on the nightly news. A similar pattern can be found in the print media. For the *New York*

Times in the 1960s, the vast majority of the news stories (91 percent) were descriptive. By the 1990s, the vast majority (84 percent) were interpretative (Patterson 1994, 82; see also Gilens, Vavreck, and Cohen 2007). Rather than direct communication from politicians, much of what the public hears today is the analysis of journalists.

The Fragmentation of the Media

Thanks to deregulation and technological innovation the actual number of media outlets has skyrocketed over what was available just a few years ago. Cable and satellite TV gave rise to channels like MSNBC, CNN, and the Fox News Network, which cover the political news twenty-four hours a day, seven days a week. The Internet revolution, offers unlimited access to political information any time of day. Political Web sites proliferate, often with a decided ideological tilt. Anyone can set up his or her own political blog, and some have become quite popular and even profitable. Depending on one's preferences, there is news with a liberal slant and news with a conservative slant.

Figure 8.1 shows the dramatic decline in two sources of political news—daily newspapers and the networks' evening news shows on broadcast television. Measured on a per household basis, newspaper circulation and the audience for the traditional network evening news shows have both declined by about half since 1980. The bulk of the defectors have moved to the newer media sources, such as cable television and the Internet. Table 8.1 offers further details of the change in audience, based on Pew surveys, where people are asked where (if anywhere) they

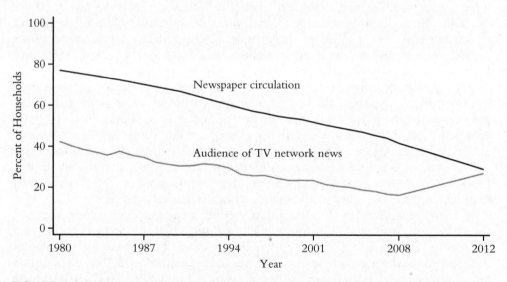

FIGURE 8.1 Downward trends in the audience for two traditional media sources of news.

Source: Based on the data compiled from Tables 4.1 and 4.2 in Harold W. Stanley and Richard G. Niemi, *Vital Statistics on American Politics 2013–2014* (Washington: CQ Press, 2013), augmented by data from *Editor and Publisher* and Pew Web sites.

TABLE 8.1 Audience for Traditional Media and New Media

	1991	1996	2000	2004	2008	2012
Watch news on TV %	68	58	56	69	57	55
Read a newspaper %	56	50	49	43	35	29
Listen to the radio %	54	44	43	42	34	33
Get online/mobile news %				24	34	39

Question: Which of these did you do yesterday?

Source: Based on Pew Research Center, "In Changing Landscape, Even Television Is Vulnerable" (September 27, 2012), http://www.people-press.org/2012/09/27/section-1-watching-reading -and-listening-to-the-news-3/.

got their news the previous day. It should not surprise that fewer now get their news from newspapers than either the radio or the Internet.[3]

These trends have been ongoing. The percentage of households subscribing to a daily newspaper peaked in 1950. The percentage getting news from the network television peaked in 1970 (West 2001, 131). Meanwhile, the first cable news channel came online in 1980. Talk radio was not a major factor for political discourse until 1988, when it was reinvented by Rush Limbaugh. And no one got his or her news from the Internet prior to the mid-1990s.

It is also important to understand that television as a news source is not so much in decline as simply fragmented. There is now a wider menu from which to choose. Even today, more people watch local TV news than watch network news than watch cable news. Heavy viewers, however, focus on cable news shows. The proportion of households who watch any cable news over the course of a month is 38 percent (Olmstead et al. 2013). Over a given month, more households will have tuned at least once to CNN than Fox News or MSNBC, but they do not always stay for long. The Fox political audience is the most loyal, often sticking with the network for long sittings. For this reason Fox's political commentary and news programs have the highest ratings of all cable news networks. While about a third watch cable news at some point during a month, the amount of attention is often slim. At any given moment during prime time only 1 percent of U.S. households are tuned in (Prior 2013). It is a small but a politically attentive audience.

The fragmentation of news media outlets has had several important effects on how people get the news. One consequence of the greater competition among news outlets may be the quality of news reporting and the amount of information about current events that people receive. With twenty-four-hour news channels and Internet news sources, interested news consumers can catch up with current events at a speed previously unimaginable. Yet, despite the new diversity of choices and contrary to American culture's celebration of the virtues of competition, some observers conclude that the fragmented media have actually lowered the quality of the news. John Zaller (2004b) presents evidence that in-depth coverage of issues decreases as competition increases. He concludes that journalists produce better-quality news when insulated from market pressures.

The diversity of choices has had further consequences. Today's consumer of television news can choose from a menu of cable all-news outlets—Fox on the right, CNN more mainstream, and MSNBC with mainly liberal commentary.[4] For more information, opinion, and analysis, the avid news consumer can turn to the incredible diversity of the Internet, where each network and major newspaper has its Web page, or to sites for political opinions and analysis of all ideological stripes. In a fragmented media market, people have the ability to ideologically customize their sources of political information. Not surprisingly, studies show that the audience for Fox News is predominantly Republican, while the audience for CNN and especially MSNBC leans Democratic.[5]

The ability of people to ideologically customize their sources of political information contributes to the increasing ideological polarization of the electorate discussed previously. Before cable television and then the Internet, everybody who watched the news on television observed a common content from the assertively nonpartisan network news programs. Now when people can rely solely on news sources that fit their ideological niche, they become less open to alternative viewpoints. As a result, initial opinions intensify and are reinforced, possibly contributing to rancor in public discourse that had previously been absent (Mutz 2007).

Paradoxically, the expansion of the media menu may contribute to a decline in political information—at least in some segments of society. At one time the evening news had a monopoly on television viewing. There was no competition for the nightly news, so a person either watched nothing or watched the news. In the current media environment, the news has to compete with entertainment for its audience. The result is that those most interested in politics with access to cable/satellite TV and the Internet have many choices, resulting in high levels of political information. Those with access to cable/satellite TV and the Internet with little or no interest in the news can avoid it entirely and turn to strictly entertainment channels.

The result is an increased division of information levels between the politically interested and knowledgeable on the one hand and the disinterested and voluntarily ignorant on the other. Prior (2007) demonstrates that for those without cable or Internet access, interest in politics has little relationship to political knowledge. But among those with access to the Internet, cable/satellite TV, or (especially) both, interest leads to increased knowledge and disinterest leads to increased ignorance. The least informed of Prior's subjects were those with potential access to many sources of information but who were uninterested in politics. With Internet and cable/satellite, this group was able to tune out politics in favor of other pursuits.[6]

A related consequence of the fragmented media is a decline in the power of the president and other leaders to hold people's attention (Baum and Kernell 1999; Cohen 2008). Cable/satellite TV had ended the "golden age" of presidential influence via television. The multiplicity of media options has significantly diminished the president's ability to reach a large national audience. Previously, when presidents chose to address the nation, they had a monopoly on prime-time television. Viewers could either watch the address or seek entertainment other than television. In 1969, a routine press conference of President Richard Nixon drew 59 percent of the potential national TV audience. In 1995, a major prime-time news conference by President Clinton attracted only 6.5 percent of households with television. While access to cable news may allow greater attention to the details of contemporary politics, television viewers are freed from reliance on the broadcast networks. Analyzing the 1996 presidential debates, Baum and Kernell found, when controlling for key background variables, those without cable television—a captive audience— were 7 percent more likely to have watched the first debate and 9 percent more likely to have watched the second debate than those with cable television.[7] This fragmentation is not lost on network executives, who appreciate that the cost of carrying a prime-time presidential address is the loss of audience share to cable competitors. "Going public" had become an important leadership tool for the modern presidency. The current focus on audience share and profits may mean the president has lost an asset that will be difficult to replace (Baum and Kernell 1999).

It is widely believed that the rise of the Internet has one important victim— the American newspaper. Although newspaper circulation rose by 6 percent in 2012 with its intense presidential race, this was the first annual circulation gain in a decade (Newspaper Association of America 2013). Newspapers have adapted by developing their own Web sites, and, as a result, paradoxically, some are now actually reaching more readers than ever before. But by generally offering free access on the Web, newspapers online must make money by advertising on their Web sites, which to date has yielded disappointing revenue. As a result, news content suffers, reporters are laid off, and a downward spiral persists. News media decision makers are vexed by this set of circumstances. For now, readers on the Internet enjoy wide access to newspaper content. But over time the content of what they read will suffer in quality unless newspapers can find an alternative revenue model.

8-2 Bias and Negativity in the News

In the Era of the New Media it is important to make a distinction between professional journalists and news commentators. The evening news anchors like Brian Williams at NBC or Diane Sawyer at ABC are expected to be scrupulously fair, as are the reporters in the major newspapers. On the other hand, news commentators like Bill O'Reilly (Fox) and Rachel Maddow (MSNBC) are not expected to be objective. They are "news entertainers" not professional journalists.

Although professional journalists pride themselves on the fairness of their news coverage, critics from both the left and the right complain that the "hard news" media, even though staffed by professionals, are biased and lack objectivity. Could it be the case that the media *are* seriously biased, or are ideological critics too quick to blame the messenger when they dislike the message? *Objectivity* has proven notoriously difficult to define. Like beauty, it is very much in the eye of the beholder. Objectivity is so elusive that it was dropped from the code of ethics by the Society of Professional Journalists. It was replaced in the ethics code by "truth, accuracy and comprehensiveness" (Bennett 2003, 192). One reason is that objectivity can imply passing along messages from government officials without subjecting them to critical scrutiny—a practice some would say on its face is nonobjective, given the ability of those in government to dominate the news. But to what extent do the media cover the news with truth, accuracy, and comprehensiveness? Given the complexity of the question, it is not surprising there is no agreed-upon answer.

Critics on the political left charge that as business operations are dependent on business advertising for their profits, the media tilt their coverage to the right. Critics on the political right see a liberal bias to the media, with liberal journalists slanting the news to the left. Both liberals and conservatives have nonprofit organizations with Web sites devoted exclusively to exposing press bias. Accuracy in the Media (http://www.aim.org) and Newsbusters.org (http://newsbusters.org) are two Web sites devoted to exposing liberal bias in the news. On the other side of the spectrum, Fairness and Accuracy in Reporting (http://www.fair.org) and Media Matters (http://mediamatters.org) are designed to ferret out bias in the conservative direction. Neither side lacks compelling examples. On the other hand, the academic literature has concluded—at a minimum—there is no systematic and pervasive ideological bias in the media to the advantage of one side or the other (Patterson 1994; Groeling and Kernell 1998; Farnsworth and Lichter 2011; D'Alessio 2012).

Criticism of the mainstream media is occasionally subtle and can extend beyond blanket charges of bias based on ideology. Some say because the mainstream media try to appeal to the broadest possible audience, they constrict the flow of ideas in the safe middle range (Bennett 1980, 304–44). Yet others argue the reverse. They claim that much of what is presented in the news are the views of the far left and the far right, each given about equal time in the interest of fairness. According to this view, rigorous in-depth reporting and analysis of the news has mostly disappeared.[8] Some see the media as too uncritical of government officials out of a need to protect their access to news sources (Hertsgaard 1988; Press and Verburn 1988). But others again see the reverse, with journalists giving a particularly hard time to incumbent officeholders (Patterson 1994). As we will discuss, one of the more serious charges against the media is that to maintain the interests of their audience, news outlets promote an overly cynical outlook as they focus excessively on negative news.

In this section we discuss two sorts of claims about the content of the media. First, is the news biased in a liberal or conservative direction? Second, as some charge, are the news media unduly negative in their reporting?

Liberal Journalists

Is there a liberal bias to the news media? One foundation for the claim that the news is biased in a liberal direction comes from the fact, confirmed by many studies, that journalists themselves tend to be much more liberal and Democratic than the American public as a whole. Further, the most liberal and most Democratic journalists tend to work for the prestige news sources, such as the *New York Times* or network news (Weaver and Wilhoit 1996). Shown in Table 8.2 are data contrasting the opinions of journalists and everyday citizens from a 1985 *Times-Mirror* survey and a 1992 survey sponsored by the Freedom Forum (see also Dautrich and Deneen 1996). Although the findings may seem dated, there is no reason to believe that the distinctions shown between journalists and the public have narrowed. A 2004 Pew survey of the press found liberals outnumbering conservatives by a margin of 33 to 7 percent (with the remainder mainly self-described "moderates") (Pew 2004).

TABLE 8.2	Views of General Public and Journalists on Selected Issues		
		Public	**Journalists**
Consider self	Left (liberal)	18%	47%
	Right (conservative)	34	22
Consider self	Democrat	34	44
	Republican	33	16
Sympathize with	Business	33	27
	Labor	32	31
Government should reduce income inequality	Favor	55	50
	Oppose	23	39
Increase defense budget	Favor	38	15
	Oppose	51	80
Allow women to have abortions	Favor	49	82
	Oppose	44	14
Prayer in public schools	Favor	74	25
	Oppose	19	67
Death penalty for murder	Favor	75	47
	Oppose	17	47

Source: David H. Weaver and G. Cleveland Wilhoit, *The American Journalist in the 1990s* (Mahwah, NJ: Erlbaum, 1996), pp. 15–18; William Schneider and I.A. Lewis, "Views on the News," *Public Opinion* 8 (August–September 1985), p. 7.

Journalists are particularly more liberal than the public on cultural issues like abortion and the death penalty, as can be seen in Table 8.2. However, journalists may be more conservative than the public when it comes to economic issues. At a time when only 23 percent of the public opposed government action to reduce income inequality, 39 percent of the journalists were opposed (Schneider and Lewis 1985). The national press corps in Washington is relatively highly paid, and these data may reflect their class interest.

It is interesting to speculate why journalists lean to the left politically. Although some conservatives might argue differently, there is no evidence that news organizations reward reporters and other workers based on their political ideology. The reason news employees show a liberal political tendency is not that conservative aspirants are cast aside for their political views. To some extent, the liberalism of journalists, especially outside the economic sphere, simply reflects the values of young urban college-educated professionals—the class from which journalists are drawn. Another factor may be that journalism attracts people with liberal personality traits, much the same way that a military career attracts conservative personalities.

Conservative Ownership

If some claim that the media are biased to the left because of the political views of news media employees, what about the opposite charge that there exists a conservative bias to the news media? The foundation for the claim of conservative bias starts with media ownership. Newspapers are businesses whose owners are most interested in the financial bottom line. Gilens and Hertzman (2000) found significant differences in how newspapers covered congressional debate on the 1996 Telecommunications Act, designed to ease restrictions on corporate ownership of multiple media outlets. The newspapers owned by those who would benefit from the passage of legislation downplayed monopoly issues. The authors concluded that financial self-interest not only affected the editorial page but leaked into the straight news reporting as well. Because of newspaper owners' special interest in the fate of monopoly ownership, Gilens and Hertzman's finding of biased news coverage may be more the exception than the rule. A study by Gentzkow and Shapiro (2010) of the general ideological slant of newspapers finds news coverage to be generally unrelated to newspapers' ownership. Corporations that own multiple newspapers in different markets leave little imprint on the content. Rather, to the extent they slant their news left or right, it is toward the direction of reader opinion.

If there is a conservative tendency to the American news media, the most obvious manifestation is on the newspaper editorial pages. Unlike most television and radio stations, newspapers regularly take positions on issues. And while television and radio stations do not formally endorse candidates during election season (due to FCC rules about equal time), newspapers routinely endorse political candidates on their editorial pages. Going back at least to the 1930s, newspapers have endorsed far more Republican than Democratic candidates. This historic tendency makes it all the more remarkable that in recent presidential races most newspapers endorsed the Democratic candidates, first Kerry against Bush in 2004 and then by an even larger margin for Obama in 2008. In 2012, Romney might have had a slight edge in the number of endorsements by daily newspapers, but Obama enjoyed a major edge in terms of newspaper circulation.[9]

Two factors readily account for newspaper publishers' tradition of Republicanism and conservatism. First, newspaper publishers are businesspeople. Their conservative Republicanism is a natural extension of the prevailing orthodoxy of the business community. Second, a newspaper's advertisers also represent the conservative business community. Although major advertisers only rarely threaten to withdraw their ads from newspapers because of their political stands, newspaper publishers know they must depend on advertising for the major share of their revenue.

Biased News?

The liberalism of journalists does not necessarily mean that their ideological preferences filter into news stories, nor does the conservatism of their bosses (and newspaper editorial pages) necessarily spill over into the reporting of the news. It is plausible that both the liberalism of journalists and the conservatism of their bosses influence the presentation of the news, with each offsetting the other. Objective measurement of possible bias is difficult, complicated by loud voices on the left and right claiming to quantify the existence of bias by the other side.

The public discussion of bias tends to bog down in narrow debates between competing protagonists, with each side presenting its own mostly anecdotal evidence. For instance, the conservative former CBS newsman Bernard Goldberg (2001) claims to have identified one way in which TV newscasts promote liberalism as the mainstream. He charges that network newscasts repeatedly label conservative political figures as "conservatives" while leaving their liberal counterparts unidentified ideologically. Goldberg claims the networks see liberal positions as the norm and identify those taking positions on the right as "conservative" to alert viewers they are out of the mainstream. Liberal media critic Eric Alterman (2003) dissents, saying Goldberg presents only anecdotal evidence to support his contention. Alterman cites counterevidence where the networks label conservatives and liberals evenhandedly. Even if it were true that network newscasts disproportionately pin ideological labels on conservative politicians more than liberal politicians, this would fall far short of proof that the network newscasts, or the media at large, routinely distort the news to favor the liberal point of view. On the other hand, critics say this tendency is simply one sign of a much larger problem.

Academic studies of presidential campaign network news coverage suggest that the networks attempt to achieve balance. Network news shows devote roughly equal time to both major party candidates, and network journalists insist that their news judgment is unaffected by personal political preferences. But are they evenhanded in the tone of their stories about presidential candidates?

Pew's Journalism Project (a.k.a. the Project for Excellence in Journalism) has rated the tone of a sample of print and broadcast media about the candidates for the four presidential elections held in the twenty-first century. The data are summarized in Table 8.3. The tone tilts toward the negative. Averaging the media tone of these four elections, 43 percent of the media comments about the candidates were negative, with just 21 percent being positive (the rest were neutral).[10] The Republican and Democratic candidates got about the same negative coverage in 2000 and 2012, with the Republican getting more hostile treatment in 2004 and 2008.

In evaluating claims of bias or favoritism in the news, we must consider that an observable tilt in the tone to favor one candidate over the other could represent the actual reality of the news rather than a bias by the media. It important to understand that "good" news for one candidate and "bad" news for the other can

---

TABLE 8.3 General Election News in Media: Tone of Coverage, 2000–2012

	2000	2004	2008	2012
Democrat nominee positive %	13	34	36	19
Democrat nominee negative %	56	25	29	30
Republican nominee positive %	24	14	14	15
Republican nominee negative %	49	59	57	36

Source: Based on Pew Research Journalism Project; http://www.journalism.org/numbers/tone-of-media-coverage-of-bush-and-gore-debates-2000/; http://www.journalism.org/numbers/tone-of-media-coverage-of-bush-and-kerry-debates-2004/; http://www.journalism.org/2008/10/22/barack-obama/; http://www.journalism.org/2012/11/02/winning-media-campaign-2012/.

easily represent the reality of campaign events. For instance, candidates who do well in debates (e.g., Bush in 2000 and Kerry in 2004) get scored with more favorable media treatment (see also Farnsworth and Lichter 2007). In 2012, the Pew data showed that following Obama's flat performance and Romney's strong performance in the first debate, the tone of media coverage tilted in Romney's favor. Of course, the most plausible causal interpretation is that the debate performances generated changes in the tone of the media narrative. It is not plausible that media tone simply changed for no discernible reason. Presumably, no one would argue the press should shy away from positive coverage about a candidate who seems to capture public enthusiasm or manufacture good news about a candidate who falters.

In another investigation of bias, Groseclose and Milyo (2005) examined the "think tank" and advocacy groups cited as sources over a ten-year period by the print and broadcast media. They scored the left–right ideology of policy think tanks and advocacy groups based on the ideology of Congress members who cited these sources in the *Congressional Record*. Then they counted the frequency with which the various media cited these sources in their news coverage. The bottom line is that media outlets more often cited liberal sources than conservative sources. Policy advocacy groups favored by conservatives in Congress are relatively ignored as sources by the media. The authors conclude that the news media interpret the news with a liberal slant (see also Groseclose 2011).

Not surprisingly, Groseclose and Milyo's study has been criticized for its own possible ideological bias. What the study does show is a fact with multiple interpretations. One rival interpretation is that instead of indicating bias, Groseclose and Milyo's results arise because congressional conservatives cite conservative sources with inferior intellectual credentials. If so, the media are not likely to use them as sources.

In a more recent paper, Gentzkow and Shapiro (2010) scored phrases used by members of Congress by the ideological leanings of those who used them. Based on these same phrases, they then scored several newspapers by the "slant" of their news coverage based on the extent the same political phrases were found in the news pages. While their research shows that newspapers slant their coverage in accord with readership ideological taste, they find little evidence of a general pattern of bias to either the left or the right.

The search for an overall bias in the media is a difficult if not fruitless quest (see Groeling 2013 on the challenges). For example, all studies show that Fox News Hour is to the right of the broadcast networks' evening news shows. The argument is over the location of a possible neutral point. And we should pause before using the preferences of the average Congress member as the standard. The goal of a free press ought not be the successful mirroring of government preferences.

Whatever the final verdict on bias in news reporting, there exists no even balance when we turn from the reporting of the news to opinion or commentary. Any liberal favoritism in news reporting is offset by the conservative tilt of media commentary. Thus, as one meta-analysis of bias studies concluded, maybe when the full range of voices is considered, the net bias of the news media balances out to "zero" (D'Alessio 2012).

Particularly in the Era of Fragmented Media, conservative voices have come to significantly outnumber liberal voices. To the conservative dominance of newspaper editorial pages, which has long been in place, one must add talk radio and cable news punditry. Talk radio, in particular, is dominated by conservatives. Every one of the top ten radio talk shows has a conservative tilt.[11] On national radio there are no liberal equivalents to Rush Limbaugh, Laura Ingraham, and Michael Savage. The tilt is not as pronounced on cable news channels. But Fox News's stable of conservative commentators—Bill O'Reilly and, farther on the right, Shawn Hannity—consistently draw larger audiences than MSNBC's Rachel Madow and others on the left.

The Public's View of Media Bias

Among the general public, many believe that the media are not entirely objective in covering the news. When people were asked about "bias in the media" in a 2013 Gallup poll, 46 percent said the "news media" were "too liberal," while only 13 percent said they were "too conservative" (37 percent said it was "about right"). Similar numbers were recorded in 2013 when Pew respondents were asked whether the news media are best described as "liberal" (46 percent), "conservative" (26 percent), or "neither" (19 percent). When people are asked if press criticism does more good than harm, surveys from the Reagan to Obama administrations show opinion depends on which party is in power. Those who share the partisanship of the incumbent president are always the least likely to applaud media criticism, although typically majorities within both parties say it does more good than bad.

Some degree of skepticism about the media is probably healthy. Still, if taken too far it can undercut the ability of the press to credibly inform the public in a fashion necessary for citizens to hold elected officials accountable. Despite the numbers, there is reason to doubt that the situation is as gloomy as it might appear. There is a tendency for partisans to see any unfriendly criticism as media bias, and, as we saw earlier, criticism is the norm in today's news. Provocatively, Dalton, Beck, and Huckfeldt (1998) demonstrated there is virtually no connection between the liberal–conservative tilt taken by newspapers and reader perceptions of that tilt. Dalton and his colleagues used content analysis and a representative sample of newspapers in forty counties to measure the actual ideological slant of the news and a survey to measure the perception of that slant by newspaper readers. They found no meaningful correspondence. What they did find was that in the 1992 presidential race, strong Republicans saw their paper as slanted toward Clinton and strong Democrats saw their paper as slanted toward Bush.

The results reported by Dalton and his associates are consistent with a good deal of experimental research on the hostile media phenomenon, which holds that people are predisposed to see bias when the press covers topics important to them. In one study, two groups on opposite sides of the Middle East issue (either pro-Arab or pro-Israeli) were given a news story about conflict in the area and asked to evaluate it. Both sides tended to see the story as biased against their position. However, the two sides read exactly the same account (Vallone, Ross, and Lepper 1985).

As we detail in the following section, it is apparent why some people at both ends of the political spectrum might see the news as biased. Much of the content of the media is negative in tone. As citizens look at media content through the colored glasses of partisanship, it is easy to conclude that one's own political values are not getting a fair share.

Negativity in the News

While there remains disagreement about ideological bias in the news, a much stronger case can be made that in recent years the tone of the media has turned profoundly negative, and not just in campaign coverage by network news. According to Thomas Patterson, the real bias in the media is an "ingrained cynicism" (Patterson 1996). In an analysis of stories in *Time* and *Newsweek* about presidential campaign coverage, Patterson (1994) found the negative content of this coverage increased dramatically beginning in 1980. In 1960, only 25 percent of the stories were negative, but by 1976, 40 percent were negative. Over half were negative in 1980, and in 1992, 60 percent of the stories were negative. According to Groeling and Kernell (1998), in 1991 when the popularity of George H.W. Bush reached 90 percent in some polls, barely half his media coverage was positive.

Why has the press become more negative toward politicians over recent decades? One explanation holds that relations between politicians and the press have become increasingly adversarial. In recent years, politicians have aggressively tried to control the flow of the news, which detracts from the ability of journalists to do their job. A mutual dislike has arisen, resulting in the negative coverage of political personalities (Zaller 2004b). A second explanation is economic. The conviction in financial quarters that the news must be entertaining to be profitable has led to a focus on sensational stories, scandal (real or imagined), and "gotcha" news coverage of those in public life (Sabato, Stencel, and Lichter 2000; Farnsworth and Lichter 2011).[12] Whatever the reason, the media are a good deal more aggressive in exposing potentially embarrassing actions by public officials than they were in the past.

While there is agreement that cynicism in the news has increased substantially when compared to the past, there is disagreement about how this trend affects public opinion. Some make the controversial claim that the decline in political trust and/or the continuing low levels of political trust can largely be blamed on the negative media (Patterson 1994, 22; but for a different view, see O'Keefe 1980). Experimental studies show that people exposed to negative stories about government are more likely to be distrusting than an equivalent control group (Cappella and Jamieson 1997), as are people exposed to the "incivility" currently so common on cable television's political talk shows (Mutz and Reeves 2005; Mutz 2007; Sobieraj and Berry 2011). Basing their findings on survey evidence, others claim that the more one is exposed to the political news, the greater the mistrust of government (Hetherington 2001). Another claim is that the approval rate of Congress suffers due to relentless negative portrayals of the institution in the media (Mann and Ornstein 1994, 4). About nine out of ten media evaluations of Congress are negative. Hibbing and Theiss-Morse (1998) found that the greater the exposure to the media, the more likely people had a negative emotional reaction to Congress.

Has increased negativity in the media caused a decline in political trust? Not all are convinced. While the decline in political trust coincides with the rise in media negativity, cause and effect have yet to be clearly demonstrated. And, before getting unduly concerned about alleged harm from a negative press, we should stop to consider the opposite problem. Would the public be better served by a docile press that goes out of its way to report only happy news about politicians and their antics? Some media critics complain precisely about such an imbalance, objecting that the press is overly timid and overly reluctant to challenge the political leaders to whom it owes its access (Cook 1998; Fritz, Keefer, and Nyhan 2004). The media's acquiescence with the Bush administration in spring 2003 on the rationale for the Iraq War is a case in point.

8-3 Models of Media Effects

In the 1938 radio broadcast "War of the Worlds," Orson Welles described an invasion of New Jersey by Martians from outer space. Although the story was fiction, many believed it to be true, causing something of a panic in the New Jersey area. For many scholars, this was an example of the powerful sway the media can have over citizens. The use of media propaganda by Benito Mussolini in Italy and Adolf Hitler in Germany to gain and hold political power was seen as another example of pervasive media effects. This model of media influence has been dubbed the *hypodermic effect*, as it is similar to getting a drug injection. The effect is immediate and powerful. However, with the advent of scientific public opinion surveys, scholarly consensus shifted in the opposite direction. Early studies found media influences in political campaigns to be trivial, giving rise to a new perspective, called the *minimal effects model*. In recent years, the minimal effects model has also fallen into disfavor. Current media scholars favor a more nuanced approach that emphasizes the search for subtle but meaningful consequences of media exposure, including some that are easy to overlook.

The Minimal Effects Model

The first attempts to examine empirically the political influence of the mass media were the early studies of voting behavior: panel studies of voters in Erie County, Ohio, in 1940 and voters in Elmira, New York, in 1948 (Lazarsfeld, Berelson, and Gaudet 1948; Berelson, Lazarsfeld, and McPhee 1954). These early studies presented a viewpoint regarding the influence of the media that has since become known as the minimal effects model of media influence. Perhaps because the researchers for these projects moved into voting research from market research, they expected to find campaign messages in the mass media (at that time, essentially newspapers and radio) to be quite influential on individual voters. They envisioned voters waffling in their choice of candidates somewhat in the way a consumer might change his or her choice of toothpaste from purchase to purchase, depending on the effectiveness of the latest advertising.

These early researchers on presidential choice, however, made three discoveries that seemed to dismiss the mass media's influence. First, they discovered the anchor of partisanship. A substantial number of citizens interviewed as early as May of election year had already decided how they were going to vote in November. This suggests that most voters had a "product loyalty" to one or the other of the two major political parties. Second, the researchers discovered perceptual screening. Voters paid particular attention to the messages from the candidate they preferred, which served to maintain their "product loyalty." They avoided exposure to campaign messages for the opposition, even misperceiving these messages when exposure was unavoidable. Third, the researchers discovered the importance of personal conversations. When someone was about to change his or her viewpoint due to a persuasive message in the media, that person would often return to the original opinion after talking to others who shared that original opinion.

For these reasons, the messages on the mass media are less influential than they might appear. Because people's political views are anchored by their past beliefs, perceptual screening, and interpersonal communications, it is not likely that any particular revelation in the evening news will create massive changes in people's political likes and dislikes. Two interesting examples are the responses to President Reagan's Iran-Contra scandal in 1986 and 1987 and the scandal involving President Clinton and Monica Lewinsky in 1998 and 1999.

In late 1986, the American public was first shocked to learn that President Reagan was selling arms to Iran and then shocked again to learn that one purpose was to illegally fund the Contras in Nicaragua. The national media gave this scandal the coverage and the treatment usually reserved for a constitutional crisis on the order of Watergate. In one month, popular approval of Reagan's performance dropped about 20 percentage points, which (until 9/11) perhaps defines the outer limit of how quickly public opinion can respond in the short run. Twenty percentage points is the greatest one-month drop in presidential approval ever recorded. Yet, if one sets a high threshold regarding what constitutes a "major" opinion change, an upper limit of 20 percentage points may seem like not much at all. At least two-thirds of those who approved of Reagan before the scandal continued to do so despite the Iran-Contra revelations.

The 1998 Lewinsky scandal surpassed the Iran-Contra scandal in shock value. Within days of the first revelations, pundits were discussing whether the president would be or should be impeached. The news being reported appeared disastrous for the president at a time when Clinton was basking in the glow of a record level of popularity for a president so late in his presidency. Given the new revelations involving sex, lies, and audiotape, most political experts were sure that Clinton's standing with the public would plunge like a rock. Instead, it rose. In fact, over the first week of the scandal, Clinton's approval rating rose 10 points, close to a record for short-term presidential gain. What occurred was a seeming disconnection between the negative media stories and the public's evaluation of the president—a development that remains far from fully understood (Zaller 1998; Cohen 2008). What is clear from this episode is that public opinion does not automatically flow in the direction of the news. People judged the facts of the Lewinsky case in a way that allowed them to support the president in spite of negative revelations and speculation in the media.

Contemporary Perspectives on Media Effects

The Iran-Contra and Lewinsky examples illustrate the obvious limits of the media's power. Consistent with the minimal effects interpretation of media influence, shifts in public evaluations are limited even in response to one-sided news stories, and sometimes not even in the expected direction. However, many mass media researchers reject the minimalist interpretation. They concede the media have limited ability to change vote preferences in partisan elections or change opinions deeply rooted in partisanship or group identification. Instead, they search for more modest influences on political beliefs that perhaps can be detected only by experimental designs, imposing complex statistical controls on the data, or by isolating influences that exist only under restricted circumstances (e.g., see Bartels 1993; Finkel 1993; Arceneaux and Johnson 2013).

It is well understood that media effects are circumscribed because message awareness and message acceptance push in opposite directions. Consider that the possibility of opinion change in response to a new political message depends on both the likelihood of becoming aware of the message and the likelihood of accepting it once becoming aware. For many people, when the likelihood of accepting a message from the media is high, the likelihood of hearing it is low—and vice versa. Individuals most susceptible to media effects are those with moderate levels of political sophistication—sufficiently interested to be aware of media content but lacking the sophistication to completely resist media messages (Converse 1962; Zaller 1997).

Finally, there is a recognition that the net influence of the mass media so often seems to be slight because it represents a balance among conflicting points of view (Zaller 1992, 1996). If the media messages were truly one-sided, like the flow of propaganda in a nondemocratic regime, their cumulative impact might well be substantial. Even in a democratic society, there is often a consensus at the elite level that results in a one-sided media message. Examples include the president's honeymoon period and rally effects following crises, both discussed in Chapter 4. In these instances, presidents receive exceptional popularity levels because media voices are uniformly supportive (Brody 1991).

Contemporary thinking about media effects focuses on three processes by which the media are believed to influence public opinion: (1) agenda setting, where the media influence the issues citizens think are most important; (2) priming, which influences how citizens use these issues to evaluate political figures; and (3) framing, which can influence opinion by the way issues are presented to the public.

Agenda Setting

The potential influence of the mass media on political thinking is not limited to influence on policy preferences. As Bernard Cohen famously remarked, the media "may not be successful much of time in telling people what to think, but it is stunningly successful in telling [people] what to think about" (Cohen 1963).

Ever since a pioneering study by McCombs and Shaw (1972) of the 1968 presidential election, it has been known that people talk about the same issues that are being discussed in the media at the time (see also McCombs 2013). Is this media manipulation, or are the media and the citizens simply reacting to the same salient events when they occur?

Ideally, the best way to ascertain a causal inference whereby the mass media influence the agenda is to experimentally manipulate what people read or watch. This approach was used by Iyengar and his associates (Iyengar, Peters, and Kinder 1982; Iyengar and Kinder 1987) in a classic study of the network news. Ordinary citizens were divided into four groups, and for six consecutive days they watched the nightly news. Unknown to the subjects, each group saw a different version. For one group, a news story about defense preparedness was edited into each news program. For the second, a news story about pollution was inserted. The third group saw an economic inflation story, and the fourth group saw an unedited version of the news. Thus, each group got a weeklong dose of messages concerning one particular problem.

The most interesting result was the set of responses to the "most important problem" question before and after the experiment. Those given pollution stories and those given defense stories registered significant increases in concern about pollution and defense, respectively. The inflation group did not change much, apparently because they already expressed a strong concern about inflation in their questionnaires prior to the experiment and could hardly increase the level of their response. Further analysis suggested that the subjects in each group began to evaluate President Carter according to how they saw Carter's handling of their manipulated topic.

An important issue is how individual political sophistication relates to agenda setting. Iyengar, Peters, and Kinder (1982) report that their least sophisticated respondents were the most responsive to experimental manipulation of the agenda. This finding seems reasonable, as less sophisticated people lack the stored information that helps discount messages in the media at odds with their current opinions. However, the subjects were shown news programs under artificial experimental conditions. Would they have been as attentive and persuaded in a natural setting? As we noted earlier, at least a moderate level of political sophistication seems necessary for the media to lead. To be persuaded by the media requires some minimal attention to the media. In a natural setting, that attention apparently does not exist among the least sophisticated.

It is now understood that when an issue becomes the subject of media attention, the net public opinion change will be slight as long as both sides of the issue are presented (although people on each side may become more polarized). When the media present only one side of an issue, public opinion responds to the dominant message (Zaller 1992; Baumgartner and Jones 1993; Jacobs and Shapiro 2000; Sniderman and Theriault 2004; Gershkoff and Kushner 2005). The door is thus open for possible media manipulation. However, objective circumstances mostly drive the media agenda. For example, the media cover inflation when inflation is high and therefore newsworthy.

Priming

The concept of "priming" political attitudes was introduced by Iyengar and Kinder (1987). By setting the agenda, the media not only increase the perceived importance of an issue but can also "prime" the public by directing them to consider certain aspects of the question and not others when they make their political evaluations. For example, when the 1991 Gulf War was in the daily headlines, the popularity of the first President Bush soared to record heights. The public was being primed by the media to evaluate Bush based on how he was handling the war. However, by November 1991 the attention of the media shifted to the economy. By placing the economy at the top of the public agenda, the media were priming the public to evaluate Bush not on his past successes in the Persian Gulf but on an allegedly stalling economy (Krosnick and Brannon 1993; Hetherington 1996). When the media shifted their focus from the war to the economy, the president's approval rating rapidly declined (Zaller 1994).

There are two ways priming might work. First, it can increase the accessibility of information in short-term memory. When the media focus attention on combating terrorism, "considerations" about the war on terrorism rise to "the top of the head." Second, when the media focus attention on an issue, they make clear, either explicitly or implicitly, that reporters and editors feel this issue is important. It is not unexpected that many people come to share this media perspective—at least if they place some minimal level of trust in the media. Once a person comes to believe an issue is important, it is only natural to place significant weight on that issue when evaluating the president (Miller and Krosnick 2000).

Framing Issues

A media frame provides meaning to unfolding events. It is the central or organizing theme or story line in a news report. A frame highlights what is important about an issue, such as its causes, morality, the people involved, and proposed solutions (Price, Nir, and Cappella 2005; Chong and Druckman 2007, 2013). While agenda setting and priming concern the importance the media place on an issue, framing concerns the way media present the issue content to the public. A frame determines what is in the picture and what is left out. According to the framing hypothesis, the slant or angle journalists take on newsworthy issues that can affect opinions about these issues. We are all familiar with the way news stories can be framed. News about poverty programs can stress a "helping hand" or a "government handout." Combatants in foreign conflicts can be "freedom fighters" or "terrorists." Antiabortion protestors can be portrayed as idealists committed to the sanctity of life or as religious zealots intent on enforcing their views on everyone else.

One example of a powerful and successful frame concerns the war in Iraq. When the United States went to war on March 19, 2003, it was supported by more than 70 percent of the population—despite opinion polls showing Americans expected a long, costly war with significant adverse economic consequences that in the short-term would likely increase rather than reduce terrorism. The best explanation for the high level of support is that the Bush administration was able to frame the Iraq invasion as an extension of the war on terrorism. This view went unchallenged by Democrats and quickly became the dominant media frame, which had a major influence on political attitudes regarding the war (Gershkoff and Kushner 2005). Once critics began to challenge the evidence for weapons of mass destruction, the old frame was quickly undermined, as was the approval of the president. This example illustrates that frames left unchallenged can powerfully shape public opinion. But once frames are challenged by counterframes, their initial effect can be greatly undermined (Tedin, Rottinghaus, and Rodgers 2011; Rottinghaus and Tedin 2012).

Mediating Media Influence

We should be careful not to overstate the influence of the mass media on political beliefs. We saw in Chapter 3 a distinction between the long-term stability of peoples' political dispositions and the volatility of their responses to survey questions, as the nature of the stimuli affects the short-term response. This note of caution applies here. For instance, experimental studies that involve manipulation of media presentations rarely report effects to be long lasting (e.g., Mutz and Reeves 2005; Dilliplane, Goldman, and Mutz 2013). Arguably, evidence of framing and priming is little more than a demonstration that one can influence what bubbles to "the top of the head" (Zaller 1992) without generating a long-term impact. And we should always keep in mind that the relationship between the journalistic source and the recipient does not go unfiltered. People immunize themselves from media influence not only by their personal belief systems but also by talking to others (Druckman and Nelsen 2003; Druckman 2004).

Moreover, we must recognize the source of agenda setting, priming, and framing is not some mass media monolith. News stories are prepared by journalists who themselves are influenced by the competing voices clamoring for their attention—such as competing politicians and interest groups trying to get their story out to the public. Finally, it must be recognized that if the mainstream media ever could keep the gates closed regarding what people think or think about, that is no longer possible in the age of the Internet. Political stories often appear first on political blogs. When they draw interest, they force the mainstream media to give them attention.

8-4 Media Content and Political Opinions

While the minimal effects model holds that the media do little more than reinforce preexisting opinions, recent research has demonstrated meaningful media effects on political opinions among those who regularly follow politics on television and talk radio and in the newspapers. In this section we discuss the findings of some of these studies.

Television Network News

In an ambitious study, Page and Shapiro (1992) estimated the influence of television news reports on the content of public opinion. They collected eighty instances from the late 1960s into the early 1980s where the same survey question about an important question of public policy was administered to national samples over a period of years. They then determined whether television news content between the two surveys could account for the observed change in public opinion. This exercise involved extensive monitoring and coding for more than a decade's worth of network news programs.

On the average, opinion did not change much in the short run of even a few years. But when change occurred, the direction tended to be consistent with the preponderant direction of the messages on network news. The authors examined the impact of many sources of information on network news (e.g., presidents, the opposition party, interest groups). The source that best predicted opinion change was television commentary—from anchorpersons, reporters in the field, and special commentators. According to the estimates, each viewpoint presented in a commentary could bring about as much as 4 percentage points of opinion change. But Page and Shapiro are cautious when interpreting why television commentary predicts opinion change. They do not claim that individual newscasters are themselves the major source of opinion change. Rather, their message frequently overlaps or reinforces the dominant elite message that filters to the public via the media. Or news commentators and others with whom they agree may be perceived as simply reflecting an agreed-upon consensus that may strongly influence the formation of citizen opinions (Page and Shapiro 1992).

In other words, when the messages on television news are predominantly one sided and advocate a particular change of policy, it is a good bet that public opinion will change at least modestly in the same direction. Another possibility, however, is that both televised messages and public opinion are *responding* independently, but in a common direction, to the same events. In this way, public opinion and messages from the media could be moving in tandem but with neither causing the other.

The Fox News Effect

Now of course, less of our news viewing is from network news and more is from the cable news outlets. With its conservative slant, Fox News has grown to be the most heavily watched cable news channel. Because of Fox News's success at attracting viewers, it would seem obvious that its entry into the news field has had a significant impact on public opinion.

One ambitious and careful study has attempted to measure just that. The Fox News Channel did not exist until October 1996, when it began its twenty-four-hour news service in a few scattered cable markets. By 2000, it had become available to about 20 percent of the U.S. public. The pattern of its spread was idiosyncratic. DellaVigna and Kaplan (2008) examined the voting trends between the presidential elections of 1996 and 2000 in the towns where Fox News became available by 2000 with the trends in comparable towns where cable viewers were not yet able to receive Fox News. To get the best estimates, they compared towns with the Fox News Channel with towns in the same county where it was not yet available and utilized further statistical controls.

What they found was a small but quite statistically significant effect of about one-half of a percentage point on the vote. Republican George W. Bush would have received about half a percent fewer votes had Fox News been absent. Half a point may not seem like much, although like any factor it could have been decisive in the close 2000 election. But to see why this impact is impressive, consider the size of the pool of potential converts available for Fox to push toward Bush. Where Fox became available, only some potential viewers subscribed to cable and, of these, not all found their way to the upstart Fox News Channel. Of these, roughly half were going to vote for Bush anyway. Thus, one-half of 1 percent of all voters being swayed represent a much more sizeable chunk of would-be Gore voters who had cable and followed the campaign on Fox News.

In its early days, new viewers to Fox News might have been more influenced by its conservative tilt because they were not yet aware of its conservative reputation. Today, television viewers are generally aware of Fox News's conservative slant, and this awareness can inoculate them from the full impact of its content. Undoubtedly, Fox News continues to influence its most faithful conservative viewers by reinforcing their already conservative beliefs. Others who are aware of Fox News's reputation but are not particularly predisposed toward its conservatism may use this knowledge to discount its conservatism when they do watch it or to ignore it by switching to rival news channels. Further studies of the impact of the diverse choices people have of cable news channels would be welcome (see Arceneaux and Johnson 2013.)

Talk Radio

In recent times, nowhere has the merger of the news and entertainment been more successful than talk radio. According to Arbitron ratings, more than nine in ten Americans say they tune into radio weekly, and talk shows provide about 12 percent of the radio audience. The preponderance of successful talk radio shows has opinionated hosts from the political right and sometimes the far right and rarely from the left (and even more rarely from the center). One factor that may contribute to this imbalance is that most conservatives believe that most media are biased against their cause. Talk radio is an outlet for this frustration (Berry and Sobieraj 2011).

The audience for talk radio tends to be older white males—particularly in the case of conservative talk radio. For the media's best-known personality, Rush Limbaugh, 67 percent of listeners are male, 45 percent are over fifty years old, and 95 percent are white. Those who listen to talk radio tend to be more conservative than nonlisteners, but not by a large margin. Davis and Owen (1999, 168–70) found that 57 percent of listeners call themselves conservative, compared to about 40 percent of their public sample. The fact that talk show hosts are generally a good deal more conservative than their audiences leads some analysts to conclude that entertainment is as big a drawing card as is political content (Lee and Cappella 2001).

The audience for talk radio leans to the right mainly because conservatives self-select to listen. Talk show hosts are essentially preaching to the choir. Mostly, that is the correct conclusion. Talk radio content rarely changes political opinions. However, in some unique circumstances, talk radio hosts can have an independent influence on the thinking of their audience. One instance was in 2000, when Rush Limbaugh came out early in favor of George W. Bush in the Republican presidential primary over his principal opponent, Senator John McCain (who Limbaugh said was not a "real" Republican). Using a design where respondents could be tracked over time, Barker (2002) found the more one listened to Limbaugh, the more likely was a change toward a favorable opinion of Bush and an unfavorable opinion of McCain. Because the sample was entirely composed of Republicans and tracked change over time, one can reasonably rule out the alternative explanation of self-selection. And, important to understand is that Limbaugh was trying to convince his conservative audience who, among two conservative candidates, was the best for the cause.

Newspapers

In principle, political reporting in newspapers is not supposed to reflect an ideological position. Professional ethics dictate that journalists not let their own political feelings color their reporting. However, for the editorial pages, that is neither the expectation nor the case. Here, columnists such as conservative George Will and liberal Paul Krugman analyze political events through an ideological prism. In addition, the owners and managers of newspapers often endorse candidates for public office—a rare practice for the owners of television and radio stations. Because they use the public airwaves, radio and television stations would have to provide equal time for other candidates to respond.

As in the case of television and talk radio, there is evidence that the editorial content of newspapers can affect the political opinions of its readers. One reason is that editorial opinion can leak from the editorial page to straight news coverage.

For example, in an analysis of media coverage of seventy-nine senate races between 1988 and 1992, Kahn and Kenney (2002) found that when a newspaper endorsed an incumbent senator on its editorial pages, the tone of its campaign coverage of that senator was significantly more positive than when it made no endorsement. Thus, to the extent there is spillover from the editorial pages to the straight news, the potential is greater for newspapers to influence political opinions (but see Dalton, Beck, and Huckfeldt 1998 for a somewhat different take).

Various researchers (Erikson 1976c; Entman 1989; Kahn and Kenney 2002; Druckman and Parkin 2005) have examined public opinion surveys to search for possible evidence that the newspapers people read influence their opinions or vote. With statistical controls for the influence of other variables, these analyses reveal evidence of newspaper influence. Interpretation should be cautious, however, because even the most careful statistical analysis might not be able to control fully for selective exposure—the tendency to select reading material based on ideological affinity. Also, newspapers tend to offer the slant their readers want to read (Gentzkow and Shapiro 2010).

Gerber, Karlan, and Bergen (2009) avoided the selective-exposure problem by conducting a field experiment. Prior to the 2005 Virginia governor's election, they randomly assigned treatments of newspaper subscriptions to either the liberal *Washington Post* or the conservative *Washington Times*. Control subjects got neither. Surprisingly, they found that newspaper reading from either paper led to a boost in support for the Democratic candidate compared to the control group. They probably obtained this result because the flow of the news during this period (post-Katrina) was generally favorable to Democrats and critical of the Bush administration. Apparently, even conservative newspapers were not immune—another indicator of minimal media effects.

The Internet

With the Internet era still in its adolescence, we have learned a few things (Nie et al., 2010; Farrell 2012), but much is yet to be discovered about its impact on political attitudes. It should first be stated that politics is only one aspect of Internet content. For instance, tracking data show that pornographic Web sites gather three times the traffic of news sites and a full 100 times the traffic of strictly political sites (Hindman 2009). Still, as we shall see, the Internet obviously is a major source of political news for many people.

Internet political content—news sources and blogs—can be found on both the political left and the right. But as if to counterbalance talk radio as the comfort zone of the political right, the Internet provides a haven for the political left. Left-wing blogs have more traffic than those on the right, and liberals read far more about politics on the Internet than do conservatives (Hindman 2009). Just as with talk radio, the ideological tilt can be partially explained by demographics—heavy Internet users are younger, more educated, and more Democrat than the average Internet user or nonuser (Smith 2009).

As discussed earlier, the Internet creates an opportunity for people to focus only on sources of information that are ideologically congenial with their current political beliefs. The net effect is a growth in polarization. Indeed, research shows that most people who read political blogs read mainly those that fit their ideological taste, which serves to reinforce their political predispositions. The division between blog readers on the left and on the right is greater than between the viewers of "mainstream" television news (who tilt left) and Fox News viewers on the right. Further, one can argue that the two groups of blog readers are more polarized ideologically than even Democrats and Republicans in Congress (Lawrence, Sides, and Farrell 2009).

8-5 Media Change and the Quality of Electoral Decision Making

In political campaigns, the public must rely on the news media for their information. Over the past half century there have been important changes in how and where the electorate has sought campaign news and as well as in the content of campaign coverage provided by the media. In this section we examine this change and its possible consequences.

News Consumption During Presidential Campaigns

Earlier in this chapter, we documented the general changes in news media consumption. Here we expand this discussion to focus on attention to the media during presidential campaigns, going back to 1992. Starting in 1992, the Pew Research Center asked respondents if they followed the campaign news in newspapers, television, radio, magazines, and starting from 1996 the Internet. The responses are shown in Figure 8.2.

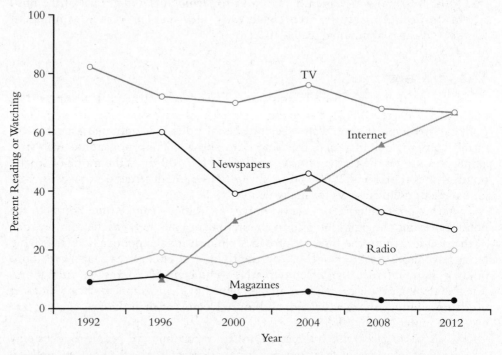

FIGURE 8.2 How do People Get Most of Their News about the Presidential Election Campaign?

Source: Based on the data from http://www.pewresearch.org/fact-tank/2013/10/16/12-trends-shaping-digital-news/ actually dated Oct. 18 2013.

The data show the now-familiar decline in the dependence on newspapers (dropping from 57 to 27 percent). The other print media, magazines, showed a similar decline. Television remained dominant, down from 1992 but still a healthy 67 percent. In 1996 Pew began asking about the Internet. Starting at a meager 10 percent in 1996, the Internet, at 67 percent in 2012, had caught up with television. Interestingly, the oldest medium—radio—showed an uptick of 12 to 20 percent.

Do people who follow the campaign closely on television tend to be the same people who follow the campaign closely in print, whether in print via newspapers or online via the Internet? We can answer that question with the 2012 ANES. The data show that regular television viewing and newspaper reading go together. They also tend to correlate positively with political interest and political information. The more attention to these news sources, the more people are interested politically and correctly informed about where the candidates stand on the issues. Striking is the difference that following politics on the Internet seems to make. Among those who said they read or heard two or fewer political stories on the Internet, just 16 percent said they followed the presidential campaign closely, compared to 63 percent who said they followed "a good many" political stories on the Internet. In addition, those following a "good many" Internet stories about politics are also quite able to correctly place where the candidates stand on the issues.

However, we need to be careful about the direction of cause and effect. While monitoring the media can stimulate interest and the growth of information, it is also possible that *a priori* interested and informed citizens seek out media information to a much greater extent than those with only a passing interest or no interest at all.

The Content of Television Campaign News

We might ask whether the fact that television (and now the Internet) has surpassed newspapers as a source for campaign news has made the electorate any less capable citizens. The minority of citizens for whom politics is a passion now gain more information (and reinforce their biases) by consuming shows on cable news channels or political Internet sites. But what about the majority of citizens who follow politics more passively? It is commonly believed that people learn more about politics by reading newspapers than by watching television (e.g., Weaver and Drew 1993; Druckman 2005). The reasons are several. First, newspapers can carry far more in-depth information than brief newscasts can. Second, it is possible to browse the newspaper (and now the Internet) for detailed information in a way that is not possible or practical with television. Third, as the proportion of the voters who watch network news has declined by about half, people get their news from even less informative sources such as local news programs or entertainment shows. Fourth, as discussed later in this chapter, television has focused increasingly on covering campaigns as horse races, at the expense of presenting the candidate's actual campaign activities and policy proposals. Are voters worse off as a result?

Some say that the media tend to frame the campaign not as a clash of ideas but as a strategic game. Issues are seldom covered, and even less often covered in any depth. Rather, the news media are fixated on the game of politics—the "horse race." A consistent finding for elections in the past thirty years is that the primary focus of the network news is on who is leading, who is gaining, and who is losing electoral support, with stories often supported by polling data.[13] Since television news pays little attention to issues, it is not surprising that viewers gain little substantive knowledge. As Larry Bartels (1988, 32) notes, "In covering a presidential campaign, the media tell us more about who is winning and losing than they do about who is fit to be president."

Horse-race journalism has not always characterized the media campaign coverage. Until the 1970s, reports on candidate issue positions more than held their own with reports of campaign conduct (Iyengar, Norpoth, and Hahn 2004). The most frequently identified reason for this change is the need the media have for novelty, currency, appealing pictures, and human interest stories—all of which feed into the corporate requirement to maximize profits. The proliferation of public opinion polls has accentuated this tendency. As we noted in Chapter 2, two-thirds of all campaign stories include information from polls.[14] The evidence is mixed on whether the public really prefers horse-race journalism or wants the media to focus more on issue substance. On the one hand, Farnsworth and Lichter (2007) cite a number of polls and other evidence supporting the claim that people really want more substance. On the other hand, Iyengar, Norpoth, and Hahn (2004) find that when given an unambiguous choice in a real-world setting, more people prefer strategic information than issue information.

8-6 Political Advertising

Much of what people learn about political campaigns is incidental—from political advertisements that interrupt entertainment and news shows alike on television (and radio). The typical complaint about political ads is that they are overly negative. But, as we will see, some say that the ads actually are educational—and might even tell the voters more about political candidates than the voters learn from television news.

Negativity in Political Ads

Negative ads are not new but seem to have increased significantly since 1980. By one account, only about 10 percent of paid ads were negative in 1960; by 2008 the percent of ads that were negative soared to 60 percent (West 2014). Still, coding an ad as "negative" is very subjective, and percentages vary considerably from one study to another (Lau et al. 1999). In particular, there is often a fine line between "contrast ads" in which candidates are compared and "negative ads" in which opponents are personally attacked.

The study of negative advertising was pioneered by Ansolabehere and Iyengar (Ansolabehere et al. 1994; Ansolabehere and Iyengar 1995). They came to very harsh conclusions about the effect of negative ads on the public, asserting that negative ads lead to political cynicism and lower efficacy because "people infer from negative advertisements that the entire process, not the just the targeted candidate, is deeply flawed." According to their data, negative ads account for a 5 percent decrease in voter turnout.

The original work on negative ads has spawned a cottage industry of elaborations and refutations (prominent examples are Freedman and Goldstein 1999; Kahn and Kenney 1999; Sigelman and Kugler 2003; Lau and Pomper 2004; Mutz and Reeves 2005; Geer 2006; Krasno and Green 2008). Some studies make the counterclaim that negative ads actually increase turnout by signaling to voters that election is about something important. Other replications have failed to detect decreases in efficacy, political trust, and turnout due to negative ads (Finkel and Geer 1998; Freedman and Goldstein 1999). Sigelman and Kugler (2003) found almost no overlap between the way academics code negative ads and the extent to which citizens actually perceive advertising as negative in real-world electoral contests. Lau and his associates (1999) conducted a "meta-analysis" of fifty-five studies on the effect of negative political advertising.[15] When integrating the results of these fifty-five studies, they found no support for any of the effects attributed to negative ads—including increasing likes or dislikes of the competing candidates. A 2007 follow-up confirms these findings (Lau, Sigelman, and Royner 2007).

Ads and Political Information

Surprising as it may seem at first glance, citizens learn more about substantive policy issues from the content of paid candidate campaign ads than they do from television news coverage. The superior issue content of political ads was first claimed by Thomas Patterson and Robert McClure in a study of the 1972 presidential campaign and was reconfirmed in studies of the 1992 and 2000 elections (Brians and Wattenberg 1996; Freedman, Franz, and Goldstein 2004). Patterson and McClure (1976) found that people who claimed to regularly watch the network news increased their knowledge of candidate issue positions by 28 percent on average between September and November 1972. But people who claimed to not watch network news at all gained about as much, 25 percent, indicating the network news had almost no effect. On the other hand, those who (by self-report) watched "many" political ads gained 36 percent in awareness of candidate issue positions, compared to 25 percent among those who watched only "a few" ads.

While cynics often charge that political advertising is without substance and designed simply to fool the voters, research indicates that ads provide considerable information about candidate policy positions. Based on a study of the almost 1 million television ads run in the 2000 election, Freedman, Franz, and Goldstein (2004) make an even bolder claim for the pedagogical merits of campaign commercials, calling them the "multivitamins" of American politics. They note that 95 percent of all presidential ads and 90 percent of all general election ads contained issue content. Campaign advertising, they claim, "is rich in informational content." Comparing those most exposed to these ads with those least exposed, they found exposure significantly increased political information, political interest, and voter turnout. And importantly, exposure had its greatest effect among those least politically engaged.

Gilens, Vavreck, and Cohen's (2007) analysis of ANES electoral data from 1952 through 2000 finds surprising evidence for the positive impact of ads. The more political ads were shown on television, the more the public focused on policy issues. The more advertisements accented policy differences between the candidates, the more voters evaluated candidates based on their policy positions. Extending this analysis to strictly negative ads, John Geer (2006) has made the provocative claim, backed by large data base over twelve elections, that negative ads enrich the political knowledge of the electorate—more so than positive ads or contrast ads. One reason is that negative ads require more supporting evidence than do positive ads in order to be credible, and that negative ads contain more issue-based information as they must in order to be effective. Whether this positive aspect significantly rehabilitates the negative ad remains a matter of spirited dispute.

Battleground Versus Nonbattleground States   Because of the Electoral College's winner-take-all feature at the state level, presidential candidates concentrate their ads in "battleground" states where the vote is expected to be closest and largely ignore the other "blackout" states. About one-third of the nation is exposed to an unrelenting barrage of ads, while the remainder receives virtually none. Researchers are beginning to explore what difference this barrage makes for the quality of electoral decisions.

Gimpel, Kaufman, and Merkowitz (2007) find that battleground state residents, because they are exposed to more ads, become more interested and engaged in the campaign, especially low-income voters. Panagopoulos (2009) finds that over the campaign, candidate preferences are more volatile in battleground states, where they are exposed to most of the information. In effect, by their exposure to the campaign, battleground state residents sometimes shift their aggregate preferences, while blackout state residents rarely do so. And Gilens, Vavreck, and Cohen (2007) find that voters focus on issues more in battleground states than in blackout states. Urban and Niebler (2014) find similar effects of campaign exposure on campaign contributions. They study voters in nonbattleground states who were subject to little television advertising. Those who were exposed to spillover ads from television stations in neighboring battleground states were more likely to make campaign contributions than those not exposed.

For the 2012 election, we can see the information effect of living in a battleground state from a simple analysis of data from the 2012 American National Election Study. Recall from Chapter 3 our information scale, where we scored ANES respondents based on the number of issues on which they correctly scored Obama to the left of Romney. Scores ranged from zero to a maximum of seven (the mean is 4.8). With statistical controls for income and education levels, ANES respondents from battleground states scored 0.3 points higher on average information levels than respondents from nonbattleground states. This nudge on information levels is slight as expected, but highly statistically significant.[16]

Do Political Ads Work?

In recent years political advertising has reached high levels of technological sophistication, especially at the presidential level (Issenberg 2012; Sides and Vavreck 2013). The conventional wisdom is that ads make a difference. But do they? The correct answer is elusive, because candidates tend to place ads in media markets where they think they can harvest the most votes. Even if ads are placed where there is the great chance to gain votes, it might be that the size of the potential vote harvest lures the ad makers rather than the ads win more votes. To estimate the power of ads, how does one overcome this "selection" problem?

Huber and Arceneaux (2007) get around the problem with the aid of a natural experiment—the spread of ads to unintended targets—residents of blackout states who reside in media markets centered in battleground states. (An example would be Kentuckians [not in a nonbattleground state] receiving Ohio television from the Cincinnati market in battleground Ohio.) What they find in 2000 is the more ads there were for Bush relative to Gore, the better Bush did among accidentally exposed nonbattleground state voters.

In an influential study, Gerber et al. (2011) conducted a field experiment in which ad buys were randomly determined. In 2006, Governor Rick Perry of Texas was facing a Republican primary challenge. In March of that year, he spent about 2 million dollars on TV ads. To assess the effect his campaign team used random assignment of their ads to Texas media markets. Some markets got ads; others did not. Whether a TV market got the ads (the treatment) or not (the control) was left to chance. To estimate the effects, the Perry campaign conducted a tracking poll. The Gerber team found the ads did have a detectable although small effect on vote choices. But the effects were detectable only in the short run, perhaps a matter of days. Then any trace disappeared.

It is not clear, however, that the effects of political ads (or any political messages) have only a short-term impact. Consider that if every political message left a visible imprint on the recipient, the exposure to multiple messages would leave people bouncing all over the place politically, and we know that does not happen. The best interpretation is that political messages have both a short-term and a long-term component. The short-term component may be visible but is transient; the long-term component is tiny but permanent (or nearly so), and therefore hard to detect. At the end of the day (say Election Day), the net attitude is the sum of a series of tiny long-term influences. This model fits presidential campaigns, whereby events appear to affect vote intentions in the short-term but also leave a long-term residue. On Election Day, the cumulative long-term effects matter, along with any short-term effects that are closely proximate to Election Day (Erikson and Wlezien 2012a).[17]

8-7 The Media and Political Polarization

Consider the change in the mass media over the years. From the 1950s into the 1990s, Americans got their news from a set of common sources that were politically neutral in tone—their daily newspaper and the nightly television news. This has changed with the advent of, first, cable news and then the Internet. Now, much of the news people learn is partisan in tone and highly fragmented, with people having a new set of choices regarding which sources to follow and which sources to believe.

It is commonly argued (e.g., Jamieson and Cappella 2008; Sunstein 2009) that this new fragmentation and diversity of media shares much of the responsibility for the polarization of American public opinion. The subtleties of this argument are considerable (Prior 2013; Arceneaux and Johnson 2013). People are not blank slates. They rarely wander into the lair of an ideology-ladened news source expecting unbiased neutrality. And when they want an ideological viewpoint, they know how to find it. And even when people have favorite sources on the left or right, they often shop around by changing channels or checking a diversity of Web sites.

One consequence of today's media environment is that those who like to follow politics can find it. In the process, because of self-selection, they tend to become stronger ideologues or more intensely engaged. In some ways, the opportunity is present for people to consume more politics than may benefit the collective good. At the same time, the greater availability of alternative entertainment outlets on the Internet and on TV allows people not inclined to follow politics to ignore it to a degree not previously possible—again perhaps not to the benefit of the collective good.

Like citizens and politicians, the media have a crucial role to play in the American democracy. Self-government depends on the free exchange of ideas among reasonably well-informed men and women. How the media provide the necessary information for this exchange of ideas in the years to come will have important consequences for democratic accountability in the United States. The advent of multiple sources of political information can certainly be the cause for optimism. At the same time, the negativity, the emphasis on the political horse race, and the strident ideological tone of much of the commentary all are reasons for pessimism. With rapid advances in technology and some human ingenuity, it may yet be possible to make the political news appealing and profitable while genuinely informative. However, even under the best of circumstances, one should not overestimate the influence of the media for either good or bad. While the minimal effects model, taken to its extreme, is certainly not correct, the realistic alternative could perhaps be labeled something like *minimal effects plus a little bit more*.

Critical Thinking Questions

1. People of various political orientations often claim that there is bias in the news. But what does this mean, and can we scientifically identify politically biased media reporting when it exists? Could you imagine steps to reduce bias?
2. Like any other occupational group, journalists have their unique characteristics that distinguish them from others. In what ways might this matter, or should we not be worried in terms of the quality of political news?
3. With the growth of opinionated cable TV news networks and the spread of political Web sites, people can now receive a variety of differing political viewpoints. Do you see any risks for American democracy in these recent media trends?

Endnotes

1. We adopt West's (2001) timeline with some modifications.
2. There is still debate over what actually sunk the *Maine*. The most plausible explanation is that the ship hit a mine, causing its munitions to explode. Others believe the cause was internal; perhaps its munitions were ignited by a spark from its boilers.
3. As the size of the audience for traditional news sources declines, the remaining audience grows older. In Pew's 2012 survey, only 6 percent of young respondents aged eighteen to twenty-four reported having read a print newspaper the day before and only 29 percent reported watching news on television. The comparable numbers for seniors over age 65 were 48 percent (newspapers) and 72 percent (television). The youngest group did, however, lead the seniors in getting news off the Internet, 52 to 28 percent.
4. In 2012, among those regularly watch CNN 50 percent identified as Democrats,16 percent as Republicans. Among those who regularly watch Fox 22 percent are Democrats

and 40 percent are Republicans. Among those who regularly watch MSNBC 58 percent are Democrats and 16 percent are Republicans (Pew Research Center).

5. According to Arceneaux and Johnson's (2013, 44) analysis of Pew data from 2010, regular Fox News viewers are more than six times more likely to call themselves Republicans than Democrats. Regular MSNBC viewers tilt Democratic by more than 3 to 1. These differences are also reflected in ideological identification and stands on specific issues.

6. In the new fragmented media, one strategy candidates increasingly use to reach those with low political interest is appearing on entertainment talk shows or even Jon Stewart's fake news, *The Daily Show*. One bonus for these appearances is that the tone of the coverage they receive is overwhelmingly positive.

7. While households not wired for cable comprise a captive audience for television networks, the amount of news presented by broadcast networks has declined appreciably. Much political news of the type once reported by broadcast networks (e.g., coverage of party conventions) is now relegated to cable news networks.

8. http://www.goodreads.com/quotes/tag/flat-earth.

9. See the American Presidency Project's "2012 General Election Editorial Endorsements by Major Newspapers," http://www.presidency.ucsb.edu/data/2012_newspaper_endorsements.php.

10. We averaged the positive tone for the Democratic and Republican candidates for each year and then averaged those over the four elections shown in Table 8.3.

11. *Talkers Magazine*, October 2013, http://www.talkers.com/top-talk-radio-audiences/.

12. Still another contributing factor to the news media's increased negativity is that they take the lead from the increased negativity of candidate advertising. As candidates increasingly run negative campaigns attacking their opponents, these attacks become part of the news story and hence reported by the media.

13. Pew has tracked the degree to which prime time news shows cover the horse race. In 2008, 53 percent of all prime time news stories about the presidential campaign focused on horse-race coverage. The proportion fell to 38 percent in 2012 according to Pew but was not matched by compensatory increases in coverage of candidate policy positions.

14. One downside of the media's reliance on polls is inaccurate reporting, as reporters often misinterpret poll results. Stephanie Larson (2001) gives a number of examples of how reporters come to wrong conclusions based on polling data.

15. A *meta-analysis* is a study of the findings of all work in a specific area. The results of each study are quantified and entered into a database. Standard statistical tests are used to determine if the studies taken as a whole support a particular conclusion.

16. With controls for education (dummies not beyond high school and for college graduates) and income (richest and poorest tertile), the information gain from living in a battleground state is significant at the .005 level. The estimated knowledge gap increases with the number of controls.

17. In the 2012 presidential race, the two campaigns followed different strategies for timing their ads. The Obama campaign struck early and often, persistently attacking Romney for the allegedly predator practices of the company he once headed, Bain Capital. The idea was that this campaign tactic would have a cumulative effect to erode Romney's standing with the voters. Romney saved his fire for a blitz of ads late in the campaign in the hope that they would create a large if short-term effect that would last until Election Day. See Sides and Vavreck's (2013) interesting analysis of the ad wars and their effects in 2012.

CHAPTER 9

Elections as Instruments of Popular Control

LEARNING OBJECTIVES

- Describe the *normal vote*
- Describe the effect of political information on voter volatility

- Describe *issue voting* and alternative explains for apparent issue voting
- Explain key public opinion factors that determine election outcomes

In a democracy, the public supposedly controls the behavior of its public officials by exercising its influence at the ballot box in a rational fashion—in accordance with what we call the *rational-activist model*. Ideally, each voter selects the candidate who best represents his or her views on matters of public policy. At least in a two-candidate election, the collective choice is then the candidate who is closer to most voters on the issues. The policy result is the closest correspondence possible, given the choice of candidates, between the collective preferences of the electorate and government policy.

But representation of the public interest via democratic elections is not as simple in practice as it is in theory. It is possible, for instance, to hold elections in which none of the candidates on the ballot offer policy choices that voters find attractive. Even when the candidates present a relevant menu of policy choices, the electorate may—through some combination of misguidance, ignorance, and indifference—vote "irrationally" by voting into office a candidate who does not represent its interests. Also, if officeholders perceive that the electorate is not watching, or that it does not care, they may feel free to make policy decisions without consideration of public opinion.

Looking at the matter positively rather than negatively, we can state the conditions that *do* allow elections to be an effective instrument for inducing policy decisions that are responsive to public opinion. First, the candidates should offer a meaningful choice of policy options that appeal to voters, and once elected, the winner should try to carry out campaign pledges. Second, the voters should be informed about the issues that separate the candidates and vote for the candidate who best represents their own views. Clearly, the fulfillment of each of these conditions depends on the other. For example, political leaders pay the greatest attention to public opinion when they believe the public is alert enough to throw them out of office if they do not. Similarly, voters have the greatest opportunity to vote intelligently on the basis of policy issues when the politicians act on the assumption the public is going to do so.

In this chapter, we examine the behavior of the electorate when it carries out its assigned responsibility. In Chapter 10, we examine the responsiveness of political elites to public opinion.

9-1 Political Campaigns and the Voter

During every political campaign, voters are bombarded with news and propaganda about the candidates who seek their favor. Judging by the attention politicians give to the voters at election time, one might conclude that the voter reacts to campaign stimuli in the same fluid manner as a consumer reacting to advertising stimuli in the mass media. Just as the person about to purchase a product, such as a detergent, might vacillate in his or her choice of brands until the moment of purchase, so might the voter waver between the candidates until entry into the voting booth forces a final decision. But, as we saw in Chapter 8, this image of the voting process underestimates the voter's ability to resist political messages.

As discussed in Chapter 3, most American voters have a more or less permanent attachment to either the Republican or the Democratic Party. It is through this filter of party identification that most voters view the partisan aspects of the political world. The anchor of party identification prevents voters from changing the party they vote for from one election to the next and from wavering in their choice of candidates during a campaign.

From one election to the next, only a small minority of those who vote both times switch sides. Converse (1962) reports 20 percent changed the party of their presidential vote from 1956 to 1960 among the ANES's 1956–1960 panelists. In the ANES's 1992–1996 panel the percent switching sides deflates to 11 percent if third-party votes for Perot are excluded. And in the ANES 2000–2004 panel, of those who voted in both presidential elections, only 10 percent switched their presidential vote from Republican to Democratic or vice versa. Over the past half century, voters have become more polarized in their vote choice.

On a day-to-day or week-to-week basis over a campaign, vote choices are even more stable. The periods when there is most change are (1) the primary election season in the spring, when voters are becoming familiar with the eventual party nominees, (2) the national party convention season, and (3) the final week of the campaign, when some voters finally focus on the choice. The period of least change is the fall campaign itself, with few voters shifting their choice between Labor Day and the campaign's final week (Erikson and Wlezien 2012a).

The ANES presidential polls interview their respondents both before and after the election. About one-fourth of the initial interviews take place from forty-five to sixty days before the election—at the early stage of the fall campaign. Over a half century of polling, over 3,000 from this set of respondents offered a preelection preference for a major-party candidate and then reported voting for a major-party candidate when reinterviewed after the election. These respondents offer a window regarding the degree of switching over in the final two months of the campaign. From 1952 to 2008, only 7 percent switched their vote preference between the preelection interview and Election Day. The polarizing Obama–Romney campaign of 2012 appeared to harden choices even further. Only 2 percent of the ANES interviewees who held a major-part choice both during preelection and on Election Day changed sides. Ninety-eight percent stuck with their initial choice rather than find themselves influenced to shift by the barrage of campaign propaganda.[1]

Below the presidential level, the percentage of voters who stick with their party's choice can be even higher. For lower offices, the amount of information that reaches voters is often too slight to give them any reason to go against their party. Only in nonpartisan elections and primary contests (where party identification cannot be a criterion of choice) do voters vacillate in an erratic manner. In fact, vote preferences in primary contests are so fluid that pollsters have great difficulty predicting outcomes, even when they monitor opinion as late as a day or two before the election.

Of course, if party identification were the sole determinant of how people vote, election results would simply reflect the balance of Democratic and Republican identifiers. And since the ratio of Democratic to Republican identifiers changes only modestly in the short run, election results would be almost identical from one election to the next. In fact, election results often depart considerably from the voter division that would occur with a strict party-line vote.

When an election is decided on a party-line basis, the result is called the *normal vote*. At one time, the normal vote was considered a constant of politics. The calculation was that assuming a 50–50 split by Independents and a balanced, minimal defection rate by partisans (about 10 percent on each side), the nation-level normal vote would be a narrow Democratic win by about 54 percent Democratic to 46 percent Republican (Converse 1966; see also Petrocik 1989). This calculation reflects the Democratic edge in party identification that more than counterbalances the higher turnout rate among Republicans than Democrats.

Figure 9.1 presents a sixty-four-year approximation of the normal vote, between 1948 and 2012, derived from the national division of party identification.[2] Note

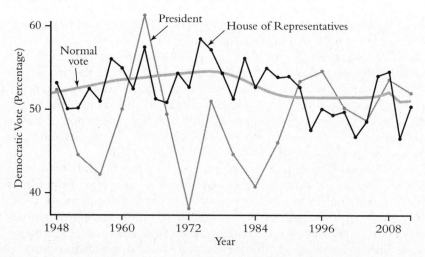

FIGURE 9.1 The national two-party vote (percent Democratic), 1948–2012.

Source: Compiled by the authors.

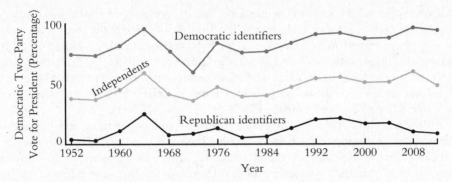

FIGURE 9.2 Party identification and the vote for president, 1952–2012.

Source: Based on American National Election Studies election data.

the disappearance of the Democrats' once-dominant edge over the Republicans. Nationally, the normal vote is approximated by the national vote in congressional elections. As Figure 9.1 shows, the national House vote between 1948 and 1992 never varied from between 50 and 59 percent Democratic, averaging at the expected 54 percent Democratic. The Democrats' prior large advantage in party identification thus explains why the Democrats controlled the House of Representatives (and usually the Senate) for forty years running, from 1954 to 1994. In 1994 the Republicans suddenly gained control of the House after their forty-year drought. This could not have happened without a change in the normal vote brought about by Republican gains in party identification.

The difference between the actual vote and the normal vote represents the *short-term partisan forces* of the election. National-level short-term forces are modest for congressional elections, so party control of Congress is largely determined by the normal vote. But for the presidency, short-term forces can be of major importance. As Figure 9.1 shows, the national vote for president often departs significantly from the normal vote. In fact, during the post–World War II era, the presidency has been won by the Republicans as often as by the Democrats.

Deviations of election results from the normal vote do not signify that the usual role of party identification in shaping election results has broken down. Instead, one finds that the party favored by short-term forces is the beneficiary of most of the short-term party defections, and it also wins the majority of the Independent vote. Figure 9.2 shows this pattern over the sixteen presidential elections from 1952 through 2012.

When short-term forces favor the Republicans, Democrats defect beyond their usual rate; Republicans are even more loyal to their party than usual, and Independents vote overwhelmingly Republican. With pro-Democratic short-term forces, the pattern is the reverse—with unusually frequent Republican defections and a Democratic trend among Independents.

Short-Term Forces Below the Presidential Level

For state and local elections, the normal vote reflects the partisan balance of the particular state or local constituency rather than the nation as a whole. Due to the kinds of people who reside in the area, the local normal vote is often one sided in favor of the Republicans or Democrats. Election results reflect the local normal vote plus any short-term forces that carry over from national politics (or from higher-level state or local contests). In addition, the local vote reflects the short-term forces generated by the local candidates and their campaign. One way of thinking about local short-term forces is as the personal vote generated by the candidates themselves (Cain, Ferejohn, and Fiorina 1987).

Although candidates for local office run less visible races than presidential candidates, their own campaigns help determine their electoral fate. The importance of local campaigns is indicated by the fact that as many as half the voters in a national election report that they split their ticket rather than vote for one party's candidate for all offices (Burden and Kimball 2002). Because of this ticket splitting, the same constituency often votes the Democratic candidate into one office and the Republican candidate into another.

As for president, election outcomes below the presidential level depend in large part on the short-term forces of the specific campaign. By one estimate, short-term forces for the statewide offices of governor and U.S. senator are about as large as for president (Erikson, Wright, and McIver 1994, ch. 9). The implication is that statewide (and perhaps local) outcomes readily depart by 10 or 15 percentage points from the state (or local) normal vote. Even where one party dominates, the disadvantaged party often can win when it fields the stronger candidate.

Who Are the Floating Voters?

Election outcomes are the result of both the normal vote and short-term partisan forces of the campaign. Voters whose choice is determined by the campaign rather than a long-term partisan commitment are called *floating voters*. An important question remains: How informed are the floating voters? If the floating voters were more politically informed than the average, we would think that election trends are essentially the response of the most politically alert segment of the public. But if the reverse is true—that floaters are *more* politically *ignorant* than the average—then we might be pushed toward the more dismal conclusion that election trends are largely the result of campaign propaganda of the sort that appeals to the voters least capable of making an informed evaluation.

Thanks to a classic article by Converse (1962) and an elaboration by Zaller (1992, 2004a; see also Alvarez 1997), we have a good but complicated theory regarding floating voters. Consider a candidate's decision to pitch the campaign at inattentive and unsophisticated voters or at attentive and sophisticated voters. On one hand, the more attentive voters are easier to reach with new campaign messages. On the other hand, these attentive voters are more hardened in their views. Their accumulated storage of political information helps bolster their initial views against intruding information. For example, a Republican who is highly informed about politics is better equipped to discount Democratic propaganda than one who is more politically ignorant. Less attentive voters are more easily swayed, but only if new information reaches them.

Given these complications, the information level of floating voters depends considerably on the intensity of the campaign and the flow of information. When the information flow is low, the least attentive voters are so uninformed that they lack any basis for switching between candidates. They vote according to their initial partisan predisposition, if they vote at all. Attentive voters, meanwhile, although more resistant to influence from campaign propaganda, sometimes change their candidate choice when new information reaches them. However, when the information flow is high, even the least attentive voters receive some information. Because these least attentive voters are the most influenced by new information they receive, they contribute disproportionately to electoral volatility.

The battle for the presidency attracts great interest and large voter turnout, with almost all voters receiving some campaign exposure. The universal intake of new information during a presidential campaign loosens a great number of voters from their partisan moorings—particularly among the least attentive voters. The tiny fraction of presidential voters who manage completely to avoid the campaign maintain stable candidate preferences throughout. But setting these few cases aside, partisan defections and preelection wavering in candidate choice are most frequent among voters with the least exposure to presidential campaign information.

Table 9.1 illustrates the relationship between our information scale, introduced in Chapter 3 and defined in Appendix, and partisan defection in the 2012 presidential election. Defectors are partisans who vote against their party. First, let us consider the Democratic identifiers in 2012. Although the vast majority voted for Obama, the few defectors were drawn mainly from "low"-information voters;

TABLE 9.1   Vote for President, 2012, by Information Level and Party Identification*

	Information		
	Low	Medium	High
Democratic identifiers			
Obama	88%	94%	96%
Romney	12	6	4
	100%	100%	100%
Independent identifiers			
Obama	53%	48%	39%
Romney	40	52	61
	100%	100%	100%
Republican identifiers			
Obama	17%	8%	5%
Romney	83	92	95
	100%	100%	100%

*Information scale based on the correctness of relative placement of candidates on issues. For details, see Appendix.

Source: Based on American National Election Studies, 2012 election data.

"high-information" Democrats were the most steadfast for Obama. Among Republicans, similarly, the few defections were mainly among the less-informed voters. In general, low-information partisan voters were three or more times more likely to defect than their high-information counterparts. (Overall, Republicans defected at a slightly lower rate than Democrats in 2012; Romney's loss is because of fewer Republican identifiers than Democrats.)

Table 9.1 also shows the voting behavior of self-proclaimed Independents in the 2012 presidential election. In 2012, Independent voters were fairly evenly divided (slightly pro-Romney) but with a clear difference based on the level of information. Following the usual pattern, the least-informed Independent voters flocked disproportionately to the winner, Obama. In 1992, 1996, and 2008—all clear Democratic presidential triumphs—the Democratic presidential candidate did well among all Independents, particularly the least informed. In 1988, the last time a Republican won a decisive presidential victory, the first President Bush did well among the Independents, especially the least informed.

Knowledgeable voters tend to sort as Democratic and Republican partisans based on their beliefs and stick to them. Less-informed voters enter the campaign as relatively blank slates, available to persuasion by the short-term forces of the campaign. We see this when we follow the vote over the presidential elections from 1984 to 2012 separately for high-information voters and low-information voters. Among the ANES's "highly informed" presidential voters (by criteria similar to those used here for the 2012 election), the 1984–2012 trend in the two-party vote was slight:

	1984	1988	1992	1996	2000	2004	2008	2012
% Dem. among high-information voters	46%	48%	56%	48%	48%	48%	47%	46%

But among ANES's low-information voters, we see considerable volatility:

	1984	1988	1992	1996	2000	2004	2008	2012
% Dem. among low-information voters	44%	48%	61%	77%	63%	50%	60%	58%

As Converse (1962, 578) argues, it sometimes seems that "not only is the electorate as a whole quite uninformed, but it is the least-informed members within the electorate who seem to hold the critical 'balance of power' in the sense that alternatives in the governing party depend disproportionately on shifts in their sentiment."[3]

We might even be tempted to conclude that the most effective presidential campaign would be one aimed directly at the voter who is normally inattentive and uninformed about politics. But recall that the inattentive voter is a less accessible target of campaign messages. Note, too, the tendency of the least informed to dilute their influence by not voting. Based on self-reports, the 2012 voter turnout within the least- and most-informed categories was as follows:

	Low Information	High Information
Voted	68%	93%
Did not vote	32	7
	100%	100%

The electoral contribution of the least-informed citizens is diluted by their low motivation to vote.

9-2 Policy Issues and Voters

Despite our current knowledge about voting behavior, scholars do not fully agree on the precise role of policy issues in elections. From what we know about the capabilities of average American voters, we are not surprised that many scholars are skeptical of the capacity of candidates' policy proposals and ideological leanings to affect many voter decisions. Among the most pessimistic are the authors of *The American Voter*, undoubtedly the single most influential book on voting behavior. They found the electorate almost wholly without detailed information on the issues of the day, unable to judge the rationality of government policies, and unable to appraise the appropriateness of the means necessary to arrive at desirable ends (Campbell et al. 1960, 543).

The American Voter, however, was based on the two Eisenhower elections from the quiescent 1950s. Several studies of subsequent elections—with titles such as *The Changing American Voter* (Nie, Verba, and Petrocik 1976), *The New American Voter* (Miller and Shanks 1996), and *The American Voter Revisited* (Lewis-Beck et al. 2008)—offer a rather different interpretation of the capabilities of the American voter. Beginning with the Johnson–Goldwater election of 1964, political issues and political ideology have become increasingly important as determinants of the vote in the United States. The reason for this growth of issue voting is that parties and candidates have become more polarized on liberal versus conservative lines. But just how important issues have become remains controversial.

For voters to be influenced by policy issues when they cast their ballots, two conditions must be met. First, the voters must be aware of the differences between the policy views of the candidates. Second, the voters must be motivated to vote on the basis of the issues that divide the candidates. Evidence of issue voting is strongest when the divergence between the candidate stances is strong and the issue is of considerable importance to the electorate.

Here, we examine the evidence of policy voting in presidential elections. Most of the data analysis that follows is from the ANES survey of the 2012 presidential election. The 2012 contest saw an exceptional amount of issue voting—even more than in other recent elections in the current era of partisan polarization.

Voter Perceptions of Candidate Differences, 2012

A necessary condition for voting on the basis of candidates' policy positions is that the voters perceive actual policy differences between the candidates. Following their usual procedure, in 2012 the ANES researchers asked respondents for their perceptions of the presidential candidates' positions on a series of seven-point scales representing several issues. Table 9.2 arranges these data to show how voters rated the Democratic victor, President Barack Obama, relative to his Republican opponent, Mitt Romney, on five issues.

Individuals could rate Obama to the left of Romney (correct), rate Romney to the left of Obama (incorrect), or place the two candidates in a tie (presumably incorrect). Additionally, on each issue scale some voters (generally around 10 percent) gave incomplete ratings, claiming not to know the position of one or both of the major candidates. We also scored responses as incomplete in all instances where the respondent had no opinion on the issue.

Table 9.2 shows voter perceptions of the candidates' relative positions on issues where Obama and Romney clearly differed. On all these issues, a majority of voters ordered the candidates correctly. Obama was seen as to Romney's left by anywhere from 61 to 82 percent of the respondents who said they voted; meanwhile, from 5 to 14 percent mistakenly placed Romney to the left of Obama.

The five respondent ratings of candidate ideology shown in Table 9.2 were among the seven ratings that contributed to our classification on our information index. Among voters in the 2012 election, a respectable 34 percent were "high-information" scorers, meaning they saw Obama to Romney's left on all seven items. "Low-information" scorers constituted 27 percent of the voting total, as they correctly identified the relative placement of the candidates on no more than four of

---

TABLE 9.2 **Voter Perceptions of Issue Differences Between Presidential Candidates, 2012**

	Obama Left of Romney	Romney Left of Obama	Same or Incomplete Ratings
Liberal–conservative ideology	78%	14%	8%
Domestic spending	82	8	10
Defense spending	61	18	21
Standard of living	81	8	11
Aid to blacks	69	8	23
Abortion	82	5	13
Medical Care	82	7	11

Source: Based on National Election Studies, 2012 election data. Each percentage is based on voters only. Relative positions are determined by voters' responses on a seven-point scale, except for the abortion issue, where the question presents a four-point scale. For full question wording, see Appendix.

the seven issues. The remaining 37 percent were in between. Thus, roughly speaking, one-third of active presidential voters are clearly tuned in to the candidates' ideological differences and about one quarter are not, with the remainder somewhere in between. As usual, our picture of the electorate is mixed.

Policy Issues, Ideology, and Votes, 2012

In order to vote on the basis of policy issues, it is not enough for voters to become aware of the candidates' policy differences. In addition, they must find these choices sufficiently important to influence their vote choices. With policy voting, we would observe people voting for the candidate closest to their own views. This would usually mean liberals voting Democratic and conservatives voting Republican.

Table 9.3 presents a simple evidence of policy voting in the 2012 presidential election. This table shows that over a variety of issues, voters who prefer the liberal position gave the most support to Obama, while voters preferring the conservative position gave the most support to Romney. Of these ten issues, what divided the electorate most in terms of influencing its vote choice (with vote gaps in the 50 percent range) were the Affordable Care Act (Obamacare), defense spending, and domestic spending. Farther behind were a guaranteed standard of living, aid to blacks, taxing the rich more, and gay marriage. Trailing in importance were the so-called cultural issues of abortion, immigration reform, and gun control.

It is typical that voters vary most on the basis of economic issues and less on the basis of cultural issues. Foreign policy can also intervene, depending on the circumstances. From 2004 to 2008, the war in Iraq interjected itself as a salient issue. The strong influence of foreign policy on the campaign was unusual, in that in normal times voters supposedly do not put foreign policy as their top priority. But a war and nation-building in the Middle East during the midst of a war on terror are not normal times.

It is worth noting also the polarization on gay marriage, which of course is a prime cultural issue. During the 2012 campaign, Obama offered his endorsement of gay marriage. It emerged as an issue to divide people's votes.[4]

Because so many issues seem to matter, we should be able to improve our vote predictions by taking into account voter positions on many issues simultaneously rather than one issue at a time. Table 9.4 shows the relationship between general liberal–conservative ideology and the 2012 vote in two different ways. First, the table shows the vote as a function of ideological self-identification, where ideological identification is measured using the full seven-point scale from "extremely liberal" to "extremely conservative." Ideological identification predicts fairly well, particularly for voters on the liberal side of the spectrum. Of the 23 percent who placed themselves at one of the three positions on the liberal side of the spectrum, 93 percent voted for Obama over Romney. Of the 37 percent on the conservative side, 82 percent chose Romney over Obama. Thus, for the vast majority of voters with an ideological leaning, the presidential choice was in line with their ideological preference. But not all voters identify with one of the ideological sides. Of the 44 percent of voters either moderate or without an ideological preference, almost two-thirds chose Obama over Romney.

TABLE 9.3 **2012 Presidential Vote by Policy Opinions**

Policy	Obama (%)	Romney (%)	(%)	Difference
Obamacare				
Favor	84	16	= 100%	+71
Oppose	13	87	= 100%	
Defense spending				
Less	78	32	= 100%	+45
More	32	68	= 100%	
Domestic spending				
More	81	19	= 100%	+59
Less	22	78	= 100%	
Aid to blacks				
Favor	88	12	= 100%	+54
Oppose	34	66	= 100%	
Guaranteed job, standard of living				
Favor	81	19	= 100%	+48
Oppose	33	67	= 100%	
Legalize gay marriage				
Favor	74	26	= 100%	+41
Oppose	33	67	= 100%	
Raise taxes on rich				
Favor	65	35	= 100%	+45
Oppose	20	80	= 100%	
Abortion				
Permit	70	30	= 100%	+30
Restrict	40	60	= 100%	
Path to citizenship				
Favor	62	38	= 100%	+26
Oppose	36	64	= 100%	
More gun control				
Favor	74	26	= 100%	+36
Oppose	38	62	= 100%	

Source: Based on National Election Studies, 2012 election data. Votes for minor-party candidates are ignored.

The second part of Table 9.4 shows the vote as a function of the ten-item composite liberal–conservative index introduced in Chapter 3. Here the degree of prediction is, if anything, even better. The ten-item scale has a twenty-one-point range from +10 (perfect liberal) to −10 (perfect conservative). Among the 22 percent on the far left, from −5 to −10, 97 percent voted for Obama over Romney. Similarly, among the 19 percent who are on the far right, from +5 to +10, 98 percent chose Romney.

TABLE 9.4   Presidential Vote by Two Summary Measures of Liberalism–Conservatism, 2012

| | Self-Identification on Ideological Scale | | | | | | | |
| | Extremely Liberal | | | | | | Extremely Conservative | |
	1	2	3	4	5	6	7	None
Obama (%)	98	97	86	62	26	12	7	66
Romney (%)	2	3	14	38	74	88	93	34
(Percentage of voters)	(2)	(12)	(8)	(22)	(15)	(18)	(3)	(18)

Ten-Item Composite Issue Index*

| | Most Liberal | | | | | | Most Conservative |
	−10 to −8	−7 to −5	−4 to −2	−1 to +1	+2 to +4	+5 to +7	+8 to +10
Obama (%)	100	96	81	56	22	2	0
Romney (%)	0	4	19	44	78	98	100
(Percentage of voters)	(5)	(17)	(19)	(22)	(19)	(15)	(4)

*For construction of the ten-item composite issue index, see Appendix.

Source: Based on American National Election Studies, 2012 election data.

From this demonstration, voters with consistently liberal or conservative views are highly predictable in their vote choice. But most voters are not at either ideological extreme. Nearly one-fourth (22 percent) are near the exact center—in the −1 to +1 range on the ten-point scale—and must be described as decidedly moderate or centrist. Many others appear only vaguely liberal or conservative, and their votes do not always follow from their ideological direction.[5]

In part, the predictability of votes from ideology as shown in Table 9.4 is due to voters simply responding to their partisan background. Liberals tend to identify with the Democratic Party and conservatives with the Republicans (Chapter 3). Thus, just by voting their party identification, voters tend to support the candidates closest to their views. Issue voting is further enhanced by party defections and issue voting by Independents. Table 9.5 illustrates this tendency by showing the relationships between ideology and the vote within the three categories of party identification. Conservative Democrats and liberal Republicans, while rare in today's polarized political climate, are the partisan groups most prone to defect in their presidential voting. Meanwhile, Independents present the clearest example of issue voting. Neutral in terms of partisanship, they generally vote Democratic if liberal and Republican if conservative.

TABLE 9.5   **2012 Presidential Vote by Ideology with Party Identification Controlled**

	Democrats			Independents			Republicans		
	Ideological Self-Identification								
	Lib.	Mod.	Con.	Lib.	Mod.	Con.	Lib.	Mod.	Con.
Obama (%)	97	84	93	91	59	16	21	20	6
Romney (%)	3	16	7	9	41	84	79	80	94
(Percentage of voters)	(19)	(10)	(4)	(7)	(13)	(16)	(1)	(4)	(25)

	Democrats			Independents			Republicans		
	Ten-Item Issue Index*								
	Lib.	Center	Con.	Lib.	Center	Con.	Lib.	Center	Con.
Obama (%)	96	90	61	93	42	14	11	20	4
Romney (%)	4	10	39	7	58	86	89	80	96
(Percentage of voters)	(24)	(12)	(1)	(10)	(15)	(12)	(1)	(9)	(16)

*Ideology scale collapsed so −10 to −3 = liberal; −2 to +2 = center; +3 to +10 = conservative.

Source: Based on American National Election Studies, 2012 election data.

Information and Ideological Voting

As one would expect, ideological voting is most prevalent among voters who are highly informed about candidate positions. In surveys, the observed relationship between ideology and vote choice becomes most pronounced when we select the most informed voters (Knight 1985; Jacoby 1991). Figure 9.3 illustrates how issue voting rises with information, illustrating with 2012 ANES data.

For voters in both the high-information and low-information categories, the figure shows how presidential voting varied with issue positions. For each group, Figure 9.3 shows the relationship between the ten-item index of respondent liberalism–conservatism and the vote. Graphed percentages represent the Obama proportion of the two-party vote.

The graph shows that the sharpness of the tendency for liberals to vote Democratic and conservatives to vote Republican varies with the voters' level of information. Among the "high-information" voters, there were few exceptions to the rule that liberals voted Democratic and conservatives Republican. In fact, 98 percent of highly informed liberals in the −5 to −10 range on the twenty-one-point ideology scale voted for Obama and 98 percent of highly informed conservatives in the +5 to +10 range voted for Romney. Informed ideologues almost never voted for the ideologically "wrong" candidate. (Together, these groups comprised about 14 percent of all voters.)

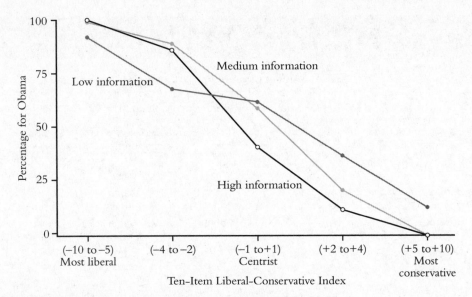

FIGURE 9.3 Issue voting by level of information, 2012.

Source: Based on American National Election Studies election data.

Among "low-information" voters, the figure shows a milder tendency toward ideological voting. But it is remarkable that most of these voters with little information about the issues found ways to vote "correctly" based on their issue positions.[6]

Issue Voting and Candidate Advantage

So far we have seen evidence of ideological and issue voting whereby the most liberal voters based on a survey item or set of items vote Democratic while the most conservative vote Republican. We might also wonder which issues help or hurt the various candidates. On a given issue in 2012, who did the voters see as closer to them: Obama or Romney? To set up the test, we analyze responses to the 2012 ANES items regarding ideological leanings plus four issues where the candidates took divergent stands and on which the voters were asked to place the candidates on the same scale as the voters. On most issues, these scales were the ANES seven-point scales where voters were asked to rate themselves and the candidates from 1 (liberal) to 7 (conservative). We identified respondents who were closer to Obama or Romney based on these scales. Many respondents of course placed themselves equidistant between the candidates or assigned identical scale scores to the two candidates and thus could not be counted as closer to one candidate over the other on the particular issue. Others were excluded due to missing data on one or more of the three necessary scale scores needed for a comparison. Importantly, even if a voter's ratings indicated a greater proximity to one candidate over the other, we excluded the relative rating if the voter mistakenly scored Romney to the left of Obama on the issue. The argument behind this exclusion is that voters who assign the "wrong" relative positions to the candidates are mainly "guessing" (and guessing wrong) and would not likely have been influenced by the issue in the election.

TABLE 9.6   Presidential Vote Choice and Relative Closeness of Voters to Candidates, 2012

	Percent Closer to		Vote of Those Closer to	
	Obama	**Romney**	**Obama**	**Romney**
Liberal–conservative ideological identification	41	52	97% Obama 3% Romney	10% Obama 90% Romney
Domestic spending	44	50	92% Obama 8% Romney	14% Obama 86% Romney
Defense spending	45	46	91% Obama 9% Romney	9% Obama 91% Romney
Government versus private health care	43	50	89% Obama 11% Romney	17% Obama 83% Romney
Abortion rights	59	33	75% Obama 25% Romney	22% Obama 78% Romney

Note: Respondents scored in terms of closeness only if they perceived Romney to the right of Obama on the issue.

Source: Based on American National Election Studies, 2012 election data.

Table 9.6 shows the results. For each item, the table presents the proportion of voters closer to each candidate by the criteria outlined plus each group's vote choice. On the five issues, from 91 to 94 percent of the voters saw themselves as closer to one candidate than the other. Romney held a slight edge on ideological identification. (More voters saw themselves as closer to Romney's conservatism than to Obama's liberalism.) Slight pluralities also saw themselves closer to Romney on domestic government spending, defense spending, and health care. However on abortion, voters preferred Obama's pro-choice position more than Romney's pro-life position by about two to one. The right-hand side of Table 9.6 shows the electoral consequences of these beliefs. Varying slightly by the issue (most on ideological identification, least on abortion policy), there was about a 87- to 53-percentage-point differential in the vote choices of those who saw themselves closer to Obama versus those seeing themselves closer to Romney. Thus, even analyzed separately, positions on these issues provided a fairly useful litmus test for how 2012 voters cast their presidential ballots.

Overall, a perusal of Table 9.6 would suggest a very close contest in terms of which candidate was, on balance, closer to the voters. Romney wins on closeness except on abortion, where Obama's position is decisively favored. We can consider voters' net balance on the five items shown in Table 9.6. Summing across issues, we find that 45 percent of all voters in the 2012 ANES sample saw themselves as closer to Obama and 90 percent of them cast their ballots for Obama. On the other side of the ledger, the identical 45 percent saw themselves closer to Romney and 90 percent of this group voted for Romney. Meanwhile, a pivotal 10 percent were in the middle when summing across issues, and they supported Obama by a 64 to 36 ratio. In terms of wooing voters on issues, the contest between Obama and Romney was very close.

Obama may owe his reelection to other factors, such as general likeability. We should be somewhat cautious, however, in assigning one candidate with the advantage in terms of issue proximity. Note how relative closeness depends on the item under discussion. How we do the scoring depends on survey researchers' decisions regarding which issues are sampled.

Prediction and Causation

Policy issues, ideological identifications, group attitudes, retrospective evaluations, candidate evaluations, and party identifications all seem to predict the vote. The more variables we take into account, the better the prediction. To see that most votes can be predicted, let us simultaneously predict year 2012 presidential votes from the three best predictors: (1) party identification, (2) the ten-issue ideological scale, and (3) net candidate evaluations. Net candidate evaluations are based on the voter's relative scoring of the two candidates on an eleven-point likeability scale.[7] (Obama outpolled Romney on the eleven-point scale 54 to 40.) We simply score each predictor as pro-Democratic, neutral, or pro-Republican and sum them to make a scale from −3 (liberal Democrats who like Obama better) to +3 (conservative Republicans who like Romney better). The results are shown in Table 9.7.

Table 9.7 scores 9 percent at zero with balanced positions on the three predictors; these seemingly neutral voters gave a slight margin to Obama over Romney, 53 to 47 percent, close to an even split. For the remaining 89 percent with a partisan tilt to their relevant attitudes, the vast majority—98 percent—voted in accord with the direction of their partisan attitudes. At the extreme, 35 percent of the voters found all three relevant attitudes in partisan agreement; they were either liberal Democrats who liked Obama better or the slightly smaller group of conservative Republicans who liked Romney better. All of this set—over a third of the voting

---

TABLE 9.7 Predicting 2012 Presidential Votes from the Summary of Partisan Attitudes

	Pro-Obama			Neutral		Pro-Romney	
	−3	−2	−1	0	+1	+2	+3
Obama (%)	100	97	80	47	16	3	0
Romney (%)	0	3	20	53	84	97	100
(Percentage of voters)	(20)	(20)	(8)	(9)	(14)	(12)	(15)

Note: Index scores represent sum of partisan direction. (+ = Republican, − = Democratic) on party identification, the ten-point left–right scale, and net candidate evaluations. −3 voters are liberal Democrats who like Obama better. +3 voters are conservative Republicans who like Romney better.

Source: Based on American National Election Studies, 2012 election data.

electorate—voted consistent with their partisan attitudes. The lesson to be learned is that when voters possess consistent reasons to vote one way or another, their votes are usually consistent with those reasons.[8]

We must be cautious, however, in attributing causal connections. Voters have a need to maintain cognitive consistency between their partisan attitudes and their vote. Of course, the obvious way to achieve this consistency is to vote according to one's partisan attitude. The problem is that when people decide whom to vote for, they may also rearrange their political attitudes to fit their vote decision. Once citizens decide to vote Democratic, for example, they tend to develop new attitudes even more favorable to the Democratic point of view. Thus, when a 2012 Obama supporter asserted the economy was prospering, that Obama was a great leader, or that Obama was right on the issues, we might suspect that some of these attitudes are generated to support the vote choice rather than the reverse.

Consider the voter whose views are initially out of alignment—for example, the voter might have liberal views combined with an initial attraction to the more conservative Republican candidate. How this voter would resolve this dilemma depends on which of the three elements—perceptions of the candidates, policy views, and candidate preference—is the weakest link. If the voter feels strongly about his or her policy views and is certain the favored candidate opposes them, the voter could resolve the dilemma by reversing the candidate choice. This would be an example of policy voting. If the candidate's stands are only vaguely known, the easiest way out might be to shift his or her estimate of the candidate stances. This process, known as *projection*, is a frequent way out of the dilemma. Voters who see conservative candidates as liberals or vice versa are often projecting their favored views onto their favored candidates (or projecting views they dislike onto candidates they dislike).

A third possible resolution would be for the voter to change a relatively weak policy stance to make it consistent with the position of the favored candidate. Because of such *rationalization*, it becomes impossible to disentangle fully the causal process that produces a correlation between voters' policy views and their candidate choice. Consider, for example, the many voters observed to be both liberals and Obama supporters. Presumably liberals supported Obama because they were attracted to his liberalism. But in theory, part of the explanation could be that liking Obama—for whatever reason—made his supporters think better of his policy positions.

Does rationalization seriously contaminate survey analyses of the vote? In an analysis of panel data from various electoral contexts, Lenz (2012) finds several instances of voter rationalization. One clear instance involved the issue of social security in the close 2000 presidential campaign. George W. Bush campaigned hard in favor of allowing social security recipients to invest their funds in the stock market; his opponent Al Gore emphasized the dangers of this approach, offering the metaphor of insuring the funds in a "lockbox." This distinction became clearer over the campaign, especially when the two candidates emphasized their positions in their first debate.

Over the 2000 campaign, voters increasingly became aware of the candidates' divide on the social security issue and their vote choices became increasingly consistent with their personal preferences on social security (Johnston, Hagan, and Jamieson 2004). This of course is consistent with the notion that upon learning the candidates' positions voters shift their candidate choice based on this new information. But no such shift occurred. Instead, Lenz found that voters shifted their positions on social security to become consistent with their candidate choice; Bush supporters increasingly saw the investment plan as a good idea while Gore voters saw it as increasingly risky. This was a classic example of voter rationalization, revising their views on issues to make them consistent with their candidate choice.

Every report of a relationship between voter attitudes and voter decisions should be read cautiously with an eye to the possibility that the seeming evidence of policy voting may be contaminated by widespread voter projection or rationalization. Still, we should consider the context. The social security example involved complex considerations—a "hard" issue—upon which most voters lacked expertise. Thus voters rarely switched their candidate choice based on a candidate's social security spiel. The result would be different if the voter learning involved candidate positions on an "easy" issue like race or whether government should spend more to help poor and middle-class voters. Besides, we should remember that voters tend to stand firm in their candidate choice during a campaign. Thus we should not expect that new information about candidate issue positions would change many minds. Partisanship in particular keeps voter choice grounded in their policy preferences. As a standing decision, liberals generally vote Democratic because their ideology leads them to the Democratic Party and conservatives generally vote Republican because their ideology leads them to the Republican Party.[9]

9-3 Explaining Election Outcomes

Explaining election outcomes requires a different level of analysis than explaining voter decisions. At the microlevel, analysts try to account for why people vote the way they do. At the macrolevel, analysts try to account for short-term forces and electoral trends—for example, why Obama defeated McCain in 2008 and Romney in 2012, whereas Bush had won in 2004. In this section, we explore the sources of electoral change. We identify four sets of influences for our discussion: the electorate's partisanship, the economy and other aspects of government management, the relative attractiveness of the candidates, and the ideological (issue) proximity of the candidates to the voters.

Partisanship

As we discussed in Chapter 4, the partisanship of the national electorate (often called *macropartisanship*) changes over time, but usually in small increments. For most of the post–World War II period, the Democrats had a numerical edge over the Republicans in macropartisanship. This Democratic advantage declined in fits and starts beginning in the early 1980s and by the early part of the twenty-first century became virtually nonexistent, leaving the two parties in a state of virtual parity in terms of their allegiance by the general public. Starting about 2006, the trend switched again, with a decline in Republican allegiance following the unpopularity of George W. Bush during the later years of his presidency. The Democrats grew their lead in "party i.d." but by no means to the level it once was in the 1960s and 1970s. Future trends, of course, are unpredictable.

We have seen in this chapter that party identification matters mightily in the accounting of individual votes: Everything else being equal, Democrats usually vote Democratic and Republicans vote Republican. We see the importance of partisanship at the macro level ("macropartisanship") when we turn to elections for the House of Representatives. For nineteen straight elections spanning forty years—from the 1954 to the 1994 elections—the Democrats won the most votes and controlled the most seats. During this period, the Democrats were the dominant party as the nation's "normal vote" favored the Democrats. With minimal short-term forces interfering with the national vote for Congress, a Democratic House (and almost always a Democratic Senate) was guaranteed. Following the forty-year Democratic reign, the Republicans enjoyed twelve years of firm but narrow control of the House (and, usually, the Senate), helped greatly by the more even division of the electorate's party preferences. The year 2006 ushered in the brief return of Democratic control of Congress that lasted until the Republican surge in 2010. It would seem that party control of Congress now is in regular contention.

As discussed in section 9-1, for one party to hold the edge in terms of the normal vote is not necessarily a guarantee of electoral success. In elections for governor, for example, both the Democrats and the Republicans are competitive in most states even when one party holds the edge in terms of party identification. At the national level, the Democratic edge in partisanship and the normal vote has not prevented the Republicans from winning their share of presidential elections. The lesson is that the minority party can overcome its electoral handicap by choosing candidates and programs that appeal to the electorate.

Retrospective Performance Evaluation: The Economy and Wars

Recall that voters are often motivated by their reaction to the nature of the times—their personal evaluation of government performance and their attribution to the presidential party. The electorate's net evaluation of the nature of the times is partially captured by its evaluation of the president. Especially when the incumbent president runs for reelection, a useful electoral predictor is simply the incumbent president's popularity as Election Day approaches. An axiom of politics is that when presidents seek reelection, an approval rating above 50 percent (Eisenhower, Johnson, Nixon, Reagan, Clinton) is followed by victory, while an approval rating below 50 percent (Ford, Carter, the first Bush) augurs defeat. George W. Bush and Barack Obama's approval ratings were only about 50 percent throughout their reelection campaigns, and they won their second terms only by narrow margins in the popular vote.

As we saw in Chapter 4, foreign policy helps drive presidential approval. Presidents gain popularity when they are seen as coping with foreign policy crises. George W. Bush's boost in the aftermath of 9/11 is the most visible example. However, prolonged wars (e.g., Vietnam and Iraq), prolonged crises (e.g., the Iran hostage crisis), and foreign policy folly (Iran-Contra) certainly do not help. It is a reasonable proposition that George W. Bush would have won a larger victory in 2004 if the fighting in Iraq had been contained or if the war had not been fought at all.

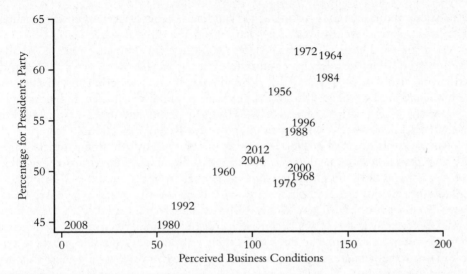

FIGURE 9.4 Presidential vote by perceptions of business conditions, 1956–2012.

Source: Compiled by the authors.

The perceived management of the economy is a particularly important aspect of presidential popularity (see Vavreck 2009). Beyond its effect on presidential popularity, the degree of economic prosperity is a key determinant of presidential election results. Prosperity on Election Day benefits the incumbent presidential party regardless of whether the president seeks reelection.

The effects of the economy on presidential elections can be observed directly. For fifteen post–World War II elections, Figure 9.4 graphs the vote (for the incumbent party) as a function of public perceptions of the degree of economic growth (or its absence) over the previous year, as measured by the University of Michigan's Survey of Consumers. Clearly, the healthier people see the economy, the more they vote for the president's party.

The 2012 election provides an interesting case regarding economic effects. Economic recovery had been slow following the sharp recession that hit in 2008 on George W. Bush's watch as president. Despite the sluggish recovery even as late as 2012, voters appeared hesitant to blame Obama. In fact, as Figure 9.4 shows, the electorate's perception of the recent economy was slightly more positive than average. On the eve of the 2012 election, people saw a growing economy as a hopeful sign of the future.[10]

Candidate Evaluations

One important source of changing short-term electoral forces is the changing cast of candidates. For election to any level of office, the personal attractiveness of the major-party candidates can be a decisive factor. At the presidential level, the electorate's attraction to the Republican and the Democratic candidates can vary dramatically from one election to the next. Using multivariate statistical techniques, analysts have shown these evaluations of candidate personalities and capabilities (based on a series of questions about likes and dislikes of the candidates) constitute a major determinant of electoral change (Stokes 1966; Kagay and Caldeira 1980; Erikson 2002).[11]

As mentioned earlier, Obama's electoral success was helped by his likeability. The most popular presidential candidate as recorded by the ANES's "likes-and-dislikes measure" was Dwight "Ike" Eisenhower, elected twice in the 1950s as the Republican standard-bearer. Eisenhower was a popular World War II general who engaged the voters with his warm smile. His basic popularity was a major factor in his landslide victories as a Republican in an era of Democratic dominance.

Are elections greatly determined simply by which candidate the people seem to like as personalities and leaders? It is not easy to disentangle the electorate's collective reactions to the candidates' personal attributes from the candidates' ideological reputations. Two of the candidates with the least personal appeal were Barry Goldwater (Republican, 1964) and George McGovern (Democrat, 1972). Were these candidates seen as unattractive because they lacked personal charm and leadership? Or were voters responding to cues from their political environment, as these two candidates were persistently vilified as ideological extremists during their runs for the presidency? Similarly, was Eisenhower's popularity due in part to the fact that his ideological imagery was that of a moderate? Was Reagan popular because of or despite his conservatism? It is to the candidates' ideological closeness to the voters that we turn to next.

Issue Positions of Candidates and Voters

Changing candidates provide more than a revolving set of personal attributes for the voter to judge. Each new candidate also brings a unique ideological tone and a new set of policy positions. Moreover, candidates (like the parties they represent) can shift their positions in response to the times. And candidates sometimes change their positions as well. Each shift of candidate positioning or shift in the electorate's preference can change the equation regarding which candidate is closest to the electorate's net preferences and in turn affect the election outcome. Let us examine how.

Part of the popular lore of politics is that in a two-person race, the candidate who stakes out the middle ground of the political spectrum will win by virtue of appealing to the moderate voter. In terms of their personal views, candidates tend to be more liberal (Democrat) or conservative (Republican) than their electorate. Yet the belief that moderate voters decide elections pushes candidates toward the center of the spectrum.

This logic is spelled out in a model of the vote developed by Anthony Downs (1958, Chapter 8) and illustrated in Figure 9.5. This figure presents voter positions as a bell-shaped distribution on the liberal–conservative spectrum. The Downs model assumes policy voters who prefer the candidate closest to their views on this spectrum. If both candidates are stationed near the center, as in Figure 9.5(a), neither will have the policy edge. But if one candidate veers toward one of the ideological extremes—as does the conservative in Figure 9.5(b)—then policy voters in the middle will support the opponent, giving that more moderate candidate the victory.

The Downs model predicts that Democratic candidates get more votes when they take moderate rather than liberal positions and that Republican candidates get more votes when they take moderate rather than conservative positions. These

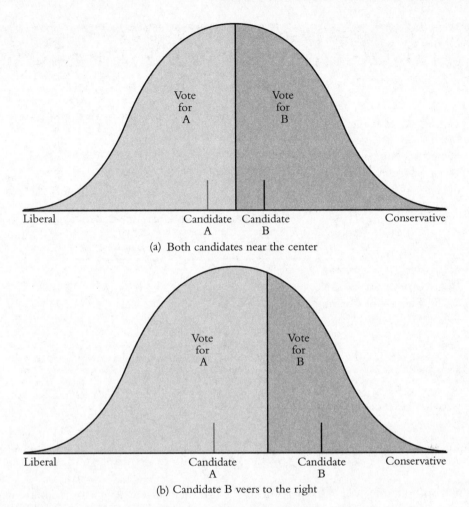

FIGURE 9.5 Candidate ideology and voter responses (hypothetical).

Source: Compiled by the authors.

hypotheses have received considerable support in research on congressional (U.S. House and Senate) elections (Erikson 1971; Wright and Berkman 1986; Erikson and Wright 2001; Canes-Wrone, Brady, and Cogan 2002; Erikson and Wright 2013).

Legislators create their own record of roll-call votes, which can be arrayed on a scale from extreme liberal to extreme conservative. Both Democrats and Republicans usually get ideological satisfaction from voting with their party's ideological extreme, but they gain electoral benefit from moderation. By one estimate, Congress members in the middle of the ideological spectrum generate as many as 10 percentage points more of the vote than they would at their party's ideological extreme (Erikson and Wright 2001).

Table 9.8 offers a simple illustration. Nationally in 2012, the major-party vote divisions for the House of Representatives and the presidency were very similar. The Democrats won 50.4 percent of the House vote (although only a minority of

| **TABLE 9.8**   Vote for House Incumbent Candidates (as Lead over Presidential Ticket) by Incumbent Roll-Call Ideology, 2012 |||

	Republican Incumbents' Roll-Call Ideology		
	Most Conservative	**In Between**	**Most Moderate**
Mean % for Rep. incumbent	63.4	61.4	59.3
Mean% for Romney in district	61.3	59.0	54.0
Mean % lead over Romney	**2.1%**	**2.4%**	**5.3%**
(*N* in parentheses)	(62)	(62)	(62)
	Democrat Incumbents' Roll-Call Ideology		
	Most Liberal	**In Between**	**Most Moderate**
Mean % for Dem. incumbent	74.1	71.0	63.1
Mean % for Obama in district	72.6	68.6	58.4
Mean % lead over Obama	**1.5%**	**2.4%**	**4.7%**
(*N* in parentheses)	(45)	(44)	(45)

Note: Ideology is measured as the weighted mean of the first- and second-dimension DW-NOMINATE scores, where the second dimension is weighted .35 times the first. This index measures the relative liberalism and conservatism of members of the House of Representatives and is based on their roll-call votes in 2011 and 2012. See Poole and Rosenthal (2007) for a discussion of DW-NOMINATE methodology. For each party, the members with contested elections are divided into roughly three equally sized groups based on ideological positions.

Source: Compiled by the authors.

seats), and Obama won 52.0 percent of the presidential vote. We can compare extremist and moderate Congress members of each party to see how they fared in the 2012 election compared to their presidential ticket; that is, by how much did their personal vote margins exceed or fall below those of their party's presidential ticket in their district. For a Republican, the question is how much did the representative lead (or lag) Romney. For a Democrat, the question is how much did the representative lead (or lag) Obama.

Table 9.8 shows the data where for each party incumbent representatives are grouped according to the ideological tendency of their roll-call votes. Each party's incumbent candidates are divided into three based on their roll-call voting—most extreme (conservative for Republicans, liberal for Democrats), in between, and (relatively) most moderate. For each party we see that the most extreme members have slimmer leads over their presidential running mate than do their more moderate counterparts. In 2012, for both Republican and Democratic House members, the modest ideological difference between belonging to their party's most extreme or moderate third was worth about 3 percentage points at the polls.[12]

If congressional contests can be decided by candidate ideology, the same must certainly be true for presidential elections. We have already seen that citizens' votes are determined by their personal positions on the left–right scale. Presidential election outcomes are partially determined by both the voters and the candidates' ideological positions—which candidates (and which parties) best reflect the preferences of the voting electorate.

To shed some light, we can examine ANES survey data. Since 1972, respondents have been asked not only to place themselves on the seven-point version of the ideological scale but also to locate the two major presidential candidates. Figure 9.6 traces the historical record, comparing the mean positions over time of the electorate and also the candidates as they are perceived by the ANES voters.

Of the eleven elections shown in Figure 9.6, the 1972 contest stands out as one clear case where most voters were closer ideologically to one candidate than the other. In 1972, Richard Nixon was decisively reelected over the Democratic nominee, George McGovern, who most voters saw as too liberal. Figure 9.6 also shows that in elections since 1972, the average voter was close to the midpoint between the mean perceptions of the two candidates' positions. A close scan of the figure also shows that in all but one contest (1980), voters were slightly closer ideologically to the Republican than to the Democratic candidate. But this may be deceptive. Voters comfortable with ideological language tend to vote Republican and on average are about as Republican as their relative ideological proximity from the candidates suggests. Some voters do not rate themselves or the candidates ideologically in ANES surveys. Those voters tend toward liberal positions on specific issues, and vote Democratic.

If we look at voter evaluations of candidate positions on specific issues rather than general ideology, they give the edge to the Democrats on some issues (e.g., abortion) and to the Republicans on others (e.g., affirmative action). The depiction in Figure 9.6, based on ideological perceptions alone, presents a rather static portrayal of Democratic and Republican candidates' relative proximity to the voters over time. Greater volatility can be obtained by measuring voter preferences and actual party positions over specific issues. *The Macro Polity* (Erikson, MacKuen, and Stimson 2002) measures the rival candidates' proximity to the voters in terms of the ideological distance between the liberalism–conservatism of the party platforms and the liberalism–conservatism of the electorate measured by Stimson's policy mood. Perhaps out of necessity to overcome their numerical handicap, it was the Republicans who took positions closer to the voters for most of the elections from the 1950s through the 1980s. Starting with Clinton, however, the Democrats have been the more moderate party. According to *The Macro Polity*, ideological proximity is a powerful predictor of presidential election outcomes once the electorate's partisanship is controlled.[13]

In the final analysis, what can we say about the role of issues and ideology in deciding election outcomes? Most political analysts and candidates believe that ideological issues divide Americans and that voters evaluate the ideological positions of candidates when they go to the polls. Because issues and ideology matter, ideological mood swings by the public and the ideological responses of candidates and party leaders contribute to the relative fortunes of the Democratic and Republican parties in American politics. Moreover, the belief that issues and ideology matter drives politicians to respond to changes in public preferences when they become visible. We examine how politicians respond to public opinion in the next chapter.

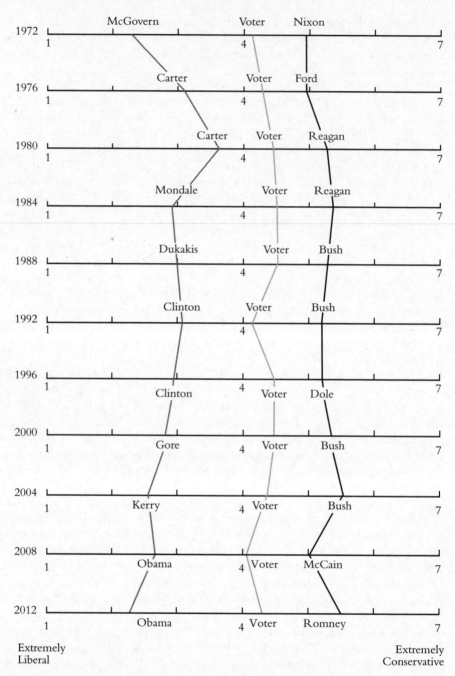

FIGURE 9.6 Mean ratings by voters of their own positions and candidates' positions on seven-point liberal–conservative scales, 1972–2012.

Source: Based on American National Election Studies data.

9-4 Conclusion

When the rational-activist model is fulfilled, elections are decided by voters choosing candidates on the basis of their policy views. By this standard, the record of recent presidential elections is mixed. Tracing back to the 1964 presidential election, Democratic and Republican presidential candidates have polarized on liberal versus conservative grounds sufficiently to give the voters a clear ideological choice. At the microlevel, many individual voters are motivated by the ideological menu when they cast their ballots. But they are also motivated by nonpolicy considerations. At the macrolevel, the electorate's collective reactions to candidate positions help shape their electoral verdict, but in conjunction with other considerations.

Apart from policy issues and ideology are additional determinants of the vote. As we have seen, people sometimes vote for or against the incumbent party on the basis of its past performance. One would find difficulty condemning this behavior as irrational. In addition, two important predictors of individuals' votes are their party identification and their evaluation of the personal characteristics of the candidates. To the extent that people vote on the basis of a party identification that is grounded in policy or ideological considerations (as when a staunch conservative is committed to the Republican Party) and to the extent that the candidates are ideologically typical of their party (see Chapter 10), party voting can be viewed as rational.

But what about voting on the basis of the candidates' personal characteristics? One of the best predictors of a person's vote is simply whether the voter likes the personal qualities of the Democratic candidate more than the Republican. We may be tempted to view voting on such a nonissue (or even apolitical) basis to be voting on the basis of irrelevant considerations. But this view may be mistaken. Writing over a quarter century ago, Morris Fiorina puts the question well:

> Various authors have suggested that voting on the basis of candidate qualities is irrational, or at least of lower order of rationality than voting on the issues.... Such suggestions apparently stem from the erroneous belief that attitudes toward the candidates reflect no more than Ike's smile, Nixon's beard, or Kennedy's accent. Actually, the bulk of the citizenry's impressions of the candidates focuses on qualities which are of legitimate relevance to the latter's capacity to govern: experience, leadership ability, and so on.... Why should a candidate's intelligence, administrative ability, etc., be any less a legitimate issue than where he stands on Medicare or aid to Israel? (1977, 618)

That voters choose the candidate they find to have the greatest character, competence, or trustworthiness is quite reasonable, even if their candidate is not the one who is closest to the voters on policy issues. Unfortunately, however, voters do not always have the necessary information to make good judgments about a candidate's character until after the candidate is elected president.

The collective decisions voters make at election time contain elements of both stability and change. That most voting decisions are based on long-standing partisan loyalty adds an element of stability. Electoral shifts are normally only temporary because voters shifting toward the advantaged party or candidate do not change their identification in the process. Consequently they may surge in the opposition partisan direction in a subsequent election, or even do so when voting in another contest held on the same date. Yet it is also true that partisan loyalties continually evolve, in part due to the entry of new voters and the departure of old and in part due to partisan conversions (see Chapters 4 and 5). In extreme, the change is sufficiently major to be labeled an electoral realignment. The most recent such realignment period, centered in the 1930s, produced a change from a considerable Republican advantage in national voting loyalties to a long-term Democratic edge in party identification that has persisted until recently. If another realignment is on the near horizon, it could restore the Republican Party to the predominant position it once held before the New Deal era of the 1930s. Or, it could restore the Democratic dominance of the later twentieth century. Also possible is a major change in the focus of the issues that separate the two parties but without any net change in the distribution of party loyalties. If any of these possibilities comes to pass, the public will have arranged its partisan loyalties as a long-term electoral response to the decisive issues of the day.

Critical Thinking Questions

1. People usually vote for candidates who are closest to them on policy issues. But are people's votes really caused by their positions on political issues, and if so how would we know?
2. Some people say they vote for the person, not the party. Others vote a straight party ticket. Which do you think is best for democratic accountability?
3. It may be a fantasy to think that voters generally select candidates based on their issue positions. But suppose it were true. How might politicians behave differently before an attentive, issue-oriented public?

Endnotes

1. Like all data presentations from the 2012 ANES face-to-face survey, the reported findings are based on the properly weighted sample.
2. In Figure 9.1, the normal vote is constructed as the prediction of the House vote from regressing the vote on macrolevel party identification in quarter three of the election year and then smoothing the trendline via the LOWESS procedure.
3. The reader might be curious regarding information level and the rate of switching sides during the campaign. As discussed earlier, only six percent of ANES respondents switched their presidential choice over the final sixty days of the campaign. The switching rate was only 1 percent among those high in political knowledge but 11 percent among those in the lowest-knowledge category. Clearly late changes were mainly among the least informed.
4. The relative importance of the issues as shown in Table 9.3 is maintained if one predicts the vote from positions on the ten issues in a multivariate probit analysis. The probit equation estimates the impact of each variable, while holding the others statistically constant.
5. For more on ideology and the vote through the years, see Knight (1985), Tedin (1987), and Miller and Shanks (1996).
6. Issue voting by low-information voters can be seen as an instance of low-information rationality, as discussed in Chapter 3.

7. When respondents were scored as having a differential of four or more points in favor of a candidate, they were scored as liking their favored candidate better. Otherwise they were scored as relatively neutral.

8. It has long been recognized that it is easy to predict voting decisions from known attitudes; for instance, see Campbell, Gurin, and Miller (1954) and Kelley (1983). The best statistical procedure for predicting vote decisions from multiple attitudes is via a probit equation. Some readers may be interested in the probit equation predicting the presidential vote from our three (three-point) attitudinal predictors used to construct the scale in Table 9.7. Using the McKelvay–Zavoina procedure for estimating a pseudo-R squared, the three variables together account for 89 percent of the variance in the latent dimension that accounts for vote decisions.

9. Our discussion of voters and campaigns scratches only the surface in terms of the available literature. In addition to the literature cited elsewhere in this chapter, see Campbell 2008, Lau and Redlawsk 2006, and Hillygus and Shields 2008.

10. Figure 9.4 shows that elections are somewhat predictable from the *subjective* economy—the one in voters' minds. Most models of economic voting predict from objective indicators, typically the growth rate of per capita GDP or personal income. In 2012, these models did not perform as well as usual. In part this may be because the "blame" for the sluggish economy was ambiguous. See Erikson and Wlezien (2012b) and Hibbs (2012).

11. In past elections (though not 2012), the ANES asked voters to record their many likes and dislikes about presidential candidates and then recorded the content of these remarks. The partisan direction of the comments about candidate personality varied more over the years than did comments about policy. The degree of relative favorability for one party's candidate over the other's was seen as an important electoral predictor.

12. The findings of Table 9.8 are supported by regression analyses predicting the House vote from the district presidential vote and the member's ideology, typically measured as scores on the first- and second-dimension DW-Nominate scores. For 2012 elections (the 2011–2012 Congress), the second dimension is particularly important as a predictor of congressional voting. In Table 9.8, ideology is measured by the weighted average of the member's DW-Nominate score on dimensions 1 and 2, where scores on the second dimension are weighted .35 as much as scores on the first dimension.

13. In Erikson, MacKuen, and Stimson (2002), the median voter's position and candidate-party positions are measured on different scales—Stimson's mood and platform ratings by McDonald, Budge, and Hofferbert (1999). The problem of comparing apples and oranges is solved by treating both variables separately in a regression analysis predicting the vote. The more liberal the mood and more conservative the two party platforms, the stronger is the Democratic vote.

CHAPTER 10

The Public and
Its Elected Leaders

LEARNING OBJECTIVES

- Explain the sharing model for voter-elected official opinion congruence
- Explain how political parties promote voters to elect politicians who share their preferences

- Describe the *delegate model* and how it prompts politicians to follow the public opinion
- Account for when elected officials need to follow or not follow public opinion

As shown in the previous chapter, voters often use elections as a policy expression, as prescribed by the rational-activist model. Voters tend to reelect officeholders who show evidence of policy competence (e.g., presidents who produce economic prosperity or foreign policy success). Moreover, voters generally support candidates who are close to them in terms of their policy positions. By sorting candidates for office into winners and losers, voters do their part to achieve agreement between public preferences and public policy.

The degree of policy representation depends on the behavior not only of voters but also of politicians. The rational-activist model is one of five models of linkage between public opinion and policy that were introduced in Chapter 1. In this chapter, we consider the four additional models by which public opinion translates into policy: the sharing model, the political parties model, the delegate model, and the interest groups model. To understand these models, our focus is on politicians and their relationship with the public.

By the sharing model, representation is achieved because politicians are drawn from the same culture as their constituents. By the parties model, Republican and Democratic politicians diverge ideologically to provide the convenient cue of party affiliation, allowing voters to vote rationally using their habit of party identification. By the delegate model, politicians are sufficiently fearful of public opinion that they follow public opinion in their policies in advance of the next election. By the interest groups model, politicians respond to public opinion when they respond to articulated interest group opinion.

10-1 Opinion Sharing Between Policymakers and the Public

In this section, we consider political leaders as a class. We ask how different they are from the general public. If leaders (elected officials) and followers (the general public) are essentially alike in their interests and preferences, it matters less whether leaders' decisions follow from their own preferences or from trying to satisfy public opinion. In the extreme, public opinion and leader opinion could be the same thing.

The simplest form of linkage between public opinion and the policy decisions of political leaders is the simple sharing of common opinions by followers and leaders. Consider, for example, the result if we elected members of the House of Representatives by lottery. Just as a randomly selected sample of survey respondents is representative of the general population within a certain margin of error, so would an assembly of 435 randomly selected people acting as a House of Representatives be representative of the population. If such an assembly could act without being distracted by the demands of powerful interest groups or the actual rules of Congress that impede change, then—for better or worse—its decisions would reflect public opinion. In actuality, the Congress (and other legislatures) is less representative than a random sample, if for no other reason than that members are supposedly chosen for their superior capabilities rather than their typicality.

How then do members of Congress and other political leaders differ from the general population? To answer this question, we must find the traits that motivate some people but not others to pursue a political career and the traits that favor success in achieving this goal. When people who are active in politics—whether as a local party official or an elected legislator—are interviewed, they often report that a spur to their political career was a politically active family. The consensus, based on several early studies, is that about 40 percent of the people who are presently politically active grew up in politically active homes. Thus, assuming only 10 percent of the public (at the most) is active in politics, almost half of our political leaders come from the 10 percent of the nation's families that are most politically active (Prewitt 1970). Current evidence suggests that the influence of political upbringing on office-seeking persists. In their study of the causes of political ambition, Fox and Lawless (2005) find growing up in a politically active family to be a major cause of interest in a career in politics.

Intense political interest alone cannot push a person into a political leadership role. It helps to be recruited by others. To contest an election seriously, the would-be political leader must attract the base of support necessary to win. In some cases, the political leader is a self-starter who, because of his or her political interest and ambition, announces candidacy and is then able to accumulate support. In other cases, the future leader is selected by the local business or party elite for the task of getting elected.[1]

Because the wealthiest and best educated people are most likely to be politically interested and articulate and have the visibility to be tapped for a leadership role, we are not surprised that these are the people who become some of our political leaders. Put simply, there is an upper-status bias to the political leadership opportunity structure. For example, as Figure 10.1 shows, the occupations of the members of Congress are predominantly professional or managerial. In a society where only 18 percent of the workforce is engaged in such occupations, lawyers and businesspeople are particularly overrepresented in Congress. Lawyers and businesspeople are somewhat

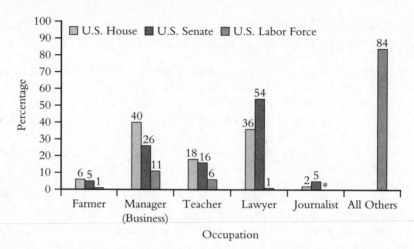

FIGURE 10.1 Occupations of Members of Congress compared with the Public, 2008 (in percentages).

Source: Based on data from Table 5.5 in Members of Congress: Seniority and Occupation, 2001–2011, in Harold W. Stanley and Richard G. Niemi (Eds.), *Vital Statistics on American Politics 2011–2012* (Washington, DC: Congressional Quarterly Press, 2011). Retrieved from http://library.cqpress.com/vsap/vsap11_tab5-5.

overrepresented in state legislatures as well. In addition, greater percentages of legislators are white, male, Protestant, and middle-aged than in the general adult population.[2]

In part, the overrepresentation of the affluent and educated in the councils of government stems from the middle-class leadership structure of the two major political parties. Even the Democratic Party—supposedly the more representative of the working class—draws its leaders from the middle class. By contrast, in many other democracies, the presence of a Socialist or Labor Party draws working-class people into greater political activity. Although Socialist and Labor parties do not draw their leaders exclusively from the working class they represent, they do at least open the door for the political recruitment of blue-collar workers, a door that is rather closed in the United States.

The disproportionate concentration of political leadership skills in the hands of the better educated and prosperous may make the class bias all but inevitable. For example, delegates to Democratic National Conventions are better educated and more affluent than the general population, even though representative on the basis of race, sex, and age. Even movements of economic protest draw their leaders from the most affluent strata within the protest group. For example, Lipset (1950, 166) discovered that within agricultural protest movements: "the battle for higher prices and a better economic return for their labor has been conducted by the farmers who need it least."

The status bias to the leadership structure does not necessarily mean that the views of political leaders typify their class instead of that of the general public. For example, Democratic Convention delegates do not express the prevailing views of the economically comfortable. Still, a general consideration is that whatever their individual ideology, the generally affluent leaders might resist wealth-redistribution legislation that would work against their self-interest. For example, a study of the attitudes of national convention delegates (in 1956) found that one of the few issues on which delegates of both parties were clearly more conservative than the public was their resistance to making the rich pay a greater share of taxes (McClosky, Hoffman, and O'Hara 1960).

Of course, one could argue that virtually all political viewpoints found in the general population are also shared by some of the prosperous and better educated—and these might be our leaders. Those who run for office do not always represent the political views of their economic group. Thus, one can hope there is sufficient diversity of viewpoint among the candidates for office from which the people make their selections at the polls. And if not, there is still the possibility that electoral pressure can divert the behavior of political leaders from unrepresentative personal preferences.

We can try a direct approach to the question of whether political leaders and the general public share opinions by comparing the political attitudes of the two groups. In Chapter 6 we already discussed one difference between public and leadership attitudes—leaders' greater support for civil liberties. For routine policy issues, however, only a few sets of data exist from which to assess the correspondence between the policy views of the public and its elected leaders.

Measuring the personal policy preferences of politicians is made difficult because politicians take what are called "electorally induced" positions. That is, the public positions such as roll-call votes are influenced by the electoral consequences of their policy stands as well as their personal views. Politicians' public and private positions are difficult to separate. But we can try.

To find studies that compare the political views of leaders and the public, we must go back several decades. One opportunity derives from CBS/*New York Times* polls that compare public and congressional responses to current political issues: in 1970 (by CBS) and in 1978 and 1982 (by CBS/*New York Times*). Examples for 1978 are shown in Figure 10.2. For both the 1970 and 1982 surveys, the distributions of responses by the public sample and by U.S. House members generally differ by only a few percentage points.[3] Small differences between the views of the public and their elected officials were also found by Herrera, Herrera, and Smith (1992) in their later public versus Congress comparison and by Uslaner and Weber (1983) in their study of state legislators.

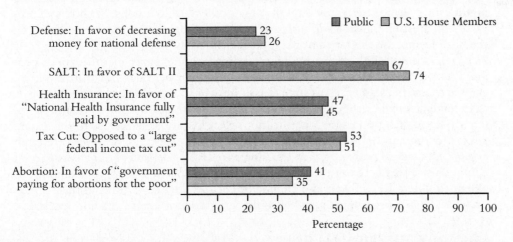

FIGURE 10.2 Comparison of Public and Congressional Opinion on Selected Policy Issues, 1978 (in percentages).

Source: Based on data from Kathleen A. Frankovic and Laurily K. Epstein, "Congress and Its Constituency: The New Machine Politics," paper delivered at American Political Science Association Meeting, Washington, DC, September 1979.

That the public and its elected leaders have similar opinions on a variety of issues may seem a surprise, given the differences of the two groups in income, education, and other background characteristics. The biases of leadership selection could have us expect that elected officials would share the opinions of the affluent and most educated rather than the opinions of the public as a whole. Instead, the apparent absence of bias in leadership opinions suggests that electoral politics works to weed out political candidates whose views are incongruent with public opinion.

10-2 Political Parties and Representation

So far we have compared politicians generally with the voting public. Averaged out, politicians might approximate a mirror image of the electorate. But this similarity can be misleading in that U.S. politicians come in two dominant and distinct flavors—as Democrats and as Republicans. In this section we look at this partisan distinction with an eye to determining the choice it affords voters.

According to the political parties model, party labels clarify the political choices available to the voters, allowing them to cast informed ballots with minimal search for information about candidates. Based on the history of their parties' behavior, Democratic politicians earn reputation as liberals and Republican politicians earn reputation as conservatives. These stereotypes then provide useful cues regarding what Democrats and Republicans will do once in office. This simplifies the task of the policy-oriented voter. Instead of monitoring each candidate's campaign statements and hoping they reflect what he or she would do if elected, the voter need only learn the differences between the parties and use party labels as a cue to rational voting.[4]

As we have seen earlier (Chapter 3), ideological considerations compete with other factors (such as family history) as motivations for party choice. Increasingly, citizens are polarizing ideologically, with liberals as Democrats and conservatives as Republicans. This trend is present when comparing aggregated constituencies as well as individual citizens, with a growing tendency for local electorates to use ideology as their basis of partisan sorting. Figure 10.3 shows this ideological sorting among state electorates as measured in the 2008 state exit polls. With few exceptions, the most liberal states in terms of ideological identification also tended to be the most Democratic in terms of party identification.[5]

Just as individuals tend to vote according to their party identification, geographic constituencies tend to vote according to their net party identification. We can see this at the state level, as state electorates are strongly influenced by their partisan tendencies when they select their U.S. senators. Table 10.1 shows that predominantly Republican states (in identification) elect mainly Republicans to the Senate while predominantly Democratic states elect mainly Democrats. Whether voters can achieve ideological representation by using party labels depends on the existence of actual differences between the programs of the two parties. Next we examine the extent to which Republican and Democratic leaders actually differ in their policy presences, in the programs they offer to the voters, and in their behavior in office.

Ideology and Party Leaders

In Chapter 3 we saw that ideology is an increasingly important source of partisan division between ordinary Republican and Democratic Party identifiers.

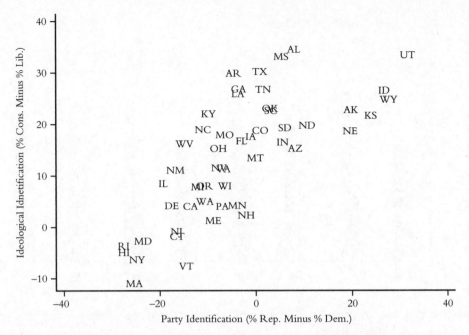

FIGURE 10.3 Partisanship and ideology of state electorates, 2008.

Source: NEP Exit Polls.

TABLE 10.1 Partisanship of Senate Delegations by Partisanship of State Electorates

Partisanship of State Senate Delegation, Post-2012 Election	Partisanship of State Electorate		
	Republican States (Ten or More Point Republican Lead in Party Identification)	Competitive States (Parties Within Ten Points of Each Other in Party Identification)	Democratic States (Ten or More Point Democratic Lead in Party Identification)
Both Republicans	5	7	1
Split	2	13	2
Both Democrats	0	4	15

Note: Numbers in cells represent the number of states. Party identification is from the states' 2008 NEP Exit Poll.

Source: Compiled by the authors.

Especially among those highly aware of party differences on issues, ordinary voters sort themselves ideologically, with liberals identifying as Democrats and conservatives as Republicans. Among political activists and politicians, ideology is an even stronger motivation force. When a strong ideology motivation spurs an individual to political activism, the individual usually develops an affinity for the ideologically appropriate party.

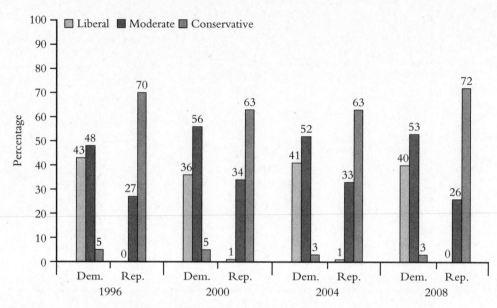

FIGURE 10.4 Ideological Identification of National Convention Delegates, 1996–2008.

Source: Based on data from CBS News/*New York Times* polls as reported in Harold W. Stanley and Richard G. Niemi, *Vital Statistics of American Politics, 2011–2012* (Washington, DC: Congressional Quarterly Press, 2013). Retrieved from http://library.cqpress.com/vsap/vsap11_tab1-28.

For instance, in studies of delegates to the national conventions going back to 1956, each party's delegates are more ideologically extreme than the party rank and file. Republican delegates are to the right of Republicans in the electorate and Democratic delegates are to the left of Democrats in the electorate (McClosky, Hoffman, and O'Hara 1960; Miller and Jennings 1987). In terms of ideological identification, Democratic delegates tend to be liberal or moderate, but rarely conservative; Republican delegates tend to be conservative or moderate, but rarely liberal. Figure 10.4 displays these patterns for delegates over six sets of national conventions.

Political parties obtain their political energy from their activists. But while the classic role of party leader is to balance the ideological preferences of the activists with the pragmatism necessary for winning elections, party activists may be more concerned with ideological correctness than with electoral victory. Starting with the decline of traditional party organizations and the growing openness of party conventions and the dominant role of party primaries beginning in the early 1970s, activists with very liberal and very conservative ideologues have increasingly dominated party leadership positions. There is an irony here. As the leadership structures of the political parties have become more internally democratic, the potential for greater policy choice between the parties is created. This increases the conflict between the parties' policies and the more moderate preferences of their less active rank-and-file supporters.

Public Opinion Relative to the Public's Perceptions of the Parties

Here we examine party differences through the eyes of ordinary citizens as they perceive their personal positions in relation to the parties. As discussed in Chapter 3,

TABLE 10.2   Public Perceptions of Their Policy Positions Relative to the Two Major Party Candidates, 2012

Respondent's Perceived Position	Strong Dem.	Weak Dem.	Ind.	Weak Rep.	Strong Rep.	All Cases
Respondent left of Obama	36%	13%	10%	0%	0%	**13%**
Respondent same as Obama	28	6	5	0	0	**8**
Respondent in between the two candidates	36	81	65	56	29	**52**
Respondent same as Romney	0	0	3	23	23	**9**
Respondent right of Romney	0	0	16	20	48	**18**
	100%	100%	100%	100%	100%	100%

Source: National Election Studies, 2012 election data. Based on respondent's (voters only) perceptions of self and candidate positions on ideology, domestic spending, defense spending, and health care. Includes only "high-information" voters who saw Obama (the Democrat) to the left of Romney (the Republican) on all seven issues.

about one-third of the respondents in the 2012 ANES survey were scored as in the "high-information" category, due to their recognizing Obama to the left of Romney on all seven of the selected issues. For this group, who hold a correct recognition of the candidates and parties' positions on the liberal–conservative continuum, we can place their personal issue positions relative to the two candidates.

We examine averages over five issues—liberalism–conservatism, domestic spending, defense spending, health care, and abortion rights. On each issue, 2012 ANES respondents were asked their own position, Obama's position, and Romney's position. Selecting only respondents who saw Obama to Romney's left on all issues tested, we ascertained whether the respondent saw his or her position as, on average, to the left of both parties, to the right of both parties, exactly at one of the two party's positions, or in between.

Table 10.2 displays the relevant data. Overall, slightly more than half of those who correctly order the major presidential candidates ideologically see themselves as between the Democrat on their left and the Republican on their right. About 15 percent see themselves as exactly at one of the party positions. The remainder—almost one-third—are about evenly split between conservatives who see themselves even to the right of the Republican and liberals who see themselves even to the left of the Democrat.

Table 10.2 also shows perceptions of candidate positions broken down by party identification. The most interesting groups are the "strong Republicans" and "strong Democrats." Forty-eight percent of the strong Republicans were sufficiently conservative as to see themselves to the right of both Obama and Romney. Similarly, 36 percent of the strong Democrats saw themselves to the left of both candidates. The two parties need to satisfy these polarized partisans, but they also need to woo the portion of the electorate—mainly weak partisans and Independents—in the middle of the ideological spectrum.

Each party's strong identifiers are typical of the party's primary electorate. Activists tend to dominate low-turnout party primaries, with an important segment urging the party in a more extreme ideological direction. But to the extent the primary electorate chooses extreme candidates over moderates, the party risks alienating voters in the center. Each party's more moderate candidates may have the greatest chance to become general election winners, but they face the problem first in securing the nomination from a hostile primary electorate.[6]

And what of that majority of the relevant electorate who appears ideologically located between the two parties? These centrist voters seemingly face a distasteful choice of giving power either to a party that is too conservative or to a party that is too liberal. However, these voters also have the opportunity to split their ticket, voting for a balance of Democrats and Republicans. The desire of moderates for an ideological balance of party power may help explain the frequent pattern of divided party control. Arguably, moderate voters should prefer the ideological balance of one party controlling the presidency and the other controlling Congress over unified control by either party (Fiorina 1992; Alesina and Rosenthal 1995).

The Relevance of Party Platforms

At national conventions every fourth year, each party devotes considerable time to spelling out the details of its platform in order to detail the party's official position on the issues of the day. Party platforms are often dismissed as mere ritualistic documentation because they are rarely read, quickly forgotten, and not officially binding on a party's candidates. Nevertheless, as research by Gerald Pomper with Susan Lederman (1980, Chapters 7 and 8) shows, careful reading of party platforms provides clues to what the parties would do if they came to power.

Pomper examined the content of the Democratic and Republican platforms from 1944 to 1976. He found about half the platform statements to be relatively meaningless rhetoric ("The American Free Enterprise System is one of the greatest achievements of humankind") or statements about the issues that are too vague or broad to be meaningful ("The Anti-Trust Laws must be vigorously enforced"). About another quarter of the platform statements qualify as policy approval ("In the Nuclear Test Ban Treaty, we have written our commitment to limitations on the arms race"). Finally, about one-quarter are detailed policy statements like "The Security of the American Trade Unions must be strengthened by repealing 14B of the Taft-Hartley Act." Although people rarely read party platforms directly, platform statements reach voters indirectly "through interest groups, mass media, candidates' speeches, and incomplete popular perceptions" (Pomper and Lederman 1980, 152).

Of particular relevance is whether parties keep their policy promises once in office. Pomper finds that about two-thirds of the winning presidential party's pledges become at least partially fulfilled during the next four years. Somewhat over half the pledges of the nonpresidential party do as well. When both parties offer the same pledge in their platforms, the pledge is fulfilled in some fashion about 80 percent of the time. Pomper concludes, "We should take platforms seriously, because politicians take them seriously" (1980, 176). An analysis of more recent platform data through 2004 by Lee Payne (2008) finds that both major parties continue to act consistently with platform promises the vast majority of the time.

A statistical analysis by Ian Budge and Richard Hofferbert (1990) also showed the impact of party platforms. They were able to connect changing federal expenditure patterns to changing priorities in party platforms, particularly the platform of the presidential party (see also McDonald, Budge, and Hofferbert 1999). And the ideological messages in platforms reflect the party positions revealed to voters. The more moderate a party's platform (as opposed to representing the party's ideological extreme), the stronger is the party's showing in presidential elections (Erikson, MacKuen, and Stimson 2002).

Party Voting in Legislatures

Ideally, from the standpoint of the political parties model, the electorally dominant party not only would articulate a program that achieves voter approval but would also be in a position to enact that program once in power. The dominant congressional party, for example, would be able to enact its preferred legislation, particularly if the president is of the same party and gives encouragement.

As is well known, events do not always work out this way in the American political system. About as often as not, the presidency and Congress are controlled by different parties, leading to the potential for gridlock or stalemate. Even when the president's party is in the congressional majority, the president still has difficulty pushing his proposals through Congress. For instance, President Clinton was unable to pass his health care legislation in 1993 and 1994, even though the Democrats held a healthy majority in both the House and the Senate. With similar congressional majorities, President Obama barely got his Affordable Care Act (a.k.a. Obamacare) passed by Congress in 2010.

This discussion may seem to suggest that party labels are not relevant in Congress. However, that is far from the truth. In fact, party affiliation is the single best predictor of roll-call voting in Congress. As is well known, the degree of party polarization in Congress is increasing rather than decreasing (McCarty, Poole, and Rosenthal 2006; Theriault, 2008).

Figure 10.5 shows visually the differences between the two parties' roll-call voting in the U.S. House of Representatives for the 112th Congress (2011–2012).

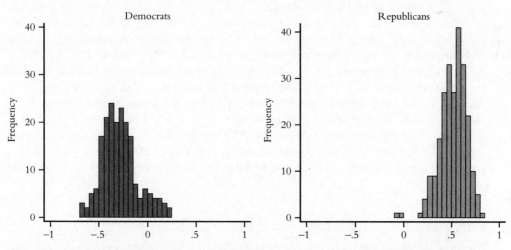

FIGURE 10.5 Party differences in roll-call liberalism–conservatism, U.S. House of Representatives and Senate, 2011–2012. Roll-call ideology is measured as the weighted average of dimension 1 and dimension 2 of DW-Nominate scores, where dimension 2 is weighted 0.35 that of dimension 1.

Source: Keith T. Poole and Howard Rosenthal, http://voteview.com.

The ideology measure is a blend of individual members' voting records along two dimensions known as DW-Nominate scores (Poole and Rosenthal 2007).[7] The dominant first dimension represents traditional left–right issues that divide the parties, such as the role of the federal government. It may exaggerate somewhat the parties' ideological differences because it captures in part procedural issues within Congress (such as voting on amendments) as well as matters of substance to voters. Roll-call voting on the second dimension is unrelated to party but still taps aspects of liberalism–conservatism. This second dimension captures congressional voting on certain issues involving civil liberties or reform, such as campaign finance reform. Fewer roll-call votes are cast on the second dimension than the first dimension.

Because the first dimension (e.g., liberal–conservative) is so dominant in terms of explaining how members vote on roll calls, the second dimension is often ignored in political science analysis. But because variation along the second dimension does appear to matter to voters (and to the representation process), we consider it here. A useful working assumption is that voters weigh Congress members' behavior along the second dimension about 0.35 times as much as they do their behavior on the first dimension. Thus, in the analysis that follows (and of voters' congressional voting in Chapter 9), we compress congressional voting records to one dimension, but as a blend of one part dimension 1 and 0.35 parts dimension 2. We call it, simply, liberalism–conservatism.

State legislatures show a considerable variation in their degree of party polarization (Aldrich and Coleman Battista 2002). At one extreme, Nebraska elects its legislators on a nonpartisan basis, with the result being a noticeable lack of ideological structure to roll-call votes (Wright and Schaffner 2002). At the other extreme, some state legislative parties behave as disciplined units, resulting in parties even more polarized than the U.S. Congress.

The source of the growing party polarization in Congress is the subject of considerable debate among political scientists, just as is the debate about the growth of polarization within the electorate. Some say the visible increase in party differences reflects an increase in party discipline, as party leaders pressure members to support their position (Cox and McCubbins 1993, 2004; Aldrich and Rohde 2001; Aldrich, Berger, and Rohde 2002). Others say rather than the product of coercion, the polarization simply reflects the growing differences of opinion between Democratic and Republican activists (Krehbiel 1993, 1999, 2000). Resolving this debate empirically has been particularly challenging (Theriault, 2008). In any event, it is clear that the polarization of congressional parties provides voters with an ideological choice.

Party Labels as a Basis for Policy Choice

Although elected leaders from the Democratic and Republican parties differ ideologically, one might think this results simply because Democrats and Republicans represent distinct geographic constituencies rather than ideological competition within constituencies. What is required by the parties model is that prospective voters are provided a choice within specific constituencies. In this section, we examine the ideological choice provided by the Republican and Democratic parties at the constituency level. Our focus is on candidates in individual contests for the U.S. House of Representatives.

In U.S. House races, the electorate's choice is not between the typical congressional Democrat and the typical congressional Republican because (as we will demonstrate) congressional candidates often adjust their issue stances according to the prevailing constituency views. A liberal district is generally given a choice between a relatively liberal Democrat and a relatively liberal Republican. Similarly, a conservative district is given a choice between Democrat and Republican candidates who are both relatively conservative for their party. We are interested in the extent to which candidates at the district level diverge and give the constituency voters a meaningful choice.

It is no understatement to say that almost always, when a constituency's congressional candidates differ on important issues, the Democrat is more liberal than the Republican. For instance, a study of congressional candidates in 2002 found the Republican to the right of the Democratic candidate in all 168 districts sampled (Erikson and Wright 2005), with no exceptions (see also Ansolabehere, Snyder, and Stewart 2001). The expectation is that similar patterns would be found in most U.S. Senate elections (and for state legislature and most local offices).

A congressional voter has an easy decision rule for casting a partisan ballot: To help elect the most conservative candidate, vote Republican; to help elect the most liberal candidate, vote Democratic. When the public desires a more conservative or liberal Congress, it can simply elect more Republicans or Democrats accordingly. On the one hand, changes in the party composition of Congress are often attributed to such factors as economic conditions, presidential coattails, and Watergates—not to changes in policy preferences by the public. On the other hand, one can marshal statistical evidence that the over-time variation in the numbers of Republicans and Democrats in Congress is partially due to ideological shifts by the public (Erikson, MacKuen, and Stimson 2002). The mechanism of choice is available for the public to create a policy shift in Congress—and in state legislatures and other political arenas as well.

The Importance of Party Competition

The importance of parties is evident under circumstances in which parties cease to play a major role—when elections are held on a truly nonpartisan basis, as in many American cities and sometimes for state offices. Reformers once saw nonpartisan elections as ideal because they weaken the role of corrupt political parties. But it is now generally believed that nonpartisan elections make it more difficult for voters to get their preferred policies enacted and to hold leaders accountable for their actions (Cassel 1986).[8]

When both major parties compete effectively for the electorate's favor, we would expect close elections. Sometimes, however, party competition breaks down and one party enjoys a monopoly. This has not happened at the national level since the Era of Good Feelings—which was around 1820. Often at the state and local levels, however, one party becomes so dominant that it wins almost every election.

In theory, the effect of strong party competition should be to enhance representation. With election outcomes uncertain, each party has an added incentive to woo the marginal voter who otherwise would be ignored. The opposite result occurs under one-party dominance. The dominant party does not need to make policy appeals to a public whose loyalty (or apathy) it has already won.

V.O. Key (1949) argued that the lack of party competition in the American South allowed the once-dominant Democratic Party to ignore public opinion, with the result that the haves enacted public policy at the expense of the have-nots. There is, largely as a result of Key's position, a conviction among political scientists that parties become more responsive to public opinion when there exist two strong parties competing for votes. When the parties are evenly matched in the contests for control of governorships and state legislatures, this can only be a positive step in terms of the political parties model, yielding increased influence in the political process by everyday citizens.

Does Party Control Matter?

Readily following from our discussion, which party controls the levers of power can have important policy consequences. We have already seen that elected politicians do often turn party platform pledges into law. We can also see different policies under different types of party control. Liberal innovations in domestic policy, for example, are most frequent when Democrats control Congress and, especially, when the Democrats hold the White House (Kiewiet and McCubbins 1985; Browning 1986; Erikson, MacKuen, and Stimson 2002). Statistically speaking, unemployment (a major concern of the less affluent) is more likely to decline under Democratic presidents. And inflation (a major concern of the more affluent) is more likely to decline under Republican presidents (Hibbs 1987, Chapter 7; Alesina and Rosenthal 1995). There is also statistical evidence that the income gap between the rich and the poor goes up under Republican presidents and down under Democratic presidents (Hibbs and Dennis 1988; Bartels 2008).

Of course there are important limits to the policy consequences of party control. The U.S. system of separation of powers and checks and balances slows the connection between policy proposals and policy enactment. For citizens with a radical perspective, the choices between the policies of the Democrats and Republicans can be viewed as merely slight variations on the status quo. If one's taste runs toward policies like government ownership of industry, legalization of all drugs, or abandonment of the public school system, one will not be represented by either major party.

Actually, many see the major problem with today's parties as not the lack of choice but rather that they are too ideologically polarized. Faced with a choice between liberal Democrats and conservative Republicans, the moderate voter in the middle can achieve ideological satisfaction only by massive ticket-splitting. In theory, either party could gain votes by moving toward the center. But the parties do not do so, possibly because of the ideological extremism of primary voters or the parties' ideological reputations are so hardened that party leaders believe that voters will not respond to centrist gestures. Still, individual politicians sometimes move from the dominant ideological position of their party, moderating their policy positions in order to stay elected rather than pleasing their parties' ideological constituents. We turn to this aspect of democratic representation next.

10-3 Politicians' Responsiveness to Public Opinion

When in office, politicians face the choice of pursuing their personal policy agenda or following the dictates of the voters who elect them. In this section we ask whether politicians, even as partisan ideologues, respond to public opinion in a way that overrides their own policy taste. When they do respond to public opinion rather than personal taste, they play the role of the people's delegate or agent. This is the delegate model at work. By this model, politicians anticipate the next election, responding to public opinion in advance of the potential fury of the voters.

Officeholders are driven by two often conflicting motivations: to win elections and to make good policy (as they see it). How strongly they respond to public opinion depends both on the relative strengths of these two motivations and on how strongly they believe their reelection goals are affected by their behavior. Suppose, counterfactually, that voters are incapable of responding to the policy choices candidates present. If voters ignore what politicians do, even electorally sensitive politicians are free to ignore the nominal policy preferences of the public when they make policy. On the other hand, suppose, again counterfactually, that voters are hypersensitive to candidate policy choices, always electing the candidate closest to their views. If voters care only about policy choices, even policy-centered politicians are compelled to follow the public's wishes because that is the only way to win elections.

In truth, citizen attention is highly variable—on average somewhere between no attention and full attention. Thus, the responses of politicians—with their mixed goals of election and policy—are also in between. They try to follow public opinion but are also guided by their personal policy preferences.

For the delegate model to work, the representative must have an incentive to choose the public's preference over his or her own. While this incentive may be the representative's belief that following public opinion is ordinarily the right thing to do, more likely it is the representative's fear that electoral defeat would be the consequence of ignoring public opinion. For reelection to properly motivate, the elected official must believe the public is watching. The official must also want to be reelected. Finally, for the model to work well, the representative must know what public opinion is, a task made easier by modern public opinion polling.

Political Ambition

The belief that their reelection chances hinge on how well they represent constituency opinion will not influence officeholders much unless they care about being reelected. When officeholders retire rather than seek reelection, the fear is that they shirk their responsibility to represent constituency opinion (Rothenberg and Sanders 2000). As Joseph Schlesinger (1966, 2) described the positive functions of political ambition, "no more irresponsible government is imaginable than one of high-minded men unconcerned for their political futures."

Politicians at the top of the political ladder usually try to continue in office as long as possible. For example, presidents normally want to stay in office for their constitutional allotment of two full terms. Even Truman and Johnson, who both opted for retirement in the spring of their reelection years, did so only after the results of the first presidential primaries indicated that even renomination by their party would have been a hurdle.

Most governors (about 75 percent) also seek reelection when not constitutionally prohibited by term limits. Ambition also runs high for Congress members. When up for reelection, about 80 percent of senators and 90 percent of House members try for another term (see Davidson, Oleszek, and Lee 2014, for historical details). Even when Congress members retire, they rarely leave political life; most House members who decline to run again for their congressional seat do so to seek another political office or to serve as highly paid lobbyists in Washington.

Preoccupation with reelection is a persistent theme in studies of congressional behavior. Douglas Arnold (1990) claims that staying elected is the dominant congressional motivation. Kingdon (1973) shows that representatives aim to please constituency interests even on routine legislation, while Fenno (1978) finds that representatives spend much of their time in their districts explaining their roll-call votes to constituents. Mayhew (1974) argues that the structural organization of the House of Representatives is best understood as a collective response to the members' need to stay elected, while Adler (2002) shows how the reelection concern has thwarted reform of the House committee system. Of course the desire to stay elected is not the sole congressional motivation. Parker (1992) reminds us that representatives focus on generating safe reelection prospects to free themselves in order to pursue their policy agendas.

Promoters of term limits for officeholders argue that the continuous preoccupation with staying elected detracts from the policymaking function. One concern is that elected officials may overrespond to the less enlightened aspects of public opinion. As V.O. Key (1961a, 490) observed, "Public men often act as if they thought the deciding margin in elections was cast by fools; moreover, by fools informed enough and alert enough to bring retribution to those who dare not demonstrate themselves equally foolish."

Interestingly, the inclination to hold onto office for several terms is a relatively recent phenomenon. In the nineteenth century, House and Senate members quite frequently returned to private life after a term or two (Price 1971). This is the pattern in many state legislatures even today, particularly in states offering low legislative pay (Squire 1988, 1992). With variation from state to state, perhaps one-fifth of state legislators retire before each election (Jewell and Breaux 1988; Montcrief 1999). Many retirements actually are to pursue alternative electoral opportunities.

Having strong policy goals does not free representatives from electoral concerns. Surely, many politicians are strongly motivated to advance their conception of the public interest. But this pursuit of accomplishments only feeds their ambition for further public service, which requires reelection. This reasoning suggests the hypothesis that the political leaders with the strongest policy motivations tend to feel the most electoral pressure to satisfy public opinion—at least on matters that concern them least.

Following Public Opinion

The legislator's role is as an agent, serving the interests of the constituency. The classic question is whether the legislator should serve these interests as the legislator thinks best (as a "trustee") or should the legislator heed public opinion and follow the wishes of the constituency (the "delegate" model). Ascertaining politicians' concern about public opinion is difficult. As V.O. Key lamented in 1961, "We have practically no systematic information about what goes on in the minds of public men as they ruminate about the weight to be given to public opinion in governmental decision" (Key 1961a, 490). If we take seriously the reported attitudes of politicians and the public when they are surveyed, it would seem that neither puts much credence in the delegate model. When asked, politicians are more likely to claim they act in their constituents' best interests as they see them rather than by slavishly following constituency preferences (Friesema and Hedlund 1981). Similarly, citizens are more likely to claim they prefer their politicians to be of independent mind rather than asking them (the voters) what to do (Hedlund 1975).

Citizens and politicians alike claim to reject the notion that elected officials should follow the wishes of their constituents even if those wishes are contrary to their own. To be sure, many legislators would find it too humiliating to admit to being merely the voice of others. Indeed, most of us applaud the courage of the statesmanlike legislator who votes with his independent judgment rather than pander to the views of his constituency—particularly when we agree with that judgment.

Politicians from today's polarized parties generally take positions to the left (if a Democrat) and to the right (if a Republican) from the median voter. Examining what elected representatives do rather than what they say produces strong circumstantial evidence that politicians follow district preferences (are delegates), at least in terms of broad ideological outline. Numerous studies have examined the statistical relationship between constituency opinion on one hand and legislative behavior on the other. For instance, Snyder (1996) was able to compare the votes cast in the California state legislature with constituency choices on several referenda issues. He found a strong statistical connection between constituency preferences and legislative behavior. For U.S. House districts, we have no direct measure of constituency opinion, although the constituency's vote for president is a serviceable indicator of district ideological preferences. For members of each party, district presidential voting correlates strongly with the ideological tendencies of the member's roll-call behavior; the more Democratic the district, the more liberal the member (Erikson and Wright 2001; Clinton, 2006). Figure 10.6 shows this pattern for roll-call voting in the 110th Congress (2007–2008). Each party's most ideologically extreme members represent districts that voted one-sidedly for their party's candidate for president. Safe districts allow ideological voting, while competitive (moderate) districts require moderation of issue positions for electoral survival.

In the U.S. Senate, we can measure constituency preferences directly from the liberal–conservative preferences in statewide surveys. State-level liberalism–conservatism in surveys is strongly related to roll-call liberalism by the states' senators (Wright and Berkman 1986; Erikson 1990; Wood and Anderson 1998),

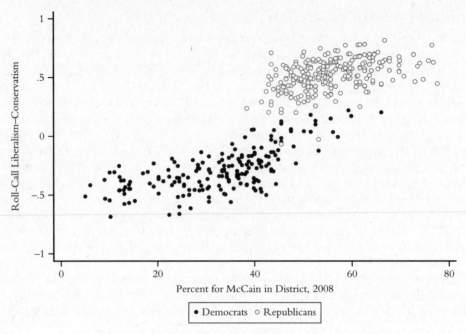

FIGURE 10.6 House of Representatives roll-call liberalism, 2011–2012, by district
2008 presidential vote, by party of representative. Roll-call ideology is measured as the weighted average of dimension 1 and
dimension 2 of DW-Nominate scores, where dimension 2 is
weighted 0.35 that of dimension 1.

Source: Keith T. Poole and Howard Rosenthal, http:// voteview.com.

even after controlling for the senator's party. Figure 10.7 summarizes this pattern
for 2011–2012. For both Democrats and Republicans, the more liberal the state's
opinion as measured by the 2008 exit polls, the more liberal is the senator's roll-call
liberalism as measured by our DW-Nominate-based index of legislative liberalism.
Thus, despite the general tendency for senators to be ideologically polarized by party,
they moderate their views when faced with an ideologically adverse constituency.[9]

Although Congress members moderate when faced with a moderate constituency, there is a limit to their responsiveness to constituency opinion. This is not
surprising since today's politicians generally are liberal or conservative ideologues
themselves. But it is worth keeping in mind that while Congress members are pulled
toward the center by constituency opinion, they typically remain more ideologically
extreme (liberal for Democrats, conservative for Republicans) than even their own
party's median constituent (Bafumi and Herron, 2010).

We can find evidence of responsiveness to public opinion when comparing the
paths of public opinion and congressional legislation over time (Erikson, MacKuen,
and Stimson 2002). Controlling for the presidential party and party composition of
Congress, Congress enacts more liberal legislation when public opinion (lagged) is
in a liberal mood. Similarly, policy conservatism follows from public conservatism.
The response is slow, however, and not immediate. Still, the electorate's ideological

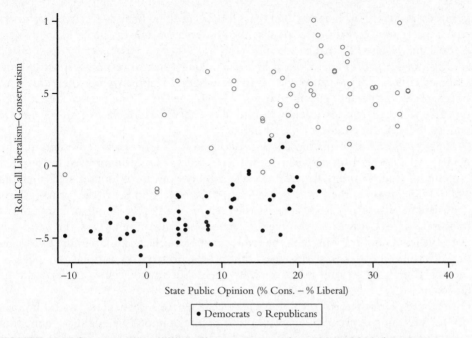

FIGURE 10.7 Senate roll-call liberalism-conservatism, 2011–2012, by state opinion (2008 NEP Exit Polls), by party of senator. State opinion = percent conservative minus percent liberal in ideological identification in state exit polls. Roll-call ideology is measured as the weighted average of dimension 1 and dimension 2 of DW-Nominate scores, where dimension 2 is weighted 0.35 that of dimension 1.

Source: Keith T. Poole and Howard Rosenthal, http://voteview.com.

mood not only helps determine election outcomes (e.g., electing Republicans when conservative); in anticipation of electoral sanctions, Congress also takes public opinion into account when it legislates.

Electoral Timing

The alert reader will notice the circumstantial nature of much of our evidence of responsiveness to constituencies. While politicians' positions correlate with constituency preferences (while holding party affiliation constant), there are other possible sources besides legislator attentiveness (the delegate model). The source could be simply the sharing of interests by constituents and representatives (the sharing model). The reason that each party's most conservative politicians represent conservative districts, for instance, could be that they are drawn from their constituencies and share their values rather than (or in addition to) a response to constituency concerns.

A further reason that legislators seem responsive to constituency opinion is that the constituencies can be the enforcers, via the rational-activist model (Chapter 9). By voting into office the candidate closest to its collective views, an attentive constituency becomes the source of consistency between its opinions and the policy preferences of its representative. For instance, one reason there are few liberal Congress members from conservative constituencies is that the conservative constituencies usually reject liberal candidacies at the ballot box.

For the delegate model we would like a stronger test of responsiveness to constituency concerns. One test might be to see whether responsiveness increases with the approach of the next election. Another is whether or not politicians adapt ideologically when their constituency boundaries change. Here we examine evidence from state legislators and the U.S. Congress.

In a study of California legislators, Kuklinski (1978) assessed representation by means of the correlation between constituency liberalism (as expressed in frequent referendum results) and the legislator's roll-call liberalism. He found that California assembly members in the lower house—who face reelection every two years—show a consistent pattern of responsiveness throughout the years examined. For California state senators, however, who face reelection only every four years, the pattern is more cyclical, more responsive in the two years before election than in the two years after election. These examples suggest that representatives do respond to perceived electoral threats by seeking to better reflect their constituents' views as election time approaches.

The six-year senatorial term makes the U.S. Senate a particularly useful laboratory for watching elected leaders respond to public opinion. We might presume that senators act more constrained by opinion in their state late in their six-year term, as reelection time approaches, than early in the six-year cycle just after being elected. Democratic senators, whose personal beliefs are generally more liberal than those of their statewide constituencies, would act less liberal as their term progresses but then return to more liberal positions once reelected. Republican senators, whose personal beliefs generally are more conservative than those of their statewide constituencies, would act less conservative as their term progresses but then return to more conservative positions once reelected. In a study of Senate roll-call voting, Martin Thomas (1985) reports exactly these patterns. Both Democratic senators and Republican senators moderate their roll-call record as reelection time approaches. This is true, however, only for senators who seek reelection. Interestingly, Thomas shows that senators who do not run again moderate their views through the fifth year and then return to their original positions in the sixth year when the retirement decision has been made.[10]

With their two-year term, U.S. House members must continually try to stay elected. Although we cannot watch their behavior change with the election cycle, an opportunity is sometimes present to watch them change when their constituency changes. U.S. House constituencies change every ten years following the U.S. Census, as district lines must be redrawn to reflect population changes. Amihai Glazer and Marc Robbins (1985) have statistically demonstrated that U.S. House members respond to these district changes in their roll-call voting. They measure changes in constituency opinion by comparing the past presidential voting of the new and the old district. By this measure, when the House member gets a more liberal district, the member usually becomes more liberal; when the member gets a more conservative district, the member usually becomes more conservative (see also Stratmann 2000).

Legislators are not the only politicians who respond to the electoral cycle. Brandice Canes-Wrone (2006) offers a "conditional pandering theory" to explain the behavior of U.S. presidents as a function of the election cycle. For presidents in their first term, the closer to the election, the more their stands are consistent with ("pander to") public opinion. The tighter the reelection battle seems to be according to advance indicators, the greater the pandering late in the election cycle. If they succeed to a second term and thus become ineligible for reelection, the election cycle no longer governs a president's behavior (Canes-Wrone, Herron, and Shotts 2001; Canes-Wrone and Shotts 2004; Canes-Wrone 2006).

This latter observation reminds us that electoral timing works two ways. Politicians can move in the direction of their constituents when Election Day approaches. But if they plan to retire or become ineligible for reelection, they can move in the other direction—away from their constituency toward their party's extreme. Snyder and Ting (2003) have conducted the most rigorous investigation of this phenomenon, technically known as "last period shirking." They find that when Republican House members retire they shift to the right, whereas when Democrats retire they shift left. In each case this is what we expect from ideologically motivated politicians once liberated from constituency pressure.

Political Leaders as Educators

When we observe policy agreement between constituencies and their elected officials, it is natural to assume that the causal mechanism is public opinion influencing the officials' position. Consider again the dilemma of public officials torn between their personal beliefs about good public policy and the contrary sentiment of public opinion. Their options are not limited to following public opinion or ignoring it altogether. A tempting alternative is to try to educate the public about their point of view. When this strategy works, the opinion–policy connection is instigated by the politicians rather than the public they represent. Just as public opinion can influence politicians, so too can politicians influence public opinion.

Politicians who can influence voters toward their point of view enjoy a win–win situation. They win on policy and electorally. Lawrence Jacobs and Robert Shapiro (2000) document this educating behavior among the contestants in the battle over national health care in the early Clinton administration. Rather than pandering to public opinion, both supporters and opponents of national health care drew their positions based on principle and then tried to influence the public. (The opponents won the battle.) More generally, when we observe Democrats and Republicans challenging each other with ideological rhetoric, they are not pandering to the median voter's point of view; they are trying to shift the median position in their direction. That politicians engage in this behavior in no way detracts from the importance of public opinion in the electoral process. They try to influence public opinion precisely because public opinion decides their electoral fates.

10-4 Do Elected Officials Need to Follow Public Opinion?

We have seen that politicians apparently try to consider public opinion when making decisions—partly from fear of electoral retribution if they do not. Actually, one might suspect public officials do not need to weigh public opinion heavily in order to be reelected. Incumbent officeholders do not lose reelection bids at a rate that stimulates electoral anxiety. Furthermore, most people do not monitor their leaders' policy with sufficient attention to produce massive voter reactions. Could it be that elected officials have more freedom from public opinion than they realize?

Incumbency

Judging from their reelection rates, it may seem that elected politicians have little reason to fear the wrath of the voters. In the 2000s, 95 percent of U.S. House incumbents who sought reelection were returned to office. For U.S. senators, the reelection rate was only slightly lower (Davidson, Oleszek, and Lee 2014). State legislators are also secure, with reelection rates above 90 percent—but with important variations among states (Jewell and Breaux 1988).

There are five clear reasons incumbents almost always win reelection. First, many elections are partisan contests, decided along partisan lines. Consequently, elections tend to favor the locally dominant party. Where one party dominates the other, even an officeholder with a low personal standing can win repeated victories. District lines for legislative elections are typically carved in a way that creates one-party districts that are safe for incumbents. Statewide elections are far more competitive than district-level elections, accounting for the greater electoral vulnerability of U.S. senators and state governors.

Second, incumbents generally win because the status of incumbency gives them an advantage over their opponents. In U.S. House elections, incumbents gain 5 percent or more of the vote between their first victory and their first reelection attempt (Alford and Brady 1993). State legislators enjoy a similar incumbency advantage (Barry, Berkman, and Schneiderman 2000). The process that accounts for this incumbency advantage is not fully understood, but it seems House members and state legislators are able to exploit their office in terms of constituency service and easy publicity. Interestingly, the more visible U.S. senators and state governors do not seem to gain much of an advantage from incumbency status.

Third, incumbents generally win due to electoral selection. Candidates with strong personal appeal tend to win elections. Winners in one election tend to be strong candidates in future elections. So when winners seek reelection as incumbents, they generally do well due to their personal appeal. In other words, winning creates incumbency status in addition to the other way around.[11]

Fourth, incumbents gain votes by scaring off strong challenges. Potentially strong candidates tend not to run in elections they are likely to lose. Thus, potentially strong challengers avoid challenging strong incumbents, preferring to wait until the incumbent retires. In addition, the weaker candidates who do run against strong incumbents have few resources at their disposal, as potential supporters prefer not to concentrate their time and money on contests with little hope of success (Jacobson and Kernell 1983; Cox and Katz 1996).

A final reason that incumbents rarely lose is that anticipation of defeat makes incumbents more likely to retire. Candidates are most likely to retire when their reelection prospects are at a low ebb, due, for instance, to scandal or the prospect of a strong challenger (Fukumoto 2009). Representatives are most prone to retire when their party's national election prospects are at a low ebb (Wolak 2007).

The retirement of vulnerable incumbents in advance of potential voter wrath helps lower the observed rate of incumbent defeat. Far more incumbents would lose if they were forced to seek reelection rather than take their graceful exit by quitting.

The electoral success of incumbents may signal both something wrong and something right about the status of representation. When elected officials are repeatedly returned to office because people vote for the dominant party or because people vote for the security of the familiar incumbent, they can act unbound by constituency opinion. Under these circumstances, representation suffers. But there is also a positive side. Part of the reason for incumbent success is that candidates who do things to please voters are allowed to stay in office. Incumbents who represent their constituencies on policy issues are allowed to stay in office the longest.[12]

The Public's Attention to Policy Positions

To what extent do citizens react to the content of their leaders' policy decisions and policy proposals for the future? In the previous chapter we saw evidence of policy voting, particularly at the presidential level. But especially in subpresidential contests, the public's information is usually too low to allow the expectation of much policy voting. The best data in this regard concern people's awareness of the U.S. House of Representatives and their particular representative. Let us consider how visible House members' actions are to their constituents.

First, the local news media rarely give much coverage to the roll-call stands of members of Congress or to the substantive issues of congressional campaigns. Consequently, even if more people had the urge to follow the congressional politics of their district, they would have great difficulty in doing so (Hutchings 2003).

Less than half the public can recall the name of their congressional representative. Similarly, at election time only about half claim to have read or heard anything about their representative in Washington or the opposing candidate. When interviewers probe to find out what respondents have read or heard about the incumbent congressional candidate, the answer is typically a vague reference such as "he (or she) is a good person," or "he (or she) knows the problems." In the National Election Studies, only about 15 percent express reactions to their U.S. House member in terms of positions taken on specific legislation (Jacobson 1987).

On even hotly debated congressional issues, few people know where their Congress member stands. Consider the following examples. After Congress's passage of the 1991 resolution authorizing the first President Bush to conduct the first Gulf War, ANES respondents were asked how their individual House member had voted on this contentious issue. Fifty-six percent correctly identified their member's position, while 30 percent got it wrong (Alvarez and Gronke 1996; Lapinski 2001).[13] In one of the biggest congressional votes of Clinton's presidency, Congress narrowly assented to Clinton's tax-raising, budget-balancing Budget Resolution of 1993. Following the vote, ANES respondents were asked about their House member's vote. Sixty-three percent reported their member's vote correctly on this highly partisan issue, while twenty-one percent got it wrong (Lapinski 2001). More recently, respondents in a 2005 poll were asked their representative's positions on a proposed constitutional amendment banning gay marriage and a bill banning partial birth abortions. The percent correct and incorrect were thirty-eight and twenty, respectively, on gay marriage and forty-eight and fifteen, respectively, on partial birth abortions. Assuming as many were guessing the correct answer as gave the wrong answer, still less than half knew their Congress member's positions on these important votes (Ansolabehere and Jones 2010).

Looking at these survey findings, one might well wonder whether the representatives need to pay attention to the views of their constituency when they weigh the alternatives of each legislative decision. As Warren Miller and Donald Stokes (1963, 54) observed in a pioneering study, "Congressmen feel that their individual legislative actions may have considerable impact on the electorate, yet some simple facts about the representative's salience to his constituents imply that this could hardly be true."

Indeed, we may have a major political linkage between mass opinion and leader response that is generally overlooked—although the public is not watching, leaders sometimes do what they think the public wants because they mistakenly believe the public is paying attention! If this is true, then leaders' responsiveness to public opinion would quickly evaporate once somebody points out to them that surveys show the public to be rather indifferent to what they do. On the other hand, maybe the politicians do not exaggerate the importance of their record to their electoral fate as much as the polls seem to suggest. Let us explore the reasons officeholders must tread carefully when they consider violating public opinion.

First, the high reelection rate of incumbent officeholders does not actually provide much security because the officeholder may want to win not only the next election but also several thereafter. Consider the case of U.S. House members, who have a success rate of over 90 percent per reelection attempt. Most survive their next election, but in the long run about one-third eventually leave office via an electoral defeat (Erikson 1976a). Such odds on long-term electoral survival can give House members reason to pay special attention to constituency desires.

Second, the easiest way for citizens to become aware of their elected leader's record is for it to be exploited by an opponent as a stand against public opinion. Therefore, although name recognition generally wins votes, lack of public knowledge of a political leader's policy stands may sometimes actually be a sign of successful representation. Put another way, if members of Congress became more casual in their consideration of constituency views—for example, if representatives of liberal districts started acting like conservatives and vice versa—the polls might show much more evidence of constituency awareness, and on Election Day, more incumbents would be defeated. David Mayhew explains it this way:

> When we say "Congressman Smith is unbeatable," we do not mean there is nothing he could do that would lose him his seat. Rather we mean, "Congressman Smith is unbeatable as long as he continues to do the things he is doing." If he stopped answering his mail, or stopped visiting his district, or began voting randomly on roll calls, or shifted his vote record eighty points on the ADA scale, he would bring on primary or November election troubles in a hurry. (1974, 37)

Third, one should note that there does exist a sprinkling of informed voters who shift their political weight according to the policy views of the candidates. Even if these alert voters compose a tiny fraction of the total, their opinion leadership allows them to influence election outcomes to an extent beyond what their number would indicate. As information about the representative diffuses downward from relatively informed opinion leaders to the mass public, many voters may "get simple positive or negative cues about the Congressman which were provoked by his legislative actions but no longer have a recognizable policy content," as Miller and Stokes (1963, 55) suggest. By responding to such cues, a significant number of voters may act as if they are relatively informed about their representative's record. As a result, the collective electoral decisions in congressional contests may be more responsive to roll-call records than our knowledge about individual votes would indicate.

In the previous chapter, we saw the result of this process is visible in election returns. Members of Congress lose votes when they take ideologically extreme public positions. Normally such vote loss due to policy stands is not sufficient for defeat, as the representative is often protected by a modest incumbency advantage and a one-party district. But the few who do lose can often blame their own policy stands for their misfortune.

10-5 Interest Groups and Democratic Representation

Public opinion is generally treated as a passive input for the consideration of elected officials, with politicians absorbing the costs of interpreting public preferences from polls and other indicators. But public opinion can take on an active voice when people try to gain attention by such actions as protesting, ranting on the Internet, and lobbying officials. Often people coordinate their activity so it becomes group activity. Then, politicians pay extra attention due to the power of numbers. At its best, this is the interest groups model at work.

Like the political parties model, the interest groups model allows for an intermediate agent (in this case, organized groups) between individuals and their government leaders. Group members need not engage in extensive activity themselves but can instead rely on their group's leaders and lobbyists to represent their interest. Members may be called on, however, to contribute to the group's strength by giving money, writing letters to officials, participating in demonstrations, or voting for the group's endorsed candidates. Elected leaders, according to the model, satisfy public opinion when they respond to (and anticipate) group pressures. To the extent the interest groups model is working, the influence of different interest groups reflects their membership and the intensity with which their views are held. When conflicting demands of different interest groups collide, the policy result is a compromise, with each side getting its way in proportion to the strength of its membership support.

Interest Groups Opinion as Public Opinion

By organizing as political interest groups, people take the initiative to get the attention of politicians. An argument can be made that organized interest groups facilitate the representation of public opinion. Policymakers want to be informed about public opinion so they can act without electoral surprises. Thus, they listen to spokespersons for the various groups with interests in the matter at hand. Without organized groups to facilitate their understanding of the varying interests of the public, politicians would be operating from ignorance. In the ideal case, the aggregation of group opinion represents public opinion.

Politically active interest groups include business groups (e.g., the National Association of Wholesale Distributors), labor unions (e.g., the United Auto Workers), professional groups (e.g., the American Nurses Association), issue advocates (e.g., the National Rifle Association), identity groups (e.g., National Organization of Women), and ideological groups (e.g., various "Tea Party" groups). Some claim to represent the interests of the public generally (e.g., Common Cause). This diversity masks the challenge that the various groups holding a political interest do not face equal costs of organizing or enjoy equal persuasive powers when they do. In fact, the startup costs for group action are considerable. As elaborated in Mancur Olson's (1968) classic argument, the advantage goes to the groups organized in advance. When organized, some groups are more influential than others. When groups have become institutionalized in political life, as when the NRA is identified as representing gun owners or when the AARP is identified as the group spokesman for retired people, politicians pay the most attention (Grossman, 2012).

When interest groups lobby the government, we might assume that they readily get their way. Yet there is no guarantee of the result. In some instances, opposing group interests lead to stalemate or compromise. In many others, when groups lobby government for new policies, the outcome is no change at all (Baumgartner et al. 2009). With over 3 billion dollars spent annually on lobbying in Washington alone, one can ask whether this is money well spent. The answer is probably yes on the grounds that lobbying professionals know what they are doing (Leech, 2010).

One common concern is that the wealthy and educated people gain an advantage in influencing via the group process. Studies repeatedly find that citizens at the high end of the socioeconomic ladder belong to more political groups than those at the low end (e.g., Schlozman, Verba, and Brady 2012). The wealthy and educated gain a further advantage because officeholders tend to empathize more with higher-status citizens. For instance, elected officials are more likely to attend to the concerns of business leaders than to those of advocates for the homeless. Besides, they know that compared to the business community, politicians believe that the poor are too distracted to pay attention.

Implicit in any discussion of interest group success is the group's power to dispense or withhold rewards to elected officials. The most obvious source of reward or punishment is the group's vote on Election Day. Yet it is not always clear that group leaders speak for their members' interests or whether their endorsements of candidates can influence voters (Lupia and McCubbins 1998).

Groups may lobby most effectively on issues outside the public spotlight. Generally, a group is successful if its goal would greatly benefit the group and cost little to others. Examples of such benefits include tax breaks, agricultural subsidies, oil import quotas, veterans' benefits, and land tariffs on commodities. Unfortunately, from the standpoint of the interest groups model, the beneficiaries of such policies are special interests that cannot claim to represent public opinion. Narrow but specialized interests have an advantage not only because they have a unity of purpose but also because the public is often not aware of their activities. Meanwhile, groups that depend on a large mass membership for support are often handicapped when their members become satisfied by public relations gestures and symbolic rewards (Edelman 1965).

Money, PACs, and the Electoral Process

Interest groups have additional political resources besides the power of the vote. For instance, they are often able to offer the government their technical expertise. Most important of all, interest groups dispense cash to finance politicians' campaigns. While most campaign contributions originate with individual citizens directly rather than groups, organized groups' Political Action Committees (PACs) play a special role in campaign financing by drawing money from their membership base, bundling it, and dispersing it to political candidates. By law, citizens are limited in the amounts they can contribute to political campaigns or to PACs. The Supreme Court's 2010 *Citizens United vs. Federal Elections Commission* decision, however, has complicated matters further. On freedom-of-speech grounds, the Court ruled that corporations, unions, and other groups could not be limited in their spending on political advocacy as long as they acted independently of the formal political campaigns. Since *Citizens United*, money has flowed without limits into advocacy groups known as Super-PACS. Critics see these developments as further biasing the interest group system in favor of the wealthy.

The role of PACs in campaign finance is widely regarded as giving too much power to well-financed groups at the expense of ordinary citizens. More is involved than simply the effect of money on election outcomes. The argument goes as follows. Contributors give to campaigns not as philanthropic generosity to the deserving class of righteous politicians but as policy investments. Otherwise, why would groups contribute so much to unopposed candidates or concentrate their contributions on electorally safe members of congressional committees that must vote on legislation relevant to the group? Although contributions are often given in gratitude for legislative support of the group's positions in the past rather than for explicit future favors, legislators can enhance their expectation of future group support if they support the group position in advance. Once they receive a PAC's support, individual legislators become even more receptive to the group's position. A legislator who votes against a PAC's interest can find its future contributions withdrawn or even given to an electoral opponent. Even when a PAC mistakenly backs the losing horse in an election, the PAC often recovers influence by funding the winner. In fact, PACs often spread their investment by contributing to both candidates in an election.

With reelection rates of over 90 percent, and with evidence showing that the money they spend in a campaign is rarely crucial to their reelection, we might ask why members of Congress could not boldly act independently of PAC influence. One argument is that politicians do not like to take electoral chances they can avoid. Certainly many politicians take PAC money without being influenced by it, and many others avoid all PAC money on principle. But there can be little doubt that PAC money buys access if not actual influence. Elected officials generally pay extra attention to the views of those who give them money.

Does PAC activity distort the political process in favor of groups with advantages in resources? Political scientists tend to be somewhat cautious in their conclusion because testing for statistical evidence of PAC influence is not easy. The test would seem to be whether elected leaders give more weight to contributor opinion than their overall voting record, constituency preferences, and party affiliation would suggest. Although it stands to reason that people who give money to campaigns expect something in return (Snyder 1992), the statistical evidence suggests elected officials rarely take abrupt U-turns in policy in response to bursts of campaign cash (Wawro 2001). While corrupt deals undoubtedly occur behind closed doors, the evidence is elusive regarding the influence of political money on roll-call voting (Ansolabehere, de Figueirido, and Snyder 2003). Of course, the challenge is that lobbyist influence most likely would occur at a different stage of the process than when officeholders cast public roll-call votes.

Many informed observers doubt that significant reform of campaign financing would greatly diminish the overall role of interest groups in the policy process because organized groups would still possess the advantages of information, expertise, and direct monitoring of government officials—which the general public does not possess. The hoped-for change would be that a group's bankroll would play a smaller role in determining its degree of influence. When elected leaders respond to potential votes rather than potential cash, the different organized groups compete on a more level-playing field.

Interest Groups: An Assessment

Because the positions voiced by influential organized groups do not necessarily correspond to even the most strongly held views within the general public, the actual group process seldom follows the prescription of the interest groups model. If group activity were the sole input into governmental decision, the result would be a distortion of public opinion. The problem is that the group process results in some opinions carrying more weight than others.

Although some people obtain more representation from group activity than others, this does not mean that interest groups' freedom to operate in the political arena works against the public interest. A fact of political life is that some people—particularly the wealthy, educated, articulate, and already politically powerful—are in the best position to advance their political preferences. This fact is made clearer only when we examine the role of interest groups in politics.

One could conduct a mental experiment of imagining a political world where all interest group access to government officials is somehow eliminated. While the "special interest" would lose access, so would the spokespersons for the general public. Rather than wishing for the wholesale reduction in interest group influence, perhaps we should concentrate on ways to make the process of interest group access more equitable.

10-6 Conclusion

This chapter has explored sources beyond the direct mechanism of elections for additional linkages between public opinion and public policy. Four models were explored. The sharing model generates representation because politicians are drawn from the same community as their voters. The parties model generates representation because parties provide voters with an easy cue to cast rational ballots. The delegate model generates representation because elected leaders anticipate the need to please future voters. Finally, although it can lead to distortion, the interest groups model generates representation because the politicians' response to group interest can indirectly reflect the opinions of the general public.

A public that is not well informed gets its policy views represented by government, perhaps to a degree greater than it seems to deserve. In the next and final chapter, we assess the net influence of public opinion on policy in the United States, and we discuss possible ways to make the public's influence stronger.

Critical Thinking Questions

1. Observers are divided on the value of political parties to electoral politics. In some instances at the state or local level, elections are conducted on a nonpartisan basis and people run for office without party labels. Would nonpartisan elections enhance democracy or perhaps make it less workable? Why or why not?
2. The public seems to like the idea of term limits for politicians. How might strict term limits for all elected leaders affect the conduct of politics? Would the public get what it wants if strict term limits were implemented?
3. Once elected, politicians have the freedom to ignore the views of the people who elected them. Why then might politicians want to pay heed to the views of their constituents?

Endnotes

1. In an early study of nonpartisan city councils, Kenneth Prewitt (1970) found many "lateral entrants" who were encouraged by friends and associates to run for office. In an early study of the partisan Connecticut legislature, James Barber (1965) identified many "reluctants"—serving not because of their raw ambition or political interest but because of the insistence of others.
2. In 2012, women comprised only 17 percent of both the House and the Senate. Ten percent of House members were African-American, and 5 percent were Hispanic. The Senate contained no African-Americans but two (2 percent) Hispanics. Only 5 percent of the House members were under forty years of age. No senator was under forty years (Stanley and Niemi 2013, Table 5.2). Women and minorities are less likely than white males to consider political careers in the first place, even when they have the occupational stature that normally leads to political success. See Fox and Lawless (2004, 2005).
3. Comparing opinions of the mass public with those of the elites is difficult because the results of the comparison can depend on the issues that are chosen. In 1982, the CBS/*New York Times* survey included questions about school prayer and a constitutional amendment to balance the budget. Elites appear more liberal on these issues because they are more aware of the complexities than the mass public, who treats questions about prayers and balanced budgets as referenda on God and the virtue of thrift, respectively. On the practical issues of what Congress should spend its money on, the 1982 mass and congressional samples were remarkably similar.
4. Ansolabehere and Jones (2010) find strong survey evidence that voters often use their Congress member's party affiliation as a cue regarding their votes on important bills.

5. As recently as 1988 there had been virtually no statistical relationship between state-level ideology and state-level partisanship (Erikson 2001). Much—but not all—of the change in the states has been due to conservative Southern states converting to the Republican Party.

6. Although the image of primary elections as driven by the preferences of ideologues of the left (for Democrats) and right (Republicans) is a common one, support from survey analysis is elusive; see Norrander (1989) and Abramowitz (2008). See also Hirano et al. (2010), on the historical sequencing of primaries and polarization.

7. DW-Nominate scores can be obtained from the Web site http://voteview.com.

8. If nonpartisan officials are generally less responsive to public opinion, an exception to this conventional wisdom can be found in the judicial branch. Caldarone, Canes-Wrone, and Clark (2009) show that elected state supreme courts are most responsive to state opinion on abortion rights when they are elected on a nonpartisan basis. The argument is that nonpartisan judicial candidates must pander to public opinion, whereas partisan candidates are protected from scrutiny by the reputations of their party labels.

9. For the House of Representatives, the correlations between the presidential vote and our roll-call liberalism measure are .84 (all cases), .69 (Democrats), and .43 (Republicans). For senators, the correlations between roll-call liberalism and our measure of state opinion are .71 (all cases), .70 (Democrats), and .46 (Republicans). Overall, our composite index incorporating dimension 2 as well as dimension 1 of the DW-Nominate scores correlates more strongly with measures of constituency opinion than scores on either dimension treated separately.

10. It is not only legislators who modify their behavior in election years to respond to an anticipated public opinion. Huber and Gordon (2004) find that elected judges (in Pennsylvania) rule more punitively in criminal cases during years when they are up for reelection.

11. The original use of the term *electoral selection* as a source of incumbent electoral strength was probably found in Erikson and Wright (1997). Zaller (1998b) presents the analogy from boxing. Champion boxers generally defeat their challengers. It would be foolish to attribute their success to their incumbency advantage. Rather, their ability to repeat as champion is due to their skill in the ring.

12. For further discussion, see Erikson and Wright (2001).

13. Voter knowledge of positions on the first Gulf War was equally slim regarding senators and representatives (Alvarez and Gronke 1996).

CHAPTER 11

Public Opinion and the Performance of Democracy

According to democratic theory, the health of a democracy depends on the existence of a politically informed and active citizenry. By carefully monitoring government affairs, citizens can develop informed opinions about policies that represent their interests. By working for and voting for candidates who represent their views, and by making their views known to elected leaders, citizens can collectively translate their policy preferences into government action. The resulting set of policies that governments enact represents a reasonable compromise between competing claims of equally powerful and informed citizens. This description is the democratic ideal. In this concluding chapter we assess the degree to which American democracy approaches the ideal and speculate about possible ways to achieve improvement.

11-1 Assessing the Impact of Public Opinion on Policy

We have discussed five models that have the potential to provide public policy consistent with what the public prefers. By voting for leaders who share their views, the public can fulfill the basic needs of the rational-activist model. If reliable voting cues are furnished by political parties, policy-oriented voters can fulfill the political parties model by choosing the party platform most compatible with their views. Aside from voting, people can influence policymakers by bringing the preferences of the group to which they belong to bear on officials, thus fulfilling the interest groups model.

In addition, when policymakers try to follow public opinion and perceive that opinion accurately, the delegate model is fulfilled. Finally, because leaders and followers share many political beliefs, the sharing model provides political linkage.

By itself, each of these sources of political linkage may provide only a small increase in the degree to which officials are responsive to the public. Their total effect may in fact be slight, as to show that public opinion can influence policy is not a demonstration that public opinion is followed all or even most of the time. Perhaps the evidence we need is some sort of counting of the frequency with which government policies are in accord with public opinion. A truly definitive study following this design would require information at the national, state, and local levels across a broad range of policies as to whether the process of political linkage results in public policy consistent with public opinion. We would want to be able to say which of the linkage models proves most viable, and on what issues. We would want to assess the consequences of linkage failure for the public's opinions about its government, for its participation in political affairs, and, ultimately, for political stability. Unfortunately, such a study does not exist.

Because presently available evidence of the frequency of political linkage is limited, conclusions based on it must be tentative—perhaps limited to the specific issues studied, the level of government considered, and the period involved. Moreover, congruence of majority opinion and government policy may not always be the best indicator of political linkage, as government decisions can be responses to the intense opinions of a minority rather than the preferences of the majority. Also, as we have seen, majority opinion on an issue fluctuates with the exact wording of a survey question. Keeping these cautions in mind, let us see what the evidence shows about the congruence of public opinion and government policy.

Evidence at the National Level

If acts of Congress were determined by the demands of public opinion, then Congress would act whenever public opinion built to majority support or higher behind a proposed program. Because polls do not regularly monitor opinions on specific proposals before Congress, we often do not know how much the public supports a policy before its enactment. However, polls can offer clues to how well Congress serves the broad policy guidelines preferred by the public.

To develop a strong statistical argument that policy corresponds to (or seems to follow) public opinion, we must find a consistent pattern of congruence over many issues. One form of congruence would be a pattern of policy changes in the direction of majority opinion. Even stronger evidence would be both opinion and policy changing in the same direction as when public opinion shifts and policy change follows.

Alan Monroe (1979, 1998) has examined opinion–policy congruence over the period from 1960 to 1974 and again from 1980 to 1993. For a variety of poll questions, Monroe ascertained whether or not the public preferred a specific change in national policy. For each issue, he then determined whether the public's preferred policy change eventually took place. His findings for the earlier period are shown in Figure 11.1. On the seventy-four issues for which the public favored the status quo, the desired outcome of no change occurred 76 percent of the time.

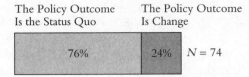

When a Majority of the Public Prefers the Status Quo

The Policy Outcome
Is the Status Quo

The Policy Outcome
Is Change

76%   24% $N = 74$

When a Majority of the Public Prefers Change

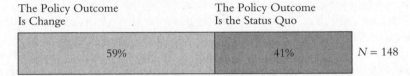

The Policy Outcome
Is Change

The Policy Outcome
Is the Status Quo

59%   41% $N = 148$

FIGURE 11.1 Congruence of Policy Preference Among the Mass Public and Policy Outcomes at the National Level.

Source: Based on data from Alan D. Monroe, "Consistency Between Public Preferences and National Policy Decisions," *American Politics Quarterly* 7 (January 1979), p. 9. Copyright © 1979 by Sage Publications.

On the 148 issues on which the public preferred change, the desired change outcome occurred 59 percent of the time. Evidently, the public is less likely to get its way when it prefers change than when it prefers the status quo. Of course, that the American political system tends to be status-quo-oriented has often been observed—that is, an intense minority (e.g., opponents of gun control) can often block change. But in either case, the public's preference becomes policy more often than not. Over all cases—preferences for change and preferences for the status quo—Monroe finds policy corresponding to public opinion almost two-thirds of the time. For the later period (1980–1993), the rate of policy correspondence was somewhat lower for reasons that are not clear.

In a related study, Page and Shapiro (1983) examine over 300 instances of opinion change recorded by polls between 1935 and 1979. They find a healthy correspondence between the direction of change in public preferences and the direction of change in public policy. In the 231 instances where opinion and policy both changed, they changed in the same direction 66 percent of the time. Page and Shapiro do not entirely rule out the possibility of some spurious relationship: Political elites could educate the public on the policies they prefer and then convince the public of their merit. Support for the inference that opinion causes policy is strengthened, however, by the fact that observed policy changes almost always followed the change in opinion rather than the other way around.

The relationship between national opinion and national legislation seems to have weakened in the past decade or two. Monroe's 1998 report shows a linkage that is weaker than that in his earlier 1978 study. Jacobs and Shapiro (2000) concur that the relationship between opinion and policy on specific issues has become frayed. A case in point is the relationship between opinion and policy on raising the minimum wage. (Because the minimum wage is not indexed, congressional action is required to keep up with inflation.) Polls consistently show decisive majorities favoring further increases, and until the 1990s, Congress responded willingly. Then eleven years went by, from 1996 to 2007, without a minimum wage increase even though Gallup polls in 2001 and 2005 showed more than 80 percent of the public favoring an increase. When the minimum wage was finally increased in 2007 (from $5.15 to $7.15 an hour), it had been at its lowest in terms of real dollars since the early 1950s.

The slow incremental change in the minimal wage illustrates the fact that while opinion might be an influence on national policy, the many institutional choke points in Congress (e.g., the filibuster) serve to favor the status quo (Clinton 2011). Congress may delay acting or fail to act at all in passing legislation favored by the public. But rarely does Congress act against the clear objection of the American public. With the arguable exception of the passage the Affordable Care Act (Obamacare), it is difficult to find instances of Congress passing major legislation even though the polls say the public disapproves.[1] One cannot say the same about legislation that is obscure. Burstein (2006) shows that on issues mostly invisible to the public, the nominal views of the public as expressed in polls have little bearing on policy.

Scholars have explored long-term relationships between opinion and national policy in search of statistical evidence of opinion influencing policy, with several positive results reported. The clearest evidence is for defense spending, with changes in defense spending seemingly following from shifts in public perceptions of need (Bartels 1991; Hartley and Russett 1992; Wlezien 1995b). Spending levels for domestic purposes also appear responsive to public preferences (Wlezien 1995a). Statistical evidence even suggests that Supreme Court decisions respond to shifts in public opinion (Mishler and Sheehan 1996; Flemming and Wood 1997; McGuire and Stimson 2004; Giles, Blackstone, and Vining 2008; Casillas, Enns, and Wohlfarth 2011; Epstein and Martin 2011).[2]

Time-series evidence of an opinion–policy linkage at the national level can also be presented in terms of the electorate's ideological mood on the one hand and a composite of national policies on the other. As our measure of public opinion, we use Stimson's "mood" indicator of public liberalism. Recall (Chapter 4) that mood represents a composite of trends over several survey questions regarding national policy. As a measure of national policy, we count the number of major liberal laws minus the number of major conservative laws for each Congress, 1953 to 2012.[3] Figure 11.2 overlays public opinion (mood) and policy (laws) over the last half of the twentieth century, revealing a connection between public opinion and policy. When public opinion turns more liberal or conservative, the index of national policy appears to follow: the more liberal the national mood, the more major laws in the liberal direction. And, although not directly evident from Figure 11.2, the passage of liberal laws lessens the demand for liberal legislation as measured by mood, while conservative legislative records raise it (Erikson, MacKuen, and Stimson 2002).

At its best, representation occurs because lawmakers respond to public opinion, but also public opinion adjusts its demands in response to new legislation. For instance, if the public demands new liberal legislation, demands for new liberal polices lessen. The politicians stay elected, and the people are satisfied. This feedback process is called the *thermostatic* model (Wlezien 1995b; Soroka and Wlezien 2010).

In Figure 11.2, one clear break in this pattern appears at the end of the time series. The G.W. Bush administration's conservative policies pushed mood in the liberal direction, generating a bigger gap than usual between mood and laws

FIGURE 11.2 Public opinion (mood) and policy liberalism (laws) over time.

Source: Updated from Erikson, MacKuen, and Stimson (2002, Figure 9.1).

in the early twenty-first century. This pent-up liberal demand set the stage for the election of President Obama in 2008, and the Democrats poised to pass the liberal agenda that included Obamacare.[4] The thermostatic response was of course a conservative reaction and more conservative policies following the return of Republican control of the House of Representatives.

Evidence at the State Level

At the state level, the opinion–policy linkage can be analyzed by seeing whether the policy preferences of state electorates are related to the actual policies in the states. One such approach is to compare the general policy preferences of the state (e.g., the population's relative liberalism–conservatism) to the general ideological tone of state policy. For a broad analysis of state policy, Erikson, Wright, and McIver (1994) pooled several CBS/*News York Times* surveys from the 1976–1988 period. Pooling of several surveys provided over 100,000 national respondents and large samples within states. Their measure of state opinion is based on the ideological self-identification (liberal, moderate, or conservative) of the state samples. Their measure of state policy is a composite of eight policies with a liberal versus conservative content. They find a strong correlation (.81) between the opinion measure and the policy measure.

This relationship is shown in Figure 11.3, where the ideological tendency of state public opinion and the ideological tendency of state policy are seen to almost always go together. The most liberal states enact the most liberal policies, and the most conservative states enact the most conservative policies. Although we cannot be certain about the causal direction, these data strongly suggest that public opinion matters when states make important policy decisions.

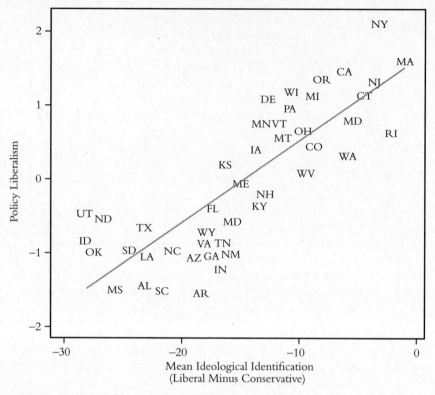

FIGURE 11.3 State policy liberalism and public opinion.

Source: Robert S. Erikson, Gerald C. Wright, and John P. McIver, *Statehouse Democracy* (New York: Cambridge University Press, 1994).

Other studies have examined the relationship between state opinion on specific topics and state policymaking on that topic. Recent years have seen research on the opinion–policy connection in the states on specific policies—notably abortion rights (Wetstein 1993; Norrander and Wilcox 1999; Lax and Phillips 2012), capital punishment (Mooney and Lee 2000; Norrander 2000), environmental policy (Johnson, Brace, and Arceneaux 2005), gay rights (Haider-Markel and Kaufman 2006; Lax and Philips 2009), health policy (Lax and Philips 2012; Pacheco 2012), and spending for education and welfare (Pacheco 2013). These studies find modest to strong relationships between state opinion on the specific topic and relevant state policy.[5] And at a lower-level government, Berkman and Plutzer (2006) find evidence that local preferences on school spending influence school boards' spending policy.

An Opinion–Policy Connection

Although the evidence is certainly incomplete, the few relevant studies that test for an opinion–policy linkage suggest that public opinion is far from inconsequential. At the national level we find that opinion and national policy are in agreement more often than not. At the state level we find that state opinion can be a good predictor of state policy. These findings should not be surprising because, as we have seen, several linkages work to translate even feebly voiced public opinion into policy. This information, however, should not be the cause for complacency about the current state of American democracy. Other forces besides public opinion shape government decisions—and we must keep in mind that collective public opinion at best moves incrementally and is often simply uniformed.[6]

We should of course be wary of assigning the United States an inflated grade for its current level of responsiveness to public opinion. It is sometimes suggested that observed correlations between public opinion and policy are not what they seem. In some instances when the electorate's preferences are statistically related to policy outcomes, it is conceivable that the true causal connection is reversed—that is, that politicians are educating the public rather than the public influencing the politicians (Page 2002; Hurley and Hill 2003). Certainly the political and economic leadership—the elite—plays a role in shaping public opinion. To contend that public opinion influences policy does not require that the driving force of politics must be some sort of populist will of the masses that arises independent of elite influence. When public opinion changes course, it usually follows the lead of elite discourse. A case in point is public attitudes toward homosexuality and gay rights. Over recent decades, public opinion became increasingly acceptant, and legislation is proliferated to advance the rights of homosexuals. There is no doubt that it took a shift in elite opinion to drive the public's growing tolerance toward homosexuality (Zaller 1992). But there can also be no doubt that public opinion responded and will determine how far policy will go in terms of advancing the agenda of the gay rights movement.[7]

Do All Opinions Count Equally?

Although legislators' policy positions are highly predictable from constituency opinion (Chapter 10) and policy direction is often predictable from public opinion (here in Chapter 11), we must ask whether this is evidence that elected politicians respond to public opinion generally or just to the opinions of a selected few. In other words, all opinions may not count equally. As we saw in Chapter 3, the opinions of the informed are often different from those of the less informed. These informed opinions are likely to have disproportionate influence, which of course means that many are underrepresented (Althaus 2003). Those with "no opinion" in surveys may be the most powerless of all (Berinsky 2004). As we saw in Chapter 9, it is the most informed about and interested in politics who vote and cast votes based on issues. As we saw in Chapter 10, politicians listen to these voices to stay elected. According to one recent study, despite strong statistical evidence that the opinions of a state's voters influence its senator's roll-call behavior, senators appear to ignore the views of their states' nonvoters (Griffin and Newman 2005).

Considerable attention has been focused on the gap between the political influence of the rich and the poor. One must ask, why hasn't the United States' growing income gap been corrected by government responsiveness to public opinion (Bonica et al. 2013)? One reason is the advantage that the affluent have over the poor in terms of political information. They also have greater access to elected leaders. Politicians listen to those who finance their campaigns, and of course campaign contributors are wealthier than others. And politicians listen most attentively to people like themselves, which usually means the affluent.

Based on a detailed analysis of state public opinion and Senate roll-call voting, Bartels (2008) has compared the responsiveness of senators to their constituents at different income levels. He finds that senators respond more to the views of the rich than to those of the poor. In an ambitious study, Gilens (2005, 2012) compares the preferences found in almost 2,000 opinion polls with subsequent policy outcomes—except that he performs this exercise separately for respondents at different income levels. He finds that the richer are more likely to receive their desired policy changes. Similarly, at the state level, Rigby and Wright (2010) find that policy responds more to the views of the affluent than those less well off. And on foreign policy, a domain where the influence of public opinion has been understudied, Jacobs and Page (2005) find that the influential voices are those of business leaders and other elites—and not public opinion at all (see also Kelly 2009).

Other statistical analyses find less evidence of unequal representation across income groups (Ura and Ellis 2008; Bhatti and Erikson 2010; Stimson 2010; Enns and Wlezien 2011). One challenge is that opinions of the rich and the poor are often similar and move in tandem, making their effects hard to disentangle. The truth might be that by attending to the rich, the politicians do not depart much from the wishes of the poor. If so, the puzzle shifts. The usual assumption is that the poor would demand more liberal policies, particularly those that involve some redistribution of resources. But, as we saw in Chapter 7, the income divide in terms of policy preferences is weaker than one might think. From the perspective of the political left, the first question is why don't the poor better understand their own political interests? Second, what can be done to awaken them sufficiently that the politicians heed their views?

11-2 Interpreting the Public's Role in Democracy

As we have seen throughout this book, the public generally does not live up to its prescribed activist role. Moreover, while public opinion can often influence government policy, in reality it is not the sole determinant of policy outcomes. Why not? Public control of government decisions depends on both the extent to which people actually participate in politics and the equality of people's resources for effective participation. The first point is obvious: It seems logical that the more people participate in politics, the more they can influence government decisions. But some people can participate more effectively than others because they command a greater share of the necessary resources, such as money, information, articulateness, and access to decision makers. How inequitable one views the distribution of these political resources can determine one's view of how democratic the political system actually is. Some observers see effective political power concentrated in the hands of an elite that controls policy outcomes for its own interests. Others more optimistically see the inequality in the distribution of power limited basically to the different political skills that individuals have and their interest in using them.[8] Because this debate over the equality of the distribution of political power is not easily decided by scientific inquiry, we do not enter it directly here. But, taking into account that the tools of effective political participation are not equally distributed, how can we assess the less than active political role of the public? We discuss four plausible conclusions.

Public Apathy as Mass Political Incompetence

Perhaps the easiest view of the public's limited role in government affairs is that people are simply incapable of doing better. We have seen that many people are inattentive or ignorant about politics and fail to hold coherent political opinions or even understand the ongoing liberal–conservative dialogue. All this could lead one to conclude that people generally lack the skills necessary to make sophisticated judgments about their political leaders and policies. Worse yet, the political views that people do hold may be intolerant, naive, or simply wrong. Viewed from this perspective, an increase in public participation would only make the situation worse because "bad" public opinion would drive "good" policymakers toward undesirable acts.

If the mass public is viewed as being inherently incapable of playing a useful role, then the remedy of trying to uplift public opinion becomes ineffective. Instead, one might have to rely on the proper training or careful recruitment of political leaders as a means of producing desired outcomes. If such desired outcomes include the preservation of the substance of democracy, then one must prescribe both a limited public role and the instillation of a heavy dose of democratic values among political elites. Louis Schubert, Thomas Dye, and Harmon Ziegler (2014), who arrive at this position, call it the "irony of democracy."

Public Apathy as Rational Disengagement

Possibly the reason most people do not allow politics to intrude far into their lives is that to do so would be irrational. From a strict cost–benefit standpoint, one should not follow public affairs closely because the investment would get one nowhere. One person's vote is useless because it is fantasy to assume that a single vote can decide an election's outcome except in the most extraordinary circumstances. Even when an individual's economic interest is directly at stake in the political arena (which may be rare), organizing like-minded people for collective political pressure is irrational because the costs of organization outweigh the possible benefits one could expect (Olson 1968). The cynic might also suggest that increased public knowledge of governmental affairs would produce only greater political withdrawal, as people who learn about their leaders' corruption and unresponsiveness would feel even more helpless at the prospect of changing things.

If this logic is correct, then people who participate in politics are usually motivated by something other than tangible personal gains. Perhaps they "irrationally" participate in order to gratify a felt obligation or civic duty, or out of concern for others besides themselves (altruism) (Edlin, Gelman, and Kaplan 2007). If the major determinant of an individual's sense of obligation to participate is preadult political socialization, then a reformer might hope to increase public participation by improving the training of the next generation of citizens. Alternatively, one might hope to eliminate rational withdrawal from politics by somehow increasing the rewards of political participation.

Public Apathy as Elite Manipulation

One can also interpret the public's low participation in politics as the result of manipulation by leaders and their allies (Domhoff 2002; Page 2002). When one observes political docility on the part of people who seemingly should have strong reasons for political protest, one can easily draw the conclusion that the individuals are being misled by elite propaganda. By this view, people are quiet and content because a ruling elite distracts them with bread and circuses.

One need not believe in a complex conspiracy in order to view political quiescence as the result of elite manipulation. Because most political events are remote from people's everyday lives, people willingly view these events through the interpretation of their leaders. Also, because people want to believe their political system is benign rather than corrupt or evil, they readily find reassurance from optimistic interpretations of the existing order and resist the voices that tell them otherwise (Edelman 1965).

If one sees people as unwilling to accept the "truth" because they do not want to disturb their cherished beliefs, the obvious remedy would appear to be heavy doses of correct information. But how to make this remedy effective remains unclear.

Public Apathy as Public Contentment

Rather than viewing public apathy as a sign that the classical democratic model does not hold, one can interpret apathy as an indicator of public contentment. If people do not concern themselves with political matters, then they must not have any additional demands to make on their government. Conversely, when many people do participate in politics, it is a distressing signal either that government has ignored public needs or that conflicts between societal groups are no longer being successfully resolved by political leaders.

Actually, the view that public apathy means public satisfaction rests on the assumption that the public is rather politically sophisticated. It assumes that people know their own interests, are capable of articulating grievances, and believe their expression of grievance would be effective if exercised. Only if these assumptions are made can one conclude that the lack of political participation indicates that people's needs are met by the proper working of a democratic system.

Evaluation

Although they contradict one another, each of these four possible explanations of the public's lack of political participation contains a grain of truth. For example, the public may not be capable of participation in all government decisions, particularly when the decision depends on proper evaluation of advanced technical knowledge. Equally obvious is that people can take only limited time from their personal affairs to participate in politics. Moreover, people may decide not to participate because they feel (perhaps mistakenly) they can trust their political leaders. Finally, people may retire from the political arena because they indeed have no grievances.

Simply holding these explanations up to the light of scientific evidence cannot determine which of the explanations for low participation in politics is most valid, as individual observers will view the evidence through the filter of their own preconceptions and values. How observers view such matters as human nature, people's basic interest, and the benevolence of government can shape whether they conclude that political inactivity signifies incapability, rational withdrawal, manipulation, or contentment. Similarly, the extent to which observers see their own opinion in harmony with majority opinion might influence their views of whether public control of government should increase or decrease.

11-3 The Expansion of Political Participation

Whether or not increased public political participation is desirable also depends on the type of political participation. Few would applaud increased mass participation that results in civil war or mass mobilization in support of an antidemocratic movement. But few would fear an increase in informed, democratic participation—particularly if we ignore possible disagreement over what *informed democratic participation* means. When there is little mass participation, the burden of responsibility falls on the political elites—both to ensure the continuation of the democratic rules and to make policy decisions that are fair and equitable. But if one agrees that the purpose of democracy is to ensure political leaders are held accountable to the people, one can hardly applaud when people do not actively seek to protect their own interests. Are there ways to increase the number of active participants while ensuring this participation is rational and democratic?

Seemingly, part of the answer involves some way of creating a more politically informed public. The public can hardly be blamed for its political ignorance when it is given little information with which to make political judgments. One can readily endorse more thorough political reporting by news media and other efforts to induce a more informed public. Hopes should not be set too high, however, because information campaigns do not always reach the people most in need of them. Also, we must recognize the possible side effects produced by increased public knowledge, such as greater public cynicism or an intensification of conflicts among politically aroused mass groups.

However difficult the task of boosting information might be, we can readily imagine that a more informed public would be better able to serve its function in the American democracy. Furthermore, we can speculate about how different the opinions of a truly informed public would be from the actual public we know. Increasingly, political scientists are taking this matter seriously, asking in what ways an informed public would act differently and how a more informed public might be achieved (Delli Carpini and Keeter 1996; Bartels 1996, 2008; Lupia and McCubbins 1998; Althaus 1998, 2003; Gastil 2000; Gilens 2001; Luskin 2003; Fishkin 2011; Mansbridge et al. 2012).

Answering these questions is difficult. A particular challenge is that the public may not want to be thrust into the policymaking spotlight. Citizens see their job as keeping a watch over the rascal politicians at the helm rather than taking the helm themselves (Hibbing and Theiss-Morse 2002).

Apart from inducing the development of a more informed public, a related and equally daunting task is to induce more people to participate in politics. The most obvious way of doing so would be to legislate changes that lower the costs and burdens of participation. For instance, motor-voter legislation and other reforms reduce or eliminate the initial barriers to voter registration. If we register the unregistered, maybe they will vote and maybe they will become informed and cast informed votes. We await the evidence. Today's voting rate (among eligible voters) is lower than the voting rate half a century ago. This is a disturbing phenomenon made all the more puzzling because most of the entry costs for voter participation have been removed. Almost half of American adult citizens chose to be nonparticipants. Political scientists have failed to understand this trend and its underlying causes.

Perhaps the existing methods for translating public opinion into government policy are inaccurate relics of a technically primitive time when ballot casting, face-to-face communication, and geographic representation were the only feasible conduits for public expression. New methods might be tried to encourage greater citizen participation, giving people greater opportunity to participate directly in local decisions, including perhaps more participatory democracy in nongovernmental groups such as the workplace, school, and religious organizations. Also, people could play a more direct role by deciding policy questions in referenda instead of letting their elected leaders decide them. Finally, it is now technologically feasible to allow people to vote in referenda via the Internet from the comfort of their home.

There is no question that greater citizen participation is a desired democratic value. But it is debatable whether additional opportunities to participate would lead to wiser government decisions than those elected leaders currently make. While proposals for expanding participation deserve serious consideration, their practicability and desirability remain uncertain.

Critical Thinking Questions

1. Some studies show that government policy generally follows the preferences of public opinion, at least in terms of general ideological (liberal vs. conservative) direction. How could this be the case, given the limited political understanding of many Americans?
2. It would seem that not everyone's opinions count equally when elected officials make policy. Some opinions, like the opinions of the wealthy, seem to matter more. Can you justify a system in which some opinions count more than others?
3. The American public participates less in politics than the supposed democratic ideal. But how could we boost public interest? If people who currently don't care about politics start participating, what differences might we see?

Endnotes

1. The Affordable Care Act is major legislation that was passed with large Democratic majorities in Congress, but weak public support. In polls, opponents clearly outnumbered supporters. However, as described in Chapter 4, a large swath of the opposition was on the grounds that the new law did not go far enough to insure health care rather than that it went too far.

In retrospect, it is sometimes said that the landmark Voting Rights Act (VRA) of 1965, which helped to ensure the exercise of voting rights by African-Americans and other minorities, was an instance of Congress passing major legislation even though it was unpopular in its day. This is incorrect. The VRA received majority support in polls at the time of passage. Similarly, passage of its companion civil rights bill, the Public Accommodation Act of 1964, was eased by the fact that it received majority support in the polls. In Chapter 4, we considered the case of the Bush tax cuts, a major legislation that received majority support in most polls, but arguably by the manipulation of question wording. The TARP economic rescue plan in 2008 passed Congress only once it seemed to garner majority support from the public. Although strictly speaking not in the category of "legislation," one clear instance of Congress acting against public opinion is the impeachment of President Clinton by the House of Representatives in 1998. The Republicans suffered electorally in the short term.

2. The Supreme Court can respond directly to public opinion when it takes public opinion into account when making its rulings. Or, of a less dramatic nature, public opinion can influence the Court indirectly when a conservative electorate elects a conservative president who appoints conservative justices. The evidence points to the former process as well as the latter.

3. The measurement of the laws index is an update of the methodology in Erikson, MacKuen, and Stimson (2002). The biennial measure of mood is the two-year average. Important laws are from David Mayhew's Web site http://davidmayhew.commons.yale.edu/.

4. Earlier, less visible gaps between mood and policymaking occurred in the early 1960s, when a liberal mood led to the Kennedy–Johnson administrations and eventually the great society, and then in the late 1970s, when the conservative tone of mood led to the conservatism of the Reagan presidencies.

5. To estimate state opinion requires drawing large samples from within states. To do so, studies that estimate state opinion typically pool multiple surveys and collect state-level subsamples. Back in the 1930s, the Gallup poll collected much larger state-level samples than national polls do today. This allowed the testing of the relationship between state opinion and policy on selected issues—capital punishment, women on juries, and the failed child labor amendment to the Constitution. On each of these three issues, opinion on the issue was strongly related to state policy. Opinion from the 1930s on capital punishment was also related to state capital punishment policy in the 1970s (Erikson 1976b).

6. As an example of opinion based on misinformation, consider opinion on crime. Public perceptions of the severity of the crime problem do not track well with the objective crime rate (Sharp 1999).

7. For a thorough review of the literature on policy and representation, see Shapiro, 2011.

8. The debate is framed by two classic studies, now decades old: Mills (1956), claiming rule by a "power elite," and Dahl (1961), arguing for the presence of pluralism.

The American National Election Study and the General Social Survey Questions

Two major national surveys, designed specifically for academic analysis, are conducted on a regular basis. These are the American National Election Study (ANES), done by the Center for Political Studies at the University of Michigan (conducted in even-number years), and the General Social Survey (GSS), done by the National Opinion Research Center at the University of Chicago (usually conducted yearly). For academic purposes, these surveys are usually more valuable than surveys done by commercial polling organizations. One reason is that the interviews are done in person rather than over the phone. Another is that the questionnaires are quite lengthy, usually including hundreds of items administered over a period of more than one hour. Also, many items are repeated over time, allowing for the analysis of changes.

In recent years, surveys conducted by the Pew Research Center have also proved valuable for academic analysis. Pew will usually do several surveys a year focused on a specific topic that has sufficient questions for academic analysis. Also, commercial surveys such as Gallup or ABC News have increased in value as they now have repeated many questions over a sufficient period of time to allow for inferences about opinion change. However, the ANES and GSS remain our principal sources of data.

Throughout this book, responses to opinion questions asked by various survey organizations have been examined. As their content usually appears in abbreviated form, the complete wordings for the most frequently used questions in the book are presented here. Where appropriate, responses are labeled as [L] for liberal and [C] for conservative, according to how these terms are applied to the response alternative within the text.

A-1 Questions from the American National Election Studies

1. Party Identification

Two questions are used to measure party identification. First, respondents are asked:

> Generally speaking, do you usually think of yourself as a Republican, a Democrat, an Independent, or what?

This basic question provides the division between the three kinds of partisans. For the second question, partisans are probed regarding the strength of their partisanship, and Independents are probed to see whether they lean toward one of the major parties.

Republicans and Democrats are asked:

> Would you call yourself a strong Republican [Democrat] or not so strong Republican [Democrat]?

Independents are asked:

> Do you think of yourself as closer to the Republican Party or to the Democratic Party?

Independents who choose a party are called *Independent Leaners.* Many Independents respond that they lean toward neither party. They are often called *Pure Independents.*

The net result is a seven-point scale of partisanship.

1. Strong Democrat
2. Not so strong (or "weak") Democrat
3. Independent, leaning Democrat
4. Pure Independent
5. Independent, leaning Republican
6. Not so strong (or "weak") Republican
7. Strong Republican

Unless otherwise noted, we use the simpler three-way division: Democrats (1 and 2), Independents (3, 4, and 5), and Republicans (6 and 7).

2. Liberal/Conservative Ideology

People are asked to choose an ideological position on a seven-point scale. Respondents are first asked:

> We hear a lot of talk these days about liberals and conservatives. Here is a seven-point scale on which the political views that most people might hold are arranged from extremely liberal to extremely conservative.

Then they are asked:

> Where would you place yourself on this scale, or haven't you thought much about it?

1. Extremely liberal
2. Liberal
3. Slightly liberal
4. Moderate, middle-of-the-road
5. Slightly conservative
6. Conservative
7. Extremely conservative
8. Don't know
9. Haven't thought much about it

Where we show the basic division between self-identified liberals and conservatives, we combine responses 1, 2, and 3 as *liberal* and 5, 6, and 7 as *conservative.*

In recent years, the ANES has used the following variation of the seven-point scale for many of its issue questions. Respondents are first presented with two extreme positions on the issue. Then they are asked to place themselves with regard to the issue on a scale ranging from 1 to 7. Shown the scale, respondents are asked: "Where would you place yourself on this scale, or haven't you thought much about it?" The scale position 1 generally represents the extreme liberal viewpoint, and scale position 7 generally represents the extreme conservative viewpoint. For convenience, we often compress the scale, combining the responses 1, 2, and 3 as *liberal* responses and 5, 6, and 7 as *conservative* responses, with neutral "4" respondents and those who admit they "haven't thought much about it" combined as "nonopinion holders."

Following are the four seven-point issue scales used in our ten-item index of respondent liberalism–conservatism.

3. Government Services/Spending Scale

> Some people think the government should provide fewer services, even in areas such as health and education, in order to reduce spending. . . . Other people feel it is important for the government to provide many more services even if it means an increase in spending. . . . Where would you place yourself on this scale? . . .

> [C] Government should provide many fewer services, reduce spending a lot.
> [L] Government should provide many more services, increase government spending a lot.

(On this one item, ANES scores 1 to 7 as conservative to liberal. We reverse the polarity so that 1 represents the liberal and 7 the conservative end of the scale, consistent with the other items.)

4. Government Job and Standard of Living Scale

> Some people feel the government in Washington should see to it that every person has a job and a good standard of living. Others think the government should just let each person get

ahead on his own. . . . Where would you place yourself on this scale? . . .

[L] Government should see to a job and a good standard of living
[C] Government should let each person get ahead on own

5. Aid to Blacks Scale

Some people feel that the government in Washington should make every effort to improve the social and economic positions of blacks. . . . Others feel that the government should not make any special effort to help blacks because they should help themselves. Where would you place yourself on this scale? . . .

[L] Government should help blacks
[C] Blacks should help themselves

6. Defense Spending Scale

Some people believe that we should spend much less for defense. . . . Others feel that spending should be greatly increased. . . . Where would you place yourself on this scale? . . .

[L] Greatly decrease defense spending
[C] Greatly increase defense spending

Items 3–6 are used as a part of our ten-item composite index of liberal–conservative policy positions from the 2012 ANES Survey. For this composite scale, each component item is added as a −1 (liberal), +1 (conservative), or 0 (other or in between). The remaining six issues for the composite scale are the following six items from the 2012 ANES Survey.

7. Affordable Care Act (Obamacare)

Do you favor, oppose, or neither favor nor oppose the health care reform law passed in 2010? This law requires all Americans to buy health insurance and requires health insurance companies to accept everyone.

[L] Favor
[C] Oppose

8. Tax the Rich

Would you favor, oppose, or neither favor nor oppose a plan to reduce the federal budget deficit if it included the following. . . . Raise personal income taxes for those earning over $250,000?

[L] Favor
[C] Oppose

9. Gun Control

Do you think the federal government should make it more difficult for people to buy a gun than it is now, make it easier for people to buy a gun, or keep these rules about the same as they are now?

[L] More difficult
[C] Make it easier or keep the same

10. Immigration

Which comes closest to your view about what government policy should be toward unauthorized immigrants now living in the United States?

1. Send them back to their home country
2. Have a guest worker program that allows them to remain
3. Allow unauthorized immigrants to remain . . . if they meet certain requirements
4. Allow unauthorized immigrants to remain in the United States without penalties

For purposes of ideological classification, responses 1 and 2 are coded as [C] and responses 3 and 4 are coded as [L].

11. Gay Marriage

Should same-sex couples be allowed to marry, or do you think they should not be allowed to marry?

[L] Favor
[C] Oppose

12. Abortion

Do you favor, oppose, or neither favor nor oppose abortion being legal if the woman chooses to have one?

[L] Favor
[C] Oppose

13. Political Information Scale

For some items, the ANES asked respondents to locate the positions of the major presidential candidates on the same scale. We used the candidate placements for five items listed above (liberal/conservative ideology to defense spending) to form the political information scale used in Chapters 3, 9, and 10. Two additional items were a four-item scale about abortion rights and a seven-item scale about government versus private health insurance. To construct the political information scale, every correct answer (Romney to the right of Obama) was scored as 1. All others were scored as zero. These scores were summed to create a composite knowledge score ranging from 0 (none correct) to 7 (all correct).

A-2 Questions from the General Social Survey

14. Abortion

Please tell me whether or not you think it should be possible for a pregnant woman to obtain a legal abortion.

a. If there is a strong chance of a serious defect in the baby?
b. If she is married and does not want any more children?
c. If the woman's own health is seriously endangered by the pregnancy?
d. If the family has very low income and cannot afford any more children?
e. If she became pregnant as a result of a rape?
f. If she is not married and does not want to marry the man?
g. If the woman wants it for any reason?

15. Political Tolerance

The GSS asks tolerance questions with a variety of groups as the target. The general form of the question, using a Muslim clergyman as the target group, is

There are always some people whose ideas are considered bad or dangerous by other people. Now consider a Muslim clergyman who preaches hatred of the United States . . .

a. If such a person wanted to make a speech in your community preaching hatred of the United States, should he be allowed to speak, or not?
b. Should such a person be allowed to teach in a college or university, or not?
c. If some people in your community suggested that a book he wrote which preaches hatred of the United States be taken out of the public library, would you favor removing this book, or not?

16. Political Trust

Since 1958 the ANES has been asking questions about trust in government. The following are the three ANES questions we used to measure political trust.

a. How much of the time do you think you can trust the government in Washington to do what is right—just about always, most of the time, or only some of the time?

("Never" is a volunteered answer.)

b. Would you say the government is pretty much run by a few big interests looking out for themselves or that it is run for the benefit of all the people?
c. Do you think that people in government waste a lot of the money we pay in taxes, waste some of it, or don't waste very much of it?

REFERENCES

Abrajano, Marisa A., and Ramon Michael Alverez. 2012. *New Faces, New Voices: The Hispanic Electorate in the United States*. Princeton, NJ: Princeton University Press.

Abramowitz, Alan I. 1994. "Issue Evolution Reconsidered: Racial Attitudes and Partisanship in the U.S. Electorate." *American Journal of Political Science* 38 (Feb.): 1–25.

———. 2008. "Don't Blame Primary Voters for Polarization." *The Forum* 5: Article 4.

———. 2010. *The Disappearing Center: Engaged Citizens, Polarization and American Democracy*. New Haven, CT: Yale University Press.

Abramowitz, Alan I., and Kyl L. Saunders. 1998. "Ideological Realignment in the U.S. Electorate." *Journal of Politics* 60: 634–652.

Abramson, Paul R. 1983. *Political Attitudes in America*. San Francisco: Freeman.

Achen, Christopher H. 1975. "Mass Political Attitudes and the Survey Response." *American Political Science Review* 69 (Dec.): 1218–1231.

Adler, Scott E. 2002. *Why Congressional Reforms Fail: Reelection and the House Committee System*. Chicago: University of Chicago Press.

Adorno, Theodore W., Else Frenkel-Brunswick, Daniel J. Levinson, and R. Sanford Nevitt. 1950. *The Authoritarian Personality*. New York: Harper.

Aldrich, John H. 2003. "Electoral Democracy During Politics as Usual—and Unusual." In *Electoral Democracy*, eds. George Rabinowitz and Michael B. MacKuen. Ann Arbor: University of Michigan Press, 279–309.

Aldrich, John H., Mark M. Berger, and David W. Rohde. 2002. "The Historic Variability in Conditional Party Government, 1877–1994." In *Party, Process, and Political Change in Congress*, eds. David W. Brady and Matthew D. McCubbins. Stanford, CA: Stanford University Press.

Aldrich, John H., and James S. Coleman Battista. 2002. "Conditional Party Government in the States." *American Journal of Political Science* 46: 164–172.

Aldrich, John H., and Richard Niemi. 1995. "The Sixth American Party System: Electoral Change, 1952–1992." In *Broken Contract?* ed. Stephen Craig. Boulder, CO: Westview Press.

Aldrich, John H., and David W. Rohde. 2001. "The Logic of Conditional Party Government: Revisiting the Electoral Connection." In *Congress Reconsidered*, 7th ed., eds. Lawrence C. Dodd and Bruce I. Oppenheimer. Washington, DC: Congressional Quarterly Press.

Alesina, Alberto, and Edward L. Glaeser. 2004. *Fighting Poverty in the U.S. and Europe*. Oxford: Oxford University Press.

Alesina, Alberto, and Howard Rosenthal. 1995. *Partisan Politics, Divided Government, and the Economy*. New York: Cambridge University Press.

Alford, John R., and David W. Brady. 1993. "Personal and Partisan Advantage in U.S. Congressional Elections." In *Congress Reconsidered*, 5th ed., eds. Lawrence C. Dodd and Bruce I. Oppenheimer. Washington, DC: Congressional Quarterly Press.

Alford, John R., Carolyn L. Funk, and John R. Hibbing. 2005. "Are Political Orientations Genetically Transmitted?" *American Political Science Review* 99 (May): 153–169.

Alford, John R., Peter K. Hatemi, John R. Hibbing, Nicholas G. Martin, and Lindon J. Eaves. 2011. "The Politics of Mate Choice." *The Journal of Politics* 73 (Apr.): 362–379.

Almond, Gabriel A., and Sidney Verba. 1963. *The Civic Culture*. Boston, MA: Little, Brown.

Altemeyer, Bob. 1981. *Right Wing Authoritarianism*. Winnipeg, MB: University of Winnipeg Press.

———. 1988. *Enemies of Freedom: Understanding Right Wing Authoritarianism*. San Francisco: Jossey-Bass.

———. 1997. *The Authoritarian Spector*. Cambridge, MA: Harvard University Press.

Alterman, Eric. 2003. *What Liberal Media?* New York: Basic Books.

Althaus, Scott L. 1998. "Information Effects in Collective Preferences." *American Political Science Review* 92 (Sep.): 545–558.

———. 2003. *Collective Preferences in Democratic Politics*. Cambridge, UK: Cambridge University Press.

Althaus, Scott L., and Devon M. Largio. 2004. "When Osama Became Saddam: Origins and Consequences of Change in America's Public

Enemy #1." *PS: Political Science and Politics* 37 (Oct.): 795–799.

Alvarez, R. Michael. 1997. *Information and Elections*. Ann Arbor: University of Michigan Press.

Alvarez, R. Michael, and John Brehm. 2002. *Hard Choices, Easy Answers: Values, Information, and American Public Opinion*. Princeton, NJ: Princeton University Press.

Alvarez, R. Michael, and Paul Gronke. 1996. "Constituents and Legislators: Learning About the Persian Gulf Resolution." *Legislative Studies Quarterly* 21: 105–127.

Alwin, Duane F., Ronald L. Cohen, and Theodore M. Newcomb. 1991. *Political Attitudes over the Life Span*. Madison, WI: University of Wisconsin Press.

Anderson, David D. 1981. *William Jennings Bryan*. Boston, MA: Twayne.

Andolina, Molly W., Krista Jenkings, Cliff Zukin, and Scott Keeter. 2003. "Habits from Home, Lessons from School: Influences on Youth Civic Engagement." *PS: Political Science and Politics* 36 (Apr.): 275–280.

Ansolabehere, Stephen, John de Figueirido, and James Snyder. 2003. "Why Is There So Little Money in U.S. Politics?" *Journal of Economic Perspectives* 17 (Winter): 105–130.

Ansolabehere, Stephen, and Shanto Iyengar. 1995. *Going Negative*. New York: Free Press.

Ansolabehere, Stephen, Shanto Iyengar, Adam Simon, and Nicholas Valentino. 1994. "Does Attack Advertising Demobilize the Electorate?" *American Political Science Review* 88 (Sep.): 829–838.

Ansolabehere, Stephen, and Phillip Jones. 2006. "Constituents Policy Preferences and Approval of Their Member in Congress." Cooperative Congressional Election Study Working Paper 6-01, downloaded from web.mit.edu.polisci/port1/cces/material/ansolabehere_jones.pdf.

Ansolabehere, Stephen, and Philip Edward Jones. 2010. "Constituents' Responses to Congressional Roll-Call Voting." *American Journal of Political Science* 54(3): 583–597.

Ansolabehere, Stephen, Nathaniel Persily, and Charles Stewart, III. 2010. "Race, Region and Voter Choice in the 2008 Election: Implications for the Future of the Voting Rights Act." *Harvard Law Review* 123: 1385–1436.

Ansolabehere, Stephen, James Rodden, and James M. Synder, Jr. 2008. "The Strength of Issues: Using Multiple Measures to Gauge Preference Stability, Ideological Constraint, and Issue Voting." *American Political Science Review* 102 (May): 215–232.

Ansolabehere, Stephen, James Snyder, and Charles Stewart. 2001. "Candidate Positioning in House Elections." *American Journal of Political Science* 45 (Jan.): 136–159.

Arceneaux, Kevin, and Martin Johnson. 2013. *Changing Minds or Changing Channels? Partisan News in the Age of Choice*. Chicago: University of Chicago Press.

Arceneaux, Kevin, and Robin Kolodny. 2009. "Educating the Least Informed Group: Experiments in a Grassroots Campaign." *American Journal of Political Science* 53 (Oct.): 755–770.

Arnold, Douglas. 1990. *The Logic of Congressional Action*. New Haven, CT: Yale University Press.

Arterton, F. Christopher. 1974. "The Impact of Watergate on Children's Attitudes Toward Authority." *Political Science Quarterly* 89 (June): 269–288.

Avery, P. G. 2002. "Political Tolerance, Democracy, and Adolescents." In *Education for Democracy: Contexts, Curricula, Assessments,* ed. Walter C. Parker. Greenwich, CT: Information Age Publishing, 113–130.

Bafumi, Joseph, and Michael C. Herron. 2010. "Leapfrog Representation and Extremism: A Study of American Voters and Their Members in Congress." *American Political Science Review* 104: 519–542.

Baker, C. Edwin. 2006. *Media Concentration and Democracy*. Cambridge, UK: Cambridge University Press.

Banks, Antoine, and Nicholas A. Valentino. 2012. "Emotional Substrates of White Racial Attitudes." *American Journal of Political Science* 56 (Apr.): 286–297.

Barabas, Jason. 2004. "How Deliberation Affects Policy Opinions." *American Political Science Review* 98 (Nov.): 687–701.

Barabas, Jason, and Jennifer Jerit. 2009. "Estimating the Causal Effects of Media Coverage on Policy Specific Knowledge." *American Journal of Political Science* 53 (Jan.): 73–89.

Barbaranelli, Claudio, Gian Vittorio Capara, and Michele Vecchione. 2007. "Voters' Personality Traits in Presidential Elections." *Personality and Individual Differences* 42 (May): 1199–1208.

Barber, James D. 1965. *The Lawmakers*. New Haven, CT: Yale University Press.

Barker, David C. 2002. *Rushed to Judgment: Talk Radio, Persuasion, and American Political Behavior*. New York: Columbia University Press.

Barker, David C., Jon Hurwitz, and Traci L. Nelson. 2008. "Of Crusades and Culture Wars: 'Messianic' Militarism and Political Conflict in the United States." *Journal of Politics* 70 (Apr.): 307–323.

Barker, David C., and James D. Tinnick. 2006. "Competing Visions of Parental Roles and Ideological Constraint." *American Political Science Review* 100 (May): 249–265.

Barry, William D., Michael B. Berkman, and Stuart Schneiderman. 2000. "Legislative Professionalism and Incumbent Reelection: The Development of Institutional Boundaries." *American Political Science Review* 94: 859–874.

Bartels, Larry. 1988. *Presidential Primaries and the Dynamics of Public Choice*. Princeton, NJ: Princeton University Press.

———. 1991. "Constituency Opinion and Congressional Policy Making: The Reagan Buildup." *American Political Science Review* 85 (June): 457–474.

———. 1993. "Messages Received: The Political Impact of Media Exposure." *American Political Science Review* 87 (Mar.): 267–286.

———. 1996. "Uninformed Voters: Information Effects in Presidential Elections." *American Journal of Political Science* 40: 194–230.

———. 2000. "Partisanship and Voting Behavior, 1952–1996." *American Journal of Political Science* 44: 35–51.

———. 2005. "Homer Gets a Tax Cut: Inequality and Public Policy in the American Mind." *Perspectives on Politics* 3 (Mar.): 15–31.

———. 2008. *Unequal Democracy*. Princeton, NJ: Princeton University Press.

Baum, Matthew A., and Samuel Kernell. 1999. "Has Cable Ended the Golden Age of Presidential Television?" *American Political Science Review* 93 (Mar.): 99–114.

Baumgartner, Frank R., Jeffrey M. Berry, Marie Hojnacki, David C. Kimball, and Beth L. Leech. 2009. *Lobbying and Policy Change: Who Wins, Who Loses, and Why*. Chicago: University of Chicago Press.

Baumgartner, Frank R., Suzanna L. De Boef, and Amber E. Boydstun. 2008. *The Decline of the Death Penalty and the Discovery of Innocence*. Cambridge, UK: Cambridge University Press.

Baumgartner, Frank R., and Bryan D. Jones. 1993. *Agendas and Instability in American Politics*. Chicago: University of Chicago Press.

Bawn, Kathleen. 1999. "Constructing 'US': Ideology, Coalition Politics, and False Consciousness." *American Journal of Political Science* 43: 303–334.

Beck, Paul Allen. 1977. "The Role of Agents in Political Socialization." In *Handbook of Political Socialization*, ed. Stanley A. Renshon. New York: Free Press.

Beck, Paul Allen, and M. Kent Jennings. 1991. "Family Traditions, Political Periods, and the Development of Partisan Orientations." *Journal of Politics* 53 (Aug.): 742–763.

Beckwith, Jon, and Corey A. Morris. 2008. "Twin Studies of Political Behavior: Untenable Assumptions." *Perspectives on Politics* 6 (Dec.): 785–791.

Bennett, Stephen. 1996. "Why Young Americans Hate Politics, and What We Should Do About It." *Politics and Political Science* 30 (Mar.): 47–52.

———. 1997. "Why Young Americans Hate Politics, and What We Should Do About It." *PS: Politics and Political Science* 39 (March): 47–52.

———. 1998. "Young Americans Indifference to Media Coverage of Public Affairs." *Political Science and Politics* 31 (Sep.): 535–541.

———. 2003. *News: The Politics of Illusion*. New York: Longman.

Bennett, W. Lance. 1980. *Public Opinion in American Politics*. New York: Harcourt.

Berelson, Bernard, Paul Lazarsfeld, and William McPhee. 1954. *Voting*. Chicago: University of Chicago Press.

Berinsky, Adam J. 1999. "The Two Faces of Public Opinion." *American Journal of Political Science* 43 (Oct.): 1209–1230.

———. 2004. *Silent Voices: Public Opinion and Political Participation in America*. Princeton, NJ: Princeton University Press.

———. 2009. *In Time of War*. Chicago: University of Chicago Press.

Berkman, Michael B., and Eric Plutzer. 2006. *Ten Thousand Democracies*. Washington, DC: Georgetown University Press.

Berry, J. M., and S. Sobieraj. 2011. "Understanding the Rise of Talk Radio." *PS: Political Science and Politics* 44: 762–767.

Best, S. J., and B. S. Krueger, eds. 2012. *Exit Polls: Surveying the American Electorate, 1927–2012*. Los Angeles, CA: CQ Press.

Bettig, Ronald V., and Jeanne Lynn Hall. 2003. *Big Media, Big Money*. New York: Rowan-Littlefield.

Bhatti, Yosef, and Robert S. Erikson. 2010. "How Poorly Are the Poor Represented in the U.S.

Senate." In *Who Gets Represented?*, eds. Peter Enns and Christopher Wlezien. New York: Russell Sage, 223–246.

Biemer, Paul, Ralph Folsom, Richard Dulka, Judith Lessler, Babu Shah, and Marchael Weeks. 2003. "An Evaluation of Procedures and Operations Used by the Voter News Service for the 2000 Presidential Election." *Public Opinion Quarterly* 67 (Spring): 32–45.

Bishop, George F. 2005. *The Illusion of Public Opinion*. Boulder, CO: Rowman & Littlefield.

Bishop, George F., Robert W. Oldendick, Alfred J. Tuchfarber, and Stephen E. Bennett. 1980. "Pseudo-Opinions on Public Affairs." *Public Opinion Quarterly* 44 (Summer): 198–209.

Bloch-Elkon, Yaeli, and Robert Y. Shapiro. 2005. "Deep Suspicion: Iraq, Misperception, and Partisanship." *Public Opinion Pros* (June). www.PublicOpinionPros.com.

Block, Jack, and Jeanne H. Block. 2006. "Nursery School Personality and Political Orientations: Two Decades Later." *Journal of Research in Personality* 40(5): 734–749.

Blumberg, Stephen, and Julian V. Luke. 2012. "Wireless Substitution: Early Release of Estimates from the National Health Interview Survey, July–December 2011." Center for Disease Control and Prevention (June 20). http://www.cdc.gov/nchs/data/nhis/earlyrelease/wireless201206.pdf.

Blumer, Herbert. 1948. "Public Opinion and Public Opinion Polling." *American Sociological Review* 13 (Oct.): 542–554.

Bobo, Lawrence, and David Johnson. 2004. "A Taste for Punishment." *Du Bois Review* 1(1): 151–180.

Bogart, Leo. 1972. *Polls and the Awareness of Public Opinion*, 2nd ed. New Brunswick, NJ: Transaction.

Bond, Jon R., Richard Fleisher, and B. Dan Wood. 2003. "The Marginal and Time-Varying Effect of Public Approval on Presidential Success in Congress." *Journal of Politics* 65: 92–110.

Bonica, Adam, Nolan McCarty, Keith T. Poole, and Howard Rosenthal. 2013. "Why Hasn't Democracy Slowed Rising Inequality?" *Journal of Economic Perspectives* 27(3): 103–124.

Boudreau, Cheryl. 2009. "Closing the Gap: When Do Cues Eliminate Differences Between Sophisticated and Unsophisticated Citizens?" *Journal of Politics* 71 (July): 964–976.

Bowler, Shaun, and Todd Donovan. 2002. "Democracy, Institutions, and Attitudes About Citizen Influence over Government." *British Journal of Political Science* 32 (July): 371–390.

Bowman, Karlyn, Andrew Rugg, and Jennifer K. Marsico. 2013. *Polls on Attitudes on Homosexuality and Gay Marriage*. Washington, DC: American Enterprise Institute.

Box-Steffensmeier, Janet, Suzanna L. De Boef, and Tse-min Lin. 2004. "The Dynamics of the Partisan Gender Gap." *American Political Science Review* 98 (Aug.): 515–528.

Box-Steffensmeier, Janet, Kathleen Knight, and Lee Sigelman. 1998. "The Interplay of Macroideology and Macropartisanship: A Times Series Analysis." *Journal of Politics* 60: 131–149.

Brady, Henry E., and Paul M. Sniderman. 1985. "Attitude Attribution: A Group Basis for Political Reasoning." *American Political Science Review* 79 (Dec.): 1061–1078.

Brady, Henry E., Sidney Verba, and Kay Lehman Schlozman. 1995. "Beyond SES: A Resource Model of Political Participation." *American Political Science Review* 89 (Mar.): 271–292.

Brehm, John, and Wendy Rahn. 1997. "Individual-Level Evidence for the Causes and Consequences of Social Capital." *American Journal of Political Science* 48 (Aug.): 999–1023.

Brewer, Paul R., Kimberly Gross, Sean Aday, and Lars Willnat. 2004. "International Trust and Public Opinion About World Affairs." *American Journal of Political Science* 48 (Feb.): 93–112.

Brians, Craig L., and Martin P. Wattenberg. 1996. "Campaign Issue Knowledge: Comparing Reception from TV Commercials, TV Shows, and Newspapers." *American Journal of Political Science* 40 (Feb.): 172–193.

Brody, Richard A. 1991. *Assessing the President*. Stanford, CA: Stanford University Press.

Brody, Richard A., and Lee Sigelman. 1983. "Presidential Popularity and Presidential Elections: An Update and Extension." *Public Opinion Quarterly* 47 (Fall): 325–328.

Brooks, Clem, and Jeff Manza. 2013. *Whose Rights? Counterterrorism and the Dark Side of American Public Opinion*. New York: Russell Sage Foundation.

Browning, Robert X. 1986. *Politics and Social Welfare Policy in the United States*. Knoxville: University of Tennessee Press.

Bryce, James. 1900. *The American Commonwealth*. New York: Macmillan.

Budge, Ian, and Richard I. Hofferbert. 1990. "Mandates and Policy Outputs: U.S. Party Platforms and

Federal Expenditures, 1950–1985." *American Political Science Review* 84 (Mar.): 248–261.

Bullock, John G. 2011. "Elite Influence on Public Opinion in an Informed Electorate." *American Political Science Review* 106 (Aug.): 486–515.

Burden, Barry C., and David C. Kimball. 2002. *Why Americans Split Their Tickets: Campaigns, Competition, and Divided Government.* Ann Arbor: University of Michigan Press.

Burnham, Walter Dean. 1970. *Critical Elections and the Mainsprings of American Politics.* New York: Norton.

Burstein, Paul. 2006. "Why Estimates of the Impact of Public Opinion on Public Policy Are Too High: Empirical and Theoretical Implications." *Social Forces* 84: 2273–2289.

Cain, Bruce, John Ferejohn, and Morris Fiorina. 1987. *The Personal Vote.* Cambridge, MA: Harvard University Press.

Caldarone, Richard P., Brandice Canes-Wrone, and Tom S. Clark. 2009. "Partisan Labels and Democratic Accountability: An Analysis of State Supreme Court Abortion Decisions." *Journal of Politics* 71 (May): 560–573.

Campbell, Andrea. 2010. *How Americans Think About Taxes: Public Opinion and the American Fiscal State.* Princeton, NJ: Princeton University Press.

Campbell, Angus, Philip E. Converse, Warren E. Miller, and Donald E. Stokes. 1960. *The American Voter.* New York: Wiley.

Campbell, Angus, Gerald Gurin, and Warren E. Miller. 1954. *The Voter Decides.* Evanston, IL: Row.

Campbell, David E. 2005. "Voice in the Classroom: How an Open Classroom Environment Facilitates Adolescents' Civic Development." Circle Working Paper 28. Downloaded from www.civicyouth.com/

Campbell, David E. 2008. "Voice in the Classroom: How an Open Classroom Climate Fosters Political Engagement Among Adolescents." *Political Behavior* 30: 437–454.

Campbell, David E., John C. Green, and Geoffrey C. Layman. 2011. "The Party Faithful: Partisan Images, Candidate Religion, and the Electoral Impact of Party Identification." *American Journal of Political Science* 55 (January): 42–58.

Campbell, James B. 2008. *The American Campaign,* 2nd ed. College Station: Texas A & M University Press.

Canes-Wrone, Brandice. 2006. *Who Leads Whom? Presidents, Policy, and the Public.* Chicago: University of Chicago Press.

Canes-Wrone, Brandice, David W. Brady, and John F. Cogan. 2002. "Out of Step, Out of Office: Electoral Accountability and House Members Voting." *American Political Science Review* 96: 127–140.

Canes-Wrone, Brandice, Michael C. Herron, and Kenneth W. Shotts. 2001. "Leadership and Pandering: A Theory of Executive Policymaking." *American Journal of Political Science* 43: 532–550.

Canes-Wrone, Brandice, and Scott de Marchi. 2002. "Presidential Approval and Legislative Success." *Journal of Politics* 64: 491–509.

Canes-Wrone, Brandice, and Kenneth W. Shotts. 2004. "The Conditional Nature of Presidential Responsiveness of Public Opinion." *American Journal of Political Science* 48 (Oct.): 690–706.

Cantril, Albert H. 1991. *The Opinion Connection.* Washington, DC: Brookings.

Cantril, Albert H., and Susan Davis Cantril. 1999. *Reading Mixed Signals: Ambivalence in American Public Opinion About Government.* Baltimore, MD: Johns Hopkins University Press.

Cantril, Hadley. 1951. *Public Opinion 1935–1946.* Princeton, NJ: Princeton University Press.

Caplan, Bryan. 2007. *The Myth of the Rational Voter.* Princeton, NJ: Princeton University Press.

Cappella, Joseph, and Kathleen Jamieson. 1997. *Spiral of Cynicism: The Press and the Public Good.* New York: Oxford University Press.

Carmines, Edward G., and James A. Stimson. 1980. "The Two Faces of Issue Voting." *American Political Science Review* 74 (Jan.): 78–91.

———. 1989. *Issue Evolution: Race and the Transformation of American Politics.* Princeton, NJ: Princeton University Press.

Carney, Dana, John T. Jost, Samuel D. Gosling, and Jeff Potter. 2009. "The Secret Lives of Liberals and Conservatives: Personality Profiles, Interaction Styles, and the Things They Leave Behind." *Political Psychology* 29(6): 807–840.

Carsey, Thomas M., and Geoffrey C. Layman. 2006. "Changing Sides or Changing Minds? Party Identification and Policy Preferences in the American Electorate." *American Journal of Political Science* 50 (Apr.): 464–477.

Carter, Amy, and Ryan L. Teten. 2002. "Assessing Changing Views of the President: Revisiting Greenstein's Children and Politics." *Presidential Studies Quarterly* 32 (Sep.): 453–462.

Casillas, Christopher J., Peter K. Enns, and Patrick C. Wohlfarth. 2011. "How Public Opinion

Constrains the Supreme Court." *American Journal of Political Science* 55: 74–78.

Cassel, Carol A. 1986. "The Non-Partisan Ballot in the United States." In *Electoral Laws and Their Consequences*, eds. Bernard Grofman and Rend Lipjart. New York: Agathon.

Chadwick, Andrew. 2005. *Internet Politics: States, Citizens, and New Communication Techniques.* Oxford: Oxford University Press.

Charney, Evan. 2008. "Genes and Ideologies." *Perspectives on Politics* 6 (June): 299–319.

Charney, Evan, and William English. 2012. "Candidate Genes and Political Behavior." *American Political Science Review* 106 (February): 579–594.

———. 2013. "Genopolitics and the Science of Genetics." *American Political Science Review* 107 (May): 382–395.

Childs, Harwood. 1965. *Public Opinion: Nature, Formation and Role.* Princeton, NJ: Van Nostrand.

Chong, Dennis. 1993. "How People Think, Reason, and Feel About Civil Liberties." *American Journal of Political Science* 37 (Aug.): 867–899.

———. 2006. "Free Speech and Multiculturalism in and Out of the Academy." *Political Psychology* 27 (Jan.): 29–54.

Chong, Dennis, and James N. Druckman. 2007. "Framing Theory." *Annual Review of Political Science* 10: 103–126.

———. 2013. "Counterframing Effects." *Journal of Politics* 75 (Jan.): 1–16.

Clinton, Joshua D. 2006. "Representation in Congress: Constituents and Roll Calls in the 106th House." *Journal of Politics* 68: 397–409.

———. 2011. "Congress, Lawmaking, and the Fair Labor Standards Act, 1971–2000." *American Journal of Political Science* 56: 355–372.

Clinton, Joshua D., and Steven Rogers. 2013. "Robo-Polls: Taking Cues from Traditional Sources?" *PS: Political Science and Politics* 46: 333–337.

Cobb, Michael D., and James H. Kuklinski. 1997. "Changing Minds: Political Arguments and Political Persuasion." *American Journal of Political Science* 41 (Jan.): 88–121.

Cohen, Bernard. 1963. *The Press and Foreign Policy.* Princeton, NJ: Princeton University Press.

Cohen, Jeffrey E. 2008. *The Presidency in the Era of 24 Hour News.* Princeton, NJ: Princeton University Press.

Coley, Richard J., and Andrew Sum. 2012. "Faculty Lines in Our Democracy: Civic Knowledge and Civic Engagement in the United States." Educational Testing Service. www.ets.org/research.

Conover, Pamela J., and Donald D. Searing. 2000. "A Political Socialization Perspective." In *Rediscovering the Democratic Purposes of Education*, eds. Lorraine M. McDonnell, P. Michael Timpane, and Roger Benjamin. Lawrence, Kansas: University of Kansas Press, 91–124.

Converse, Jean. 1987. *Survey Research in the United States: Roots and Emergence 1890–1960.* Berkeley: University of California Press.

Converse, Philip E. 1962. "Information Flow and the Stability of Partisan Attitudes." *Public Opinion Quarterly* 26 (Winter): 578–599.

———. 1964. "The Nature of Belief Systems in Mass Publics." In *Ideology and Discontent*, ed. David Apter. New York: Free Press.

———. 1966. "The Concept of the Normal Vote." In *Elections and the Political Order*, ed. Angus Campbell, Philip E. Converse, Warren E. Miller, and Donald E. Stokes. New York: Wiley.

———. 1987. "Changing Conceptions of Public Opinion in the Political Process." *Public Opinion Quarterly* 51(Spring): 12–24.

———. 1990. "Popular Representation and the Distribution of Information." In *Information and Democratic Processes*, eds. John Ferejohn and James Kuklinksi. Urbana: University of Illinois Press.

Converse, Philip E., Aage R. Clausen, and Warren E. Miller. 1965. "Electoral Myth and Reality: The 1964 Election." *American Political Science Review* 59 (June): 332–335.

Converse, Philip E., and Gregory B. Markus. 1979. "Plus Ça Change: The New CPS Election Study Panel." *American Political Science Review* 73 (Mar.): 32–49.

Cook, Timothy E. 1998. *Governing with the News: The News Media as a Political Institution.* Chicago: University of Chicago Press.

———. 2007. *Governing with the News: The News Media as a Political Institution*, 2nd ed. Chicago: University of Chicago Press.

Cox, Gary, and Jonathan N. Katz. 1996. "Why Did the Incumbency Advantage in the U.S. House Grow?" *American Journal of Political Science* 40: 478–497.

Cox, Gary W., and Matthew D. McCubbins. 1993. *Legislative Leviathan: Party Government in the House.* Berkeley: University of California Press.

———. 2004. *Setting the Agenda*. Cambridge, UK: Cambridge University Press.

Craig, Stephen G. 1993. *The Malevolent Leaders*. Boulder, CO: Westview.

Crespi, Irving. 1988. *Pre-Election Polling: Sources of Accuracy and Error*. New York: Russell Sage.

Cress, Donald A., and David Wootton. 2011. *Jean Jacques Rousseau: The Basic Writings*. Indianapolis, IN: Hackett Publishing.

Curtin, Richard, Stanley Presser, and Eleanor Singer. 2005. "Changes in Telephone Survey Nonresponse over the Past Quarter Century." *Public Opinion Quarterly* 69 (Spring): 87–98.

Dahl, Robert A. 1961. *Who Governs?* New Haven, CT: Yale University Press.

———. 1971. *Polyarchy*. New Haven, CT: Yale University Press.

———. 1982. *Democracy in the United States*. Chicago, IL: Rand McNally.

———. 1989. *Democracy and Its Critics*. New Haven, CT: Yale University Press.

D'Alessio, David W. 2012. *Media Bias in Presidential Election Coverage*. New York: Lexington Press.

Dalton, Russell J. 2008. *The Good Citizen*. Washington, DC: CQ Press.

Dalton, Russell J., Paul A. Beck, and Robert Huckfeldt. 1998. "Partisan Cues and the Media: Information Flows in the 1992 Presidential Election." *American Political Science Review* 92 (Mar.): 111–126.

Daniel, Jonnie. 2012. *Sampling Essentials: Practical Guidelines for Making Sampling Choices*. Thousand Oaks, CA: Sage.

Daves, Robert P. 2000. "Who Will Vote? Ascertaining the Likelihood to Vote and Modeling a Probable Electorate in Preelection Polls." In *Elections Polls, the News Media and Democracy*, eds. Paul J. Lavrakas and Michael W. Traugott. Chatham, NJ: Chatham House.

Dautrich, Kenneth, and Jennifer Necci Deneen. 1996. "Media Bias: What Journalists and the Public Say About It." *Public Perspective* 7: 7–19.

Davidson, Roger H., Walter J. Oleszek, and Frances E. Lee. 2014. *Congress and Its Members*, 14th ed. Washington, DC: Congressional Quarterly Press.

Davis, Darren. 2007. *Negative Liberty: Public Opinion and the Terrorist Attacks on America*. New York: Russell Sage Foundation.

Davis, Darren, and Brian Silver. 2004. "Civil Liberties Versus Security: Public Opinion in the Context of the Terrorist Attacks on America." *American Journal of Political Science* 48: 47–61.

Davis, James A. 2005. "Did Growing Up in the 1960s Leave a Permanent Mark on Attitudes and Values? Evidence from the General Social Survey." *Public Opinion Quarterly* 68 (Summer): 161–183.

Davis, Richard, and Diana Owen. 1999. *New Media and American Politics*. New York: Oxford University Press.

Dawson, Michael C. 1994. *Behind the Mule: Race and Class in African-American Politics*. Princeton, NJ: Princeton University Press.

Delhey, Jan, and Kenneth Newton. 2003. "Who Trusts: The Origins of Social Trust in Seven Societies." *European Sociological Review* 21 (Dec.): 311–327.

DellaVigna, Stefano, and Ethan Kaplan. 2008. "The Fox News Effect: Media Bias and Voting." *Quarterly Journal of Economics* 122 (Aug.): 1187–1234.

Delli Carpini, Michael X. 1986. *Stability and Change in American Politics: The Coming of Age of the Generation of the 1960s*. New York: New York University Press.

Delli Carpini, Michael X., Fay Lomax Cook, and Lawrence R. Jacobs. 2004. "Public Deliberations, Discursive Participation, and Citizen Engagement: A Review of the Empirical Literature." *Annual Review of Political Science* 7: 315–344.

Delli Carpini, Michael X., and Scott Keeter. 1996. *What Americans Know About Politics and Why It Matters*. New Haven, CT: Yale University Press.

Deutscher, Irwin. 1973. *What We Say/What We Do*. Glenview, IL: Scott.

Dietz, Janna L., and Keith Boeckelman. 2012. "Simulating 2008: A Mock Presidential Election's Impact on Civic Engagement." *PS: Political Science and Politics* 45 (Oct.): 743–747.

Dilliplane, Susanna, Seth K. Goldman, and Diana C. Mutz. 2013. "Televised Exposure to Politics: New Measures for a Fragmented Media." *American Journal of Political Science* 57 (Jan.): 236–248.

Dillman, Don A. 2008. *Mail and Internet Surveys: The Tailored Design Method*, 2nd ed. New York: John Wiley.

Djupe, Paul A., and Christopher P. Gilbert. 2002. "The Political Voice of the Clergy." *Journal of Politics* 64 (May): 596–609.

Dolan, Kathleen. 2011. "Do Women and Men Know Different Things? Measuring Gender Differences in Political Knowledge." *Journal of Politics* 73 (Jan.): 97–107.

Domhoff, G. William. 2002. "The Power Elite, Public Policy and Public Opinion." In *Navigating Public Opinion*, eds. Jeff Manza, Fay Loxmax Cook, and Benjamin I. Page. Oxford: Oxford University Press.

Downs, Anthony. 1958. *An Economic Theory of Democracy*. New York: Harper.

Drezner, Daniel. 2008. "The Realist Tradition in American Public Opinion." *Perspectives on Politics* 6: 51–70.

Druckman, James N. 2004. "Political Preference Formation: Competition, Deliberation, and the (Ir)relevance of Framing Effects." *American Political Science Review* 98 (Nov.): 671–686.

———. 2005. "Media Matter: How Newspapers and Television News Cover Campaigns and Influence Voters." *Political Communication* 22: 463–481.

Druckman, James N., and Kjersten R. Nelsen. 2003. "Framing and Deliberation: How Citizens' Conversations Limit Elite Influence." *American Journal of Political Science* 47 (Oct.): 729–745.

Druckman, James N., and Michael Parkin. 2005. "The Impact of Media Bias: How Editorial Slant Affects Voters." *Journal of Politics* 67: 1030–1049.

Duckitt, John, and Chris G. Sibley. 2009. "A Dual-Process Motivational Model of Ideological Attitudes and System Justification." In *Social and Psychological Bases of Ideology and System Justification*, eds. John T. Jost, Aaron C. Kay, and Hulda Thoprisdottir. New York: Oxford University Press, 292–370.

Dudley, Robert L., and Alan R. Gitelson. 2003. "Civic Education, Civic Engagement, and Youth Civic Development." *Political Science and Politics* 36 (Apr.): 263–267.

Easton, David. 1965. *A Systems Analysis of Political Life*. New York: Wiley.

Easton, David, and Jack Dennis. 1969. *Children and the Political System*. New York: McGraw.

Edelman, Murray. 1965. *The Symbolic Uses of Politics*. Urbana: University of Illinois Press.

Edlin, Aaron, Andrew Gelman, and Noah Kaplan. 2007. "Voting as a Rational Choice: Why and How People Vote to Improve the Well-Being of Others." *Rationality and Society* 19: 293–314.

Edwards, George C. 2003. *On Deaf Ears: The Limits of the Bully Pulpit*. New Haven, CT: Yale University Press.

Ellis, Christopher, and James Stimson. 2012. *Ideology in America*. Cambridge: Cambridge University Press.

Enns, Peter K., and Christopher Wlezien. 2011. "Group Opinion and the Study of Representation." In *Who Gets Represented?* eds. Peter K. Enns and Christopher Wlezien. New York: Russell Sage Foundation, 1–26.

Entman, Robert M. 1989. "How the Media Affect What People Think: An Information Processing Approach." *Journal of Politics* 51 (May): 347–370.

Epstein, Lee, and Andrew D. Martin. 2011. "Does Public Opinion Influence the Supreme Court? Probably Yes (But We're Not Sure Why)." *University of Pennsylvania Journal of Constitutional Law* 13: 263–281.

Erikson, Robert S. 1971. "The Electoral Impact of Congressional Roll Call Voting." *American Political Science Review* 65 (Dec.): 1018–1032.

———. 1976a. "Is There Such a Thing as a Safe Seat?" *Polity* 8 (Summer): 613–632.

———. 1976b. "The Relationship Between Public Opinion and State Policy: A New Look at Some Forgotten Data." *American Journal of Political Science* 20 (Feb.): 25–36.

———. 1976c. "The Influence of Newspaper Endorsements in Presidential Elections: The Case of 1964." *American Journal of Political Science* 20 (May): 207–234.

———. 1979. "The SRC Panel Data and Mass Attitudes." *British Journal of Political Science* 9 (Jan.): 89–114.

———. 1990. "Roll Calls, Reputations, and Representation in the U.S. Senate." *Legislative Studies Quarterly* 15: 623–642.

———. 1993. "Counting Likely Voters in Gallup's Tracking Poll." *Public Perspective* 4 (Mar./Apr.): 22–23.

———. 2001. "The 2000 Election in Historical Perspective." *Political Science Quarterly* 116 (Spring): 29–52.

———. 2002. "National Election Studies and Macro Analysis." *Electoral Studies* 21: 269–281.

Erikson, Robert S., Michael B. MacKuen, and James A. Stimson. 1998. "What Moves Macropartisanship? A Reply to Green, Palmquist, and Schickler." *American Political Science Review* 92 (Dec.): 901–912.

———. 2002. *The Macro Polity*. New York: Cambridge University Press.

Erikson, Robert S., Costas Panagopoulos, and Christopher Wlezien. 2004. "Likely (and Unlikely) Voters and the Assessment of Campaign Dynamics." *Public Opinion Quarterly* 68 (Winter): 588–601.

Erikson, Robert S., and Laura Stoker. 2011. "Caught in the Draft: The Effects of Vietnam Draft Lottery Status on Political Attitudes." *American Political Science Review* 105 (May): 2221–2237.

Erikson, Robert S., and Kent L. Tedin. 1981. "The 1928–1936 Partisan Realignment: The Case for the Conversion Hypothesis." *American Political Science Review* 75 (Dec.): 951–962.

Erikson, Robert S., and Christopher Wlezien. 1999. "Presidential Polls as a Time Series: The Case of 1996." *Public Opinion Quarterly* 63 (Summer): 163–178.

———. 2012a. "The Objective and Subjective Economy and the Presidential Vote." *PS: Political Science and Politics* 45 (Oct.): 620–625.

———. 2012b. *The Timeline of Presidential Elections: How Campaigns Do (and Do Not) Matter.* Chicago: University of Chicago Press.

Erikson, Robert S., and Gerald C. Wright. 1997. "Voters, Candidates, and Issues in Congressional Elections." In *Congress Reconsidered*, 6th ed., eds. Lawrence C. Dodd and Bruce I. Oppenheimer. Washington, DC: Congressional Quarterly Press.

———. 2001. "Representation of Constituency Ideology in Congress." In *Continuity and Change in Congressional Elections*, eds. David Brady and John Cogan. Stanford, CA: Stanford University Press, Chapter 8.

———. 2005. "Voters, Candidates, and Issues in Congressional Elections." In *Congress Reconsidered*, 8th ed., eds. Lawrence C. Dodd and Bruce I. Oppenheimer. Washington, DC: Congressional Quarterly Press, 77–106.

———. 2013. "Voters, Candidates, and Issues in Congressional Elections." In *Congress Reconsidered*, 10th ed., eds. Lawrence C. Dodd and Bruce I. Oppenheimer. Washington, DC: Congressional Quarterly Press, 91–116.

Erikson, Robert S., Gerald C. Wright, and John P. McIver. 1994. *Statehouse Democracy: Public Opinion and Policy in the American States.* New York: Cambridge University Press.

Erskine, Hazel. 1962a. "The Polls: Race Relations." *Public Opinion Quarterly* 26 (Winter): 137–148.

———. 1962b. "The Polls: Attitudes." *Public Opinion Quarterly* 26 (Winter): 293.

———. 1975. "The Polls: Health Insurance." *Public Opinion Quarterly* 39 (Spring): 128–143.

Farnsworth, Stephen J., and S. Robert Lichter. 2007. *The Nightly News Nightmare*, 2nd ed. New York: Rowman-Littlefield.

———. 2011. "The Contemporary Presidency: The Return of the Honeymoon: Television News Coverage of New Presidents, 1981–2009." *Presidential Studies Quarterly* 41 (July): 590–603.

Farrand, Max. 1961. *The Records of the Federal Convention of 1787*, vol. 1. New Haven, CT: Yale University Press.

Farrar, Cynthia, James S. Fishkin, Donald P. Green, Christian List, Robert Luskin, and Elizabeth Levy Paluck. 2010. "Disaggregating Deliberation's Effects: An Experiment Within a Deliberative Poll." *British Journal of Political Science* 40 (Apr.): 333–347.

Farrell, Henry. 2012. "The Consequences of the Internet for Politics." *Annual Review of Political Science* 15: 35–52.

Fearon, James. 1999. "Electoral Accountability and the Control of Politicians: Selecting Good Types Versus Sanctioning Poor Performance." In *Democracy, Accountability, and Representation*, eds. Adam Przeworski, Susan C. Stokes, and Bernard Manin. Cambridge, UK: Cambridge University Press, 55–97.

Feaver, Peter D., and Christopher Gelpi. 2004. *Choosing Your Battles.* Princeton, NJ: Princeton University Press.

Federico, Christopher M. 2006. "Race, Education, and Individualism Revisited." *Journal of Politics* 68 (Aug.): 600–610.

Federico, Christopher M., Emily L. Fisher, and Grace M. Deason. 2011. "Political Expertise and the Link Between the Authoritarian Disposition and Conservatism." *Public Opinion Quarterly* 75 (Fall): 686–708.

Feldman, Kenneth, and Theodore M. Newcomb. 1969. *The Impact of College on Students*, vol. 2. San Francisco: Jossey-Bass.

Feldman, Stanley. 1988. "Structure and Consistency in Public Opinion: The Role of Core Beliefs and Values." *American Journal of Political Science* 32 (June): 416–440.

———. 1989. "Reliability and Stability of Policy Positions: Evidence from a Five-Wave Panel." *Political Analysis* 1: 25–60.

———. 2003. "Enforcing Social Conformity: A Theory of Authoritarianism." *Political Psychology* 24: 41–74.

Feldman, Stanley, and Leonie Huddy. 2005. "Racial Resentment and White Opposition to Race-Conscious Programs: Principles of Prejudice?" *American Journal of Political Science* 49 (Jan.): 168–183.

Feldman, Stanley, and Karen Stenner. 1997. "Perceived Threat and Authoritarianism." *Political Psychology* 18: 741–769.

Fenno, Richard F., Jr. 1978. *Home Style: House Members in Their Districts*. Boston, MA: Little, Brown.

Ferejohn, John. 1999. "Accountability and Authority: Toward a Theory of Political Accountability." In *Democracy, Accountability, and Representation*, eds. Adam Przeworski, Susan C. Stokes, and Bernard Manin. Cambridge, UK: Cambridge University Press, 131–153.

Ferree, G. Donald. 1993. "Counting Likely Voters: A Reply to Erikson." *Public Perspective* 4 (Mar./Apr.): 22–23.

de Figueiredo, Rui J. P., and Zachary Elkins. 2003. "Are Patroits Bigots? An Inquiry into the Vices of In-Group Pride." *American Journal of Political Science* 47 (Jan.): 171–188.

Finke, Roger, and Rodney Stark. 1994. *The Churching of America, 1776–1990*. New Brunswick, NJ: Rutgers University Press.

Finkel, Steven E. 1993. "Reexamining the Minimal Effects Model of Recent Presidential Campaigns." *Journal of Politics* 55 (Feb.): 1–21.

Finkel, Steven E., and John G. Geer. 1998. "A Spot Check: Casting Doubt on the Demobilization Effect of Attack Advertising." *American Journal of Political Science* 42 (Aug.): 573–595.

Finkel, Steven E., Edward N. Muller, and Karl-Dieter Opp. 1989. "Personal Influence, Collective Rationality, and Mass Political Action." *American Political Science Review* 83 (Sep.): 885–903.

Fiorina, Morris P. 1977. "An Outline for a Model of Party Choice." *American Journal of Political Science* 21 (Aug.): 601–625.

———. 1981. *Retrospective Voting in American National Elections*. New Haven, CT: Yale University Press.

———. 1992. *Divided Government*. New York: Macmillan.

Fiorina, Morris P., and Samuel J. Abrams. 2009. *Disconnect. The Breakdown of Representation in American Politics*. Norman: University of Oklahoma Press.

Fiorina, Morris P., Samuel J. Abrams, and Jeremy C. Pope. 2011. *Culture War: The Myth of a Polarized America*, 3rd ed. New York: Longman.

Fischer, Claude S. 1975. "Toward a Subcultural Theory of Urbanism." *Social Forces* 53 (Mar.): 420–432.

Fishkin, James S. 1997. *The Voice of the People: Public Opinion and Democracy*. New Haven, CT: Yale University Press.

Fishkin, James S. 2011. *When the People Speak*. Oxford: Oxford University Press.

Fitzgerald, Jennifer. 2011. "Family Dynamics and Swiss Parties on the Rise: Exploring Party Support in a Changing Electoral Context." *Journal of Politics* 73 (July): 783–796.

Flemming, Roy B., and B. Dan Wood. 1997. "The Public and the Supreme Court: Individual Justice Responsiveness to American Policy Moods." *American Journal of Political Science* 41: 468–498.

Fowler, James H., Laura A. Baker, and Christopher T. Dawes. 2008. "Genetic Variation in Political Participation." *American Political Science Review* 102 (May): 233–248.

Fowler, James H., and Christopher T. Dawes. 2008. "Two Genes Predict Voter Turnout." *Journal of Politics* 70 (Aug.): 579–594.

———. 2013. "In Defense of Genopolitics." *American Political Science Review* 107 (May): 258–271.

Fox, Richard L., and Jennifer L. Lawless. 2004. "Entering the Arena? Gender and the Decision to Run for Office." *American Journal of Political Science* 48: 264–280.

———. 2005. "To Run or Not to Run for Office: Explaining Nascent Political Ambition." *American Journal of Political Science* 49: 642–659.

Frankel, Martin R., and Lester R. Frankel. 1987. "Fifty Years of Survey Sampling in the United States." *Public Opinion Quarterly* 51 (Winter): S127–S138.

Frankenberg, Erica, and Rebecca Jacobson. 2011. "The Polls: Trends in School Integration." *Public Opinion Quarterly* 75 (Winter): 788–811.

Franklin, Charles H., and John E. Jackson. 1983. "The Dynamics of Party Identification." *American Political Science Review* 77 (Dec.): 957–973.

Frankovic, Kathleen. 2003. "Horserace Polling and Survey Method Effects: An Analysis of the 2000 Campaign." *Public Opinion Quarterly* 67 (Summer): 244–264.

Free, Lloyd A., and Hadley Cantril. 1967. *The Political Beliefs of Americans*. New York: Simon and Schuster.

Freedman, Paul, Michael Franz, and Kenneth Goldstein. 2004. "Campaign Advertising and Political Citizenship." *American Journal of Political Science* 48 (Oct.): 723–741.

Freedman, Paul, and Kenneth Goldstein. 1999. "Measuring Media Exposure and the Effects of

Negative Campaign Ads." *American Journal of Political Science* 43 (Nov.): 1189–1208.

Freeman, Gary P., Randall Hansen, and David Leal. 2012. *Immigration and Public Opinion in Liberal Democracies*. New York: Routledge.

Fried, Amy. 2006. "The Forgotten Lindsay Rogers and the Development of American Political Science." *American Political Science Review* 100 (Nov.): 555–562.

Fridkin, Kim L., Patrick J. Kenney, and Jack Crittenden. 2006. "On the Margins of Democratic Life: The Impact of Race and Ethnicity on the Political Engagement of Young People." *American Politics Quarterly* 34: 605–626.

Fried, Amy. 2012. *Pathways to Polling: Crisis, Cooperation and the Making of Public Opinion Professions*. New York: Routledge.

Friesema, H. Paul, and Ronald D. Hedlund. 1981. "The Reality of Representational Roles." In *Public Opinion and Public Policy*, ed. Norman R. Luttbeg. Itasca, IL: Peacock.

Fritz, Ben, Brian Keefer, and Brendan Nyhan. 2004. *All the President's Spin*. New York: Touchstone.

Fritz, Sara, and Dwight Morris. 1992. *Handbook of Campaign Spending*. Washington, DC: Congressional Quarterly Press.

Fukumoto, Kentaro. 2009. "Systematically Dependent Competing Risks and Strategic Retirement." *American Journal of Political Science* 53 (Aug.): 740–754.

Fukuyama, Francis. 1995. *Trust: Social Virtues and the Creation of Propriety*. New York: Free Press.

Gaines, Brian J., James H. Kuklinski, Paul J. Quirk, Buddy Peyton, and Jay Verkuilen. 2007. "Same Facts, Different Interpretations Partisan Motivation and Opinion on Iraq." *Journal of Politics* 69: 967–974.

Gallup, George, and Saul Rae. 1940. *The Pulse of Democracy*. New York: Simon.

Galston, William A. 2004. "Civic Education and Political Participation." *PS: Political Science and Politics* 32 (Apr.): 263–266.

Gamble, Barbara. 1997. "Putting Civil Rights to a Popular Vote." *American Journal of Political Science* 32 (Jan.): 245–269.

Gamson, William. 1968. *Power and Discontent*. Homewood, IL: Dorsey.

Garcia, F. Chris. 1973. *Political Socialization of Chicano Children*. New York: Praeger.

Gartner, Scott S., and Gary M. Segura. 1998. "War, Casualties, and Public Opinion." *Journal of Conflict Resolution* 42 (June): 278–300.

de la Garza, Rodolfo O., Angelo Falcon, and F. Chris Garcia. 1996. "Will the Real Americans Please Stand Up: Anglo and Mexican-American Support of Core American Political Values." *American Journal of Political Science* 40(2): 335–351.

de la Garza, Rodolfo O., and Seung-Jin Jang. 2011. "Latino Public Opinion." In *The Oxford Handbook of Public Opinion and the Media*, eds. Robert Y. Shapiro and Laurence C. Jacobs. New York: Oxford University Press, 505–519.

Gastil, John. 2000. *By Popular Demand: Revitalizing Representative Democracy Through Deliberative Elections*. Berkeley: University of California Press.

Geer, John G. 1996. *From Tea Leaves to Opinion Polls*. New York: Columbia University Press.

———. 2006. *Attacking Democracy: A Defense of Negativity in Presidential Campaigns*. Chicago: University of Chicago Press.

Gelman, Andrew, David Park, Boris Shor, Joseph Bafumi, and Geronimo Cortina. 2008. *Red State, Blue State, Rich State, Poor State: Why Americans Vote the Way They Do*. Princeton, NJ: Princeton University Press.

Gelpi, Christopheri, Peter D. Feaver, and Jason Reifler. 2005–2006. "Casualty Sensitivity and the War in Iraq." *International Security* 30: 7–46.

Gentzkow, Mathew, and Jesse M. Shapiro. 2010. "What Drives Media Slant? Evidence from U.S. Daily Newspapers." *Econometrica* 78 (Feb.): 35–71.

Gerber, Alan S., Gregory A. Huber, David Doherty, Conor M. Dowling, and Shang E. Ha. 2010. "Personality and Political Attitudes: Relationships Across Issue Domains and Political Contexts." *American Political Science Review* 104 (Feb.): 111–133.

Gerber, Alan S., James G. Gimpel, Donald P. Green, and Darren R. Shaw. 2011. "How Large and Long-Lasting Are the Persuasive Effects of Televised Campaign Ads? Results from a Randomized Field Experiment." *American Political Science Review* 105: 135–150.

———. 2012. "Personality and the Strength and Direction of Partisan Identification." *Political Behavior* 34: 653–688.

Gerber, Alan S., Dean Karlan, and Daniel Bergan. 2009. "Does the Media Matter? A Field Experiment Measuring the Effect of Newspapers on Voting Behavior and Political Opinions." *American Economic Journal: Applied Economics* 1(2): 35–52.

Gerbner, George. 1998. "Who Is Shooting Whom? The Content and Analysis of Media Violence."

In *Bang Bang, Shoot Shoot! Essays in Guns and Popular Culture*, eds. Murray Pomerance and John Sakeris. Needham Heights, MA: Simon and Schuster.

Gershenson, Carl, Patrick Glaser, and Tom W. Smith. 2011. "The Polls: Trends in Surveys on Surveys." *Public Opinion Quarterly* 75 (Spring): 165–191.

Gershkoff, Amy, and Shana Kushner. 2005. "Shaping Public Opinion: The 9/11-Iraq Connection in the Bush Administration's Rhetoric." *Perspectives on Politics* 3 (Sep.): 525–538.

Gibson, James L. 1986. "Pluralistic Intolerance in America." *American Politics Quarterly* 14 (Oct.): 267–293.

———. 1987. "Freedom and Tolerance in the United States." NORC (unpublished codebook, University of Chicago, Chicago, IL).

———. 1988. "Political Intolerance and Political Repression During the McCarthy Red Scare." *American Political Science Review* 82 (June): 512–529.

———. 1996. "The Paradoxes of Political Tolerance in the Process of Democratization." *Politikon: South African Journal of Political Science* 23: 2–21.

———. 2008. "Intolerance and Political Repression in the United States: A Half Century After McCarthyism." *American Journal of Political Science* 52 (Jan.): 96–108.

Gibson, James L., and Richard D. Bingham. 1985. *Civil Liberties and the Nazis: The Skokie Free-Speech Controversy*. New York: Praeger.

Gibson, James L., and Gregory A. Caldeira. 2009. "Knowing the Supreme Court? A Reconsideration of Public Ignorance About the High Court." *Journal of Politics* 71 (Apr.): 429–441.

Gibson, James L., and Kent L. Tedin. 1988. "The Etiology of Intolerance for Homosexual Politics." *Social Science Quarterly* 69 (Sep.): 587–604.

Gilens, Martin. 1999. *Why Americans Hate Welfare: Race, Media, and the Politics of Welfare Policy*. Chicago: University of Chicago Press.

———. 2001. "Political Ignorance and Collective Policy Preferences." *American Political Science Review* 95: 379–398.

———. 2005. "Inequality and Democratic Responsiveness." *Public Opinion Quarterly* 69: 778–796.

———. 2012. *Affluence and Influence: Economic Inequality and Political Power in America*. Princeton, NJ: Princeton University Press.

Gilens, Martin, and Craig Hertzman. 2000. "Corporate Ownership of News Bias: Newspaper Coverage of the 1996 Telecommunications Act." *Journal of Politics* 62 (Aug.): 369–389.

Gilens, Martin, Lynn Vavreck, and Martin Cohen. 2007. "The Mass Media and the Public Assessment of Presidential Candidates." *Journal of Politics* 69 (Nov.): 1160–1175.

Giles, Michael, Bethany Blackstone, and Richard L. Vining, Jr. 2008. "The Supreme Court in American Democracy: Unraveling the Linkages Between Public Opinion and Judicial Decision Making." *Journal of Politics* 70: 293–306.

Gilliam, Frank D., and Shanto Iyengar. 2000. "Prime Suspects: The Influence of Local Television on the Viewing Public." *American Journal of Political Science* 44 (July): 560–573.

Gilljam, Mikael, and Donald Granberg. 1993. "Should We Take Don't Know for an Answer?" *Public Opinion Quarterly* 57 (Fall): 348–357.

Gimpel, James G., Karen M. Kaufman, and Shanna Pearson Merkowitz. 2007. "Battleground States Versus Blackout States: The Behavioral Implication of Modern Presidential Campaigns." *Journal of Politics* 64 (Aug.): 786–797.

Gimpel, James G., J. Celeste Lay, and Jason E. Schuknecht. 2003. *Cultivating Democracy*. Washington, DC: Brookings Institution Press.

Ginsberg, Benjamin. 1982. *The Consequences of Consent: Elections, Citizen Control and Popular Acquiescence*. Reading, MA: Addison-Wesley.

———. 1986. *The Captive Public*. New York: Basic.

Glazer, Amihai, and Marc Robbins. 1985. "Congressional Responsiveness to Constituency Change." *American Journal of Political Science* 29 (May): 259–273.

Glynn, Adam N. 2013. "What Can We Learn with Statistical Truth Serum? Design and Analysis of the List Experiment." *Public Opinion Quarterly* 77: 159–172.

Goidel, Kirby. 2011. "Public Opinion Polling in the Digital Age: Meaning and Measurement." In *Political Polling the Digital Age: The Challenge of Measuring and Understanding Public Opinion*, ed. Kirby Goidel. Baton Rouge: Louisiana State Press.

Goldberg, Bernard. 2001. *Bias in the News*. Washington, DC: Regnery.

Goldstein, Robert. 1978. *Political Repression in Modern America: From 1870 to the Present*. Cambridge, MA: Schenkman.

Gomez, Brad T., and J. Mathew Wilson. 2006. "Rethinking Symbolic Racism: Evidence of Attribution Bias." *Journal of Politics* 68 (Aug.): 611–625.

Goren, Paul. 2004. "Political Sophistication and Policy Reasoning: A Reconsideration." *American Journal of Political Science* 48 (July): 462–478.

———. 2005. "Party Identification and Core Political Values." *American Journal of Political Science* 49 (Oct.): 881–896.

Green, Donald P., Peter M. Aronow, Daniel E. Bergan, Pamela Greene, Celia Paris, and Beth I. Weinberger. 2011. "Does Knowledge of Constitutional Principles Increase Support for Civil Liberties? Results from a Randomized Field Experiment." *Journal of Politics* 73 (Apr.): 463–476.

Green, Donald P., and Bradley Palmquist. 1994. "How Stable Is Party Identification." *Political Behavior* 16(4): 437–464.

Green, Donald P., Bradley Palmquist, and Eric Schickler. 1998. "Macropartisanship: A Replication and Critique." *American Political Science Review* 92: 883–899.

———. 2002. *Partisan Hearts and Minds: Political Parties and the Social Identities of the Voters*. New Haven, CT: Yale University Press.

Green, John C. 2007. *The Faith Factor: How Religion Influences American Elections*. Westport, CT: Praeger.

Greenberg, Edward. 1970. "Black Children and the Political System." *Public Opinion Quarterly* 34: 335–348.

Greenstein, Fred. 1965. *Children and Politics*. New Haven, CT: Yale University Press.

Greer, Christina M. 2013. *Black Ethnics: Race, Immigration, and the Pursuit of the American Dream*. New York: Oxford University Press.

Griffin, John D., and Brian Newman. 2005. "Are Voters Better Represented?" *Journal of Politics* 67: 1206–1227.

Groeling, Timothy. 2013. "Media Bias by the Numbers: Challenges and Opportunities in the Empirical Study of Partisan News." *Annual Review of Political Science* 16: 129–151.

Groeling, Timothy, and Samuel Kernell. 1998. "Is Network News Coverage of the President Biased?" *Journal of Politics* 60: 1063–1087.

Groseclose, Timothy. 2011. *Left Turn: How Liberal Media Bias Distorts the American Mind*. New York: MacMillan.

Groseclose, Timothy, and Jeffrey Milyo. 2005. "A Measure of Media Bias." *Quarterly Journal of Economics* 120(4): 1191–1237.

Gross, Neil. 2013. *Why Are Professors Liberal and Why Do Conservatives Care?* Cambridge, MA: Harvard University Press.

Grossman, Matt. 2012. *Not So Special Interests: Interest Groups, Public Representation, and American Governance*. Stanford: Stanford University Press.

Groves, Robert. 2006. "Nonresponse Rates and Nonresponse Bias in Household Surveys." *Public Opinion Quarterly* 70 (Winter): 646–675.

Groves, Robert, Floyd J. Fowler, Mick P. Couper, James M. Lepkowski, Eleanor Singers, and Roger Tourangeau. 2009. *Survey Methodology*. New York: Wiley.

Guth, Mathew. 2009. "Religion and American Public Opinion: Foreign Policy Issues." In *The Oxford Handbook of Religion and American Politics*, eds. Corwin E. Smidt, Lyman A. Kellstedt, and James L. Guth. Oxford: Oxford University Press, 243–265.

Hacker, Jacob S., and Paul Pierson. 2005. "Abandoning the Middle: The Bush Tax Cuts and the Limits of Democratic Control." *Perspectives on Politics* 3 (Mar.): 33–53.

Haider-Markel, Donald P., and Matthew S. Kaufman. 2006. "Public Opinion and Culture Wars. Is There a Connection Between Opinion and State Policy on Gay and Lesbian Issues?" In *Public Opinion in State Politics*, ed. Jeffrey E Cohen. Stanford, CA: Stanford University Press, 161–182.

Haidt, Jonathan. 2012. *The Rightious Mind; Why Good People Are Divided by Politics and Religion*. New York: Vintage.

Hainmueller, Jens, and Michael J. Hiscox. 2010. "Attitudes Toward Highly Skilled and Low-Skilled Immigration: Evidence from a Survey Experiment." *American Political Science Review* 104 (Feb.): 61–84.

Hand, Learned. 1959. *The Spirit of Liberty: Papers and Addresses*. New York: Knopf.

Hand, Michael. 2011. "Should We Promote Patriotism in Schools?" *Political Studies* 59: 328–347.

Hansen, John Mark. 1998. "Individuals, Institutions, and Public Preferences over Public Finance." *American Political Science Review* 92 (Sep.): 513–531.

Harris, Frederick C. 2011. "The Contours of Black Public Opinion." In *The Oxford Handbook of Public Opinion and the Media*, eds. Robert Y. Shapiro and Laurence C. Jacobs. New York: Oxford University Press.

Harris, Louis, and Alan F. Weston. 1979. *The Dimensions of Privacy*. Stevens Point, Wisconsin: Sentry Insurance.

Hartley, Thomas, and Bruce Russett. 1992. "Public Opinion and the Common Defense: Who Governs

Military Spending in the United States?" *American Political Science Review* 86 (Dec.): 905–915.

Harvey, O. J., and G. Beverly. 1961. "Some Personality Correlates of Concept Change Through Role Playing." *Journal of Abnormal and Social Psychology* 27 (Mar.): 125–130.

Harvey, G. Ted. 1972. "Computer Simulation of Peer Group Influence on Adolescent Political Behavior." *American Journal Political Science* 16 (Nov.): 588–621.

Hatemi, Peter K., John Hibbing, John Alford, Nicholas Martin, and Lindon Eaves. 2009. "Is There a Party in Your Genes?" *Political Research Quarterly* 62: 584–600.

Hatemi, Peter K., Sarah E. Medland, and Lindon J. Eaves. 2009. "Do Genes Contribute to the Gender Gap." *Journal of Politics* 71: 262–276.

Healy, Andrew, and Neil Malhotra. 2013. "Childhood Socialization and Political Attitudes: Evidence from a Natural Experiment." *Journal of Politics* 75 (Oct.): 1023–1037.

Hedlund, Ronald D. 1975. "Perceptions of Decisional Referents in Legislative Decision-Making." *American Journal of Political Science* 19 (Aug.): 527–542.

Herbst, Susan. 1993. *Numbered Voices: How Public Opinion Has Shaped American Politics*. Chicago: University of Chicago Press.

Hero, Alfred O. 1973. *American Religious Groups View Foreign Policy: Trends in Rank and File Opinion, 1937–1969*. Durham, NC: Duke University Press.

Herrera, Cheryl Lin, Richard Herrera, and Eric R. A. N. Smith. 1992. "Public Opinion and Congressional Representation." *Public Opinion Quarterly* 56 (Summer): 185–205.

Herrera, Richard. 1992. "The Understanding of Ideological Labels by Political Elites: A Research Note." *Western Political Quarterly* 45 (Dec.): 1021–1035.

Herson, Lawrence J. R., and C. Richard Hofstetter. 1975. "Tolerance, Consensus, and Democratic Creed." *Journal of Politics* 37 (Dec.): 1007–1032.

Hertsgaard, Mark. 1988. *On Bended Knee: The Press and the Reagan Presidency*. New York: Farrar.

Hess, Robert D., and Judith V. Torney. 1967. *The Development of Political Attitudes in Children*. Chicago, IL: Aldine.

Hess, Stephen. 2000. "Poll Stories Are Often Wrong. The Hess Report on Campaign Coverage in Nightly Network News." The Brookings Institution (Oct. 29).

Hetherington, Marc J. 1996. "The Media's Role in Forming Voters National Economic Evaluations in 1992." *American Journal of Political Science* 40 (May): 372–395.

———. 1999. "The Effect of Political Trust on the Presidential Vote, 1968–1996." *American Political Science Review* 93 (June): 311–326.

———. 2001. "Declining Trust and Shrinking Policy Agenda: Why Media Scholars Should Care." In *Communication in U.S. Elections: New Agendas*, eds. Roderick P. Hart and Daron R. Shaw. Lanham, MD: Rowman-Littlefield.

———. 2005. *Why Trust Matters: Declining Political Trust and the Demise of American Liberalism*. Princeton, NJ: Princeton University Press.

———. 2006. *Why Trust Matters: Declining Political Trust and the Demise of American Liberalism*. Princeton, NJ: Princeton University Press.

Hetherington, Marc J., and Jason A. Husser. 2012. "How Trust Matters: The Changing Political Relevance of Political Trust." *American Journal of Political Science* 56 (Apr.): 312–325.

Hetherington, Marc J., and Thomas J. Rudolph. 2008. "Priming, Performance, and the Dynamics of Political Trust." *Journal of Politics* 70 (Apr.): 498–512.

Hetherington, Marc J., and Jonathan D. Weiler. 2009. *Authoritarianism and Polarization in American Politics*. Cambridge, UK: Cambridge University Press.

Hibbing, John, and Elizabeth Theiss-Morse. 1998. "The Media's Role in Public Negativity Toward Congress: Distinguishing Emotional Reactions and Cognitive Evaluations." *American Journal of Political Science* 42 (May): 475–498.

———. 2002. *Stealth Democracy: Americans' Beliefs About How Government Should Work*. Cambridge, UK: Cambridge University Press.

Hibbs, Douglas A., Jr. 1987. *The American Political Economy: Macroeconomics and Electoral Politics in the United States*. Cambridge, MA: Harvard University Press.

———. 2012. "Obama's Reelection Prospects under 'Bread and Peace' Voting in the 2012 U.S. Presidential Elections." *PS: Political Science and Politics* 45 (Oct.): 635–640.

Hibbs, Douglas A., Jr., and Christopher Dennis. 1988. "Income Distribution in the United States." *American Political Science Review* 82 (June): 467–490.

Highton, Benjamin. 2009. "Revisiting the Relationship between Educational Attainment and Political

Sophistication." *Journal of Politics* 71 (Oct.): 892–911.

Hilderbrand, Robert. 1981. *Power and the People: Executive Management of Public Opinion in Foreign Affairs*. Chapel Hill, NC: University of North Carolina Press.

Hillygus, D. Sunshine. 2005. "The Missing Link: Exploring the Relationship Between Higher Education and Political Engagement." *Political Behavior* 27: 25–45.

Hillygus, D. Sunshine, and Todd G. Shields. 2008. *The Persuadable Voter*. Princeton, NJ: Princeton University Press.

Hilmer, Jeffrey D. 2011. "Social Science, Political Science and Democracy Today." *New Political Science* 33 (June): 239–248.

Hindman, Mathew. 2009. *The Myth of Digital Democracy*. Princeton, NJ: Princeton University Press.

Hippler, Hans J., and Norbert Schwarz. 1986. "Not Forbidding Isn't Allowing: The Cognitive Basis of the Forbid-Allow Asymmetry." *Public Opinion Quarterly* 50 (Spring): 87–96.

Hirano, Shigeo, James M. Snyder, Jr., Stephen Ansolabehere, and John Mark Hansen. 2010. "Primary Elections and Partisan Polarization in the U.S. Congress." *Quarterly Journal of Political Science* 5: 169–191.

Hitchens, William. 1992. "Voting in the Passive Voice." *Harpers* 284 (Apr.): 45–53.

Hoffman, Beth R., Peter R. Mone, Chich-Ping Chou, and Thomas W. Valente. 2007. "Perceived Peer Influence and Peer Selection on Adolescent Smoking." *Addictive Behaviors* 32: 1546–1554.

Holbrook, Allyson L., Jon A. Krosnick, and Alison Pfent. 2008. "The Causes and Consequences of Response Rates in Surveys by the News Media and Government Contractor Research Firms." In *Advances in Telephone Survey Methods*, eds. James Lepkowski, Clyde Tucker, Michael Brick, Edith Leeuw, Lilli Japec, Paul Lavrakas, and Rioberta Snagster. New York: Wiley Interscience, 499–528.

Holsti, Ole. 2004. *Public Opinion and American Foreign Policy*. Ann Arbor: University of Michigan Press.

———. 2011. *Public Opinion on the Iraq War*. Ann Arbor: University of Michigan Press.

———. 2012. "The Coalition of the Willing: United States." In *Public Opinion and International Intervention: Lessons from the Iraq War*, eds.

Richard Sobel, Peter Furia, and Bethany Barratt. Washington, DC: Potomac Books, 12–34.

Hopkins, Daniel J. 2009. "No More Wilder Effect, Never a Whitman Effect: When and Why Polls Mislead About Black and Female Candidates." *Journal of Politics* 71 (July): 769–781.

Huber, Gregory A., and Kevin Arceneaux. 2007. "Identifying the Persuasive Effects of Political Advertising." *American Journal of Political Science* 51: 957–977.

Huber, Gregory A., and Sanford C. Gordon. 2004. "Accountability and Coersion: Is Justice Blind When It Runs for Office?" *American Journal of Political Science* 48 (Apr.): 247–263.

Huber, Gregory A., Seth J. Hill, and Gabriel S. Lenz. 2012. "Sources of Bias in Retrospective Decision Making: Experimental Evidence on Voters Limitations in Controlling Incumbents." *American Political Science Review* 106 (Sep.): 720–741.

Huber, Gregory A., and John H. Lapinski. 2006. "The 'Race Card' Revisited: Assessing Racial Priming in Policy Contents." *American Journal of Political Science* 48 (May): 375–401.

Huber, Gregory A., and Neil Malhotra. 2012. "Political Sorting in Social Relationships." (unpublished manuscript, Stanford Graduate School of Business, Stanford, CA).

Huddy, Leonie, Stanley Feldman, Charles Taber, and Gallya Lavhav. 2005. "Threat, Anxiety, and Support of Antiterrorism Policies." *American Journal of Political Science* 49 (July): 593–608.

Huddy, Leonie, and Nadia Khatib. 2007. "American Patriotism, National Identity, and Political Involvement." *American Journal of Political Science* 51 (Jan.): 63–77.

Hugick, Larry, and Guy Molyneux. 1993. "The Performance of the Gallup Tracking Poll: The Myth and the Reality." *Public Perspective* 4 (Jan./Feb.): 12–14.

Huntington, Samuel P. 1991. *The Third Wave: Democratization in the Late Twentieth Century*. Norman: University of Oklahoma Press.

———. 2004. *Who Are We?* New York: Simon and Schuster.

Hurley, Patricia A., and Kim Quaile Hill. 2003. "Beyond the Diamond-Input Model: A Theory of Representational Linkages." *Journal of Politics* 65(2): 304–326.

Hurwitz, Jon, and Mark Peffley. 2005. "Playing the Race Card in the Post-Willie Horton Era." *Public Opinion Quarterly* 69 (Spring): 99–112.

Hutchings, Vincent L. 2003. *Public Opinion and Democratic Accountability*. Princeton, NJ: Princeton University Press.

Hutchings, Vincent L., and Ashley E. Jardina. 2009. "Experiments on Racial Priming in Political Campaigns." *Annual Review of Political Science* 12: 397–402.

Inglehart, Ronald. 1990. *Culture Shift*. Princeton, NJ: Princeton University Press.

———. 1997a. *Modernization and Postmodernization*. Princeton, NJ: Princeton University Press.

———. 1997b. "Postmaterialist Values and the Erosion of Institutional Authority." In *Why People Don't Trust Government*, eds. Joseph S. Nye, Philip D. Zelikow, and David C. King. Cambridge, MA: Harvard University Press, 217–236.

Inkeles, Alex. 1961. "National Character and the Modern Political System." In *Psychological Anthropology: Approaches to Culture and Personality*, ed. Francis L. K. Hsu. Homewood, IL: Dorsey.

Issenberg, Sasha. 2012. *The Victory Lab: The Secret Science of Winning Elections*. New York: Crown Publishing.

Iyengar, Shanto, and Donald R. Kinder. 1987. *News that Matters*. Chicago: University of Chicago Press.

Iyengar, Shanto, Helmut Norpoth, and Kyu S. Hahn. 2004. "Consumer Demand for Election News: The Horserace Sells." *Journal of Politics* 66 (Feb.): 157–175.

Iyengar, Shanto, Mark D. Peters, and Donald R. Kinder. 1982. "Experimental Demonstrations of 'Not-So-Minimal' Consequences of Television News Programs." *American Political Science Review* 76 (Dec.): 848–858.

Jackman, Mary R., and Robert W. Jackman. 1983. *Class Awareness in the United States*. Berkeley: University of California Press.

Jackman, Mary R., and Michael J. Mulha. 1984. "Education and Intergroup Attitudes: Moral Enlightenment, Superficial Democratic Commitment, or Ideological Refinement." *American Sociological Review* 49 (Aug.): 751–769.

Jackman, Robert W. 1972. "Political Elites, Mass Publics, and Support for Democratic Principles." *Journal of Politics* 54 (Aug.): 753–773.

Jackman, Robert W., and Robert A. Miller. 1996. "A Renaissance of Political Culture?" *American Journal of Political Science* 40 (May): 632–659.

Jackman, Simon, and Paul Sniderman. 2006. "The Limits of Deliberative Discussion: A Model of Everyday Political Arguments." *The Journal of Politics* 68: 272–283.

Jacobs, Lawrence R., and Robert Y. Shapiro. 2000. *Politicians Don't Pander: Political Manipulation and the Loss of Democratic Responsiveness*. Chicago: University of Chicago Press.

Jacobs, Lawrence R., and Benjamin I. Page. 2005. "Who Influences U.S. Foreign Policy?" *American Political Science Review* 99: 107–123.

Jacobson, Gary C. 1987. *The Politics of Congressional Elections*, 2nd ed. Boston, MA: Little, Brown.

———. 2007. *A Divider, Not a Uniter: George W. Bush and the American People*. New York: Longman.

Jacobson, Gary C., and Samuel Kernell. 1983. *Strategy and Choice in Congressional Elections*, 2nd ed. New Haven, CT: Yale University Press.

Jacoby, William G. 1988. "The Impact of Party Identification on Issue Attitudes." *American Journal of Political Science* 32 (Aug.): 643–661.

———. 1991. "Ideological Identifications and Issue Attitudes." *American Journal of Political Science* 35 (Feb.): 178–205.

Jamal, Amaney, and Irfan Nooruddin. 2010. "The Democratic Utility of Trust: A Cross-National Analysis." *Journal of Politics* 72 (Jan.): 45–59.

Jamieson, Kathleen Hall, and John N. Capella. 2008. *Echo Chamber*. Oxford: Oxford University Press.

Jaros, Dean, Herbert Hirsch, and Frederick Fleron. 1968. "The Malevolent Leader: Political Socialization in an American Sub-Culture." *American Political Science Review* 62 (June): 564–575.

Jelen, Ted G. 1992. "Political Christianity: A Contextual Analysis." *American Journal of Political Science* 36 (Aug.): 662–692.

Jennings, M. Kent. 1987. "Residuals of a Movement: The Aging of the American Protest Generation." *American Political Science Review* 81 (June): 365–381.

———. 1992. "Ideological Thinking Among Mass Publics and Political Elites." *Public Opinion Quarterly* 56 (Winter): 419–441.

———. 2002. "Generational Units and the Student Protest Movement in the United States: An Intra- and Intergenerational Analysis." *Political Psychology* 23 (June): 303–325.

———. 2004. "Political Socialization." In *The Oxford Handbook of Political Behavior*, eds. Russell Dalton and Hans-Dieter Klingman. Oxford: Oxford University Press.

Jennings, M. Kent, and Ellen Ann Andersen. 1996. "Support for Confrontational Tactics Among AIDS Activists: A Study of Intra–Movement Divisions." *American Journal of Political Science* 40 (May): 311–334.

Jennings, M. Kent, and Gregory B. Markus. 1984. "Partisan Orientations over the Long Haul: Results from the Three-Wave Political Socialization Panel Study." *American Political Science Review* 78 (Dec.): 1000–1018.

Jennings, M. Kent, and Kenneth P. Langton. 1969. "Mothers Versus Fathers: The Formation of Political Orientations Among Young Americans." *Journal of Politics* 31 (Nov.): 724–741.

Jennings, M. Kent, and Richard G. Niemi. 1968. "The Transmission of Political Values from Parent to Child." *American Political Science Review* 62 (Mar.): 1579–1592.

———. 1974. *The Political Character of Adolescence.* Princeton, NJ: Princeton University Press.

———. 1982. *Generations and Politics.* Princeton, NJ: Princeton University Press.

Jennings, M. Kent, and Laura Stoker. 1999. "The Persistence of the Past: The Class of 1965 Turns Fifty." Paper presented at the Midwest Political Science Convention, April 1999. Chicago, IL.

———. 2004. "Social Trust and Civic Engagement Across Time and Generations." *Acta Politica* 39 (July): 342–379.

Jennings, M. Kent, Laura Stoker, and Jake Bowers. 2009. "Politics Across Generations: Family Transmission Reexamined." *Journal of Politics* 71 (July): 782–799.

Jensen, Richard. 1968. "American Election Analysis: A Case of History and Methodological Innovation and Diffusion." In *Politics and Social Science*, ed. Seymour Martin Lipset. New York: Oxford University Press.

Jerit, Jennifer, and Jason Barabas. 2006. "Bankrupt Rhetoric: How Misleading Information Affects Knowledge About Social Security." *Public Opinion Quarterly* 70 (Fall): 278–303.

Jewell, Malcolm E., and David Breaux. 1988. "The Effect of Incumbency on State Legislative Elections." *Legislative Studies Quarterly* 13 (Nov.): 495–514.

Johnson, Martin, Paul Brace, and Kevin Arceneaux. 2005. "Public Opinion and Dynamic Representation in the States: The Case of Environmental Attitudes." *Social Science Quarterly* 86 (Mar.): 87–108.

Johnston, Richard, Michael G. Hagan, and Kathleen Hall Jamieson. 2004. *The 2000 Presidential Election and the Foundation of Party Politics.* Cambridge, UK: Cambridge University Press.

Joslyn, Mark R. 2003. "The Determinants and Consequences of Recall Error About Gulf War Preferences." *American Journal of Political Science* 47: 127–139.

Jost, John T. 2009. "Elective Affinities: On the Psychological Bases of Left-Right Differences." *Psychological Inquiry* 20: 129–141.

Junn, Jane, Takku Lee, S. Karthick Ramakrishnan, and Janelle Wong. 2011. "Asian-American Public Opinion." In *The Oxford Handbook of Public Opinion and the Media*, eds. Robert Y. Shapiro and Laurence C. Jacobs. New York: Oxford University Press.

Kagay, Michael R., and Gregory A. Caldiera. 1980. "A 'Reformed' Electorate? Well, At Least a Changed Electorate, 1952–1976." In *Paths to Political Reform*, ed. William Crotty. Lexington: Lexington Books, 3–33.

Kahn, Kim Fridkin, and Patrick J. Kenney. 1999. "Do Negative Campaigns Mobilize or Suppress Turnout? Clarifying the Relationship Between Negativity and Participation." *American Political Science Review* 93: 877–889.

———. 2002. "The Slant of the News: How Editorial Endorsements Influence Campaign Coverage and Citizens' Views of Candidates." *American Political Science Review* 96 (June): 381–394.

Kahne, Joseph, and Joel Westheimer. 2006. "The Limits of Political Efficacy: Educating Citizens for Democratic Society." *PS: Political Science and Politics* 39 (Apr.): 289–298.

Kaiser Family Foundation. 2012. "Kaiser Tracking Poll—March 2012." (March 14).

Kam, Cindy D., and Donald R. Kinder. 2007. "Terrorism and Ethnocentrism: Foundations of American Support for the War on Terrorism." *Journal of Politics* 69 (May): 320–338.

Kanthak, Kristin, and Barbara Norrander. 2004. "The Enduring Gender Gap." In *Models of Voting in Presidential Elections*, eds. Herbert F. Weisberg and Clyde Wilcox. Stanford, CA: Stanford University Press.

Karp, Jeffrey A. 1995. "Support for Legislative Term Limits." *Public Opinion Quarterly* 59 (Fall): 373–391.

Kaufmann, Karen M. 2006. "The Gender Gap." *PS: Political Science and Politics* 39: 447–453.

Kaufmann, Karen M., and John R. Petrocik. 1999. "The Changing Politics of Men: Understanding the Source of the Gender Gap." *American Journal of Political Science* 43 (July): 864–887.

Keele, Luke. 2005. "The Authorities Really Do Matter: Party Control and Trust in Government." *Journal of Politics* 87 (Aug.): 872–886.

Keeter, Scott. 2011. "Public Opinion Polling and Its Problems." In *Political Polling the Digital Age: The Challenge of Measuring and Understanding Public Opinion*, ed. Kirby Goidel. Baton Rouge: Louisiana State Press, 38–53.

Keeter, Scott, Juliana Maenasce Horowitz, and Alec Tyson. 2008. "Gen Dems: The Party's Advantage Among Young Voters Widens." Pew Research Center (Apr.). http://pewresearch.org/pubs/813/gen-dems.

Kelley, Stanley. 1983. *Interpreting Elections*. Princeton, NJ: Princeton University Press.

Kelly, Nathan J. 2009. *The Politics of Income Inequality in the United States*. New York: Cambridge University Press.

Kenski, Kate, and Kathleen Hall Jamieson. 2000. "The Gender Gap in Political Knowledge: Are Women Less Knowledgeable Than Men About Politics?" In *Everything You Think You Know About Politics and Why You Are Wrong*, ed. Kathleen Hall Jamieson. New York: Basic Books.

Kenski, Kate, and Natalie Jomini Stroud. 2006. "Connections Between Internet Use and Political Efficacy, Knowledge, and Participation." *Journal of Broadcasting and Electronic Media* 50 (June): 173–192.

Kerlinger, Fred N. 1984. *Liberalism and Conservatism*. Hillsdale, NJ: Erlbaum.

Kernell, Samuel. 1978. "Explaining Presidential Popularity." *American Political Science Review* 72 (June): 506–523.

———. 2006. *Going Public: New Strategies for Presidential Leadership*, 4th ed. Washington, DC: Congressional Quarterly Press.

Key, V. O., Jr. 1949. *Southern Politics in State and Nation*. New York: Knopf.

———. 1961a. *Public Opinion and American Democracy*. New York: Knopf.

———. 1961b. "Public Opinion and the Decay of Democracy." *Virginia Quarterly Review* 37 (Autumn): 481–491.

Kiewiet, D. Roderick, and Matthew D. McCubbins. 1985. "Congressional Appropriations and the Electoral Connection." *Journal of Politics* 47 (Spring): 59–82.

Kinder, Donald R., and Cindy D. Kam. 2010. *Us Against Them: Ethnocentrism Foundations of American Opinion*. Chicago: University of Chicago Press.

Kinder, Donald R., and D. Roderick Kiewiet. 1979. "Economic Grievances and Political Behavior: The Role of Personal Discontents and Collective Judgments in Congressional Voting." *American Journal of Political Science* 23 (Aug.): 495–527.

———. 1981. "Sociotropic Politics." *British Journal of Political Science* 11 (Apr.): 129–161.

Kinder, Donald R., and Lynn M. Sanders. 1996. *Divided by Color*. Chicago: University of Chicago Press.

Kingdon, John W. 1973. *Congressmen's Voting Decisions*. New York: Harper.

Kirscht, John P., and Ronald C. Dillehay. 1967. *Dimensions of Authoritarianism: A Review of Research and Theory*. Lexington: University of Kentucky Press.

Klemmersen, Robert, Peter K. Hatemi, Sara Binzer Bobolt, Ingre Petersen, Axel Skytthe, and Asbjorn S. Norgaard. 2012. "The Genetics of Political Participation, Civil Duty, and Political Efficacy Across Cultures: Denmark and the United States." *Journal of Theoretical Politics* 24 (July): 409–427.

Knight, Kathleen. 1985. "Ideology in the 1980 Election: Political Sophistication Matters." *Journal of Politics* 47 (Aug.): 828–853.

Kobus, Kim. 2003. "Peers and Adolescent Smoking." *Addiction* 98(Suppl. 1): 37–55.

Kohut, Andrew, and Bruce Stokes. 2006. *American Against the World. How We Are Different and Why We Are Disliked*. New York: New York Times Books.

Kornhauser, William. 1970. *The Politics of Mass Society*. Chicago, IL: Markham.

Krasno, Jonathan S., and Donald P. Green. 2008. "Do Television Presidential Ads Increase Voter Turnout: Evidence from a Natural Experiment." *Journal of Politics* 70 (Jan.): 245–261.

Krehbiel, Keith. 1993. "Where's the Party?" *British Journal of Political Science* 23: 235–266.

———. 1999. "The Party Effect from A to Z and Beyond." *Journal of Politics* 61: 832–841.

———. 2000. "Party Discipline and the Measures of Partisanship." *American Journal of Political Science* 44: 212–227.

Kriner, Douglas L., and Francis X. Shen. 2012. "How Citizens Respond to Combat Casualties: The Differential Impact of Local Casualties on Support for the War in Afghanistan." *Public Opinion Quarterly* 76 (Winter): 761–770.

Kroh, Martin, and Peter Selb. 2009. "Inheritance and the Dynamics of Party Identification." *Political Behavior* 31: 559–574.

Krosnick, Jon A., and Laura Brannon. 1993. "The Impact of the Gulf War on the Ingredients of Presidential Evaluations: Multidimensional Effects of Political Involvement." *American Political Science Review* 87 (Dec.): 963–975.

Krosnick, Jon A., and Matthew K. Kerent. 1993. "Comparisons of Party Identification and Policy Preferences: The Impact of Survey Question Format." *American Journal of Political Science* 37 (Aug.): 941–964.

Kuklinski, James H. 1978. "Representatives and Elections: A Policy Analysis." *American Political Science Review* 72 (Mar.): 165–177.

Kuklinski, James H., Michael D. Cobb, and Martin Gilens. 1997. "Racial Attitudes in the New South." *Journal of Politics* 59 (May): 323–349.

Kuklinski, James H., Paul J. Quirk, Jennifer Jerit, and Robert Rich. 2001. "The Political Environment of Citizen Competence." *American Journal of Political Science* 41 (Oct.): 410–429.

Kull, Steven, Clay Ramsey, and Evin Lewis. 2003–2004. "Misperception, the Media, and the Iraq War." *Political Science Quarterly* 118: 369–398.

Ladd, Everett Carl. 1970. *American Political Parties: Social Change and Political Response.* New York: Norton.

———. 1989. *The American Polity.* New York: Norton.

———. 1998. *America's Social Capital: Change and Renewal in Civil Life.* New York: Free Press.

Lane, Robert. 1962. *Political Ideology.* New York: Free Press.

Langer, Gary. 2002. "Trust in Government." *Public Perspective* (July/Aug.): 7–10.

Lapinski, Daniel. 2001. "The Effect of Messages Communicated by Members of Congress: The Impact of Publicizing Their Votes." *Legislative Studies Quarterly* 26: 81–100.

Larson, Stephanie G. 2001. "Poll Coverage of the 2000 Presidential Campaign on the Network News." Paper delivered at the annual meeting of the American Political Science Association, September. San Francisco, CA.

Lasswell, Harold D. 1951. "Democratic Character." In *The Political Writings of Harold D. Lasswell.* Glencoe, IL: Free Press.

Lau, Richard R., and Gerald M. Pomper. 2004. *Negative Campaigning: An Analysis of U.S. Senate Elections.* New York: Rowland and Littlefield.

Lau, Richard R., and David P. Redlawsk. 2006. *How Voters Decide: Information Processing During Election Campaigns.* New York: Cambridge University Press.

Lau, Richard R., Lee Sigelman, Caroline Heldman, and Paul Babbit. 1999. "The Effects of Negative Political Advertisements: A Meta-Analytic Assessment." *American Political Science Review* 93 (Dec.): 851–876.

Lau, Richard R., Lee Sigelman, and Iry Brown Royner. 2007. "The Effects of Negative Political Campaigns: A Meta-Analytic Reassessment." *Journal of Politics* 69 (Nov.): 1176–1209.

Lavine, Howard, Milton Lodge, and Kate Freitas. 2005. "Threat, Authoritarianism, and Selective Exposure to Information." *Political Psychology* 26: 219–244.

Lawrence, Eric, John Sides, and Henry Farrell. 2010. "Self-Segregation or Deliberation: Blog Readership and Polarization in American Politics." *PS: Perspectives on Politics* 8 (Mar.): 141–157.

Lax, Jeffrey R., and Justin H. Philips. 2009. "Gay Rights in the States: Public Opinion and Policy Responsiveness." *American Political Science Review* 103 (Aug.): 367–376.

———. 2012. "The Democratic Deficit in the States." *American Journal of Political Science* 56: 148–166.

Lazarsfeld, Paul, Bernard Berelson, and Hazel Gaudet. 1948. *The People's Choice.* New York: Columbia University Press.

Lebo, Mathew, and Andrew O'Green. 2011. "The President's Role in the Partisan Congressional Area." *Journal of Politics* 73 (Aug.): 718–734.

Lee, Gahgheong, and Joseph N. Cappella. 2001. "The Effects of Political Talk Radio on Political Attitude Formation: Exposure Versus Knowledge." *Political Communication* 18: 369–394.

Leech, Beth. 2010. "Lobbying and Influence." In *The Oxford Handbook of American Political Parties and Interest Groups*, eds. L. Sandy Maisel and Jeffrey M. Berry. Oxford: Oxford University Press.

Lenz, Gabriel. 2012. *Follow the Leader? How Voters Respond to Politicians Policies and Performance*. Chicago: University of Chicago Press.

Lepkowski, James M., Clyde Tucker, J. Michael Brick, and Eeith D. De Leeuw. 2008. *Advances in Telephone Survey Methodology*. New York: Wiley Interscience.

Levendusky, Mathew W., and Jeremy C. Pope. 2011. "Red States vs. Blue States: Going Beyond the Mean." *Public Opinion Quarterly* 75 (Summer): 227–248.

Levendusky, Stephen. 2009. *The Partisan Sort: How Liberals Became Democrats and Conservatives Became Republicans*. Chicago: University of Chicago Press.

Lewis-Beck, Michael S., and Mary Stegmeier. 2000. "Economic Determines of Electoral Outcomes." *American Journal of Political Science* 44 (Aug.): 183–219.

Lewis-Beck, Michael S., William S. Jacoby, Helmut Norpoth, and Herbert F. Weisberg. 2008. *The American Voter Revisited*. Ann Arbor: University of Michigan Press.

Lewis-Beck, Michael S., and Tom Rice. 1982. "Presidential Popularity and the Presidential Vote." *Public Opinion Quarterly* 47 (Winter): 534–537.

Light, Paul C., and Celinda Lake. 1985. "The Election: Candidates, Strategies, and Decision." In *The Elections of 1984*, ed. Michael Nelson. Washington, DC: Congressional Quarterly Press.

Lindeman, Michael. 2002. "Opinion Quality and Policy Preferences in Deliberative Research." In *Research in Micropolitics: Decision-Making, Deliberation and Participation*. Greenwich, CT: JAI Press.

Link, Michael W., and Jennie W. Lai. 2011. "Cell-Phone-Only Households and Problems of Differential Nonresponse Using an Address-Based Sampling Design." *Public Opinion Quarterly* 75 (Winter): 613–635.

Lippmann, Walter. 1922. *Public Opinion*. New York: Harcourt.

———. 1925. *The Phantom Public*. New York: Harcourt.

Lipset, Seymour M. 1950. *Agrarian Socialism*. Berkeley: University of California Press.

———. 1959. "Some Social Requisites of Modern Democracy: Economic Development and Political Legitimacy." *American Political Science Review* 53 (Mar.): 69–105.

———. 1960. *Political Man*. Garden City, NY: Doubleday.

Lodge, Milton, Marco R. Steenbergen, and Shawn Brau. 1995. "The Responsive Voter: Candidate Information and the Dynamics of Candidate Evaluation." *American Political Science Review* 89 (June): 309–331.

Lodge, Milton, and Patrick Stroh. 1993. "Inside the Mental Voting Booth: An Impression-Driven Process." In *Explorations in Political Psychology*, eds. Shanto Iyengar and William J. McGuire. Durham, NC: Duke University Press.

Lodge, Milton, and Charles S. Taber. 2013. *The Rationalizing Voter*. New York: Cambridge University Press.

Lottes, Ilsa L., and Peter J. Kuriloff. 1994. "The Impact of College Experience on Political and Social Attitudes." *Sex Roles* 31: 31–54.

Ludeke, Stephen G., and Robert F. Krueger. 2013. "Authoritarianism as a Personality Trait: Evidence from a Longitudinal Behavior Genetic Study." *Personality and Individual Differences* 55 (Dec.): 480–484.

Lupia, Arthur, Adam Seth Levine, Jesse O. Manning, and Giesela Sin. 2007. "Were Bush Tax Cut Supporters 'Simply Ignorant'? A Second Look at Conservatives and Liberals in 'Homer Gets a Tax Cut'." *Perspectives on Politics* 4 (Dec.): 773–784.

Lupia, Arthur, and Mathew D. McCubbins. 1998. *The Democratic Dilemma: Can Citizens Learn What They Need to Know?* New York: Cambridge University Press.

Luskin, Robert C. 1987. "Measuring Political Sophistication." *American Journal of Political Science* 31 (Nov.): 856–899.

———. 2003. "The Heavenly Public: What Would a Fully Informed Citizenry Be Like?" In *Electoral Democracy*, eds. George Rabinowitz and Michael B. MacKuen. Ann Arbor: University of Michigan Press.

Luskin, Robert C., James Fishkin, and Roger Jowell. 2002. "Considered Opinions: Deliberative Polling in Britain." *British Journal of Political Science* 32: 455–487.

Luttbeg, Norman R. 1968. "Political Linkage in a Large Society." In *Public Opinion and Public Policy*, ed. Norman Luttbeg. Homewood, IL: Dorsey.

MacDougall, Curtis D. 1966. *Understanding Public Opinion*. Boston, MA: Little, Brown.

MacKuen, Michael B., Robert S. Erikson, and James A. Stimson. 1989. "Macropartisanship." *American Political Science Review* 83 (Dec.): 1125–1142.

———. 1992. "Peasants or Bankers? The American Electorate and the U.S. Economy." *American Political Science Review* 86 (Sep.): 597–611.

MacMullen, Ian. 2011. "On Status Quo Bias in Civic Education." *Journal of Politics* 73 (Aug.): 872–886.

Manin, Bernard, Adam Przeworski, and Susan C. Stokes. 1999. "Elections and Representation." In *Democracy, Accountability, and Representation*, eds. Adam Przeworski, Susan C. Stokes, and Bernard Manin. Cambridge, UK: Cambridge University Press, 29–54.

Mann, Sheilah. 1999. "What the Survey of American College Freshman Tells U.S. About Their Interest in Politics and Political Science." *PS: Political Science and Politics* 32 (June): 263–268.

Mann, Thomas E., and Norman J. Ornstein, eds. 1994. *Congress, the Press, and the Public*. Washington, DC: Brookings.

Mansbridge, Jane. 2003. "Rethinking Representation." *American Political Science Review* 97: 515–528.

Mansbridge, Jane, James Bohman, Simone Chambers, Thomas Christiano, Archon Fung, John Parkinson, Dennis F. Thompson, and Mark E. Warren. 2012. "A Systemic Approach to Deliberative Democracy." In *Deliberative Systems*, eds. John Parkinson and Jane Mansbridge. Cambridge, UK: Cambridge University Press, 1–26.

Manza, Jeff, and Clem Brooks. 1999. *Social Cleavages and Political Change: Voter Alignments and U.S. Party Coalitions*. New York: Oxford University Press.

Marcus, George E., W. Russell Neuman, and Michael B. MacKuen. 2000. *Affective Intelligence and Political Judgment*. Chicago: University of Chicago Press.

Markus, Gregory B., and Philip E. Converse. 1979. "A Dynamic Simultaneous Equation Model of Public Choice." *American Political Science Review* 73 (Dec.): 1055–1070.

Masuoka, Natalie, and Jane Junn. 2013. *The Politics of Belonging: Race, Public Opinion and Immigration*. Chicago: University of Chicago Press.

Mayhew, David R. 1974. *Congress: The Electoral Connection*. New Haven, CT: Yale University Press.

———. 2002. *Electoral Realignments: A Critique of the American Genre*. New Haven, CT: Yale University Press.

McCarty, Nolan, Keith T. Poole, and Howard Rosenthal. 2006. *Polarized America: The Dance of Ideology and Unequal Riches*. Cambridge: MIT Press.

McCloskey, Herbert. 1964. "Consensus and Ideology in American Politics." *American Political Science Review* 58 (June): 361–382.

McClosky, Herbert, and Alida Brill. 1983. *Dimensions of Political Tolerance*. New York: Russell Sage.

McClosky, Herbert, Paul J. Hoffman, and Rosemary O'Hara. 1960. "Issue Conflict and Consensus Among Party Leaders and Followers." *American Political Science Review* 59 (June): 406–427.

McCombs, Maxwell E. 2013. *Setting the Agenda: The Mass Media and Public Opinion*. New York: John Wiley and Sons.

McCombs, Maxwell E., and Donald L. Shaw. 1972. "The Agenda-Setting Function of the Mass Media." *Public Opinion Quarterly* 35 (Summer): 176–187.

McCrae, Robert R., and Paul T. Costa. 2012. *Personality in Adulthood: A Five Factor Theory Perspective*. New York: The Guilford Press.

McDermott, Monika L., and Kathleen A. Frankovic. 2003. "Horserace Polling and the Survey Method: An Analysis of the 2000 Campaign." *Public Opinion Quarterly* 67 (June): 244–264.

McDonald, Michael D., Ian Budge, and Richard I. Hofferbert. 1999. "Party Mandate Theory and Time Series Analysis: A Theoretical and Methodological Response." *Electoral Studies* 18: 587–596.

McFarland, Daniel A., and Reuben J. Thomas. 2006. "Bowling Young: How Youth Voluntary Associations Influence Adult Political Participation." *American Sociological Review* 71 (June): 401–425.

McGuire, Kevin T., and James A. Stimson. 2004. "The Least Dangerous Branch Revisited." *Journal of Politics* 66: 118–135.

Mearsheimer, John. 2001. *The Tragedy of Great Power Politics*. New York: W. W. Norton.

Meloen, J. D., G. van der Linden, and H. de Witte. 1996. "A Test of the Approaches of Adorno et al., Ledere and Altemeyer of Authoritarianism in Belgian Flanders: A Research Note." *Political Psychology* 17: 643–656.

Mendelberg, Tali. 2001. *The Race Card: Campaign Strategy, Implicit Messages, and the Norm of*

Equality. Princeton, NJ: Princeton University Press.

———. 2002. "The Deliberative Citizen: Theory and Evidence." In *Research in Micropolitics: Deliberation, Decision-Making and Participation*. Greenwich, CT: JAI Press.

———. 2008. "Racial Priming Revived." *Perspectives on Politics* 6 (Mar.): 109–123.

Mellow, Nicole. 2013. "Voting Behavior: How the Democrats Rejuvenated their Coalition." In *The Elections of 2012*, ed. Michael Nelson. Los Angeles: Sage.

Merelman, Richard. 1997. "Symbols and Substance in National Civics Standards." *PS: Political Science and Politics* 29 (Mar.): 53–56.

Metz, Edward, and James Youniss. 2003. "A Demonstration that School-Based Required Service Does Not Deter—But Heightens—Volunteerism." *PS: Political Science and Politics* 36 (Apr.): 281–286.

Milburn, Michael A., S. D. Conrad, and Sheryl Carberry. 1995. "Childhood Punishment, Denial, and Political Attitudes." *Political Psychology* 16: 447–478.

Milgram, Stanley. 1969. *Obedience to Authority*. New York: Harper.

Miller, Joanne M., and Jon A. Krosnick. 2000. "News Media Impact on the Ingredients of Presidential Evaluations: Politically Knowledgeable Citizens Are Guided by a Trusted Source." *American Journal of Political Science* 44 (Apr.): 301–315.

Miller, Warren E., and M. Kent Jennings. 1987. *Parties in Transition: A Longitudinal Study of Party Elites and Party Supporters*. New York: Russell Sage.

Miller, Warren E., and J. Merrill Shanks. 1996. *The New American Voter*. Cambridge, MA: Harvard University Press.

Miller, Warren E., and Donald W. Stokes. 1963. "Constituency Influence in Congress." *American Political Science Review* 57 (Mar.): 45–56.

Mills, C. Wright. 1956. *The Power Elite*. New York: Oxford University Press.

Mirels, Herbert L., and Janet B. Dean. 2006. "Right-Wing Authoritarianism, Attitude Salience, and Beliefs About Matters of Fact." *Political Psychology* 27 (Dec.): 839–866.

Mishler, William, and Richard Rose. 2005. "What Are the Political Consequences of Trust?" *Comparative Political Studies* 38 (Nov.): 1050–1078.

Mishler, William, and Reginald S. Sheehan. 1996. "Public Opinion, the Attitudinal Model, and Supreme Court Decision Making: A Micro Analytic Perspective." *Journal of Politics* 58: 169–200.

Mondak, Jeffery J. 2010. *Personality and the Foundations of Political Behavior*. Cambridge: Cambridge University Press.

Mondak, Jeffery J., and Mary Anderson. 2004. "The Knowledge Gap: A Reexamination of Gender-Based Differences in Political Knowledge." *Journal of Politics* 77 (Aug.): 492–512.

Monroe, Alan D. 1979. "Consistency Between Public Preferences and National Policy Decisions." *American Politics Quarterly* 7 (Jan.): 3–21.

———. 1998. "Public Opinion and Public Policy: 1980–1993." *Public Opinion Quarterly* 62: 6–28.

Montaigne, Michel de. 1967. *The Complete Works of Montaigne*. Stanford, CA: Stanford University Press.

Montcrief, Gary. 1999. "Recruitment and Retention in U.S. Legislatures." *Legislative Studies Quarterly* 24: 173–208.

Mooney, Christopher Z., and Mei-Hsien Lee. 2000. "The Influence of Values on Consensus and Contentious Morality Policy: U.S. Death Penalty Reform, 1956–1982." *The Journal of Politics* 62: 223–239.

Moore, David W. 1992. *The SuperPollsters*. New York: Four Walls, Eight Windows.

———. 2008. *The Opinion Makers*. Boston, MA: Beacon Press.

———. 2013. "Annual Top Ten Dubious Polling Awards, 2013." iMediaEthics. www.imediaethics.org/News/3722.

Moore, Stanley W., James Lare, and Kenneth A. Wagner. 1985. *The Child's Political World*. New York: Praeger.

Mueller, John E. 1973. *War, Presidents, and Public Opinion*. New York: Wiley.

———. 1977. "Changes in American Attitudes Toward International Involvement." In *The Limits of Military Intervention*, ed. Ellen Stern. Beverly Hills, CA: Sage.

———. 1994. *Policy, Opinion, and the Gulf War*. Chicago: University of Chicago Press.

———. 1996. "Fifteen Propositions About American Foreign Policy and Public Opinion in an Era Free of Compelling Threats." Paper presented at the National Convention for the International Studies Association, April 16–20. San Diego, CA.

———. 2005. "The Iraq Syndrome." *Foreign Affairs* 84: 44–54.

Muller, Edward N., and Thomas O. Jukam. 1983. "Discontent and Aggressive Political Participation." *British Journal of Political Science* 13 (Apr.): 159–179.

Muller, Edward N., and Karl-Dieter Opp. 1986. "Rational Choice and Rebellious Collective Action." *American Political Science Review* 80 (June): 471–488.

Muller, Edward N., and Mitchell A. Seligson. 1987. "Inequality and Insurgency." *American Political Science Review* 81 (June): 425–452.

Murphy, Mike, and Mark Mellman. 2007. "The Heisenberg Primaries—Candidates and Media Beware: You Can't Measure What Hasn't Happened." *Los Angeles Times* (July 5).

Mutz, Diana C. 2007. "Effects of 'in-your-face' Television Discourse on Perceptions of Legitimate Opposition." *American Political Science Review* 101 (Dec.): 621–636.

Mutz, Diana C., and Byron Reeves. 2005. "The New Videomalaise: Effects of Televised Incivility on Political Trust." *American Political Science Review* 99 (Feb.): 1–16.

Nacos, Brigitte L., Yaeli Block-Elkon, and Robert Y. Shapiro. 2011. *Selling Fear: Counterterrorism, the Media, and Public Opinion.* Chicago: University of Chicago Press.

Newspaper Association of America. 2013. "The American Newspaper Media Industry Revenue Profile 2012." http://www.naa.org/Trends-and-numbers/newspaper-Revenue/newspaper-media-Industry-Revenue-Profile-2012.aspx.

Newton, Kenneth. 2007. "Social and Political Trust." In *The Oxford Handbook of Political Behavior*, eds. Russell Dalton and Hans-Dieter Klingemann. Oxford: Oxford University Press.

Neyman, Jerzy. 1934. "On the Two Different Aspects of the Representational Method: The Method of Stratified Sampling and the Method of Purposive Selection." *Journal of the Royal Statistical Society* 558: 217–234.

Nie, Norman H., Jane Junn, and Kenneth Stehlik-Barry. 1998. *Education and Democratic Citizenship in America.* Chicago: University of Chicago Press.

Nie, Norman H., Darwin W. Miller, Saar Golde, Daniel M. Butler, and Kenneth Winneg. 2010. "The World Wide Web and the U.S. Political News Market." *American Journal of Political Science* 54 (Apr.): 428–430.

Nie, Norman H., Sidney Verba, and John R. Petrocik. 1976. *The Changing American Voter.* Cambridge, MA: Harvard University Press.

Niemi, Richard G., and Jane Junn. 1998. *Civic Education: What Makes Students Learn.* New Haven, CT: Yale University Press.

Norrander, Barbara. 1989. "Ideological Representatives of Presidential Primary Voters." *American Journal of Political Science* 33 (Aug.): 570–587.

———. 2000. "The Multi-Layered Impact of Public Opinion on Capital Punishment Implementation in the American States." *Political Research Quarterly* 53: 771–794.

Norrander, Barbara, and Clyde Wilcox. 1999. "Public Opinion and Policymaking in the States: The Case of Post-Roe Abortion Policy." *Policy Studies Journal* 27 (Dec.): 707–722.

Norris, Pippa. 1988. "The Gender Gap: A Cross-National Trend?" In *The Politics of the Gender Gap*, ed. Carol M. Mueller. Beverly Hills, CA: Sage.

———. 2006. "The Feminist Challenges to the Study of Political Engagement." In *The Oxford Handbook of Political Behavior*, eds. Russell Dalton and Hans-Dieter Klingemann. Oxford, England: Oxford University Press.

Norris, Pippa, and Ronald Inglehart. 2004. *Sacred and Secular: Religion and Politics Worldwide.* Cambridge, UK: Cambridge University Press, 724–743.

Nunn, Clyde Z., Harry J. Crockett, Jr., and J. Allen Williams, Jr. 1978. *Tolerance for Nonconformity.* San Francisco: Jossey-Bass.

Nye, Joseph S. 1997. "The Decline of Confidence in Government." In *Why People Don't Trust Government*, eds. Joseph S. Nye, Philip D. Zelikow, and David C. King. Cambridge, MA: Harvard University Press, 1–20.

Nye, Joseph S., Philip D. Zelikow, and David King. 1997. *Why People Don't Trust Government.* Cambridge, MA: Harvard University Press.

O'Keefe, Garrett J. 1980. "Political Malaise and Reliance on Media." *Journalism Quarterly* 57: 122–128.

Olmstead, Kenneth, Mark Jurkowitz, Amy Mitchell, and Jodi Enda. 2013. "How Americans Get TV News at Home." Pew Research Journalism Project. http://www.journalismorg/2013/10/11/how-Americans-get-tv-news-at-home.

Olson, Mancur, Jr. 1968. *The Logic of Collective Action.* New York: Schocken.

Orren, Gary. 1997. "Fall from Grace: The Public's Loss of Faith in Government." In *Why People Don't Trust Government*, eds. Joseph S. Nye, Philip D. Zelikow, and David C. King. Cambridge, MA: Harvard University Press, 77–108.

Owen, Diana. 2013. "The Campaign and the Media." In *The American Elections of 2012*, eds. Janet M. Box-Steffensmeier and Steven E. Schier. New York: Routledge.

Pacheco, Julianna. 2012. "The Social Contagion Model: Exploring the Role of Public Opinion on the Diffusion of Antismoking Legislation Across the American States." *Journal of Politics* 74: 187–202.

———. 2013. "The Thermostatic Model of Responsiveness in the American States." *State Politics & Policy Quarterly* 13: 306–332.

Page, Benjamin. 1996. *Who Deliberates*. Chicago: University of Chicago Press.

———. 2002. "The Semi-Sovereign Public." In *Navigating Public Opinion*, eds. Jeff Manza, Fay Loxmax Cook, and Benjamin I. Page. Oxford: Oxford University Press 325–344.

———. 2006. *The Foreign Policy Disconnect*. Chicago: University of Chicago Press.

Page, Benjamin I., and Lawrence Jacobs. 2009. *Class War*. Chicago: University of Chicago Press.

Page, Benjamin I., and Robert Y. Shapiro. 1983. "Effects of Public Opinion on Public Policy." *American Political Science Review* 77 (Mar.): 175–190.

———. 1989. "Foreign Policy and the Rational Public." *Journal of Conflict Resolution* 32 (June): 211–247.

———. 1992. *The Rational Public*. Chicago: University of Chicago Press.

Palmer, Paul A. 1936. "The Concept of Public Opinion in Political Theory." In *Essays in History and Political Thought*, ed. Carl F. Wittke. London: Oxford University Press.

Panagopoulos, Costas. 2009. "Campaign Dynamics in Battleground and Nonbattleground States." *Public Opinion Quarterly* 73 (Spring): 119–129.

Parker, Glen R. 1992. *Institutional Change, Discretion, and the Making of the Modern Congress*. Ann Arbor: University of Michigan Press.

Pascarella, Ernest T., and Patrick T. Terenizi. 2005. *How College Affects Students*. New York: Jossey-Bass.

Patterson, Thomas E. 1989. "The Press and Its Missed Assignment." In *The Election of 1988*, ed. Michael Nelson. Washington, DC: Congressional Quarterly Press.

———. 1994. *Out of Order*. New York: Vintage.

———. 1996. "Bad News, Period." *PS: Political Science and Politics* 29 (Mar.): 17–20.

———. 2002. *The Vanishing Voter*. New York: Alfred A Knopf.

———. 2005. "Of Polls, Mountains: U.S. Journalists and Their use of Election Surveys." *Public Opinion Quarterly* 69 (Special Issue): 716–724.

Patterson, Thomas E., and Robert D. McClure. 1976. *The Unseeing Eye*. New York: Putnam.

Payne, Lee. W. 2008. "Responsive and Responsible Parties: Public Opinion, Polarization, and Platform Promise Keeping." (Ph.D. dissertation, Department of Political Science, University of Houston, Houston, TX).

Peterson, B. E., L. E. Duncan, and J. Pang. 2002. "Authoritarianism and Political Impoverishment: Deficits in Knowledge and Civic Disinterest." *Political Psychology* 23: 97–112.

Peterson, B. E., K. A. Smirles, and P. A. Wentworth. 1997. "Generativity and Authoritarianism: Implications for Personality, Political Involvement, and Parenting." *Journal of Personality and Social Psychology* 72: 1202–1216.

Petrocik, John R. 1989. "An Expected Party Vote: New Data for an Old Concept." *American Journal of Political Science* 33 (Feb.): 44–66.

———. 2007. "Political Knowledge and Current Affairs Little Changed by News and Information Revolution." Pew Research Center for People and the Press (Apr. 15). http://people-press.org/report/319.

Pettinico, George. 1996. "Civic Participation Alive and Well in Today's Environmental Movement." *Public Perspective* 31 (June/July): 27–30.

Pew Research Center for the People and the Press. 2004. "Bottom-Line Pressures Now Hurting Coverage, Say Journalists." (May 23). http://people-press.org/report/214/.

———. 2012. "In Changing News Landscape, Even Television Is Vulnerable: Trends in News Consumption: 1991–2012." www.people-press.org/2012/09/27/in-changing-news-landscape-even-Television-is-vulnerable.

Pew Research Journalism Project. 2012. "Winning the Media Campaign 2012." www.journalism.org/2012/11/02/winning-media-campaign-2012.

Peytchev, Andy. 2013. "Consequences of Survey Nonresponse." *The Annals of the American Academy of Political and Social Science* 645 (Jan.): 88–111.

Peytchev, Andy, and Benjamin Neely. 2013. "RDD Telephone Surveys: Toward a Single-Frame Cell-Phone Design." *Public Opinion Quarterly* 77 (Spring): 283–304.

Pinkleton, Bruce E., Erica Weintraub Austin, and Kristine K. J. Fortman. 1998. "Relationships Between Media Use and Political Disaffection to Political Efficacy and Voting Behavior." *Journal of Broadcasting and Electronic Media* 42: 34–49.

Plomin, Robert. 1997. *Behavioral Genetics.* New York: W. H. Freeman.

Plutzer, Eric, and Michael Berkman. 2008. "Trends: Evolution, Creationism, and the Teaching of Human Origins in Schools." *Public Opinion Quarterly* 72 (Fall): 540–553.

"Political Tolerance, Democracy, and Adolescents." In *Education for Democracy: Contexts, Curricula, Assessments,* ed. Walter C. Parker. Greenwich, CT: Information Age Publishing, 113–130.

Pomper, Gerald M., with Susan S. Lederman. 1980. *Elections in America: Control and Influence in Democratic Politics,* 2nd ed. New York: Longman.

Poole, Keith T., and Howard Rosenthal. 2007. *Congress: A Political-Economic History of Roll Call Voting.* Oxford: Oxford University Press.

Popkin, Samuel L. 1991. *The Reasoning Voter.* Chicago: University of Chicago Press.

Press, Charles, and Kenneth Verburn. 1988. *American Politicians and Journalists.* Boston, MA: Scott.

Prewitt, Kenneth. 1970. *The Recruitment of Political Leaders: A Study of Citizen Politicians.* New York: Bobbs-Merrill.

Price, H. Douglas. 1971. "The Congressional Career—Then and Now." In *Congressional Behavior,* ed. Nelson W. Polsby. New York: Random.

Price, Vincent. 1992. *Public Opinion.* Newbury Park, CA: Sage.

Price, Vincent, Lilach Nir, and Joseph N. Cappella. 2005. "Framing Public Discussion of Gay Civil Unions." *Public Opinion Quarterly* 69 (Summer): 179–212.

Prior, Markus. 2002. "Political Knowledge After September 11." *PS: Political Science and Politics* 35 (Sep.): 523–529.

———. 2007. *Post-Broadcast Democracy.* New York: Cambridge University Press.

———. 2013. "Media and Political Polarization." *Annual Review of Political Science* 16: 101–127.

Prior, Markus, and Arthur Lupia. 2007. "Money, Time, and Political Knowledge: Distinguishing Quick Recall and Political Learning Skills." *American Journal of Political Science* 52 (Jan.): 169–183.

———. 2008. "Money, Time, and Political Knowledge: Distinguishing Quick Recall and Political Learning Skills." *American Journal of Political Science* 52 (Jan.): 169–183.

Putnam, Robert D. 1995a. "Bowling Alone: America's Declining Social Capital." *Journal of Democracy* 6: 65–78.

———. 1995b. "Tuning In, Tuning Out: The Strange Disappearance of Social Capital in America." *PS: Political Science and Politics* 28: 664–683.

———. 2000. *Bowling Alone: The Collapse and Revival of American Community.* New York: Simon and Schuster.

Putnam, Robert D., and David E. Campbell. 2010. *American Grace: How Religion Divides and Unites U.S.* New York: Simon and Schuster.

Putz, David. 2002. "Partisan Conversion in the 1990s: Ideological Realignment Meets Measurement Theory." *Journal of Politics* 64: 199–209.

Rapoport, Ronald B. 1982. "Sex Differences in Political Expression: A Generational Explanation." *Public Opinion Quarterly* 46 (Spring): 86–96.

———. 1985. "Like Mother, Like Daughter: Intergenerational Transmission of DK Response Rates." *Public Opinion Quarterly* 49 (Summer): 198–208.

Ray, John J. 1988. "Why the F Scale Predicts Racism: A Critical Review." *Political Psychology* 9: 671–679.

Rector, Robert, and Rea Hederman. 2004. "Two Americas: One Rich, One Poor?" The Heritage Foundation. Downloaded from www.heritage .org, Nov. 29, 2005.

Rentfrow, Peter, John T. Just, Samuel D. Gosling, and Jeffrey Potter. 2009. "Statewide Differences in Personality Predict Voting Patterns in 1996–2004 U.S. Presidential Elections." In *Social and Psychological Bases of Ideology and System Justification,* eds. John T. Jost, Aaron C. Kay, and Hulda Thorisdottir. Oxford: Oxford University Press, 314–347.

Richard G. Niemi, John Mueller, and Tom W. Smith. (1989). *Trends in Public Opinion.* New York: Greenwood.

Rigby, Elizabeth, and Gerald C. Wright. 2010. "Whose Statehouse Democracy? How State Policy Choices Align with the Preferences of Poor, Middle-income and Wealthy Segments of the Electorate." In *Who Gets Represented*, eds. Peter Enns and Christopher Wlezien. New York: Russell Sage, 189–222.

Robinson, Claude. 1932. *Straw Votes: A Study of Political Predicting*. New York: Columbia University Press.

Rogers, Lindsay. 1949. *The Pollsters: Public Opinion, Politics, and Democratic Leadership*. New York: Alfred A. Knopf.

Rohde, Paul W., and Koleman S. Strumpf. 2004. "Historic Presidential Betting Markets." *Journal of Economic Perspectives* 18: 127–142.

Rokeach, Milton. 1960. *The Open and Closed Mind*. New York: Basic.

Rose, Arnold M. 1964. "Alienation and Participation." *American Sociological Review* 27 (Dec.): 151–173.

Rosenberg, Milton J., Philip E. Converse, and Howard Schuman. 1970. *Vietnam and the Silent Majority*. New York: Harper.

Ross, E. Wayne. 2004. "Negotiating the Politics of Citizenship Education." *PS: Political Science and Politics* 32 (April): 249–251.

Rothenberg, Lawrence C., and Mitchell S. Sanders. 2000. "Severing the Electoral Connection: Shirking in the Contemporary Congress." *American Journal of Political Science* 44: 316–326.

Rottinghaus, Brandon. 2007. "Following the 'Mail Hawks': Alternative Measures of Public Opinion on Vietnam in the Johnson White House." *Public Opinion Quarterly* 71 (Nov.): 367–391.

Rottinghaus, Brandon, and Kent L. Tedin. 2012. "Presidential 'Going Bipartisan:' Opposition Reaction and the Consequences for Institutional Approval." *American Behavioral Scientist* 56(12): 1696–1717.

Rotunda, Ronald D. 1986. *The Politics of Language: Liberalism as Word and Symbol*. Iowa City: University of Iowa Press.

Rudolph, Thomas J., and Jillian Evans. 2005. "Political Trust, Ideology, and Public Support for Government Spending." *American Journal of Political Science* 49 (July): 660–671.

Ruttenberg, Jim. 2005. "Pollsters Faulted for Failure to Predict Edward's Surge and for Subsequent News Coverage." *New York Times*, Feb 19: A19.

Saad, Lydia. 2013. "In U.S., 71% Back Raising Minimum Wage." *Gallup Politics* (March 6).

Sabato, Larry J. 1993. *Feeding Frenzy: How Attack Journalism Has Transformed American Politics*, 2nd ed. New York: Free Press.

Sabato, Larry J., Mark Stencel, and S. Robert Lichter. 2000. *Peep Show: Media and Politics in an Age of Scandal*. Lanham, MD: Rowman-Littlefield.

Saez, Emmanuel. 2013. "Striking It Richer: The Evolution of Top Incomes in the United States: Updated with 2012 Preliminary Estimates." (unpublished paper, Department of Economics, University of California, Berkeley).

Sapiro, Virginia. 2004. "Not Your Parents' Political Socialization." *Annual Review of Political Science* 7 (May): 1–23.

Schafer, Chelsea E., and Greg M. Shaw. 2009. "The Polls—Trends: Tolerance in the United States." *Public Opinion Quarterly* 73 (Summer): 404–431.

Schlesinger, Joseph. 1966. *Ambition and Politics*. Chicago, IL: Rand.

Schlesinger, Mark, and Caroline Heldman. 2001. "Gender Gap or Gender Gaps? New Perspectives on Support for Government Action and Policy." *Journal of Politics* 63 (Feb.): 59–92.

Schneider, William, and I. A. Lewis. 1985. "Views on the News." *Public Opinion* 8 (Aug.–Sept.): 6–11, 58–59.

Schoen, Harald, and Siegfried Schumann. 2007. "Personality Traits, Partisan Attitudes, and Voting Behavior: Evidence from Germany." *Political Psychology* 28(4): 471–498.

Scholz, John T., and Mark Lubell. 1998. "Trust and Taxpaying: Testing the Heuristic Approach to Collective Action." *American Journal of Political Science* 42 (Apr.): 398–417.

Schlozman, Kay, Sidney Verba, and Henry E. Brady. 2012. *The Unheavenly Chorus: Unequal Political Voice and the Broken Promise of American Democracy*. Princeton, NJ: Princeton University Press.

Schubert, Louis, Thomas R. Dye, and Harmon Zeigler. 2014. *The Irony of Democracy: An Uncommon Introduction*, 14th ed. Boston: Wadsworth.

Schuman, Howard. 2008. *Method and Meaning in Polls and Surveys*. Cambridge: Harvard University Press.

Schuman, Howard, and Stanley Presser. 1996. *Questions and Answers in Attitude Surveys*. Thousand Oaks, CA: Sage.

Schwartz, Sandra K. 1975. "Preschoolers and Politics." In *New Directions in Political Socialization*, eds. David C. Schwartz and Sandra K. Schwartz. New York: Free Press.

Sears, David O., and Carolyn L. Funk. 1990. "Self-Interest in Americans Political Opinions." In

Beyond Self-Interest, ed. Jane J. Mansbridge. Chicago: University of Chicago Press.

———. 1999. "Evidence of the Long-Term Persistence of Adults' Political Predispositions." *Journal of Politics* 61 (Feb.): 1–28.

Sears, David O., Carl P. Hensler, and Leslie K. Speer. 1979. "Whites' Opposition to Busing: Self Interest or Symbolic Politics." *American Political Science Review* 73 (June): 369–384.

Sears, David O., and Donald R. Kinder. 1971. "Racial Tensions and Voting in Los Angeles." In *Los Angeles: Viability and Prospects for Metropolitan Leadership*, eds. W. Z. Hirsch. New York: Praeger.

Sears, David O., and Richard R. Lau. 1983. "Inducing Apparently Self-Interested Political Preferences." *American Journal of Political Science* 27 (May): 223–252.

Sears, David O., and Sheri Levy. 2003. "Childhood and Adult Political Development." In *Oxford Handbook of Political Psychology*, eds. David O. Sears, Leonie Huddy, and Robert Jervis. New York: Oxford University Press.

Sebert, Suzanne K., M. Kent Jennings, and Richard G. Niemi. 1974. "The Political Texture of Peer Groups." In *The Political Character of Adolescence*, eds. M. Kent Jennings and Richard G. Niemi. Princeton, NJ: Princeton University Press.

Segovia, Francine, and Renatta Defever. 2010. "The Polls: American Public Opinion on Immigrants and Immigration Policy." *Public Opinion Quarterly* 74: 375–394.

Shapiro, Michael J. 2002. "Post-Liberal Civil Society and the Worlds of Neo Tocquevillean Social Theory." In *Social Capital: Critical Perspectives on Community and 'Bowling Alone*, eds. Scott L. McLean, David A. Schultz, and Manfred B. Steger. New York: New York University Press.

Shapiro, Robert. 2011. "Public Opinion and American Democracy." *Public Opinion Quarterly* 75 (Winter): 982–1017.

Sharp, Elaine B. 1999. *The Sometimes Connection: Public Opinion and Social Policy*. Albany: State University of New York Press.

Shaw, Greg M., and Laura Gaffey. 2012. "Trends: American Public Opinion on Economic Inequality, Taxes and Mobility: 1990–2011." *Public Opinion Quarterly* 76 (Fall): 576–596.

Sheehan, Colleen A. 2004. "Madison v. Hamilton: The Battle over Republicanism and the Role of Public Opinion." *American Political Science Review* 98 (Aug.): 405–424.

Shingles, Richard D. 1981. "Black Consciousness and Political Participation: The Missing Link." *American Political Science Review* 75 (Mar.): 76–91.

Shultziner, Doron. 2013. "Genes and Politics: A New Explanation and Evaluation of Twin Study Results and Association Studies in Political Science." *Political Analysis* 21: 350–367.

Sidanius, Jim, Shana Levin, Colette Van Laar, and David O. Sears. 2008. *The Diversity Challenge: Social Identity and Intergroup Relations on a College Campus*. New York: Russell Sage Foundation.

Sides, John, and Kimberly Gross. 2013. "Stereotypes of Muslims and Support for the War on Terror." *Journal of Politics* 75 (July): 583–598.

Sides, John, and Lynn Vavreck. 2013. *The Gamble: Choice and Chance in the 2012 Presidential Election*. Princeton, NJ: Princeton University Press.

Sigelman, Lee. 1981. "Question-Order Effects on Presidential Popularity." *Public Opinion Quarterly* 45 (Summer): 199–207.

Sigelman, Lee, and Mark Kugler. 2003. "Why Is Research on the Effects of Negative Campaigning So Inconclusive? Understanding Citizens' Perceptions of Negativity." *Journal of Politics* 65 (Feb.): 142–160.

Sigelman, Lee, Steven A. Tuch, and Jack K. Martin. 2005. "What's in a Name? Preference for 'Black' Versus 'African-American' Among Americans of African Descent." *Public Opinion Quarterly* 69 (Fall): 429–438.

Sigelman, Lee, and Susan Welch. 1991. *Black Americans' View of Racial Inequality: The Dream Deferred*. Cambridge, UK: Cambridge University Press.

Silbiger, Sara S., 1972. "Peers and Political Socialization." *Youth and Society* 5 (Mar.): 169–178.

Skocpol, Theda, and Vanessa Williamson. 2013. *The Tea Party and the Remaking of Republican Conservatism*. Oxford: Oxford University Press.

Smidt, Corwin E., Kevin R. den Dulk, Bryan T. Froehle, James M. Penning, Stephen V. Monsma, and Douglas L. Koopman. 2010. *The Disappearing God Gap: Religion in the 2008 Presidential Election*. New York: Oxford University Press.

Smidt, Corwin E., Lyman A. Kellstedt, and James L. Guth. 2009. "The Role of Religion in American Politics: Explanatory Theories and Associated Analytical and Measurement Issues." In *The Oxford Handbook of Religion and American*

Politics, eds. Corwin E. Smidt, Lyman A. Kellstedt, and James L. Guth. Oxford: Oxford University Press, 3–42.

Smith, Aaron. 2009. "The Internet's Role in Campaign 2008." Pew Internet and American Life Project (Jan. 11). http://www.pewinternet ·.org/Reports/2009/6—The-Internets-Role-in-Campaign-2008.aspx.

Smith, Eric R. A. N., and Peverill Squire. 1990. "The Effects of Prestige Names in Question Wording." *Public Opinion Quarterly* 54 (Spring): 97–116.

Smith, Kevin, John R. Alford, Peter K. Hatemi, Lindon J. Easves, Carolyn Fund, and John R. Hibbing. 2013. "Biology, Ideology, and Epistemology: Do We Know Political Attitudes Are Inherited and Why Should We Care." *American Journal of Political Science* 56 (Jan.): 17–33.

Smith, M. B., J. S. Bruner, and R. W. White. 1956. *Opinions and Personality*. New York: Wiley.

Smith, Tom W. 1984. "Nonattitudes: A Review and Evaluation." In *Surveying Subjective Phenomena*, vol. 2, eds. Charles F. Turner and Elizabeth Martin. New York: Russell Sage.

———. 1990. "The First Straw? A Study of the Origins of Election Polls." *Public Opinion Quarterly* 54 (Spring): 21–36.

Sniderman, Paul M. 1975. *Personality and Democratic Politics*. Berkeley: University of California Press.

Sniderman, Paul M., and Edward G. Carmines. 1997. *Reaching Beyond Race*. Cambridge, MA: Harvard University Press.

Sniderman, Paul M., Gretchen C. Crosby, and William G. Howell, 2000. "The Politics of Race." In *Racialized Politics: The Debate About Racism in America*, eds. David O. Sears, Jim Sidanius, and Lawrence Bobo. Chicago: University of Chicago Press, 236–279.

Sniderman, Paul M., and Thomas Piazza. 1993. *The Scar of Race*. Cambridge, MA: Harvard University Press.

Sniderman, Paul M., and Edward H. Stiglitz. 2012. *The Reputational Premium*. Princeton, NJ: Princeton University Press.

Sniderman, Paul M., Philip E. Tetlock, James N. Glaser, Donald Philip Green, and Michael Hout. 1989. "Principled Tolerance and the American Mass Public." *British Journal of Political Science* 19 (Feb.): 25–45.

Sniderman, Paul M., and S. M. Theriault. 2004. "The Structure of Political Argument and the Logic of Issue Framing." In *Studies in Public Opinion*, eds.

W. E. Saris and P. M. Sniderman. Princeton, NJ: Princeton University Press, 133–165.

Snyder, James M., Jr. 1992. "Long-Term Investments in Politicians, or Give Early, Give Often." *Journal of Law and Economics* 35 (Apr.): 15–44.

———. 1996. "Constituency Preferences: California Ballot Propositions, 1974–1990." *Legislative Studies Quarterly* 21: 463–488.

Snyder, James M., Jr., and Michael Ting. 2003. "Roll Calls, Party Labels, and Elections." *Political Analysis* 11: 419–444.

Sobieraj, Sharah, and Jeffrey M. Berry. 2011. "From Incivility to Outrage: Political Discourse in Blogs, Talk Radio, and Cable News." *Political Communication* 28 (Feb.): 19–41.

Somit, Albert, and Steven A. Peterson. 1997. *Darwinism, Dominance, and Democracy: The Biological Bases of Authoritarianism*. Westport, CT: Praeger.

Soroka, Stuart, and Christopher Wlezien. 2010. *Degrees of Democracy and Politics, Public Opinion and Policy*. Cambridge, UK: Cambridge University Press.

Spitz, Elaine. 1984. *Majority Rule*. Chatham, NJ: Chatham House.

Squire, Peverill. 1988. "Why the Literary Digest Failed." *Public Opinion Quarterly* 52 (Spring): 123–133.

Squire, Peverill. 1992. "Changing State Legislative Careers." In *Changing Patterns in State Legislative Careers*, eds. Gary F. Moncrief and Joel A. Thompson. Ann Arbor: University of Michigan Press, 175–194.

Stanley, Harold W., and Richard G. Niemi. 2012. *Vital Statistics of American Politics, 2011–2012*. Washington, DC: Congressional Quarterly Press.

Stanley, Harold, and Richard G. Niemi, eds. 2013. *Vital Statistics on American Politics 2013–2014*. Thousand Oaks, CA: Congressional Quarterly Press.

Steeh, Charlotte, and Maria Krysan. 1996. "Trends: Affirmative Action and the Public, 1970–1995." *Public Opinion Quarterly* 60 (Spring): 128–158.

Stein, Robert M., and Greg Vonnahme. 2008. "Engaging the Unengaged Voter: Vote Centers and Voter Turnout." *Journal of Politics* 70 (Apr.): 487–497.

Stenner, Karen. 2005. *The Authoritarian Dynamic*. New York: Cambridge University Press.

Stevens, Daniel, Benjamin G. Bishin, and Robert R. Barr. 2006. "Authoritarian Attitudes, Democracy, and Policy Preferences Among Latin American

Elites." *American Journal of Political Science* 50 (July): 606–620.

Stimson, James A. 1975. "Belief Systems: Constraint, Complexity, and the 1972 Election." *American Journal of Political Science* 19 (Aug.): 393–417.

———. 1999. *Public Opinion in America: Moods, Cycles, and Swings,* 2nd ed. Boulder, CO: Westview.

———. 2004. *Tides of Consent.* New York: Cambridge.

———. 2010. "The Issue of Representation." In *Who Gets Represented?* eds. Peter Enns and Christopher Wlezien. New York: Russell Sage, 347–360.

Stoker, Laura. 2001. "Citizen Value Judgments." In *Citizens and Politics,* eds. James H. Kuklinksi. New York: Cambridge University Press.

Stoker, Laura, and Jackie Bass. 2011. "Political Socialization: Ongoing Questions and New Directions." In *The Handbook of American Public Opinion and the Media,* eds. Robert Shapiro and Lawrence Jacobs. Oxford: Oxford University Press.

Stoker, Laura, and M. Kent Jennings. 2005. "Political Similarity and Influence Between Husbands and Wives." In *The Social Logic of Politics,* ed. Alan S. Zuckerman. Philadelphia: Temple University Press.

———. 2008. "Of Time and Partisan Polarization." *American Journal of Political Science* 52 (July): 619–635.

Stokes, Donald E. 1966. "Some Dynamic Elements of Contests for the Presidency." *American Political Science Review* 60 (Mar.): 19–28, 453–470.

Stonecash, Jeffrey M. 2000. *Class and Party in American Politics.* Boulder, CO: Westview.

Stouffer, Samuel A. 1949. *The American Soldier.* Princeton, NJ: Princeton University Press.

———. 1955. *Communism, Conformity, and Civil Liberties.* New York: Doubleday.

Stratmann, Thomas. 2000. "Congressional Voting over Congressional Careers: Shifting Careers and Changing Constraints." *American Political Science Review* 94: 665–676.

Strauss, Claudia. 2012. *Making Sense of Public Opinion: American Discourses About Immigration and Social Programs.* Cambridge: Cambridge University Press.

Streb, Mathew J., Barbara Burrell, Brain Frederick, and Michael A. Genovese. 2008. "Social Desirability Effects and Support for a Female American President." *Public Opinion Quarterly* 72 (Spring): 76–89.

Stroud, Natalie J. 2011. Niche News: *The Politics of New Choice.* New York: Oxford University Press.

Sturgis, Patrick, Caroline Roberts, and Nick Allum. 2005. "A Different Take on the Deliberative Poll: Information, Deliberation, and Attitude Constraint." *Public Opinion Quarterly* 69 (Spring): 30–65.

Sullivan, John L., James E. Piereson, and George E. Marcus. 1982. *Political Tolerance and American Democracy.* Chicago: University of Chicago Press.

Sundquist, James L. 1973. *Dynamics of the Party System.* Washington, DC: Brookings.

Sunstein, Cass R. 2009. *Going to Extremes: How Like Minds Unite and Divide.* New York: Oxford University Press.

Surowiecki, James. 2004. *The Wisdom of Crowds.* New York: Doubleday.

Tarman, Christopher, and David O. Sears. 2005. "The Conceptualization and Measurement of Symbolic Racism." *Journal of Politics* 67 (Aug.): 731–761.

Tarrow, Sidney. 1996. "Making Social Science Work Across Space and Time: A Critical Reflection on Robert Putnam's Making Democracy Work." *American Political Science Review* 90 (June): 389–397.

Tate, Katherine. 1993. *From Protest to Politics: The New Black Voters in American Elections.* New York: Russell Sage.

Tedin, Kent L. 1974. "The Influence of Parents on the Political Attitudes of Adolescents." *American Political Science Review* 68 (Dec.): 1579–1592.

———. 1980. "Measuring Parent and Peer Influence on Adolescent Political Attitudes." *American Journal of Political Science* 24 (Feb.): 136–154.

———. 1987. "Political Ideology and the Vote." In *Research in Micro-Politics,* vol. 2, ed. Samuel Long. Greenwich, CT: JAI Press.

———. 1994a. "Mass Support for Competitive Elections in the Soviet Union." *Comparative Politics* 27 (Apr.): 241–271.

———. 1994b. "Self Interest, Symbolic Values, and the Financial Equalization of the Public Schools." *Journal of Politics* 56 (Aug.): 628–649.

Tedin, Kent L., Richard E. Matland, and Gregory R. Weiher. 2001. "The Politics of Age and Race: Support and Opposition to a School Bond Referendum." *Journal of Politics* 63 (Feb.): 270–294.

Tedin, Kent L., and Richard W. Murray. 1979. "Public Awareness of Congressional Representatives: Recall Versus Recognition." *American Politics Quarterly* 7: 509–517.

Tedin, Kent L., Brandon Rottinghaus, and Harrell Rodgers. 2011. "When the President Goes Public: The Consequences of Communication Mode for Opinion Change Across Issue Types and Groups." *Political Research Quarterly* 64 (Sep.): 506–519.

Tedin, Kent L., and Gregory R. Weiher. 2004. "Racial/Ethnic Diversity and Academic Quality as Components of School Choice." *Journal of Politics* 66 (Nov.): 1109–1133.

Tedin, Kent L., and Oi–Kuan Fiona Yap. 1993. "The Gender Factor in Soviet Mass Politics: Survey Evidence from Greater Moscow." *Political Research Quarterly* 46 (Mar.): 179–211.

Terman, Lewis M., and Melinda H. Oden. 1959. *Genetic Studies of Genius V: The Gifted Group at Midlife.* Stanford, CA: Stanford University Press.

Theriault, Sean M. 2008. *Party Polarization in Congress.* New York: Cambridge University Press.

Thomas, Martin. 1985. "Electoral Proximity and Senatorial Roll Call Voting." *American Journal of Political Science* 29 (Feb.): 96–111.

Tocqueville, Alexis de. 1966. *Democracy in America,* eds. J. P. Mayer and Max Lerner. New York: Harper.

Torney-Purta, Judith, and Jo-Ann Amadeo. 2003. "A Cross-National Analysis of Political and Civic Involvement Among Adolescents." *PS: Political Science and Politics* 36 (Apr.): 269–274.

Traugott, Michael W., and Mee-Eeun Kang. 2000. "Push Polls as Negative Persuasive Strategies." In *Election Polls, the News Media, and Democracy,* eds. Paul J. Lavrakas and Michael W. Traugott. Chatham, NJ: Chatham House.

Traugott, Michael W., and Paul L. Lavrakas. 2008. *The Voter's Guide to Election Polls,* 4th ed. Lanham, MD: Rowan and Littlefield.

Treier, Shawn, and D. Sunshine Hillygus. 2009. "The Nature of Political Ideology in the Contemporary Electorate." *Public Opinion Quarterly* 73 (Winter): 679–703.

Turner, Charles, and Elizabeth Martin. 1984. *Surveying Subjective Phenomena.* New York: Russell Sage.

Ura, Joseph Daniel, and Christoper R. Ellis. 2008. "Income, Preferences and the Dynamics of Policy Responsiveness." *PS: Political Science and Politics* 41 (Oct.): 785–794.

Urban, Carley, and Sarah Niebler. 2014. "Dollars on the Sidewalk: Should Presidential Candidates Advertise in Uncontested States?" *American Journal of Political Science* 58 (April): 322–366.

Uslaner, Eric M. 2002. *The Moral Foundations of Trust.* New York: Cambridge University Press.

Uslaner, Eric M., and Ronald E. Weber. 1983. "Policy Congruence and American State Elites: Descriptive Representation Versus Electoral Accountability." *Journal of Politics* 45 (Feb.): 183–196.

Valentino, Nicholas A., and David O. Sears. 2004. "Old Times There Are Not Forgotten: Race and Partisan Realignment in the Contemporary South." *American Journal of Political Science* 49 (July): 672–688.

Vallone, Robert, Less Ross, and Mark Lepper. 1985. "The Hostile Media Phenomenon: Bias Perception and Perceptions of Media Bias in Coverage of the Beirut Massacre." *Journal of Personality and Social Psychology* 49 (Sep.): 577–588.

Vavreck, Lynn. 2009. *The Message Matters: An Economic Theory of Campaigns.* Princeton, NJ: Princeton University Press.

Verba, Sidney. 1996. "The Citizen as Respondent: Sample Surveys and American Democracy." *American Political Science Review* 90(1): 1–7.

Verba, Sidney, and Norman H. Nie. 1972. *Participation in America.* New York: Harper.

Verba, Sidney, Kay Lehman Schlozman, and Henry E. Brady. 1995. *Voice and Equality: Civic Voluntarism in American Democracy.* Cambridge, MA: Harvard University Press.

Verhulst, Brad, Lindon J. Eaves, and Peter K. Hatemi. 2012. "Correlation and Not Causation: The Relationship Between Personality Traits and Political Ideologies." *American Journal of Political Science* 56 (Jan.): 34–51.

Visser, Penny, Allyson Hobrook, and Jon A. Krosnick. 2008. "Knowledge and Attitudes." In *The Sage Handbook of Public Opinion Research,* eds. Wolfgang Donsbach and Michael Traugott. Thousand Oaks, CA: Sage.

Wahlke, John, Heinz Eulau, William Buchanan, and LeRoy C. Ferguson, 1962. *The Legislative System.* New York: Wiley.

Wald, Kenneth D., Dennis E. Owen, and Samuel S. Hill. 1989. "Churches as Political Communities." *American Political Science Review* 82 (June): 532–548.

Warren, Mark. 1999. "Democratic Theory and Trust." In *Democracy and Trust,* ed. Mark Warren. London: Cambridge University Press.

Wattenberg, Martin P. 2011. *Is Voting for Young People,* 3rd ed. New York: Longman.

Wawro, Gregory. 2001. "A Panel Probit Analysis of Campaign Contributions and Roll Call Votes." *American Journal of Political Science* 45: 563–579.

Weatherford, Stephen. 1987. "How Does Government Performance Influence Political Support?" *Political Behavior* 9(1): 5–27.

Weaver, David H., and Dan Drew. 1993. "Voter Learning in the 1990 Off-Year Election: Did the Media Matter?" *Journalism Quarterly* 70: 356–368.

Weaver, David H., and G. Cleveland Wilhoit. 1996. *The American Journalist in the 1990s*. Mahwah, NJ: Erlbaum.

Weissberg, Robert. 1998. *Political Tolerance: Balancing Community and Diversity*. Thousand Oaks, CA: Sage.

West, Darrell M. 2001. *The Rise and Fall of the Media Establishment*. Bedford, MA: St. Martin's Press.

———. 2014. *Air Wars: Television Advertising in Election Campaigns, 1952–2012*, 6th ed. Washington, DC: Congressional Quarterly Press.

Westheimer, Joel. 2007. *Pledging Allegiance: The Politics of Patriotism in America's Schools*. New York: Teachers College Press.

Wetstein, Matthew E. 1993. "A LISREL Model of Public Opinion on Abortion." In *Understanding the New Politics of Abortion*, ed. Malcolm Goggin. Newbury Park, CA: Sage.

Wheaton, Sarah. 2013. "For First Time on Record, Black Voting Rate Outpaced Rate for Whites in 2012." *New York Times*, May 8: A16.

Wilcox, Clyde, and Patrick Carr. 2010. "The Puzzling Case of the Abortion Attitudes of the Millennial Generation." In *Understanding Public Opinion*, 3rd ed., eds. Barbara Norrander and Clyde Wilcox. Washington, DC: Congressional Quarterly Press, 123–142.

Williams, J. Allen, Jr., Clyde Z. Nunn, and Louis St. Peter. 1976. "Origins of Tolerance: Findings from a Replication of Stouffer's Communism, Conformity, and Civil Liberties." *Social Forces* 44 (Dec.): 394–408.

Wilson, J. Mathew. 2009. "Religion and American Public Opinion: Economic Issues." In *The Oxford Handbook of Religion and American Politics*, eds. Corwin E. Smidt, Lyman A. Kellstedt, and James L. Guth. Oxford: Oxford University Press, 191–216.

Wilson, Thomas C. 1985. "Urbanism and Tolerance: A Test of Some Hypotheses Drawn from Wirth and Stouffer." *American Sociological Review* 50: 117–123.

Wittkopf, Eugene R. 1990. *Faces of Internationalism: American Public Opinion and Foreign Policy*. Durham, NC: Duke University Press.

Wlezien, Christopher. 1995a. "Dynamic Representation: The Case of U.S. Spending on Defense." *British Journal of Political Science* 26: 81–103.

———. 1995b. "The Public as Thermostat: The Dynamics of Public Preferences for Spending." *American Journal of Political Science* 39: 981–1000.

Wlezien, Christopher, and Robert S. Erikson. 2000. "Temporal Horizons and Presidential Election Forecasts." In *Before the Vote: Forecasting American National Elections*, eds. James E. Campbell and James C. Garand. Thousand Oaks, CA: Sage, 103–118.

———. 2002. "The Time Line of Presidential Campaigns." *Journal of Politics* 64: 969–993.

Woessner, Mathew, and April Kelly-Woessner. 2009a. "I Think My Professor Is a Democrat: Considering Whether Students Recognize and React to Faculty Politics." *PS: Political Science and Politics* 42: 342–352.

Woessner, Mathew, and April Kelly-Woessner. 2009b. "Left Pipeline: Why Conservatives Don't Get Doctorates." In *The Politically Correct University: Problems, Scope, and Reforms*, eds. Robert Maranto, Richard E. Redding, and Frederick M. Hess. Washington, DC: AEI Press, 38–59.

Wolak, Jennifer. 2007. "Strategic Retirements: The Influence of Public Preferences on Voluntary Departures from Congress." *Legislative Studies Quarterly* 32 (May): 285–308.

Wolak, Jennifer, and Michael McDervitt. 2011. "The Roots of the Gender Gap in Political Knowledge in Adolescence." *Political Behavior* 33(3): 505–533.

Wolff, Edward N. 2012. *The Asset Price Meltdown and the Wealth of the Middle Class*. New York: New York University Press.

Wong, Janelle, and Vivian Tseng. 2007. "Political Socialization with Immigrant Families: Challenging Parental Socialization Models." *Journal of Ethnic and Migration Studies* 34(1): 151–168.

Wood, B. Dan, and Angela Hinton Anderson. 1998. "The Dynamics of Senatorial Representation, 1952–1991." *Journal of Politics* 60: 705–736.

Wright, Gerald C., Jr., and Michael Berkman. 1986. "Candidates and Policies in United States Senate Elections." *American Political Science Review* 80 (June): 567–588.

Wright, Gerald C., Jr., and Brian F. Schaffner. 2002. "The Influence of Party: Evidence from the State Legislatures." *American Political Science Review* 96: 367–380.

Wyer, Robert S., Jr., and Victor C. Ottati. 1993. "Political Information Processing." In *Explorations in Political Psychology*, eds. Shanto Iyengar and William J. McGuire. Durham, NC: Duke University Press, 264–295.

Yang, Soon Joon, and Richard D. Alba. 1992. "Urbanism and Nontraditional Opinion: A Test of Fischer's Subcultural Theory." *Social Science Quarterly* 73 (Sep.): 596–609.

Zaller, John. 1992. *The Nature and Origins of Mass Opinion*. Cambridge, UK: Cambridge University Press.

———. 1994. "Elite Leadership of Mass Opinion: New Evidence from the Gulf War." In *Taken by Storm: The Media, Public Opinion, and U.S. Foreign Policy in the Gulf War*, eds. William L. Bennett and David L. Paletz. Chicago: University of Chicago Press, 166–209.

———. 1996. "The Myth of Massive Media Impact Revived: New Support for a Discredited Idea." In *Political Persuasion and Attitude Change*, eds. Diane C. Mutz, Paul M. Sniderman, and Richard A. Brody. Ann Arbor: University of Michigan Press.

———. 1997. "A Model of Communication Effects at the Outbreak of the Gulf War." In *Do the Media Govern? Politicians, Voters, and Reporters in America*, eds. Shanto Iyengar and Richard Reeves. Thousand Oaks, CA: Sage.

———. 1998a. "Monica Lewinsky's Contribution to Political Science." *PS: Political Science and Politics* 31: 182–189.

———. 1998b. "Politicians as Prize Fighters: Electoral Selection and Electoral Advantage." In *Politicians and Party Politics*, ed. John Geer. Baltimore, MD: Johns-Hopkins Press.

———. 2004a. "Floating Voters in U.S. Presidential Elections, 1948–2000." In *Studies in Public Opinion*, eds. Willem E. Saris and Paul M. Sniderman. Princeton, NJ: Princeton University Press.

———. 2004b. "A Theory of Media Politics." (unpublished manuscript, University of California, Los Angeles).

Zaller, John, and Stanley Feldman. 1992. "A Simple Theory of the Survey Response: Answering Questions and Revealing Preferences." *American Journal of Political Science* 36: 579–616.

Zipp, John F., and Rudy Fenwick. 2006. "Is the Academy a Liberal Hegemony? The Political Orientations and Educational Values of Professors." *Public Opinion Quarterly* 70: 304–326.

Zmerli, Sonja, and Kenneth Newton. 2008. "Social Trust and Attitudes Toward Democracy." *Public Opinion Quarterly* 72 (Winter): 706–724.

Zukin, Cliff, Scott Keeter, Molly Andolina, Krista Jenkings, and Michael X. Delli Carpini. 2006. *A New Engagement*. Oxford: Oxford University Press.

INDEX